The New Emperors

The New Emperors

China in the Era of Mao and Deng

Harrison E. Salisbury

LITTLE, BROWN AND COMPANY
BOSTON   TORONTO   LONDON

First Edition

Library of Congress Cataloging-in-Publication Data

Salisbury, Harrison Evans, 1908-
   The new emperors : China in the era of Mao and Deng / Harrison E.
Salisbury.
         p.   cm.
   Includes bibliographical references and index.
   ISBN 0-316-80910-1
   1. Mao, Tse-tung, 1893-1976.   2. Teng, Hsiao-p'ing, 1904-
3. Heads of state — China — Biography.   4. China — History — 1949-
I. Title.
DS778.A1S426   1992
951.05'092 — dc20
   [B]   91-31017

10 9 8 7 6 5 4 3 2 1

MV NY

Printed in the United States of America

For the young people of China,
in whose hands its future rests.

Anyone who is able to prevent violence and remove harm from the people so that men's lives are protected, who can reward good and punish evil and thus avoid disaster — such a man may be called an emperor.
— *The General Mirror for the Aid of Government,* eleventh century

Contents

Illustrations follow page 176 and page 368.

Maps appear on the following pages: China, page xiv; Beijing and Zhongnanhai, page 5.

About Emperors

HUNDREDS OF MEN have borne the title of emperor, *huang-ti,* in China's long history. Few have exercised more power, personal and political, than Mao Zedong and Deng Xiaoping, true *huang-ti*.

The first *huang-ti* was the Yellow Emperor, the legendary ruler who founded China on the rich loess floodplains of the Yellow River. Mao led his Red armies, with Deng at his side, out of these plains to found his New China at Tiananmen in 1949.

The concept of emperor in China is intimately associated with that of the dragon. China's dragons, guardians of the throne, are unlike those of the West. They are benign and protective but can turn like terrible emperors on the people. If they do so, it is the fault of the people, not the dragons. They breathe fire and thrash their tail only if betrayed, a convenient concept for an emperor.

In Chinese custom, dynasties and bloodlines are not so important as power. The great Chinese dynastic scholar Zhang Zhi says of Mao, "He founded the first peasant dynasty in six hundred years." In Chinese history a capable minister or victorious general has often won the Mandate of Heaven. Deng Xiaoping fit the concept perfectly. Both men earned the title of *huang-ti* despite the fact that both considered themselves Marxists. Both were Sons of Heaven, rulers by a kind of divine right.

In the words of the preeminent scholar Derk Bodde: "In China more perhaps than in any other country a knowledge of the past is essential for an understanding of the present."

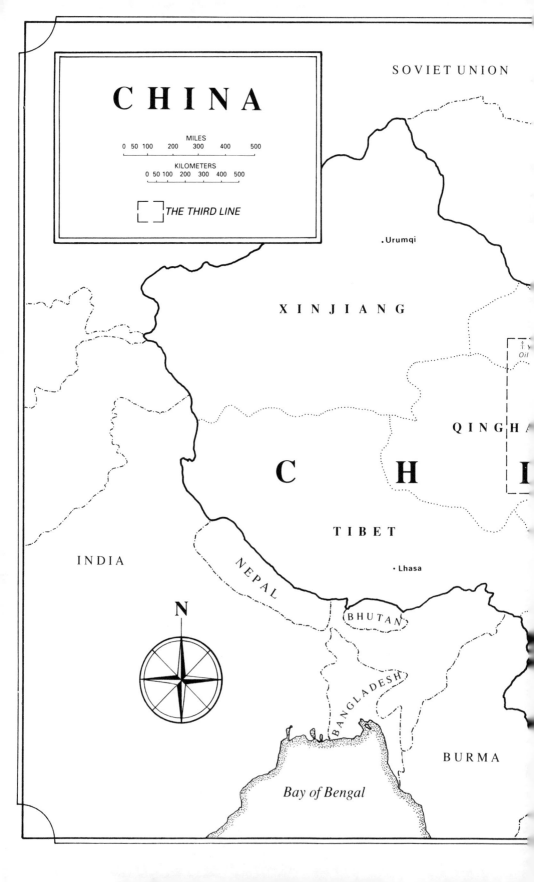

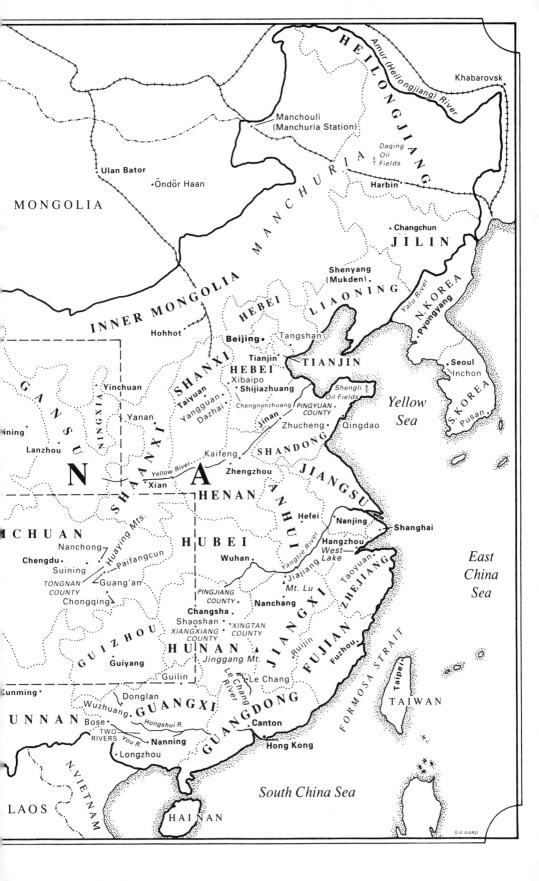

PART 1

THE BIRTH OF NEW CHINA

1

The Old Capital

THERE IS NO SIGN of it today, but near the southwest corner of the Forbidden City long ago stood the Tower of Yearning, where in the eighteenth century the Fragrant Concubine, Ke Fei, spent many hours. She would climb two flights to a window and gaze for hours on the Moslem bazaar and mosque that Emperor Qian Long had built to ease her heartache for Kashgar, where she was born. Ke Fei was called the Fragrant Concubine because, it was said, when she lay with her lover her body gave off an exotic essence.[1]

Today only the tower gate stands, quiet, inconspicuous, unmarked, imperial red columns, gold leaf, jade green lacquer. Even the name is gone. In the days of Republican China it was changed to the Gate of New China. Not for years had it attracted attention until in 1989 student demonstrators in Tiananmen Square tried to break through its heavy doors.

Often passing through Tiananmen at night, as I did in the spring of 1972, I saw two soldiers standing guard at the gate under the tangerine shadows of fat Chinese lanterns. In my imagination I saw Mao Zedong beyond that portal, consulting the ancient classics that filled his study.

No one told me that Mao's chambers could be found behind the red lacquer door, but, in fact, my fancy did not play me false. When, years later, I passed into the secret world of the Forbidden City, I discovered that the Gate of New China *did* lead to Mao's quarters.

Through the gate lay Zhongnanhai, a hidden fairyland of lakes and parks and palaces where Marco Polo strolled and Kublai Khan built his pleasure domes; where emperors and empresses, concubines and eunuchs, took their leisure within walls more forbidding than those of the Forbidden City itself.

Not until I had seen this unsuspected enclave, which had endured since the days of the great emperor Qian Long, did I begin to grasp the extraordinary blend of ancient China and contemporary Marxism that occupies the heart of the enigmatic state created by Mao Zedong and inherited by Deng Xiaoping. Debate will persist for centuries as to the proportions of Ming and Marx, of China eternal and dialectic empiricism, that constitute what Mao called the New China and Deng has changed radically but called the same.

Within the Gate of New China Qian Long's parks stand a bit faded, but remarkably well preserved. Mao made no important change. Here are three imperial lakes, a diadem of crystal waters a mile long, fed by the Jade Fountain, a spring in the Fragrant Hills beyond the Summer Palace.[2]

These waters, so the Chinese believed, possessed an aphrodisiac, partaking of the male and female principles, yang and yin. They called the lakes the Pools of Great Fertilizing Spume, and around them for centuries prevailed total privacy. On the shores were built the Sea Palaces: the Pavilion of Perpetual Southern Melodies, to honor the emperor Shun, who (perhaps) lived more than two thousand years before Christ; the Palace of Sublime Wisdom; and a hundred others. No place more Chinese, more steeped in the aura of the world's most ancient society, could be found.

Mao Zedong, high priest of China's Communism, would in 1949 make his sanctuary and settle about him his commanders and commissars, the princes and the philosophers — and their ladies — of his new utopia within a walled cloister at the heart of a walled city in a China whose most renowned achievement was the Great Wall, the only object made by man visible from the moon.

In the early days of 1949, after three years of war, Mao knew that his armies stood on the verge of victory over Chiang Kaishek's Nationalists. Yet he did not seek the spotlight. To the outside world — and even to China — he seemed to have disappeared. He had abandoned the Yanan stronghold in Shaanxi Province where he had spent ten years. His armies seemed to be fighting everywhere, but he had hardly been sighted since 1946, when war with Chiang Kaishek broke out again. But this was an illusion. Nothing was more dangerous than to take Mao at face value. If he retreated, it was to lure his enemy into

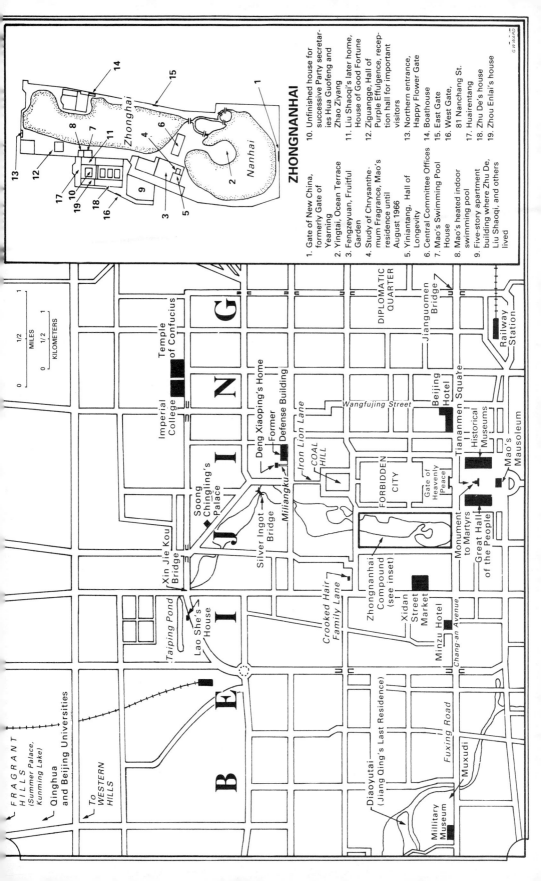

ZHONGNANHAI

1. Gate of New China, formerly Gate of Yearning
2. Yingtai, Ocean Terrace
3. Fengzeyuan, Fruitful Garden
4. Study of Chrysanthemum Fragrance, Mao's residence until August 1966
5. Yiniantang, Hall of Longevity
6. Central Committee Offices
7. Mao's Swimming Pool House
8. Mao's heated indoor swimming pool
9. Five-story apartment building where Zhu De, Liu Shaoqi, and others lived
10. Unfinished house for successive Party secretaries Hua Guofeng and Zhao Ziyang
11. Liu Shaoqi's later home, House of Good Fortune
12. Ziguangge, Hall of Purple Effulgence, reception hall for important visitors
13. Northern entrance, Happy Flower Gate
14. Boathouse
15. East Gate
16. West Gate, 81 Nanchang St.
17. Huairentang
18. Zhu De's house
19. Zhou Enlai's house

Zhonghai

Nanhai

G.W.WARD

B E I J I N G

FRAGRANT HILLS
(Summer Palace, Kunming Lake)

Qinghua and Beijing Universities

To WESTERN HILLS

1/2 0 1 MILES

0 1/2 1 KILOMETERS

Temple of Confucius

Imperial College

Deng Xiaoping's Home
Former Defense Building

Iron Lion Lane

COAL HILL

Wangfujing Street

Beijing Hotel

DIPLOMATIC QUARTER

Jianguomen Bridge

Railway Station

Historical Museums

Mao's Mausoleum

FORBIDDEN CITY

Gate of Heavenly Peace

Tiananmen Square

Soong Chingling's Palace

Xin Jie Kou Bridge

Silver Ingot Bridge

Miliangku

Monument to Martyrs

Great Hall of the People

Crooked Hair Family Lane

Zhongnanhai Compound (see inset)

Xidan Street Market

Minzu Hotel

Chang-an Avenue

Taiping Pond

Lao She's House

Diaoyutai (Jiang Qing's Last Residence)

Fuxing Road

Muxudi

Military Museum

a trap. If he smiled, beware, as friend and foe learned to their cost. No man lived in greater peril than one whom Mao designated his heir apparent.

It was Mao who ordered his army to give up the Yanan redoubt in 1947 and vanish deep into the countryside. It was Mao who had conceived a strategy of feint and deceit that seemed to place him everywhere and nowhere. It was Mao and his partner, Zhu De, who had invented this mobile, many-fronted war behind which they massed armies that would demolish Chiang Kaishek.

As Liu Bocheng, "One-Eyed Liu," a veteran commander, put it: "It was high time that we ate meat; we had had enough bones. We took one piece of meat in our mouth, held another in our chopsticks, and kept an eye on a third. You must have a good appetite to take three pieces of meat at one time."[3]

Mao and his men had that appetite. He had set up secret headquarters late in May 1948 in a village called Xibaipo on the southwest approach to Beijing. There his men lurked, about 175 miles from the capital, diligent as beavers, cutting away the last supports that propped up Chiang's rickety regime.[4]

Invisible Mao might be to the world, but to his generals, the men who Major General David Barr, the top U.S. military observer, swore would do credit to any army in the world, he was omnipresent.[5]

By late 1948 Mao, from his dusty hideout in the north China hills, was engaged in operations — some of the greatest military campaigns the twentieth century had seen — that would change the face of China: Lin Biao, Mao's brilliant if sinister general, was mopping up Manchuria, besieging Beijing, and capturing Tianjin; Peng Dehuai and He Long were cutting Beijing's connections with the rest of China; Liu Bocheng, Deng Xiaoping, and Chen Yi were launching the extraordinary Huai-Hai operations, which would cost Chiang a million men and seal his doom.

"So quietly and gently that one is hardly aware of it, yet inexorably, the 'red tide' draws near," Derk Bodde, a Fulbright scholar in Beijing, noted in his diary on December 12, 1948.[6]

That was the day the Communist Northeast Field Army, led by Lin Biao, began to close in on Beijing.[7] Two days later John Melby of the American embassy flew up from Nanjing for what would be a final glimpse of the old capital before the Communist takeover. He was lunching with Colonel David Barrett, the deputy U.S. military attaché, who had lived there much of the time since the 1920s. They were talking in Barrett's courtyard home in the thin sunshine of Beijing's winter when they heard heavy cannon fire. The Communists had taken the Fragrant Hills and were shelling the airport. If the Americans wanted to get out, they had better run. They ran. Next day Derk Bodde learned that Qinghua and Yenching universities, to the northwest, had been cut off. The city was surrounded. As of December 17, Beijing was under siege.[8]

It lasted six weeks. Sometimes a small plane got in or out; not much more. Behind-scenes negotiations for surrender went forward. Mao told Lin Biao not to hurry. Filth piled up in the streets. The Forbidden City teemed with Chiang's troops. They blew up historic buildings and hacked down three-hundred-year-old trees to create fields of fire. Night soil rose in odoriferous mountains — the honey carts could not get past the city gates. Food vanished. Water was down to a trickle. Trenches were dug in the Forbidden City, ancient stones heaped in careless barricades. Thousands toiled at turning a polo field east of the Forbidden City into a small airfield. Barbed wire stretched across promenades. Horses stabled in old Manchu palaces, Bodde recalled.

The surrender of Beijing was agreed to on January 21, 1949, effective at 6:00 P.M., January 22.[9] By this time the streets were littered with garbage. Fortunately, Bodde commented, the weather was cold. The pleasure gardens behind the Gate of Yearning were a shambles. Not until March could the Forbidden City reopen. Of the three lakes only Beihai, the Northern Sea, once again admitted the public. Rubble cluttered paths, and the lake was a muddy stink. It had been drained for a thorough scrubbing. The other lakes, Zhonghai and Nanhai, stayed closed.[10] Forty years passed. In 1991 they were still closed.

The first Communist detachments marched into Beijing about 4:00 P.M. on January 31, 1949, holding aloft red flags and portraits of Mao Zedong and Zhu De, Mao's great commander. Many peasants thought the Revolution was led by one man, named Zhu Mao. The troops moved up ancient Wangfujing Street, Palace Well Street, and into the heart of the city.[11] Palace Well Street had been renamed years earlier to honor a famous British correspondent, Dr. George Morrison. That name was quietly abandoned.

At the edge of the Forbidden City outside the American consulate stood Mariann Clubb, wife of the U.S. consul-general, O. Edmund

Clubb. A young soldier, ruddy-cheeked, his uniform dusty, asked for a cup of water. "Let me get you some boiled water," she said. "Oh, we don't need boiled water now," he said. "We're in Beijing."[12]

In Beijing! So the young soldier was, and so soon would be thousands of other Communist soldiers and Party cadres.

There was a victory parade on February 3 amid a dust storm so heavy you could hardly see the troops with their American trucks, American guns, American artillery, American tanks, American armored cars, even American uniforms, all captured from the Nationalists. "Chiang Kaishek was our supply officer," Mao once said.[13]

Still no sight of Mao. Not until late March would Mao move his headquarters from remote rural Xibaipo to the Fragrant Hills, northwest of Beijing. He was still lying low. There was no clue to his whereabouts except, perhaps, a hint in the tight security that descended on the Hills and the Summer Palace.[14]

In the early hours of March 25, Mao slipped through Beijing like a ghost. No one saw him come. No one saw him go. Not a word in the newspapers. Preparations for Mao's journey had been made with excruciating care. A working team had been sent six weeks earlier under Li Kenong, a top Party security man. Party and army staffs had been lectured on discipline and security. Zhou Enlai ruled that no one was to enter the city for three months except on urgent missions.

Because of Mao's obsession with enemy agents and secret plots, he ordered that headquarters be set up outside Beijing in the Fragrant Hills. One hundred security agents were picked to protect the area around the Xiangshan Temple (it had been a hotel for some years), which had been selected as headquarters for the Party and the People's Liberation Army.[15]

Mao's column started from Xibaipo on March 23, a long convoy of captured American jeeps with a security detachment ahead. Each leader had his own jeep — Mao, Liu Shaoqi, Zhou Enlai, Zhu De, Ren Bishi, and Lin Boqu, all members of the Politburo, the ruling body of the Party's Central Committee. The top army commanders followed them. Wives rode beside their husbands.

They got under way shortly after noon. Mao had worked late into the night — his custom. He awoke about 11:00 A.M., ate a bowl of rice and some Chinese pickles, and the group set off.[16] Baggage had been sent ahead, but Mao's bodyguards had packed a few books to take along, two Chinese encyclopedic dictionaries, *Lexicon of Words (Ci Hai)* and *Origin of Words (Ci Yuan)*, and two dynastic works of great distinction, studied and annotated by emperors, statesmen, and scholars for hundreds of years. One was called *Records of the Historian (Shi Ji)* and covered the period from the semimythical Yellow Emperor, China's founding father, and into the Han dynasty until about a hundred years before Christ. The other, *The General Mirror for the Aid of Government (Cu Chi Tang Qian)*, covered thirteen hundred years of history and had been compiled in the eleventh century. It was designed as a practical handbook for the emperor, telling him how his predecessors had handled difficult questions. No text by Marx or Lenin.

Mao had studied these massive historical tomes for years. The first contained 130 chapters, the second, 294 chapters. He was learning his trade — how to rule the world's largest country — and he had gone to China's roots. If he was to rule the empire, he must be guided by the wisdom of the past emperors.[17]

Mao's cavalcade took a roughly paved road into the mountains to the northeast. Spirits were high. Mao joked that it was like going to Beijing to take the imperial examination. Zhou Enlai said that they must try to get a good grade. "There is no going back," Mao proclaimed. "We shall never be like Li Zicheng," a general who took over Beijing when the Manchus were toppling the Ming dynasty. He got to Beijing and seized power but lost it after two days.[18]

The Mao party had expected to overnight at Baoding, seat of the Hebei provincial government, but had to stop at the village of Shin, in Tangxian County, because Ren Bishi's jeep broke down. They got to Baoding about noon on March 24. Mao conferred with Lin Tie, the Hebei Party secretary. He warned Lin Tie that the methods used against landlords and rich peasants in the villages (confiscation of property and public executions) must not be applied to capitalists in the cities. Zhou Enlai asked that local Party chiefs publicize the Party policy of protecting urban capitalists, so that the national bourgeoisie would cooperate with the new regime "for a long time to come."

Mao, Zhou, and the others had been pondering how to handle Beijing once they came to power. They knew the tactics that had been so successful in winning the peasants would not do for the more sophisticated metropolis.[19]

By 3:00 P.M. Mao had gotten to Zhuoxian, a junction point on the railroad south of Beijing. There he met Chief of Staff Ye Jianying and Teng Daiyuan, who had come out from Beijing. Ye reported that all was going smoothly in the old capital. No problem with saboteurs.

There had been no incidents. Communist troops were patrolling the Legation Quarter. The city was quiet and peaceful. Mao's special train waited until 2:00 A.M., March 25, before starting;[20] the security men thought a night passage would be safer.

Mao's mind was busy with problems of the new order. He told his associates, as they remembered, that the most urgent task was to "learn how to administer urban affairs" and how to conduct "economic work." Mao's words would echo down the decades. Forty years later the prime concern of Deng Xiaoping would be economic and urban affairs, and there would be massive evidence that neither Deng nor his critics, be they reactionary stalwarts or idealistic students, had learned these lessons well. The Party leadership both in 1949 and in 1989 was rooted in the countryside, not the cities. It was commanded by men who knew the Chinese peasant but were strangers in Beijing and Shanghai. As one urban Party chief put it in 1988, "They are all peasants. They think that if people have a cement floor instead of a baked mud one on which to sleep they should be happy."[21]

As the train moved through Beijing's western outskirts, Mao's eyes stared out the window. Turning to his companions, he offered a glimpse of his thoughts. More than thirty years had passed since he had first come to Beijing, seeking "the truth to save the country and the people," as he said. He was lucky, he recalled, to have met Li Dazhao, "a good true person" who had been very kind to him and "who had been my teacher in the full sense of the word." A revealing remark. Li Dazhao had been librarian of Beijing University when Mao arrived in 1918 and had given the penniless student a job as a clerk, in which he sorted books, brought them to readers, returned them to the stacks. Li Dazhao was China's first Marxist and, with Mao, a founder and leader of the early Communist Party. It was Li Dazhao's primitive notion of Marxist theory that Mao embedded in what later came to be called Mao Zedong Thought.[22]

Mao got off the train at 11:00 A.M. at the Qinghua station, just south of the Summer Palace and the Fragrant Hills. Here he was met by Lin Biao and Nie Rongzhen, commanders of the North China Military Area; Peng Zhen, secretary of the Beijing Party (and forty years later, past the age of ninety, still a power in the city); and Li Kenong, the security officer who had made the arrangements.

Mao drove to the Summer Palace in a bullet-proof Dodge limousine made in Detroit for Chiang Kaishek in the 1930s. At the palace Ye Jianying, one of China's great military leaders, later defense minister and key man in the downfall of the Gang of Four and the rise of Deng Xiaoping, offered lunch to Mao in the Great Hall of the Palace of Benevolent Longevity. Here behind a silken screen, near the end of the nineteenth century, the old dowager empress Ci Xi had received visitors and ruled China.[23]

At five that afternoon Mao drove over to Xiyuan Airport. He had changed from the bullet-proof Dodge to a captured olive-drab U.S. jeep. As a band played *"Qi Lai"* (Rise Up, or The March of the Volunteers), Mao took the salute of infantry, artillery, and armored and tank troops. A mortar battery set the sky over the Western Hills ablaze with five hundred star shells.[24]

When the fireworks died away Mao had dinner with representatives of non-Communist democratic parties. He was worried about support and eager to enlist the non-Communists and lure them into a coalition government. They talked until midnight about a future government embracing Communist and non-Communist elements.

That night Mao slept for the first time in Shuang Jing, the Villa of the Two Wells, just below the great Xiangshan Temple. The villa was very quiet. Its compound once had been known as the "garden within the garden."[25] Mao was a night owl. Filled with the day's excitement, looking at Beijing's lights from the terrace of his villa, he had little inclination for sleep. There was so much to think about — the village of Shaoshan, deep in the Hunan countryside, where he had been born in 1893; his greedy peasant father, an arrogant man clawing his way upward, a grain merchant and a moneylender; his devout Buddhist mother, who brought him into her traditional faith; the Long March, in which he had led his armies over six thousand miles in the grueling retreat of 1934–35, over, as he had said, ten thousand rivers and one thousand mountains; the battles with Japan; and the victories against Chiang Kaishek. Just ahead awaited the full triumph of Communist power in China.

Mao's guards had stacked beside his bed the volumes that he was reading. He picked up *The General Mirror for the Aid of Government* and began to turn the pages. He had passed through the old capital that day. It had been called Peking — Beijing in the pinyin transliteration — for a millennium. But under the Nationalists it went by the name of Peiping, Northern Peace. Already it had won back its old name. It was Beijing, the Northern Capital. A small start. There were so many lessons he must study about how to rule China. Fortunately, he had the ancients and the wisdom of all of China's emperors to guide him.[26]

2

The Poet
of the Fragrant Hills

BEFORE MAO LEFT XIBAIPO he had made a decision — he would plant his new red banner in China's historic capital of Beijing, the old capital, as he called it. Today Mao's decision seems inevitable, but the choice was not obvious in 1949, and it set in train historical and social consequences of a magnitude that cannot easily be quantified.

China has had many emperors and many capitals. Chiang Kaishek made his headquarters at Nanjing, the traditional southern capital. Mao was strongly attracted to Nanjing. He confessed that he would have liked to live at Wuxi, halfway between Nanjing and Shanghai. The soft Nanjing climate was more suitable to his taste than Beijing's winter dust and cold. But he rejected Nanjing because he saw it as too dangerous, the seat of American power in China. Beijing was not the only alternative, however. Chiang had moved his wartime capital to Chongqing, on the cliffs of the Yangtze, far from Japanese threat. Some two thousand years earlier Emperor Qin had unified China and put his capital at Chang-an, present-day Xian. Dr. Sun Yatsen had set up shop at Canton.

The choice of a capital is no light thing. Peter the Great of Russia built St. Petersburg and moved his capital there from Moscow to dramatize Russia's opening to the West. The American founding fathers invented the capital of Washington as a visible symbol of their new republic.

There was debate among Mao's comrades over where to put the capital of New China. Some were opposed to Beijing. But Mao stood firm. He had based his choice on the legitimacy Beijing gave him. Over centuries the capital had returned to Beijing again and again. In the days of Kublai Khan and Marco Polo, Beijing was the capital, with the name of Dadu. During the Liao dynasty (986–1135) it had been called Yenching.

The argument against Beijing was ideological. Opponents felt that New China should make a clean break with the old. Beijing's traditions would taint the Revolution. The nation should start afresh. Some even proposed Lanzhou, the emerging industrial center to the north, close to the Soviet frontier.

But these lines of reasoning seemed to most of the leaders theoretical. Lanzhou was hundreds of miles from railheads. Its connections with the rest of China were weak. The opposition to Beijing petered out, but it left a vague sense of unease among thoughtful Mao supporters, a twinge, perhaps, of memory of new dynasties that wound up so much like the old.[1]

There is no evidence that Mao considered these ideas. The factor that tipped the scales, some associates believed, was Mao's fear that the United States might intervene and try to crush the infant Communist state in its cradle, as England and France had tried to stifle Lenin's Soviet in its swaddling clothes.

American military might cast a strong shadow over China in Mao's mind and would continue to do so over the years. Mao interpreted the mission of General George C. Marshall to mediate between the Nationalists and the Communists in 1945–46 as a hypocritical U.S. maneuver to bring Chiang Kaishek into power. Mao believed that American airlifts in support of Chiang and American transfers of arms and military matériel were part of the pattern. He felt certain that at some point the United States would intervene on the Asian continent — as so many influential Americans, especially Republicans, were demanding — and try to settle the score with the Communists.

Mao's fears were fanned by Josef Stalin, who warned Mao repeatedly to beware of America's might. Prudence, thus, as well as tradition, dictated to Mao that he pick Beijing. It was close to the Soviet border, a flight of only two to three hours. Better play it safe.

Publicly, Mao had sailed in the face of the American threat and, in effect, thumbed his nose at Stalin's warnings as well. In 1946, when Chiang Kaishek began preparing an all-out drive against the Communists, Stalin urged Mao to enter into a coalition with Chiang and take a secondary role. Resistance, Stalin contended, might lead to World War III. For many years Stalin had demonstrated his preference for Chiang, as Mao bitterly knew. Stalin had supported Chiang even after he turned on the Communists in the 1927 massacre at Shanghai.

Only with the greatest reluctance had Stalin shifted his backing from Chiang Kaishek in Shanghai to the Communists and left-wingers in Wuhan. During the United Front period of the 1930s, Stalin sent Chiang planes, arms, and military advisers (some of whom had escaped the 1927 massacre by a hair's breadth). To Mao he sent only a planeload of propaganda leaflets. When Hitler attacked the Soviets in June 1941, Stalin asked Mao to down arms against Chiang and launch a suicide offensive against Japan in Manchuria. Mao refused.[2]

Mao had no illusions about whom Stalin preferred. As a contemporary Soviet historian commented: "Stalin favored a two-Chinas policy." Stalin felt Chiang was weak and posed no danger to Moscow. He did not trust Mao.

In 1946 Mao had ignored Stalin's advice to avoid conflict with Chiang.[3] Mao paid no heed to a proposal from Stalin that he turn over to Chiang U.S. military supplies that fell into his hands (but the Soviets did turn over vast stores to Chiang).[4] Mao kept all the U.S. stores he could grab. They helped him mightily.

Now, despite (or was it because of?) the success of Mao's armies, Stalin made a last-minute effort to keep them from destroying Chiang. Around year's end 1948, he sent Anastas Mikoyan to Xibaipo with a message asking Mao to halt at the Yangtze; let Chiang have south China. It was too dangerous to wipe him out. If Mao destroyed Chiang, the United States would come in and world war would break out. Mao must remember that America still had military personnel in China.

Mao was not moved. He laid out his plans to Mikoyan. They were so good they won Mikoyan over (or so Mao thought) and were bound to convince Stalin (they didn't).[5] As if to remove all doubt of his intentions, Mao published a New Year's declaration on December 30, 1948, saying that China would "never take pity" on Chiang Kaishek and his "snakelike scoundrels": "No one is [our] true friend who guilefully says that pity should be shown." The only course, he said, was to destroy the Nationalists and expel the "aggressive forces of U.S. imperialism."[6] Nothing could be more blunt.

This is the version that Mao gave to his associates, according to General Yang Shangkun, for many years director of the General Office of the Communist Party and by 1988 China's president.[7] Yang remembered Mikoyan's coming to Xibaipo "after the three major campaigns," which would place his visit in late December 1948 or early January 1949. Mao, said President Yang, had emphasized his determination by his New Year's declaration. He would cross the Yangtze and follow Chiang wherever he fled, expel him from the mainland or exterminate him.

Professor Wang Fangming of Beijing People's University heard Mao make the following remarks in 1957 and recorded his words:

> Even in 1949 when we were about to cross the Yangtze River, *someone* [emphasis added] still wanted to prevent us. According to him we should under no circumstances cross the Yangtze. If we did so America would send troops to China and become directly involved in China's Civil War and the South and North dynasties would reappear in China.
>
> I did not listen to what they [sic] said. We crossed the Yangtze. America did not send troops to China and there were no South and North dynasties. If we really had followed his words surely there would be a situation of South and North dynasties.
>
> Later on I met that person who intended to prevent us from crossing the Yangtze. His first words in our conversation were: "The victor bears no blame."
>
> I had not listened to him. As a result he not only did not blame me. On the contrary, he recognized me as the victor. It is very important that one should analyze and solve problems on one's own and always seek truth from facts.

The "someone" to whom Mao referred was, of course, Stalin.[8]

Perhaps Stalin's opposition to Mao's plans was the reason that the Soviet Union, alone among the foreign powers, sent its ambassador along with Chiang when he fled Nanjing, his capital. All the other ambassadors remained in Nanjing in preparation for Mao's takeover.[9] As Mao himself told André Malraux, "The Russians' feelings were for Chiang Kaishek. When he escaped from China, the Soviet ambassador was the last person to wish him goodbye."[10]

Independent Mao was; foolhardy he was not. There was a chance that Stalin might be right about the Americans. Far safer to take some precautions in setting up the new regime. Mao would set up his new capital in Beijing, where he could make a quick getaway if needed. After plans for the new government were approved at a plenary session of the Seventh Party Congress at Xibaipo, March 5 to 13, 1949, Mao took out a little more insurance against the American threat.[11]

John Leighton Stuart, the U.S. ambassador, had remained behind in Nanjing, like all the other ambassadors. With Mao's approval, and probably at the instigation of Zhou Enlai, Stuart was invited back to Beijing for commencement exercises at Yenching University, of which he had been president.

Stuart told Yenching he would be delighted to come if the Communists would permit his trip, and he asked Washington for permission to go. Stuart hoped this would give him an opportunity for informal talks with the Communists and suspected this was what Zhou Enlai and Mao desired. (He was right.) But Washington vetoed the trip. Stuart was told he must have nothing to do with the Communists, officially or unofficially.[12]

One more very unofficial move was made. The U.S. consul-general, O. Edmund Clubb, had remained in Beijing. He received private word that Zhou wanted to meet with him. The hint was so vague Clubb never felt sure that it was real. In the end nothing came of it.

Once the devilish winds of spring had blown away the dust, Mao could see from the Xiangshan Temple compound all the way to the beautiful marble-posted bridge over which Marco Polo and early travelers passed, entering Beijing from the southwest. Close by stood the dreamlike White Cloud Temple, the Taoist shrine where travelers stopped to refresh themselves before entering the imperial capital.

Of the temple, it was said:

> There are three monkeys who cannot see their faces
> There is a bridge but no water
> There are windows but they do not open
> There is a tablet but no words
> There is a mirror but you cannot see your face
> There is a gate but no one passes through.

It was a riddle Mao had known from early days. He also knew it was a riddle that had no answer.

A stone's throw from Mao's retreat stood the Summer Palace and Kunming Lake, where the dowager empress Ci Xi in the 1890s built a marble frigate instead of using the funds, as appropriated, to outfit a navy to oppose the European squadrons.

In April and May 1949, while Mao was enjoying this dynastic splendor, the north slopes of the Fragrant Hills, as an American woman wrote, shimmered in "white with blossoming fruit trees, breathtakingly lovely." But it was over "so quick you must be there at the right moment; one day they are scarcely open and two or three days later the wind has caught them and the branches are bare."[13]

Mao was a poet as well as a politician; a philosopher as well as a polemicist. His days should have been filled with military calculations, political arrangements, and prosaic details of creating a new Communist government. But this was not entirely true. His poetry gave an insight into the mind of this revolutionary with his deep-set, aching eyes. A month after he took up residence in the Villa of the Two Wells, a month after he had begun to stroll in Emperor Qian Long's Garden of Peacefulness and sit in the Retreat for Revealing the Mind, Mao wrote some lines to an old friend and fellow poet, Liu Yazu, with whom he had last exchanged poems in wartime Chongqing, in 1944.[14] Liu Yazu was turning his back on Mao's revolution and thinking of going back to his home village and spending his life in contemplation, just as had the classic poet Yan Guang, of the later Han dynasty, who had retired to the Fuchan River and become a fisherman.

Don't do it, Mao implored his friend. In this "season of falling flowers" (as the eighth-century poet Tu Fu had called spring), Mao wrote that he had returned to Beijing after thirty-one years, back to "the old capital." Look to the future, Mao urged his friend, "range your eyes over long vistas." It was better to watch the fish at play in Kunming Lake than in the far-off Fuchan River.[15]

For hundreds of years the mountains, the vistas, the flowers, the legends, of the Fragrant Hills had inspired poets and refreshed emperors. Spring in the Hills was long and cool, a parade of blossoms. Toward the end of April, winter jasmine and the rosy petals of peaches painted the face of Longevity Hill. Then came the white drift of plums and the pinkish petals of the almonds, flowering crabapples, and intoxicating lilacs. It was a time for slow walks on paths carved out centuries ago, a time for lovers to stroll hand in hand, a time for romance, a time for dreams.

Mao tarried. His words to Liu Yazu might have been directed to himself. This was a delicious moment in a life as dramatic as any Mao read of in his favorite historical work, *Romance of the Three Kingdoms*. Not only did Mao tarry because of the scenic vistas, but because romance seems to have entered his life, perhaps for the last time. He showed no inclination of abandoning the Fragrant Hills. He may even have toyed with the idea of making his capital there. He journeyed to Beijing rarely, for obligatory meetings, but hurried back to the alluring atmosphere of the cool mountaintop, the half-ruined temples — and his new inamorata. These enticements held him fast week after week, and not until November did he abandon his poetic life and come down to Beijing to take up an emperor's role in Zhongnanhai.[16]

3

"Don't Underestimate
That Little Fellow"

NOT FOR LIU BOCHENG, Deng Xiaoping, Chen Yi, Nie Rongzhen, and Mao's field commanders the romance of the Fragrant Hills. Deng Xiaoping had not seen Mao since Xibaipo in early 1949. He was not in Beijing when Lin Biao led the Red Army on its triumphal entry into the city. The field commanders were too busy fighting Chiang Kaishek's Kuomintang (KMT) to relax amidst the settings of empire. During the winter and spring of 1948–49, Deng Xiaoping hardly had time to change his rumpled tunic, saturated with sweat and powder smoke.

The Red Army did not possess a commander smaller than Deng. He stood less than five feet high, shorter than Napoleon. In his early Party photographs he looks like a schoolboy, but by 1949 he was coordinating the Central Front in the biggest battles ever fought in China. They changed the course of China's history and the lives of hundreds of millions. As Zhang Zhen, president of the National Defense University in Beijing in 1988 and a member of the Huai-Hai command staff in 1949, recollected: "We captured enough KMT generals to form two companies of infantry."[1]

During an argument in 1957 with Nikita Khrushchev, Mao Zedong pointed to Deng and warned the Soviet leader, "Don't underestimate that little fellow. He destroyed an army of one million of Chiang's best troops." Then Mao added: "He has a bright future ahead of him."[2]

As 1949 opened, that "little fellow" and his Central Plains Army were completing the feat to which Mao referred, the destruction of 25 Nationalist corps, 5 armies, and 56 divisions in sixty-six days.[3] Between September 12, 1948, and January 11, 1949, the Communists destroyed 1.5 million Nationalist troops — 12 armies and 149 divisions.[4]

Deng was then and would continue for years to be a favorite lieutenant of Mao's, both in war and in peace. He remained relatively unknown abroad because he fought distant battles and in peacetime was deep in the countryside waging industrial campaigns, often top-secret ones. Year by year his responsibilities and his reputation grew inside, if not outside, China.

It would be a mistake, however, to suppose that before the estab-lishment of the People's Republic he was regarded as a likely successor to Mao Zedong. Any poll of popular opinion would have produced a consensus on Zhou Enlai or Liu Shaoqi as a more likely successor. A bit earlier there might have been some votes for Zhu De, because of his towering popularity and his military prowess. Deng was seen as a promising figure but of a younger generation.

In the days before Beijing, Mao did not stand on ceremony. He and his men — Zhu De, his alter ego in "Zhu Mao," a bluff bear of a man; the little jumping jack Deng Xiaoping; the jovial One-Eyed Liu; Chen Yi, a man so brave he once roped himself to a tree so he would not shake with pain while he poured Tiger Balm medicine into a putrid wound in his thigh; and the enigmatic Lin Biao — had fought together since the late 1920s. They had made the Long March. They were, as the survivors attested, a band of brothers. Mao was the elder brother, not yet a Jove hurling bolts of lightning. They had lined up to piss together after a banquet or a battle, Lin Biao standing a bit to one side. They had dropped their pants and squatted in a row, emptying their bowels over a muddy ditch, Mao's veins bulging from his temples as he strained against chronic constipation.

Mao's bowel problems were severe, and they had political as well as physical consequences. When Mao's constipation had not been relieved for four or five days he became testy and irritable. His frus-tration caused him to strike back sharply. His target could be a close aide or a foreign envoy.

Mao's bodyguards knew his bowel problems intimately. Often he was so constipated they had to put their fingers up his anus and pry his feces out. Mao preferred to go out to the fields alone to relieve himself. Toilets were "too stinky," he complained. His chief body-guard, Li Yinqiao, noticed that when Mao went into the fields he often picked up a piece of human sewage, which was used as fertilizer, and smelled it before squatting down. The guard couldn't understand Mao's action.

"Well," Mao told him, "I like to sit and think while I'm relieving myself. If it smells too bad I can't think."[5]

It took a good battle, Mao used to say, to loosen his gut. In Yanan when after eight or nine days Mao's frustration came to an end, word would spread: "The chairman's bowels have moved! He has had a good shit!" But Mao's trouble seemed to ease after a great upholstered chair encasing a Western porcelain toilet bowl was installed in his quarters at Zhongnanhai.[6]

Relations among these men were easy. The veteran general Su Yu conceived the Huai-Hai campaign but on its eve asked Mao to appoint someone with more experience to lead the battle. Mao put One-Eyed Liu and Deng Xiaoping in charge and added Chen Yi and his Third Communist Field Army to beef up the force. No hard feelings. In those days Deng could tell Mao that his plan for an offensive must be changed because the selected terrain was too marshy, the troops would bog down. Mao accepted that. "Mao was quite modest," General Zhang Zhen recalled, marveling a bit that this could have been true. "He took the advice of his commanders." This attitude would vanish in the mid-1950s.

It was a rough-hewn company; almost all except the suave and brilliant Zhou Enlai had their roots in peasant China. That was one reason they moved so effectively over China's vast spaces. Later, as Mao sensed on the approach to Beijing, that peasant heritage would reveal a negative side.

Some commanders came from well-off rural families, like Mao and Deng. Chen Yi once told an American that he didn't have a proletarian background. "The others will tell you they came from the peasantry or urban poverty; I come from the bourgeoisie and I'm not going to hide that." Others, like Zhu De and tough old Peng Dehuai, knew the brutal face of starvation, slavery, beatings, and opium.

A few of the leaders had seen a bit of the world (mostly the factory slums of Paris and Berlin) and gotten a whiff of Bolshevism in the early heady days in Moscow, but Mao was not one of them. He had helped organize a work-study group for France but had left his comrades at pier side, staying behind in China. Why was never quite clear — lack of money, lack of confidence, a deep instinct that China, not Europe, was his world, a sense so common to Chinese that China *was* the world.

Mao's men had won their spurs in battle. Whatever their titles, they were actually military commanders. They had braved death a hundred times. Some had started life as mercenaries in warlord armies and then joined Mao's Red Army. They were the backbone of the Communist movement. They lived in a military world and they followed military rules. An order was an order. It was to be obeyed precisely and instantly. No questions. Later on, after the battle, questions could be asked. The fierce discipline of Mao's commanders was reinforced by that of the Communist Party, to which they all belonged.

These were men who had earned their positions under fire. They served the Party, and the Party served them. If they were wounded, the Party made every effort to save their life. If they died, it cared for their family. If they were captured, it tried to rescue them on the battlefield. If not rescued, a commander took his own life rather than reveal secrets under torture. They were bound by an oath of secrecy as binding as the Sicilian *omertà*.

Their oath was holy, and it admitted them to the sanctum sanctorum of the order. The word of the Party was supreme and Mao was its oracle. Therein lay the strength of the movement. And its weakness.

But Mao was not yet sacrosanct. Before a decision or after a battle questions could be, and were, raised by these tough soldiers. They had not — yet — suspended judgment on ordinary matters. Had they not been realistic, observant men they could not have won their battles. But they were good soldiers. They obeyed even the mistaken orders and argued afterward. They supported each other. The rule was one for all and all for one. That was the brotherhood. In spite of terrible casualties on the Long March among men and lower officers, the top men and women, the cadres, as the Party called its professionals, suffered an astonishingly low death rate.

These were men who had begun their careers as mountain guerrillas or in the jungle of the Shanghai underground. A single false move, an incautious word, meant death. They had come through the six thousand miles of the Long March, sometimes so ill they were carried over cliffs and down hills in litters, sometimes tied to a mule's back. They had sat at Mao's feet in Yanan and relearned the catechism of his Communism until they could recite it in a sleep-drugged coma. They had fought the Japanese. They had been booby-trapped by Chiang Kaishek's men. They had survived. They were not merely brothers — they were blood brothers. They formed a quasireligious order like the Knights of Malta, all for the goal of revolution.

Now these bullet-tempered men were coming to the end of their battlefield crusade and about to tackle the complex chores of directing the world's largest nation, one steeped in ignorance, superstition, and medieval ways, beset by every disease known to man (and some never before seen by modern physicians), illiterate, with millions and tens of millions having lived in slavery or its equivalent for thousands of years.

Mao had some glimmer of the task. Not so his generals. Their confidence was founded on winning battles, not solving thousand-year-old problems. No one knew the strength of unity and discipline better than Mao. The Revolution had almost been wrecked by the split between Mao and the Russians in the late twenties and early thirties. Mao had won that battle and stamped his philosophy on Party and army (indistinguishable at that time). He had won another battle for leadership, over Zhang Guotao, at the end of the Long March. All his days Mao believed Zhang Guotao, leader of the rival Fourth Field Army, would have deposed and killed him had not Mao swiftly slipped from his grasp. Walking with American journalist Edgar Snow in Yanan in 1937, Mao pointed to Bo Gu, who had deposed Mao as Party leader five years earlier (and been deposed in turn by Mao in 1935), and said: "That man tried to kill me." And, speaking to body-guard Li Yinqiao in July 1948, he pointed to Wang Ming, an associate of Bo Gu's and leader of the Moscow-oriented faction of the Chinese Communist Party, and said: "He wanted to kill me."[7]

The impressions of what Mao believed was a life-and-death struggle for control of the Party never left him. He had spent much time at Yanan reimposing his views on his comrades in a rigorous "rectification campaign."

Unity, unity, unity. This was Mao's credo. Now, with the Party and the army taking over all of China, and Mao preparing to pick up the reins of government in late 1949, he felt more wary than ever. By absorbing millions of Chiang's soldiers into the Red Army (now called the People's Liberation Army), he would dilute discipline and Party strength.

Nationalists, Japanese, and warlords had run the country for years. There were a hundred different attitudes among the population. Assuming control of China was not like taking over a peasant village or a peasant province. Here were urban metropolises marching to different drums, capitalists, bourgeoisie, intellectuals of every variety, small traders, professionals, soldiers.

The need was obvious: Discipline. Don't take chances. China was a new and dangerous sea, not the comfortable countryside where everything was so familiar. Mao and his men must hang together or they would hang separately.

If these were the concerns of Mao, they were far from the mind of Deng Xiaoping, busy writing orders for the last big campaign, the crossing of the Yangtze, the water barrier that divided the wheat-and-steamed-bun north from the rice-bowl south, for the drive to seize Chiang's capital of Nanjing and for the capture of the international city of Shanghai.

In these days convoy after convoy of Nationalist trucks rolled to the wharves of Nanjing. Chiang and his generals were pulling out and packing their gold and their concubines, their troops and their guns, onto riverboats that silently slipped downstream in the night.

On April 21, 1949, Mao issued his first proclamation from Beijing (he was, of course, still in the Fragrant Hills). It was a summons to the army to "advance bravely and annihilate resolutely, thoroughly, wholly and completely all the Kuomintang reactionaries within China's territory and sovereignty." Then he added: "Pay special attention to arresting the bandit chieftain Chiang Kaishek."

For twenty years Chiang had called Mao and his men bandits and put a price on their heads as though they were robbers and pickpockets. Mao did not forget or forgive.[8]

Even before the fog lifted on the morning of April 21, hundreds of thousands of troops from Liu Bocheng and Deng's Second and Chen Yi's Third Communist Field armies were clambering into dinghies, sailboats, junks, barges, rafts, and paddle wheelers and crossing the Yangtze on a three-hundred-mile front stretching from a point northeast of Nanchang to Jiangyin, ninety miles upstream from Shanghai.

Deng observed the operations through his field glasses. In the words of a Chinese commentator, it was a crossing "unprecedented in history." All of south China now lay open to the Communists. Chiang had threatened to destroy the dikes to prevent the crossing, an action that would have drowned hundreds of thousands and, by wiping out the rice crop, condemned millions to starvation. Instead he ran away. Nanjing surrendered on April 24 without a fight. Hangzhou fell on May 5, Nanchang on May 22.

But Shanghai, Chiang Kaishek swore, would be different. His forces concentrated there. The troops built a wooden wall fifteen miles long around the city, ten feet high and an inch or two thick. Foreigners mocked it as the "Great Wall of Shanghai." West of the city, houses and buildings along Hongqiao Road were cleared for "a field of fire." You could save your house from destruction only by a well-placed bribe.

Proclamation after proclamation announced the city would be defended to the death. Political prisoners — and ordinary citizens — were executed in public squares, maybe six hundred in all. But Chen Yi's Third Field Army moved in steadily, and by May 14 the city was encircled. Nationalist troops and officers began evacuating by ship to Taiwan. On May 24 the manager of the Columbia Country Club, on Shanghai's outskirts, telephoned a friend that there was rifle fire around the tennis courts. "I guess I'll have my tiffin on the front lines," he said.[9] Next day, the Nationalists held a "victory parade" along the Bund, army trucks and soldiers, soon to vanish aboard ship for Taiwan. Amos Landman, an American reporter, drove on May 26 down Nanking Road, Shanghai's main street. He passed four or five trucks of Nationalist soldiers parked outside the Wing On department store. A block farther around a curve he found six or eight soldiers, weary, uniforms grimy, huddled in a doorway. They were the *ba lu*, the PLA, inching forward. Neither group knew that only two hundred yards separated them.

Later that day a brief, fierce encounter erupted at the Garden Bridge across Soochow Creek, right at the little park famous for its sign "Chinese and Dogs Not Allowed." Shots rang out. Some Nationalist fire whizzed into the office of American consul-general John Cabot. Cabot was indignant. The Nationalists, he growled, should have known that the American consul-general was not harboring Communist snipers. Shanghai's conquest was completed on May 27 — the greatest city in China was now in Communist hands.[10] The triumph of Mao and the defeat of Chiang were established. The advance had been so fast that Liu Bocheng, Deng Xiaoping, and the Second Field Army had hardly been able to keep pace. Now they began to shift emphasis and muster the forces to clean up China's great southwest. This would take a little time, but by December 10, 1949, Chiang had abandoned the mainland and fled to his refuge in Taiwan.

4

The Sunshine Boy

IT IS INTRIGUING to speculate that the paths of Mao Zedong and Deng Xiaoping might have crossed in childhood. There were similarities in the background of Mao and his energetic lieutenant. Both grew up in backcountry China under better-than-normal conditions. Both came of well-to-do families and got better educations than the average rural boy.

But their home villages were situated several hundred miles apart, Mao's in Hunan and Deng's in northern Sichuan. They spoke different dialects, and at the turn of the century the villages might have been on opposite sides of the Pacific Ocean as far as contact was concerned.

There were no roads leading to Shaoshan, Mao's village, nor to Paifangcun, the hamlet outside Guang'an town where Deng was born. There was hardly a road in all of Sichuan and Hunan — only narrow footpaths up and down the mountains, "little roads," as the Chinese called them. Every bag of rice, every catty of grain, had to be carried on the back of a man or a woman or, sometimes, a mule.

Mao and Deng were not typical country boys. Mao's father was on the rise. Two generations earlier the Mao family had been poor and landless in the clan village of Shaoshan, where everyone's name was Mao.[1] Mao's grandfather had begun to climb, and Mao's father, as money-grubbing, tight-fisted a peasant as could be found in all of China (the kind the Russians called *kulaks,* or fists), was bursting out of his low class.

It is possible that Mao's forebears had been more prosperous in the deep past. An elaborate family tree tracing Mao's ancestry to the Yuan dynasty was compiled during his lifetime but kept secret for years after his death. It purports to follow the Mao line back to a warrior named Mao Dehua, who settled during the Ming dynasty in Hunan Province, in Xiangxiang County, adjacent to Mao's birthplace of Shaoshan. Two of Mao's closest collaborators — Liu Shaoqi and the great old warrior Peng Dehuai, both harried to terrible deaths in the Cultural Revolution — were born in the same area. The Mao genealogy presents him as a twentieth-generation descendant of Mao Dehua. There is no reason to believe that the Mao family tree has any more basis than the charts offered at ten dollars to show you are descended from the "Kings of Ireland." But Mao seems to have possessed the same yearning for roots as many American immigrants.

The Mao genealogy, however, is much more elaborate than the embossed scripts proclaiming a link to the kings of Ireland. It comes in twenty volumes and was originally put together during the reign of the famous Qing emperor Qian Long (1736–96), he of the Fragrant Concubine. The earlier version of the document traced the Mao family to the son of the emperor Zhou Wen, a prince named Mao Bozhang. There are only about one hundred family names in China. Of China's 1.2 billion population probably 200 million are named Mao. The commercial possibilities of selling Mao genealogies are apparent.

Mao kept his genealogy under lock and key during his lifetime, but in 1988 the Jilin People's Publishing House published it for the first time.[2] Mao once said he thought his family originally came from northern Shaanxi.[3]

Mao's father expanded the family's landholdings. He became a moneylender and grain merchant. He squeezed his neighbors. He was illiterate, tough, grasping, mean-spirited, and domineering. Before his death he had amassed 10,000 silver dollars in addition to his property, a fortune in those days, and a tidy sum in China twelve years after his son's death.[4] He envisioned his young son as a bookkeeper and partner; he needed someone who could read and write, do the accounts, and figure the usurious interest.

Mao grew up hating his father, sympathizing with his mother, educating himself in his own way, becoming a teacher and almost a scholar. He was not a happy youngster. He was brooding, talented, ambitious, and a Chinese patriot, at war with his father, at war with the world, and at war with himself. He was twenty-three years old before he heard of Karl Marx. His first hero was the great American guerrilla George Washington, from whom he learned some of the tactics that he used in the Long March. Mao's bodyguards called him Lao Tu, the Old Peasant. Mao didn't mind that. He said: "I am *tu*. I am too vulgar. I am the son of peasants and I have the peasants' living habits."[5]

*   *   *

Deng grew up in a region just as isolated as Shaoshan. But he was born into a totally different kind of family. The Dengs had some inherited wealth and, more important, cherished a tradition of scholarship, public service, and leadership. They had been responsible citizens for generations.

Deng was a happy child. No one remembered him sulking, no one remembered him rebelling against anything. He was a sunshine boy, bright, happy-go-lucky, smart at his lessons. All Chinese children have a string of names. Deng's reflected him in the mirror of his father's eyes. His formal name was Xiansheng, which means To Be a Saint. His birth name was Xixian, which means Hoping to Be a Saint. His nickname was Xianwa, Good Boy.[6] A saint he was not, but everyone remembered him as a good boy.

Deng's family was in the old-fashioned patriarchal style of the Chinese rural gentry. The firstborn son was the heir apparent, the paragon of virtues in his parents' eyes. The earliest recollection some townsfolk had of Deng was of him turning somersaults. At the age of seven or eight he would somersault from the courtyard of the Deng house down the worn footpath almost all the way from Paifangcun to Xie Xing, perhaps a li (about a quarter mile) distant. Then he would turn around and somersault back home, his small body going end over end, sometimes vanishing in the deep ruts.

Deng loved to climb the memorial arch at the entrance to Paifangcun. He would shinny up the columns and wave from the top. Paifangcun, Village of the Arch, was named after this monument.

No trace of the arch remained in 1988. It had been dedicated to the memory of Deng's ancestor Deng Shimin, five generations back. Deng Shimin won the rank of Hanlin scholar in the imperial examinations, which meant entrance to the Hanlin Academy and close relations with the imperial court and even the emperor. This occurred during the reign of Emperor Qian Long, and the arch bore a plaque with an inscription in the emperor's own brushwork. But arch and plaque vanished in 1966 when Red Guards descended on peaceful Paifangcun, intent on destroying every relic of the "Olds," particularly those related to Deng Xiaoping, who had taken, in Mao's words, the "capitalist road" and betrayed the Revolution. The arch had been smashed, the plaque hurled into a ditch, and the very name of the village wiped out. A sign proclaiming the village to be the "Anti-Revisionist

Brigade" went up. In 1988 neither the arch nor the plaque had been restored but, as I found on a visit, once again it had become the Village of the Arch.

From the mid-eighteenth century the Deng family had been first in the village. The Dengs had migrated to remote north Sichuan from Jiangxi or Guangdong during the Ming dynasty. They were Hakka, or guest people, displaced from their native lands.[7]

In the nineteenth century the family had fallen in economic status but lived in a comfortable gentry house, still standing in 1988. It differed little in style from the Mao home in Shaoshan. Each had packed earthen floors. The Deng home as seen in recent years is a one-story house with a main section and two parallel wings at right angles, a pleasant, spacious dwelling.

The Dengs were a traditional Chinese family. Deng's father, Deng Wenming, had four wives. The first, named Zhang, bore no children. She was still alive when Deng Wenming took his second wife, named Dan, the mother of Deng Xiaoping.

Deng Xiaoping was born in 1904 in a graceful mahogany bed still standing in 1988 in the old house. He was the first son and second child of Deng Danshi (to give her the old-fashioned Chinese name of the time; in those days women took their husband's name, retaining their family name as a second name and adding to it the suffix "shi" to indicate it was a family name). Deng Danshi bore four children, all in the mahogany bed where she slept until her death, in 1927, of tuberculosis. The first child was Deng Xianli, Deng Xiaoping's older sister, living in Chongqing in 1989; then came Deng Xiaoping; and then his two natural brothers, Deng Ken, a Party man and a veteran of Yanan who later became mayor of Chongqing and vice governor of Wuhan, living there in retirement in 1990, and Deng Shiping, a suicide during the Cultural Revolution, one of the countless victims of that mindless anarchy.

When Deng's mother died, his father married again, this time to a woman named Xiao, who bore a son, Deng Xianqing. In 1988 he was working in the Sichuan provincial government office. Deng Xiaoshi died within three years, and Deng's father married for the fourth time, to Xia Bogan, who was to become an intimate member of the family of Deng Xiaoping. She bore three daughters. The first was Deng Xianfu, who was working on the Sichuan Provincial Party Committee in 1988. For a time she and her husband taught school at Guang'an

Middle School Number 2, which Deng Xiaoping had attended. The second daughter was Deng Xianrong, who died of illness in 1949. The third was Deng Xianjun, living in Beijing in 1989. In all there were eight children. The grandchildren are numerous.

Not far from the courtyard house in 1988 stood the carefully tended hillside tomb of Deng's mother, with an inscription by her sons, who had erected it (and later had repaired the damage done to it during the Cultural Revolution).[8]

Middle School Number 2 in Guang'an bulges with bright-eyed youngsters not too different from those with whom Deng studied seventy years earlier. The study hall where he pored over his books, a nook in an overhead passageway above the stone steps leading to the school, still stands.

By the twentieth century the Dengs no longer held Mandarin status, but Deng's father, Deng Wenming, was captain of the town militia, a literate man well liked by the townsfolk, dedicated to education, culture, and the betterment of China. He was no revolutionary, perhaps not even a liberal, and could easily have been painted as the prototype of the gendarmes upholding the imperial regime (as no doubt he would have been in primitive propaganda). But, in fact, he saw to the education of his children and encouraged them to take up the cause of China.

Deng's father was a religious man, a Buddhist but probably not so dedicated as was the mother of Mao Zedong. Like men of his class, the elder Deng made pilgrimages to Buddhist shrines, and Deng Xiaoping, like Mao, was raised as a Buddhist.

Although it is said that Deng's secondary-school grades have long been lost, his contemporaries remember him as brilliant and mischievous. His elderly uncle Dan Yixing, the brother of Deng's mother, called Deng "a very wise child." Sitting in 1988 in the sunshine beside three broody hens on the steps of his new home (he had lived in the old Deng house until 1987), Dan cleared his throat with a mighty hawk and declared that as a child Deng Xiaoping could read a book three times and recite it from memory. Yes indeed, Dan said, Deng was a very good boy.[9] An old schoolmate, Yang Erhe, eighty-six years old in 1988 but brisk and lucid, remembered Deng playing coin games with his younger brother, Yihe. Deng was very good at *bing ban ban* (heads or tails) and *ba peng qian* (hitting one coin with another). If you hit the coin you won it; if you missed you lost your fen. Deng got a lot more hits than misses.[10]

It was Deng's father and his uncle Deng Shaosheng who helped to put young Deng Xiaoping on the path that, with many a tumble from grace, finally led him to leadership of the New China.

The corner of Sichuan whence Deng sprang was like a picture postcard of Old China. The doors of the houses were protected against evil spirits by red-and-gold-painted fairytale champions, wielding swords and clad in armor, ready to battle any demons to the end. The houses were half plaster and half timber, a bit like those of medieval England. Haycocks were different from those elsewhere in China; they were shaped like shaggy haymen. It was a land of legend, of lazy warlords and slow streams, remote from the fierce winds of challenge springing up in China. But Deng was hardly into his teens when he was carried to the more lively channels of Chongqing and Chengdu.

Deng Xiaoping, like his brothers, was tutored at home. He went to Guang'an High School Number 2 as a boarding student in 1915, and late in 1916 took a small wooden boat, propelled by oarsmen, carrying a dozen passengers down the river Qu. The boat tied up at a wharf at night, and the passengers slept at inns.[11] After three days Deng arrived at Chongqing. He was accompanied by Deng Shaosheng. Deng spent some time in Chengdu, then settled down to study in a tutorial in Chongqing run by an old revolutionary, Wu Yuzhang, which prepared young Chinese for a work-study program in France.[12] For most students this program was an initiation into revolutionary activity. But if Deng took part in the famous May 4, 1919, student demonstrations that established the tradition of student movements and led straight to the 1989 Tiananmen manifestation, there is no record of it. Nor did his mentor, Mao Zedong, take part in this seminal event.

Deng learned a bit of French at the Chongqing school and in 1920 sailed with his uncle on the liner *André Lebon,* of the old Messageries Maritimes, for France. Deng didn't study much in France because he had to work hard to survive. He was employed at the Creusot Iron and Steel works and the Renault auto plant and as a locomotive fireman, though he was hardly as tall as his shovel. He lived on a glass of milk and a croissant a day (he thought his skimpy diet contributed to his short stature). He met Zhou Enlai, lived in his flat for a while, and became a Communist in 1925. In 1926 he went to Moscow, returning to China at the end of that year. When Deng represented China at a United Nations meeting in New York in 1974, he stopped off in Paris on his way back and bought a hundred croissants, which he took to Beijing for Zhou Enlai and other comrades of his Paris days.[13] Perhaps it was no accident that the Beijing Hotel began to serve croissants for breakfast after Deng came to power.

Deng's father was on intimate terms with Yang Sen, one of the three warlords who ruled Sichuan. Although a warlord, Yang Sen was also a fairly progressive man, almost a radical in the contemporary political landscape.[14] He firmly supported the reformist objectives of the day. He opposed traditional Chinese Confucianism and favored reform of education and learning from advanced Western society — all objectives inherent in Dr. Sun Yatsen's vision of the New China.

These goals were shared by Deng Wenming, a more progressive man than his warlord patron, and with the support of Yang Sen, he became chief of the county militia and ultimately leader of the militia of eight counties, commanding a force of more than seven hundred soldiers. The function of this force was to maintain law and order and protect the property and estates of the gentry. Deng's father was, in effect, high sheriff.[15]

There was more money now. The thatched roof of the courtyard house was replaced with tile, paid for, it was said, by townsfolk in recognition of Deng's father's service to the community. At this time eight or nine people lived in the Deng house, all members of the family.

When Rewi Alley, the longtime New Zealander sympathizer with the Chinese Communists, visited the house in 1981, it was jammed with nine families, numbering fifty-one individuals, including Deng Xiaoping's uncle Dan Yixing and his wife. In 1987 they were moved out, and the province undertook some rehabilitation preparatory to turning the building into a small museum. Dan Yixing was not happy about being moved out of the old homestead. He saw no sense in renovating the house. If they wanted to build a fine new brick house — well, that would make some sense.[16]

After the right wing of the house was taken down, money ran out and work stopped. Then a peasant from Gansu who had vastly benefited from Deng's policy of letting farmers make money came on a pilgrimage to Paifangcun and donated 5,000 yuan. The work was resumed.

Deng's father was remembered as kindly, thoughtful of his neighbors. He owned and worked about 80 mu (13 acres) of land, a goodly farm by local reckoning. Some land had to be sold after his death to pay funeral and other expenses. He was regarded as a learned man.

He had a good education, studied law and political science, and the family traditionally was a cultured one. Deng Senior had maintained good relations in Guang'an and the countryside, often visiting local teahouses and soliciting the views of all, whether they were rich or poor, peasants or landowners, officials, plain people, or gentry. He was remembered by his peers as well liked.

Deng Wenming's brother Shaosheng was equally well educated, as was a third brother, who took the lead in educational work and held a post in Chengdu. His career was handicapped because he became an opium addict.

When rumors circulated in 1933 that the Red Army was headed for Paifangcun and was killing all landlords, Deng's father took to his heels. But the Red Army failed to arrive, and he returned home. The Red Army force was Zhang Guotao's Fourth Army, not the First Front Army, in which Deng Xiaoping served.

In 1987, over the lintel of the Deng house, county officials put up a sign in red letters: "Deng Xiaoping's Old Home." On either side of the door they pasted long yellow and red strips of ceremonial paper on which an homage to Deng was inscribed. He had saved his country at a critical juncture, it said, and his great deeds would cast glory on Guang'an County "for thousands of years." His genius was proclaimed as having "defeated danger, overcome difficulty, stabilized the country and consolidated the nation."

"Longevity," declared the door strips, "for the great man is the wish of millions of people."

In Mao's time the door strips on countless peasant homes proclaimed:

You	You
Owe	Owe
Your	Your
Happy Life	Happiness
to	to
the Communist	Chairman
Party	Mao

Every word painted on Deng's door strips violated his own rule. Sickened by the deification of Mao, his glorification in song, in word, in statues, in portraits, Deng barred any cult of personality. His portrait was not permitted in public buildings. Pictures of him were not sold in shops. No political biographies were published. He gave no press interviews, and only on rare occasions did personal articles about him appear in the press.

But apparently he could not halt the local authorities from turning his old home into a shrine. Nor could he halt the people in Guang'an who carefully tended a garden laid out on a hillside centuries earlier by Wang De, a minister in the Ming dynasty who was dismissed and exiled to this spot. He lived quietly until the emperor realized he had made a mistake: Wang De, in fact an honest, able minister, was recalled to Beijing. People saw in him a parallel to Deng, who was dismissed by Mao and then recalled in 1973, when, as the people thought, Mao Zedong realized his mistake. Not an exact parallel, but close enough for the citizens of Guang'an.

The local people were fond of omens. They associated Deng's rise with the blooming of a century plant, a cactus shrub called *tie,* or iron tree, almost identical to its American cousin. It was supposed to bloom every hundred years. In 1979, the year Deng came into full power, it bloomed for the first time. The good folk of Guang'an took this to be a favorable portent.[17]

From the courtyard of the old Deng house, three low, rounded hills are visible. These are seen by some as symbolic of the three major ups and downs in Deng's political life. They are viewed by others as symbolic of the Chinese pen rack, which has this shape and which denotes a well-educated man.

There is a mystery about the death of Deng's father, which occurred in 1940. He was murdered less than a mile from his home as he was returning from a pilgrimage to Suining, where he had worshiped at a Buddhist temple. The villagers do not like to discuss it. The murder was brutal: Deng Wenming's head was chopped off, his body hacked almost in two. Deng Xiaoping, then in Yanan, did not return for his father's funeral. Some residents have speculated that a breach between the rising Communist leader and his landlord father, who was intimately associated with the local warlord, may have arisen.

The circumstances of Deng Wenming's death, occurring so close to home, have aroused curiosity. Several possibilities have been suggested — that the murder was committed by enemies of the warlord Yang Sen; that it might have arisen from a local quarrel; or that it might have been carried out by Communist guerrillas based in the nearby Huaying Mountains.[18]

Like all foresighted Chinese of his generation, Deng's father had selected a site for his grave. As the funeral party moved toward the site, with the coffin borne by half a dozen pallbearers, a dark cloud passed over, the wind rose, and rain hurtled down. The coffin bearers fled in fright. When the rain halted and they returned, they found they could not move the coffin; it was heavy as lead. So Deng Wenming was buried right there. The superstitious took this as God's will.

When Deng Xiaoping became chief of state, the citizenry examined the burial place with care. It seemed to be shaped like a swan, and they decided the swan had carried Deng Wenming straight to heaven. Therefore, they reasoned, his son, Deng Xiaoping, must be a great man. An old Chinese superstition holds that if your father is buried in an appropriate spot, you surely will become a great leader.

After Deng left Paifangcun in 1916, he never came back — not when his mother died, in 1927, not when his father died. But he kept in touch with his family and particularly with his stepmother Xia Bogan, whom he had never met. She was a capable woman and held the family together after the death of her husband.

Although Deng never went back to his hometown, his emissaries occasionally visited Paifangcun. In 1986 Deng visited Chengdu, and his uncle and aunt came to see him there. Uncle Dan said he had told Deng he was doing a good job but qualified the statement by quickly assuring his interviewer that "there are many good leaders in China."[19] Dan had seen enough political change (he and his wife had been given a hard time during the Cultural Revolution) to want to throw a small anchor to windward.

When Deng Xiaoping spent a vacation in Guilin, in Guangxi Province, in 1986, the governor-general tried to persuade him to visit his old home, even offering to take him there by helicopter. Deng refused as he had before. "Guang'an is in Sichuan," he said. "So Sichuan is my native place."

In 1987 Deng sent his uncle Dan a message that he was not to ask the government for favors.[20]

Paifangcun seems not to have changed much between 1916 and 1988. The road from Guang'an to Deng's home, a four-mile stretch, had been black-topped; a black-topped parking lot had been laid down close by the Deng house. Visitors were anticipated when the restoration had been completed.

Guang'an had grown to a county seat of fifty thousand in a county with a population of more than a million. Overpopulation was a problem. Posters on the highway asserted: "To Have One Child Is Glorious." A good many families, it seemed, had passed up glory for the sake of one or two extra boys with the potential of making the family richer. (An earlier slogan had been "To Get Rich Is Glorious.") Guang'an produced so much corn it liked to call itself the Golden County, but it was out of the mainstream in 1916, when Deng left, and remained so in 1988. But change was on the way. Foreign entrepreneurs had begun to sniff around for possible ventures. There were also the natural beauty of the Huaying Mountains and the fame of Deng. Japanese and French cities proposed to establish city-to-city relations with Guang'an. And in the spring of 1988 *The Color Purple* was being shown at the local movie house.

5

Into the Wilderness

DENG XIAOPING was forty-five years old when his troops crossed the Yangtze and advanced on Shanghai. He was a civilian, a political commissar, a Party man. But for twenty years he had never been without a revolver on his hip or a rifle in his hands. He had fought in the Shanghai underground, taught rudimentary tactics in a warlord's military academy, and learned the soldier's trade, as had his comrades, in guerrilla war in the jungle and mountains.

Deng learned war at first hand. At the first stage of his military life he had to invent his own tactics, turn peasants into soldiers, and make decisions hundreds or thousands of miles from Party or military superiors. He was on his own in the wilderness; there were no communication lines. Whether Deng and his men survived or perished depended on his judgment as a twenty-five-year-old Party leader living by his wits in hostile jungle and mountain hideouts.

Deng had formed his own "armies" and commanded them in battle, but to the end of his days he never wore an insignia of rank or bore a formal military title. He was never a general, a marshal, or even a colonel. Just a commander.

As years went by Deng shared command of the PLA's 129th Division, its finest. He went on to direct field armies and groups of armies. He gave orders to tens and then hundreds of thousands of men. Yet even after coming to power as China's emperor-to-be in the late 1970s, Deng felt he had to apologize to the marshals for taking the lead in military affairs. They deferred. "We have always considered you one of us," they said. Well they might. There was little about war that Deng did not know and had not learned in the field.

Deng embarked on his military career in 1929, when he was sent into the sweltering backcountry of Guangxi Province, west of Canton, on a mission of desperation. Deng had been working in the Shanghai Communist underground, a hunted man, in danger day and night of being ferreted out by Chiang Kaishek's secret police. There had been a peasant revolt in Guangxi, the Two Rivers Uprising, and the Shanghai underground ordered Deng and half a dozen other young Communists into the hinterland to find and organize the peasants into a military force. The idea was to lead them in a campaign to capture the southern metropolis of Canton and other big cities.

It was a wild notion, but the Shanghai Communists were desperate. Their movement had almost been wiped out by Chiang. Every maneuver had been smashed since the terrible 1927 massacre of Communists in Shanghai conducted by Chiang and his underworld allies. A Communist uprising at Nanchang in August 1927 had petered out. Mao himself — against his better judgment — had led the Autumn Harvest Uprising in an effort to capture Changsha. It sputtered out. So had a revolt at Canton. The Communists were in disarray and clutching at any straw to demonstrate that they were still a viable force.

Just at this time Moscow sent them exhortation after exhortation to capture *big cities,* to get the Revolution blazing again. Like dutiful soldiers, the young Communists, reinforced by a band of Moscow-trained Chinese, diligently were trying to carry out Moscow's orders. What they did not know was that Moscow's demand for revolutionary fervor in China was a complex move on the chessboard of a struggle between Josef Stalin and Leon Trotsky. Trotsky was claiming that Stalin had "lost" the China revolution. Stalin was eager to show that his China tactics were correct and that the Revolution was still alive. He had to prove that he was a better world revolutionary than Trotsky.

The Kremlin could care less what sacrifices it might be imposing on the fledgling Chinese Communist band. It needed results, big ones that would make the headlines.

In this atmosphere Shanghai pinned its hopes on the Guangxi peasants — and Deng. Deng and his companions dutifully took on the assignment, Deng under the name he was using at that time, Deng Bin. They slipped aboard a ship in Shanghai and cruised down the south China coast, making their way to Longzhou, on the Chinese–French Indochinese border. A small revolt was going on then in Indochina, led by a man named Ho Chi Minh. Whether Deng met Ho in Longzhou is not certain, but the two had been acquainted in Paris and had also been in Moscow together.

Deng and his companions pushed deep into the mountains, where there were no roads, only narrow footpaths. They walked. Occasionally Deng found a horse to ride, but not often. The paths were too narrow for carts. Wheelbarrows were the only wheeled transport.[1]

The land exuded an eerie quality. Eroded limestone hills like the mushroom-shaped domes of Guilin marched northwest in irregular order. Neither Deng nor his companions had any notion of the Kremlin politics that had propelled them into this wasteland. Nor had any of them the slightest experience in guerrilla war.

Deng had picked up a little knowledge of military tactics and strategy in Moscow and at the military academy of the "Christian general" Feng Yuxiang near Xian, where he taught briefly on his return to China. But for the most part he had to rely on his native wit.

The country through which Deng passed was a land drained of color and reduced to rusty browns and dull grays. Nothing had changed here for five hundred years, perhaps not for a millennium. Farmers hacked out a starvation crop of corn on hillside terraces and drove their plodding gray water buffalo through the rice paddies. Leprosy was common; so were scurvy and opium. Bandits roamed the hills. Once a few of them captured Deng on a lonely trail. One stuck his bayonet into Deng's cheek until it bled. Deng thought his days had ended. But the robbers wanted money, not his life. He gave them the few silver dollars in his pocket and they let him go.[2]

Deng worked hard with the peasants and earned their respect as he did his best to turn them into an effective guerrilla force. Years later they remembered him for his common touch. He never gave himself airs, they said, and he had a great asset for a military man — he could bellow like a bull. His voice was so loud they could hear him wherever they were standing, and his words, they said, flowed like the water of a river in flood.[3]

An eighty-four-year-old veteran named Ya Meiyuan later remembered once telling Deng that some people thought he was "a little bit radical." Deng asked why. "Because after the battle you killed some landlords who didn't need to be killed." Deng replied: "How could we have peasants share the property of the landlords without killing some of them?"[4]

To Deng, life was a coin to be spent for political ends. He encouraged the peasants to kill the landlords and share their land and possessions. Doing so gave poor men and women a direct stake in the Revolution. Once they had killed a landlord, they knew their own lives would be in peril, if the other side came back. The bloodshed put them in pawn to the Revolution. Once in, never out.

This was a philosophy that Deng acquired early on. He would abide by it to his last days, believing that blood could and should be shed for political ends. His view was shared by Mao and the other Red Army leaders. This same philosophy would underlie the decision of Deng and his council of elders in ordering the army to carry out the Tiananmen massacre in 1989.

The killing of landlords by the peasants and the seizure of land and property — be they spontaneous or incited by the Communists — were to become the hallmarks of the rural revolution of Mao Zedong. On this point there was no difference between the views of Mao and Deng.

The peasants of the Two Rivers region had been holding meetings in the local temple, called Bai Di, located beneath a huge stone outcropping on a mountainside. Under its shelter several thousand men could assemble. The peasants took over the temple and rechristened it Lenin's Cave. Here Deng exhorted the peasants. He organized them into units and did his best to teach them tactics. They had little in the way of arms, most carrying spears, sickles, pitchforks, and long poles sometimes studded with iron. There were eight or nine thousand peasant guerrillas in all.

Deng whipped these raw recruits into the best shape he could, formed them into what he euphemistically called the Seventh and Eighth armies, and tried to lead them out to capture "big cities," as he had been instructed. Actually, he didn't have enough men to capture small cities. In any engagement the ratio of troops against him was always three or four to one. Naturally, he lost almost every battle he fought. He pulled back from others where he knew the odds were too long against him. He didn't come close to capturing Canton or Guilin, and for a long time even Longzhou and Bose eluded him.

Still, Shanghai kept pressing him to fight big battles for big cities. Shanghai was, of course, just repeating Moscow's instructions. This was a no-win situation for Deng, and before long he was yanked back to Shanghai and threatened with court-martial and loss of Party membership, relieved of his military-political responsibilities, and subjected to a Party inquiry.

For Deng it was the first — but hardly the last — of the political reverses he would suffer. (He was knocked down so often in his career and bounced back so strongly that he came to be called an India rubber ball by many Chinese.) He escaped with little more than a reprimand, and since he was not labeled a saboteur or a traitor, his recall from Two Rivers was far from a major setback. In the end Shanghai sent Deng back to Two Rivers; it couldn't find anyone else who would take the rickety command.[5]

By the time Deng eased his way through the Nationalist lines and back into Two Rivers, his force had largely been dissipated in reckless adventures, trying vainly to win some flashy victories. His first task was to find the remnants of his troops. That took several weeks. There were so few left they were now called the 56th and 58th regiments, and even those were grandiose designations for the tattered band.

Deng set up operations in a hamlet called Wuzhuang, putting his headquarters in the Big Dipper Pagoda, a strange building that looked more like the campanile of an Italian Renaissance church than a Chinese shrine. It rose high over the rice paddies, and from his tower Deng could see enemy troops approaching from miles away. He worked night after night, often until after midnight, pulling the elements of his force together. He wrote articles on policy, defending himself against "leftists" who said he was following a "rich peasant policy" because he did not confiscate the property of middle peasants but took only from the rich.

Late in 1930 Deng led his men north and east with the idea of joining Mao Zedong and Zhu De at their base on Jinggang Mountain. How many men Deng then had is uncertain; probably not more than a few thousand. They husbanded their strength, fought no battles. By the time they joined the Red Army they were down to little more than a thousand.

One time they were caught in a snowstorm at a place called Jinghua, in Hunan. The men were wearing tropical shorts. They joked that

"God is sending us cotton," but it was not funny. They were freezing. Deng gave them permission to confiscate warm clothes from the local landlords. Most of the coats were women's and "very loud," one veteran remembered; "we looked like a troupe of actors." Deng refused to don a bizarre costume.[6]

Long before the juncture with the Red Army, Deng left his men at Le Chang River, near the Jiangxi border. He was called back once again to Shanghai. He never returned to his troops. Just why is unclear. According to one version, Deng set out with some bodyguards to try to contact Mao and Zhu De, then found himself separated by large KMT forces and was unable to slip through to his own command.[7] Deng left in mid-February 1931, turning over his command to his aides. He moved with one convoy of guards after another through the dangerous countryside, finally reaching Shanghai.

During the Cultural Revolution, Red Guards prowled about Guangxi looking for evidence that Deng had been a traitor, had fled and abandoned his men. The Guards terrorized many ordinary soldiers but were unable to trump up any charges.

The scenario is still not entirely certain, but we do know that Deng Xiaoping plunged directly from dead-end Guangxi into the embattled camp of Mao Zedong. Deng had left Shanghai and by August 1931 was in Ruijin, capital of the Central Soviet Zone of Jiangxi. Mao and Zhu De controlled the zone, but the Chinese supporters of the pro-Soviet, anti-Mao line, who favored big battles for big cities and a concentration on urban proletarian goals, were working to undermine Mao and take over the area.[8]

Deng was an articulate and able supporter of Mao's doctrine that the revolutionary war could be won only by guerrilla tactics, organization of the peasant population, and use of small military resources to inflict crushing defeats on exposed units of Chiang's larger, better-equipped armies.

In Ruijin Deng was made Party secretary of Ruijin County, an important post for a young newcomer, but many posts were open because of an ongoing witch-hunt. Several thousand Party members had been arrested, and many had been executed, as members of the AB conspiracy. The initials *AB* supposedly stood for "anti-Bolshevik," and the conspiracy was said to be aimed at overthrowing the Communists. Supposed conspirators were persecuted with devilish cruelty. One group of local Party leaders was paraded through a village street, each man led by a rusty wire that penetrated his testicles. At the village square all were shot.[9]

Deng, using his down-to-earth wits, brought the arrests to an end. He ran an inquiry, released almost all those who had been detained, held a few for further investigation, and ended the reign of terror. In a few weeks Ruijin was back to normal. Fifty years into the future, after the death of Mao Zedong, Deng would do much the same, on a far wider scale, to liquidate the paranoid legacy of the Gang of Four. He quickly separated sheep from goats, liberating and rehabilitating Party victims by the million.

The entire Party apparatus, everyone from Shanghai, the young supporters of Moscow, began to gather in Ruijin. It was the only place in China where a Communist did not face twenty-four-hour-a-day danger of arrest and execution. Zhou Enlai arrived there shortly after Deng. He observed Deng's commonsense work and instantly approved it.

Soon after the proclamation on November 7, 1931, of an "interim" Chinese soviet government and the designation of Ruijin as the "Red Capital," Deng was railroaded out of Ruijin and sent to Huichang County; he was given responsibility for Xunwu and Anyuan counties as well. It sounded important. It wasn't. All three counties had just been liberated and were precariously held.

The anti-Mao faction, encouraged by the Comintern military adviser Otto Braun, began to cut into Mao's power. The faction did not feel secure enough to attack Mao openly, but Deng was a convenient stand-in.[10]

Deng was sent to the General Political Department of the Red Army in Ruijin to be "struggled against" (as he was again during the Cultural Revolution in 1966). This was not a struggle of minds and ideas but "an attack without mercy and a struggle with brutality," as specified by a notice in the Party Central organ, *Struggle*. This statement was signed by Lo Man (the Party nickname of Li Wiehan), secretary of the Party organization bureau. Brutal and without mercy the struggle was. One day the kindhearted wife of Lu Dingyi, deputy premier, met Deng as he was being taken by his guards to his cell after a struggle session. "I'm so hungry," Deng told her. "I don't get enough to eat." She took a silver dollar, bought two chickens, cooked them, and told the guards to bring Deng to her house, where she gave him a chicken dinner. She wrapped up the other chicken for him to take back to his cell. Perhaps that was why, when the Red Army left on the Long March, she was left behind.

Deng wrote a couple of self-criticisms but refused to go far enough to satisfy his critics. "I cannot say more," he insisted. "What I say is true." It was the same stubborn insistence on reality that he was to display during the Cultural Revolution.

Lo Man, chief accuser of Deng, was a big, handsome, deliberate man. At the height of the struggle A Jin (known before joining the Party as Jin Weiying), Deng's wife, divorced him and married Lo Man. Later, in Yanan, Lo Man and A Jin were divorced.[11]

The unrepentant Deng was now, in General Yang Shangkun's words, "sent down to the grass roots." He was exiled to Nancun in Le'an County, far from Ruijin and only partially controlled by the Communists. It was a no-man's-land where troops of both sides roved "all tangled together," as one military man put it. After nightfall bandits reigned. Some believe Deng was sent there in the hope he would be killed.

Deng's stay was short, not more than ten days. Someone in Ruijin had second thoughts. Suppose Deng went over to the KMT? He was whisked back and tucked into the Red Army Political Department as general secretary under Wang Jiaxiang, a badly wounded Red Army veteran, then an opponent of Mao's but a man who eventually came over to Mao. This job lasted two or three months. Then Deng — at his own request, it was said — became an ordinary political worker.

Deng started the Long March in October 1934 in the ranks, carrying his own pack, his rice bag, his bullet bag, and his rifle, a load of about sixty pounds. At that time Deng, like Mao, was an outcast. The Long March was in the hands of the Russian-trained Party people and the military adviser Otto Braun.[12]

The "Russians" didn't last long. The Red Army went from defeat to disaster. It lost two thirds of its original strength of eighty thousand. By December 1934 Mao's military associates had had enough. They rallied around Mao, ousting Braun and the Soviet-trained men. Mao took over. His peppery supporter Deng Xiaoping got a job and a horse to carry his gear. At the Zunyi conference of January 1935, when leadership was voted to Mao, Deng was present, sitting in a corner and taking notes for the army paper, *Red Star,* of which he had just become editor.[13]

It was a decisive moment. Deng's wagon henceforth would be hitched to Mao's star. Even during Mao's dementia of the 1970s, after he had ousted Deng, subjected him to humiliation, torture, imprisonment, and exile, he would look back on those days in Jiangxi and on the Long March and his face would light up with warmth for the little fighter who had stood at his side and never lost heart.

This had been the first of Deng's great political falls, and it was the first of his remarkable political rebounds. He had been sent into the wilderness in the hope that an enemy bullet would end his life. Instead he bounced back, the small, ever-ready, eager, infinitely energetic, and faithful supporter of the new leader, Mao. In his downfall and rise he had taken the first great step that would, in 1978, bring him to the leadership of New China.

PART 2

THE SECRET LIFE OF ZHONGNANHAI

6

The Study
of Chrysanthemum Fragrance

AS MAO ENJOYED the spring and summer in the Fragrant Hills in 1949, he turned over to his commanders the task of putting the nation in order and preparing the foundations for the New China. The pacification and absorption of many regions was far from complete, particularly in the great southwest, where Liu Bocheng and Deng Xiaoping were still hard at work. The complex problems of Shanghai had been placed in the capable hands of Marshal Chen Yi and his Third Army. In Beijing the principal questions were being handled by Marshal Ye Jianying.

The northern warlords, the Japanese, and Chiang Kaishek's lieutenants, in their successive rules before Mao and his army assumed power, had set up municipal offices in some of the buildings of Zhongnanhai. Marshal Ye took over these quarters and soon recommended that Mao and the government follow his example and make this quiet, secure (as he believed), and attractive enclave the seat of empire.

Mao hesitated. Not only did he find the Fragrant Hills much to his taste, but he had not overcome his fears about the security of Zhongnanhai and, indeed, of Beijing itself. The Nationalists had held it, as had the Japanese. How many secret assassination squads, fifth columnists, and provocateurs had been left behind? Not to mention spies and terrorists, booby traps and land mines.

The security problems had been turned over to the devious Kang Sheng and the Party security chief, Li Kenong. Police units had been put in charge of every block and every *hutong,* or alleyway.[1] Mao was in no hurry to come down from the Fragrant Hills. Let the city be cleansed of human detritus as well as night soil.

He did not make an immediate decision on Marshal Ye's suggestion. There was a shortage of space, no doubt of that. There simply wasn't room for the spawning bureaucracies, and the question of razing the Forbidden City was broached. It spread over 720,000 square meters; half the grounds were occupied by palaces, the remainder by parks. The buildings were rambling and grandiose, hardly suited to the use of clerks and commissars. If they were torn down, a vast area in the heart of Beijing would be opened up for quick slab construction to provide endless corridors for the new masters.

The proposal was not only pragmatic. What more dramatic way to signal that a new order had been born than to blast from the earth the most famous symbol of ancient empire? Had not the Mongols razed the palaces of the Sung dynasty and put up their own? Had not the Ming emperor Yong Le razed the capital of the Yuan dynasty?

For a time the Forbidden City teetered on the brink. Zealous ideologues detested it as a monument of feudal decadence. There may, too, have been some clear-eyed Party men who remembered the fate of past dynasties that had swept into the imperial city, slaughtered the princes, and then succumbed to the culture of their victims, until in the end the new was inextricably tainted by the eternal old.

Mao had a superstition about the Forbidden City. He did not set foot there, and in later years when the idea of his taking it as the seat of his dynasty was raised by his courtiers he rejected it. "I am just a grand dragon," he said. "I am not a sky dragon." In Chinese mythology the ruler of the imperial city was called a sky dragon, the supreme power.[2]

The idea of a new Red City died quickly. Mao said no. "There's only one sun in the sky," he observed.[3]

For the time being the government bureaucrats would have to make do with what was available. Skeleton ministries appropriated available buildings. The Beijing Hotel, a block from Tiananmen, was requisitioned by the Foreign Ministry. It housed diplomats, government envoys, distinguished Party guests. The nearby Hôtel des Wagons-Lits was first given to Marshal Ye and then to the Foreign Ministry.[4]

After careful inspection of Zhongnanhai, suitable quarters for Mao Zedong were selected and approved by Mao himself. Zhongnanhai had been a quiet, neglected corner for years, largely uninhabited since the time of the northern warlords of the late teens and twenties.[5] A small school was housed in one small palace. There were municipal offices in another. The complex was run-down, with many palaces vacant and shabby.

An exquisite Qing palace dating to the seventeenth century (and probably with origins earlier, in the Ming dynasty) was picked for Mao. It was one of several in the Garden of Abundance, Fengzeyuan, which took its name from a small plot where each spring the emperor carried out the sowing rites, putting his gloved hands to a plow and, while servitors scattered seed, guiding a pair of gentle oxen down a short furrow. The ceremony, it was hoped, would ensure an abundant harvest. Mao never indulged in the ancient ritual, but there would be years when he would have given a good deal for a bigger harvest.

Within the Garden of Abundance stood Yiniantang, a palace erected by the great Qing emperor Kang Xi. He called it the Hall of Respect for Elegance. In the Republican era it became the Hall of Friendly Talks. When Mao moved in, it was renamed the Hall of Longevity.

A wing of the splendid structure, still boasting the russet red of the dynasty and an imperial yellow tile roof with swallow wings, was known as the Study of Chrysanthemum Fragrance. It had sometimes been used as an imperial library. This residence was meticulously refurbished for Mao's use.[6]

In this compound, perfumed with the scent of jasmine and osmanthus, with wide windows giving onto a pillared terrace and a flat stone courtyard, Mao took up residence. Here peace was sublime. No sound penetrated, day or night, save the piping of Beijing magpies or the haunting voices of cranes on the Nanhai shore or, occasionally, the footfall of an armed sentry.

Security was intense. Diplomatic guests, received in the Hall of Purple Effulgence, just to the north, might or might not enter through the New China Gate just beyond Tiananmen Square or through a side entrance at 81 Nanchang Street. Mao and his closest associates more often swung back of the Forbidden City, through Beihai Park, and entered (as I did) through Baoguangmen, the Gate of Magic Light, and proceeded down a back lane to a rear door.

Mao's quarters were fitted to his taste. Along the north wall, so that the southern sun would flood the broad windows, was a study through which one passed into his bedchamber, the biggest of his rooms. Beside the courtyard windows stood his bed, a square wooden bed, the legs mounted on sturdy wooden blocks, bigger than the great *kang,* or oven-bed, in his parents' home in Shaoshan, bigger than many a room in the new flats of Beijing — not a king-sized bed, an emperor-sized bed.[7] Mao reposed on a hill of pillows. Half his bed, as long as he lived, was piled with papers, books, the slender sheaves of the Chinese classics that he read and reread from boyhood to old age. As for the other half of the bed, it was to have many and varied occupants.[8]

A pair of brass bracket lamps were mounted on the wall behind Mao's bed, eight feet from the floor. More bracket lights were fixed between the windows. On tables beside his bed and at its head stood gooseneck lamps, flexible to adjust to his angle of sight. The walls of the bedroom and study were lined with books and document boxes filled with reports, correspondence, and possibly some items from the special library collected for Mao by the secret police specialist, Kang Sheng.[9] The floor was covered with a Chinese carpet of apple green.

A member of the Central Committee was charged with filling Mao's shelves with the books he would need and want. A colleague dropped in to inspect the work. He saw shelf after shelf of China's great literary and historical works, not much foreign literature in translation. All his life Mao tried to learn English but never succeeded.[10] The visitor spotted a notable omission: very little Marx, Engels, Lenin. Not a single book by Stalin.

"Don't you think," the visitor asked the committee member, "you should reserve a little space for the Marxist classics — for the sake of appearances if nothing else?" The omission was corrected.[11]

Mao's new quarters awaited him at Zhongnanhai. But still he did not budge from the Fragrant Hills. Not that he did not recognize the serious tasks that lay at hand. One day an old friend, Zhu Zhongli, wife of Wang Jiaxiang and a physician who had made the Long March with Mao, called on him. She remarked that the long struggle was coming to an end; most of the country had been liberated.

Mao took issue. "We have just taken the first step on our Long March. It is the beginning, not the end. To build a new socialist state will involve a hard struggle, too."

Zhu Zhongli did not argue. She took Mao's blood pressure. It was 130 over 70; his pulse was normal. His weight was 187 pounds. He had gained about twenty pounds in the Yanan years and would keep on adding weight until the last years of his life.[12]

Mao Zedong well understood the symbolism of moving into Zhongnanhai. Perhaps this was one reason he approached the move so carefully and cautiously. All was ready for him at the Study of Chrysanthemum Fragrance by October 1, 1949, the date of the founding of the People's Republic. Many of his colleagues already occupied their new palaces. Not Mao. Once he entered Zhongnanhai there could be no backward step.

To sleep in an emperor's chamber was the exercise of power. When a dynasty fell it was said that the Mandate of Heaven had been withdrawn. The Mandate of Heaven was the smile of the gods, and it ordained the new emperor as the rightful successor. By being emperor he was emperor. Mao had no doubt he was that emperor, leader of a nation of how many hundreds of millions he did not then know, more than inhabited any other country. All the other Chinese dynasties were history. He was the present, and he believed he was the future.

Mao Zedong was fifty-six years old. He had never known luxury. He spent his first fourteen years in a courtyard house with hard dirt floors. He had never seen a newspaper. He did not know what running water was. There had been no electricity in his village.

For years he lived on the run, a guerrilla in the mountains. He fought Chiang's troops for a year on the Long March — also battling fog, rain, snowy mountain peaks, blazing deserts, bottomless bogs, hunger, cold, fever, pain, and peril. If he had a door stripped from a peasant hut to sleep on, he counted himself lucky. He worked all night, night after night, slept in the day swinging in a litter carried by sturdy soldiers. In Yanan he lived in a cave dug into the yellow loess hills. He had lived a solider's life, subsisting on a bowl of rice per day, sleeping in his clothes, picking off the lice and cracking them between his white teeth. He was lean as a wolf and one of the finest poets in China.

The fire of revolution kept Mao alive. He ate, slept, breathed revolution and would die leading a revolution against his own revolution. He had acquired absolute pitch for the rhythm of China's peasants.[13] He knew them better than they knew themselves. He did not know how many years it would take, but he knew his revolution would win. He did not think much about the world; China was his world.

While he considered himself a proletarian (in theory), he was obviously a peasant in practice, guided, as events would disclose, more by China's philosophical heritage than by Marx, Lenin, Stalin, or even *The Communist Manifesto,* although this he would never concede. The Hegelian dialectic was not his strong point, and he was more familiar with Sun Tzu's *Art of War* than with Clausewitz. Mao worried more about what President Harry Truman and the enigmatic United States would do than about the dire predictions of Malthus. Second only to his concern about the United States was that over what Stalin (whom he hated and feared) might be plotting. And he was far from clear what to do with China now that he had won it.

Long before, Mao had gone on a walking trip deep into the Hunan countryside with his friend and classmate Siao You. The young men encountered a lively young woman at an inn who possessed the power of reading physiognomy. She predicted that Mao might become a great officer, a prime minister, or a bandit chief.

"You could kill ten thousand or even a hundred thousand people without blinking an eye," she said.[14]

And there had been a more recent prophecy. Mao had, so it was told, visited the great Qingliming monastery on the banks of the Yellow River, forty miles due east of Yanan. A Taoist monk prostrated himself at Mao's feet and declared: "You are a Zhen Long Tianzi, a real Dragon Son of Heaven." Mao asked the monk to tell his fortune. The monk predicted that Mao would go to Beijing and found his dynasty on October 1.[15] It was a prophecy right out of *Romance of the Three Kingdoms,* the ancient Chinese classic.

Did Mao dream this ancient Chinese dream of the dragon throne? We have no positive answer, but some who were close to him believed he took these prophecies seriously.[16] Mao kept no record of his secret thoughts. All that his secretaries ever found were brief scribbles on his desk pad tabulating how many hours he had slept, how many hours he had swum each day, and possibly other physical statistics.[17] But clearly Mao's eyes were focused on the present and the future. He did not lament the past, but he believed he could learn from it. He had won the Long March and the war against Chiang Kaishek by studying the strategy and tactics of *Romance of the Three Kindgoms* and by reading the military philosophy of *The Art of War.*

Now he must learn the art of ruling China, the art of holding the Mandate of Heaven. It was no accident that he arrived in the Fragrant Hills with the two great works on Chinese dynastic rule — *Records of the Historian* and *The General Mirror for the Aid of Government* — in his baggage.

One of Mao's first acts on entering the Study of Chrysanthemum Fragrance was to repair an omission in his library. He sent for the Twenty-four Books, the Annals of the Dynasties, which compose the great history of Chinese empire. These are huge tomes, not single volumes, but sets of volumes, scores, hundreds of books in which are recorded the annals of all that has gone before, the record of each emperor as compiled by his successor, the mother lode of Chinese statecraft and tradition, the accumulated wisdom of a hundred Chinese Machiavellis and their princes.

The Annals of the Twenty-four Dynasties were placed in a special sandalwood cabinet in Mao's bedchamber. There he lay on his heap of pillows, his gooseneck lamps focused on the rice paper pages, and pored over the Annals from beginning to end — not once, but twice, on the evidence of China's most respected historian of the Mao period.[18]

Not all Mao's survivors believed that he had read so widely in the history of how princes won kingdoms and emperors lost them, of how the Mandate of Heaven was passed from one emperor to the next.

"I don't see how he could have read the whole text of the Annals," said Li Rui, who of all the survivors of the Mao era probably understood him best. He served Mao as personal secretary for a period in the 1950s, wrote a striking study of Mao's early life, and studied Mao for years, many of them spent in the prison where Mao had confined him. Although Li Rui did not believe Mao had time after moving into Zhongnanhai to read the whole of the Annals, he said, "I am prepared to believe that he did read a good deal, particularly those passages discussing how each man came to the throne and how he came to leave it."

Mao, said Li Rui, was interested in the change of dynasties. He kept the annals of the third-century Three Kingdoms by his bedside over the years. Li Rui believed Mao had studied the transition from the Ming to the Qing dynasty with great care and, perhaps, segments of the period when China was divided into regimes of the north and of the south, during the fifth and sixth centuries.[19]

After I visited Zhongnanhai, the picture of Mao, sprawled on his enormous bed, turning the pages of ancient documents, reading on and on into the record of hundreds of years, seemed entirely plausible. It was, after all, the traditional duty of the new emperor to read the annals of what had gone before.

Mao, it seems clear, never stopped reading the Annals. In his last years, when his eyesight was fading, a special edition was printed by the Xinhua News Agency in large ideograms especially for Mao's use.[20] The more Mao studied China's past, the greater — or so it finally began to seem — his problems in handling China's present.

7

The Gate of Heavenly Peace

THE GATE OF HEAVENLY PEACE, Tiananmen, for hundreds of years has been the main entrance to China's Forbidden City.

On this gate on October 1, 1949, under a clearing autumn sky, stood Mao Zedong, dressed in a fine gray tunic, the pea-sized wen on his chin visible and prominent, with his comrades of the Long March, the men on whom Mao would call to build the new Communist China. The gate rises thirty feet high and forty feet thick, its roof a hundred feet from the ground. Mao and his comrades gathered on the terrace behind the balustrade, a scarlet and gold reception hall where tea, orange pop, shrimp chips, peanuts, and cigarettes refreshed them during the long ceremonial.[1]

Below the balustrade, mounted on marble columns, stood a pair of *hou,* small mythical lion-dogs whose role was to make certain that the emperor did not while away his time with pleasant ladies. The *hou* did not bark; they cried out in human voices, "Oh, great sir, Your Majesty! Don't spend so much time in pleasure. Come back and attend to your official duties." The myth testified to the eternal problem posed by the pleasure domes of the Forbidden City. It is not likely that the distinguished assembly on this October day paid heed to these archaic survivals. This, perhaps, was a mistake.

The great gate had been repainted in the traditional imperial purple, a color that commoners were forbidden to use, an off shade of carmine. The origins of the color were almost forgotten by 1949. In ancient China the North Star was seen as the center of the celestial universe and was believed to have a violet shade. The imperial city, the center of the world, therefore also bore the celestial color violet.

A portrait of Chiang Kaishek, painted on a vast sheet of flattened gasoline tins soldered together, had adorned the gate until recently. This had been removed, and the gate stood clean and proud, as in the time of the Mings. But a huge portrait of Mao had been hoisted on the wall beside it. In front of the gate a flagpole had been erected. One imaginative observer commented that the flagpole had "pierced the old city to its cosmic heart."[2] Ten-foot silken Chinese lanterns hung under the red-and-golden-lacquered eaves of the gate.

Groves of silk trees, which had adorned the square, had been chopped down, and new cement and asphalt laid. Everywhere blossomed the red-painted slogans "Long Live Chairman Mao" and "Long Live the People's Republic of China."[3]

In past centuries emperors had posted their edicts at the gate. Here the abdication of the last Qing emperor, Puyi, was proclaimed in 1912. Here the Japanese hammered up a notice establishing their "East Asia Co-Prosperity Sphere" in the occupation years preceding the 1945 surrender. Here citizens had come with petitions. They had passed through the gate to audiences with the emperor. It was China's place of authority, the symbol of the power of the great throne. Here on May 4, 1919, China's university students had shown their anger at the Chinese statesmen at Versailles who signed away China's rights at the World War I peace conference. The demonstrators of May 4 set in train the students' movement that would play its role in Mao's revolution and later.

Here in the Cultural Revolution would mass a million Red Guards, filling the square and vowing fealty to Mao Zedong, who stood before them, his face waxy as the moon. At the gate on June 3–4, 1989, would occur the Tiananmen massacre.

Now, on that sunshine-and-showers day of 1949, the decay of the years and past humiliations were forgotten. This was the day of Mao's declaration of the People's Republic, of the raising of the new flag, of the designation of *"Qi Lai"* (The March of the Volunteers) as the national anthem, and of the introduction of the Christian calendar in place of the hallowed calendar of the dynasties. Gone, or so it was thought, were the Year of the Dragon, the Year of the Snake, and all the others.

"Thus begins a new era in the history of China," Mao proclaimed. "We, the four hundred and seventy-five million people of China, have now stood up."[4]

Some one hundred thousand people stood jammed into the walled enclosure before Tiananmen, which was cluttered with old imperial cubbyhole offices and foreign legations, brazen signs of alien power. The wireless tower of the U.S. consulate was silhouetted higher than the walls of the Forbidden City.

The great east-west artery of Chang-an and the hundred-acre stone prairie of Tiananmen Square had not yet been cleared. Neither the stubby column to the martyrs of the Revolution nor the clear plastic jumbo that was to house the catafalque of Mao yet existed.

In the eight months since the fall of Beijing, Mao had laid the foundations of his new state. The marshals and generals were being converted into proconsuls, just as Rome had converted her generals. They had been assigned the great tasks of building New China. On October 1 Mao proclaimed himself chairman; Zhou Enlai, foreign minister; Zhu De, commander-in-chief; Liu Shaoqi, vice chairman (soon to be president). The State Council was a roster of the men who had won the Revolution, a roll call of the Praetorian guard.

Chen Yi had assumed the post of chief of Shanghai. Mao had tried to get Deng Xiaoping to take the job, but Deng insisted that it go to Chen Yi. Although the troops of the Second Field Army would have liked to stay and enjoy the luxury of Shanghai, Deng would not have it. When the October 1 celebration was over, Deng and One-Eyed Liu Bocheng took the train back to the southwest, to direct their force deeper into the region.

Ultimately Deng would become Mao's proconsul for all of southwest China, a region of extreme importance as Mao's fears of American attack rose, especially after the start of the Korean War, in June 1950.

This danger gave birth in Mao's mind to the notion of creating a strategic stronghold, self-sufficient and impervious to American assault. It came to be called China's Third Line, in the mountains and deserts of the remote southwest. The complications, costs, dangers, and strains of this ill-judged endeavor would burden China — and Deng Xiaoping — with extraordinary problems.

But in the joyful mood of October it would not be imagined how difficult New China's birth agonies would be. Who could guess that danger of war with Communist Russia one day would haunt Communist China? That Stalin would plot to detach Manchuria from the People's Republic? Or that a conflict of brother against brother, of the men who had brought victory to the Communist cause, would leave a train of death, of revolutionary heroes in prison cells, hospital rooms, detention pens? Or that men who stood now arm in arm, comrades all, would be bludgeoned or tortured to death on public stages?

Did anyone on that high platform remember the fate a hundred years earlier of the Taipings, who, confused and superstitious, turned

China upside down and clutched at the Mandate of Heaven, only to lose it in a torrent of blood that incarnadined the Dadu River? Not likely. The men of October 1949 were profoundly confident of the future. It belonged to them. They had won it.

They were all there that day — or almost all. There was Lin Biao, architect of the stunning conquest of Manchuria, Beijing, and Tianjin, standing a bit aloof, as always. He was not a mixer, not one for the endless toasts of *maotai* with which his fellow generals celebrated their victories and their manhood. His comrades were used to Lin Biao. He was reserved, shy on the dance floor. This was his style; he was seemingly more thoughtful, more introspective, perhaps a hypochondriac. But this had never seemed to harm his military leadership. Lin Biao would remain a key figure, close to Mao and always wanting to be closer. He would die in 1971 in a mysterious plane crash in Outer Mongolia, trying to escape, it was said, after plotting to assassinate Mao and take over China.

Close to Lin stood Gao Gang, to whom Mao had entrusted the prize of Manchuria. Gao Gang was Mao's Manchurian proconsul, and he had already been to Moscow and signed his own separate treaty of trade with Stalin. Gao Gang and Deng Xiaoping, it was said later, were Mao's favorites at the time. They always accomplished whatever assignments he entrusted them with.[5] No one could have guessed that charges of treason and suicide lay ahead for Gao Gang. Liu Shaoqi, veteran of the Long March, stood at ease, a crushed khaki campaign cap on his head. He had played a role in the dangerous underground work in the "white" areas (those controlled by the KMT), behind Chiang Kaishek's lines. Mao would soon pick him to be China's president. No one on Tiananmen that day would die a more harrowing death. Zhu De, his broad face all smiles, was Mao's oldest military collaborator. He and Mao had invented the Red Army's tactical style on Jinggang Mountain in the guerrilla days of 1927–28. Zhu De had suffered many a hardship on the Long March. Worse lay ahead for him.

Deng Xiaoping, a man who always seemed to be in a hurry, stood restlessly with his co-commander, One-Eyed Liu, both eager to get back to the southwest, to complete their sweep. Soon Mao would give Deng authority over Chongqing and the southwest, and Liu would be sent to Nanjing to preside over the new military academy. No future seemed more secure than theirs, their lives and careers dedicated to building the New China.

*   *   *

Many of his colleagues still thought of Deng as "young Deng," but he was now in mid-career, despite his youthful look. In fact, there was little in the complex political spectrum of the New China that his quick eyes did not take in. Deng's favorite game in these days was poker. He played to win. If he took a chance, it was because he knew the odds and knew the men he was playing against, knew their strengths and weaknesses.

This was a lesson he had begun to learn in the hills of Guangxi and had perfected in the long days when the Red Army again and again had to fight as an underdog. In those times Mao had started a catalogue of the KMT, a dossier on every commander and every military unit, down to battalion level, sometimes even to company grade. Every Red Army officer contributed his observations and information. It was a tool of extraordinary utility. Deng studied these reports night after night. He knew the KMT commanders and their units better than they knew themselves.

This enabled Deng to make decisions swiftly and accurately. He knew whom he was fighting; which commanders were quick to break and run; which units were badly trained and would fall apart under a hard blow; which generals were professionals and not likely to make an error.

Deng and his partner, One-Eyed Liu, read identical intelligence files, so why, Liu once asked, was Deng, not a graduate of a military school, not a professional soldier, more self-assured in his decisions, more quick to respond to challenge, and more frequently correct than Liu himself?

Liu answered his own question: It was because Deng made himself more familiar with every detail of the enemy situation. "He knows the enemy commanders at every level," a fellow commander, Zhang Zhen, remembered Liu's saying.[6] Deng, in short, was a quicker reader than Liu, and his mind retained what he read.

Deng and Liu had worked together for years, a comfortable professional and personal relationship. Several times Mao tried to get rid of Liu Bocheng but was blocked by Deng's stubborn support of his partner.[7]

During the war against the Japanese, Deng and Liu shared leadership of the 129th Division, the best in the PLA, which was then expanded into the Second Field Army in the civil war against Chiang Kaishek. The Liu-Deng partnership's first great success was the One

Thousand Li campaign, in which, at great cost, they compelled Chiang to divert troops to fight them in the Dabie Mountains, opening the way for Mao to cut other KMT units to bits.

One-Eyed Liu never got over his amazement at Deng's inexhaustible energy. "Oh, God!" Liu exclaimed one night. "How can you be so energetic? You work all day and then you play cards far into the night."

In the days of the Huai-Hai campaign, Deng discovered billiards and began to play the ivories as well as poker. He lugged a billiard table around the backcountry so he could play at night.[8]

Some orthodox Party people raised their eyebrows at Deng's love of cards. "It's good for my brain," Deng insisted in later years, after becoming a world-class bridge player.[9] "It keeps it going and shows that I have not lost my mind." Deng was acutely aware of his mental ability. He was determined not to hang on into the senility that overtook Mao Zedong.[10]

Like Mao, Deng was a great swimmer. He said, "I like to swim and that shows that my body still functions."[11] In the summer of 1988, beset with economic and political problems, Deng managed to swim almost every day at the seaside resort of Beidaihe. This was real swimming, not just putting his toe in the water. President Yang Shangkun bragged to Korean leader Kim Il-sung in 1988 that Deng had swum thirty-nine times during his vacation stay, ninety minutes or more each time.[12]

On Tiananmen that October 1949 day, Peng Dehuai, the lion of the Red Army, as always was posted beside Mao, his craggy face looking out on the crowd. He was the most redoubtable of Mao's commanders (only Lin Biao's skills rivaled his) and was headed to the top of the military ladder as minister of defense. The men on the platform would have roared obscenities had anyone suggested that the future held any break between Mao and his toughest general. Others might fall; never Peng Dehuai.

Also on the rostrum was Yang Shangkun, a strong, compact man who had been at Mao's side from the early days in Jiangxi, before, during, and after the Long March, efficient, knowledgeable, a man of all talents in the inner Party circle. No one matched his political know-how, but Mao would teach him some unpleasant lessons. Chen Yi, the Third Field Army commander, already designated proconsul of Shanghai, and He Long, the Robin Hood general who plundered from the landlords to give to the poor peasants, heroes of the people, surveyed the crowd with pleasure. The day would come when heroism would not save them from the inferno.

There were dozens of others, but none so worldly, so skilled in court diplomacy, so kind and thoughtful, as Zhou Enlai. He had placed his head and heart at Mao's disposal during the Long March of 1934–35, and his course had never varied. He would die in tragedy in January 1976, eight months before Mao.

They were, to put it simply, gathered under the banner of Heavenly Peace. If Heavenly Peace did not prevail in every heart, surely there was not among them one who could have imagined that twenty years ahead they would live in the shadow of nuclear attack from their comrade Communists in Moscow; that their own ranks would be bloodied and torn; and that their land would be rent to the verge of chaos.

The demonstration atop Tiananmen Gate was not entirely male. There was one woman, Soong Chingling, widow of Dr. Sun Yatsen, the founder of Republican China, and one of the three famous daughters of Charlie Soong, Sun Yatsen supporter and businessman. Soong Chingling took her place by right. She had steadfastly supported the Communist cause after her husband's death in 1925 and had refused the blandishments of Chiang (who wanted to marry her) and his Nationalists. In the stormy days of the late twenties and thirties she had maintained — at great risk — the old Sun Yatsen residence on Shanghai's Rue Molière as a safe house for Communist Party couriers.[13]

Madame Soong despised Beijing and loved Shanghai, but, radiant and beauteous, she left her Rue Molière home for the October ceremonial. After a few days she returned to Shanghai. Although she was later named vice president of the new regime and given an old Manchu palace as her official residence, only in the ill health of her last years did she take up permanent residence in Beijing.

In the crowded square people cheered Mao. They shouted: "Mao Zedong, *zhuxi, wan sui!* Long live Chairman Mao!" This was a day for all China. The New China had not yet established diplomatic relations. A small group of Russians had been shunted into a corner. No snapshots of them on Tiananmen. A handful of diplomats, their status uncertain, remained in Beijing. There were some foreign students, some missionaries not yet sifted out, a few businessmen. It was, after all, a Chinese celebration, of, by, and for the Chinese. People were jammed together, cheering every word from Mao and Zhu De and the others. Mao shouted: "Long live the People's Republic!" They responded: "*Wan sui! Wan sui!*" Men pushed their grandchildren in little wooden prams fitted with wooden bars to keep the babies from falling out. Young people, stern, earnest, sat talking on benches. The city was dressed for the celebration: red bunting, flags, autumn flowers, posters, strings of colored lights, colored paper lanterns.

In Tiananmen Square there were music and drums and dancing of the *yangko* — a peasant rice-planting dance, it was said, but actually of Mongol origin.

An American, David Foot, had lived in Beijing for several years as a Fulbright scholar and had married a young Chinese woman. The couple, hand in hand, came down to Tiananmen. They had no passes, and the guards wouldn't let them through. But a friendly PLA man helped them climb onto the cab of his truck. They could see the crowds, dimly hear the speaking, and later on watch the fireworks.

As the sky darkened to dusk the young couple saw hundreds of paraders bearing lanterns on long bamboo poles suddenly converge to form a huge fiery ship — the Chinese ship of state, as they imagined, riding on glowing blue-green waves.[14]

Outwardly it was a happy day, a pleasant day. True, the Revolution had displaced many people; lives had been lost or disrupted, fortunes seized, rich or suspected rich Chinese imprisoned, tortured, or killed. The peasants had been instigated (many needed little prompting) to rise against landlords, burn their houses, seize their grain, bludgeon the greedy and the plunderers to death. Years later an educated Chinese, asked if there was not such a thing as a *good* landlord, gasped in astonishment at the idea. To *be* a landlord was to be evil. It was like asking if there were not such a thing as a good devil in hell.[15]

Mao's China began life on that October day in 1949, and he predicted it would have a long and stormy passage. He did not exaggerate. That evening when the festivities were over, the last toast drunk in fiery *maotai,* the 160-proof alcohol that Mao's Red Army had discovered at the town of that name in northwest Guizhou, Mao made his way back to the Fragrant Hills, since the Study of Chrysanthemum Fragrance was not yet ready for his use or, more likely, Mao was not yet ready for his emperor's bed.

8

A Missing Face

ONE FACE was missing from the joyous group that stood atop Tiananmen on that founding day of October 1, 1949. It was that of Jiang Qing, thirty-five years old, wife of Mao Zedong for the last eleven years.

There exists a famous photograph of Mao riding a white pony, leading a Red Army column out of Yanan when he abandoned his Communist sanctuary in March 1947.[1] Chiang Kaishek had mustered powerful forces to crush Mao in his base. Instead, Mao packed up his headquarters, gathered his troops, and slipped away into the endless loess hills of Shaanxi without a battle, opening a war of maneuver, sudden retreats, and quick advances, which in less than two years led to the total defeat of Chiang's armies.

In the photograph Jiang Qing is seen on the second pony behind Mao, a boyish figure with a pert face, her cloth Red Army cap tucking in her hair, wearing army tunic and uniform. For years the photograph was distributed by the New China News Agency. No longer. The picture is still provided to customers, but the boyish figure of Jiang Qing has vanished, airbrushed from the print.

No one airbrushed Jiang Qing in 1949. Or did they? There is reason to believe that she herself — or someone — airbrushed a whole episode out of the life of this complicated woman. Her ultimate ambition, it would become clear, was to make herself empress of China in the pattern of the old empress dowager Ci Xi, who brought the Qing dynasty to an end, or, more aptly, that of the remarkable empress Wu, who founded her own Zhou dynasty (a subdynasty of the Tang) in the seventh century after intrigue and murder that took many lives, including those of two or three of her own sons.

Jiang Qing was in eclipse during the birth of the People's Republic. Not only was she absent from the Gate of Heavenly Peace, she was far from China, deep in the Soviet Union, quite possibly confined against her will in one of Stalin's medical spas. Or she may have been making her way slowly back to China from such confinement. Quite a few wives of high-ranking Chinese Communists, not to mention some leaders, found themselves in similar circumstances. Stalin provided the facilities, the Chinese paid the bills. The medical gambit was well known, and in fact, on the eve of the Long March, in 1934, some young Moscow supporters among the Chinese Communists had proposed shipping Mao off to Russia, but the Comintern, Russia's international revolutionary arm, turned down the idea, saying that it could not do without Mao's prestige.[2]

From the time Mao and Jiang Qing mounted their ponies and left Yanan in the spring of 1947, they spent a full year in the arid wastelands of Shaanxi. Jiang Qing was often separated from Mao. The country was difficult. Quarters were rough, infested with lice and bedbugs. She had her small daughter, Li Na, to look after. Even when Mao settled down in Xibaipo, on May 27, 1948, he had little time for his wife.

In the remarkable thirty-hour interview that Jiang Qing gave to Roxane Witke, the American scholar, in 1972, Jiang had not a word to say about staying in Xibaipo. Nor did she mention the Fragrant Hills, to which Mao repaired from Xibaipo. She did not say she went there with her husband. In view of her obsessive detail about almost every other phase of her life, the omissions are significant.

All Jiang said was that, simultaneous with Mao's going "to Beijing," she was placed on a railroad train in March 1949 with an entourage of nurses and bodyguards and shipped off to the Soviet Union. The decision, she said, was not her own or that of Chairman Mao but that of "some leading comrades." The notion that any comrade, leading or not, could send the chairman's wife to Russia without the chairman's approval is ridiculous.

Jiang Qing made no attempt to identify the "leading comrades," nor did Roxane Witke ask who they were. Jiang said that her health had been so worn down by the years away from Yanan that "they" felt she must be treated. Stalin obliged by putting Russian medical facilities at Chinese disposal. She made no substantive reply to a question by Witke as to what facilities the Russians had that the Chinese did not possess.[3]

Jiang Qing's remarks to Witke about Moscow and her absence before returning to China in autumn 1949 were contradictory. But she exposed more than she realized. She said that by April 20–21, 1949, when the Chinese fired upon the British gunboat *Amethyst* in the

Yangtze near Nanjing, she was under treatment on the Black Sea, at the Crimean resort of Yalta. Here she heard the news. She was thrilled, she said, at Chairman Mao's declaration that the Chinese people had stood up. In fact, Mao's announcement of the *Amethyst* affair does not contain this statement, which was made instead in his October 1, 1949, proclamation from Tiananmen.[4] It is tempting to believe that Jiang Qing heard both the chairman's April 30 statement and his October 1 declaration over the radio in the Soviet Union.

Mao's bodyguards recalled Mao's inveighing against Jiang Qing in those spring days when he was still at Xibaipo, about to leave for the Fragrant Hills. Mao and Jiang Qing had a fierce quarrel, bodyguard Li Yinqiao remembered. It started over a seventeen-year-old baby-sitter for their daughter, Li Na. Jiang cursed the baby-sitter and said she was stupid. Mao flared up: "You just can't correct your bourgeois egotism and selfishness." In light of Mao's liking for teenage girls, there may have been more behind the outburst than baby-sitting.[5]

They had another row, about Jiang Qing's shadowy past in Shanghai. Jiang wanted Mao to speak up for her. He refused. "History is history," he snapped. "If you were so radical and revolutionary in Shanghai, why do you need me to say things for you?"

"This marriage is a failure," the bodyguards also recalled Mao's saying. "If she was my secretary I would have thrown her out long ago." Now he couldn't simply divorce her. She had committed no "big mistake." Divorce would cause controversy among the leaders. "But if I don't divorce her I will always carry a political burden. I'm helpless. I must manage to live with her."[6]

Jiang Qing, Mao said, was very jealous. She could not tolerate those who did things better than she. She liked to swim but would never go in the pool if Wang Guangmei, Liu Shaoqi's wife, was there, because Wang Guangmei could swim properly while Jiang Qing could only dog-paddle.

"She has a sharp mouth and a sharp tongue," Mao said, "and she will always make trouble. A week after I die people will kill her."[7]

No wonder Jiang had nothing to say about these times. There is good evidence that her fate was hanging in the balance. During this period — or at some point in 1949 — Mao told his associates that he was ready to give up Jiang Qing. Later on he was to say that he had been persuaded by Party associates not to divorce her.[8]

Jiang Qing's background was tawdry. Born in the town of Zucheng, not far from Qingdao, the old German treaty port of Shandong Province, Jiang had for a father a carpenter and small tradesman, a drunkard, a man who beat both wife and child. Her mother was his concubine, in fact, little more than a prostitute who continued to ply her trade. Nonetheless, Jiang Qing, forlorn, often neglected, seemingly headed for the gutter, got a surprisingly good schooling.

Later on there would be tales about her and security chief Kang Sheng, known variously as "that devil," as the nonagenarian New Zealander Rewi Alley called him years after Kang's death,[9] and "that man of depravity" in his relationship with Jiang Qing, as Hu Yaobang once remarked when he was secretary-general of the Communist party.

One story was that Jiang had been sold into Kang Sheng's family as a pubescent slave and teenage prostitute. "All the men in the family used her," Rewi Alley insisted.[10] Neither of Jiang Qing's American biographers, Roxane Witke and Ross Terrill, credits this version — which is widely believed in Beijing — but Terrill does concede that there was probably a sexual connection between Jiang and Kang Sheng. Of Kang Sheng's aid in introducing Jiang Qing to higher Party echelons there is no doubt. He helped get her into Yanan, where she could meet Mao. Kang Sheng stayed close to her and would be her partner in the nightmare of the Cultural Revolution.

There were to be scores of men in Jiang Qing's life. During her Shanghai days as a B-class actress, she picked them up, used them (or they used her), and discarded them. One man, a brilliant countryman named Yu Qiwei, or Huang Qing, or David, an erratic and quixotic figure, touched her deeply.

David, as he was called by Edgar Snow and his first wife, Helen, met Jiang Qing in 1932 as a student at Shandong University. A passionate love affair sprang up, and the two were married — no ceremony. They were radical young people who rejected the old conventions. Some Chinese believe Kang Sheng introduced Jiang Qing to David.

If Kang Sheng was an evil man (as surviving Party leaders agree), David was an idealist who came to Communism and revolution from pure patriotism and a desire to save his country. He became an underground hero and eventually was arrested in 1933 and held under threat of execution. His uncle, a high Nationalist official, quietly rescued him, but Jiang Qing lost her husband. He went to Beijing in 1934, leaving Jiang Qing behind. Before long he was helping Edgar and then Helen Snow make their separate ways to Mao Zedong's northern Shaanxi enclave.[11]

During Jiang Qing's Shanghai days, she tried in every way (and her ways were quite diverse) to advance herself in the theater and films. She became active in radical circles of Shanghai's Hollywood. With the help of David and/or Kang Sheng, Jiang Qing got to Yanan in 1937. By this time Edgar Snow's account of his trip to Mao's Shaanxi base, *Red Star over China,* began to be published in translation in Chinese newspapers and in book form. It swept China like a typhoon, touching off a migration of young Chinese to Yanan. By May 1938 more than twenty-five hundred students and other young people had made their way to the Communist area, many, like Jiang Qing, from Shanghai.[12]

It is not true, as some gossipy Chinese have said, that David or Kang Sheng deliberately maneuvered Jiang Qing into Yanan's Lu Xun Arts and Literature College in order to place her in Mao's bed. But it is true that Kang Sheng eased her into the college when Chen Yun, the strict Party man who lived to become a leading conservative critic of the Deng Xiaoping reforms, turned her down. And it is also true that Mao lectured there, spotted Jiang Qing in the front row, all eyes and awe, and soon thereafter they were sleeping together. All Yanan knew it because Jiang announced to her classmates one day that "you will be happy to know I am now sharing the bed of Chairman Mao."[13]

The way for the consummation of Jiang Qing's ambition to make it with *somebody* (not necessarily Mao) was helped by both David the good and Kang Sheng the evil. But the hypothesis posed by some that the conjunction of Mao and Jiang had been conceived, encouraged, and advanced by David in order to place his own woman in a position of extraordinarily intimate access to Mao cannot be sustained. What happened, more likely, is that Jiang Qing had positioned herself so that she could seize an opportunity if it knocked. And knock it did.

Several saucy ladies, newly arrived in Yanan from Shanghai, had taken advantage of the free habits of Yanan (well hidden from the public by an opaque screen of pious puritanism) to persuade Party leaders to discard their veteran wives of the Long March in favor of their own more lively companionship. Lin Biao was one of these leaders, He Long another. Mao's wife of the time, He Zizhen, became outraged at Mao's participation in these flirtations. Her nerves cracked, her health impaired by repeated childbearing on the Long March, still recovering from shrapnel wounds, she threw Mao over. Supposedly she went off, unhappily, to Moscow, but it probably was more complex than anyone now will admit. In the words of Liu Ying, wife of Zhang

Wentian (also known as Luo Fu), who knew them both, "Jiang Qing didn't push He Zizhen out of the picture. He Zizhen left Mao's bed empty. Jiang Qing just moved into it."[14]

Mao's marital record was complex. During his early youth his parents, in the Chinese tradition, arranged a marriage for him to an older woman. Mao objected violently, and the marriage was never consummated. His first wife was Yang Kaihui, daughter of Professor Yang Changji, Mao's mentor in Changsha and Beijing. Mao and Yang Kaihui married in 1920. She was executed in Changsha by the Nationalists in 1930. Mao was then already living with He Zizhen on Jinggang Mountain, where they had met in 1927. The break with He Zizhen came in 1937, when she left or was sent (depending on the witness) to Moscow. Mao then married Jiang Qing.

He Zizhen suffered tragedy after tragedy in Moscow. In 1949, with Communist victory at hand, she was able to return to China. It had taken a long time to get permission. Jiang Qing, firmly married to Mao (or was she?), had seen to that.[15] In an odd quirk, Mao's second wife was returning to China just as wife number three was leaving for Russia. Their trains may have passed each other in Siberia.

In time David would become a senior member of the Party, sharing the full confidence of Mao and the elders. His health was poor. Some said he suffered from a bad heart, others that he had had a bout of tuberculosis. But he held important Party posts, and when Mao moved his base to Shijiazhuang in May 1948, David was nearby, serving as mayor of Zhangjiakou, a city to the north. David had a beautiful and highly intelligent sister, an actress named Yu Shan. Some said the two were as close as twins. The sister, by David's arrangement, made her way to Mao's headquarters city to perform in the theater. She sang Beijing opera, which Mao loved, and David introduced her to Mao.[16]

Speculation has been advanced that this was a new strategy by David. Embittered or disappointed by his protégée and former wife, Jiang Qing, David decided to seduce Mao with a new partner, one who he felt was Jiang's superior in every respect — cultural acumen, intelligence, refinement, attractiveness. David had become convinced that Jiang Qing could not become a fit spouse for a new Chinese ruler. She did not possess the qualities needed to share the life of an emperor. She had neither the savoir faire nor the diplomatic skills.

This is speculation. True, David's sister possessed the characteristics mentioned. True, she went to Shijiazhuang. True, David introduced her to Mao. And, most important, there was the rift between Mao and Jiang Qing starting in the late forties. Certainly Jiang Qing would not have taken lightly the appearance of her former husband, the man who knew her secrets, and the man who had unlocked some of the doors that led her into Mao's bedroom. Jiang Qing was already worn, drawn, uneasy, nervous, and upset. The sudden arrival of David's sister, beautiful, sophisticated, was bound to cause an upset.

This would seem to be the reason Jiang Qing was put on the train for Moscow in 1949. Official accounts have always indicated that Mao moved to Beijing from the Fragrant Hills toward the end of June or early July. No specific date had been offered. But in 1990 a visitor to Mao's Villa of the Two Wells, Shuang Jing, in the Fragrant Hills noticed a descriptive note posted on the wall. It said Mao had occupied the villa from March 25, 1949, to November 1949. Mao's dalliance in the Fragrant Hills was considerably longer than had been known. It coincided exactly with the period of Jiang Qing's absence from China.

Did Mao spend these long months with David's beautiful sister? There seems little reason otherwise for his extended absence. Whatever the case, a permanent relationship did not ensue. Despite Yu Shan's qualifications, her beauty, her potential skills as empress, she may not have entirely pleased Mao. As time went on, it became clear that his tastes in bed were earthy. Few of his ladies would have qualified for the upper ranks of imperial concubinage. His preference seemed to be for harem girls, peasants, and pickups.

The episode explains why Jiang Qing was not on the terrace of the Gate of Heavenly Peace on October 1, 1949, and why, when she finally did move into Zhongnanhai, it was not into the Study of Chrysanthemum Fragrance but into what were delicately called "adjoining" quarters.

When the hypothesis that David — a pure, principled, idealistic, dedicated, self-sacrificing young student willing to make any contribution for the Revolution — was, at the same time, a Machiavelli willing to use the body of his sister in a complex intrigue for power was presented to several old revolutionaries, they exploded in outrage. This was not their David. They had known him well, in good times and bad, in danger and in difficulty. This image of David was repugnant, a libel, a slander on a man whom they worshiped as the pure spirit of the Revolution, a man who had, in Mao's words, made China stand up.

The violence of their response, the clarity with which they limned David's portrait, gave me pause. The sleazy picture of a man who might have inhabited the court of the Borgias must be wrong, a filthy caricature.

Then by chance I mentioned David to a woman who possessed all of the characteristics with which David was endowed by his friends, a woman who had gone through fire; who had placed her life on the line time and again with the guerrillas; who was so bold that the KMT put a price of 5,000 silver dollars on her head; who had endured the phobic years of Mao's Cultural Revolution. I was puzzled by the curious expression on her face when I mentioned David's name. Finally, at the urging of her daughter, the old revolutionary told me a story.

In 1943 she had been in the hospital to have her appendix removed. There she met David, then using the name of Huang Qing. He was, she said, completely mad. He refused medication. He would take no drugs, believing the doctors were trying to kill him. They wanted to give him acupuncture. David repulsed them with such strength they could do nothing. Finally they told him that Mao Zedong had sent an order that he was to have acupuncture. With this assurance he permitted them to treat him.[17]

She had, the old revolutionary said, heard a great deal about David at that time. She knew that he had known Jiang Qing in Shandong and later in Shanghai and that he had a sister, a famous actress in the 1930s. There was much else, but she did not want to talk about it. However, she confirmed that after treatment David recovered his mental balance and went on to become mayor of Tianjin, a post of major importance. His death at the age of forty-seven was attributed to heart disease.[18]

David's wife at the time of his death was Fan Jin, a brilliant journalist who was to become deputy mayor of Beijing. During the Cultural Revolution, Fan Jin was tortured with exceptional ferocity on a public stage before an audience that included Jiang Qing. Many others associated with David and Fan Jin were relentlessly tracked down (as was charged in Jiang Qing's trial). Fan Jin went mad under torture but survived and in 1988 had in large measure recovered.[19]

There would be those who saw in the tragic story of David (true or not) a metaphor of the Revolution itself, its mixture of good and evil, lofty ideals and miserable depths. David was a manic-depressive with severe symptoms of paranoia, so like the Revolution, with its highs, its lows, its loves, its suspicions, its hates, its scenes of total chaos, of degradation of innocent men and women, its exaltation of noble conduct, its raving mobs savagely beating their victims, dragging them from village to village, until finally they used their picks and shovels to sever heads from bodies, to gouge out eyes and tear away limbs.

A revolution, as Mao liked to say, is not a tea party.

9

Saturday Night Dances

LIFE IN ZHONGNANHAI quickly began to establish its own pattern. Living and working amid the faded splendors of empire had more effect on the life-style of the Party than Mao may have realized. This was no encampment along the Dadu River or cave city in northern Shaanxi. It was a secret compound of palaces and villas such as existed nowhere else in the world.

Mao and his comrades strolled the corridors of the dynasties. Magnificent surroundings enveloped them as they pondered the future of a land still starving and destitute. They held their meetings — public assemblies — in gold and carmine buildings, and they used the Sea Palaces of Emperor Guangxu for exhibitions and rallies. The living quarters were exquisite. They could choose from among the treasures of thousands of years. Zhongnanhai bore scars of foreign cannon and foreign looting, but unless you knew what had been destroyed you would not miss it amid riches beyond compare.

Mao and his men (and women) boated on the lakes of Zhongnanhai. They could see in the distance the ordinary people of Beijing boating and swimming in Beihai Lake, the Northern Sea. There was no mixing.

Zhongnanhai housed the Central Party Committee offices, and hundreds of clerks, but nowhere in China was access more tightly guarded, sentries more strict, security more rigid.

                    *   *   *

The children of the leaders went to special schools. They called Mao
"Uncle"; Zhou Enlai's wife, Deng Yingchao, "Auntie" or "Deng
Mama"; and Zhu De's wife, Kang Keqing, "Kang Mama."[1] General
Yang Shangkun, who was in charge of the General Office of the
Communist Party, seemed to have more free time than most of the
adults. The children of Liu Shaoqi remembered him taking them to
the movies and buying them ice cream. Liu Shaoqi was so busy, their
mother recalled, that they spent more time playing with "Uncle Mao"
than with their own father. Tingting as a tot even called Mao "Daddy."

There was a kindergarten on the western shore of Zhonghai, the
Middle Sea, for children of cadres. It was run by the mother of Wang
Guangmei, wife of President Liu Shaoqi. In the western suburbs was
a grade school for children of cadres, called Yu Cai (Bringing Up
Talents). Almost all of the children of high Party officials were taught
at this school. A middle school called the August 1 School was located
near Beijing University.[2]

The parents drew stipends from the state, but they seldom carried
money in their pockets. Everything was bought by their "bodyguards,"
a group now rapidly growing from the two or three men of Yanan
to bigger and bigger companies and finally regiments, one for each
important leader.

Mao had a fetish about money. He refused to carry it and refused
even to touch it. As his bodyguard Li Yinqiao recalled, Mao was
willing to shake hands with his deadliest enemy, Chiang Kaishek, but
he would not soil his hands with a yuan note. He wouldn't even look
at money. "You know I never touch money," he told Li.[3]

Mao had fallen in love with Western dancing in the Yanan days. Hand-
wound portable Victrolas and old-fashioned red-label records had
made their way to Yanan. There has been some controversy over
whether Western dancing was brought in by Agnes Smedley, an American Communist sympathizer, in the late 1930s or by the American
military Dixie Mission during World War II. Some Chinese insisted
they imported it themselves (from Shanghai), but whatever its origin,
its popularity had been established long before Mao left Yanan. There,
Saturday night dances were held in the Date Garden, a broad clay-
packed floor outside the caves. Americans like Jack Service and Colonel
David Barrett danced there and watched eager-eyed young Chinese
girls approach Chairman Mao and Zhu De and say, "Please dance

with me." Then they were swung around the floor in ecstasy. Brooks Atkinson, the *New York Times* correspondent and drama critic, remembered meeting Jiang Qing at the Date Garden. He was not impressed; she seemed like just another young Shanghai woman. Lin Biao and Zhou Enlai were the best dancers. Marshal Ye Jianying was assiduous on the dance floor, but his interest was, perhaps, more in acquiring new bed partners than in the etiquette of Terpsichore. No one remembers seeing Deng Xiaoping on the dance floor. Maybe he thought he was too short. Most of the girls were taller.

Mao's dancing style was compared by one observer to that of a reluctant bear. He approached his partner, arms extended, body stiff, straight and a bit apprehensive, leaving a lot of distance between himself and the woman. Mao had no ear for music or any interest in what was played. He danced to Beijing opera songs, humming and singing as he propelled the young ladies around the floor in relentless circles.[4]

Hardly had Mao moved into the Study of Chrysanthemum Fragrance than he suggested resuming the pleasant custom of Saturday night dances. Mao, in a way, was reviving an ancient Zhongnanhai pastime. The last and most decadent of the Mongol emperors of the Yuan dynasty in the fourteenth century had amused himself and his guests by creating a group of dancing girls called the Fourteen Heavenly Devils. These young ladies, resplendent in lavish brocades and magnificent jewels, engaged in erotic dances and scandalous conduct in the guise of performing Lamaist rituals. The Han Chinese had professed to being shocked by such goings-on. However, they were not too upset to jot down precise anatomical descriptions of the scenes.

All had been arranged for Mao's Saturday night dances to begin when a hitch arose — where to get dancing partners for Mao? For security reasons, they couldn't just round up a bunch of pretty girls from the street. The crisis was resolved by requisitioning wives and female workers from the Foreign Ministry, which Zhou Enlai had set up in the old Hôtel des Wagons-Lits, just down the street from the Beijing Hotel. The Foreign Ministry women filled in until an "art ensemble" was put together, vetted for security, and established in residence in Zhongnanhai, so there would always be girls on tap if Chairman Mao needed one.[5]

The Yuan emperor's dancing girls performed water ballets around the Zhongnanhai lakes as the emperor and his guests viewed the spectacle from imperial barges. Mao's pursuits lacked the grace and grandeur of his predecessor's. His dances were held indoors at the

Hall of Diligent Governing, an ugly building erected by Yuan Shikai, the warlord who usurped power from Dr. Sun Yatsen and named himself emperor, only to fall within six months.[6]

A large outdoor swimming pool had been built in 1933 on the western shore of Zhonghai.[7] No spot in Beijing was more popular in summer in the 1930s. There were tables set along the shores; tea and light lunches of fried rice and French pastries were served. It was a place so pleasant that George Kates, the author of *The Years That Were Fat*, often whiled away a whole day, lazily gazing on the scene and trying to memorize Chinese characters from the ideograph cards he always had at hand.[8]

The swimming pool was located just south of the Hall of Purple Effulgence, which had been used by Manchu emperors for military assemblies and competitions in archery and horseback riding. For years the hall was neglected, set in a grove of ill-tended silk trees, but Mao would restore it, using it for the reception of foreign diplomats (as had the late Manchus) and for important gatherings, sometimes of a military nature.

Mao loved to swim, as did Deng Xiaoping and some of the other leaders. The pool was promptly declared out-of-bounds to the public and reserved for the use of Mao and of the top Party leaders and their families. No longer would the gilded youth of Beijing loll through lazy summer days beside the Zhonghai pool. No one in Mao's group noticed that the young people who now swam and played in the swimming pool were, in effect, kin of their predecessors: young, well born (into the Party), privileged, set apart from the common folk, and, like their parents, an elite — a new elite that would with the years take on more and more characteristics of the old.

There was a drawback to the Zhonghai pool. It was unheated and could be used only in summer. Mao confessed in later years that he was not a real swimmer when he moved into Zhongnanhai, but the more he used the pool, the more he liked swimming. In the winter of 1954 he decided to become a real swimmer. The only heated indoor pool in Beijing was at Qinghua University. For three months he went out to Qinghua every evening with his swimsuit and towel in a valise, put on his trunks, and, as he said, "without interruption I studied the nature of the water."[9] General Yang Shangkun accompanied Mao on these expeditions. They went incognito, it was said. How Mao could have disguised his great pumpkin head, his moon face, and his bulky body was not explained. In 1958–59 Mao had a new pool built in

Zhongnanhai, Olympic-size, this one enclosed and heated so that he could swim whenever he wanted, summer or winter.[10]

And, as time went by, many of China's great cities built grandiose guesthouses set in lavish parks — often they took over large central public parks for the purpose — reserved for Mao's use, should he chance to visit. They were kept up, fully staffed, ready at any moment to be placed at his disposal. Each had a big swimming pool (most of them indoor and heated) and a permanent "art ensemble," just in case. Some of these establishments stood unused until Mao's death; he had never gotten around to visiting them. Many ultimately were turned into rambling, unprofitable tourist hotels. This was true of the big Welcome Zedong Hotel and the Zedong Park in Taiyuan. Zhou Enlai stayed there, but Mao never made it.[11]

The imposing trappings of Zhongnanhai did not develop at once, and not all the Party leaders moved in immediately. The Defense Ministry took over the old Iron Lion Lane mansions of previous regimes but kept the military establishment in the Fragrant Hills. Zhu De, the PLA commander-in-chief, moved in when Mao did, occupying a palace with his rifle-toting wife, Kang Keqing, only a hundred yards from Mao. Zhou Enlai occupied a quiet palace called Western Elegance up a narrow lane from Mao's. Zhou's widow, Deng Yingchao, still occupied it in 1990. Kang Keqing moved from the Zhu De house to a villa in the Western Hills after her husband died.

Liu Shaoqi moved into a house close to Mao's in late August 1949. Deng was a latecomer. His assignments in Chongqing and the southwest kept him out of Beijing until 1952.

Of Mao's fondness for Zhongnanhai there was no doubt. In the early days its atmosphere was quite easygoing. Liu Shaoqi and his family settled comfortably into the communal life. When Deng Xiaoping finally arrived, he did not take to it so readily. He strolled with his wife and children on Sundays in the parklike rambles. Staying in Zhongnanhai was a bit like living in Central Park with no ordinary citizens about.

When Deng came into his own after Mao's death, he did not move back to Zhongnanhai and recommended that his associates not do so either. It wasn't safe, he insisted. One bomb could destroy the whole Politburo, and a coup could capture them all. He took a residence behind the Forbidden City, just east of Coal Hill in the old grain warehouse district. Located down a very narrow *hutong* wide enough for only a single car, the home was very secure. It had been the residence of Li Kenong, the security specialist. It was rebuilt for Deng's use with steel-plated walls and bullet-proof windows. The house could hardly be seen from the street behind its courtyard, strong steel gates, and sturdy masonry pillars.[12]

Another who felt uneasy in Zhongnanhai was Lin Biao, the enigmatic general. Instead of a Zhongnanhai palace, he picked a lovely and treasured Old China house, the home of the Yus, an ancient Han family of great wealth and tradition. The Yu residence sprawled over several acres in the Yellow, or West, City, close by West Four Arch at 3 Crooked Hair Family Lane.[13] It had been built in the time of the third Ming sovereign, on an old temple site, and possessed one of the loveliest gardens in Beijing, as well as an ancient pool, a handsome Hall of Harmonious Virtues, and seven large tiled courtyards connecting its buildings.

After the Revolution the Yu family sold the establishment to the new Ministry of Finance for fifteen thousand dollars. It took two hundred carts to empty the place of furniture. The Finance Ministry was headed by Bo Yibo, ultimately one of Deng's elders, following a bold guerrilla career. The ministry did not use it as Bo's residence, as it had promised, but filled in the pool and turned the garden into a parking lot and the house into a clinic.

Lin Biao took the estate over from the Finance Ministry and, since it had deteriorated badly, refurnished it, in a Hong Kong mixture of modern Chinese and Western styles. Lin also had a tunnel built between his home and Zhongnanhai. He occupied the Yu residence until he fled to his death in September 1971.[14]

Another Party leader who preferred to live outside Zhongnanhai was Kang Sheng, the security operative. He was out of Beijing for a long period, turning his native Shandong Province into a police state. When he came back he moved into a tasteful Manchu prince's palace on a tiny lane close by the Silver Ingot Bridge and the Rear Lake, north of Zhongnanhai. In the rock garden of his courtyard he possessed a cave where, it was said, he kept victims for private torture. After the deaths of Kang Sheng and Mao, the house was turned into a small hotel, the Bamboo Gardens, for conferences and meetings.[15]

Perhaps it is a commentary on changing times that by the 1980s the younger generation of the Beijing elite, the sons and daughters, grandsons and granddaughters of the elders, had begun to detest Zhongnanhai. They didn't care for imperial grandeur and the ever-present guards. Zhongnanhai's old-fashioned style didn't suit the new generations, so many of whom had lived and traveled widely in the West, particularly the United States. They didn't care for the security checks on their friends and the ban on jazz, contemporary rock, the latest dances from New York, Los Angeles, and London. They had begun to move out of the privileged park into more relaxed environments.

The celerity with which the princes of Mao's new regime occupied the dwellings of those whom they had displaced was extraordinary for a group that preached the universality of men, egalitarian society, and privilege for none.

Within months of moving into the old capital the commissars had acquired many of the material conveniences of the rich and powerful without, it could readily be said, acquiring the artistic tastes that went with their rank. Because Mao himself had been the leader in choosing an imperial setting and because of his extraordinary authority, there was no debate of this tendency and no opposition.

Some leaders did not follow the pattern. Zhou Enlai continued to live a modest life, as did his wife. They occupied a simple palace, with few servants, no lavish feasts. Zhou was the host at many official dinners but usually ate a bowl of noodles in the kitchen of the Beijing Hotel before dinners at the Great Hall of the People so he could devote his attention to his guests. His tunics and suits were often threadbare and sometimes missing buttons.[16] Jiang Qing once called his attention to the fact that the soles of his cotton slippers had worn through and he was walking in his white cotton socks.[17]

Deng Xiaoping was another who never lost his soldier's simplicity. His manners were plain and so was his taste. His children grew up well behaved and unused to special favors, except for the ice cream that Yang Shangkun treated them to.

Mao must have realized that they were moving away from the simplicity of the Long March and the informal life of Yanan. In the old days, if Mao was asleep in his cave when his fellow commanders wanted to talk to him, they would yank the blanket off his bed, start him up, stark naked, and begin the conference. On the Long March, Mao and his men ate, more or less, from a common rice bowl. No food was taken from the peasants without money or an I.O.U. being offered in return. The penalty for rape or robbery was being shot on the spot. The strength of the Revolution lay in the conduct of the army and its cadres. In the Old China it was said that you did not use good iron to make nails or good men to make soldiers. The Red Army completely reversed that adage, and its moral conduct won the peasantry and won China.

*   *   *

If these earlier days of the Revolution were in some ways less complicated, they were also a battleground for the war for sexual equality.

At the turn of the century China was still a feudal society. Women had hardly more rights than cattle; they were bought and sold. Marriages were arranged. The woman was considered subordinate to the husband and her husband's family, a slave of her mother-in-law. If her husband died, she had little chance of remarriage and was kept as a chattel in the household of her husband's family. Her only escape was into prostitution.

The life of married couples in the Red Army was originally regulated by boarding-school rules. Couples were permitted to be together only one night a week — Saturday night.

Then foreigners appeared in Yanan: revolutionary sympathizers, American women like Agnes Smedley, Anna Louise Strong, and Helen Snow. Agnes Smedley had incendiary views about women's rights; she believed women should love when, where, and how they liked.

In addition, there had been an influx of young Chinese women into Yanan, many of them attractive, sexually active women like Jiang Qing. They came from the artistic and theatrical worlds of Shanghai. Some were women of great stature, like Ding Ling, China's most famous radical writer. Ding Ling believed a woman possessed the absolute right to use her body as she wished. Any restriction was "bourgeois morality."

At first, Mao made women's rights his leading cause. He believed in freedom from sexual constraints. He and his two best friends, the brother and sister Cai Hesen and Cai Chang, agreed to ban the "Three Nos" from conversation: prostitution, gambling, and money.[18] They cherished high moral values. They signed a compact pledging that they would never marry. Of course, none of them kept the promise, but it was a measure of their feeling about marriage. When Mao and his first wife, Yang Kaihui, fell in love, they simply announced that they were living in a "trial marriage," a marriage founded on romantic ideals. Mao created the slogan "Women Hold Up Half the Heavens" to propagandize women's rights.

Soon a dichotomy between Mao's ideals and conduct began to develop. When Yang Kaihui was imprisoned by Chiang Kaishek's minions and was awaiting execution in Changsha, Mao began living with He Zizhen on Jinggang Mountain. He married He Zizhen shortly after hearing, he said, news of Yang Kaihui's death.[19] To his last days he mourned Kaihui, writing his most moving poem about "my proud poplar."[20]

Mao had a bad conscience about Yang Kaihui. He told his bodyguards that he would always feel guilty. He said that he married He Zizhen in 1928, believing that Kaihui was dead, and did not realize she was held in prison until 1930. It was a thin excuse. Official accounts of Mao and He Zizhen always have indicated they met on Jinggang Mountain in 1927 but did not marry until after Kaihui's death.[21]

Young revolutionary women believed marriage turned women into property and that it was nothing but a contract for exploiting sexual access. They believed as did the famous Russian revolutionary Alexandra Kollontai, who proclaimed that "love is like a glass of water," to be indulged in whenever you were thirsty. She carried her argument to Lenin, who rejected it (although he himself lived for years in a ménage à trois). Ding Ling had the same argument with Mao in Yanan. He listened sympathetically, teased her about the number of concubines the emperors had, holding her hand and counting them off on her fingers and his own, then came down on the side of bourgeois morality, solely, in the view of his biographer Li Rui, for political reasons. Mao was catering to the "moral majority" of the peasants, to whom free love was anathema.[22] The turmoil aroused in Yanan by Agnes Smedley, Ding Ling, and the ardent young Shanghai ladies set off shock waves. Mao and his party chiefs sent Smedley away and banished several Chinese women in an effort to restore peace to paradise.

When Mao wanted to marry Jiang Qing, his associates were reluctant to approve. They permitted the marriage after Mao claimed Jiang was essential to his physical well-being, but banned her from politics — a ban that was maintained for about twenty years.

Amid the turmoil about relations between the sexes, Deng Xiaoping was untouched. No hint of scandal was to rise over his marriage to Zhuo Lin. They had been married in Yanan, and fifty years later were still married, as comfortable a couple as China possessed.

But the Deng marriage was one of the exceptions in Zhongnanhai. Not much of the early idealism was left. No longer did men and women profess commitment to each other in the romantic terms of eternal love. Now they spoke of a bed partner as the "loved person," *ai ren*. The term does not imply a fixed or abiding relationship. It smacks of impermanence, love on the fly, one-night stands, a loosening of principles. In this, Mao, with his secret troupes of "dancing partners," was the leader, as he was in all else.[23]

Milovan Djilas, the Yugoslav Communist leader, had summed it all up in 1957 in his indictment of Communist leadership, called *The New Class*. The Communists had come to power in Yugoslavia, as they had in the Soviet Union and China. They had destroyed and displaced the old ruling class, denouncing its riches and its privileged way of life. Then, as fast as they could, they had replicated the privileges, the same elite style of living, and become almost instantly a new ruling class, differing from the old only in terminology and in a more naked power system.

In some ways Mao never was able to accommodate himself to Zhongnanhai. He sensed that there was something wrong. But he never changed his style of governance in the compound or abandoned it for a new headquarters. He complained that "nobody tells me anything" in Beijing. It wasn't like the old days of free and easy communication. Beijing, he often said, is just a processing center; all the materials come from the countryside.[24] He would have to see for himself what was happening. He traveled a lot, but usually to Hangzhou, Guangzhou, Chongqing, from one palace to another, from one set of bureaucrats to another, until finally it didn't really matter whether he left Zhongnanhai or not. Mao complained to his guards: "Wherever I go they prepare for me. I can't find out the truth."

He staged surprise attacks, in which he would suddenly order his special train to halt at an obscure village, leap out, and hurry to the Party office, hoping to catch the residents unaware. But his guards had orders to alert local authorities, and by the time Mao got there the villagers were struggling into their best clothes, sweeping out their houses, and preparing feasts (sometimes with food supplied by the guards).

Finally, Mao took to sending his guards out to the countryside to report on conditions in their home villages. But the guards were chary of telling him the truth because, despite what Mao claimed he wanted, bad news enraged him.

"On the one hand Mao wanted to discover the truth," said bodyguard Li Yinqiao, "but on the other hand he could not tolerate anyone who dared to tell the truth."[25]

PART 3

THE DUEL OF DICTATORS

10

Mao's Feud with Stalin

JIANG QING was not the only absentee from the high platform of Tiananmen on October 1, 1949.

The Soviet ambassador, Lieutenant General N. V. Roshchin, former military attaché at Chongqing, was not present. This was no accident. He had been glued to the side of Chiang Kaishek throughout the civil war and was still at Canton awaiting orders.[1]

Despite Roshchin's absence there was a quiet Soviet presence at Tiananmen, almost invisible to the naked eye. Early in the morning of October 1 a Soviet "cultural" delegation, headed by the writers Aleksandr Fadeev and Konstantin Simonov, arrived at Beijing's Central Railway Station from Manchuria. At the station to greet them was S. L. Tikhvinsky of the consul-general's staff. The Soviets had taken over the old Russian building in the Legation Quarter, which sprawled at the foot of Tiananmen.

As Tikhvinsky waited he was startled to see Zhou Enlai approaching along the platform. Zhou's face was sheet-white, his eyes were closed, his feet shuffled inertly, and he was supported on either side by burly bodyguards who were, in fact, carrying his unconscious body. An aide hurriedly explained that Zhou was literally out on his feet. He had worked four days and nights without rest preparing for the big day and overseeing the People's Consultative Assembly meeting. He had insisted on obeying protocol for the reception of the Soviet group. As the train pulled in, Zhou's aides shook him awake. He roused himself, greeted the Russians with his usual courtesy, and excused himself.

At Tiananmen Zhou seemed his normal self, lively and alert, but

Russia was still on his mind. Tikhvinsky and the delegation were sitting in a temporary wooden stand below Tiananmen. Amid the ceremonies Tikhvinsky received a note from Zhou. An important message from the Chinese government had been delivered at the consulate, but there was no one to receive it.

Tikhvinsky slipped off the platform, made his way to the consulate, only two hundred feet away, and found a formal notification of the establishment of the Chinese People's Republic. The note said China hoped to establish diplomatic relations with the Soviet Union and other friendly countries. Tikhvinsky fired off a cable to Moscow and went on to the official reception at the Beijing Hotel. Next morning Foreign Minister Andrei A. Gromyko sent Moscow's formal recognition of the new government. An order was sent to Roshchin to proceed to Beijing and present his credentials.[2]

"Cool" is too weak a word to describe the nature of Soviet-Chinese and Stalin-Mao relations over those years. Again and again Mao had been compelled to pay lip service to Stalin. Mao had a keen ear for insults and a long memory. He had not forgotten the times since 1926 that he had been forced by the Soviets to eat humble pie, the reprimands, the expulsions from Party and office because he had failed to follow Moscow's orders, or the mistaken policies Soviet advisers had insisted the Chinese carry out at the cost of death and disaster.

Mao well remembered Stalin's paroxysm when Chiang Kaishek in 1927 massacred the Chinese Communists in Shanghai. Stalin ordered the overnight roundup and arrest of every Chinese in Moscow, including Chinese members of the Comintern and Chinese students being instructed at the Comintern-run University for the Toilers of the East. True, he later released most of them, but this was only the beginning. Thousands of Chinese were later sent to Stalin's gulags or simply shot out of hand. A survivor of Vladivostok's large Chinese colony called it "simple genocide." A high percentage of dedicated Chinese revolutionaries who had the misfortune to be in the Soviet Union paid with their lives. There had been heavy Chinese populations in many eastern Siberian cities — several hundred thousand in all. They vanished. The official explanation was that they had been "repatriated." Actually, many turned up in the camps of Vorkuta, Solovetsky, and Kolyma, where they soon died.[3]

Nothing would erase from Mao's mind the peremptory telegram he got from Stalin in December 1936 ordering him to see that Chiang Kaishek was safely released. Chiang had been kidnapped at Xian by the Young Marshal of Manchuria, Zhang Xueliang, in a quixotic plot to compel him to make peace with the Communists and join a common front against Japan. Mao had hoped to put Chiang on public trial, disgrace him, and possibly execute him. Stalin ordered Chiang freed immediately, threatening that he would otherwise break off all relations with China and publicly denounce Mao. Painfully Mao had complied, but he never forgot.[4]

Mao had a prodigious memory for detail, but he had swallowed all this because he was convinced Communist China was not strong enough to survive without diplomatic, economic, and military protection. He had hoped in World War II that the United States would be his protector and had sent a personal message in January 1945 to President Franklin Roosevelt saying he and Zhou Enlai were ready to come to Washington and negotiate an arrangement. He had never gotten a reply. He did not know that the message had been intercepted by U.S. ambassador Patrick J. Hurley and reached FDR only in distorted form.[5]

Even before General George C. Marshall abandoned his doomed post–World War II effort to negotiate a truce between the Nationalists and the Communists, Mao had concluded that he would have to do business with Stalin — hardly a pleasing prospect. In August 1945, a week after Japan's surrender to the Allies, Stalin had ordered Mao to engage Chiang Kaishek in peace talks and not fight a civil war that would risk total ruin for China.[6] Stalin recalled telling the Chinese "bluntly that we considered the development of the uprising has no prospects and that the Chinese comrades should seek a modus vivendi with Chiang Kaishek, that they should join the Chiang Kaishek government and dissolve their army."

Mao therefore had no illusions that Stalin would be a cooperative partner, and he was not made more comfortable by the fact that the Russians were still trying to help Chiang Kaishek survive or, at rock bottom, to detach China's western province of Xinjiang. The Russians had been interested in Xinjiang since the mid-nineteenth century. Now that interest was whetted by the discovery that Xinjiang possessed rich uranium deposits.

Mao was well aware that China might have to go it alone, faced with hostility both in Moscow and Washington. The prospect was daunting, but Mao had taken at least a few precautions. As early as 1946 and the winter of 1947 he had engaged in a series of remarkable conversations with the American revolutionary Anna Louise Strong, a fervent supporter of the Chinese Communists and follower of their line. Strong's great regret was that the Chinese Communists would never admit her to Party membership. (Nor, in fact, would the American and Soviet parties; they regarded her as too eccentric.) Despite Strong's shortcomings, Mao decided to use her to carry to the West the first outline of his independent personal philosophy, differentiating the Communism of China from that of Moscow.

It was in the conversations with Strong that Mao enunciated his belief that the United States (like other capitalist states) was a "paper tiger." He advanced the theory that the atom bomb would not be decisive in warfare. He continued talking with Strong until the eve of his evacuation of Yanan, in March 1947. Strong wanted to stay, but he insisted that she leave, go to the West, and publicize his views. He enjoined her to carry them to both the Communist and the non-Communist worlds — except for Moscow. It was not necessary for her to go to Moscow. He did not say why.

In her talks with Communists, Mao stressed, she was to tell them that he expected to be in power in China within two years. In talking with non-Communists she was to offer this as her personal opinion rather than Mao's.

Much against her will Strong left Yanan, went to Beijing, took a room at the Beijing Hotel to start writing, then traveled to Shanghai and back to America. She composed a book containing a section on Mao's views, which she called "The Thought of Mao Zedong."[7] Her book was published in the United States and other non-Communist countries and attracted enormous interest in Eastern Europe, where plans were made to publish it in most of the Communist regimes.[8] In Eastern Europe, not yet under Stalin's control, there was obvious interest in a China whose Communist leader was advertising an "independent" brand of Communism. Keenly aware that the enmity between himself and Stalin could easily worsen, Mao was making public in a subtle but unmistakable way that China and "The Thought of Mao Zedong" represented an alternative to Stalin and Stalinism. Mao could not foresee the repercussions of Stalin's purges and police tactics in Eastern Europe, but he wanted to sound a note that might attract discontented Communist leaders and states to his banner. It was a delicately nuanced operation, and in the hands of the ebullient but erratic Strong it was totally deniable.

Strong did not understand Mao's cryptic remarks about Moscow. He told her that he expected her back in China in two years and that it was "not necessary" to return via Russia; better come via Hong Kong. That went over Strong's head. She perceived herself as riding the crest of the wave of the soon-to-succeed Chinese revolution. She went back to Moscow in the autumn of 1948, full of loud talk about China. She announced that once she had a chance to meet Stalin she would persuade him to drop all this nonsense about a split with Tito. She was annoyed but not disturbed at the failure of the Russians to give her a transit visa for China.

Her loose talk so frightened old Moscow friends that they refused to meet with her. Her oldest associate, Mikhail Borodin, the man whom Stalin and Lenin had sent to China to advise Dr. Sun Yatsen, gently tried to persuade her to curb her tongue. She did not. The result: In early January 1949, Strong was arrested by Stalin's police, thrown into the Lubyanka, and branded an agent of the CIA. Borodin was arrested, as well as the entire staff of the English-language *Moscow News,* which he had founded with Strong after they escaped from China in 1927. Most of Russia's China specialists were also arrested, many of them to die in prison camps. Only Strong's arrest was announced. The rest were kept secret.[9]

There could hardly have been a more dramatic demonstration of Stalin's sensitivity (and fear) of Mao's independence. Mao must have gotten the message. Strong, however, released after five days in the Lubyanka and thrust over the Soviet border into Poland, came back to the United States in bewilderment. She was denounced by every Communist organ, including the *Daily Worker* of New York, which had been serializing her book about Mao. She apparently believed her arrest was all a mistake by "Stalin's underlings." Not until March 1955, two years after Stalin's death, did *Pravda* finally publish a note saying that there were no grounds for the case against Strong. And not until 1956 did Strong admit, in a letter to the author, that she had received a veiled warning from Mao to stay away from Moscow and to avoid traveling to China via Moscow. It was so nuanced, she said, that she did not quite comprehend its significance. Now, however, she understood that she had been meddling in politics far beyond her depth. She had thrown her full strength into publicizing Mao and his thoughts, even addressing the Varga Economic Institute in Moscow on the subject. "Boy, did I ever do a job for Mao!" she recalled in glee.[10] Yan Mingfu, Mao's Russian interpreter of the day, had no doubt that Mao's veiled admonitions arose from fear the Russians would arrest Strong.

There was no way for Mao to know all the details, but he knew enough to perceive the danger signs. By early March 1948 he had become convinced that he would have to go to Moscow for a showdown with

Stalin. When Mao arrived at the Chengnanzhuang headquarters of his great commander Nie Rongzhen, en route to Xibaipo, he decided no more time was to be lost. It was a season of extraordinary turbulence in the Communist world. Tito's independence had sent Stalin into a paroxysm. He saw enemies everywhere. He was making plans to attack Tito with his tanks (he ultimately backed off, fearing U.S. intervention), and his secret police were turning Eastern Europe into a killing ground, rooting out the old regimes, arresting Communist Party leaders, staging show trials, and instigating a rule of terror. Stalin was becoming convinced that Mao might follow Tito's path and might even be conniving with Tito. With Mao in power, Stalin had begun to imagine the prospect of a hostile forty-five-hundred-mile border in Siberia and the Far East, with hundreds of millions of yellow men and their intransigent leader, Mao Zedong, confronting him.

How acutely Mao understood Moscow's paranoia cannot be established. But he decided he could afford no more delay, and he threw himself into preparations. He wrote two new pamphlets for his troops and began to organize a mission, headed by himself, to make its way to Moscow and establish a basis for future relations with the Russians.

He picked a small party to accompany him and proposed to go by jeep to the Soviet-Chinese frontier, probably near Manchouli. There he would either connect with the Trans-Siberian Railroad or be picked up by a Soviet transport plane and flown to Moscow.[11]

When Mao communicated his plans to Stalin he got a testy rebuff. This was no time for Mao to leave his revolution, Stalin claimed; the military situation was too precarious (it wasn't). If there was a need for consultation, Stalin would send a trusted member of the Politburo to meet with Mao.[12]

It was this initiative that ultimately led to the dispatch by Stalin of Anastas Mikoyan to China in late 1948 or early 1949. The delay was attributed by the Russians to the lack of physical security of Mao's headquarters complex at Shijiazhuang, Xibaipo, and Chengnanzhuang.[13] Although there had been occasional Nationalist bombings of Xibaipo after Mao's move there in May 1948, the area had been secure for nearly a year. It is impossible to avoid the suspicion that Stalin was deliberately letting Mao twist in the wind.

Mao told Liu Shaoqi that Stalin no longer would even talk with him. This impression was deepened by the lengthy pause before Mikoyan actually arrived. Mao saw Soviet hostility as the reason Moscow continued to oppose his plans for crossing the Yangtze, persisted in suggesting that he enter into some arrangement with the Nationalists,[14] and refused to discuss the status of Mongolia, which Mao (like Chiang Kaishek) regarded as within the Chinese sphere of influence.[15]

The Anna Louise Strong affair coincided with the Mikoyan trip to China, but what Mikoyan told Mao about it or what Mao knew is not clear. There was no indication of Chinese support, private or public, for Strong. Although rumors long circulated that China made some gesture in behalf of Borodin, such an action seems dubious in light of Mao's antipathy to Borodin and his disagreement with Borodin's strategy and advice.

Mao knew how the press of the world was reacting to the Communist successes, the conquest of Manchuria, the steady, irresistible sweep of the Red forces through north China, the fall of Beijing and Tianjin, the massing at the Yangtze crossings. These events were sending tremors through Europe, Asia, and North America, creating big headlines, commentaries, speculation about the change in world balance. Everyone was watching China — or so it seemed — except Moscow. There was no Soviet reaction to these tremendous developments and, besides a snippet on the back page of *Pravda* and a few paragraphs inside *Izvestia,* no editorial comment or analysis in either of these newspapers.

To Soviet eyes nothing was happening, or at least nothing of note. The word "China" hardly appeared. No lectures were given, no doctoral theses defended, and Chinese studies vanished from the universities. Library readers found the China section of the shelves empty. No one in Moscow had any way of finding out that one of the greatest revolutionary events since Karl Marx issued *The Communist Manifesto* in 1848 was taking place. To those who knew what was happening, it could hardly have been more apparent that something was wrong between Moscow and Beijing.[16]

Banned, as he believed, from Moscow, Mao launched a secondary probe. Liu Shaoqi, his right hand of the day, had worked and studied in Russia, knew the language, got on well with Russians. Mao took Liu up on an offer to help and sent him to Moscow in July 1949. Liu stayed there well over a month, meeting with Stalin and engaging in preliminary negotiations.

To Liu Shaoqi, Stalin offered his first apology for misjudging China. He confessed he had invited the Chinese to the Kremlin in 1946 to warn them against trying to seize power by force. "Our idea was incorrect," he said. "Your idea was right."[17] For a man like Stalin it was a remarkable and gracious gesture. It seemed to mark a turn in

Soviet policy, a strong hint, at least, that in the presence of a fait accompli, that is, a new China, Stalin would shed his deep hostility and work on friendly terms.

Later there were those who wondered how much Stalin's words counted. Liu Shaoqi did not go alone to Moscow. He was accompanied by a large and special delegation headed by Gao Gang, Mao's newly appointed viceroy for the "Special Manchurian Economic Region." Because of "special conditions" — i.e., the fact that Moscow still maintained formal friendly relations with Chiang Kaishek — the Soviet Union would violate diplomatic protocol if it entered into direct talks with Mao's government. The fiction of an agreement with Gao Gang's Manchurian economic region was just a cover, it was said, to start Sino-Soviet negotiations.

But in 1955, after the death of Stalin, after the execution of Stalin's police chief, Lavrenty Beria, China suddenly announced that Gao Gang was a traitor who had plotted to set up his own "independent kingdom" in northeast China. He was arrested and charged with high treason. He compounded his guilt with an even more heinous deed: Before he could be brought to public trial and the full record of his nefarious conduct exposed to the multitudes, he cheated the executioner and took his own life.

Gao Gang vanished into the land of nonpersons, those whose existence is no longer mentioned. Not a word was spoken in Beijing of Gao Gang's partner, Stalin, in the conspiracy of this private kingdom, not a word of the trips to Moscow, the deals and the treaties with Stalin.

Not so on the Russian side. When, after 1959–60, polemics became the order of the day between Moscow and Beijing, Gao Gang was hailed in Moscow as a true Chinese statesman. Eulogies and articles about his career were published. Mao was condemned as a criminal for bringing to an end the life of this brave Chinese, a true friend of the Soviet Union.[18]

Moscow did not have to say another word. It was clear to anyone who bothered to examine the evidence that in the summer of 1949, when Mao was so concerned over his relations with the Soviet Union, Stalin and Beria were not only putting puppets into parts of Eastern Europe, they had secretly acquired their own man in Manchuria, the most strategic stronghold in all of China, ready to stab Mao in the back at their command. Paranoia indeed!

The blunt truth was that the two Communist overlords were as devious and deadly as the princes of *Romance of the Three Kingdoms*. Stalin's addiction to treachery had already been exposed by his infamous deal with Adolf Hitler, which had set the stage for World War II. Stalin had hoped to double-cross Hitler and win the world. Hitler had double-crossed Stalin and come within an ace of wiping out Stalin and his empire. Now Stalin was ready for another roll of the dice, this time against his confederate in pseudo-Marxism, Mao Zedong. Mao knew the slippery ground on which he was playing but felt he had no alternative. That Mao understood how cunningly and carefully Stalin was preparing his trap seems dubious.

11

Stalin's Birthday Party

NINETEEN FORTY-NINE had not been a good year for the Kremlin, and Stalin was paranoid, more nervous about the Communist world than ever before. His fear and suspicion of Mao were great. All the Communist regimes in Europe now possessed new leaders, handpicked by Stalin or his secret police, all except Yugoslavia, Albania, and East Germany. Stalin had excommunicated Tito. "If I shake my little finger Tito will fall," he had proclaimed. But Tito had not fallen. Stalin was even more angry about Albania. His attempt to overthrow the Albanian chiefs by having his agents bribe the Albanian navy had failed. And, as he kept warning his intimates, Mao could be another Tito.

During World War II, Stalin had abolished his international revolutionary organization, the Comintern, to win favor with Churchill and Roosevelt. Now Stalin revived it under a new name, the Cominform. But it didn't help much. He had shot almost all the old

Comintern operatives, and the new crew was a poor lot. Although Stalin had embarked on a reign of terror, it didn't make him feel secure.

China's Mao — Stalin was beginning to think it would take some time to get rid of this Asian who he liked to say wasn't even a Communist, nothing but a "margarine" Communist, not the real Red article. Despite all the help Stalin had given Chiang Kaishek, Mao was on the verge of total power in China. It was not a prospect that pleased the Kremlin.

New maps had gone up at the U.S. State Department and the European foreign offices after October 1, 1949. They showed the world a solid splash of red from the Elbe River east to the tip of the Bering Strait. Impressive. All Communist. A big red star marked Moscow. There had been nothing like it before — not under Victoria, not under Napoleon, not under Alexander the Great or Genghis Khan. Three quarters of a billion people, revolutionary, armed to the teeth, waiting for the word to march on the "Free World."

No such maps hung on the walls of Stalin's monastic office in the great Kremlin Palace — just the same old portraits of Marx, Lenin, and the czarist military heroes Aleksandr Suvorov and Mikhail Kutuzov — or in Mao's Study of Chrysanthemum Fragrance. Had there been maps on the walls of Stalin's and Mao's offices they would have shown in sharp relief the frontiers between China and Russia. Mao's would have shown those areas of China taken by Russia in the eighteenth and nineteenth centuries. The question of lost territories was never to vanish from the Chinese agenda. It remained there, unresolved, in 1990.

A bit after noon on a frosty December 6, 1949, Mao Zedong, in fox fur cap, mink-lined overcoat, a "Mao tunic" and trousers, his bulky body encased in long wool underwear, boarded a meticulously clean train, its exterior gleaming in fresh green and gold paint, its locomotive black with fire-engine-red wheels, to start the long journey to Moscow.

The underground siding to Zhongnanhai was not completed, and the party entrained at the Central Railway Station, the platform sealed off by a brigade of security officers. The security was intense. Mao had never gone abroad before, and Li Kenong and the security men were taking no chances. This was no ordinary train. It was Chiang Kaishek's special armored train, the one he had used in shuttling between Nanjing and Shanghai.

Mao was escorted by the Soviet ambassador, General N. V. Roshchin, and Nikolai Fedorenko, a young Russian specialist in Chinese literature who acted as an interpreter.[1]

Fedorenko remembered their leaving Beijing on a bright, sunny winter day, the air clear of the yellow Gobi dust that so often sweeps down from the northwest. Mao was exhilarated at the prospect of his first journey outside China. For some distance the train ran alongside the Great Wall. Mao could hardly tear himself from the window of his compartment.

There was a drawback — no heat. It was so hot on the Nanjing-Shanghai run and the train so heavy with its sheet armor that no heating pipes had been installed. Before Mao got to Tianjin the water in his carafe was solid ice. His aides scurried about with portable kerosene heaters. They helped very little. Mao was furious. He was already nervous about leaving China. Now he was more so.

They got to Shenyang (called Mukden before 1949) the next morning. Mao planned to spend the day sightseeing. At least he would be warm. But he found Shenyang decorated with huge portraits of Stalin and none of himself. More angry than ever, he reboarded the icy train and headed north for the border crossing at Manchouli. There he entered the well-heated Trans-Siberian cars for the seven-day trip to Moscow. Li Kenong went back to Beijing on the refrigerator train.[2]

On the long trip across Siberia, a landscape of endless snow, Fedorenko recalled, Mao was moved by the vastness and the cold of the taiga. Lake Baikal, the largest body of fresh water in the world, was just freezing, boiling in turbulence and sending into the air clouds of fog that covered everything for miles around with hoarfrost.

Fedorenko joined Mao in his compartment, and they engaged in discussions of Chinese classical literature. The young Chinese scholar was impressed by the depth of Mao's knowledge and came to have great respect for Mao's poetry and calligraphy.[3]

Mao's entourage was devoid of specialists who would have made up a negotiating delegation. There was a reason for this. Mao was going to Moscow at long last, but his stated purpose was to pay respects to Stalin on his seventieth birthday, December 21, 1949. To emphasize the ceremonial and not the business side, Mao had left Premier Zhou Enlai and his experts at home. He was eager to set a precise tone.

To say that Stalin's seventieth birthday posed a difficult problem for Mao is an understatement. Mao knew that many people would interpret the visit as a tribute-bearing mission in the style of the

Chinese dynasties, and he weighed every detail. He did not bring a retinue of "princes and generals of the realm," as *The General Mirror for the Aid of Government,* the dynastic commentary he had been studying, described past rulers doing.

In fact, Mao's delegation included only one real specialist, his principal interpreter, Shi Zhe. A most unusual man, Shi Zhe had gone to the Soviet Union in the late 1920s, sent by General Feng Yuxiang, the "Christian" general who was then very friendly with the Soviets. Feng was the general for whom Deng Xiaoping briefly worked at Xian on his way back from Moscow in 1927. Shi Zhe had stayed in Russia for years, returning to China only in the later Yanan days. There wasn't much about Russia he didn't know.[4] Mao's secretary, Chen Boda, accompanied him. No other major advisers made the trip.

Most important was the question of Mao's gift to Stalin. Mao had not wanted to take a present of great worth, which would seem to the Chinese a tribute. He wanted his gift to be personal and simple.

Trusting the solid judgment of General Yang Shangkun, he put him in charge of preparing a suitable array of gifts. There was a discussion in which Jiang Qing intervened. As a native of Shandong Province, Jiang Qing proposed that Mao present Stalin with a selection of Shandong vegetables, which she insisted were the best in the world — particularly an onion called *dacong,* a green onion so succulent that if you gave it to an enemy his anger melted as he savored the delicate tuber. To this was added a wagonload of Shandong turnips, cabbage, marinated garlic, and radishes. Some raised their eyebrows and wondered whether Jiang's venom for Stalin after her long, unhappy stay in Russia had anything to do with her choice. But Mao went along with her and added crates of a special variety of Chinese kumquat, so tart he felt it had no equal. Mao may have approved the market garden offering on the theory no one could accuse him of bearing tribute.[5]

The gifts chosen by General Yang were more conventional and, some thought, more appropriate. They included tea, porcelain, and an example of Hunan embroidery, a full-length portrait of Stalin including an inscription composed by Mao: "May you live a life as long as the southern mountains survive."[6]

There is no evidence that Mao's gifts had the desired effect — or any effect whatsoever. The assiduity with which Stalin's secret police guarded their master against any attempt at poisoning was such that the miraculous onions and kumquats probably went out of the Kremlin with the day's garbage.[7] Between December 1949 and March 1951, *Pravda* printed a daily list of gifts to Stalin, which totaled in the thousands. They were displayed in the Russian Pushkin Museum (the masterpieces were relegated to the cellar). When the list finally ceased and the presents were packed off to some warehouse where they probably still repose, no mention had been made of Mao's cabbages and onions.

The trip from Beijing lasted ten days. Mao caught a severe cold in Sverdlovsk, probably because he had been hopping off the train and stretching his legs on station platforms all across Siberia, regardless of the subzero temperatures. Fedorenko recalled that Mao almost lost consciousness from the severe cold and that doctors had to be called.

The train made a perfectly timed arrival in Moscow on December 16. It pulled into Yaroslav Station just as noon was chiming from the Kremlin's Spassky bell tower. Because Mao was still unwell, welcoming ceremonies were curtailed and he was whisked out to one of Stalin's nearby guesthouses, or dachas, in the countryside.[8]

Stalin received Mao in the Kremlin at 6:00 P.M. the same day. The meeting did not go well. Mao arrived three minutes early. The Kremlin guards kept the doors closed until six sharp, then threw them open to disclose Stalin and the full Politburo waiting. Stalin showered Mao with compliments and began to quiz him on what he hoped to do in Moscow. Mao said he would like to accomplish something: "It must be delightful to the eye and agreeable to the taste." Shi Zhe knew these words wouldn't make sense to the Russians. He tried to explain that Mao wanted to achieve something that would be handsome in form yet have substance and flavor. The Russians shook their heads. Lavrenty Beria, the police chief, blurted out a rude exclamation that Shi Zhe thought it better not to translate.

Mao said that he'd like to have Zhou Enlai come to Moscow a bit later. What for? Stalin asked. Mao didn't reply. Later Stalin telephoned Mao several times to ask why Zhou was coming. Mao told him to wait and see.[9]

There was one extraordinary moment. Stalin had just told Mao: "You are a good son of China. We hope you are well and strong forever."

Mao began to reply, saying he had "long been attacked and pushed out. I have had nowhere to turn," perhaps thinking of the times Stalin's men had expelled him from the Party or turned against his leadership.

Stalin cut in quickly, saying, "Winners allow no accusations. Victory is everything. Winners accept no accusations. That is common practice."

Mao said not another word. Nor did Stalin.[10] As Fedorenko recalled, neither man alluded to their many past differences and Stalin became quite cautious.[11]

On December 21 Mao attended the official birthday ceremony at the Bolshoi Theater, where *Krasny Mak* (The Red Poppy), a Soviet ballet dedicated to the Chinese revolution, was presented as a special mark of Sino-Soviet friendship. The ballet dated to the 1920s but had been restaged for the occasion. The corps de ballet danced a Russian version of the *yangko,* the dance that the Communists had made synonymous with the Revolution.

Shi Zhe sat between Stalin and Mao in the state box at the center balcony of the great gilt and crimson opera house, "just where the czars sat," Shi recalled. The box was curtained in such a way that it was not possible for the audience to see who, if anyone, was sitting there. Stalin was handsome and smiling in his generalissimo's uniform, with its gold braid and golden epaulets. Mao wore his best dove-colored tunic.

Mao and Stalin, not ballet fans, left after the celebratory speeches. Shi Zhe, Chen Boda, and others stayed, but before the curtain rang down Chen Boda and his companions, offended by the subject matter and interpretation, walked out. The ballet, set in Shanghai in 1927, dealt with one of the great tragedies of the Chinese revolution, the massacre by Chiang Kaishek's thugs of thousands of Shanghai workers and Communists, many of whom had their heads hacked off by great Chinese scimitars. The ballet glorified the heroism of the Soviet sailors who rushed from their ships to help their Chinese comrades, an imaginary event. The sailors were the stars of the ballet.

Even worse to the Chinese was the title. "Red poppy" to the Chinese meant the curse of their nation — opium. To present the poppy as the symbol of the Revolution was like a prostitute presiding over a mass. Whatever may have been the Russian intention, it seemed to the Chinese — particularly to Mao, once he was told about it — like a deliberate insult.

Whether Stalin intended this or whether the Russians were simply ignorant and insensitive is beyond discovery. The Chinese did not conceal their indignation. The Soviet hosts expressed surprise and regret. The ballet was removed from the repertoire — for a while.[12]

It was not the best of starts for the state visit.

Many Chinese have described Mao's days in Moscow as marked by great tension. One old associate called the visit "most unpleasant." Shi Zhe took a different view. He said the problem was boredom. Stalin failed to provide a program. All he did was send Mao some old biographical films to watch, mostly dedicated to Stalin's glory. There were no meetings. The Chinese were confined to the dacha under heavy guard. The only distraction was a billiard table.

"There was not enough to do," Shi Zhe recollected in 1988. "It was dull. We had no contact with our opposites."

It was a puzzle. Neither foreign correspondents nor diplomats in Moscow could figure it out. Mao simply vanished from public view. Moscow had a rigid protocol for state visits, but it was not being followed. Nothing appeared in *Pravda* or *Izvestia*. One American correspondent ventured to the Chinese embassy to see what he could find out. He was received politely — until it was discovered that he was American. Then he was ushered out with equal politeness.

Finally a London newspaper published a story that Stalin had put Mao under house arrest. This produced action. Stalin ordered a *Pravda* reporter to interview Mao. Mao was grumpy. "All I do here is sleep," he said.[13] "I have nothing to do but eat and shit."[14] If they continued to treat him like this, Mao said, he would pack and go back to Beijing in the morning. It was at this point, Nikita Khrushchev later reported, that Mao was so fed up that he would have left Russia and signed up with the United States, had not his relations with Washington been so bad. Stalin, Khrushchev said, treated Mao like a second-rate colonial governor.[15]

Mao's words got action. Stalin decided he had let Mao hang long enough in the breeze. He proposed that the two issue a joint communiqué saying that Mao would go sightseeing in Russia and that the two would then sign a treaty. Mao knew from previous hints that Stalin was eager to get his signature on a treaty. Mao telegraphed Zhou Enlai, asking him to come to Moscow. Then he set off on a tour of Leningrad.

Mao spent five days in Leningrad. They were hardly a success. Mao was put up at the Smolny Institute, the former noblewomen's school where Lenin made his headquarters in 1917. Rare indeed was the guest who had been privileged to stay here, but there is no sign this made an impression on Mao.

The first place he was taken to was Kronstadt, the great naval fortress island in the Gulf of Finland, equally rare for a visitor to be shown. It was here that Soviet sailors rose against the revolution in 1921 and, at Lenin's order, were slaughtered by Bolshevik troops in a battle to the death on the ice. What Mao knew of this event is uncertain. What is certain is that as he walked out on the ice he was as excited as a small boy.

"Here I am," he told his comrades, "in the Baltic Sea and the Atlantic Ocean. Next time I visit the Soviet Union I'll go to Vladivostok [he never did] and the Pacific Ocean and then I will go to the Black Sea and finally I'll go to the Arctic Sea. I'm getting to know the Soviet Union!"[16]

It was Mao's first walk on ice. And his last.[17]

Mao showed no interest in anything else he was shown. He was taken to the Winter Palace and the Hermitage Museum but strolled past the great collections of Rembrandts, Van Dycks, Michelangelos, and Leonardo da Vincis. His pace was brisk; no sideward glance, no questions, no comments. He was taken to the great Peterhof Palace, still in ruins from Nazi destruction, the Catherine Palace, the Cameron Gallery. Not a flicker of interest. One morning he was escorted to a battlefield on Leningrad's outskirts. The great Nazi underground emplacements, the siege guns, the tunnels — all still in place. An officer began to explain the action. Mao waved him away airily. "Oh, I understand all this," Mao remarked. "We have been through war ourselves." But never, the officer might have told Mao, anything like the nine-hundred-day siege of Leningrad, with its 1.5 million deaths in a city of 3.5 million. There had been nothing like it in the world. No evidence exists that the escort officers told Mao anything of the siege or that Mao asked about the frozen bodies piled in mountains at the gates of cemeteries, the bravery, the self-sacrifice, the starvation, the freezing. Nor did his hosts tell him that Stalin had just carried out a purge that took the lives of almost all the Party chiefs who had defended Leningrad.[18]

Whether Mao's disinterest was feigned or real, a response to Stalin's bad manners or sheer ignorance, none could say. Mao spent his allotted five days in Leningrad, then returned to Moscow on the Red Arrow, the magnificent old mahogany and brass train of the French Wagons-Lits Company, and telephoned Zhou Enlai, who had arrived at Novosibirsk en route to Moscow. The line was so poor they could not understand each other. Mao tried again when Zhou had reached Sverd-lovsk. This line worked, and he spent an hour and a half telling Zhou what he wanted in the treaty with the Soviets so Zhou could start work on it.[19]

A day or so later Zhou arrived in Moscow and moved in with Mao at his dacha, Mao on the first floor, Zhou on the second.[20] The Russians had been working on their draft, and with Zhou overseeing every word, the two drafts were put together.[21]

The treaty was composed of three principal documents: agreements on defense, friendship, and mutual aid. It was ostensibly directed against Japan, which had yet to sign a peace treaty with either the Soviet Union or China. The treaty provided that China and the Soviet Union would come to each other's aid in the event of aggression by Japan or any nation allied with Japan (i.e., the United States). It retained, in effect, Soviet rights to Port Arthur and Dairen (lost to Japan in the Russo-Japanese War of 1905) and to the South Manchurian Railroad (lost by Russia at the same time) and gave Russia mineral rights in Xinjiang, China's westernmost province. The mineral deposits were uranium, but this was not mentioned. The treaty also provided $300 million in credits to China over a five-year period, a piddling sum. Devaluation of the dollar knocked 20 percent off the total within the year. The United States was then providing more aid per year to Ecuador. The documents were signed February 13, 1950.[22]

There was one last touch — a reception given for Stalin by Mao in the Metropol Hotel, the talk of Moscow when it was completed in 1908. It was located halfway up Lubyanka Hill, halfway between KGB headquarters and the Kremlin. To one who lived there in those times the event was mind-boggling, because Stalin never left the sanctuary of the Kremlin. Once during World War II he had attended a dinner in the British embassy, across the Moskva River from the Kremlin, given by Churchill, who offended Stalin by showing up in his light blue "sireen" suit, the zippered coveralls he had adopted for London air shelter dress. Stalin was demanding an Allied second front in Europe, and Churchill chose this way of emphasizing that England was fighting a deadly enemy, too, the Nazi Luftwaffe.

Stalin demurred when Mao proposed his party, saying he would have to get Politburo permission, which he seemed dubious would be forthcoming. But ultimately the Politburo "agreed." Security precautions were extraordinary. A number of Russian guests were moved out of the hotel. The lobby was turned over to plainclothes police.

All interior doors to the Metropol's grand dining room were guarded by armed men. Only the street entrance on the Lubyanka side was left open.

At 6:30 P.M. on February 14, Mao, Stalin, and their colleagues swept up in curtained black Zis limousines. They entered the marble-columned portals of the dining hall, with its fountain and fish pool where live sturgeon and carp sported before being lifted out to become the evening's dinner; its bandstand where Moscow's jazz bands had cavorted until Stalin rounded them up and sent them to Central Asia. This was the hall where Rasputin occupied a balcony loge and entertained his bare-breasted noble ladies, often displaying his extended organ over the rail or mounting his guests without bothering to draw the curtain; the hall where young officers of the imperial guards on the eve of revolution sometimes tossed their last gold coins into the lap of a gypsy singer, pulled out revolvers, fired a few shots into the blue and gold ceiling frescoes, and emptied the last into their brains.

In this singular setting Mao toasted his Soviet counterpart in the finest Chinese *maotai*, proclaiming "*Ganbei*," and J. V. Stalin returned the honor in vintage vodka. A movable glass wall had been put up to separate the leaders from the several hundred guests. When the toasts were offered, the guests could not hear and crowded up next to the elite enclave. Zhou Enlai had the wall removed so the guests could hear. Zhou spoke for China, predicting future generations of Sino-Soviet friendship. Stalin spoke for the Soviet Union. "In unity," he said, "there is strength."[23]

By 9:00 P.M. the hall was cleared, the guests gone, the back doors unlocked, and the security guards scattered, leaving only plainclothes *spiki*, the ordinary police shadows, dozing in their black leather chairs in the Egyptianesque Metropol lobby.[24]

On February 17 Mao and his party boarded a special train for the long ride back home. Vyacheslav Molotov, then Soviet premier, saw them off and gave Mao one last bit of advice from Stalin: "Pay close attention to security and never be careless in this regard."

To the young interpreter Nikolai Fedorenko the visit of the Chinese had been a nightmare. He did not know from minute to minute what crisis might next arise, and he was possessed by anxiety. It seemed to him that Stalin was wearing a mask and acting out a calculated role, speaking softly and genially, but what was going on in Stalin's mind he could not guess. It was a play, but only Stalin knew the plot. Even the places for the talks — Stalin's dacha and his Kremlin suite — seemed to Fedorenko like stage settings for a sinister drama.

Fedorenko was haunted by fear. One misstep, he believed, and his career — if not his life — would be forfeit. There was no telling from what quarter danger might come. During one meeting Mao asked him why Stalin had two carafes of wine, white and red, before him at the table and drank alternately from them. Fedorenko confessed he did not know, suggesting that Mao ask Stalin. But Mao thought that tactless. Stalin noted the mumbled conversation and pounced on Fedorenko: "What are you talking about?" Fedorenko thought his career had ended. Mao had forbidden him to raise the question, and now Stalin was demanding an answer. Fedorenko told Stalin what they were talking about. To his relief Stalin explained amiably that he liked both red and white wines and drinking them together enhanced their taste.

Fedorenko sighed with relief. But a new crisis emerged. The Kremlin chef summoned him. Mao's chef was refusing to accept the carp Stalin had ordered them to provide for Mao's dinners. Fedorenko hurried to Mao's dacha. The Chinese chef said Mao had specified that he was to cook only live fish. "How do I know when these carp were killed?"

Fedorenko straightened that out by ordering that only live fish be delivered to the Chinese.

Then yet another danger arose. In the middle of a meeting Mao was describing to Fedorenko a critical moment in the battle against Chiang Kaishek. A Red Army unit had been encircled and could not fight its way out. The commander told his men they must try again and not to fear death; death was only a return to their beginnings. Fedorenko was not sure he understood correctly. Mao's explanation only muddied the matter.

To his horror Fedorenko heard Stalin say: "How much longer are you going to be occupied with this *conspiracy?*"

The word sent an electric shock through Fedorenko's body. This was it. He knew all the stories about Stalin's suspiciousness. Now Stalin thought he was "conspiring with Mao." Oozing guilt, he tried to explain that he was just clarifying a point.

"Why don't you ask Mao what he means?" Stalin said in a cold voice.

"I have," Fedorenko said, "but he hasn't been able to explain."

"Well, go ahead with your secret talks," Stalin said. Fedorenko now saw Beria fix his eyes on him like a vulture. The eyes did not blink.

Finally Mao explained and Stalin relaxed. But not Fedorenko. He felt his head had rested on the guillotine. Who could say whether he would safely escape the next crisis? The aura of paranoia, the waves of suspicion that enveloped the two dictators, were palpable.[25]

After the Chinese-Soviet treaties were announced, the world resounded with bulletins reporting that China had subjected itself to the Soviets. Stalin had taken over. Mao had signed away his sovereignty. It was one big Communist plot. The capital was the Kremlin, Stalin the Red Emperor. This was the interpretation of the event put forward by the CIA and merchandized by the State Department.

What Mao thought of this absurdity is not known. In a sense, such an interpretation served his purposes since, if it meant anything, it indicated that the West would be reluctant to attack China, believing that a nuclear response from Moscow would follow. (Moscow had announced its first nuclear test in October 1949.) This assessment of the Chinese-Soviet treaties was swallowed whole by the United States, and almost all of the Western world. To the United States, as Dean Rusk would write in 1950, there could be no question of recognition of Beijing and diplomatic relations. Mao was a mere puppet of Stalin. As Rusk put it, "The regime does not pass the first test. It is not Chinese."

Neither Stalin nor Mao publicly challenged this interpretation. Each for his own purposes simply let it pass, preferring not to place on record the fact that arrayed against the West was not, as it believed, a unified colossus, but two very testy, mutually antagonistic powers.

12

The Triple Cross

THE SUN was blazing hot on Sunday, June 25, 1950, by the time Mao Zedong's bodyguards entered the Study of Chrysanthemum Fragrance, pulled back the silvery curtains that screened the wide windows, and brought Mao his tea. Mao's bed was rumpled. He sweated heavily, which he thought was healthy. There was no air-conditioning in Mao's study. In summer he kept his suite hot, and in winter he preferred it cold, habits stemming from the health faddism of his youth.

Mao looked a bit of a slob on this hot morning. Since moving into the emperor's quarters he had become more careless of appearance. He described his habits as "freedom" and urged his companions to dress as they pleased. In general he disliked constraints. "Liberate yourselves," he would say, lolling on his bed, his sheet hunched up to his armpits. Not until his last years did he wear nightclothes. He customarily slept naked.[1]

Mao thought nothing of trailing about his quarters half-dressed. But he never walked about nude. Some residue of prudishness caused him to draw the line at that.[2] His habits were not too different from those of Lyndon Johnson, who used to summon visitors to his side while he squatted on the toilet, or of Winston Churchill, who stalked about his bedchamber totally naked.

Now, Mao lay back on a pile of pillows, his eyes blinking in the sunlight. He had worked at night for years and still did not rise until noon unless compelled by a state meeting. As the Chinese liked to say, he turned the sun into the moon and the moon into the sun.[3]

Like most of his Long March companions, Mao was addicted to sleeping pills. He could not live without them, and he slept little enough with them. His guards estimated he got no more than thirty hours of sleep a week. One week he slept thirty-five hours, a record. If Mao had a burst of bad temper — as was not infrequent — nine times out of ten, in the opinion of chief bodyguard Li Yinqiao, it was the result of lack of sleep. Li often massaged Mao to relax him. Mao also liked Li to comb his hair, saying it restored his strength, so Li would run the comb through Mao's receding hair again and again. (It probably made Mao more wide awake; a simple and quick way to send a charge of adrenaline through the body is to yank the hair.) Mao drank tea from the time he woke up until he finally dozed off, and he ate the tea leaves from each cup. This huge consumption of caffeine was enough to nullify all the sleeping pills he ingested.[4]

Mao's aides did their best not to schedule meetings before 1:00 P.M. None had been arranged for this Sunday. Cold tubs had been the habit of Mao's mentor, Professor Yang Changji, whose daughter, Kaihui, had been Mao's first and beloved wife. Yang, as staunch an advocate of cold baths as any Puritan New Englander, plunged into a cold tub every morning. He suffered a heart attack and died after an icy tub, but Mao still emulated him. As a youth he took rain "baths," doffing his shirt during showers, sun baths in the summer, and March "wind baths." In November he swam in cold rivers.[5] Mao's guards would remember a trip to Guangxi in February 1958 when he insisted on diving into an icy stream. They took the temperature: 14 degrees centigrade, about 57 degrees Fahrenheit. In Chicago Mao would have been a member of the Polar Bear Club.[6]

Mao believed "physical training can make one's eyes clear and one's ears good. It can even build up the health of a person sixty or seventy years old." He set forth these ideas in his first published article, "A Study of Physical Training," written for the April 1917 issue of the radical magazine *New Youth*.[7]

Mao washed in cold water and never used soap, thinking the chemicals injurious. He never used toothpaste but stuck to the tooth powder of his youth. And he did not change his toothbrush for years, even when it had lost almost all its bristles.[8] His teeth were badly stained by nicotine and tea. And despite his earlier advocacy of physical activity, by the time he entered the Study of Chrysanthemum Fragrance he had abandoned all physical exercise except swimming.

Emerging from the tub on that June Sunday, Mao knew how he was going to spend the rest of the day. He would go over to the pool in Zhonghai, swim his usual fifty laps, and lounge in and out of the water all day. If the heat spell continued he might have the guards pack up and take the train down to West Lake, in Hangzhou. There was no place he loved better. He had been fond of West Lake and its gardens and palaces since his first visit there, after the founding of the Chinese Communist Party in Shanghai, in 1921. Mao and a friend had slipped away and rambled around West Lake; he would never forget it.

Mao shuffled back to his big bedroom, bed remade, sheets replaced, pillows fresh, the night odors wafted away by the overhead fan that gently stirred the air.

He carelessly draped his cotton kimono over his shoulders, sat down on the sofa beside his bed, and began to look over the "Reference News," a bulletin he had created in the dusty, distant days of Yanan. On the Long March he had had to depend on bulletins picked up by his weak wireless and on weeks-old KMT newspapers that his troops found in village post offices. The smudgy sheets were almost worthless. He did not know what was happening in Shanghai or Beijing, let alone Moscow, London, or Washington.

When they got better wireless receivers from Moscow, Mao had his operators scan the frequencies for news. These items were typed out from the Morse code transmissions, translated into Chinese, and multigraphed on an old machine, and the end product was "Reference News."

Mao laid down a basic rule: Whatever was transmitted must be reported verbatim — no brushwork. He wanted the exact words. The transmissions were his window on the world, and he did not want the view distorted.[9] One of Jiang Qing's jobs was to read the bulletin and keep Mao up to date.[10]

On this Sunday Mao turned the pages of "Reference News" idly until his eye caught an item from Pyongyang. Korean radio reported an encounter on the 38th parallel, very heavy fighting. South Koreans were, it was said, attacking the north all along the perimeter.

Mao paused. There was constant tension on the Korean border, an incident nearly every day. This sounded serious. The Korean frontier was close to China, and Mao had not overcome his worries about the United States. He had warned his colleagues well before June 1950 that the United States might intervene in Korea.[11] This could be it.

He asked his duty secretary to check with the Foreign and Defense ministries. They had nothing, which was not surprising, since China had neither diplomatic nor military observers in Korea. Korea was a Russian fiefdom; Chinese were not welcome. Nothing had come in from Moscow or Pyongyang. Seoul radio reported fighting and blamed it on the North Koreans. The Voice of America and BBC reports were skimpy.

Mao pondered. He had no official information. He knew that Kim Il-sung had been preparing a move against the south, but he had no word on the date. This did not sound like a North Korean move. If the north was beginning a drive south, surely he would have known. Mao decided to go swimming and relax. His mind ran over the night before. What was the name of that little chicken? Ying Ying? Ding Ding? Well, what difference did it make? If news came in, his secretary could bring it over to the pool. But it didn't look like a good weekend to go to Hangzhou.

This version of events at Zhongnanhai on June 25, 1950, does not pretend to be accurate in all minor details, but there is massive evidence that the attack erupted as a surprise to Mao, with no specific advance warning.

That June Mao was in the midst of drastically cutting the size of the People's Liberation Army to improve its fighting efficiency. Plans were being drafted for two large-scale operations — one, the invasion of Taiwan, and the other, the takeover of Tibet. Both, and particularly the Taiwan operation, would require large numbers of first-class troops. No date had been fixed, but preparations for Taiwan were well advanced. Combat units had been assembled in staging areas. Landing exercises were under way. It was hardly a moment when Mao would welcome a dangerous military gamble at his doorstep. The reality was that the Soviet Union had blindsided the Chinese on Korea.[12]

Russia's deliberate exclusion of China from Korean affairs led Russell Spurr, the British historian and specialist on Korea, to conclude that it "is extremely doubtful" that the Chinese had a role in preparations for the attack. Spurr is the only Western historian who has examined Chinese war archives and interviewed Chinese participants. He speculates that Stalin and Mao must have discussed Korea at the 1949–50 Moscow conference, but in fact there is evidence that Korea got little or no attention at that time.

Clearly, President Harry Truman's surprise at the Korean attack was equaled only by that of Mao. Just two days before the fighting started, Mao told the People's Consultative Assembly (the Chinese congress) that China had now passed through the "military phase of the Revolution" and would henceforth concentrate on land reform and rebuilding the country. On June 24, twenty-four hours before the start of the Korean fighting, the assembly approved the demobilization plans. Many military units actually had already been assigned to peacetime construction and agricultural projects.

Mao was a revolutionary, but he was also prudent. The conclusion is inescapable that he was cut out of the loop in the planning and execution of the Korean conflict.[13]

Nikita Khrushchev's version of Korea is worth looking at, even though it is peppered with holes. He claimed the scheme came from Kim Il-sung, who brought it to Moscow shortly before Mao's visit in the winter of 1949 and sold it to Stalin. Kim, of course, was Stalin's protégé. He had spent most of his life in Moscow and Siberia and had secured his regime in Korea with Soviet troops.

Kim told Stalin that his army was in fine shape, having been trained and equipped by the Russians. One push and South Korea would fall into his hands. The South Koreans were eager to be liberated and would rise in his favor. The argument sounded very much like the CIA rationale for the Bay of Pigs, which held that the Cubans would rise as soon as they learned of the landing at the Bay of Pigs; it would be all over before Castro knew what was happening. The South Koreans, Kim believed, would rally to him, and it would be over before Syngman Rhee and the United States knew what was happening. Stalin liked the idea, Khrushchev said, and told Kim to go home, draft plans, and report back.[14]

Kim returned in early March 1950. Khrushchev claimed Stalin checked the idea out with Mao, got his approval, and gave Kim the go-ahead at a vodka party at his dacha.

Khrushchev added a characteristic detail. He said Stalin withdrew his military advisers from North Korea for fear one might be captured or killed, giving away Moscow's involvement.[15] A competent Soviet historian characterized Khrushchev's version as "too naive, to put it mildly." He said Stalin's involvement was much deeper.[16] The Soviet historian B. N. Slavinsky, long a believer in the theory that the south had attacked the north, finally came to the same conclusion. He quoted with approval the statement of a North Korean Party worker who was at the 38th parallel when the fighting began: "You had to be blind or an idiot not to know that Kim Il-sung started it."[17] And, in a further contradiction of Khrushchev's version, Russell Spurr in his *Enter the Dragon* paints a believable picture of Stalin freezing China out of Korean affairs.[18]

Mao seems to have been unaware of the Truman-Acheson declaration of January 5, 1950, which foreshadowed U.S. recognition of the Mao regime and banned military support for Chiang Kaishek. Nor did he seem to know of the January 12, 1950, statement in Washington, and that of March 15 in San Francisco, in which Secretary of State Dean Acheson put both Korea and Taiwan beyond the U.S. defense perimeter. Perhaps Mao did not get his "Reference News" while touring industrial centers in the Urals and Siberia on his way back to China.

These signals went right past Mao Zedong, but not Stalin. Stalin already had a stranglehold on China, a much more powerful position than Mao knew. Not only did Russia hold Outer Mongolia, it retained its naval and rail positions in Manchuria under the treaty Mao had signed in Moscow. Stalin (as evidence later revealed) had made a secret ally of Gao Gang, Mao's proconsul for Manchuria. If the Soviet Union could pick up South Korea without cost — as the Acheson pronouncement suggested — Stalin's noose around north China and Beijing would be complete.[19]

Neither Beijing nor Washington understood the real Soviet position at the outbreak of the Korean War. To Washington the invasion of South Korea looked like a Chinese move. The response of Truman and Acheson was predicated on the "Chinese" nature of the attack. They even begged Stalin to intervene with China to halt the North Koreans. A CIA report dated June 19, 1950, was exhumed twenty-four years later concluding that the Soviet Union had total political, military, and economic control over North Korea. There is no evidence that Truman and Acheson ever saw it.[20]

In the first days of the war Mao took some major precautions. He halted demobilization and ordered the establishment of a special northeast formation. It was designated the 13th Army Group, under General Deng Hua. Mao assigned four armies, three artillery divisions, and one antiaircraft and one engineering division to the group — 255,000 men in all.[21] Planning for Taiwan and Tibet went forward, as did that for reorganization of the PLA.[22]

On June 30 came another important step. China still had no representation in Pyongyang. Zhou Enlai summoned Chai Chengwen, a ranking PLA intelligence officer, to Zhongnanhai. In a post-midnight talk Zhou told Chai that Marshals Nie Rongzhen and Liu Bocheng had recommended him highly. Zhou explained that they needed someone to act as liaison with Kim Il-sung. Ni Zhiliang had been designated ambassador but was in a hospital at Wuhan. Zhou instructed Chai to go to Pyongyang as soon as possible and take two or three military attachés with him. It was July 10 before the Chinese party reached Pyongyang. The Chinese met with Kim Il-sung that evening. The war had been in progress for two weeks. Not until almost the end of July did the first Chinese reports begin to flow back to Beijing. The Chinese ambassador, Ni Zhiliang, didn't get to Pyongyang until August 6, 1950.[23]

The early stages of the war went extraordinarily well for North Korea. The south and its American allies were shoved back to Pusan, on the southeast coast, where they held on by their fingertips. The north had been well trained and moderately well supplied by the Russians.

But when the reports of Chai Chengwen began to come in, they were not so sanguine as the Pyongyang propaganda. The North Korean drive was slowing, casualties were fearsome, and efforts to liquidate the U.S. foothold at Pusan were failing.

Mao summoned his military chiefs to a meeting on August 6, 1950. Zhou Enlai and Liu Shaoqi were present. The subject was the reorganization of the PLA and its capacity for meeting the two operations that had been put on hold — the invasion of Taiwan and the occupation of Tibet. Korea was not on the agenda. The report on the PLA was presented by Peng Dehuai. The size of the PLA as of July 15 was given as 5,138,756. This figure was swollen by the absorption of 2.5 million KMT prisoners, a total far too large for China's needs. The KMT soldiers diluted the PLA's fighting quality. Peng Dehuai raised serious questions as to the army's ability, without strong reinforcement and training, to conquer Taiwan. Tibet did not present so many difficulties. A Korean operation was not discussed.

Talk centered on the shortcomings of the PLA, the need for logistics, for replacement of equipment worn out in the war with Chiang Kaishek. There were huge deficiencies in aircraft. Much of China's hardware was of World War II vintage. The generals had a healthy respect for the new American weapons supplied to Taiwan and also for the Seventh Fleet. No one thought the Taiwan option was now viable. One general said, If we're not in shape to take Taiwan, we better not think about Korea.

The military men at the conference were also concerned about domestic problems. The People's Republic had been established only ten months earlier. Everything needed to be done. China's industrial level was pitifully low. No one wanted to leave a Communist comrade in the lurch, but wasn't Russia responsible for Korea? China had no supply depots nearby, no supply routes, no communications, no roads. Korea had become an air war. China had no modern antiaircraft guns, and its warplanes were out of date. If the United States retaliated, China possessed no way of protecting its cities. America could bomb at will. And what about the A-bomb? If China entered the war it would give General Douglas MacArthur the excuse he had been waiting for — to bomb China back to the Stone Age.[24]

Mao listened and asked questions but did not express his own views. Privately he was convinced that if the United States got the upper hand, China must come to Korea's aid. If MacArthur threatened the Yalu River, China would fight. Contingency preparations must be made.[25]

About this time Mao ordered some preliminary troop dispositions, and an ad hoc headquarters was set up in an old ammunition depot in Shenyang. Zhou Enlai summoned Chai Chengwen back from North Korea on September 1 and asked him what would be the main problems if China intervened. Chai said the biggest would be transportation: Highways were very narrow, U.S. bombing was heavy, railroads had been almost obliterated by U.S. hits. Supply would be difficult. The PLA was used to replacing guns and ammunition by capturing stores from the enemy. This was not possible, Chai said, with the Americans, and because there was no food in the countryside, the army would be unable to continue its practice of living off the land and requisitioning from the peasants. The great size of the Chinese force meant all supplies would have to be brought in. And there was another handicap — lack of interpreters. The PLA would be fighting in an alien land against a foreign enemy. The Chinese did not know Korean or English.

Mao waited — even after MacArthur landed at Inchon, on September 15, and reversed the situation, beginning to drive the North Koreans back to the north. Deng Hua's 13th Army Group had been ordered to move up to positions along the Yalu River, where it awaited orders.

Chai Chengwen recalled that Gao Gang, Mao's Manchurian viceroy (and probable secret ally of Stalin's), called him in after the Inchon landing and showed him a letter from Mao stating that Inchon made Chinese intervention imperative. Chai immediately left for North Korea.[26]

Inchon convinced Mao that something had to be done. He had not made up his mind completely, but it looked as though China would have to come to the aid of Kim Il-sung. Mao summoned his military commanders and leading political associates to meet in Yinian Hall in Zhongnanhai on October 1. Kim had telegraphed Mao that day: He had to have help.

On October 1, at 1:00 A.M., Zhou Enlai called in the Indian ambassador, K. M. Panikkar, and asked him to advise the United States that if U.S. forces continued toward the Yalu River border, China would intervene. The hour of the meeting was designed to signal the importance of the warning. Truman and Acheson ignored it as "mere propaganda." MacArthur was in top gear, roaring toward the Yalu. His intelligence analysts belittled signs of Chinese troop movements, and MacArthur responded to Zhou's message with a demand for unconditional surrender of North Korean forces. Kim Il-sung turned the demand into a joke. He told the Chinese that MacArthur wanted him to put his hands up in surrender. "But we have no such custom," Kim said. He balled his fist and shook it over his head to show his response.[27]

When the meeting opened in Yinian Hall, Lin Biao was the first to speak. He totally opposed going into Korea. "In my opinion we should not go to war at the far end of the country," Lin said. "Our state has just been created. Within the country there are still bandit forces [his way of referring to Chiang Kaishek's troops]. We have not dealt with them all yet. If we take on a foreign foe as well as one at home it will only create new difficulties."

Gao Gang supported Lin Biao. The two men had worked closely in the Communist conquest of Manchuria. Gao said it was necessary to go carefully. China had been fighting for twenty years. It had just been reunified, and normal life had still not been restored. The economy wasn't strong enough to bear the burden of a new war.

Gao Gang urged that the views of Lin Biao be carefully assessed. He pointed out that the PLA's equipment was worn and outmoded and that most of it had been captured in battle (much of it U.S. Army equipment captured from the Nationalists). The Americans were much more heavily armed, Gao said, disposing at least fifteen hundred artillery pieces per army compared with fewer than three hundred for the Chinese. In tanks the ratio was even more unfavorable. The fact was, the Chinese had no modern tanks or armored units of any kind. Gao warned that the Americans would probably force the Yalu, with results that could hardly be imagined. He called not for intervention but for making every effort to fortify the northeastern frontiers.[28]

Although it was obvious that the military was strongly opposed to intervention, Mao favored it, and his vote was decisive. On October 2, Mao approved the dispatch of Chinese forces into Korea and on that day telegraphed Stalin in his own name, advising that the decision had been made to send part of China's military forces into Korea as "a volunteer army." Mao added that "we believe that analogous action [by the Soviet Union] is essential." The Chinese ambassador to the Soviet Union, Zhang Wentian, told Stalin the Chinese needed Soviet help — supplies, funds, and particularly air cover. Stalin agreed to send Soviet air force units to protect the Chinese army against U.S. air assaults and offered to equip one hundred Chinese divisions with Soviet arms.[29]

Mao first proposed to send Lin Biao to command the Chinese "volunteers"; he was experienced in the area. But Lin Biao pleaded illness and flew off to Moscow for treatment. He may have refused the command because he opposed the action. Nie Rongzhen, who had worked side by side with Lin Biao for ten or fifteen years, throughout the anti-Japanese war of 1937–45 and the liberation war, said his attitude "was really very strange. I had never seen Lin Biao frightened to this degree." Mao found Lin Biao's attitude equally strange and turned to the old, reliable Peng Dehuai to take Lin's place.[30] Mao sent a plane to Xian to pick up Peng and bring him back to Beijing. Peng got to Yinian Hall at 4:00 P.M. on October 4. He did not join the debate, since he had not heard what the others had said. Having listened to the almost unanimous opposition of his commanders, Mao said their views had weight but that when another nation was in dire straits "we would feel heavy at heart if we just stood by and watched."[31]

Mao told Peng that, despite the difficult choice, he was committing three Chinese armies to the first phase of the conflict. He knew that the war might involve hundreds of thousands of casualties and that if it went badly he would be blamed. There was even the possibility that China would face a loss of territory. If the war went poorly, he would not know how to explain it to history or to his people. He understood the concerns of his generals. But if China stood aside, how could there be any talk of a Socialist camp?

Peng Dehuai asked Mao what arrangements had been made to coordinate operations with the Soviet Union.

"That question has already been discussed with Stalin," Mao said. "Stalin agreed that the Soviet air force will take part in the war. Air operations will be the responsibility of the Soviets and land action will be our responsibility. So far as our land forces are concerned there is no problem."[32]

Peng felt a heavy responsibility. He was unable to sleep after talking to Mao. At first he thought it was the soft bed in the Peking Hotel, but when he tried sleeping on a blanket on the floor he was just as wide awake. He could not stop thinking of the war. If the Americans got to the Yalu, only a narrow river would separate them from northeast China. Already they had Taiwan, threatening Shanghai and east China. They could attack at any time. If a tiger wanted to eat a man, the timing depended only on his appetite.[33] But, thought Peng, thanks to having the Soviet Union at China's side, the nation's position was less vulnerable.

Peng flew to Shenyang, assembled and briefed his commanders. That evening he met with a representative of Kim Il-sung's. Mao issued "Order No. 1" in the name of the Central Military Committee, naming Peng commander on October 7.[34]

On October 9 a formal meeting of cadres assigned to the volunteers was convened in Shenyang by Gao Gang. Gao Gang told them the Northeast Bureau, which he headed, would be in charge of all food and supplies for the operation. He revealed that Mao had originally intended to put Lin Biao in charge, but because of Lin's illness Peng Dehuai had taken over. Peng told the workers that while there had been diverse views on the Central Committee, now they were united and would fight to the utmost "to show the character of us Chinese."

Peng left by train for the frontier town of Andong early on October 11, got to the border the morning of the twelfth, and plunged into preparations for moving the troops across. He worked all day. At 8:20 P.M. he got a telegram from Mao. It said, in effect, Hold everything. The troops were not to cross the border; they were to occupy themselves with training exercises. Peng was ordered to return to Beijing, where "the reasons for all this" would be explained.

What had happened was this. Two days earlier, October 10, in Moscow, the Soviets had called in Ambassador Zhang Wentian and given him a message for Zhou Enlai. It said that Moscow would not be able to send Soviet air units to Korea, as Stalin had promised, because the Soviet forces were not yet "properly prepared." This reversal was a staggering blow. The Chinese were fully committed. Their forces were pouring toward the Yalu border, and at this critical moment the Russians had taken themselves out of the picture.

Zhou rushed to Mao's study and read him the message. Mao's face fell. He drew deeper on the cigarette he was smoking and began to pace. For ten minutes he spoke not a word. Finally he said, "See what they have done. They have deliberately delayed with their answer until now and have only sent it after knowing that we have issued our orders and have no possibility of taking back our word."

Mao drew again on his cigarette. "We'll have to analyze this," he said to Zhou. "I am afraid you will have to go to Moscow."

Mao did not have to tell Zhou Enlai that Stalin had put Beijing in serious jeopardy. If Stalin had double-crossed Beijing by failing to inform it of Kim Il-sung's initial attack on South Korea, this was a triple cross. Having led China to believe that the intervention would be a joint venture, with the Soviets responsible for the air war and the Chinese for the land war, Stalin had lured China down a path of no return. China could not back out without a terrible loss of prestige. But it faced frightening losses, even fatal ones. There could be no question in the minds of Mao and Zhou that Stalin's conduct was deliberate. His object was to shove Mao into a war with the United States that might destroy China. No matter what the words the Kremlin used, this was the only conclusion.[35]

Later some called this the most portentous moment of Mao's career. For two days he discussed the situation with his closest associates. Then he decided to put the Korea operation on hold while Zhou Enlai flew to Moscow.[36]

Zhou was accompanied by the senior interpreter Shi Zhe, who had interpreted for Mao at the 1949–50 meetings in Moscow with Stalin. Arrangements had been made for Lin Biao, who had taken off with remarkable celerity for Moscow and medical treatment, to join the talks. Zhou was to emphasize the need not only for air support but for military equipment, munitions, transport, and even finances.

From Zhou's first meeting with Stalin, on October 11, it was plain that the Soviet dictator was not to be budged on air support. He had made up his mind, and there was no hope of changing it.[37] Zhou got the impression that Stalin was deeply disturbed at the prospect of Chinese intervention. Stalin had concluded that the Inchon landing had sealed Kim Il-sung's fate. The best thing Kim could do, Stalin argued, was to retreat across the Yalu and set up a government in exile in Manchuria on Chinese soil.

Chinese intervention, he warned, might lead to full-scale war with the United States and an American attack on the Chinese mainland. As for planes, he would be happy to train Chinese pilots and provide China with Soviet aircraft — at Chinese expense, of course.[38] He had a recommendation. If the Chinese did invade, let their force be small. A minor operation might not provoke U.S. invasion of China.

Zhou sent Mao a report on his discussion. He said it was not realistic to hope for Soviet aid.

For three days Mao did not sleep. He doubled his dose of sleeping pills. It did not help. Listeners heard him say to himself: "Stalin, Stalin!

The Socialist lands look to you. They await your help. And you will not release your air force . . . And if China pulls back her troops — what will Kim Il-sung say? We are all bound by blood ties — how can we look on quietly while people are perishing and not try to save them?"

Mao, his Chinese observer recalled, smoked a last cigarette and emerged from his bedroom, mind made up. China would go ahead — air cover or no air cover.[39] On the night of October 13, Mao dispatched a message to Kim Il-sung: China would honor its promise to come to his aid.[40]

Zhou Enlai was preparing to leave Moscow, his mission a failure. On the evening of October 13 he got Mao's telegram. He studied the message with surprise and a mounting feeling of pride. China would fight!

He had paid his farewell call to Stalin earlier. Now he appeared again at Stalin's Kremlin office. Stalin was surprised. "I thought we had said good-bye this morning," he said.

Zhou responded: "I have a telegram from Mao. Our Central Committee has decided to send troops to Korea as rapidly as possible."

It was Stalin's turn to fall silent. How can Stalin not understand, Zhou said to himself, what this decision means to the Chinese people in terms of sacrifice and bloodshed?

Finally Stalin spoke. Zhou felt that he was really talking to himself. "So, after all, the Chinese comrades are really all right. They are really all right." Stalin's surprise was obvious. What did he think? Was he calculating the odds of an American attack on China and full-scale disaster for Mao? Stalin's labyrinthine mind was beyond deciphering. What was plain and clear was that Mao had met Stalin's call and topped it.

By October 16, Peng Dehuai was back in Andong and on the nineteenth at dusk crossed the Yalu with his first troops. If all went well he would have 40,000 troops on the North Korean side in six days. He and Mao had disregarded Stalin's advice about sending in a token force, deciding that they had best get the men across while the Andong bridges still stood. Peng got four full corps and three artillery divisions, totaling 250,000 men, over the river in the first movement and built it up to six corps before the Americans spotted what he was doing. This gave him 350,000 troops to oppose the Allied 130,000 first-line forces. If the bridges went out, he had enough men south of the Yalu to win the initial engagements.[41]

Tens of thousands more PLA men were hustling north. Every train from Shanghai and Beijing northward was jammed with troops. Peng's men monitored MacArthur's wireless communications — no unusual traffic, no sign that the momentous Chinese movement had been detected through the cloud cover. Stalin or no Stalin, China's North Korean venture was under way.[42]

13

A Lovely Day in November

THE WEATHER in northern Korea in November 1950 had been miserable — chilly, with low-lying clouds, fog, drizzle, snow, sleet. Fighting conditions could hardly have been worse. Trucks bogged down in the freezing mud, tanks skidded off mountain cliffs. There was no air cover for ground troops, the visibility being too low for observation planes or fighter-bombers.

For Chinese purposes it could not have been better. Peng Dehuai was able to sandwich 350,000 Chinese troops into North Korea by early November.[1] At that time American intelligence estimated Chinese strength at fewer than 10,000 men south of the Yalu. Under cover of gloom, darkness, and mist Peng Dehuai could pick the position from which to launch his attack on the Americans.

The U.S. forces, spurred by the frenzy of General MacArthur "to finish the job," were rollicking northward with hardly an outrider to spot the enemy. MacArthur had proclaimed the mission of his troops to bring the war to an end with what he called "a massive compression envelopment."

It was true that by mid-November MacArthur was aware that Chinese troops were in North Korea. How many, he could not figure out. The Chinese had appeared in October, bloodied some South

Koreans and a few Americans, and then disappeared. The Chinese explained later that this was a "warning," designed to show the Americans they were serious about keeping an enemy force away from the Yalu. It was not a demonstration that MacArthur understood. When the Chinese vanished, he thought the way was open to drive to the Yalu and end the war.

As Thanksgiving approached MacArthur's confidence was high. He flew over the Yalu in his personal plane and landed to tell his troops they would be home for Christmas.

Just at this time a party of Chinese, new headquarters personnel, was carefully making its way southward from the Yalu. One of the men was an English-speaking interpreter. He listened to the U.S. Army radio, heard MacArthur's broadcast, and could not believe his ears. Didn't MacArthur know that hundreds of thousands of Chinese Red Army soldiers had entered North Korea? Didn't he know they were positioned to strike a terrible blow at the Americans — possibly within twenty-four hours?

When the Chinese party reached headquarters of the 13th Army Group, no one paid it the slightest attention. The headquarters seemed in trauma. Finally the interpreter found a friend who explained what had happened.

The men at headquarters had been in high spirits the day after Thanksgiving. They had heard MacArthur's boast. After weeks of drizzle the sun had come out, and the day was almost balmy. They knew what MacArthur did not know — that the next day, November 25, the Chinese would strike. Surprise should be complete.

Headquarters had been set up in an old gold-mining settlement called, in Chinese, Dayudong, some distance south of the Yalu and north of the Chungchen River. Its old caves provided excellent protection from the American fighter-bombers. But the weather was so fine that everyone had come out to enjoy a bit of sunshine. The interpreter's friend was sitting in a chair in the open air while a barber cut his hair. Then it happened. An American fighter-bomber swooped over the site, machine guns going, strafing from a low level, leaving the Chinese no time to take cover. Casualties had not been great, but one of the three officers killed was the son of Mao Zedong, Anying, twenty-eight years old. Headquarters went into shock. Anying had been assigned only a few weeks before. He was the oldest of Mao's four surviving children, son of Yang Kaihui, Mao's beloved first wife. Tall like his father, vivacious like his mother, handsome, his face narrow, not moonlike, with longish wavy black hair and an engaging smile, Anying was fond of his father but frank, no idolator, brave enough to speak his mind about the cult of personality around Mao.

Everyone in China knew Anying's story. When Mao went as a guerrilla chief to Jinggang Mountain in 1927, he had left his wife behind in Changsha with three baby sons. In October 1930 the KMT seized Kaihui with eight-year-old Anying and put them in prison. Anying was forced to look on while KMT torturers tried unsuccessfully to extract a confession from his mother. On November 14, 1930, Kaihui was executed at Changsha's Liuyan Gate. Some accounts say that the KMT made Anying watch his mother die.[2]

A few weeks later Anying was released and made his way to Bancang, outside Changsha, to the home of his grandmother and his aunt Li Chongde, Kaihui's sister-in-law. His younger brothers were already there. In late January 1931, Mao's brother Zemin sent a message asking that the three boys be brought to Shanghai to enter a kindergarten that was run by the underground for Party children, especially children whose parents had been killed.[3]

The youngsters were brought by Li Chongde to Shanghai. The evening before they left Bancang she took them to the grave of their mother. Mao had sent a small party to Changsha to see that Kaihui was properly buried and a tombstone erected. Before their mother's tomb Li spoke to the youngsters: "Remember this deep hatred and avenge her when you grow up."[4] The youngsters never forgot those words. It was a holy oath.

They were put into the Datong Kindergarten, but within the year Chiang Kaishek's secret police swooped down, arrested the teachers, and turned the children into the streets, where they became urchins, begging for a living. At one point they lived in an abandoned temple and put up a sign: "We tell stories. One cent."[5]

The youngest boy, Anlong, died suddenly, his brother Anqing recalled, of what disease he did not know. Finally the Party found the two surviving boys, smuggled them to Yanan and on to Moscow for an education. Anying proved a capable student, industrious and intelligent. He achieved a good command of Russian and learned to read and write Chinese. He'd had no education in his homeland.

When his sons returned from Moscow, Mao sent Anying to the countryside to learn the life of a Chinese peasant. He considered sending the boys to his native Hunan, but Anqing's health was precarious. For years he suffered a mental disability, possibly a result of blows to the head while begging in the streets of Shanghai.

Anying passed his father's test of work in the countryside and returned to Yanan, staying there until Mao pulled out. Mao's relations with Anying were edgy. Mao was demanding. When Anying met a young woman named Fu, fell in love, and wanted to marry her, Mao would have none of it. There was nothing wrong with being attracted to a pretty face, he told Anying, but there was no need to marry.

Mao's bodyguards sympathized with Anying. One was sitting with Anying one day as they watched a rooster chasing a hen.

"See," said Anying, "even a rooster wants to find a hen. And I'm already twenty-five."[6]

In 1948 Anying met another young woman, Liu Songlin, daughter of a Shandong Party leader who had been killed by the KMT. Liu Songlin was only sixteen, ten years younger than Anying. Mao flew into a rage when Anying told him she was eighteen. "Don't lie!" he shouted.[7]

Mao was very difficult about Anying and Liu Songlin's relationship. At one point his bodyguard Li Yinqiao feared that Mao, like Ivan the Terrible, would beat his son to death. Finally Mao calmed down and took a liking to Liu Songlin.

Anying told his father in September 1949 that he and Liu were going to marry. It was going to be simple. They didn't plan to spend any money. Mao said he'd give them a dinner. He said to tell Zhang Wenqi, Songlin's mother, that he was footing the bill. The couple gave Mao a short guest list. They had invited "Deng Mama" (Deng Yingchao, wife of Zhou Enlai) and "Kang Mama" (wife of Zhu De). Mao said they had to invite Zhou Enlai and Zhu De as well. He noticed they hadn't invited Liu Shaoqi and Liu's wife, Wang Guang-mei. "Call them up and say I'm having a friendly dinner, nothing elaborate," Mao said.

Mao gave a heavy winter overcoat to Anying as a wedding present. He told the couple they could sleep under it in winter. The mothers-in-law, Jiang Qing and Madame Zhang, gave them two pillows.[8]

Later some said that Jiang Qing had made relations between Anying and his father more difficult by her partisanship for the young man. This is difficult to document, because as Anying grew older he resented Jiang Qing. He didn't think she was an appropriate successor to his mother or to his first stepmother, He Zizhen. Jiang Qing was nervous around Anying and Mao, sensing that beneath their quarrels there was an affinity. To his bodyguards Mao seemed embarrassed at being closer to them than he was to his son.[9]

Exactly how Anying came to be stationed in Korea is clouded. Most probably the unit that he led was ordered there. By this time Anying was commander of a PLA regiment. Earlier he had served with the Soviet Red Army as a lieutenant. Jiang Qing urged Mao not to let his son go to Korea. Mao was adamant: "If he doesn't, someone else will have to." Mao insisted on no special treatment for his children. He made them dress, eat, and live like their peers.[10]

Anying went to Korea with a headquarters unit, crossing the Yalu sometime in mid-October 1950. Later there were those who said Mao never forgave Peng Dehuai for exposing Anying carelessly to danger. There seems no basis for that claim. Mao knew war, and he knew that death is its constant companion. At the height of the Soviet-Chinese polemics, in 1969–70, Moscow alleged that Mao intentionally sent his son to his death (the same screed charged Mao with deliberately abandoning Anying's mother, Kaihui, to her death in Changsha).

Mao made no public expression about his son's death — the fact was kept secret for years — but it is clear from members of the family, including the widow Songlin and even Jiang Qing, that the loss was a blow.

Mao was a man who quickly shed tears when touched, as he sometimes was, for instance, by tragic scenes in Beijing opera. He shed no tears over Anying. The tragedy, he made clear to Li Yinqiao, was much too deep.[11] Mao had become fond of Anying's wife, but for nearly three years he did not speak to Songlin of Anying's death.[12] When he finally did, he said: "It was war and war will take people's lives. Don't think that Anying should not have died for the people of China and Korea because he was my son." He added: "From now on you are my own eldest daughter."

Mao later refused to have Anying's body returned to China despite Songlin's pleas. After all, he said, tens of thousands of Chinese had died and were buried in Korea. Later on he sent Songlin to visit the grave, located on a beautiful hill surrounded by pines and cypresses at Huecang Pyongan-Namdo.[13] She took snapshots and brought them back to her father-in-law.[14]

As Mao told Songlin, they were all soldiers in a war. They were steeled to death. Each had lost close friends, brothers, sisters, fathers, mothers. Mao lost at least six members of his family: two brothers, his first wife, Anying, a cousin, and a nephew.[15]

Mao and the other leaders — Zhu De, Zhou Enlai, Peng Dehuai, Deng Xiaoping — bore these losses with the help of an iron philosophy, that death was a necessary and worthy sacrifice for the revolutionary cause. They could not make revolution if they feared death.

They did not believe, as the Taipings had, that they won instant immortality by death, ascending straight to heaven. But each man and woman killed in the struggle was adjudged a martyr. Statues and halls of remembrance were built to honor the martyrs. The lives were shed, but not in vain. It was a cruel doctrine, and by no means everyone could abide by it. Those who survived such losses strengthened their resolve by oaths such as the aunt of Anying and Anqing had made them swear at the tomb of their mother. Hate of the enemy enabled them to kill without remorse. Only out of these deep psychological drives could they fight their way across China, leaving a trail of their own and the "enemy" dead, so often landlords with heads severed and, in later years, almost anyone adjudged an "enemy of the people."

The life of Anying was only one of 450,000 to 500,000 lost by China in Korea, an extraordinary toll.[16] Some 2 million Koreans are believed to have been killed in the conflict. American casualties were about 157,000, including 54,000 deaths.

The Chinese military losses were very high — possibly even exceeding those in the anti-Japanese war and the civil war — and they were qualitatively important. Lacking artillery, devoid of antiaircraft protection, the Chinese forces again and again used "human wave" tactics to overwhelm their enemy.

Particularly in the early stages of the war these attacks were very effective. But the cost was staggering. Some of China's leading units were obliterated. Peng Dehuai was repeatedly forced to replace whole divisions, some of them the finest, most battle-tough battalions in the PLA. By the time the war simmered to occasional skirmishing, in 1952, the Chinese had paid a price that could not quickly be made good.

Everything that Zhu De, Nie Rongzhen, Lin Biao, and the other commanders had said about the state of the PLA, its need for reorganization and reequipment, had become doubly or triply true. The army had fought the United States to a standstill. But the toll in lives, top divisions, commanders, and equipment was stunning.

Thanks to tact, careful operation, and some good luck, Deng Xiaoping and Liu Bocheng had been able to occupy Tibet in the autumn of 1951 with hardly any fighting, an achievement that brought Deng congratulations from Mao when he came to Beijing for the celebration at Tiananmen of China's national day, on October 1, 1951.

But the invasion of Taiwan, Mao's number-one priority in 1949, was another thing. It had been put on hold, and it would still be on hold forty years later. Not merely the losses suffered by the PLA in

Korea deterred Mao from launching the operation. Also daunting were the barrier of the U.S. Seventh Fleet and the protective mantle that President Truman had draped over Taiwan.

Before Korea, Mao could realistically plan to invade Taiwan and take it by force. At that time, it had been specifically excluded from the U.S. defense zone. President Truman had put Chiang Kaishek on alert that the United States would not intervene to defend him.

But after Korea, Taiwan had become a full U.S. ally, and the Seventh Fleet had been assigned to fend off invasion. The whole idea of taking Taiwan was out.

Nor was this the only price Mao paid for the venture in Korea. There was the strict trade embargo imposed by the United States and its allies after the Chinese entered the war, which completely froze China out of normal commercial channels, impeded its economic development, and served as a barrier to technology transfer. The embargo was still largely intact twenty years later when President Richard Nixon visited China. There was also diplomatic isolation. China was cut off from the West and forced to turn back to its narrow, bigoted reliance on the Soviet Union, a straitjacket Mao hated. China's world had narrowed. Mao's first thoughts must have been of self-defense and whether he could trust his Soviet ally.

A few positives did emerge. The ferocity of China's fighting gave the U.S. military pause. Never again would the Joint Chiefs of Staff lightly and casually tempt fate, as MacArthur had. As Vietnam would show, the threat of Chinese intervention (however improbable) would remain at the forefront of U.S. military thinking. The Pentagon would not again beard the dragon. It was a security blanket of a sort for Mao.

An independent-minded Soviet analyst who was in China during the Korean period saw another plus for China. The war gave Mao an unequaled opportunity to rally the Chinese, on the basis of patriotism, to the support of the new and untested revolutionary regime. This observer felt that the patriotic unity achieved during the struggle was of vast assistance to Mao in unifying the country. It dampened many hostile elements that otherwise might have continued to support Chiang Kaishek, and it tended to unite the military and discourage nascent attempts at regionalism.

But there was not enough on the positive side of the ledger to balance China's huge economic losses and the setback to its development. Twenty years later, when President Nixon visited in 1972, China was still in a hostile world, its power limited by weak ties to the emerging Third World and unpredictable quarrels with the Soviet Union.

Another heritage of the Korean War — unknown to the outside world and concealed from most Chinese — was Mao's grandiose commitment that masqueraded under the ambiguous title of the Third Line. Mao had embarked upon the Third Line soon after the inception of the Korean War. Even he had only a cloudy notion of its scope, its cost, or its feasibility. But he ordered it started with the highest priority. If it worked — as he trusted it would — it might give China a chance for survival in the event that the power for which Mao cherished profound fear and dread — the United States — launched an attack on the fledgling People's Republic. He hoped for some protection from the Soviet Union, but he knew that the defense of China must basically be the task of the Chinese.

If his plan succeeded, China would gain partial security from the nightmare of the American atom bomb. Although Mao publicly had called America a paper tiger, he knew that the tiger possessed the most dangerous fangs in the world.

To the command of China's lifesaving plan Mao drafted Deng Xiaoping. No other man, Mao thought, could do the job and do it quickly. As to cost, Mao paid not the slightest heed. If your country's existence is at stake you do not haggle over the price. That the Third Line would grow and grow until it cast a secret shadow over all of China was beyond the comprehension of Mao, Deng, or anyone else at the time.

14

Deng Tackles His Biggest Job

DENG XIAOPING had unique qualifications for the tasks that Mao was preparing to place in his hands. He was Mao's viceroy for the southwest, and he knew this vast area, with its expanse of one million square miles (almost a third of the nation), as well as any man. China's "Wild West" was, in fact, his stamping ground. He had been born and raised in the northern tier of Sichuan, only seventy miles from the great southwest metropolis of Chongqing, and had gone to school there. He also knew Chengdu, the capital of Sichuan, well. He had many connections there and relatives. His family had, after all, been prominent in the affairs of northern Sichuan for generations.

It was true that Deng had not seen this part of China for many years until he and Liu Bocheng began their mopping-up operation in 1949 and he was then appointed to take charge of the whole southwest region. Deng had not gone back to his hometown since he left in 1916. For some reason he seemed to avoid his birthplace. Perhaps he had unpleasant memories of it.[1] But he had kept in close touch with conditions there through friends and relatives. He knew what people felt, and he knew the hardships and strains that had been imposed upon them by civil war, famine, and the backwardness of the country.

Mao understood Deng's special qualifications when he named him viceroy of the southwest, and he had them in mind in making Deng his choice to carry forward the extraordinary Third Line project.

Deng had crisscrossed the southwest in his viceroy's role. The southwest, as he described it, was handicapped by a "dilapidated society, a ruined economy and a wretched life for the people," the product of years of warlords, banditry, marauding KMT irregulars, machinations of secret societies, provincial political gangs, local clan infighting, general anarchy, and persistent warfare.[2]

Deng knew the heritage of the southwest and its potentials. He knew the mountains, the fast-flowing rivers torrenting down from the

Himalayas, the patchwork geography, as well as he knew the strengths and weaknesses of the Second Field Army, which Liu Bocheng and he had led across the deserts and cavern-studded mountains.

Deng had given Mao Zedong full and hearty support for the Korean project even though he knew the PLA — like his own Second Army — was hardly battle-ready, plagued as it was by worn-out equipment, tired, overstrained units, paucities of ammunition and supplies. All the more reason for throwing himself into his new assignment with the extraordinary energy for which he was already famous.

First he must complete the pacification of the southwest without delay. He must wipe out the nests of KMT troops still holding out on remote mountaintops, much as Mao himself and Zhu De had defied Chiang Kaishek on the fastness of Jinggang Mountain. Tibet was still the responsibility of himself and Liu Bocheng. They must establish Chinese power in Tibet swiftly and — if possible — with a minimum of force. If Tibet could be taken peacefully, that would be a big bonus.

The tasks Deng confronted in the southwest, as he noted later, were "monumental," nothing less than creating a new life in the just-liberated western empire.[3] But those tasks were dwarfed by Deng's new secret enterprise, the Third Line.

Mao had come to feel that the war in Korea might at any time trigger an American attack on mainland China. He believed this inevitably would take the form of a blitz like those that leveled Tokyo and Berlin. The great cities of Beijing, Shanghai, Wuhan, Chongqing, Tianjin, and the others would be wiped out, quite possibly by A-bombs. China had no air force worthy of the name and no contemporary antiaircraft guns. The cities and population would have to take it. Casualties would be mind-boggling. Mao's fears did not need to be spelled out to Deng. He knew that Korea had presented deadly peril to China.

Mao's plan to protect China from a U.S. nuclear attack did not meet the whole danger, but it might give China some chance of survival. It was built on China's experience in the anti-Japanese war. Chiang Kaishek had been compelled to move his capital from Nanjing to distant Chongqing, on the bluffs overlooking the Yangtze, deep in the interior, beyond the thrust of Japanese land forces and almost beyond Japanese air power. The move enabled Chiang and his government to exist even though the Japanese occupied China's principal cities and coastal regions.

Chongqing possessed little of the industrial and military resources needed to support a war or the huge population that flocked into the distant capital — 1.8 million by 1945. Chiang had begun to build a military-industrial complex in and around Chongqing to keep his KMT armies in the field. Chongqing already had a small arms industry. Mauser rifles — standard in the Chinese army — had been made there for years, as had light artillery. Now Chiang brought in capacity for rifles, ammunition, machine guns, hand grenades, mortars, and heavy guns. Some manufacturing plants were scattered around Chongqing and its suburbs. Others were put into the countryside. When the United States came into the war, in 1941, a few plants began to be sited in mountains and valleys difficult for the Japanese to spot and bomb. Several underground factories were installed in the vast caverns of northern Sichuan and northeast Guizhou (where some were still operating in 1984[4]).

Mao decided to follow Chiang's example on a grandiose scale. He would turn the remote Chengdu-Chongqing-Guiyang triangle into an impregnable arsenal, safe from American attack, so far away it would be almost impossible for American land forces to reach and possessing a productive capacity large enough to sustain a small-scale military effort.

There was one great problem: Chongqing had no communications with the rest of the country, none except the Yangtze River, majestic but hardly adequate as the backbone of a modern military-industrial complex. There were no railroads, no highways, and few airports. Hardly had Deng set up his headquarters in Chongqing than he was confronted with the problem of creating a rail network to link Chongqing and Chengdu with the rest of China.

The biggest single project that Deng would undertake was the rail link from Chongqing to Chengdu. It was done at breakneck speed, largely by military railroad battalions, through incredibly steep mountains and river gorges, an advanced engineering feat that set the pattern of the great southwestern rail network to be built over the next two decades. In later years Deng would account the Chongqing-Chengdu rail line, which opened on July 1, 1952, as his first major achievement in the long struggle to bring China out of its medieval morass. The construction took less than two years and set an example for the country. It provided the matrix for Mao's Third Line, not a defense line, but a redoubt that would make a defense line possible. The Chongqing-Chengdu project was to be matched only by the Chengdu-Kunming link, so difficult that it would have been built in no other country and was constructed in China only because of its extraordinary strategic importance. It was almost one long tunnel — 340 kilometers out of a total of 1,080 kilometers of rail. Not even in the Alps is there to be found so high a percentage of tunnels. It was completed in 1970.[5]

The Third Line was not confined to new facilities. It envisioned a massive shift of Chinese industry from coastal centers and exposed inland areas readily accessible to American air power to China's most remote and inaccessible regions. The task Mao handed to Deng was something like that of picking up the whole of California's high-tech industry and moving it bodily to the wilds of Montana as they existed, say, in 1880.

In contemporary times the only parallel close to what Mao had in mind was Stalin's effort in 1941 to move Russia's critical industries out of Leningrad, Moscow, and the areas of European Russia rapidly being engulfed by Hitler's attack. Stalin managed to extricate to the Urals and Siberia some war plants — aircraft assembly plants, a number of fabricating and metallurgical works — at enormous cost, disruption, and hardship. But the task of relocating basic facilities like steel plants, heavy chemical works, and petroleum complexes, the key elements of a modern economic system, was beyond Soviet abilities.

Although Mao's task would be performed in peacetime, he had only a fraction of the Russian resources. The Russians moved their factories into existing industrial sectors. Mao proposed to move his industries into an uninhabited, unpopulated, roadless wilderness. Not only did Mao decree the movement of China's prime productive facilities into "nowhere," but he ruled that all new factories of any strategic importance must be built in Third Line areas. If, Mao thought, he could tuck away military and industrial capacity in the folds and creases of Sichuan, Guizhou, Shaanxi, and Gansu, somehow China would not be lost.

No project of Mao's reign was to prove so costly, so labor-intensive, so economically unfeasible, or so disruptive as the Third Line. Nothing would so burden Deng Xiaoping. One estimate placed its cost to the economy as higher than that of the Cultural Revolution. The work was done at a dangerous pace, with scant heed to planning or safety. The tunnels, bridges, railroads, and highways were blasted out of precipitous mountainsides. Such construction took a heavy toll but was regarded as a military battle. Monuments were erected at spots where men died; they were listed as "worker-martyrs."

The Third Line, vaster than all the public works of Franklin D. Roosevelt's New Deal, bigger than Stalin's first Five-Year Plan, was unknown outside of China. Within China its dimensions were known only to a handful. It embraced one of the world's greatest oil fields,

Daqing, discovered and put into production without public knowledge. China's finest, largest, most advanced steel complex was built at Dukou, Sichuan, under total secrecy. Populations were moved from Shanghai and Tianjin, into towns that appeared on no maps, to man these plants.

The cost of the Third Line was nearly 40 percent of China's capital budget from 1963–65, 53 percent in the next five years, and 45 percent up to 1975. Expenses for rail construction were double and quadruple those of normal building — 3 to 4 million yuan per kilometer. The price tag for a dam above Lanzhou was 638 million yuan. The Dukou steel complex employed a hundred thousand construction workers and cost 3.7 billion yuan in its first phase. The total price for the Chengdu-Kunming railroad was 3.3 billion, a coal mine in Guizhou 1 billion.[6] One estimate in 1988 claimed more than 200 billion yuan had been invested in Third Line plants, including 75 percent of nuclear weapons plants and 60 percent of aeronautics. The magnitude of phasing out Mao's costly defense schemes can be judged by the costs of relocation and closing useless plants (some so badly and hurriedly built they had to be torn down and reconstructed two or three times). By 1988 relocation costs were still running 1 billion yuan or more a year. That year 2 billion yuan was allocated to relocate one hundred plants.[7]

By the time the Third Line was well advanced, China's most urgent necessity was protection not from the United States but from the Soviet Union.

Moscow-Beijing relations had seriously deteriorated by 1959. With the eclipse of Khrushchev in 1964, Sino-Soviet relations eased. But not for long. Leonid Brezhnev and the Soviet General Staff quickly moved into an even more aggressive posture toward Beijing.

By 1968–69 the two countries were approaching a prewar situation. Border clashes of unheard-of magnitude were raging. The Russians were preparing for nuclear war against China. Mao was trying to make preparations to save at least some of his population from the deadly assault.

Mao's Third Line had anchored China's critical defense industries in areas remote from possible American attack but close to the Soviet Union. They were vulnerable to nuclear or conventional weapons from Russia. It was far too late to move the great arms, chemical, steel, and power plants again. And where could Mao move them? There was no place to hide. Billions in treasure and manpower had been expended. The total probably exceeded all that China invested in industrial development, power facilities, and communications under the People's Republic. Now these complexes sat amid mountain gullies and river cliffs where Soviet missiles could methodically destroy them.

At a time when the country's attention was focused on Korea, Deng was at work night and day, probing Sichuan's mountains and the caverns of opium smugglers in Guizhou, seeking sites in which to hide Third Line factories.

No one could have displayed greater energy, imagination, speed, concentration, or more thorough devotion to the job than Deng. Mao was ecstatic about Deng's work. He sent a non-Communist philosophy professor, Liang Shuming, to observe developments. Liang Shuming reported to Mao that work was going splendidly, thanks to a man named Deng Xiaoping. Mao beamed. "Well, Mr. Liang, you have a good eye. Deng Xiaoping is capable, and whether it is politics or military affairs he does all right. He can write and he can fight. He is an able man."[8] Hardly had the formal completion of the Chongqing-Chengdu railroad been celebrated than Mao summoned Deng to Beijing. He had a place for him on the first team. In fact, he had a place for Deng as his right-hand man for the whole of China. It was a daunting task.

Deng came to Beijing in 1952, found a suitable palace in Zhongnanhai, and moved his family up from Chongqing. His wife, Pu Zhuo Lin, whom he had married in September 1939 in Yanan, was his third (after the divorce from A Jin sometime after May 1933 and the death of his first wife, Zhang Qianyuan, in labor in 1929 after eighteen months of marriage).

By the time Deng and Zhuo Lin were married she had dropped her family name, as was common among young revolutionaries. Her father, Pu Caiting, was known as the Ham King, the famous purveyor of a special Yunnan variety of ham that was as well known in south China as Smithfield ham is in Virginia. Everyone had to have a Pu ham for the spring festival feast.

Zhuo Lin's father was a wealthy man. He sent his daughter, born in 1916, to study at the principal boarding school in Kunming. After graduation she went to the Beijing Teachers College for Women, where she joined the Communist underground, coming to Yanan in 1939.[9]

At the time of moving into Zhongnanhai, the large Deng family included Deng's ten-year-old daughter, Deng Lin; his eight-year-old son, Deng Pufang; his seven-year-old daughter, Deng Nan; his six-year-old daughter, Deng Rong (Maomao); and his younger son, Deng Zhifang, just a toddler — three girls and two boys.

Deng invited his stepmother Xia Bogan, his father's capable fourth wife, to come and live in Zhongnanhai with them. Xia Bogan was to spend the rest of her life in the Deng household. Even when Deng was sent into exile in Jiangxi she was permitted to go along.[10]

It was an industrious, happy household. The children went to the special cadre kindergartens and schools. On Sundays they walked in the gardens of Zhongnanhai and sometimes picnicked on the Sea Terrace or made excursions to the Summer Palace and climbed the mountains. Deng took his youngsters boating on Nanhai and Zhonghai, and they went swimming at Beihai or in Mao's pool. They took lots of snapshots. The Zhongnanhai residents were all old friends, and they liked to walk and talk together. To the children their elders were all "Uncle" or "Auntie." Some of them got along better with Uncle Mao than with their own parents. Mao had a wry sense of humor and liked to tease the youngsters.

Quickly Mao began to entrust Deng with almost any task. He felt certain that if he turned it over to the energetic little man, it would be fulfilled. Deng came into Beijing as a vice premier dealing particularly with economic and administrative questions. By 1954 he had emerged as secretary-general of the Party Central Committee. In another year he was put into the Politburo. No one's rise was more swift and more secure than Deng's. He was Mao's golden boy, and by 1956 he was reckoned the fourth man in the Party, just after Mao, Liu Shaoqi, and Zhou Enlai. What Deng would later call "the busiest period in my life" was opening before him.[11] Deng was not a yes-man for Mao, but not once in this period, so far as the record discloses, did he seriously oppose any proposal put forward by the chairman.

In these post-Korea days Mao threw himself into the task of building a modern economy. He had no worries about the countryside; land reform moved forward, as it had under the Red Army during the civil war, with peasants taking over the fields, ousting landlords, often beheading them in public squares or clubbing them to death. How many were killed? No accurate figure will ever be found. Zhou Enlai hazarded a ballpark figure to Edgar Snow in 1960 of 830,000 "enemies of the people" killed between 1934 and 1954.[12] Mao Zedong said in 1956 that between 2 million and 3 million had been killed up to that date.[13] These are probably underestimates. Landlords permitted to live were given the most noisome tasks, such as collecting human sewage.

A Chinese cultural official, Duan Lianchen, in 1990 said with evident pride that when the Cultural Revolution had ended, 4.6 million "class enemies" were still alive. He offered no definition of a class enemy.

Mao slightly modified his policy. Land teams were instructed not to harass wealthier peasants. Their bigger crops were needed to feed the cities. Looking back, most Chinese were to call the years 1950 to 1956 the best of their lives.

Mao's leniency raised some eyebrows. Radical Party members wanted to root out all "bad elements." Among the radicals was Jiang Qing, who seemed to enjoy inciting peasants to kill the wealthy. Mao was not eager to have his wife roaming the countryside, but while he was in Moscow in 1949–50 she bullied the Party leaders of Shanghai into letting her visit the rich farming country around Wuxi. There she led propaganda teams that exhorted peasants to attack landlords, seize their property, burn their homes, and chop off their heads. She got back to Zhongnanhai just before her husband returned from Moscow.

For Mao, industry and the cities were a headache. He had no experience. There was not a line in the Annals of the Twenty-four Dynasties to give him a clue, and he couldn't get much out of Marx.

One source of know-how was the Chinese entrepreneurs. China possessed a few large industrial and banking families. Most had Nationalist connections, but some were more liberal. Mao decided to recruit what he called "national capitalists," patriotic businessmen who would support the crusade for a New China. He pointed out that Marx had decreed that all countries must pass through capitalism on the way to Socialism and Communism. China was still feudal and surrounded by imperialist powers. Capitalism was the logical next step, with no talk of an immediate leap into Socialism. Mao said nothing about how long this transitional state would last, since neither he nor anyone else had the least idea.[14] Everything was ad hoc. The only model was Russia, where the Bolsheviks had displaced a semifeudal society, albeit one considerably more advanced than China.

Mao's biggest problem was dealing with the national capitalists. Patriotic or not, many capitalists did not trust the Communists. They had seen too many colleagues come to grief, too many people murdered or driven almost naked from their estates or businesses. They were not inclined to wait to see what the future held.

A few capitalists gave Mao a hand. China's largest entrepreneurial family was the Rongs of Wuxi. They were third- or fourth-generation capitalists. Having started in flour milling and branched out into textiles, banking, and other businesses, the Rongs were still based at

Wuxi but had large interests in Shanghai, Hong Kong, America, and Europe. The Revolution dispersed the family. Some went to Hong Kong, some to Taiwan, others to San Francisco, New York, and London. But their investments in Chinese industry were great, and Rong Yiren stayed behind and became a national capitalist. He continued to run his own enterprise with light government supervision and was entitled to a large and reasonable share of profits. The rest went to the government. Mao and his associates valued him.[15]

For the future, Mao felt the best approach would be the planned economic model of the Soviet Union. Mao had discussed this with Liu Shaoqi, who agreed, as did Gao Gang, Mao's Manchurian proconsul. Mao had been hesitant to commit China to this course, but his journey back from Moscow in 1950 gave him a chance to inspect Soviet achievements in the great industrial regions of the Urals and Siberia. He stopped over in seven Soviet cities, four of them major industrial centers: Sverdlovsk, in the Urals, one of the largest Soviet steel and machinery centers; Omsk, on the river Om, a rapidly developing new factory complex; Novosibirsk, the capital of western Siberia, expanding enormously under the forced impetus of World War II; Krasnoyarsk, a Siberian power and chemicals city; Irkutsk, the old capital of eastern Siberia; Ulan-Ude, capital of the Soviet Mongol minority; and Chita, the military base for eastern Siberia. By stopping off at the Manchurian industrial centers of Harbin, Changchun, and Shenyang Mao was able to contrast the Soviet developments with Manchuria's industrial bases.

Mao not only inspected factories, power plants, and industrial installations, he visited housing developments and spent time in the universities of Siberia, gaining a comprehensive picture of Soviet development under conditions similar to those in much of China. This gave Mao a sense of inevitability. He didn't feel comfortable with the Soviet blueprint, but he could see that it worked. Until or unless some better scheme came along, he would follow the recommendations of the Russians. They were the ones with the know-how.

In fact, Mao was not interested in economic problems, perhaps as a result of his arguments with his father, who had wanted him to take an interest in his growing grain business and usurious loans to peasants. Mao refused to participate in these enterprises and was left with a prejudice against anything involving money matters and accounting. He avoided questions involving banking, budgets, and credits. They smacked of capitalism, small trade, bookkeeping. The attitude of Mao, the revolutionary, was close to that of an English aristocrat. Trade was beneath him. He had never read *Das Kapital,* which was not published in China until 1938, when he had already established himself in Yanan. No one recalls his reading it, nor did he quote from it in his speeches and writings.

Most of Mao's references to Marx were drawn from *The Communist Manifesto,* and many of his associates attested that Mao's principal interest in Marx lay in his theories of class and class warfare. Mao's belief in the importance of class warfare — even after establishment of Communist rule — persisted to his last days.[16]

Mao's mind was philosophical and poetic. He felt at home with the Chinese classics. He knew Confucius and his follower Mencius, and he knew how the Ming and the Tang and the other dynasties had handled economics. Statistics bored him. He preferred to leave these details to subordinates.[17]

Mao's great strength in the Long March and in the Revolution was his belief in the efficacy of mass action. He was convinced that there was no problem that could not be solved if he mobilized the strength of the masses. He did not literally believe in his famous parable of the old man who moved a mountain, but he did believe he knew how to direct the strength of China's huge population. With that energy there was no goal China could not attain — whether moving a mountain or creating a steel industry or wiping out the opium habit.

Tremendous tasks lay ahead. But, so far as Mao could see, although the path would be hard, the job could be done. He was not going to get much help from Stalin, yet he did not think Stalin would sabotage him. And while the United States seemed restless, the imminent danger of intervention from that quarter had faded. So it seemed.

15

Mao Zedong Tests Deng Xiaoping

THE WINTER of 1955–56 was cold in Beijing — raw, windy, the air filled with gritty dust from the Gobi. Mao Zedong spent many weeks away at his beautiful palace on West Lake, at Hangzhou. He took every opportunity to escape the Beijing winter. His throat and lungs were susceptible to cold, and in his last decade he would suffer each fall and spring from what his staff simply called "the winter disease," racking coughs that tore his body apart.[1]

In 1956 Mao relaxed as he liked to do at Hangzhou. Still winter in Beijing, it was spring in Hangzhou. Cherry blossoms put a blush on the lakeshore. Mao had pleasant dancing partners from the Hangzhou art ensemble.[2] But life was not all fox-trots and bunny hugs. He had brought to Hangzhou a small research team to work on new economic ideas. The first five-year plan — a close imitation of the Soviet model — had been completed. Its success was due, in no small measure, to the driving force of Deng Xiaoping.

The heavy material losses of the Korean War were being made good. Danger of hostilities with America seemed to have receded, and relations with the Soviet Union had improved with the death of Stalin. But Mao was restless. If it had taken the Red Army only fifteen years from the Long March to the conquest of all China, then economic development shouldn't take so long. Perhaps the trouble lay in the Soviet model they were following. Stalin had never, Mao thought, understood the irresistible power of the "mass movement," of mobilizing the whole population to build a dam, a breakwater, a new city. The mass movement, Mao believed, could build China far faster than the Soviet *pyatleka,* Stalin's Five-Year Plan.[3]

At this moment, in early March 1956, Anastas Mikoyan, the lively Armenian who was Khrushchev's political ally, arrived in Beijing. Mikoyan had been sent on so many missions to Beijing that his fellow Politburo members called him "our Chinaman."[4]

Mikoyan's visits always proved unsettling. He was sent east only when the Kremlin had something unpleasant to pass on, and this trip fit the pattern. The Twentieth Congress of the Soviet Communist Party had just adjourned in Moscow after hearing a secret speech by Khrushchev. Foreign delegates had been barred during Khrushchev's exposé on February 24–25 of Stalin's crimes. The contents of the speech were closely guarded, and Mikoyan had been sent to brief the Chinese.

The Chinese Politburo assembled in the refurbished Huairentang, or Huairen Hall, the 1880s palace built by Emperor Guangxu, ill-fated nephew of the empress dowager Ci Xi. The Communists had remodeled it as their principal assembly hall until the grandiose Great Hall of the People was put up in 1959.[5] Here the Politburo, chaired by Liu Shaoqi in the absence of Mao (still in Hangzhou), listened to Mikoyan, who spoke for three hours, relaying what Khrushchev had said. The Chinese listened in silence. There was hardly a cough or a clearing of throat. When Mikoyan finished not one Chinese offered a comment. On such a matter there could be only one opinion that mattered — that of Mao. No one would express himself until he knew what Mao thought.

Some of the Chinese, of course, had heard hints of Stalin's crimes, but the whole story came as a shock. They reacted in bewilderment and disbelief (as many Russians were to do). Liu Shaoqi suggested that Mikoyan fly south to meet with Mao. Next day Mikoyan repeated his story at Hangzhou. Mao listened quietly, then told Mikoyan that he could understand the secret speech and why it had been made. But he raised a point that the Chinese would still be raising nearly forty years later. Mao agreed that, as Khrushchev had made clear, Stalin had been guilty of terrible crimes. Yet he had also made great contributions to building Communism, and he had led the Soviets to victory in World War II. Khrushchev should have presented a more balanced portrait.

Mikoyan listened patiently and offered no rebuttal. What was important to him was that Mao had accepted the secret speech and was not going to lead the Communist world in opposition to the Soviet Union. Mikoyan was correct in the latter assumption but not in the former. As time went on, Mao's differences with Moscow grew more sharp.

Mao told his colleagues that Khrushchev was a more enlightened man than Stalin and was easier to deal with; he had a better attitude toward China. The Chinese, said Mao, should use their influence to educate Khrushchev and to widen his experience. The Soviet leader was young and new and did not always appreciate the world situation. But Mao did not remove the portrait of Stalin, which he had erected along with his own and those of Marx and Lenin in Tiananmen Square. In fact, it remained on display for years after almost every image of Stalin had vanished in the Soviet Union (except in Georgia, Stalin's birthplace). It still graced Tiananmen for thirty years after the Khrushchev speech and was taken down only in 1988.[6]

When a Soviet delegation headed by Mikoyan came to Beijing in September 1956, for the Eighth National Congress of the Chinese Communist Party, the Chinese made a point of again criticizing the lopsidedness of Khrushchev's speech.[7]

Mao believed that he must distance China's policy from that of the Soviet Union and break away from blind following of Moscow, particularly in economics. He had become more and more certain that China could do better with an original, innovative policy fashioned to its own resources, particularly its vast manpower.

It was in this mood that Mao launched in late 1956 what became known in the West as the Hundred Flowers movement, based on the slogan "Let One Hundred Flowers Bloom; Let One Hundred Schools of Thought Contend." The Chinese called it the Double Hundreds. Many Chinese and foreigners interpreted Mao's gambit as designed to draw out critical expressions in order to expose opponents and then crush them.

In reality the case was much more complex, and it is small wonder that it has been interpreted in so many ways both abroad and in China. In early stages Mao seems to have been impressed by the verdict against Stalin and to have drawn the conclusion that the time had come to loosen up the regime in China. The distinguished specialist in the study of Mao, Li Rui, himself a victim of the anti-rightist campaign of repression that followed the Hundred Flowers initiative, believed firmly that the Hundred Flowers was Mao's first step toward relaxing his regime and easing the grip of blind Soviet repressive policies.[8]

There is evidence to support Li Rui. Mao made several speeches (none of the texts have been published) in late 1956 and early 1957 on this theme. His ideas were not popular within the Party. Non-Party people reacted with extreme caution. They realized that there was a split in the Party and did not want to be crushed between the two sides.

Several important Party leaders opposed Mao on the Hundred Flowers movement. One was Liu Shaoqi, who spoke at Beijing University against the idea of letting down barriers on critical thought, as did Peng Zhen, the mayor of Beijing. Deng Xiaoping in the spring of 1957 told Qinghua University the policy was dangerous, and he later conceded his role in opposing the Hundred Flowers movement *before* Mao himself reversed the line.

After a good bit of shifting back and forth Mao was well launched on his anti-rightist campaign by 1958. It was marked by brutality. The number of victims is variously estimated. Deng himself, in 1980, offered an estimate of 500,000 repressed in 1957–58 out of 2.9 million accused of rightism. American specialists calculate the total at 400,000 to 500,000.[9]

No doubt the world situation influenced Mao. Khrushchev's secret speech had touched off upheavals in Communist countries, and Mao expressed to his intimates his concern lest the violence spread to China. It did not seem the time to experiment with a more liberal regime. Mao cautioned Khrushchev not to use force in Poland. He didn't. Mao supported armed intervention in Hungary. Khrushchev sent in the tanks. Zhou Enlai flew into Eastern Europe at Khrushchev's request, visited Warsaw, and went on to Budapest, where he made a speech supporting Khrushchev. Not likely Mao would take a softer line at home.

Perhaps because Deng had opposed the Hundred Flowers, Mao turned to him for help in his repressive drive. Some Chinese liberals have declared Deng was placed in charge of the Central Committee office that directed the anti-rightist campaign.[10] Historian Hu Hua described Mao as having put Deng in charge of what he called "small problems" of the drive. The implication was that Deng played a minor role, straightening out some cases.[11]

Deng himself took major responsibility and attempted to justify the campaign. In remarks he made at the Fifth Plenary of the Eleventh Central Committee, in 1980, he spoke out in defense of Party control, saying any relaxation would lead to chaos. He conceded that the Party had made serious mistakes but emphasized that the Party itself invariably made the corrections. Deng called himself an "activist" in the anti-rightist campaign and said he, as Party secretary-general, shared responsibility for what had been done. He evaluated his conduct as 60 percent right and 40 percent wrong. "I'll be satisfied with that," he said. He personally oversaw rehabilitation of alleged rightists and in his remarks of January 16, 1980, reiterated that "the anti-rightist campaign was necessary and correct. The struggle was not wrong. The problem was that its scope was unduly broadened."[12]

Deng's expressed attitude was consistent with his own policy toward dissent once he himself came to power, in 1978.

A year after Khrushchev's secret speech the peripatetic Anastas Mikoyan made one more flying trip to China, this time to counter the poor impression made by another Soviet diplomat. It was July 1957, the time of the crisis in Moscow over the "Antiparty Group." With the help of Marshal Georgy K. Zhukov, Khrushchev had turned the tables on his opponents — Georgy Malenkov, Vyacheslav Molotov, Nikolai Bulganin, Lazar Kaganovich, and, in fact, most of the Politburo. They had been removed from office, deprived of Party membership, and exiled to petty jobs in far-off places.

The announcement of Khrushchev's action was made to the Chinese by Pavel Yudin, the Soviet ambassador in Beijing. Yudin got a poor reception. Mao was not present. Marshal Peng Dehuai asked the only question. The Antiparty Group, he noted, was made up mostly of old revolutionaries, old Party comrades. Was there no way of dealing with them other than depriving them of Party membership? Yudin had no answer. It was a question that would reverberate when the same issue arose in the Chinese Communist Party.

When Khrushchev learned of Yudin's angry reception, he sent Mikoyan scurrying back to China. Mao was, as so frequently, in Hangzhou, where his research teams were still working out the new economic program. Mikoyan again flew to Hangzhou, and Mao received him in a small low-ceilinged room with only two small windows, no air-conditioning. The heat was sweltering, the humidity total. Mikoyan, wiry, energetic, and dark-browed, sweating like a jogger, talked for three hours. Mao sat silently, wearing his winter-weight tunic, beads of sweat rolling down his round cheeks. By the time Mikoyan finished, the interpreter's notebook was a soggy pulp.

Mao reclined like a perspiring Buddha, pondering what he had heard. Finally he spoke: "I agree with the contents of what you have said."

Mikoyan relaxed. Once again he had kept the Chinese on the reservation; Mao would not go on the warpath. The next day Mikoyan left for Moscow. The Chinese air controllers had wanted Mikoyan to take off early in the morning. It was monsoon season, and heavy rain and wind were predicted. But Mikoyan had stayed up late celebrating. It was 1:00 P.M. before his Ilyushin-14 took off into a thunderstorm. The plane tossed and shook. The pilot fought to lift it above the storm, but the cabin wasn't pressurized. He couldn't go above 10,000 or 12,000 feet.

Mikoyan stretched out on a bed. "I don't care what happens," he said. "I can die with no regrets. I've fulfilled my mission." A young Chinese interpreter, trying to brace himself in a folding chair, seethed with anger. "It was all right for Mikoyan to be prepared to meet death," he later said. "He had lived his life. I was just starting mine. I was only in my twenties. He made me very angry."

The interpreter was not the only one who lost his temper. The commander of China's air force, Liu Yalou, was directing the plane's flight at ground control. He began to jump with rage at the inability of the Russian pilot to follow his instructions. Liu had trained in the Soviet Union, and he unleashed a stream of *'mat,* mother oaths, at the pilot. "Don't just climb for altitude," he shouted. "Climb out where it is clear and get the hell away from the storm."[13] Eventually the plane escaped danger.

Mao took preparations for the Great Leap Forward to the countryside. His ideas were not yet precise, but he began to call meetings at the grass roots of local leaders, away from Beijing, where, as he correctly sensed, there was no great sympathy for his plans. He co-opted Deng to head some gatherings.[14]

This was new. Mao had not used Deng before in ideology. Deng was not a bookish person. True, he had been a good student as a youngster, but he hadn't had time for study since. In France he had to work too hard to keep himself alive to do much studying. Nor had there been time for ideological studies once he got back to China, in 1927. Deng's life was action-oriented. One big job after another, usually in the distant ends of China. Not until he wound up in detention during the Cultural Revolution would he have time for books.

Why Mao turned to his hyperkinetic deputy for these new tasks is not clear; perhaps it was a way of testing him. It may have reflected Mao's uneasiness with Zhou Enlai and Liu Shaoqi, whom he was beginning to perceive as increasingly unsympathetic to his twists and turns. Whatever the reason, Deng's leadership role began to broaden.

Mao's partiality for Deng Xiaoping had become well known by now. Mao almost seemed to regard him as a favorite son. He liked Deng's drive, his spirit, his ability to work out difficult tasks. Deng was rising rapidly in the hierarchy without unsettling his peers. He was still junior to Zhou Enlai and Liu Shaoqi, and the three got on well. Deng's new assignments did not annoy Zhou or Liu. There was no sense of rivalry, although it was apparent that Mao was deliberately expanding Deng's assignments, assessing the little man and his capabilities.

While Mao not infrequently encouraged rivalry among his underlings, seeing this as a useful way to stimulate their energies and ambitions, he did not give many outward manifestations of favor, according to bodyguard Li Yinqiao. He expected his lieutenants to do their jobs well. That did not mean that he showered them with praise. Even with Zhou Enlai, on whom Mao was dependent for the smooth running of the country, he showed no personal feelings. In fifteen years of association with Mao, attending him every day of the year, Li Yinqiao never heard a word of affection or praise from Mao toward Zhou or any of the others. It was not his way.

In the Party hierarchy Deng Xiaoping was rated number four and was so listed in the press and on posters. Number one, of course, was Mao. Number two was Zhou Enlai, and number three was Liu Shaoqi. At the important meetings it was Deng who was called upon to offer the general summary at the conclusion — at least until February 1958, when things began to change.[15]

The characteristics of Mao's lieutenants differed. Zhou Enlai was seen as Mao's probable heir. Zhou had been at Mao's side since the Zunyi conference, which had brought Mao back into power on the Long March in January 1935. Zhou inspired devotion. No one in the Party was more deeply loved. Mao was respected; Zhou was loved. Although Liu Shaoqi, with his thoughtful and careful work style, was not as charismatic as Mao or Zhou, he was widely esteemed for his total devotion to his work. There was no line of division between these men and the great commanders of the Long March, the anti-Japanese war, and the victory over Chiang Kaishek. But without question the commanders had a special attitude toward Deng. Zhu De, Peng Dehuai, Chen Yi, Liu Bocheng, Nie Rongzhen, Marshal Ye Jianying — all of them except Lin Biao — considered him "one of us." That gave Deng a special standing among the proconsuls.

PART 4

THE DRAGON THRONE
ASCENDED

16

Karl Marx Plus Emperor Qin

FROM HIS DAYS on the Long March, Mao Zedong had become fond of saying, "You fight your battle; I'll fight my battle."

This was not a casual aphorism. It represented a personal philosophy that he had evolved during the endless struggle of the Red Army against often overwhelming odds. Mao meant that he would not fight a simple reactive battle; he would not merely respond to enemy moves. He would construct his own strategy and impose it upon his enemy, by surprise, if possible, and always, he trusted, under conditions in which he could maximize his small numbers and minimize the superiority of the enemy.

Mao did not abandon this principle once the war was over and the peacetime struggle to build Communist China began. Now he used it not against Chiang Kaishek but against internal opponents, or fancied opponents within his own party, and not infrequently against those very close to him in the leadership.

As an associate once said, "Sometimes his tactics surprised people because he did something unusual and unexpected. This was not an accident. He took you by surprise just as he hoped to take the enemy by surprise. Of course, this was not always a good thing and sometimes he suffered as a result."[1]

Chen Hansheng was a man who gave almost his whole life to the Chinese revolution. He had carried out difficult and dangerous missions for the Party and was in 1987, at the age of ninety-one, almost blind (he had been deprived of drugs for his glaucoma during the Cultural Revolution). However, he retained a sharp, sardonic view of Mao and the world in which he had lived since graduating from

Pomona College, in California, and majoring in economics at the University of Chicago in the 1920s.

Chen knew Mao well. He summed up the man: Mao was a "person of hatred." He and Stalin were fundamentally the same, although neither would admit to any similarity. Mao was envious of Liu Shaoqi, and of Peng Dehuai and He Long, two of his most famous commanders. "Other people won't tell you that," Chen said. "But I will. It explains a lot."[2]

Mao by no means concealed his desire to put China's economy on a new, faster track, but the full scope of his introduction of a communal land system and of what came to be called the Great Leap Forward only gradually dawned on his associates. By 1957 Mao had lost confidence in the economic management of Zhou Enlai and Liu Shaoqi. Neither voiced opposition to Mao's new plans, but Mao believed (correctly) that they were not sympathetic to them. He did not then believe Deng Xiaoping possessed a negative attitude. Deng worked at an operating, not policymaking, level, and for a time he was thus not in the line of Mao's fire.[3] Mao put Deng in a special category. Considering him indispensable, he spoke of Deng as his "reserve force" and differentiated him from older associates like Liu.[4] Mao put Deng in charge of small regional meetings that he held to whip up support for his new schemes.[5] None of his economic plans had, as a matter of fact, been approved by the Party Central Committee or the Politburo, as required by Party statute, but Mao proceeded with them anyway. In this tactic he was much like Stalin.

Mao's associates noted that more and more he singled out for praise China's first emperor, Qin, he of the terra-cotta army at Xian. Qin's reign had lasted only eleven years, but it was one of the bloodiest in Chinese history. His cruelty was phenomenal. He killed Chinese by the tens and hundreds of thousands and destroyed much of China's recorded history, annals of past kings, storehouses of archives, great libraries. Against these acts of barbarism Mao set Qin's achievements — the unification of the Han Chinese and establishment of the first Han empire. From Qin's time China was a nation-state.

Members of the inner circle understood that Mao saw in his own feat of unifying China by smashing Chiang Kaishek a contemporary parallel with Emperor Qin's accomplishments. Mao did not say he was the latter-day Emperor Qin. That was not necessary. His colleagues knew what he thought. What they did not know was the price Mao was prepared to pay in blood to crown his achievements. Not until the Cultural Revolution would that begin to be plain.[6] The

Cultural Revolution, one of its thoughtful victims once said, equals Marx plus Emperor Qin.[7]

Later Mao's oldest associates began to ponder the significance of his choice of the Chinese tyrant as his hero. Had they been better informed about Josef Stalin they would have been made uneasy by an uncanny coincidence. About the time Stalin was well into his terror program, slaughtering old comrades and sending millions of Russians to die in his labor camps, he began to display a special interest in Russia's most brutal czar, Ivan the Terrible. He commissioned the great Russian film director Sergei Eisenstein to make a film about Ivan's success in unifying Russia and throwing off the Mongol yoke. But when Eisenstein started to make *Ivan the Terrible Part II*, dealing with Ivan's terror, Stalin killed the picture and reprimanded Eisenstein. Soon Eisenstein was dead of a heart attack — or so it was reported.

As Chen Hansheng commented, there was more similarity between Stalin and Mao than either would have acknowledged.[8]

If people had been listening closely to Mao Zedong at the Moscow conference in November 1957, they would not have been startled by the goals he later advanced. In this discussion Mao put forward the idea that the Soviet Union was on the verge of overtaking the United States and that China would catch up with England's steel production in fifteen years.[9]

Mao moved in 1958 to launch China on that "Great Leap Forward" that he believed could be achieved by "mass movement" of the people. With the stroke of his ink brush Mao placed China's vast rural population into a commune system — a bare-bones regime in which the peasants were gathered into egalitarian units. They gave up private property, even their shovels and hoes. They were housed in barracks, and their huts were torn down to provide the materials to build the new dormitories.

The peasants worked together in military formation, dressed in blue tunics and blue trousers, men and women indistinguishable at 100 feet, resembling battalions of blue ants. They shared a common poverty that made the past misery of the Chinese countryside seem like prosperity. They ate in a common mess from a common rice bowl. They owned their chopsticks — not much more.

The Chinese peasants hated the communes. They sold or butchered their pigs and cows rather than turn them over to the commune. They stuffed themselves with the communal food, since it was "free," sometimes beating their children to make them eat more of the free food and get it while they could. They did little work, because more work did not mean bigger grain allotments. They never saw any cash.

How could Mao, who had demonstrated such perfect pitch for peasant nuances, misjudge the countryside so profoundly? None of his colleagues (when they later had time to think) could understand it. Somehow, Mao, born and raised in the country, having spent his life with country people, got the idea that they preferred to labor together and live together. Some suggested his conclusion came from the ten years spent in Yanan, where the Communists, like social workers in old New York, lived with the peasants and hand led them into communal activities.

The only evidence to support Mao's notions stemmed from the fact that peasants sometimes had worked together on special projects like digging irrigation ditches or trading labor at harvesttime. Other than that, they were individualists, like peasants the world over. They planted their own crops (and the landlords') and fed their own families, without any sharing.[10]

By 1958 it was almost impossible to tell Mao anything he didn't want to hear. "Once Mao made up his mind and there was opposition," said bodyguard Li Yinqiao, "Mao would persist, and he was bound to win."[11]

Mao was as willful as a naughty boy. During an air alert at Chennanzhuang he refused to take shelter until he had a cigarette. Bombs fell nearby. "Give me my cigarette," Mao insisted. "The planes are coming in. You must take shelter," the guards said. "I don't want shelter. I want my cigarette." They tried to drag him, but he resisted until he had the cigarette.

Once in Nanning in 1958 a KMT plane came over. Mao was reading. He wouldn't go to the shelter. "If a bomb falls on my head it won't dare to explode," he said.

Nothing made him so stubborn as efforts to keep him from swimming. Luo Ruiqing, his security chief, had orders to keep him out of the water during a storm. Mao dashed into the sea regardless, leaping in the high waves, shouting, "I can catch the waves." The waves flipped him over and filled his mouth with sand. The guards rushed to save him. "Let's go again," he shouted.[12]

His capacity for self-criticism had atrophied. He had become infallible. Not one associate publicly challenged the commune plan or the Great Leap. Not Zhou, not Liu, not Deng. Mao had spoken, and Mao was never wrong. Mao would listen to suggestions only from persons too junior to be political rivals and from technicians with commonsense attitudes.[13] Zhou Xiaozhou, Hunan Party secretary, once told Mao in a tense Party debate that if those at the top preferred a particular thing, the people at the bottom "will report that it has been accomplished, essentially." Mao would not have permitted Zhou Enlai or Liu Shaoqi to say such a thing, but he accepted the Hunan man's remark with a smile.[14]

Mao maintained a fairly comfortable relationship with his secretaries and bodyguards and often talked things over with them. He did not bridle when they asked sharp questions or voiced doubts that he would never have tolerated from equals. During the Great Leap Forward, a new secretary, Li Rui, then in his twenties, questioned a production report that Mao had accepted. It asserted that a particular commune had achieved a production of 10,000 jin of wheat per mu, the equivalent of 6.5 tons per one sixth acre, an obvious impossibility. "How can you believe this report?" Li Rui asked. Mao took no offense. He replied quietly that he had read an article in which a Chinese physicist said that even without extra labor and simply by harnessing solar energy it was possible to get a yield of 10,000 jin per mu.

People around Mao gave him optimistic reports, and he accepted them. He had no background in science. He engaged in some discussions of particle physics (to better understand nuclear weapons) with the physicist Zhou Mintian and did some reading on the subject. But he possessed no independent capacity to evaluate reports and evidence from a scientific point of view.[15]

Mao's education and life experience had left great gaps in his knowledge. He knew little or nothing about capitalism beyond some primitive ideas he picked up from early readings of *The Communist Manifesto*. He accepted the need for science and modern technology because Marx said that they were necessary to construct an advanced society, but he had an imperfect grasp of technology. Perhaps this was one reason he turned so readily to things like mobilizing his population in mass efforts on a scale and style reminiscent of the Egypt of the pyramids.

His biographer Li Rui believed it was Mao's lack of background on capitalism and the West that contributed to catastrophes like the Great Leap Forward.[16] Mao had never visited the West. In his lifetime he would make only two trips outside China, both to Soviet Russia, both to Moscow. His only firsthand study of a country more advanced than China had been made in his long trip back from Moscow in early 1950 in the Urals and Siberia. He never displayed real interest in the West, unless his long and unsuccessful attempt at learning English was a symptom. Certainly Mao was not as closed to the outside as his illustrious predecessor Emperor Qian Long, who informed Lord George Maccartney, a British emissary visiting China in 1793 on a mission to open up trade, that China possessed everything it needed and that there was therefore no basis for trade between the two countries. But Mao's ignorance of the West and modern capitalism was dangerous to him and to China because he did not know that the images that he acquired from random reading did not give him a real understanding of the world.

Chen Hansheng, to whom the years had given some original views about Mao, traced Mao's approach to the peasants in the Great Leap Forward to his successes with the Red Army. Mao had spent most of his adult life as a military leader, first among the guerrillas, then as head of the vast Red Army organization.

The Red Army — like any army — was founded on universals. Its members were disciplined. They were trained to carry out specific duties. All wore the same dress. They lived in common and worked in common. In the field they lived in primitive shelters, each sharing the same hardships. They ate their meals in common, sharing the same rice pot. The differences between men and leaders were very slight. Officers wore the same uniform, no insignia of rank, no titles, no saluting — a totally egalitarian system.

Mao's army was a social system perfectly attuned to its mission. It had been a stunning success. Mao had led it to victory after victory. He had defeated Chiang Kaishek and won China. In the era of the People's Republic the PLA had faced up to the military might of the United States in Korea and fought toe to toe. It had tackled great civilian construction tasks: railroads, highways, tunnels, irrigation, flood barriers along the great rivers. It was flexible; it could be set to build a steel mill or turned out to till the fields.

The army was composed almost entirely of peasants. They had accepted army discipline and goals easily. It was natural, thought Chen Hansheng, that Mao, with his belief in the unlimited potentials of "mass action," would think in terms of the army.

Mao, Chen believed, reasoned like a peasant. He was very *tu,* as the Chinese said, earthy. He arrived at peasant solutions — simple solutions based on personal experience and the inherited lore of peasant life, which he had absorbed in Shaoshan.

The key to the commune system, Mao thought, was the common

kitchen. He did not introduce a commune system in classical Marxist terms, Chen felt. He introduced a common kitchen system, believing that people who ate together and worked together would evolve a common, unified mechanism that would be the civilian counterpart of the army.[17]

Mao was wrong. Hardly had he started the communes than he imposed upon them a special task. They would devote themselves to industry as well. They would provide the infrastructure for the Great Leap Forward under which, in fifteen years, China would match England in steel production. The medium for this leap was what came to be known as backyard steel mills. The new communes were directed to set up small smelting pots whose production, Mao fondly believed, would quickly surpass that of the few industrial steel plants China already possessed.

This was mass movement with a vengeance. By the autumn of 1958, ninety million Chinese peasants had abandoned farm work for dawn-to-dusk (or late-night) labor at ramshackle smelters set up in each commune. The peasants had no ore or pig iron to feed into the smelters.[18] Into the smelting pots instead went every piece of iron or steel they could lay hands on — picks, shovels, hoes, rakes, axes, hammers, pitchforks, crowbars, soup pots, wagon hubs, water buckets, pipes, all the iron on the farm. Galvanized iron roofs, nails, bolts, hinges, barbed wire, locks, angle irons, even small tractors were thrown in. The country looked as though it had been picked clean by iron-eating ants.

Nor was this all. There had to be charcoal to fire the smelting pots. Naturally, there was no supply in the countryside. In some areas every tree on the hillsides, every fruit tree, every shade tree, every piece of wood, was cannibalized for charcoal. Thirty years after the Great Leap the scars of its insanity disfigured slopes all over China, erosion gullies caused by the slaughter of trees that had not been replaced. For centuries erosion had been one of China's implacable problems. The Leap worsened it.

So busy were the peasants turning out "steel," they had no time to garner the harvest. In fact, Party workers told them that the new system had produced such remarkable yields of grain that they need not worry about individual harvests, because the total would be so high there would be more than enough for all. Grain rotted in the fields while clouds of smoke rose over the countryside from the jerry-built smelters.

The tools that would be needed for spring and winter plantings were blithely tossed into the smelting pots. Only here and there did a canny peasant bury his spade and rake.

Remarkable figures were reported to Mao proclaiming the mountainous production of homemade steel. So encouraging were the figures that the estimate for overtaking England in steel production was reduced from fifteen years to five, and later to three years. The nation was as dazzled by the prospect of instant transition from feudalism to advanced Socialism as the Dutch had been by the dizzy speculation of the tulip craze. Mao himself believed it was possible.[19] The sky was the limit. The mass movement, Mao believed, could attain any goal set before it. Not a word of skepticism escaped the lips of Zhou Enlai, Liu Shaoqi, or Deng Xiaoping. These sensible men were as bamboozled by Mao's sleight of hand as the sleepiest peasant from northern Shaanxi — or so it seemed. There were no reports of trouble from the countryside, only news of greater and ever-greater successes. It was a hot air balloon, but when it crashed it could bring down the whole country.

In Zhongnanhai all was quiet, all was calm. Mao busied himself with the tales of the Warring States period (475–221 B.C.). He had by no means lost his interest in dancing. His partners now seemed to be more and more youthful, gliding over the floor with panther sleekness as he lumbered along humming old Beijing opera tunes. Jiang Qing was not amused. Mao called her a spoilsport.[20]

In 1958 Kang Sheng, the shadowy police specialist, popped up in Beijing once again. He had been down in his native Shandong as party secretary, engaged in a regional reign of terror. Now Mao brought him into Beijing to "oversee higher educational institutions." Kang had been involved in some of the Sino-Soviet talks and now began to move into an intimate and deadly relationship with Mao. His lures were paranoia and sex. He knew Mao's tastes and seemed to have access to an endless roster of libidinous young women.[21]

The calm of Zhongnanhai could not long endure. Food was running out in many rural districts in late autumn 1958. Peasants were beginning to eat seed grain — if they had any. Many had none, not having bothered to harvest the fall crops. These had been described officially as bumper harvests, without precedent in Chinese history.

When the first alarm reached the high echelons of the Party and government is not certain. It was hard for a signal to work its way up through the bureaucracy. Officials at middle and higher levels had no wish to receive negative news; it might cost them their necks. If cautious alarms came from below, the reports were sent back for revision. Yields were falsified and upgraded. Even if Zhongnanhai had been alive to the danger, there would have been little evidence filtering through.

One early harbinger of the impending disaster was brought to Beijing by the older sister of Liu Shaoqi. She still lived in the family village of Ningxian, in southern Hunan, only a dozen miles from Mao's birthplace of Shaoshan. She told her brother that peasants in their home county were starving. There had already been deaths.[22] Alarming reports issued from Anhui and Sichuan. But no emergency bells rang in Zhongnanhai. Neither Zhou nor Liu nor Deng nor anyone else in a position of authority uttered any warning. The silence was deafening. Newspapers reverberated with reports of tremendous success, of incredible quantities of steel being produced. Not a word was spoken to reveal that the "steel" was so shabby its only possible use would be as scrap to go into the mix of ore fed into conventional mills. Not a word that the Great Leap had gleaned almost every farm tool from the countryside and left the peasants as incapable of cultivating their fields as newborn babes.

China was rattling toward catastrophe. No one at the top knew or dared to know what lay ahead. As for Mao, there was good reason to think that he totally believed the Great Leap had catapulted China right over the rest of the world — especially Soviet Russia — into the pure state of Communism. He could not have been more wrong.

17

At Water's Edge

TO MAO ZEDONG, Nikita Khrushchev was far preferable to
Josef Stalin. For one thing, he thought, Khrushchev did not pose a
direct menace to China. Unpredictable, gauche, not even a dedicated
Marxist (in Mao's opinion), woefully ignorant about the world
Khrushchev might be — still, it seemed to Mao that he did not
threaten China's survival as, sometimes, Stalin had.

It had hardly been the best of times for Khrushchev since his dramatic secret speech in February 1956 revealing Stalin's crimes. Mao,
not entirely happy with that document, had been considerably more
unhappy at the turbulence in the Communist world that followed in
Poland and Hungary, and at Khrushchev's political troubles at home,
the unsuccessful attempt by his own Politburo to throw him out.
There had been too much uncertainty, too much unpredictable conduct.

Khrushchev, too, was worried about the turmoil, and he proposed
to overshadow the chaos with a grandiose all-Communist summit in
Moscow to celebrate the fortieth anniversary of the Bolshevik revolution of November 7, 1917. All of the Communist states of the world
and the great Communist parties, such as those of France and Italy,
would participate. The presence of China and of Mao Zedong was
essential.

Khrushchev had worked hard to put back together the Yugoslav
humpty-dumpty Stalin had knocked off the wall. He had made a
vodka-soused pilgrimage to Canossa, a trip to Belgrade to apologize
to Marshal Tito for Stalin's attempt to overthrow him and replace him
with a Soviet puppet. Khrushchev had patched up relations with Poland and Hungary, after a fashion. All he needed was Mao's participation to make the celebration a real occasion.

Mao did not object to the gathering. He thought it was a good
idea but was reluctant to make a personal appearance, and proposed

instead to send Liu Shaoqi. Mao didn't think the celebration would provide a great show of unity unless the presence of Tito was guaranteed. Finally, when the Russians swore that Tito had promised to come, Mao agreed to take part.

Privately Mao thought Khrushchev had made a fool of himself by getting drunk in Belgrade with Tito. But if Tito was going to be in Moscow, Mao would show up. As it happened, Tito backed out at the last minute, but Mao was so deeply engaged in preparations for upstaging the Russians at their own party that he came anyway.[1]

A unity manifesto to be discussed at the summit was drafted by the Russians. They sent it to Beijing for approval. Mao thought it wasn't tough enough. He had come to believe that the Communist camp was stronger than the United States and its allies, and he wanted the manifesto to reflect his belief that "The East Wind Now Prevails Over the West Wind." Moscow's success in launching Sputnik and in producing intercontinental ballistic missiles lent credibility to Mao's thesis. Mao put some of his ideologues, headed by his longtime secretary, Hu Qiaomu, to work on revising the document. He told them to use Khrushchev's language where possible so as not to hurt his feelings.

Before his departure Mao insisted that a message be sent to Moscow to omit the welcoming ceremonies. Of course the Russians didn't comply. They turned out with a crowd of five hundred to meet Mao at Vnukovo Airport. Mao mildly objected but yielded to the Russian protocol. The Chinese party was put up at the Kremlin, where Mao was given a grand suite, especially equipped with a bathroom "with facilities to meet Chairman Mao's habits," as the translator delicately phrased it. If it matched his bathroom at the Swimming Pool House, the residence in Zhongnanhai that Mao would move to in 1966, it had a Western toilet, a Chinese squat toilet, and a urinal.

Mao's mood of the moment was for simplicity. He tried to trade his quarters for a small room occupied by his translator, Li Yueran, and a physician, Dr. Li. It took Mao's whole entourage — Yang Shangkun, Hu Qiaomu, Peng Dehuai, Deng Xiaoping — to persuade him to stay put.[2]

The chairman was in a pixieish mood. On the plane to Moscow he told Soviet ambassador Pavel Yudin that he had "an examination question" for him. Just now, Mao said, they had been at the airport. Now they were in the sky. Soon they would be on the ground again. How to explain this philosophically? Yudin was stumped. "I have never studied this," he confessed. Mao offered an answer. When the plane was parked on the ground it represented an affirmation. In the sky it was a negative. Back on the ground it was a negation of a negation. To which the ambassador replied: "Excellent! Excellent!"

In Moscow Mao regaled the writer Guo Moruo with tales of Zhuge Liang, the great Chinese general, and Cao Cao, founder of the kingdom of Wei. Mao said Beijing opera was wrong to portray Cao Cao as a villain; he was an extraordinary man. He astonished Khrushchev by declaring that he didn't want to be chairman. He wanted to be a college professor and to have more talks with young people — hardly his tone when he unleashed the know-nothingism of the Cultural Revolution.[3]

Mao had a mixed group with him. It included Deng Xiaoping, whom he designated as his chief ideological spokesman, the first time he had filled such a role. The blunt-speaking Peng Dehuai was in the group, as was the meticulous Marxist scholar Hu Qiaomu. Deng was China's principal spokesman in the debate over the text of the unity manifesto. His success in argument won Mao's lifelong admiration.

Deng argued that there must be a head of the Communist camp, someone who could act as a liaison even if he was not a leader. He challenged the Soviet position that a country could pass peacefully from capitalism to Communism. There had to be class struggle.[4]

Mao believed that Communism could triumph only by revolutionary struggle and armed confrontation, as it had in Russia and China. Peaceful solutions would never work. Blood must be shed. He and Deng polled the other Communist delegates. All agreed.

Deng proved tireless in fighting for Mao's positions. He represented China on the ten-nation committee that drafted the final manifesto. China swept the day. Mao was never to forget this. It caused him to brag about his "little guy" to Khrushchev — the man who not only bested Mikhail Suslov, the tall Soviet ideologue, but who had smashed Chiang Kaishek's army. It was a ticket that won Deng lighter treatment in the Cultural Revolution than many fellow victims. Even in the worst days, Mao would recall with pride Deng's performance in Moscow.

The Moscow meeting confirmed Mao's sense of Khrushchev's immaturity and marked the beginning of the end of fairly good relations between China and the Khrushchev regime. The first few years under Khrushchev were the best period for the two states, in the opinion of Yan Mingfu, Mao's new Russian interpreter. "The period from 1955 on was the honeymoon period in the relations of our countries," Yan Mingfu recalled. "Then there was cold war between the two."[5]

Mao emerged from Moscow with great confidence in his ability to handle world affairs. He had been freed, in a sense, from all the old constraints: the opposition of Chiang Kaishek's armies, the fear of Japan's militarists, the specter of an all-powerful America, and the menace of Stalin. Mao had taken Khrushchev's measure and no longer feared Russia. It was a time when he would take the initiative in foreign affairs.[6]

By mid-1958 this new aggressiveness helped create a crisis between Mao and Khrushchev. The Chinese had asked the Russians — in the wake of the 1957 Moscow meeting — for assistance in building a navy. On a hot July day in 1958 Mao received Soviet ambassador Yudin, who had an answer to the request. The Russians would build a navy for China, but it would be maintained under their direction. The Chinese could staff the ships, or at least some of them. It would be a "co-op" navy, and it would have the use of the harbors on the China coast. A Russian admiral would be in charge.

Mao asked Yudin to repeat his message to be certain he had heard accurately. Then he said: "We know Russia doesn't have any warm-water ports; that is what Russia has wanted since the time of Peter the Great. Now it appears that we should give you control of all the ports we have. OK. After that I will go up into the mountains and lead our guerrillas against you."[7]

Mao was fond of threatening to abandon Beijing, go up into the mountains (or down into the countryside) to raise up the peasants, and lead them against his target of the day.

The same philosophy — to raise the masses against the enemy, be it Khrushchev, Peng Dehuai, Liu Shaoqi, or the bureaucrats — underlay Mao's concoction of the Cultural Revolution.

Mao talked to the Soviet ambassador for an hour and a half. His words did not leave a pleasant impression, one of the participants recalled.[8] He had another talk with Yudin the next day. And another the day after, in which he spoke of the Soviets' "erroneous approach." He brought Liu Shaoqi, Zhou Enlai, and Deng Xiaoping into the discussion. As he told his associates, he wanted the Soviets' offer laid out clearly and fully so there could be no mistake about what they were proposing.

Yudin's reports to Moscow alarmed Khrushchev, and he asked permission to come to Beijing. Mao agreed. Khrushchev flew out in a Tupelov-104, the biggest Soviet plane of the day, something like a Boeing 707. Khrushchev landed at the military airport west of Beijing and was met by Mao and the Chinese Politburo. They drove straight to Zhongnanhai and met in the Huairen Hall. Yudin did not participate. The Chinese never saw him again. Khrushchev said the affair was simply a mistake. He had been sick and thus was unable to correct Yudin. The Soviets weren't talking about a joint navy. How could Mao imagine they had that in mind? How could he think that of him, Khrushchev, who had repaired all the insults inflicted by Stalin, had given back the positions in Manchuria and the uranium mines in Xinjiang? How could Mao think so badly of him?

Mao heard Khrushchev out, then turned Deng Xiaoping loose. Deng flew at the Soviet leader like a terrier. He accused the Russians of "Great Nation" and "Great Party" chauvinism. It wasn't only the matter of the fleet. The Russians wanted to set up long-range wireless stations in China to communicate with their fleet and particularly with their submarines in the Pacific. The Russians wanted to build, operate, and control these facilities. Deng told Khrushchev that China had no objection to long-distance wireless communications for the Soviet fleet, but they must be China-built, China-operated, China-controlled. Otherwise the Russians were demanding "military bases on Chinese soil."

Deng criticized the conduct of some of the thousands of Soviet experts based in China. He implied they were more interested in spying than in helping. He said they had made it their business to learn everything worth learning about China. Some of them were excellent, cooperative people. Others were not; they interfered in Chinese internal affairs.

Deng set it out bluntly, without diplomatic words. When he was finished it was time to break for the traditional banquet, but Mao was more angry than ever. He sent Khrushchev off to a hotel and restaurant at Jade Mountain, in the Fragrant Hills, where there was no air-conditioning. It was so hot Khrushchev moved out onto a terrace during the night and was eaten alive by mosquitoes. Next day he ruefully told Mao: "Now that we are in China even the mosquitoes are trying to help you."[9]

That day Sino-Soviet diplomatic relations careened to a zany low. Mao decreed that the parties would meet at his swimming pool. In fact, not "at" but "in" the pool. Khrushchev had never swum in his life. He was fitted out with a pair of baggy green trunks and a bulky life preserver. Mao, his boxer swimming trunks comfortably enfolding his well-developed belly, swam about like an elderly porpoise, propelling himself with a powerful sidestroke. Khrushchev was led into the water and floundered helplessly in the wake of the Chinese leader. Interpreters scurried around the rim of the pool, trying to convey Mao's husky Hunanese to Khrushchev without tumbling in themselves. Khrushchev spouted his Ukrainian-accented responses through gulps of water. The spectacle of the champions of the Communist world in their watery encounter was one never to fade from the memory of the handful of spectators.[10] (In his memoirs Khrushchev described meeting Mao Zedong *at* the swimming pool. He omitted his adventures *in* the pool.)

Finally Mao relented and permitted the sodden Khrushchev to follow him to a wooden shed beside the pool. The statesmen donned their bathrobes and were joined by the sedate Liu Shaoqi, a slightly embarrassed Zhou Enlai, and the openly smiling Yang Shangkun and Deng Xiaoping. The atmosphere became relaxed.

Mao and Khrushchev met for a third time, with the full Chinese Politburo, in Qinzhengdian, the Hall of Diligent Government. This was a formal meeting, no water sports. A joint communiqué was issued. Khrushchev had come in secret, but he departed in a fanfare of publicity.

Once again, growing Soviet-Chinese differences had been papered over. It was business as usual — but not quite. Fedorenko noted the differences: no more talk of Elder Brother and Younger Brother, no more singing of the popular song "Moskva-Beijing." No more folderol, choruses, dancing children, great illuminations. Fedorenko felt, sadly, that the eternal alliance was less than what they had hoped for.

There had been sharp exchanges on nuclear weapons. Mao had asked Khrushchev for nuclear arms or the means of making them. Khrushchev said China didn't need them, since Russia was sworn to come to China's aid if it was attacked. For China to build its own would take a long time and would employ its total power-generating capacity. There were acid exchanges about "paper tigers" — as Mao had called America and other capitalist powers. This paper tiger, Khrushchev said, "has nuclear teeth."

Mao commented on the differences in customs between Russians and Chinese. The Russians didn't like China's green tea and didn't eat the leaves (as he proceeded to do). Chinese ate rice, Europeans ate bread. And, said Mao, as if it had just occurred to him, the Chinese had had a very good harvest and possessed very generous supplies of grain. They had so much they just didn't know what to do with it.

Did Khrushchev have some advice?[11] Khrushchev had no advice for Mao. He said simply that the Soviets never had this problem. They were always short of grain.

Mao did not press the question. He perhaps was not aware that thanks to his Great Leap Forward, China was plunging into one of the greatest famines of its long history.

Andrei Gromyko, the straitlaced Soviet foreign minister, paid a visit to Beijing six weeks later, in August-September 1958 to express Moscow's concern over the Chinese shelling of Quemoy and Matsu islands in the Taiwan Strait. The Russians were afraid war might develop. The United States had moved in more naval vessels, raising the question of what it intended to do next. Mao told Gromyko he didn't think America would intervene. The shelling was just a "punitive" affair, he contended. Mao said that if the United States intervened, Gromyko recalled in his 1988 memoirs, China would evacuate its coastal zones, lure the Americans deep into the interior, and destroy them with nuclear weapons.

Yan Mingfu, the interpreter, remembered the interchange a bit differently. In his recollection, Mao told Gromyko that the Chinese would retreat inland and, when the Americans were bogged down in the marshes, strike back. Gromyko replied that China should analyze the situation closely. China must remember that the United States had nuclear weapons. Mao, as Yan Mingfu recalled, rejoined that "even if we don't have nuclear weapons now, you in the Soviet Union do have nuclear weapons."[12]

Did Mao imply that the Soviet Union should use its A-bombs to wipe out the U.S. troops? Yan Mingfu was not certain. He did not have access to the archives, which would give the precise questions and answers. He respected Gromyko as a serious statesman who would not deliberately fabricate a quotation. It seems unlikely that Gromyko or Yan Mingfu would have misunderstood Mao. More likely was it that Mao's feeling of liberation in the field of foreign affairs was leading him into a fusion of his old guerrilla tactics — luring the enemy into a killing ground — with Great Power stratagems of a global nature.

And, in fact, Mao had expressed strikingly similar sentiments in earlier conversations with Khrushchev. He had displayed a lack of concern at the casualties of nuclear war. He had said, explicitly: "So what? War is war." If China lost 300 million people, "we'll get to work producing more babies than ever before." Mao used a word more earthy than the phrase "producing babies," and this provoked laughter from Madame Soong Chingling, Dr. Sun Yatsen's widow, who was present.

Mao told Khrushchev that if the United States attacked Russia, it should fall back to the Urals — then the Chinese would enter the war and wipe out the Americans.[13]

The strategy Mao had advocated to Khrushchev was the reverse of that which he now proposed to Gromyko. To Khrushchev he advised a Russian retreat and a surprise Chinese intervention. To Gromyko it was a Chinese retreat and a surprise Soviet nuclear attack.[14]

Whatever the exact exchange, Gromyko had hardly returned to Moscow when the Soviet Union issued a declaration that an attack on China (by the United States) would be considered an attack on the USSR. Mao was overjoyed. He sent off an instant letter to Khrushchev — his first and last.[15] He felt China had moved under the protective mantle of Soviet nuclear power.

Even so, from then on the course of Sino-Soviet relations would be all downhill.

18

In the Yellow River Country

THE ROAD along the north bank of the Yellow River from Shengli runs straight and dusty across the alluvial plain, yellow, fine, fertile, and rich when the rains come, provided the river — known as China's sorrow — does not overflow and wash it all away. The road leads ultimately to Pingyuan County in northern Shandong.

For many years now the Yellow River has been corseted within massive dikes; great pipes lift water over the dikes and roads and into irrigation ditches, which crisscross the plain like the canals of Mars. The days of floods seem over, but when Mao Zedong loosed the Great

Leap Forward, Pingyuan County lay at the mercy of water and wind, as it had for thousands of years.

The written record of the county goes back three hundred years before Christ. Although once it had been a land of rice and honey, as long as tradition can say it has been poor — a poor county in a sea of poor counties.

It would be hard to find a better example than Pingyuan — a domain of the poor, the illiterate, the diseased, the ignorant, and the suffering — of what the Chinese revolution was about. This was what Mao Zedong, Zhou Enlai, Zhu De, Deng Xiaoping, and the rest had dedicated their lives to changing. The Yellow River was China's heartland, realm of the legendary Yellow Emperor and the dragon, the Middle Kingdom set a bit lower than heaven but higher than earth.

It was Mao Zedong's burning passion to lift the Pingyuans of China out of the black swamp in which they lived. This passion fired him to undertake the vast gamble of the Great Leap Forward. His impatience swept away his judgment.

The Chinese writer Deng Youmei is a native of Pingyuan County and the village known as the Deng village, a clan village in which every person is named Deng (as in Shaoshan, where everyone is a Mao). To Deng Youmei, Pingyuan was China, the real China, scarcely touched by the outside world. To write and to understand the history and social structure of China, its politics and politicians, he felt, one must know Pingyuan County firsthand. Here were the people, the burdens, here were China's past, present, and future. There were thousands of Pingyuans scattered over the face of the land. No better microcosm existed of what had been, what was, and, perhaps, what was to come.

Pingyuan village lies in the northeast corner of Shandong Province, jammed up against the shoulder of Hebei Province, far from any population center. The Deng village, the Ma village, and other clan villages are filled with people who came to Shandong from Shanxi during the Sung dynasty, about the year 1000. Shanxi Province, to the northwest, was prosperous then, but the Dengs and the Mas and the others were attracted to Shandong because it was an empty place. Its people had been slaughtered in terrible wars, and the land lay fertile, idle, and silent. The Dengs and the Mas moved in, selected good fields, empty villages, and settled down.

Their great problem was the Yellow River and its changeable habits. One year it ran to the north, the next south. Its floods, its unpredictable shifts of channel, sometimes brought riches, sometimes devastation.

The province of Shanxi was famous for nurturing kings and emperors. Shandong was the domain of the sword and the warrior, where the military tradition ran deep. Even in the day of Mao and Zhu De it boasted that it sent more generals to the Red Army than any other province (although Sichuan and Hunan were rivals).

Shandong was the home of Chinese martial arts, assiduously cherished over the centuries until they became a kind of religion. The cult is not dead. It offered fertile soil for the mystical movement of the "Heavenly Fists," or Boxers, as they were called by Westerners. The Boxer rising of 1898–1901 sought to cleanse China of foreign influence and drive out the English, the French, the Germans, the Japanese, the Americans, the Christian missionaries, and even the Manchu dynasty, which still held the throne.

In these poverty-seared Yellow River villages and the dust-silted walled towns, the rising of the Boxers had flamed like a prairie fire, only to vanish without trace after the European powers marched in. So the world supposed. But the Heavenly Fists had not vanished from Pingyuan County, the place where they were born, only twenty-five li from the county seat. Here the tradition lived on. Deng Youmei recalled that when he was a boy there was a Boxer veteran in almost every family. At evening they would sit around a fire and tell their tales, of how those of pure faith were immune to Western bullets and those who died leapt straight to heaven. Peasants possessed red-tasseled Boxer spears hidden away against the future (many dug them out when the Red Army marched through).

In Deng's youth hundreds of Boxers survived. In 1988, only one seemed to be alive, feeble and garrulous, cared for in the hospital at an age approaching, it was said, 110. But the memory of the Boxers was strong. A writer who had dedicated his life to their stories said that the people of Pingyuan respected the Boxers as national patriots. When it was suggested that they were "misguided patriots," he flared in anger: "Not misguided!" He carried a picture of Li Changsui, the founding Boxer, in his wallet.

In the twentieth century, life in Pingyuan had become more and more difficult. No one had moved into the county for a long time. It was a land of sorrow. *Everyone* was poor. There was one basic rule of village life: No one who could get away stayed. Before the Revolution there were two ways of getting out: One was to go for a soldier, the other was to join the bandits. "We had two exports — soldiers and bandits," said Deng Youmei. "Often they changed their hats." Most bandits were only part-time bandits. They joined the robbers after the harvest and always traveled twenty li away to prey on other villages, not their own. In spring they came home to plant the crops.

In the village in Deng's early years lived an old man, a friend of Deng's grandfather, who was rumored to have a fortune. For the New Year's holiday he gave the Deng family dough sticks, almost like American doughnuts but crisper. Woe to the child who took a bite. The dough sticks quickly were collected, wrapped in new red paper, and sent as gifts to those to whom the Dengs owed presents. Nor did those who received them eat them. They, too, rewrapped them and sent them on. The old man's dough sticks traveled around the whole village. Without them there would have been no New Year's.

Deng's father was fortunate. At the age of twelve he had left Ping-yuan County. He was a strong lad, and he made money by carrying people's luggage on his back. He worked his way north into Manchuria, where life was easier, got to Mukden, and became a rickshaw man. He worked for a doctor who attended the "Old Marshal" Zhang Zuolin, warlord of Manchuria, who was assassinated by the Japanese in 1928, opening the way for their takeover of Manchuria and north China. Then Deng's father went to Tianjin and worked in the harbor. Deng was born there in 1931 and went to primary school until 1942, when he went to Shandong.

Deng was eleven years old when he first saw his "native" Shandong — Chinese consider themselves natives of the place where their parents are born. By then the Japanese had occupied the great Shandong plain for five years. Deng was regarded by the villagers with awe: He could *write*. There was hardly a person in Deng village who was literate. "I wrote the peasants' letters," he recalled. "Of course I didn't write very well. But that didn't matter."

No one had new clothes in those days. Everyone wore handwoven cloth, usually linen. When girls reached the age of twelve they began to weave cloth for their dowry.

The main crops were peanuts and peanut oil. But the peasants had no oil for themselves. They sold almost every drop to pay the moneylenders and to finance the advances for food and seed they needed to carry them through the next crop year. Deng remembered how his mother treasured cooking oil. No one was permitted to use a spoon to measure it out. You held a small coin with your chopsticks and dipped it in the oil, and the drops that stuck to the coin went into the frying pan. No more.

One old villager accumulated a hundred pounds of peanuts. He was the richest man in the village. He would neither eat nor sell his peanuts, for if he diminished his hoard, he would become just an ordinary peasant. So long as his hoard existed the government treated him as gentry. He was consulted on problems of the day and given respect. He starved himself. Status came ahead of stomach.

The people of Deng village lived in huts with thatched roofs and mud-and-wattle walls. The only brick building was the temple. There were no roads, only footpaths and barrow paths. Barrows were the means of transport, not donkeys or horses. Animals were a luxury.

No one in Deng village had enough to eat. For generations, as Deng recalled, people had grown wheat and rice but had no idea what they tasted like. Their diet was coarse grains — sorghum, millet, field corn. Deng grew up with the taste of tree leaves in his mouth. Leaves, crumpled into porridge or soup or tea, were a constant supplement. The commonest kind was called *xiang chun*. Deng was over forty years old before he got the taste of *xiang chun* out of his mouth.

By the time Deng came to his village everything was changing. The Japanese had set up four houses of prostitution and a gambling den in the Ma village. A Korean was brought in to sell opium. There had never been a prostitute, a gambler, opium, or even cigarettes in the village. The men were so embarrassed they looked the other way when the prostitutes walked down the street.

Deng Youmei joined some Red Army irregulars. He was thin and too small to carry a rifle. He was what they called a Little Red Devil, a junior member of the army who served as a gofer, but he was also a spy. He got a job in Japanese headquarters as a messenger. He brought tea, ran errands, kept his eyes open. Two other underground Communists also got jobs in the headquarters.

Almost every day the twelve-year-old saw people being tortured. If the Japanese thought a Chinese had money, they would grab him, split his ribs open, and pour water into the rib cage to make him tell where the money was hidden. Sometimes they would lash a man to a sawhorse and pour water down his throat until he confessed he had helped the Red Army. Then they made his relatives pay a ransom for him.

Often the torture was only an amusement. On one occasion a small girl began screaming in terror as soon as some soldiers appeared. Taking pleasure from this, they dragged her into the street and jabbed at her with their bayonets. Her screams rent the neighborhood.

One day they mobilized a thousand peasants to build a strongpoint. When it was built they ordered the peasants to dig a wide ditch. When that was done they set up a heavy machine gun and mowed down the workers, toppling the bodies into the ditch.

"I saw all that with my own eyes," Deng said.

Finally, in 1945, Deng was allowed to join the Eighth Route Army. He served in the campaigns that were fought over the Yellow River and down to the Yangtze.

In the days of Deng Xiaoping's Huai-Hai drive, in 1948, Deng watched the endless stream of Shandong peasants hauling in their wheelbarrows the rice, the bullets, the shells, the gasoline, all the supplies for the Yangtze River assault, four hundred miles from the Yellow River. They meandered through rice fields, along muddy barrow paths, toiling around mountains, splashing through canals and streams, backs bent, muscles bulging, taking no pay for months of labor, counting it their contribution to liberation from centuries of bondage.

Deng Youmei was demobilized in 1951 and made his way back to Pingyuan. No one knew better than he what the peasants had suffered. The taste of *xiang chun* and the acid bite of peeled bark were still on his tongue. When he closed his eyes he could see the peasants and their barrows carrying loads to the Yangtze; in his ears were the screams of the little Chinese girl as the Japanese sliced her body with their bayonets.

"There was so much hatred in Shandong," he recalled. "So much. And now I felt quite sad. Liberation had come and gone, but the life of the peasants had not changed much."

The peasants were still eating bark and leaves. They were still dying of hunger. They were still wearing patches and rags. The thatch of their huts leaked, and winter winds chilled their bones as they huddled over little fires of straw. Was this what their sacrifices had brought?

The Revolution did not bring harvests that gave men and women enough food. The landlords were gone, but the people lived on in the shadows. They starved to death in the New China. Efforts to improve the countryside were being made, yet in Pingyuan people still died.

Deng paid one visit to his home village. After that, "I really could not make myself come back," he said. "Conditions were so bad." He was beginning to be known as a writer. He got letters from Deng village. They were always the same: "Please send money." "Please send grain coupons." They were asking him for a ticket to life.

All this *after* the Revolution. Deng could not save the whole population of Deng village. Worst of all, he knew that what was happening in Deng village and Pingyuan County was happening in other Chinese villages. There were exceptions — certainly not all of China was starving — but starvation had not become a casual visitor.

Conditions did not get better. In 1956 and 1957 there was a flicker of improvement. Then came the Great Leap Forward. At one bound, Mao believed, he would solve China's problem. But the Leap brought hunger and death to millions. In Deng's village the toll was a trickle, only five or ten or perhaps twenty lives a day. But this was a village of fewer than five hundred families. Everyone who could walk or hobble left — mostly men and boys. They went anywhere they could. Deng's brother went to Manchuria. Only women were left to mind the dying and bury the dead.

For a hundred years, Deng said, the people had been at war in some fashion, killing one another with guns and cannon. They had lived a life of heavy labor, the life of animals. Now, instead of finding redemption, they had been plunged into a new and lower circle of hell.

There do not seem to be statistics on how much food was available in the 1950s, but even in those days there was a steady rate of death for lack of food. By 1959 the government was sending grain to shortfall areas like Pingyuan. But the local Party secretaries were afraid to report the real figures, the truth about their failure. Pingyuan was producing only 50 pounds of grain per mu (about one sixth of an acre). If they told Beijing the truth, they could lose their jobs or their heads. So they wrote in the figure of 250 pounds per mu, five times what they had. The government accepted the 250-pound figure, and when it shipped emergency grain rations, it figured that Pingyuan had five times as much in its granaries as it actually did. The result: an allocation that brought the total grain per person to 125 grams a day — equal to a small cup of rice or two thin slices of bread.

The Pingyuan allotment was identical to that which Leningrad got in the worst days of the nine-hundred-day siege of November 1941, during World War II, the most terrible siege in modern history. The fatal ration of 125 grams is less than enough to sustain life. On 125 grams people die — fairly quickly, depending on stamina and fat reserves. In Leningrad they were gone in a week or ten days, possibly two weeks at best. Only the time span was uncertain. The outcome was certain: death. There was no possibility of escape.

In Leningrad the ration was issued in the form of 125 grams of edible grain; that is, in milled flour baked into bread in a loaf. Never mind that there was straw and grass and God knows what mixed with the flour. The Leningrader got 125 grams of something to eat. Not so his counterpart in Pingyuan and all the other Pingyuans. The Chinese ration was fed out in raw, unmilled grain, husk, stones, and all. The peasants in Pingyuan in 1959, 1960, and probably 1961 were getting the nutritive equivalent of 100 to 110 grams of edible grain a day. That was a quick-death diet. Anyone who could, got out while he possessed strength in his legs. Many died beside the narrow paths leading away from the village.

The Leningraders were subjected to the 125-gram ration for three weeks. Some 200,000 people died in that time — enough so that the ration could gradually be raised until it reached a survival level. There was no increase in Pingyuan. Only those who found enough bark and leaves and straw to fill their bellies had a fighting chance for life.

By the winter of 1960 starvation ruled the Chinese countryside. The government began shipping grain to the worst areas by truck. It was shoveled onto the highways. No ration cards. No charge. Come and get it — if you could. Anyone with strength could fill a bag or a bucket. People crawled like snakes over the torn land. They did not possess the strength to walk. Only yards away from the scattered heaps of grain many gasped and died.[1]

In the early 1960s the population of Pingyuan County began to fall precipitously. Many had died. Many had fled. Later on officials claimed the Great Leap accounted for 30 percent of the loss, and "natural causes" for 70 percent. The Pingyuan people thought the percentages should be reversed. When the peasants talk of those days, they avert their eyes so as not to reveal the horror that is still with them.

The great Chinese journalist Liu Binyan first estimated that 20 million died in the aftermath of the Leap. Gradually, as he collected reports, he raised his estimate to 30 million. A member of the brain trust run by future Party secretary Zhao Ziyang came up with an estimate of 43 to 46 million after visiting several provinces and sampling reports. A member of the Chinese Public Security Administration arrived at a total of 30 million by calculating the number of ration cards that were prepared for 1959, 1960, and 1961 but not issued because the presumptive holders had died.

The hardest-hit provinces were Anhui, Henan, Shandong, Gansu, and Sichuan. In Anhui Province, in hundreds of villages, an average of only 40 out of 200 families survived. The secretary of Gansu Province came to Beijing, went to Li Xiannian, a Politburo member, and broke into tears as he begged for help. Li managed to get him some additional grain. Death tolls were far higher in this central region than in the south or the grain-rich north. Deaths in Gansu, with a population of 8 million, were estimated at 1 million. The toll in Anhui, Henan, and Shandong was placed at at least 5 million in each province. This may be high, but the Great Leap Forward undoubtedly cost China far more lives than the terrible famine of the Yellow River bend, which took upwards of 6 million or 7 million in 1930–31.[2]

Admittedly, none of these calculations is exact, and the precise figures never will be known. Some believe that within a narrow top government echelon, information on the toll was available at the time. Mao would certainly have been privy to the data. Perhaps this is why he gave up eating pork, of which he was so fond. "For months," his guards said, "his chopsticks didn't touch pork."[3] Mao stopped eating with Jiang Qing because she insisted on serving him chicken and fish. From then on they ate separately. "Eating is the biggest thing in the world," he told Jiang. "Peasants think food is as important as God."

To give up pork was a sacrifice. Mao didn't eat, he didn't drink. He didn't touch starch. He ate no oil. He sat at the table, night after night, smoking. His feet began to swell. The guards urged him to eat. No, said Mao. The countryside had no pork; he would not eat either. His action had no effect on the starving people, but it made him feel he was one of them.[4]

Not that Mao was a peasant in his eating habits. His secretary Li Rui remembered Mao inviting him to "have lunch" about midnight one evening. "Lunch" was served in Mao's bedchamber, Mao lolling on his great bed. The year was 1958, the year the great famine started. They dined on one of China's rarest delicacies — bears' paws (not actually the paw but the membrane that joins the claws). Li had never even heard of such a dish. It was served in a small bowl, and three or four other small delicacies were offered, along with rice.[5]

There were other exotic dishes of which Mao was fond. One was called the Moon and Four Stars, which he discovered on the Long March in Guizhou: alternate layers of lamb, fish, chicken, vegetables such as taro root, dusted with rice flour. The broth was believed to cure dizziness.[6] Whether Mao permitted himself to indulge in this dish during the famine is not known.

Mao offered no public declaration of compassion, nor did he tell the people he was responsible for their suffering. To show compassion would demonstrate humanitarianism, contrary to Marxist principles.

Marx had said that kindness to the unfortunate was "capitalist bribery." During the great Volga famine in the 1890s, Lenin refused to join Russia's relief effort, led by the writer Leo Tolstoy. Even millers from Minnesota sent a shipload of flour to the starving. But Lenin opposed the effort. Let the peasants suffer, he argued; that will make them more revolutionary. China was starving, and Mao went on a private diet. This was the season in which his poetic soul was outraged at the bodyguards who swept away the winter snow without allowing, as he said, the snow's "wounds" to heal.

Deng Youmei had said he wanted a foreigner to see a real Chinese village and real Chinese life; to see what had brought about the Revolution and what the Revolution had brought to the peasants, who still constitute 80 percent of the nation's 1.2 billion people (just short of 1 billion of whom live in the countryside). Only with that image, Deng believed, could you understand China, its life before 1949, its life since 1978 in the period of Deng Xiaoping.

To be certain, Pingyuan was not China. Each county had its own problems, its own historical nature. But Pingyuan was no aberration. Through its lens you could understand what moved Mao and his revolutionary comrades, the problems that existed after the Revolution, and the heritage that Mao bequeathed to his heirs.

The Yellow River had, by tradition, given birth to China, but now the toll of human-engineered experiments was rivaling those exacted by the great river of China's birth.

19

Ascent of Mount Lu

AS FAR BACK as history records, worthy Chinese have made the pilgrimage to Mount Lu, the great peak rising six thousand feet above the mist that enfolds the Yangtze River in summer. At Mount Lu's crest, cool currents sweep away the fog. Poets fill their lungs with fresh air and commemorate the joy of untroubled peace. Philosophers ponder the morality of man.

In the nineteenth century British traders in Shanghai, Wuhan, and other cities left their Chinese compradors, or agents, to sweat over the ledgers and set out from Jiujiang, a day by steamboat from Wuhan, one of China's four "ovens," hiring bearers to carry their sedan chairs up above the heat line to Mount Lu. Missionaries followed the traders, and Mount Lu became a kind of Chautauqua-in-China, the same Wesleyan hymns, the same eleemosynary lectures and magic lantern shows. The missionaries called it Kuling, and as "Cooling" the peak became a Protestant shrine with the advent of Chiang Kaishek and his beautiful wife, Meiling.[1]

Every summer — if Chiang's war against the red bandits (Mao Zedong and the Red Army) wasn't too worrisome — Chiang and Meiling occupied the finest stone house on the mountain. Across a small stream stood a white-painted chapel where on Sundays they sang "Nearer My God to Thee" and listened to sermons by their Chinese pastor.

By the summer of 1959 Chiang and Meiling were ten years gone, established on Taiwan, but the big stone house was not empty. Mao Zedong moved in. He was as fond of the mountain as Chiang. He loved to relax in a pergola jutting out into the sea of cotton clouds and compose poems in the classic tradition.

So it was that Mao Zedong on July 1, 1959, made himself comfortable in a wicker chair looking over the poetic peaks and wrote:

I have leapt over four hundred turns to reach the green crest.
Now cold-eyed I survey the world beyond the sea. . . .

The "sea" was the broad flux of the Yangtze, and for Mao it was
a metaphor of his world, the world he now surveyed with eyes that
were icy. There was little in Mao's words to suggest quiet contemplation. It was a moment of decision, a turning point in a life that
had begun sixty-six years earlier at the Hunan village of Shaoshan.
Would Mao's reign survive?

Mao had arrived at Mount Lu (known in Chinese as Lushan) after
visiting Shaoshan for the first time in thirty-two years — not a sen-
timental journey, but a trip made with calculation. Mao had become
convinced that he was engaged in the political fight of his life, and
Shaoshan was going to play a central role. At the conference to be
held at Mount Lu, he would deliver an economic report on Shaoshan
that would devastate his enemies. Before he arrived at the little Hunan
town, he knew what he was going to say at Mount Lu: Shaoshan was
prospering under the Mao revolution. It was basking in the benign
results of the new commune policy and the Great Leap Forward. *It
had to be.*

Mao was stubborn, arrogant, self-confident, and certain of his superior wisdom. His style, as Marshal He Long had noted, was becoming more and more imperial.[2] But Mao in fact knew that China
had plunged into terrible trauma, and he knew that he was (rightly)
being blamed. He was, however, not prepared to concede that it was
his fault, nor was he ready to give up on a scheme that, as he told his
secretary Chen Boda, "exactly matched his imagination of a rural
utopia." Chen Boda had picked up the image of a rural utopia in his
speeches and in the Party journal *Red Flag,* of which he was editor.[3]

Mao had few secrets from his closest associates, his bodyguards and
his secretaries. With them he was open and remarkably frank. They
knew how troubled Mao was, how concerned over the food problem,
the agricultural crisis, the political fallout.[4]

Since midsummer 1958, when the first word of famine conditions
began to trickle in, Mao had been sending out one agent after another
to investigate. He himself had gone to Henan to inspect the commune
at Xiyiling, the first one established. The Henan Party secretary was
even whispering about famine. Before 1958 was out, Mao had sent his
most trusted private secretary, Tian Jiaying, to look into the situation.
At the same time he sent Chen Boda, who saw the communes as a
new utopia, to look at another county in Henan. Chen Boda said the

commune he visited was a miracle — "China's Sputnik." Tian Jiaying spent October 28 to November 4, 1958, at Xiyiling. His report was as black as Chen Boda's was white — an endless list of troubles.[5]

Publicly, at least, Mao opted for white over black. He presented a rosy forecast of economic achievements for 1958 and an overblown forecast for 1959. Privately he was sufficiently concerned to continue intensive monitoring of the countryside. Mao told Henan governor Wang Renzhong that "all my plans are messed up." He quoted an aphorism of the Tang dynasty: "When the country is in turmoil you need a good general."[6] Mao also told the Henan governor, "I am responsible for many things but I am afraid not everything." He recalled that after his first visit to the commune at Xiyiling, the site of the Red Flag Canal, he was interviewed by a newspaper. "I said 'Communes are good.' The headlines said 'Communes are good.' So that is my fault."[7] Mao himself began to inveigh against rural slogans like "Give Everyone a Free Meal" or "Eat As Much As You Like." No matter that these slogans had sprung up as a result of his own careless suggestions that China was leaping directly into Communism and abundance for all.

Chen Yi, the outspoken and courageous foreign minister, tried to get Mao to hold back on optimistic forecasts. He asked Mao's secretary Hu Qiaomu to pass his views along, but Hu was afraid. Hu knew which way Mao's wind was blowing, and Mao was in a "good news" pattern.[8]

Mao knew about the rising famine, and he knew that some of his associates — whatever they might say in public — knew more. This was true of his crusty Hunan comrade, Peng Dehuai. The two had worked side by side for thirty years. Peng Dehuai had gone down to the countryside, back to Hunan, to Xiangtan County, where Mao and Peng had been born. Peng had visited Wushi, his native village. He had gone to Pingjiang County, where he had led the Pingjiang Uprising in 1927.

And Peng Dehuai had gone to Shaoshan and now possessed first-hand information on Mao's own citadel. Mao feared that his report could be the bombshell that destroyed his program, particularly if Peng could show that Shaoshan's output had fallen, not risen, that it had required heavy state subsidies to stay afloat, and that famine was now lapping at the door of Mao's old home. Mao knew, too, that Liu Shaoqi also possessed damaging data. Liu came from a village just over the mountain from Shaoshan, and he had information that people were already dying of hunger in their huts.[9]

Also, Mao had evidence straight from Peng of fraud in the grain reports. Peng had repeatedly questioned the accuracy of official reports, saying they were exaggerated.

In his visit to Pingjiang County, Peng had found that officials — under pressure from the top — were faking the figures. They had taken the high results of 1957 and recorded them as those for 1958, and taken the low-yield 1958 figure and put it down as 1957's. Yields in 1959 would be sharply lower.

Peng had encountered Bo Yibo, an old-time guerrilla, now minister of finance, in Hunan. Peng told Bo Yibo about his discoveries and said that he did not think grain yields would be high enough to permit the government to buy 60 million tons of grain from the peasants to feed the cities, as was planned. The government would only have to ship grain back into the areas where it had been bought. Peng thought the program should be cut by 25 percent, and he asked Bo Yibo to send a warning to the Party Central Committee. Later Peng telegraphed Mao what he had found out.[10]

The size of the 1958 harvest had been a political hot potato for months. Peng raised the subject at a meeting at Wuchang in December. Some were proposing that a record 500-million-ton harvest be proclaimed. Peng thought that much too big. He was gently rebuked by one participant, who said: "Commander, you seem to have doubts on everything — what can we do to satisfy you?"

Peng persisted. Finally Mao resolved the argument by proposing to state the yield as 375 million tons. This was accepted, but within weeks it had to be officially lowered to 250 million tons, and even this figure turned out to be too high.[11]

Small wonder that Mao feared the damage Peng could do with a negative report on Shaoshan. But if Mao himself went to Shaoshan and brought to Lushan a bright and sunny picture of life in his home village, neither Peng Dehuai nor anyone else would dare to challenge it. Mao would command the debate and rout his opponents.

So Mao had gone back to his roots, to the town he hadn't seen since he marched off in 1927 to raise the rebellion that became known as the Autumn Harvest Uprising, not since his old home had been burned and ravaged by the KMT, not since a special squad had been sent to desecrate the graves of his parents in order to bring down on Mao, according to the superstition of peasant geomancy, terrible disasters. He was spared this fate when a wily peasant took the squad not to Mao's family plot but to that of a neighboring landlord.

*   *   *

Mao arrived by train at Shaoshan on the evening of June 25, 1959. His mood was troubled — so his guards thought. He had not been sleeping well, but that was not unusual. He never slept without sleeping pills, and even they gave him little repose. He had become, the guards knew, increasingly worried at reports from the villages. "Something has gone wrong in the countryside," he told them. "I must find out what it is. I want to go to every province and see for myself." But as he and the guards knew, even the whisper of a visit by Mao created a frenzy to fix things up, to paint houses, to fill cupboards, to bring in food, to find happy peasants to tell Mao everything was just dandy.

Mao didn't want that. He wanted the truth. Again and again he said, "I want them to tell me the truth. I want to know the truth." But did he really? The guards were not so sure. They had seen too many examples to the contrary. He would listen to them, but if Peng Dehuai told him the truth, he got angry.

Mao had ordered many high officials out on inspection trips. They were to bring back honest reports. But would they dare? The guards did not know. Mao kept sending some of the guards back to their native villages to discover what was happening. One, named Ma Wei, brought back a crust of bread from his village. It was made of unmilled sorghum, lots of husks, bitter, hard. Mao smelled it and put it in his mouth. "They are eating *this* in the village?" Tears came to his eyes.

That helped to decide him to go back to Shaoshan. He knew the village. It was blood of his blood, flesh of his flesh. There, he knew, he would find the truth and the truth would be on his side. There he would find evidence to blast away the arguments of "Old Peng," as Mao called the marshal. It was a term of endearment, of familiarity. He had been Old Peng to Mao for thirty years, and Mao had been "Lao Mao," Old Mao, to Peng for thirty years. There were only two men in the company of the Red Army, that band of brothers, who still called him Lao Mao. One was Lao Peng. The other was Chen Yi, the bravest commander in the Red Army, the foreign minister. There was not an ounce of presumption in these two marshals. Mao was Lao Mao. He had been Lao Mao for decades. He would be Lao Mao, the two marshals assumed, to the end of their days. Everyone else in China now called him Chairman Mao with eyes raised in reverence. Except for the children of the Zhongnanhai cadres: They called him Uncle Mao. (But no one called Mao's wife, Jiang Qing, Auntie Jiang.)[12]

*   *   *

Luo Ruiqing, then China's security chief, met Mao when he arrived in Shaoshan and accompanied him to a guesthouse on the mountain behind Mao's old home. Hundreds of villagers gathered in the sand-surfaced courtyard to greet Mao. Few had ever seen him before.

The cocks were crowing daybreak by the time Mao got to sleep. His guards saw candlelight flickering behind the heavy velour curtains of his bedchamber for hours. Mao stayed awake writing a poem about his return, a poem that bore a scent of nostalgia, a vague dream of the orchards he had left behind when he went out into the world. But there was also a harsh revolutionary note, hailing the serfs who had risen up with spears and red flags against the landlords. And he offered a bold challenge: He would change the moon and the sun as they coursed through the heavens. Most important was his verdict on the communes and the Great Leap Forward — offered before he had had a look at the results. They were, he declared, a success; he could see this as he gazed out over endless fields of green beans and even greener rice paddies and watched "heroes coming home in the evening haze." A self-portrait, perhaps.[13]

In the morning Mao inspected his old home. It had been rebuilt, and his neighbors asked anxiously if it had actually been like this previously. Yes, Mao said, it was exactly as he remembered, a spacious house, reflecting the prosperity of his father, with a big entrance hall, a dining room, a large room for his father and mother, separate rooms for Mao and his brothers, winter and summer kitchens, ample storage space — as good a rich peasant home as was to be found in Hunan. Mao led his escorts up the hillside to a scraggly spot where his parents were buried. He contemplated the site in silence, told the caretakers he did not wish the grave site changed in any way, promised to come again (he never did), and then went to the Shaoshan school. He had his picture taken with the children, a young girl put her red Communist kerchief around his neck, and he had a swim in the village reservoir. A newsman carefully noted that he started out with a sidestroke, switched to a backstroke, and floated lazily in the water as the villagers onshore grinned and chuckled. He met briefly with members of the Shaoshan commune, and they told him what he wanted to hear — everything was fine.[14]

"Are the communes really good?" he asked. Really good, they echoed. They gave him a piece of their bread. Mao tasted it.

"That's really good," Mao told them. "People all over China can eat your bread."[15]

A few days later, at Lushan, Peng Dehuai asked Mao if he had questioned the villagers about their harvest yields. Mao said he hadn't. Peng said afterward that he thought Mao had asked but didn't want to talk about it. Perhaps he hadn't liked the answer.[16]

It is a tricky thing to try to analyze policy by examining poetic imagery, but it was natural for Mao to express himself — if mystically — in his verses. There was a detectable shading between his homecoming poem and the one he wrote "cold-eyed" at the peak of Lushan. Mao put into his Lushan poem a reference to the great Chinese poet of the fourth century, Tao Yuanming, who retired from a government job rather than kowtow to rude and ignorant superiors whom he did not respect.

The astute China scholar Stuart Schram believed the poem was an allusion to Nikita Khrushchev and to a crisis in Sino-Soviet relations that was emerging in June and July of 1959, simultaneous with the Lushan conference. It had not been revealed, but Khrushchev on June 20 had canceled his agreement to provide China with high military technology. With his mention of Tao Yuanming, Mao was indicating his own refusal to kowtow to the Soviet Union.[17]

That Soviet-Chinese relations had taken an alarming drop at this time was observed by this writer on an extended journey to Outer Mongolia in June-July 1959. Chinese and Soviet diplomats and experts in Mongolia literally were not on speaking terms. By 1960, of course, the quarrel had gone public.

Mao's attitude toward Peng, already testy, may have been exacerbated by rumors that Peng had made known his views on the Great Leap to Moscow while touring Russia and Eastern Europe just before Lushan. He had met with Khrushchev and Marshal Kirill Moskalenko, his opposite number as Soviet defense minister, and had traveled with Marshal Ivan Konev on his return to China, Konev stopping off at Ulan Bator. There was a report — probably mistaken — that Peng had written a letter to the Soviet Party stating his objections to the Great Leap. More likely, the plain-speaking Peng simply made some sharp comments in his conversations in Russia.[18] Only a hint of a "Soviet angle" emerged in the Lushan debate. But it could explain the turbulent undercurrents.[19]

The stage was now set. All that remained was for Mao to order the curtain raised.

20

The Great Divide

THE LUSHAN CONFERENCE opened on July 2, 1959, mist
still low over the mountain. All the actors, or almost all, were assembled: Mao Zedong, Peng Dehuai, Zhou Enlai, Liu Shaoqi, Zhu De,
Lin Biao, Chen Yun, Chen Yi, the Standing Committee, the Secretariat, the Politburo, the Central Military Committee, heroes of the
Long March, the rulers of China.

There would be a delayed entrance for Deng Xiaoping and Jiang
Qing, the chairman's wife. Mao had instructed Deng Xiaoping to stay
in Beijing and oversee the day-to-day business of government while
the rest assembled on the mountaintop. It was, perhaps, a lucky break
for Deng. Mao's order kept him out of the direct line of fire in the
greatest quarrel since the founding of the People's Republic.[1]

Before it was over, Mao changed his mind and called Deng to
Lushan. The showdown was too important. Mao wanted all present
and accounted for — with him or against him. There had been another
consideration in Mao's designating Deng to stay home and mind the
store. Mao still held Deng in a special category, not hostile to Mao
and his program, not opposed to his policies. This distinguished him
in Mao's mind from Zhou Enlai and Liu Shaoqi. Mao used and needed
Zhou and Liu to keep the country running, but he identified both
(correctly) as lukewarm to the communes and the Leap. Both had
given Mao rhetorical support, and Liu had even placed the project
before the Party. But Mao was not fooled.

As for Jiang Qing no one, Mao included, expected her at Lushan.
She was still under the Party edict that banned her from any political
role. But Jiang Qing was on the brink of overthrowing that edict and
moving into the heart of China's politics, a place she would cling to
for the rest of Mao's life.

*   *   *

Deng Xiaoping, age sixteen, just before leaving for France on a work-study program in 1920.

Deng (*right*) and his uncle Deng Shaosheng, who accompanied him to France, 1920.

Near right: Deng's aunt Yang Ming Gifeng, eighty-nine in 1988.

Far right: Deng's uncle Dan Yixing, brother of Deng's mother. Dan died in 1989, at age eighty-eight.

Below: Deng's family home, in the village of Paifangcun, northeast Sichuan.

Above: Deng Xiaoping's schoolmate Yang Erhe, eighty-six in 1988.

Right: Dan Yixing with the author; at right is Wang Rougang, an interpreter.

Right: Zhou Enlai as a student in Berlin, 1922.

Below: Police and gangsters massacre workers and Communists in Shanghai, 1927.

Sketch by Huang Zhen of the Red Army crossing the Great Snowy Mountains during the Long March, 1935.

Lenin's Cave — formerly a temple — deep in Guangxi Province, where Deng Xiaoping lectured peasant guerrillas in 1929.

Red Army cavalry riding into Yanan, Communist headquarters between 1936 and 1946–47. The Yanan pagoda tops the mountain, and cave dwellings can be seen in the mountain wall.

Mao Zedong and Jiang Qing at Yanan in 1938, soon after their marriage.

Above: A victim of the Japanese bombing of Shanghai, 1937. Perhaps the most famous photograph taken in China in the twentieth century.

Left: Red Army commanders in Shaanxi Province in 1938 (*from left*): Peng Dehuai, Zhu De, Feng Xuefen, Xiao Ke, and Deng Xiaoping.

Right: Mao Zedong, riding in an American jeep captured from the KMT, takes the salute at Beijing's military airport after passing through the captured city, March 25, 1949.

Above: Mao with his son Mao Anying, 1949. Anying was killed a year later by an American bomb in Korea, where he was serving with the Chinese "volunteers."

Right: The bedroom-study of Mao Zedong in the Study of Chrysanthemum Fragrance, his palace in Zhongnanhai. It has been altered since being opened to public display after Mao's death, in 1976. Those who knew it in Mao's time say that his bed was much larger and that it was flanked by sofas and stacks of books.

Mao started Lushan off with a dreary cliché, one that he had often used when the situation was something less than satisfactory. "The achievements are great," he said, "the problems are many, the experience is abundant and the future is bright."[2]

The classic scenery of Lushan quickly faded into the background as proceedings got under way. The delegates split into working groups, with Peng assigned to the Northwest Group. Here the discussions became intense and the language often frank. It was in these small meetings that the sparks flew — not in the big assembly hall, with its dark stained-wood paneling and faintly missionary air. The groups generated position papers, recommendations, and studies. Each morning the paperwork was mimeographed and distributed to all. Gruff old Peng complained he spent so much time reading he hardly left his house, next door to that of Mao. After Lushan was over and he was trying to cope with the fallout, Peng confessed that he had never wanted to come in the first place. He was exhausted from the long Eastern European trip. He had tried to persuade his chief of staff, Huang Kecheng, to take his place, but he begged off. The Tibet mop-up was going on and he didn't want to leave it to others.[3]

Although, as he later insisted (under the torture of the Great Proletarian Cultural Revolution), Peng had no "conspiratorial" rendezvous, everyone knew that the marshal had been to Hunan, specifically to Shaoshan, and that he had found starvation there and officials who faked figures. Everyone knew that Mao had brought back a sunny picture of life in Shaoshan. A collision was certain. Neither man was the kind who backs down.

To Mao's bodyguard Li Yinqiao, the scene was like a Chinese opera — the rushing about, the whispered confidences, the misunderstandings, plot and counterplot. You could almost hear the clashing of gongs, the beating of drums, and over it all detect a sense of foreboding. Once the curtain went up the momentum toward the tragic last act could not be halted.[4]

Mao's youngest secretary, Li Rui, was in the thick of it. He had been picked by Mao less than two years earlier. Li Rui was then deputy minister of electric power, had been a newspaperman for ten years, and came from Hunan. His parents belonged to the same circle of the Changsha intelligentsia as did Mao in his years at the Changsha Normal School Number 2. Li Rui knew Mao well, if not intimately, and had become, in fact, his protégé. He had written a remarkable study of Mao's early years, a book whose brilliance fully became apparent only when it was republished, with the censored passages restored, after Mao's death.

Mao was attracted to the young man by his outspoken and forthright arguments opposing a grandiose scheme for harnessing the power of the great Yangtze River. The Three Gorges project was far beyond China's resources but had the gargantuan proportions that appealed to many new Communists. Li Rui said that it wouldn't work and that China did not possess the know-how to make it work. Mao sided with him, and the project was dropped (it surfaced again in 1991 in the minds of planners and engineers looking for one-shot cures for China's perpetual energy crisis).

Mao already had four secretaries. He took Li Rui as his fifth. Li Rui was enchanted, not realizing the dangers he now had exposed himself to. He was captivated by Mao, believed in him, trusted him, but the Great Leap and its toll of life appalled him. He threw his energies into producing evidence that would turn Mao away from it. Mao did not take this amiss, so long as it was a matter between himself and his attractive young secretary. But Lushan was different.

Zhou Enlai, the ultimate courtier, had watched the relationship evolve between Mao and Li Rui, and he warned Li against associating with Peng Dehuai. If Li became identified in Mao's mind with Peng Dehuai's "party," he would lose his unique ability to present frank and independent views to Mao. The young man did not heed Zhou and paid a heavy price. "If I had not been on the same side as Peng Dehuai," Li commented many years later, "my fate would probably have been different."[5] Although Zhou and Liu Shaoqi opposed the Great Leap, they held their tongues and managed to survive Lushan. They stood aside from the struggle. Young Li Rui plunged directly into it, openly meeting with Peng Dehuai.

The Hunan Party secretary, Zhou Xiaozhou, a fellow Hunanese and a former secretary to the chairman, who had enjoyed good relations with Mao, was another outspoken man. He was so aroused by the situation in his province that he met with Peng Dehuai before the Lushan conference and told him that the 1959 production figures had been inflated due to "pressure from the top." The real figures were rejected and called "not final." New, large, imaginary crops had to be reported.

"You should inform the chairman of these problems," Peng recalled saying. The Hunan secretary said he had already told Mao and asked Peng to do the same. Peng said military men had notified him of similar conditions. He had passed this information on to Mao as well.[6]

A prominent Long March veteran and Party leader named Zhang Wentian, better known by his underground name of Luo Fu, came to Peng's support. They took walks past the pleasant vistas of Lushan and conversed across the fence that separated their villas. They spoke, Peng recalled, of the need to convince Mao that the backyard smelters were a disaster. Luo Fu wanted to place the case in a historical perspective because of Mao's respect for the history, but Mao was concerned with the present, not the past.[7]

Luo Fu and Mao had once been political opponents. On the Long March, however, both fell ill, had to be carried on litters, and during their long, swaying progress they came to a meeting of minds. By 1959 Luo Fu had supported Mao for years and had spent a long time in Moscow as China's representative.

Luo Fu spoke frankly and critically at Lushan. Unfortunately, Nikita Khrushchev, in Moscow, chose this moment to make some pungent remarks about the Great Leap. To Mao's overheated mind the coincidence smelled of collusion. Peng had just come back from Moscow. The notion of a Moscow plot had probably already been planted in Mao's mind, and he began to suspect Peng not only was against him but was allied with his foe in Moscow.[8]

Neither Peng nor Luo Fu was exactly tactful in their discussions. One day Luo Fu said to Peng that Mao was brilliant but, like Stalin, had become "very strong-handed in rectifying people." To which Peng replied that the "first emperor in each of the Chinese dynasties had been brilliant but tough. And proletarian leaders should be tough, too."[9]

Peng had made other remarks calculated to raise Mao's ire. After his trip to Hungary he said that if the Chinese peasants had not been so disciplined they would have followed the example of the Hungarians and risen up. Marshal He Long told Mao about this. And at a Politburo meeting Peng said that if the 5 billion yuan uselessly spent for backyard steel mills had been put into consumer goods it would have made a pile higher than Mount Lu. Mao interrupted to say: "Not so high as Mount Lu." "OK," retorted Peng, "a bit lower."[10]

By Peng's account, he tried to see Mao on the morning of July 13, but when he appeared at Mao's house the guards told him Mao had just gone to bed, having, as so often, stayed up all night. That evening Peng wrote a ten-thousand-character letter (twenty-three hundred

English words) and sent it to Mao the next morning. He insisted to his last days that it was a private letter, intended only for Mao's eyes, not a political platform to rally Lushan against the chairman.[11]

Peng's letter was a coherent, terse document notable for its restraint and tactful language. Peng larded his memorandum with praise for Mao's achievements, even for the Great Leap, and found positive things to say about the miserable backyard steel mills. Again and again Peng shifted the blame from Mao to others, including himself. There was not a word to which a reasonable man could object. But Mao was neither reasonable nor objective.

And for all Peng's uncommon delicacy, flattery, and praise, the telltale strands of the case against Mao's policies did show clear and plain. The direct indictment of the Great Leap was a shocker.

Peng understood the seriousness of openly opposing Mao, no matter how he smothered his critique in compliments. But in his long relationship with Mao he had always expressed his mind freely, and so had Mao. No matter what their disagreement, they had gone forward on a basis of trust. Peng knew that Mao was changing. Peng had admitted in April 1958 to Li Rui that the Mao paean "The East Is Red" made him feel uncomfortable. Nor did he like the term "Great Leap Forward"; he preferred something like "Great Development."[12]

The next two days passed with no sign of trouble. But on the morning of July 17, Peng had a shock. His letter to Mao was published in the daily Lushan reading file under the heading "Comrade Peng Dehuai's Statement of Opinions."[13] Mao had flung down the gauntlet. Peng had to know it.

His first act was to try to get his letter withdrawn from public circulation. As he told the Northwest Group on July 18, the letter had been intended only for Chairman Mao personally. He asked that all copies be retrieved. They were not.

Events followed in quick succession. Huang Kecheng, Peng's chief of staff, arrived in Lushan on the evening of July 18, or possibly the morning of July 19, and found himself in the midst of crisis. Peng dropped by to discuss with his deputy a request for more transport for the Tibet forces. Someone said nervously: "Commander, we are only fifty paces away from being named rightists [one of the worst epithets in the Communist vocabulary]!" "Don't worry," Huang Kecheng said, "Chairman Mao will not make a mistake. The matter will be cleared up."

Huang was right. Mao was about to clear up the matter, but not in the way he imagined.[14]

Mao set about composing not a reply to Peng but a denunciation that ultimately became a formal indictment of the marshal for an "anti-Party conspiracy," a plot to overthrow Mao's regime. He would be accused of military adventurism, conspiracy with the Soviet Union, organization of a "military club" that planned a coup d'état, and slander of the Revolution. The honorable Peng Dehuai, who was born into such poverty his grandmother had to beg for rice (Peng refused to beg after going with her once), who as a youngster climbed barefoot in the snow to cut wood in the mountains, would be called a warlord, a bourgeois, an exploiter, a "black general." There was nothing in the rich repertoire of Chinese political invective that would not be thrown at him.

Hu Qiaomu, Mao's secretary of twenty years' standing, had privately sided with young Li Rui and the others who hoped to change Mao's direction. Now he warned Luo Fu: "The wind is blowing harder now." But Luo Fu and the others ignored the warning.[15]

When he finished the first draft of his denunciation of Peng, Mao hurried a copy by courier plane to Jiang Qing, who was relaxing at the Mao beach house at Beidaihe, the seashore resort on Bohai Bay, east of Beijing. Jiang Qing had been enjoying her leisure, the sunshine, the glorious beach, and the sea. When she got Mao's text she sprang into action. She put through a telephone call to Lushan and told Mao she was coming immediately; she recognized the seriousness of the crisis. "Don't come," Mao said. "The struggle is too acute." Heedless of Mao's no, Jiang Qing ordered up a plane and got to Lushan within a few hours. She sat in on the meetings from that time forward.[16]

Peng was trying to decide on his next move. The silence of Mao was deafening. Peng's supporters went ahead. They made a few speeches on July 20, backing Peng's ideas in carefully chosen words. This was true of Luo Fu; the Hunan Party secretary, Zhou Xiaozhou; and Huang Kecheng. The debates went on. But the atmosphere had turned ominous. Everyone noticed that Jiang Qing had arrived.[17]

On July 23 the chairman broke his silence. He stood on the rostrum of the assembly hall, where in other years Chiang Kaishek had spoken and in more distant days young Methodist missionaries had delivered Sunday sermons.

Mao was nervous. He looked about the hall and saw no sign of Peng Dehuai. "Why isn't Peng Dehuai here?" he asked his bodyguards.

They finally spotted him in the last row. Peng had a new haircut — very short, very military, bristling.

Mao called to him: "Why don't you sit in front with the other Politburo members?" Peng shook his head. He didn't budge. When Mao was angry he bit his lower lip. He bit it now until it nearly bled.[18]

Mao adopted a Chinese kind of good ol' boy style, half-humorous, half-apologetic, claiming that he had taken sleeping pills three times but hadn't been able to get to sleep. Now, after everyone had spoken so much, he wanted to have his say. People at the conference, he allowed, were touchy. They reminded him of Sun Fo, Sun Yatsen's son. An old comrade used to say that if you touched Sun Fo, he jumped. And so it was at Lushan: There were some comrades who were feeling the pressure, who didn't want bad things said about them, only good things. To those comrades his advice was to listen to what he had to say — that was what their ears were for.

Mao told his listeners he had been busy reading criticisms. There were so many that he hadn't yet finished. But they all had one thing in common — everyone said things were in a mess.

He joked about Lin Biao's thinness and his own and Zhu De's fatness. He ridiculed the "Communist wind," which had led many communes to seize every bit of private property (he had set it off himself, of course). Only the notorious prerevolutionary underworld gangs of Shanghai believed that what belonged to you belonged to them, that is, that all property be held in common. It was OK, he said, to seize the property of local despots, but the fat hogs and white cabbages that had been "expropriated" from the peasants must go back to them.

Everyone, himself included, should "toughen his scalp" and get ready to endure criticism. Then he got down to business. If people attacked him, Mao said, he was bound to attack them. He warned that there were comrades who had better listen to him and others who had better not "waver at a crucial time." He had noticed that some comrades' support was wavering at this very moment. A chill went through the hall as he continued.

He struck out at his critics, those who found nine things wrong out of ten. If the country continued on that course, it would certainly perish and would deserve to. In that case, "I will go to the countryside to lead the peasants to overthrow the government. If those of you in the Liberation Army won't follow me I will go and find a Red Army and organize another Liberation Army."[19] This was the official, published version. In fact, as his guards remembered, Mao told Lushan:

"If Peng Dehuai's army won't follow me then I will go down to the countryside, reorganize the guerrillas and reorganize my army."[20]

Mao was master of the scene. Peng Dehuai appeared more and more angry, and his face reddened. Mao's confidence rose as he toyed with his audience. Peng Dehuai had described himself as a "coarse fellow with no refinement." Well, Mao said, he was coarse, too, but had a certain delicacy. He conceded he knew nothing about economic construction or industrial planning and was in no position to oversee the work of the state planning specialists (all of whom had been almost driven out of their wits by his Great Leap and the commune system).

Underlying Mao's performance was a relentless dissection of Peng's criticism. Yes, said Mao, chaos had been created on a grand scale. Yes, Mao had led the country into a great catastrophe. But, as he noted, no one had halted him. All his critics of today had cheered him on. Didn't they bear some responsibility? He talked about a "big cannon" — obviously meaning Peng — who had fired big shots and missed the target. And he included a few ominous references to Moscow and its supporters. Mao took upon himself responsibility for the great crisis, but he warned: "Comrades! You must all analyze your responsibility. If you have to shit — shit! If you have to fart — fart! You will feel much better for it."[21]

By the time Mao had finished, he had created a new epoch in the Chinese revolution. The brotherhood of the Long March had ended. Now and for years to come it would be each man for himself and the devil (or Mao's minions) take the hindmost.

Peng struggled to his feet. Mao called to him, but he didn't hear or didn't want to hear. When he moved toward the door, Mao hurried after him: "Peng Zong [General Peng] — can we talk?"

Peng grew redder. "I have nothing to talk about," he snorted.

"It doesn't matter if we disagree," Mao persisted. "Can't we just sit and chat?"

Peng edged out of the room, shrugging his shoulders: "I've nothing to talk about."

Mao bit his lip again. He was as angry as Peng.[22] No one seemed to notice that neither Peng nor Mao had mentioned Shaoshan. The line had been drawn. Just as Mao's anti-rightist campaign following the Hundred Flowers movement had stifled critical expression by intellectuals, so now no one in the leadership would speak out. The penalty was too great. There would be no criticism, nothing but adulation and lies. Mao had turned his band of brothers into a claque, clapping hands and nodding heads like mechanical dolls.[23]

After Mao's speech Li Rui looked around. Everyone's face was pale. He and secretaries Chen Boda and Hu Qiaomu went for a walk. Li Rui made up a bit of doggerel:

> We have heard some thunder over the mountain
> If we ask the mountaineer — who can say if his hut
> Will still be standing in the morning.

The secretaries didn't eat lunch; they didn't feel like it. Instead they talked and talked. They thought Mao had taken a 180-degree turn. Ahead they could see only one-man rule, no more collective leadership. That evening they went to see Huang Kecheng. Huang still thought matters could be straightened out. Li Rui didn't. He told Hu Qiaomu and fellow secretary Tian Jiaying he would take on himself the responsibility for opposing Mao and siding with Peng. He swore he would not implicate Hu and Tian. Zhou Enlai and Liu Shaoqi had already talked with Huang, who had agreed to make a self-criticism. Both Liu and Zhou took the line that Peng had been actively opposing Mao for years, even in the days of the anti-Japanese war.

Hu Qiaomu and Tian Jiaying got some criticism, but Li Rui became the principal culprit. He told his critics that Mao on July 11 and 17 had spoken to him directly and encouraged him to present his views frankly — which he did.

"Oh, yes," someone said. "That's Mao's tactic. He likes for the ghosts to jump out — then he can catch them."[24]

That evening Peng Dehuai and Mao continued to debate in Mao's stone house, with the Politburo present. At one point Peng shouted at Mao: "In Yanan you fucked my mother for forty days. Now I have been fucking your mother for only eighteen days and you want to call a halt — but you won't!"[25] The debate had gone back to the peasant language of the Red Army days, in which the "fuck your mother" epithet is a literal transcription of the Chinese phrase usually rendered simply as "Fuck you." Peng's reference to forty days in Yanan concerned a long-ago row he had had with Mao.[26]

Wang Bingnan, who served Mao and the Party for years in diplomatic and secret roles, put the case this way: "After Lushan the whole Party shut up. We were all afraid to speak out. It stifled democracy. People didn't tell Mao their honest opinions. They were afraid. This led straight to the terrible times of the Cultural Revolution."[27]

Bodyguard Li Yinqiao, a bit naively, didn't think Mao really wanted a split with Peng. Nor did he think Peng wanted a split with Mao. After all, Peng's ten-thousand-character letter was only a disagreement and an opinion, not a plot or conspiracy.

But, the bodyguard observed, once Mao initiated the break with Peng, the whole Politburo and the Central Committee were bound to support him. They all quarreled with Peng, and in this Lin Biao, who would inherit Peng's position of defense minister, was the leader.[28]

With July the Lushan conference came to an end, but Mao promptly convened an extended Politburo session — still at Lushan — to finish with Peng Dehuai.

The criticism was led off on August 1 by Zhu De, although his words were very mild (he actually agreed with what his old comrade at arms had said). Mao was angry. He raised his leg and scratched the leather of his shoe, spitting out: *"Ge xue sao yang,"* meaning "You've just scratched the surface." Zhu De blushed and sat down.

Lin Biao took over. He called Peng a "careerist, a conspirator and a hypocrite." This was more to Mao's liking. Kang Sheng lent a hand, submitting two documents to Mao citing supposed precedents in Lenin and Stalin on handling "Rightist Tendencies."

The next day Lin Biao renewed his assault. Alone among the speakers he no longer called Peng "comrade." Zhou Enlai spoke, too, criticizing Peng as "disloyal to Mao."

Peng finally offered a mild self-criticism. He confessed that he had become the "bourgeois spokesman" in the Party and admitted most of the mistakes attributed to him. He promised to eradicate his errors and his "preconceived idea of Comrade Mao Zedong." But he refused to concede that he was a "careerist" or a "hypocrite." He said that he would "not commit suicide. I will not become a counterrevolutionary. I can be a farmer if I lose my Party membership."[29]

The meeting stripped Peng of his position as defense minister and put Lin Biao in his place. Huang Kecheng and the Hunan secretary, Zhou Xiaozhou, lost their jobs. A bit later Luo Fo was removed as deputy foreign secretary, and a bit earlier Li Rui had been dropped as fifth private secretary to Mao and begun an eighteen-year stint of imprisonment and forced labor.

There was a meeting in Beijing between Peng Dehuai and Mao. Peng asked permission to go down to the countryside. He wanted, he said, to return to his native Hunan. Mao did not think well of that. It wasn't safe for Peng to go to the countryside. He urged him to stay in Beijing, to take a rest, to read some books. He proposed that Peng study Lenin and suggested two pamphlets: "Two Tactics of Social-Democracy in the Democratic Revolution," which had been written in the days of Russia's 1905 revolution, and " 'Left-Wing' Communism: An Infantile Disease," written in 1917. The reader will peruse the two works in vain for a clue as to what inspired Mao's selection — the first is a rather superficial study of democracy and dictatorship, the second devoted in large measure to the tactics of the Bolsheviks in the period leading up to November 1917.[30]

Soon the security police closed in: There was a harassing, expanded Military Committee session at which Peng was shouted and yelled at — a preview of the Cultural Revolution — in an attempt to make him confess to setting up a "military club" devoted to overthrowing the government. The committee demanded that he name names and tell all about his conspiracies.

Swiftly Lin Biao slipped into the office and responsibilities of Old Peng. Lin Biao had hardly raised a voice until Mao spoke at Lushan. Then he spoke quietly, but his whisper penetrated to the ends of China.

Mao did not linger in Lushan. He proceeded to his beloved Hangzhou, the beauties of West Lake, and other pleasures. But there was a change. With him went Jiang Qing, their estrangement seemingly put aside. For the first time since she came to share Mao's bed in Yanan, Jiang Qing stood at his side openly in a political role. Not one public word was spoken against this metamorphosis. Chairman Mao's wish had now become a command. It was, as Jiang made clear to Roxane Witke, a moment to be savored.

Jiang had brought her camera to Lushan and busied herself in spare moments with taking snapshots of the misty peaks. Her prize was one that she called Faery Cave, a vista famed in legend. On the reverse side of the enlargement that she gave to Mao he wrote a quatrain about Lushan's "perilous peak."[31] Mao's words were realistic, even if the photograph was, as Ross Terrill was to assert, not of Faery Cave but of a view called Brocade Embroidered Peak; the picture had been taken from the cave, not of it.[32] By the standards of what had been said at Lushan — and what was to come — the picture caption was remarkably close to truth.

The legacy of Lushan was found not in its regard for the truth but rather in the new, ominous bond forged between Mao and Jiang Qing, the barely noticed resurgence of Kang Sheng, and the quiet ease with which Lin Biao now moved to the head of the table where sat the bewildered survivors of the Long March.

Later pondering these events, Zhu De, who had known all the comrades in good times and bad, shook his head and observed: "And to think that we once all ate out of the same rice bowl."[33]

21

Mao's Metaphor

OCTOBER 1, 1959, Tiananmen Square. Ten years since Mao Zedong stood on the high balcony and said that China had stood up. Now, on this fine day, Mao led his comrades once again to the red-and-gold-encrusted platform on the gate.

The rulers of China looked out on a new square. No more mud, dirty puddles, shabby foreground; no hated legation compound at the front gate of the Forbidden City.

Today the view was gargantuan, a paved vista of one hundred unbounded acres, the greatest central square in the world. Moscow's Red Square could comfortably fit into the northern segment; St. Peter's would not encompass the southern quadrant.

To the right Mao gazed at the titanic bulge of the new Great Hall of the People, a construct of endless assembly halls, one for each of China's provinces, sheltering an auditorium for ten thousand, a banquet hall for five thousand. The floor space exceeded that of all the palaces of the Forbidden City.

If Mao thought it the greatest palace China had ever seen, he was wrong. Kublai Khan's palace in Cambuluc, as Marco Polo called Beijing, boasted a banquet hall for six thousand, walls of marble and gold, ceiling frescoes of men, women, dragons, beasts, and birds. It was crowned by a dome lacquered in vermilion, green, blue, and yellow and could be seen for miles away. Here the khan on his birthday received twelve thousand barons and knights, the whole company clothed in silk and gold. So wrote Marco Polo. Mao's Great Hall was a shabby imitation.

To the left rose matching buildings, the new, not quite completed twin Museums of History, one of China's history, one of China's revolution. That of the Revolution was larger than that devoted to the six thousand years of China before 1949.

Trouble plagued Mao Zedong. His lieutenants Liu Shaoqi, Zhou Enlai, and Deng Xiaoping were far from comfortable. They shared a guilty secret. They knew the communes were a shambles, the Great Leap a horror. The greatest famine of contemporary China was clutching at its throat. But spread before Mao and his men — and their guest of the day, Nikita Khrushchev — was a monument to China's transformation. True, Soviet architects had had a hand in its design. Their imprint was recognizable in the banality of architecture, the pedestrian columns, and the shallowness of concept. There was no echo of the majesty of Rome or Athens. Mao's Tiananmen was anchored in Moscow's shabby world and shackled by Stalin's provincial taste. Any soaring vision had escaped the Chinese copyists.

But there was more to Tiananmen than met the eye. The square was not just bricks and mortar; it was ideology. The process of its creation bore the indelible stamp of the age of Mao. This was mass action set in concrete form. The square and its new buildings had been thrown up in a breakneck ten months, from November 1958 to September 1959. Tiananmen was built by "volunteers," a labor force of twelve thousand who worked in three shifts for up to sixteen hours a day — or until they dropped in their tracks. They died of exhaustion or in accidents. The work never halted. Around the clock under improvised floodlights the pounding of hammers, the pouring of concrete, the ceaseless trudging of wheelbarrows, the laying of brick, went on and on.

It was Mao's metaphor. He told visitors with pride that the men and women had rejected any extra pay. They would not take one fen more than the standard monthly rate of 50 yuan (they knew better than to ask). That worked out to about $15 a month. The workers ate their bowl of rice on the site, ladled from a huge caldron. They were so eager to complete the great monument to the new regime, said Mao, they just couldn't halt working.

Mao had built the new Tiananmen in defiance of predictions by

Soviet experts. They had said at the end of 1958 that it couldn't be finished for the October celebration. In June 1959 they conceded that "it might be done." In September they said "China has had a Great Leap Forward." Mao liked to quote that to his visitors.[1]

Whatever the men who gathered on the Gate of Heavenly Peace thought of Mao's metaphor, there was no doubt that Mao himself was elated. The new Tiananmen was a monument for the ages. He never tired of boasting about this triumph of Maoist mass movement. Thought of it took away the bitter taste of Lushan, the violent break with Peng Dehuai, and even the dangers of the new war that had suddenly broken out with India, possibly a sly stratagem of Lin Biao's, the new defense minister. Tiananmen helped Mao shift his thoughts from the ugly confrontation with Moscow. Khrushchev had reneged on his pledge to give Beijing atom-bomb know-how and high-tech weapons — what next? There were few smiles on the faces of Khrushchev and Mao as they stood atop Tiananmen. Each knew that the great Communist camp was tottering on the brink of dissolution.

Small wonder that Mao urged all who would listen to go have a look at Tiananmen, to let Wan Li, who had been in charge of construction, show them around. Wan Li was a deputy mayor of Beijing, an unusual man, soft-spoken and humane (he had spent many days with the lowest caste in Beijing, the honey cart drivers, the collectors of Beijing's human excrement, trying to understand their plight and inject some hope in their lives). Later, after the tortures and turmoil of the Cultural Revolution, Wan Li took charge of China's railroads and helped restore them to order. Mao didn't have a more able younger lieutenant, and he knew it. Go and see Wan Li, Mao urged his associates; let him show you how Tiananmen was built. Wan Li, Mao bragged, could run 10,000 li (about 3,000 miles) — a pun on Li's name, which literally means 10,000 li.[2]

Mao was just as proud of the great new Miyun reservoir, near the Ming tombs, northwest of Beijing, which was built at the same time, by the same kind of "volunteer" mass labor force. Mao, Liu, Deng, Zhou Enlai, the whole leadership, volunteered to spend a few hours at Miyun and, of course, have their pictures taken helping to move the tens of thousands of tons of earth. Miyun would help Beijing exist through the endless succession of dry and dusty seasons.[3]

Tiananmen and Miyun were two of Mao's "Ten Great Projects" in Beijing. All were visible advertisement of China's success under the ten years of Mao's Communist leadership.

There was more to come. Mao was already looking ten years into the future, to the celebration that would commemorate the twentieth anniversary of liberation, in 1969. Then — if all went well — Mao would reveal to the world a metaphor that would place his stamp upon China for thousands of years. The plans were being drawn for the destruction of the Forbidden City. Mao, like dynastic emperors before him, was preparing to wipe from the earth the most dramatic symbol of past reigns.

Just as had his role model — the terrible emperor Qin, who erected the new Han nation on the mountains of skulls of his rivals — so Mao would create a New China that stood on its own foundations. No longer would he be beholden to China's past. Just as he would replace his delicate and beautiful Qing Palace, the Study of Chrysanthemum Fragrance, with the mundane "Swimming Pool House," so he would give to China a new heart. He had not yet thought of what to call it — Commune Capital? China City? Might someone suggest Mao Zedong City?

Mao knew what would go into the new capital. Quietly, unofficially, the discussion about the future Forbidden City had gone on since before the Red Army entered Beijing, in early 1949.

Much had been done to destroy the landmarks that gave Beijing its fame. Most of the city walls had been struck down in 1957. Stalin had done the same in Moscow, tearing out whole sections around the Kremlin and asphalting them over. He wanted to create fields of fire so his cannon and machine guns could blast away should the people try to storm his fortress. He had opened up wide boulevards where the old city walls had stood, enabling his tanks to move swiftly from one threatened area to another.

By destroying the city walls and by opening up Tiananmen, Mao had achieved the same purpose. He had a pragmatic excuse for tearing down the walls: He wanted to build subways and underground railroads giving access to Zhongnanhai and the major government offices. Chinese technology was so poorly developed that lateral tunnels could not be bored underground. The most efficient and cheapest alternative was to dig from the surface to the level of the tunnel and then cover it over. The city walls interfered with this method. Later their stones were used in the network of underground air raid shelters, hastily dug in 1969, at the height of the fear of Soviet nuclear attack.

The plans now being drafted called for the abolition of the entire Forbidden City. There would be stupendous esplanades, government buildings to make those of Hitler's Berlin, Stalin's Moscow, and LBJ's

Washington look chintzy — great assemblages for foreign affairs, the security department, the Party Central Committee, and the Council of Ministers. There would be a skyscraper, a twenty-story department store (with what goods it would be stocked was not spelled out), a movie theater to outdo New York's Roxy or London's Palladium, with five thousand seats (or, as some suggested, ten thousand).[4]

There was in this a strong hint of the ideology that would surface in Mao's next epochal episode — the Great Proletarian Cultural Revolution. The Cultural Revolution would proclaim as its objective the destruction of China's Four Olds: old thoughts, old culture, old customs, and old habits.

What could possibly epitomize the old more perfectly than the Forbidden City?

No evidence exists that Khrushchev was affected by or even noticed Mao's symbolic charade. Nikita Khrushchev did not arrive in Beijing in a jolly mood. He was fed up with what he regarded as Mao's posturing. The memory of the swimming pool debate and the mosquito-bitten night at the Fragrant Hills had not faded. He came to Beijing with the success of his meeting with President Dwight Eisenhower ringing in his ears and the spirit of Camp David surging in his veins. He was exhilarated by his recent triumphs and had no patience for Chinese games.

From the moment his stretch Tupelov-114 touched down it was apparent that the temperature of Moscow-Beijing friendship had cooled. Had there been any doubt, Khrushchev blasted it away at the ceremonial banquet on the eve of the great October 1 festivities.

Khrushchev had written his remarks in advance and given a copy to the Chinese interpreters. The Soviets expected a copy of Mao's speech, but it was not forthcoming. They were told Mao would not speak; Liu Shaoqi would do the honors. Mao probably decided to duck after a glance at Khrushchev's text. Khrushchev opened by attacking the Chinese for provocative behavior in the shelling of Quemoy and Matsu, the Taiwanese-held islands in the Taiwan Strait. Khrushchev said it was not wise "to test the stability of Capitalism by force." He was saying that it behooved the Chinese not to twist the tail of the "paper tiger," as they liked to call the United States.[5]

There was worse to come. Khrushchev praised Eisenhower and the need for accommodation. He said that in the early days of the Soviet Union it had gotten along in friendly fashion with the Far Eastern Republic, an independent regime in Vladivostok. Later, the Soviets had peacefully incorporated the Far Eastern Republic. The implication was plain — why shouldn't Beijing get along with Taiwan and incorporate it later in a peaceful manner?

Khrushchev had a specific demand from Eisenhower to convey. The Soviet leader asked the Chinese to release two American airmen, pilots of intelligence overflights who had made forced landings in China. This, Mao felt, was outrageous interference in China's affairs.

Khrushchev launched a full-scale attack on the Chinese action in India, which he blamed (accurately) on China's intransigence. What was the purpose of this adventure? The territory — remote, uninhabitable mountain peaks — was worth nothing. India was prepared to settle the quarrel on the basis of the McMahon Line. To Mao this was even more hostile than the words about Taiwan. China had never recognized the McMahon Line, a product of British imperialism. He regarded the quarrel with India as China's own business. Khrushchev had already publicly criticized the Chinese for the conflict and was pursuing an evenhanded policy that quickly was to escalate into arms shipments and open support of India. Mao regarded this as an unconscionable violation of the relationship between members of what he liked to call the "Communist camp."[6]

Khrushchev appeared on the gate at Tiananmen beside Mao on the next day, October 1. Photos of Mao and Khrushchev at their October meeting are rare. They disappeared into closed files soon after. But one exists of the airport ceremony. Khrushchev is approaching the microphone, his head shaven almost bald, and Mao is looking sidewise at him with some apprehension. What would the ebullient Russian say next?

The talks went on for three days. Before Khrushchev flew back to Moscow he had ridiculed the Great Leap Forward, denounced the communes, questioned Mao as to what he had meant about the Hundred Flowers movement, and made clear he was not giving any more large-scale aid to China. He complained that the Chinese security police were harassing the Soviet experts, ransacking their rooms and possessions, and abusively subjecting them to vulgar racial slurs. As one Chinese participant observed: "The visit by Khrushchev ended in rather an unpleasant manner. In fact, it was a great quarrel." There was no immediate explosion in China-Soviet relations. But it was not far distant. Khrushchev's free-swinging comments in the October meeting, his praise for Eisenhower, his warnings about the nuclear might of the United States, became the subject of point two of an elaborate nine-point propaganda barrage issued by Beijing in 1963 and 1964.[7]

Peng Dehuai had dropped from sight. He had not yet lost his Politburo seat and was still vice premier. But he had been moved out of Zhongnanhai. He was absent from the October 1 celebration and the Khrushchev meetings. He lived now in an ancient abandoned park, the Wu Family Gardens, in the village of Guajiacun, in northwest Beijing, close to Beijing University.[8] It was an appropriate place. Guajiacun means Hanging Up Your Armor. It was so named for a warrior who, leading an expedition against the barbarians, paused here to rest and remove his battle dress.

The park was forlorn when Peng moved in. There were two courtyard houses. Peng and his wife, Puanxu, and two secretaries occupied one, his chauffeur and bodyguards the other. For six years he lived here in seclusion, not under house arrest but cut off from contact with politics, government, and the army. Possibly under political pressure to "draw a line," his wife divorced him.[9]

Peng occupied himself raising peaches and puttering about the garden. He made friends with the villagers. Active as he had always been, he felt at a loss. This went on until September 23, 1965, when Mao called him to Zhongnanhai and proposed to send him to the southwest to take the number-two post in building the Third Line. After a day of talks Peng accepted the assignment and went to Chongqing. He never got to work on the project. He was arrested in 1966, put in the hands of violent Red Guard torturers, beaten and beaten until his internal organs were crushed and his back splintered. He died November 29, 1974, having endured 130 "interrogations." He never gave up. "You can shoot me," he said. "I fear nothing. Your days are numbered. The more you interrogate me the firmer I become."[10] Peng lived and died a hero of the Long March.

So far as the record shows, neither Zhou Enlai nor Liu Shaoqi played any meaningful role in the case of Peng Dehuai. Nor did Deng Xiaoping. All three knew that Peng was right, that he had done nothing wrong. They held their tongues and saved their skins — for the moment.

22

Seek Truth from Facts

THE QING DYNASTY POET Zheng Banqiao was fond of wandering over the endless plains and craggy mountains of China, pausing beside a waterfall or rice paddy, sharing a bowl of rice with a farmer, taking his ease in the shade of a bamboo grove. He knew the country and the people so well that each shimmering leaf, each murmur of a willow branch, spoke to him.

"Lying in my bed in the villa," he once wrote, "I hear the rustle of bamboo leaves and imagine that it is the sighs uttered by the suffering people. I have a profound feeling for every leaf and tree in this place."

And for the people of China, enduring through the ages.

This verse was the favorite of a dedicated and thoughtful man named Tian Jiaying, who was one of Mao's secretaries.[1] Tian Jiaying was a discovery of Hu Qiaomu's, whose career as secretary for Mao was the longest of any. Tian was writing articles for the *Liberation Daily* when Hu brought him to Yanan in 1943 to help with his secretarial chores. Mao took a liking to him, and Tian began work as a secretary himself in 1948 at Xibaipo after an interview with Mao in which Tian said working for him would not be an easy task. Mao gave him a few drinks of *maotai,* the fiery Chinese liquor, to test his capacity. Tian usually held his liquor well, but he was so excited he got high on a single shot. Mao didn't like that. He sent Tian out to the northeast on a survey mission — with no instructions, neither about what to do nor what to find out. Tian's report won him his job.

Soon Mao was spending almost every evening with Tian. They discussed poetry, philosophy, Chinese classics, history. They shared a passion for calligraphy. Tian was a collector, but Mao was the greatest collector in China. Mao sometimes sent his secretaries on scouting expeditions to bring back rare examples, especially by Huai Su, a classic calligrapher. Mao would borrow calligraphy from the archives of the

Forbidden City and post them on his study walls. Once he borrowed Tian's collection and put it up in his bedroom. Tian became a close friend of Mao's son, Anying, who referred to him as "my teacher." When Mao's second son, the ailing Anqing, came back from Moscow, Mao had Tian tutor him. Tian worked with Hu Qiaomu and Chen Boda on many of Mao's research and writing projects. Together they compiled Mao's collected works but published only Mao's revised versions, making no note of what had been changed. Chen Boda took the largest role in this task.

Once when Tian Jiaying came down with the flu, Mao, greatly concerned, came to see him several times. Tian told his wife: "Mao is very emotional. He has really deep feelings for those who work for him." Tian told a friend that he and Mao were genuine confidants. He told Mao everything he knew or thought, and he believed Mao did the same with him. Of course, he told Mao's librarian, Jiang Xianzhi, "You can't be a confidant of Mao Zedong forever."[2]

Mao's bodyguards agreed about their master's emotions. Mao told He Zizhen, his second wife, that three things made him weep: the sight of poor folk crying in their misery, injury or death of a bodyguard, and the wounding of He Zizhen (she was terribly injured by bomb fragments during the Long March).[3]

Bodyguard Li Yinqiao once witnessed Mao break into tears during a performance of a Beijing opera, *The White Snake Fairy Tale*. "It was like the bawling of a calf," he recalled. Mao became so agitated while watching the opera that he forgot he was holding a cigarette until it burned his fingers. He began to call for help for the opera's heroine, shouting "We've got to have the Revolution!" When the guards sought to calm him — "Remember the audience," they whispered — he paid no heed.

Mao got more and more excited. He was completely lost in the opera. Finally he struggled to his feet, shouting for help in rescuing the heroine. As always, the bodyguards had unbuckled his belt so that the chairman, with his big belly, would be more comfortable sitting through the performance. When Mao stood up, his pants dropped from his middle before the guards could encircle his waist and fasten the belt. Tears ran like rain from his eyes. He was hardly conscious of what was going on. When the opera was finished he rushed to the stage to congratulate the singers, holding up his pants with one hand.[4]

Mao was fond of Karl Marx's aphorism "Seek truth from facts" — *Shi shi qiu shi,* as it was translated into Chinese, a phrase with the poetic lilt the Chinese loved. Mao preached it to his associates, and Tian Jiaying took the dictum literally. He believed it his duty to report his observations to Mao uncut, no varnish. He gave Mao the truth even when he knew it was a truth Mao didn't want to hear. He was the answer to Mao's oft-stated prayer for a contemporary Diogenes.

When Mao began to realize in 1958 that something was wrong in the countryside, he had turned first to Tian. He knew he would get a straight answer. He had sent him initially to Xiyiling and then to Sichuan, where Tian stayed almost six months, until the eve of the Lushan conference.

Whatever Mao said or did at Lushan, he had the no-words-spared Tian Jiaying reports. Mao knew just how bad things were — very bad, as Tian reported. So that, in fact, the views Mao gave at Lushan were nothing but lies, and Mao knew it. Not the first and far from the last time when Mao would tell a big lie and, like Hitler, use it to his political advantage.

In Sichuan, Tian had put aside Party escorts. He did not ride in the car they gave him. He plunged into the villages and walked the rice fields on the raised-up dirt paths between paddies. He took off his shoes and trudged through the mud. He helped the peasants pull their creaking carts, their wooden wheels wailing like stuck pigs for lack of grease. He slipped out of banquets to eat rice (if there was any) from the same pot as the peasants. Tian went with commune members to Chengdu to get manure and pulled the honey cart along dusty paths back to the village. He lived in peasant huts, shared the lice and the bedbugs, talked the peasants' language. There was not much he did not learn about reality.

One day he asked the leader of a production team about grain reserves. The leader told him they had 30,000 jin (a jin equals 1.3 pounds) in the granary. Tian took a look. Unmilled rice was heaped up in the bin. It looked all right, but Tian was a careful man. He picked up a bamboo pole and stabbed into the heap. The rice trickled off to one side and exposed a mound of straw lying underneath.

Tian did not denounce the peasant trick. He knew too much about the pressure that was being applied to the local leaders. "I see your rice has very long straws," he said with a grin.

Tian was a tactful man, which is why Mao kept him on when he dismissed and imprisoned Li Rui for becoming an ally of Peng Dehuai's. Mao suspected correctly that Tian Jiaying shared the views of Li Rui, Peng Dehuai, and the other critics, but he did not dismiss him, assuring him after Lushan, "Don't worry. You will still go on with your job as secretary." Unlike the others, Tian Jiaying was not named a member of the imaginary military club.

Mao seemed to accept Tian's reports — even a stark account of conditions in rich Zhejiang Province, site of Mao's beloved Hangzhou, which told of peasant starvation and incomes of *3 yuan ($1.50) a year.* Mao knew Tian had broken into tears when confronting the peasants, gaunt as Walker Evans photographs, and had denounced the Party bureaucracy for its unwillingness to tell the truth.

Tian continued doing his duty, regardless of warnings from friends. But in 1962 he argued with Mao in favor of a modified family responsibility system, which was being introduced in agriculture by Liu and Deng. Almost instantly it would begin to produce large yields and prosperity for farmers who entered the program (a primitive precursor of Deng's fabulously successful agricultural initiative of 1978). Mao caught up Tian sharply, accusing him of speaking not for himself but for someone else, meaning Liu and Deng).

That ended the relationship of confidants. As had happened with Li Rui, Tian had crossed a line, and he knew it. He begged Mao to let him go, asking to be sent to a county as Party leader. His wife could take charge of women's work. Or let him be released for historical research on the Qing dynasty. Anything to get out of the golden cage of Zhongnanhai. It was too late; Mao never let his victims escape. Tian told his wife: "The Chairman is very tough. Very tough."[5]

Tian went on working. In the spring of 1965 Mao named him to a team that he took to Hangzhou to work on preparation of six books on ideology, basic reading for Party cadres. Mao himself would prepare an introduction for a new edition of Marx's *Communist Manifesto.* But the onset of the Cultural Revolution swept the project into oblivion.[6]

In the lurid fashion that became a hallmark of Mao's treatment of his victims, he took Tian into his confidence one last time. Mao was in Hangzhou, initiating the Great Proletarian Cultural Revolution. He suddenly called in five Party workers, four radicals and Tian. The radicals were Chen Boda, soon to be the rising star of the Cultural Revolution; Hu Sheng, successor to Chen Boda as editor of the Party organ, *Red Flag;* Ai Siqi, head of a Party ideological school; and Guan Feng, member-to-be of the Cultural Revolution group and an editor of *Red Flag.*

For three hours Mao talked to the group of five, ranging over world problems. He discussed American relations, ancient Chinese history, great wars of the past, and contemporary economic conditions — he thought the outlook now was very bright. Mao said he was worried about aspects of China's cultural and social situation. He spoke of the Cultural Revolution, which he felt was needed. Mao also touched on the play "Hai Rui Dismissed from Office," which had recently been criticized ferociously in a Shanghai newspaper for its defense of a Ming dynasty official who lost his post after speaking out against misguided imperial policies. Mao said the point of the play was that the emperor had sacked Hai Rui. Since Mao had sacked Peng Dehuai, he was being portrayed as the evil emperor.

When the three hours ended, the five knew the talk was of enormous importance. A report should be drawn up and circulated to the cadres. They picked Tian Jiaying to write it. He swiftly composed a summary and submitted it to his companions, who unanimously accepted it. No one spoke of a great oddity: Tian Jiaying had not mentioned Hai Rui. As he confessed later, he hadn't thought the chairman's remark about Hai Rui was of special importance. He had seen the play several years earlier in Beijing and had not interpreted it politically. He did not think Hai Rui was Peng Dehuai or that Mao was the emperor. Tian was naive.

Without dissent the Tian Jiaying report was placed in circulation. Of the five only Guan Feng understood that Hai Rui was the key to Mao's thought. He did not mention this to Tian but promptly reported it to Jiang Qing, who in turn told Mao. Much later Hu Sheng said he didn't fault Tian for not mentioning Hai Rui. "After all," he said, "it was only a few words in an afternoon of talk."[7]

The Cultural Revolution lumbered into action. The significance of Mao's remarks was now apparent to Tian Jiaying and everyone else. Tian Jiaying continued as Mao's secretary, but no one was better aware than he, living in the heart of the storm in Zhongnanhai, how troubled the times had become.

Tian still did not count Mao an enemy. However, he knew that Chen Boda and Jiang Qing, as he told his wife, were deadly dangers. Jiang Qing, he said, was the first and only person ever to call him a "rightist" — a fatal accusation at that time. In talking of Jiang he customarily called her Miss, as though she were still a coltish actress making cheap movies in Shanghai, rather than the respected wife of Chairman Mao. He would say, "If Miss isn't under Mao's control she will come out and play." Or, "Miss wants to get out from under Mao and play her own role." Tian thought Mao would keep Jiang in check. But, as Hu Sheng noted, "it was not true after 1965." Miss had slipped the bridle.

One afternoon in late March 1966, Hu Sheng encountered Tian Jiaying just outside Zhongnanhai. He happened to have a rare piece of calligraphy with him. They unrolled the scroll and admired the Ming dynasty work, very unusual and famous, of Xu Sang.

"We both knew that dark clouds had appeared," Hu Sheng recalled. "We did not know what kind of a storm was brewing or that it would prove to be our last meeting."[8]

About midnight on May 21–22, 1966, one of Mao's secretaries, Mei Xing, arrived home from a special Party meeting and telephoned Tian Jiaying, who hurried over to hear what had happened. It was five days after a meeting at which Mao had thrown the Cultural Revolution into high gear.

When Tian Jiaying arrived at Mei Xing's house, Mei told him about this meeting. Four persons had been named as members of an "anti-Party clique" — Peng Zhen, the Long Marcher and Party boss of Beijing; Luo Ruiqing, chief of staff of the People's Liberation Army, enemy of Lin Biao's, soon unsuccessfully to attempt suicide; Yang Shangkun, for years head of the Party's General Office until quietly removed and rusticated in Canton two years earlier; and Lu Dingyi, chief of Party propaganda.

Tian Jiaying was shocked and angry. "All of those men are innocent," he said. "I know that." He added that his own record was clean. His social origins were also clean (i.e., peasant working class). "I joined the Party more than twenty years ago," he said. "I have not committed any big mistakes. *Mao knows everything about me.* I am not afraid. I am not going to betray the Party." As he left, Mei remembered, he was murmuring: "I've done nothing . . . I have done nothing wrong."

Tian Jiaying walked out into the soft May evening and back to his home in Zhongnanhai. Next day Mei Xing called his friend several times. No answer. He was worried. He did not know that on May 22 two men, criminal operatives of the Cultural Revolution, called on Tian Jiaying. One, whose name was Wang Li, would survive and surface in 1989, claiming he was a victim and not a tool of the Gang of Four.[9] The other was Qi Benyu, who fell in 1967 with Wang Li and Guan Feng and was never heard of again.

On this bright May 22 the two hit men rode high. They bore a four-part message to Tian Jiaying. First, Tian possessed, and had for a long time, a "rightist orientation." Second, his relationship with Yang Shangkun was "more than ordinary" and Yang Shangkun was a member of the anti-Party clique. Third, Tian's position as Mao's secretary was terminated as of this moment. He must write a confession and hand over all his papers. Fourth, he must move out of Zhongnanhai within twenty-four hours.

Early in the morning of May 23 Tian Jiaying departed Zhongnanhai. He swallowed a bottle of sleeping pills and ended his life. His family was not notified, but later that day they were thrown out of Zhongnanhai. Tian had been secretary to Mao for eighteen years.

Long before, Tian had spoken of how hard it was to work for Mao; how often Mao changed his mind; how quick he was to accept negative opinions (he once asked Tian to write a self-criticism about a rumor he'd heard, not bothering to ask Tian if it was true or not); how whimsical he was; how much he enjoyed compelling people to criticize their own acts.

When the day came to leave Zhongnanhai and Mao's service, Tian had said, he would tell his master three things:

First, that Mao could manage the universe but he could not manage the people around him.

Second, that he should avoid doing things that people would criticize after he was dead; as an example he would cite what Khrushchev had had to say after Stalin's death.

Third, that Mao would never accept a negative opinion. Therefore no one could tell him the truth.

Tian never got to give Mao his scorecard.

Three years after Tian's death Mao Zedong told a friend that Tian Jiaying had "no major problems." Mao's listener was not certain what Mao was trying to say — did he now miss Tian? Had he reevaluated Tian's situation? Did he now regret what he had done?[10]

To Hu Qiaomu the matter was profoundly clear. There was nothing personal about Mao's action. "It was entirely political in the higher meaning of the word," he said.

Mei Xing was soon arrested and locked up in Qincheng Prison for seven years. "During those days," he recalled, "I thought of my last meeting with Tian Jiaying millions of times."[11]

23

The Making of a State Criminal

TO A DEVOUT PARTY MAN and dedicated supporter of Mao Zedong like Tian Jiaying, the listing of Yang Shangkun as a member of an anti-Party clique could only come as a profound shock. No one had worked harder for Mao and for the Party than this unassuming, efficient man, with his easy manner and quick smile. Yang Shangkun was the epitome of dedication and loyalty.

Yang Shangkun's name did not resonate over China, but there was no one in the upper levels of the Party who did not know him and who had not worked with him for years. In practical Party matters Yang was almost Mao's alter ego. He was chief of the Party's General Office and, thus, in charge of almost every day-to-day Party activity, from distribution of Mao's edicts to getting a seat on a plane for a confidential courier on a secret mission.

There was hardly a secret Yang did not know and no one of consequence in the Party with whom he was not on familiar terms. Tian Jiaying had been accused of maintaining "more than ordinary" relations with Yang Shangkun. In a sense this was true. It was Tian's business to work closely with Yang. But as the words were phrased, they hinted at a plot. Yet, time and again, Tian and Yang had worked together at Mao's specific instructions to carry out Mao's orders. As Yang was to recall years later, "We had a working and a personal relationship. We understood each other."[1]

Tian and the inner Party circle knew that Yang had fallen out of favor with Mao in 1964 and had been demoted. But it was a hush-hush matter, and no one seemed to know why it had happened. Yang had been head of the General Office for twenty years, a low-profile job but one that, in the light of Mao's disorderly work style, could present him with almost any assignment. Yang liked people and people liked him. No one could envisage him as a plotter. In Zhongnanhai he was never too busy to pass the time of day or do a favor. Children adored him. While Liu Shaoqi and Deng Xiaoping never seemed to have time for the children, Yang Shangkun always did.

Yang Shangkun did not control access to Mao, but he made a point of knowing Mao's secretaries, Tian Jiaying and the rest, so well that he usually could advise others on when and how best to approach the chairman and on which topics could be brought up and which were to be avoided. As the years went by Yang became a walking encyclopedia of Party personnel and Party policy. He was the insider's insider.

None of Yang's expertise was sufficient to prevent Mao's wrath from descending on him. Although what motivated Mao cannot be pinpointed, it may have been Yang Shangkun's devotion to Mao's recent victim, Marshal Peng Dehuai. The association of Yang and Peng went back to the early days of the Red Army, to 1932, before the start of the Long March. Yang had come back from the Soviet Union with a group of young Chinese known as the 28½ Bolsheviks, trained sympathizers with Stalin. They had come to China with orders to bring down Mao.

Unlike the others, Yang escaped the bitter political infighting and cast his lot with the army, joining Peng Dehuai as political commissar to Peng's Third Front Army. They had fought together against Chiang Kaishek's encirclement campaigns and then on the Long March. There was not a peril the two had not shared. Fifty years later Yang still carried three metal splinters in his leg, inflicted during a Nationalist bombing on the Yunnan front in 1935. Yang had been attacked while on horseback. He and his party were all riding dull brown horses, blending into the background, except for his friend General Wu Xiuquan, who was astride a flashy white steed. The white horse caught the eye of a low-flying KMT plane, and bombs began to fall. Years later Yang Shangkun seemed to take satisfaction that the horse that attracted the bombs was killed.[2]

There was no way that Yang could conceal from Mao his empathy and affection for Peng Dehuai.[3] Nor was there anything Yang could do to help Peng once Mao got him in his sights. It would have surprised few who knew of the long, close Peng-Yang friendship if Mao had immediately targeted Yang; Mao did not. In his characteristic manner he moved circuitously. There was plenty in Yang's background that Mao might have used. The Yang family had just the kind of well-to-do affiliation that had brought doom to so many during the anti-rightist, Party rectification, and Cultural Revolution drives.

Yang was far from the only high-ranking Party man whose background did not lie among the peasantry or the proletariat. The same was true of Mao, to some extent, and of Liu Shaoqi, Deng Xiaoping, and Zhou Enlai. Like Deng, Yang sprang from the Sichuan landowning class. Both spoke the broad Sichuan dialect. Yang Shangkun's family was the wealthiest in a broad area of northern Sichuan, east of Chengdu, not distant from that of Deng Xiaoping's home. The Yangs were the first family of Tongnan County, next door to Guang'an County, where Deng was born. The Yang family seat was the town of Suining, site of a famous temple. Deng's father sometimes made pilgrimages there.[4]

It was not often in his long, active career that Yang Shangkun paused to look back over his life, and at eighty he found it hard to recapture the China of his youth. Now he was inclined to think of his rich and prosperous father as a "rather tragic figure," a man who spent much of his life and much of his treasure in a quest for a path that would lead China out of the abyss into which it had fallen.

The Yang family was large and lively. Yang's father had several wives and many children. Yang Shangkun, born in 1908, was the second child of the second wife, his mother's first son.

When Yang spoke of the "tragic figure" of his father, he was thinking of the transitional society in which his father lived, which witnessed the shift from feudal landholding to an emerging world of manufacturing, business, trade, and banking, the birth of China's long-deferred industrial revolution. Yang's father was a rich landowner with many estates and peasant serfs and a large income. But in the troubled period of his life he and his sons would lose most of these assets.

On a small scale the trials and failures of Yang's father and his brothers mirrored the trials and failures of China as a whole. The great Sichuan landowning society, so much like that of Scotland in the Elizabethan period — a land of enormous contrasts between rich and poor, of endless tracts of land and few roads, an isolated countryside whose population was ignorant, superstitious, wary of strangers, very independent of and hostile to central authority — was on the point of dissolution. It was clan country, warlord country, opium country — Texas in China. Three great warlords to whom little warlords attached themselves ruled an ever-changing complex of fiefdoms.

As Yang Shangkun entered school, explosive new ideas were coming into the Sichuan countryside from Chengdu and Chongqing.

Yang's father was a staunch believer in education and a patriotic man. He insisted on education for all of his children, sons and daughters alike, which was unusual in that time and place.

Yang Shangkun had three elder brothers, sons of his father's first wife.[5] Each in his own way, Yang felt, was imbued with optimism and ambition to bring China into the modern era. It had not worked out as they had hoped.

The eldest, number-one brother, belonged to the Tong Meng, the fraternity of warlords. With capital provided by his father, he bought a small army. Soldiers were for sale, an item of commerce, like slaves. Small warlords raised small armies and sold them to bigger warlords. It was a profitable crop. But the number-one brother didn't have enough money; his army was too small. He ended up losing so much of the family fortune his brothers called him the family black sheep.

The number-two brother was convinced China's future lay in industrialization. China must build factories, railroads, ports, bridges. He would be a builder. He entered Tangshan University, in the city the great earthquake later would destroy. Its engineering faculty was renowned. The number-two brother specialized in bridge construction. After he graduated, however, he couldn't get any contracts. He went to Japan to study law, but in the end he succeeded only in spending more of his father's money.

Brother number three was Yang Angong, and his name in the late 1980s was still well known. He went to Japan for a military education, but he got a whiff of the new currents stirring society. When he came back to Sichuan he founded a left-Kuomintang organization that was to become the matrix of the Sichuan Communist Party. For many years he was the Sichuan Party head.

Yang's father was possessed by the same spirit as his sons. He was energetic, persistent, an optimist, and not too practical. He foresaw the end of the landowning society and tried to switch into the bourgeois world. His first plunge was a shipping venture on the Yangtze. None of his sons took part, and the enterprise was a disaster. The treasurer embezzled most of the money, and Yang had to sell his business to the Lu Zuo Fu Company, an outfit with a Canadian partner and warlord backing, which had 160 ships on the Yangtze and some ocean freighters.

"It was not possible for a small capitalist to succeed without the backing of a warlord," Yang observed. "To make the transition from landlord to capitalist you had to have a warlord's protection."

Failure on the Yangtze did not discourage Yang's father. He bought some trucks in Shanghai and tried land transportation. But he was ahead of his time. He failed again.

The movies came next. The father bought a movie house, which he thought could not fail. It did. He tried a motor livery service. That failed. By now he had sold most of his land. For the rest of his life he lived on rent from his remaining real estate. He turned to acupuncture and Chinese medicine and became a licensed practitioner. He limited his practice to gentlemen and warlords. He didn't bill them, but at New Year's they sent him fine presents.

He took on one other class of patients — Party members, whom he never charged either. If they needed medication he paid for it himself.

Yang Shangkun fell under the influence of his Communist brother, Yang Angong. He was fascinated by the meetings his brother held and was permitted to stand guard at the door, then allowed in to take notes.

When Yang Shangkun went to study in Chengdu, he joined a radical reading circle. It was less than a year after the May Fourth student protest of 1919, which set off excitement all over the country. Like most young Chinese, Yang and his fellow students were attracted to anarchism. They hadn't yet heard of Communism. They began to read a mimeograph monthly called "The Guide," and this led them to Nikolai Bukharin's *ABC of Communism*. Only the first half of Bukharin had been translated. When Yang went to Chongqing in 1924 after graduating from high school, he joined the Communist Youth League and in 1926 entered the Communist Party while attending Shanghai University.

Then he took a giant leap. The Party sent him to Moscow just before the Shanghai massacre of 1927. The duel of Leon Trotsky and Josef Stalin was then in full swing. Stalin inserted a loyal follower, Pavel Mif, into the Comintern apparatus to swing the Chinese into Stalinist waters. Mif was helped by Wang Ming, who had been sent from Shanghai to represent the Chinese Party. Together they trained a group of young Chinese and sent them back to challenge Mao Zedong. In later years there would be charges that Yang Shangkun was one of these 28½ Bolsheviks. Yang dismissed the allegation as nonsense.

Yang quickly became a Mao supporter. As political commissar of the Third Army, he sat in on the Zunyi conference, in January 1935, at which the commanders restored Mao as leader. When the Red Army

settled down in 1935 and 1936 in Yanan, Yang began to widen his
horizons. He and Peng Dehuai took over the Party's northern bureau
for several years. Zhu De joined them, as did Liu Shaoqi. These men
became the nucleus of Mao's revolution. In 1944 Yang Shangkun
became director of the Party's General Office.

It was not Yang's background that cost him his job at the General
Office twenty years later. Instead it was his role in installing a tape
recorder in the reception room where Chairman Mao received foreign
guests. For years Zhou Enlai and the Foreign Ministry had been
embarrassed by declarations made by Mao to heads of state of which
they had no knowledge. Mao had a phobia about secretaries who sat
in the corner and took notes. When he saw a notebook come out he
sent its owner packing. Nor was he conscientious in reporting to his
associates what he had told his visitors. Zhou Enlai tried to be present
when Mao received visitors, but this was not always possible; Mao
did not like to have anyone listening in.

The problem got worse as Mao grew older and more unpredictable.
Finally, after much discussion, probably at Zhou's initiative, it was
decided to put in a tape recorder so the government would not be
blindsided by Mao's off-the-cuff commitments. Almost certainly Mao
himself was consulted and gave a nod or grunt of approval. It is not
likely that Zhou or the others, after thirty or forty years of working
with Mao, would attempt anything so sensitive behind his back. Tian
Jianying probably participated in discussions about the taping. There
is reason to suspect that Mao knew precisely what was going on and
used it as a pretext to bring down Yang Shangkun.[6]

Action was taken in typical Mao style. First Yang Shangkun was
relieved of his General Office post, but he was not publicly disgraced.
In 1964 he was sent to Canton, where he became second secretary of
the Party organization. It was a comedown, although in itself it did
not imply oblivion or worse. But in mid-1965 Yang was returned to
Beijing for investigation, and the charges escalated. Now he was being
investigated for a state crime, espionage. He had, in the words that
Jiang Qing was later to utter, dared to record the top-secret words of
Chairman Mao, and he was a Soviet spy, conveying to his Russian
masters the innermost thoughts of Mao Zedong. Lin Biao took a hand
in all this.

This was what was behind the allegation, reported by Mei Xing to
Tian Jiaying, that Yang Shangkun was a member of an anti-Party

clique. From such an accusation there was no escape. Prison or the supreme penalty was certain.[7]

On June 30, 1966, thirty-eight days after Tian Jiaying took his life, the doors of Qincheng high-security prison swung shut on Yang Shangkun. Who could say when — if ever — this "Soviet spy" would be released? He was placed in solitary confinement. It was years before he learned that in the cell next door was Yan Mingfu, respected high Party activist and son of one of Zhou Enlai's closest associates. Yan, too, it was charged, was a Soviet spy and traitor.

24

The Zoo Caper

TIAN JIAYING never realized that his value to Mao had been as a barometer of the economic, social, and political fallout of the Great Leap. Mao had retreated into a defensive crouch, but he was preparing a comeback. Tian provided him with a guide to the political winds.

Mao had turned over economic direction to Liu Shaoqi and Deng Xiaoping. He did this in the course of an extraordinary conclave assembled in the West Building of Zhongnanhai in January 1962, attended by seven thousand Party workers and run by Deng and Liu. Their hard-edged practicality shows through the decisions made at the conference. No more backyard steel mills. No more tacky rhetoric. Quiet, off-the-record experiments in profit motivation for the peasants (it worked like a charm but ended when Mao found out about it).

Deng and Liu acted, so it was said, under a five-year contract that Mao had agreed to under which Mao would keep his hands off economics and give them a free rein at restoring the country. It was too good to be true. But Liu and Deng had a powerful weapon. They had discovered the size of the deficit that Mao was running. China was bankrupt. The country was running on empty.

Knowledge of Mao's deficits had been acquired, as Red Guard documents were to disclose, through a secret audit of Mao's operations over the previous four years. Special attention was paid to orders and directives sent out in the name of the Party Central Committee but never discussed by or presented to that body. The telltale papers bore Mao's signature. The audit originated in 1961 with Peng Zhen, long a member of the ruling elite. Deng Xiaoping was closely associated with the enterprise. The role of Liu Shaoqi remains shadowy.

The setting of the secret audit was straight from an old kungfu movie. The investigators met in the garden of an ancient estate in northwest Beijing, close by the route followed by the dowager empress Ci Xi when she visited the Summer Palace. The estate, once the greatest park in Beijing, had fallen into disarray. In 1906 the empress turned it into a zoo, populated by a collection of birds and animals purchased in Germany for 1 million silver taels (about $200,000) and given to the old lady by a well-to-do Manchu official. The dilapidated palaces got a coat of whitewash, bars and cages were installed, and the place was opened as the Garden of Ten Thousand Animals. It had been going downhill ever since. Beijing residents displayed a lack of interest in the seedy menagerie. In 1937 Betsy, the last elephant, died, shot by Japanese marksmen. Soon the Japanese occupiers poisoned the remaining lions, tigers, and leopards as a precaution, they said, against their getting loose during an air raid. When Mao's Red Army marched into Beijing in 1949, the zoo comprised twelve monkeys, two parrots, and a blind emu. The new regime got a rehabilitation program under way, but the zoo had few visitors.

The clandestine auditing commission, guarded by a squad of soldiers, moved to a shabby zoo building, sat down on folding chairs, spread their documents out on a table, and went to work. Peng Zhen felt it unlikely Mao would hear of the unusual party at the zoo. He was right.[1]

The scope of inquiry suggested that an effort was afoot to retire Mao. When the proceedings were uncovered by the Red Guards during the Cultural Revolution, they charged that Deng Xiaoping and Liu Shaoqi indeed had this intention, and the evidence suggests that the Red Guards may have been right. Mao's status had, in fact, shrunk. He had, for reasons obscure, given up his title as president to Liu Shaoqi in 1959. Earlier he had turned over day-to-day operations to

Deng, who had proved to be a take-charge executive. The Red Guards were to allege that Deng didn't bother to consult Mao, handled everything himself, and showed little respect for Mao, a claim that Mao rather plaintively confirmed, saying he never got any reports from Deng. Throughout his career Deng was dogged by complaints that he was in too much of a hurry to bother to inform others of what he was doing.

It was no easy task to get China back on track. In the summer of 1960 Khrushchev landed another blow, announcing that the Soviet Union was pulling out all its technicians and their blueprints. This move struck deeper than China was willing to admit. The great Wuhan steelworks was dead in the water, unfinished and inoperable. A dozen years later the author found it half-deserted, most of the shops idle.[2] Han Suyin, the famous Euro-Chinese writer, reported that the Anshun coalfields were operating at 20 percent capacity because the Russians had left electrical installations, water pumps, and air blowers half-finished.[3] In every industrial town in China there were factories with smokeless chimneys, bridges half-built, buildings in disarray.

The food crisis eased a bit. Deng and Liu bought six million tons of grain on the world market and dug the money out of Mao's crippled budget to pay for it. A good many projects were put on hold as a result. Mao was furious. Grain had to be paid for in foreign exchange. It was a step backward, he felt, toward capitalism. But Deng and Liu had to have quick results. The country could not go on starving. "Communism is not poverty," Deng said. Deng was aggressive in restoring the economy. He seemed to think that if he got things moving, fed the people, started up the stalled factories, it didn't make much difference if he used profit incentives.

Deng was never good at keeping his tongue in his mouth. As early as January 1961, at the Central Committee's plenary session, he put it on the line: "Any idea which cannot be carried out and does not hold water must be rectified no matter who initiated it."[4] A clean shot at Mao.

To make his point even more plain, Deng spoke the words that were to become his trademark: "It does not matter whether the cat is black or white. So long as it catches the mouse it is a good cat."

With these words Marx went out the window. Lenin went out the window. So did Mao.

Mao had signed off on economic direction for five years. He had temporarily lost his majority in the Central Committee, the Party, and even the Standing Committee of the Politburo. But he was far from down and far from out.

There was, Mao knew, a growing movement backed by elements in the army to reverse the verdict on Peng Dehuai. If Peng was rehabilitated, if he once more could speak his blunt words in the Central Committee and the Politburo, Mao would see greater erosion of his political position.

Mao turned to the resource he knew best — Ssu-ma Ch'ien (Sima Qian in current pinyin), not the texts of Marx or Lenin or Engels or Stalin. Ssu-ma Ch'ien was the author of *Shi Ji*, the classic study of the annals of China that Mao's guards had placed by his bedside on the first night he spent within view of the old capital.

Here Mao found a text to apply to the political crisis of the day. Taking a philosophical stance, he asked his audience at the West Building on January 30, 1962, why it should be assumed that men's careers always went up and endlessly up. Why should they not go up and down and perhaps up again? Or possibly sidewise. What was wrong with that? It was good for you. Demotion and transfer built character. They strengthened revolutionary resolve. They gave you a chance to study and acquire new knowledge and new skills.

"I myself have had experience in this respect," said Mao, "and gathered a good deal of benefit." Perhaps he was thinking of the times he had been abused by Stalin. "If you do not believe me," Mao added, "try it yourself."

He quoted a passage from Ssu-ma Ch'ien. When Confucius was in trouble he compiled the *Spring and Autumn Annals,* possibly his great work. Han Fei had been imprisoned in the kingdom of Chin and was so angry he wrote a classic; Sun Tzu, author of *The Art of War,* had written it after a cruel emperor ordered his feet amputated.

In each case, said Mao, the men had been subjected to unjust punishment but had risen to make a contribution of genius. Mao did not mention that Ssu-ma Ch'ien himself had been castrated by a wrathful emperor yet went on to write his incomparable commentary.

Mao said he did not support unfair and wrongful acts; he merely wanted to demonstrate that many had risen from anguish to great accomplishment. That Mao had in mind the case of Peng Dehuai was plain to his listeners. He was implying that nothing bad would happen to Peng and that quite possibly much good would emerge. Of all Mao's hypocritical pronouncements, this proved the most specious.

But Mao achieved his short-term objective — the pressure for the restoration of Peng Dehuai faded away. Not even the doughty old warrior's recent twenty-thousand-character letter to Mao could change that.[5]

There were those in Mao's audience in January 1962 at the Tenth Plenary of the Eighth Central Committee who thought his observations on Ssu-ma Ch'ien were the ramblings of an old man approaching retirement. True, Mao would be sixty-nine in 1962, seventy by Chinese calculation. Some may have thought he was amusing when in September 1962 he recalled Peng's angry defense at Lushan of his right to challenge Mao — or, in the vernacular, to fuck his mother. "All this fucking," Mao observed, "messed up the conference and the work was affected. . . . We really mustn't do that this time."

He spoke as though Lushan had not ended with Peng removed from office, humiliated, and charged with treason. Mao continued to talk with Peng in mind. He spoke of the Party's policy on punishment and execution. The Party had a ban on executions. But if a person was guilty of sabotage or espionage (as he had claimed Peng was), he was prepared to lift that ban. However, he added, even those guilty of sabotage had not, in fact, been executed. He offered a list of convicted offenders. At least one of those he named was unjustly accused.[6]

"We must not arrest people lightly," Mao said, "and we must especially not execute them lightly. It isn't good to kill people."

He warned against "putting hats" on people; that is, labeling them capitalist roader, rightist, or revisionist. That stirred up bad feelings. It was, as it turned out, a precise prescription — in reverse — for what Mao would soon do.

He revealed that the Party had banned Peng and four others from attending the Tenth Plenary. They would not be permitted on Tiananmen Gate at the 1962 October 1 celebration.

Looking back, it was apparent that Mao had begun to set the chessboard for the Cultural Revolution. He may not yet have decided on its shape, but it was forming fast. Some Party leaders were wise enough to run for cover. One of them was Chen Yun, a senior specialist in economics, a man who had been trusted with the most confidential of missions between Moscow and the Chinese Party. Chen Yun would soon enter a Beijing hospital "for treatment." He was not really very ill; he just thought it a safer place to spend a little time.[7] Not many of Chen Yun's comrades could match him in foresight.

*   *   *

These murky moves by Mao and other top leaders were hard for the participants to follow. To the rest of the world, they remained an enigma.

Attention was focused on the growing rift within the Communist camp. There had been a brief period after the fall of Khrushchev, in 1964, when many thought the Sino-Soviet conflict would fade. The opposite had happened: The polemics had resumed more angrily than ever. The Communist world was choosing sides. The Russians had the edge. All of Eastern Europe except Albania joined Moscow. So did the important parties of France and Italy. China had only Albania, Vietnam, and North Korea. This struggle preempted the time and energy of Zhou Enlai, leaving Liu Shaoqi and Deng Xiaoping a free hand in day-to-day domestic operations.

Behind the wall of American-inspired diplomatic and trade isolation, China had become a hermit kingdom. The war with India flared up, then died down. The Hong Kong listening posts found Chinese politics too complex for analysis. Not many visitors got into China. Lord Montgomery had a long talk with Mao in 1961 and asked him who his successor would be. Mao replied that it would be Liu Shaoqi.[8] Edgar Snow, after an unexplained banishment of twenty years, got back to Beijing. Mao told him some Chinese officials thought he had become an "enemy." Snow saw Mao in 1960 and again in 1965, and Mao later told Snow that it was just after their January 1965 meeting that he decided Liu Shaoqi "must go." The day, Mao recalled, was January 25.[9]

January 25, 1965, is an arbitrary date for Mao's rejection of Liu as his successor. It represents the day of the chairman's last angry confrontation with Liu. Another of the interminable, long-winded plenaries, enlarged Politburo sessions, and work conferences was going on. Mao submitted a twenty-three-point document. Ostensibly it presented Mao's new drive, for "Four Cleansings," a general reform of the Party in economics, ideology, politics, and organization. The twenty-three points, in fact, were twenty-three articles that Mao's secretary Chen Boda had written under Mao's close supervision.

"The key point of this movement," Mao's program declared, "is to rectify those people in a position of authority within the Party who take the capitalist road." Some of these individuals, Mao asserted, were already out in the open, occupying positions in the highest echelons. Some actually harbored capitalists among their relatives (outside the mainland). It was well known that Liu Shaoqi had such relatives.

If necessary, said Mao through his amanuensis, Chen Boda, the people would take over as the capitalist roaders were rooted out. This call to the masses was Mao's favorite prescription.

"We must boldly unleash the masses," Mao proclaimed. "We must not be like women with bound feet."[10]

Liu Shaoqi, Deng Xiaoping, and Chen Yun all disagreed with Mao's capitalist-roader line. A violent row resulted in which, it was said, the quiet, normally complaisant Liu Shaoqi lost his temper. He did not know this would cost him his life.[11]

There was no sign that these men realized Mao was preparing to assign them the roles of capitalist roaders. Deng's response to Mao may have been more guarded than that of the others, for Han Suyin found evidence that Mao at this point continued to make a distinction between Liu and Deng.

Distinctions there certainly were: Liu Shaoqi was to become capitalist roader number one; Deng, capitalist roader number two. Liu was to die, Deng to survive.

Thus, starting from January 25, 1965, China's most bizarre political movement — the Cultural Revolution — would gather momentum, ultimately to encompass the whole country and all of its people.

PART 5

THE RAGE OF *LUAN*

25

Poisoned Paper

THE IDENTITY of the author of the great Chinese erotic classic, *Jin Ping Mei* (The Golden Lotus), is not known with certainty, but for three hundred years readers have believed him to be a scholar named Wang Xicheng.

The book, so legend has it, represents Wang's vengeance on the son of a man who condemned Wang's father to death after a dispute over ownership of a famous painting. The novel's hero is a recognizable caricature of Wang's enemy.

Nor is that all. As Wang wrote out his book on sheets of fine rice paper with his camel's hair brush, he squeezed a pinpoint of poison onto each page. The drop caused the sheets to stick together slightly — just enough so the reader would have to moisten a finger to turn to the next page.

Wang sent the book to his enemy, who rapidly read it cover to cover, licking his finger again and again, each time absorbing a bit of poison. As he turned the last page he fell dead.

Whatever the truth of the story, the tale of the poisoned papers has enthralled generations of readers of *Jin Ping Mei*.

Among those readers was Mao Zedong. *Jin Ping Mei* was one of hundreds (more likely thousands) of erotic books contained in the special library largely collected for Mao by his secret police specialist, Kang Sheng. The emperors of the Tang and the Ming, the Yuan and the Qing, all possessed such collections, housing them in special rooms at their palaces to which only they and sometimes their consorts had access. The Study of Chrysanthemum Fragrance had been used as a library under the Qing and possibly the Ming. It is tempting to speculate that Mao's exquisite quarters had once housed the special collections of some of his predecessors.

Mao's library, which equaled that possessed by any emperor, dated to Yanan days. Kang Sheng had been providing Mao since the late 1930s with erotica, especially hand-colored "pillow books," foldout picture guides to sexual practices.

No nation in the world, as one scholar noted, possesses richer and more varied erotica than China.[1] Among all these works *The Golden Lotus* is the greatest. It affords a panoramic view of Chinese upper-class society in the twelfth century, as well as explicit sexual passages so detailed that puritanical English scholars who made the early translations rendered page after page in Latin to discourage prurient eyes.[2]

Mao's possession of the finest collection of erotica in the People's Republic was not generally known, although his sexual proclivities hardly could be hidden from higher Party intimates. His bedroom-cum-study was as public a reception room as the bedchamber of Catherine the Great of Russia.

That Kang Sheng should have assisted Mao in forming his "dirty picture" collection was consistent with the character of this man who had insinuated Jiang Qing into Mao's circle. Kang Sheng made it his business to supply Mao with sexual partners. There is evidence that he was not the only police official who curried Mao's favor by these means. Like the establishment of art ensembles to provide Mao with dancing partners, all this was very much in the imperial tradition. As early as the Tang dynasty what was called a *qiao fang* was established, in which young girls by the hundreds were trained as dancers and palace women. Mao's establishments paled by comparison with the battalions of females assembled for possible use by earlier emperors.[3] About this time Mao, by some accounts, began to indulge in sexual water sports, filling his heated indoor swimming pool with bevies of unclad young women. Mao's taste fell far short of the beautiful erotic tableaux staged by the Mongol emperors in the Zhongnanhai lakes that so scandalized their Han servitors. The new emperor's water sports had all the subtlety of a rutting walrus.

Security considerations were never overlooked where Mao's women were concerned. Kang Sheng was ever on guard lest the Kuomintang smuggle in a female assassin. But he did not go so far as the emperor's eunuchs of bygone days who stripped the lady of the evening, wrapped her in a silken scarf, and loaded her onto the back of a stout servant, who lugged her in to the emperor. Naked, she was unable to conceal a dagger that might be employed against her imperial mate.[4]

Of course the use of sex as an avenue to power was not invented by China or Kang Sheng. He was following a well-traveled path. His mentor, Lavrenty Beria, Stalin's security boss, had employed the same tactic in ingratiating himself, and Kang Sheng had spent much time in Moscow learning the tricks of his trade.

Like those of many of his associates, Kang Sheng's origins lay not with the rudimentary Chinese proletariat or the great sea of peasantry but in the gentry. He came from a well-to-do Shandong family in Zucheng, a town of twenty thousand, about twenty kilometers from Qingdao. Kang's family was large and prosperous enough so that the widely believed story of Jiang Qing's being sold into the household as a teenage slave is at least plausible.

Kang's family lived in Zucheng at the time Jiang Qing, fourteen or fifteen years younger than Kang, was born there. It is also established that Jiang suffered poverty and hardship in her early years and that there was a connection between her and Kang, with each using the other for selfish motives.

In those days Kang Sheng looked a bit like a provincial schoolmaster, wearing round steel-rimmed glasses that gave him a vaguely unoriental appearance. His face was lean and bony, with high cheekbones, recessive eyes, and a sallow complexion. Early photographs are rare, but pictures of leadership groups in the 1950s and 1960s often show him with Mao and Zhou Enlai, usually standing to the rear, not prominent, just within the range of focus. He favored a black fedora that made him look a little like a Chinese John Foster Dulles. Many older Party members remembered something unpleasant about his smile — his lips moved but his eyes stared coldly.

Kang was born around the turn of the century, some said 1898 or 1899. Edgar Snow suggested 1903. An early recruit to Communism, he joined the Communist Youth League in Shanghai and became a Party member in 1925 or 1926. He worked in the Shanghai organization, survived the 1927 massacre, and went into the underground. By the time he went to Moscow in 1932, Stalin was planning to take over the Chinese Party and oust any Trotskyite support from its international and security divisions.

Nothing is more misty than how Kang spent his time in Moscow. Chinese associates caught glimpses of him at the Kuntsevo dacha, which Stalin put at the disposal of high-level Chinese visitors. Kang lent the Russians a hand in purging the Chinese Party of alleged Trotskyites and helped Soviet security specialists in purging some other foreign Communist parties. One of his victims was the famous Korean revolutionary Kim San.[5] Some Russian sources believe Kang Sheng was an agent of the Russian NKVD, as the security force was then called. They contend Kang played an active role in the arrest and imprisonment of Li Lisan, Chinese Party secretary, then in Moscow, and that Li Lisan and his wife were released after twenty-two months in prison only due to intervention by Zhou Enlai.[6]

Vladimir Lenin was once asked why he permitted so much corruption in the underground Bolshevik organization, employing unscrupulous men and even known criminals. Lenin made no apology. "Ours is a big business," he said. "We can use all kinds of trash." On another occasion Lenin observed, "Revolution is a dirty business. You do not make it with white gloves."[7]

The Lenin philosophy that the end justified almost any means was shared by Mao. Kang Sheng fitted Lenin's definition of revolutionary trash, and Mao found him useful. If Kang Sheng did not use the poisoned paper of the author of *The Golden Lotus,* the papers he prepared for the Party were just as deadly.

By the time Kang came to Yanan he found that Jiang Qing had arrived there with other young women of the Shanghai theater and film world. He helped her get into the Lu Xun Arts and Literature College, where she quickly met Mao. When the question of her marriage to Mao provoked angry dispute among Party seniors (and especially their wives) who felt that a second-rate actress of questionable background was hardly the person to marry the Party's chairman, Kang Sheng stepped into the breach. He defended Jiang's background, although she had confessed to him that she had forsworn the Party and signed an incriminating denunciation in order to get out of Chiang Kaishek's jail. With an airy "I know all about that. She's OK," Kang waved her into the Party and into Mao's bed.

Later Kang claimed that he had discovered "KMT elements" in the Party, and he started a purge that Mao halted. Undeterred, he dreamed up a similar "infusion of agents" in the Red Army. He was well into another purge before Mao stopped it. As the Red Army began to drive south, Kang Sheng started to ferret out "hidden capitalists" and "enemies of the people." Mao and Zhou Enlai reined him in — but not entirely.[8] Not long after the proclamation of the People's Republic, Mao sent him away to run Shandong Province.

*   *   *

When Kang Sheng returned to Beijing in 1958, he began to provide Mao with much younger partners. They now attended the chairman in couplets, triplets, or even greater numbers. "His bed was filled with young girls," an old Party member snapped.[9]

From the mid-1960s to the early 1970s, Mao's quarters sometimes swarmed with young women. It was like a latter-day harem. An important woman whose duties required her to go daily to Mao's quarters simply did not appear during these sexual saturnalia. She stayed away until things quieted down. "After Wang Hairong and Nancy Tang came in as Mao's assistants," she said, "they tried to clear the place out, not always succeeding."[10]

Kang Sheng uncovered rarities for Mao's special collection, items that had originally been in the collections of the emperors. He enlisted the assistance of antiquarians and curators, including Wu Zhongqiao of the Forbidden City museums. He built up a collection for himself as well, which by the time of the Cultural Revolution contained ten thousand works of art and more than forty thousand books. Many of these were valuable classical antiquities purloined from the Forbidden City museums. By no means all of these items were of an erotic nature. Kang Sheng acquired valuable paper from the museums, often hundreds of years old, in addition to rare books.[11]

Once the Cultural Revolution roared into high gear, with tens of thousands of ignorant teenage Red Guards pulling houses to pieces in search of the Four Olds, Kang Sheng acquired more and more valuable items. On occasion he was seen picking over heaps of manuscripts and artworks tossed into the street by the Red Guards, pulling from the piles valuable erotica before the Guards set fire to the pyres. Nor was Kang Sheng the only collector in the family. After the death of Mao and the fall of the Gang of Four, Kang's widow was accused of stealing from state museums and libraries to add to her private collections.[12]

Kang Sheng died in 1975, less than a year before his master, Mao Zedong, just early enough to get a full state funeral and escape the fate of Jiang Qing and the Gang of Four, public trial and conviction. He was posthumously expelled from the Party in 1980 and his crimes denounced. Twenty-five years after the reign of terror in which he was Mao's chief manipulator, his name was hardly known beyond China.

Nor was that of Chen Boda, Mao's personal secretary and alter ego for nearly thirty years, the man who personified Mao's most evil impulses. Chen Boda personally gave the orders that led to the death of President Liu Shaoqi and to the brutal treatment of Liu's wife, Wang Guangmei, and the rest of the family, of whom no fewer than four died and eight were imprisoned. All this was set in train by the chubby-faced tool of the chairman.[13] That Mao was a true "person of hatred," in the words of the nonagenarian Chen Hansheng, would now be demonstrated on a scale that would eclipse even the savagery of his role model, the emperor Qin.

Chen Boda was not a man to attract attention. His slablike face and figure could have been molded from *jiaozi* dough. He walked with an ambling gait and always seemed a bit out of breath, perhaps suffering from asthma. He went to work for Mao in the Yanan period. He wrote many of Mao's speeches under Mao's painstaking direction, edited papers, handled propaganda. One of Mao's principal secretaries, he specialized in ideology and politics. Chen Boda, unlike most high-ranking cadres, had not participated in the Long March and had no military experience or links to the army. Once Chen entered Mao's intimate orbit he stayed there. Mao was often reluctant to speak out himself, and in those cases Chen Boda served as his voice.

Like so many of the top echelon, Chen Boda had gone to Moscow, attending the Sun Yatsen University, and had learned to speak Russian and gotten Soviet orientation. However, according to Edgar Snow, he ducked the cutthroat politics that embroiled the Russian-trained Chinese.

For many years Chen Boda had been number two to Lu Dingyi, a senior, much-respected Party man who headed the propaganda department. Judging by Chen Boda's conduct toward Lu Dingyi during the Cultural Revolution, Chen Boda reeked with jealousy. Not much matched Chen Boda's vitriol toward his former boss.

Kang Sheng and Chen Boda were Mao's personal players in the Great Proletarian Cultural Revolution. Mao's wife took a much more visible role as she paid off old scores and dreamed of mounting the Dragon Throne. Lin Biao, the silent and gifted general, acted out another phantasmagoria — that he would vault over Mao Zedong, Zhou Enlai, Jiang Qing, and all the others to himself wear the emperor's crown.

The hard core of the Cultural Revolution was to be found in the Central Cultural Revolution Group, an ad hoc apparatus in which Jiang Qing quickly emerged as the leader. She and three fellow members evolved into what Mao later dubbed the Gang of Four. Jiang

Qing's associates were from Shanghai. A major figure in the group was Zhang Chunqiao, a heavyset veteran Party worker, an ideologue who used the Cultural Revolution to climb into Party leadership in Shanghai, an active, aggressive man in his mid-sixties. His right-hand man was the polemicist Yao Wenyuan, author of the famous Hai Rui article, a sharp-tongued, fish-eyed man of forty-six in 1966. The third member was Wang Hongwen, forty years old at the time the Cultural Revolution started, a worker in the Number 17 Cotton Textile factory, a trade unionist who advanced politically through his union. He was to blame for thousands of deaths caused by riots that he launched during the Cultural Revolution. All three men entered the Party Politburo, and two served as the inner-circle Standing Committee.

Wang Hongwen was groomed by the Gang for high office. He took over the top political job in the PLA. Mao finally was shocked by Wang's ignorance and arrogance. Wang worked hard to displace Deng Xiaoping but ultimately failed. It was rumored that Jiang Qing chose him as a lover.[14]

All four Gang members wound up in the dock after their arrest in October 1976 and were convicted. Jiang Qing was sentenced to death but the sentence, in effect, was commuted to life imprisonment. She developed cancer of the throat and was transferred to house arrest to facilitate treatment. On June 4, 1991, it was officially announced that Jiang had committed suicide in her home on May 14. She had been sunk, it was said, in a deep depression and had left a long letter denouncing Deng Xiaoping.

After it was all over — Lin Biao long since dead; Jiang Qing dead; Mao Zedong dead; Zhou Enlai dead, Zhu De dead, Kang Sheng dead and Chen Boda vanished; when the survivors of the band of brothers who made the Revolution and the Long March had reached their late eighties and early nineties — they sat around and asked how it could have happened. How could Mao have unleashed the Cultural Revolution?

Chen Yun observed, as many of his comrades had, that had Mao died in 1956 he would have been hailed as China's great — even greatest — leader. Had he died ten years later, history still would have placed him very high. But, alas, he died in 1976. What more could be said?[15] Not many survivors would quarrel with Chen Yun's words.

Why did Mao do it? The conventional explanation had been that he saw power slipping away and took a throw of the dice to win it back. But those who knew Mao best did not accept this. Some suggested that his gambit of the Cultural Revolution grew out of frustration with the Soviet Union, which he believed was moving into "revisionism" and capitalism. He was also frustrated with China's slow progress. He began to believe that his own associates had embarked on the course he felt Russia had taken. After two great revolutions, Russian and Chinese, the world was turning away from Communism. He resolved to mobilize the Chinese masses, by which he believed anything could be achieved, and lead them into a new and greater revolution.

Yan Mingfu, one of the most shrewd observers of Mao, a man who had been brought up, so to say, "in the family," who had known Yanan, whose father had belonged to the inner circle, who had watched Mao at the closest range, believed that it was the bitter and deeply emotional quarrel with Moscow that set Mao on course to his new revolution. In all of this, he felt, Kang Sheng had a major hand, reinforcing Mao's paranoia, feeding it with bits of gossip or distortions of what was happening. Once he got back to Beijing, Kang began to take a greater and greater part in all affairs concerning Russia. He accompanied Mao at some of the discussions and took every step possible to bring himself closer, slipping in his poisoned words and reports at every chance.[16]

Mao once quoted with approval a declaration by the Sui dynasty emperor Yangjian. Yangjian's father had reunited the divided north and south of China in the sixth century, and Yangjian broadened and strengthened the kingdom, building the Grand Canal to join the north and south. But foreign attacks broke out, and the upstart Tang forces closed on the emperor and his court. The emperor was badly wounded in the fighting and, realizing the end was near, called his court around him and said: "I have made this world and now I am losing this world. I have done this all myself. I have no regrets. I win and lose by my own deeds."

These words, the scholar Li Rui thought, might have been in Mao's mind as he headed into the Cultural Revolution. It was his revolution, his to win, his to lose. It was his China. He had made it.[17]

Hu Qiaomu, Mao's secretary for many years beginning in 1941 and himself a man of great complexity, felt that few observers realized the contradictions in Mao's personality. He could be strict and relaxed at the same time. Hu Qiaomu rejected Richard Nixon's analysis that Mao was "100 percent poet" and Zhou Enlai "50 percent poet." Mr. Nixon, Hu felt, made a "50 percent error." Mao was a poet all right, but he was also the leader of the army, the leader of the nation, and the leader of the Party. No poet, Hu believed, could perform all of these functions. But Mao was a poet, too, and that made a big difference. It gave him powers of imagination.

"If his imagination was misguided," said Hu Qiaomu, "it could inflict heavy losses or even disasters for his cause. And, as it happened, this was the case."

Without perceiving this overriding characteristic of Mao's personality, Hu felt, it was not possible to analyze his conduct as national leader, military chief, revolutionary leader, and the man who launched the Cultural Revolution, or to grasp the nature of his relations with his longtime colleagues.

Hu Qiaomu believed it was necessary to realize that Mao was absent from Beijing for extremely long periods, even — especially — during crises. He was still the "center of China" wherever he was. But to be the center of China in lovely Hangzhou while the crisis was in Beijing or, perhaps, Moscow was a very different thing. This resulted in many "contradictions," Hu said. Others might have used the word "aberrations."[18]

Mao was strongly inclined to "total solutions." He believed in philosophy as an instrument of change and that society was always in flux between periods of stability and periods of *luan*, chaos. Change arose from *luan*. Stability was static. In a state of upheaval, progress was made and new, capable people and ideas emerged.

The Mao scholar Li Zehou quotes Mao as saying after he read the history of China's Warring States, "It is a delight to read. But when it moves to the peaceful years I hate it. Not because I love chaos but because a time of peace is not good for the development of the people. It is unbearable."[19]

Whether all this underlay Mao's fatalistic decision will never be known. He kept no diary, and none of his secretaries was privy to all his thoughts. But there can be no question that Mao well understood his historic achievement in routing Chiang Kaishek and uniting China under the Communist banner, and he also believed that the crusade ultimately called the Cultural Revolution was an even greater enterprise. It was, in his view, a revolution not only to save his revolution but to perfect it, endangered as he believed it to be by contamination, impurities, and even treason from within. It must be saved from the men who had helped to create it. In this Kang Sheng's poisoned words played a part.

If Mao achieved success in his new campaign it would, he reckoned, be the ultimate deed of his career, overshadowing even the establishment of the People's Republic in 1949. This, he was confident, would place his name not among the great men of China but at the head of the list, as the emperor of emperors.[20]

26

"Silly Child! You Still Don't Know Anything!"

THE FAMILY of Liu Shaoqi, president of the People's Republic of China, was a very proper Communist family, close-knit, as dedicated to hard work as any Yankee household, believers in Karl Marx and loyal followers of Mao Zedong. They lived in a pleasant palace in Zhongnanhai.

Liu Shaoqi himself was a workaholic, a rather humorless father not given to romping with his four younger children. One rainy day he did teach them how to play poker, an event they remembered years later with warmth. Liu was more likely to speak to them about the Four Cleansings than to tell jokes.[1]

Liu Shaoqi followed the custom of conducting "daily life" meetings with his family and household staff. This was an old Party tradition intended to keep fresh ties to the grass roots. Liu would listen to the cooks and maids complaining that "the price of fish is too high," "we can't find any cotton cloth on the market," or "we don't understand the Party slogan about revisionism." Someone might criticize Liu himself, although this seldom happened. Liu would then offer explanations.

Early in 1966 he suffered a serious illness. When the doctor pronounced him out of danger he called his children and staff to his bedside. He was sixty-eight, and he felt that his life was drawing toward an end. He must hurry with his work. There was so much to do.

"If Karl Marx could give me ten more years," Liu said, "we could build China stronger and richer."

It was the curious conceit of atheistic Chinese Communists to say they were "going to meet Marx," as though he were God in the Communist heaven. The Chinese may have picked up this notion from their Russian cousins, who used the same figure of speech.

No one could — or so it seemed — challenge Liu Shaoqi's credentials as a pillar of Communism. He was, after all, the author of *How to Be a Communist,* the best-selling book in China by a margin of millions, until in 1966 Mao Zedong's "little red book" appeared. So far as the Liu children could remember, their father and mother showed no concern as the Cultural Revolution rather clumsily got under way in late 1965 and early 1966.[2] There is no evidence that Deng Xiaoping and his wife and family had any greater premonition.

As for Zhou Enlai — as is so often the case — it is not possible to penetrate that enigma. More than anyone else, Zhou was in a position to understand Mao. He had been as close as skin to glove with Mao since early 1935. He had, as a courtier, carefully cultivated Jiang Qing. He had known and worked with Kang Sheng. What did Zhou know or suspect? He gave no hint.

Mao had launched what he called the Four Cleansings movement in 1964; it contained the seeds of the Cultural Revolution. He had the Central Committee set up a new group to clean out writers and poets who he thought might follow the example of the Hungarian literati whose Petofi Circle had led the Budapest uprising in 1956. To head this special unit, known as the Cultural Revolution Committee, he picked Peng Zhen, the rather independent old Beijing workhorse. Little was notable about the committee except for one member: Kang Sheng. There was no outcry from Liu, Deng, or Zhou Enlai over Mao's gambit. Mao had cracked down on China's writers many times. Déjà vu prevailed.

No more sophisticated woman existed in China in 1966 than Liu Shaoqi's wife, Wang Guangmei. Daughter of a distinguished family dedicated to foreign service and international affairs, she was perfectly groomed, gifted in languages (she spoke English, French, and Russian), as chic as any woman walking in the Faubourg St. Honoré. You had only to be introduced to Wang Guangmei to know you were in the presence of a woman of self-assurance, tact, breeding, intelligence. Madame Mitterrand of France became her friend in the 1980s. She was a legend among the surviving men and women who had made the New China. This, to be certain, was very troublesome in a society dominated by Mao and Jiang Qing. No matter how gracious, how modest, how reticent Wang Guangmei might be, no one could doubt she was a great lady.

Wang Guangmei's father had been a high-ranking official in the first Republican government. He had spent time in London and Washington, and he named his son and daughter accordingly. The name Guangmei, which means Beautiful Girl of a Glorious Household, also contains a delicate reference to America, which in Chinese is called *mei guo* (beautiful country); Guangmei's father had been stationed in America when she was born. Her brother, born when her father was in London, was named Guangying, Brave Hero of a Glorious Household, which echoes the Chinese name for England, *ying guo* (heroic country). The Chinese had chosen the names for America and England to flatter the conquering powers.

Wang Guangmei had worked as a translator for the Red Chinese during General Marshall's ill-fated effort to mediate between Mao and Chiang Kaishek. She had dazzled both Chinese and Americans with her skills and intelligence. In the perverted imagination of Kang Sheng and Chen Boda this made her an American agent and possibly a Russian spy as well.

Wang was far too cosmopolitan not to understand that by her very existence she was bound to ruffle the feathers of Jiang Qing. In the Yanan days after marriage to Mao, Jiang Qing had seemed to be an ordinary housewife who whipped up plain but not untasty dinners for her husband and his guests, sometimes foreign correspondents but usually fellow cave dwellers.

It was in Yanan that Wang Guangmei and Liu Shaoqi met, during the last days there, in 1946, just before the pullout. She was twenty-five and Liu was forty-eight. His first wife had been killed in Jiangxi before the Long March. Graduating from Beijing's Furen University, Wang Guangmei had compiled a brilliant academic record. She had a master's degree in nuclear physics and probably was the best mathematics student in the history of Furen, originally a Benedictine Catholic school under American influence.[3] Stanford University and the University of Michigan each offered her a full scholarship, but at the urging of friends in the Communist underground she decided to stay in China and work for her country. She flew into Yanan in 1946 from Beijing with Marshal Ye Jianying. Although the marshal was much smitten with her, she turned him down in favor of Liu Shaoqi. She once explained to her daughter Tingting that Liu was a broader, more thoughtful man. The marshal was too military for her taste. (She probably didn't fancy being one more on his already long string of women.)⁴ She and Liu Shaoqi were married late in 1948.

When the People's Republic was established, formal political and diplomatic receptions and meetings with ambassadors, visiting dignitaries, and luminaries of the world began to give life a new gloss. Liu was vice president and attended many of these functions. In 1959 he became president, and the horizon broadened. His impeccably mannered wife began to appear at his side. The contrast with Jiang Qing, gauche, overeager, overdressed, insecure, became plain to everyone and certainly to Jiang, still hobbled by the old Party ban on her participation in politics. As Wang Guangmei began to move with her husband in international circles, it was obvious that Jiang Qing had contracted a severe case of what the Chinese call the red-eyed disease — jealousy.

It is impossible to imagine a woman like Wang Guangmei not being aware of Jiang Qing's feelings. But there is no sign that she or her husband saw this as a danger. Liu did admonish Wang protectively to remember that "you're not the First Lady."

Mao left Beijing early in the autumn of 1965. He did not wait for cold winds to send their icy message through the ill-fitting windows of Zhongnanhai. By October he and Jiang Qing had established themselves in Shanghai in his favorite residence, a tower suite on the eighteenth floor of what had been known as Cathay Mansions, the finest residential apartment in prerevolutionary Shanghai (not to be confused with the Cathay Hotel on Shanghai's bustling Bund). Now called the Jinjiang Club, it was located in the French quarter on Jinjiang Road (formerly the Rue Cardinal Mercier), across the street from the Cercle Français, a pleasant establishment surrounded by park and gardens. It was a perfect refuge for Mao and Jiang Qing, boasting a fine restaurant, an excellent chef, a pool, movie screenings, and even a dance floor for Saturday night gatherings. The club and apartments were under one management, and the whole area was cordoned off by Kang Sheng's plainclothesmen and a military detachment.

In their aerie Mao and Jiang were free from prying eyes. Except for a handful of Shanghai Party leaders, no one knew they were in town. Mao and Jiang had spent much time there. She and Mao had established close political ties with the Shanghai leadership, which included Jiang's three associates in the Central Cultural Revolution Group: Zhang Chunqiao, Yao Wenyuan, and Wang Hongwen. In his autumn of discontent Mao began to make use of these ties.

It was Mao's style to conduct political polemics through historical surrogates. Such was the case on November 10, 1965. On that day the Shanghai literary newspaper *Wenhuibao* published a full-page article called "Comments on the New Historical Play 'Hai Rui Dismissed from Office.' " The author was the hack Yao Wenyuan. Probably not more than a handful of readers had any notion what Yao was writing about. The "new play" had been performed in Beijing four years earlier and taken off the stage almost immediately. Few had seen it, few had heard of it. It was written by a man named Wu Han.

The subject of the play, Hai Rui, had been a minister under the Qing emperor Jiaqing and had lost his office because he had criticized some of Jiaqing's decisions. Herein lay the clue. As Mao and his henchmen were to point out again and again, the play was not about Hai Rui; it was about Peng Dehuai. Hai Rui represented Peng Dehuai, and the villain, the emperor, was of course Mao.

With the play thus interpreted, no politician in China could fail to understand that something more than an arcane historical debate had been engaged. Especially when they recalled that Wu Han, the author, was number-one deputy to Peng Zhen, the mayor of Beijing, and that Peng headed Mao's so-called Cultural Revolution Committee.

Nor were Hai Rui and Wu Han new characters on the political scene. Wu Han had used the analogy of Hai Rui earlier on to criticize Mao in Chinese doublespeak in the *People's Daily* in 1959, at the height of the Great Leap Forward. "Hai Rui Dismissed from Office" was no mere quirk of a historian-playwright's fancy. Wu Han had consulted his colleagues lengthily, and they included a close associate of Deng Xiaoping's. Mao's complaints that he was being made a target by upper-level Party members had solid foundations.

To anyone playing on the complex chessboard of Chinese politics, the November 10, 1965, article was a red light. Danger lay ahead. To suggest that Zhou, Liu, or Deng did not understand this is to suggest they were political cretins.

Still Peng Zhen maintained he did not get the signal. Mao called him down to Shanghai in mid-November and harangued him for three days. Peng insisted he thought the play was just a gloss on a long-standing literary-historical controversy. Peng had not instructed the Beijing papers to reprint the *Wenhuibao* article. Now he bowed to Mao's exhortations, and on November 29 the attack on Wu Han and the play was published in Beijing — and all over China. But Peng Zhen got in one (last) word. He attached an editor's note saying the article was published for purposes of literary, not political, discussion.[5]

In the autumn of 1965 Mao wrote two poems. In one he told of going back to Jinggang Mountain, where in 1927 he and Zhu De had laid the foundations of the Red Army's guerrilla war against Chiang Kaishek. The mountain had, he said, been transformed. Now "orioles sing, swallows swirl and streams murmur as the road mounts skyward." His mood was mellow, but gradually it changed, and "wind and thunder stir, flags and banners fly"; the Revolution triumphs with such power that "we can clasp the moon in the Ninth Heaven and seize turtles deep under the Five Seas." If Mao was sending a message, it was that for Red China all things now were possible.

His second poem, written at Hangzhou on the eve of the Cultural Revolution, was cryptic. He called it "Two Birds: A Dialogue." Mao wrote his poem in the style of a third-century B.C. fable about a *kun,* a great fish, that transforms itself into an equally giant bird called a *peng.* The *peng* is so large that it blacks out the sun, and a flip of its wing sets off a typhoon and stirs up a tidal wave. It can fly for six months without pause. A sparrow enters into a dialogue with the *peng.* What's the point of being so big? the sparrow asks. "I can land anytime I want — on the limb of a tree or even on the ground. Why be so big? Why fly so high and so far?" In Mao's version the sparrow is a coward. It sees gunfire exploding in the sky and shells plowing up the earth. "This is a hell of a mess," says the sparrow. It decides to fly away to a "jeweled palace in elfland" and eat goulash. The *peng* reproves the sparrow. "Stop your windy nonsense," it says. "Don't you see the world is being turned upside down?"

Some Chinese took the poem as a slap at the Russians because it contained a reference to a "triple pact" that had been signed two years earlier — the partial nuclear test-ban treaty between the United States, Britain, and the Soviet Union. But the poem could be read in a totally different way, as an attack on those in China who were opting for the "goulash" of Khrushchev's Communism, believing that the nuclear agreements between Washington and Moscow had removed the threat of world conflict. Mao almost always wrote a poem at critical moments in his life. And, in the light of what was to come, there was no doubt that he had determined to turn "the world upside down." Perhaps Mao's real point was that he himself was now a *peng.*

*   *   *

No whiff of these ominous words permeated the quiet and busy courtyard in Zhongnanhai where the Liu family lived. The three elder children — Pingping, Yuanyuan, and Tingting — were in high school. Xiaoxiao was still in grade school. But as propaganda and demonstrations mounted, the tranquillity of the Liu house began to lessen.

Lin Biao was consolidating control of the military, and one obstacle was the chief of staff, Luo Ruiqing, who was very close to Deng Xiaoping. Regarded by Jiang Qing as a personal enemy, for years Luo had held high posts controlling the security apparatus, and Kang Sheng feared him. Lin Biao got rid of him in short order. He accused Luo before a Central Committee group of crimes verging on treason. Luo was forced to make a self-criticism, and on March 18, 1966, he leapt — or was he pushed? — from a fourth-story window and was badly injured. He may have been the first of those to be "suicided," as it was called — driving a man to try to take his life as an alternative to slow death by torture and beatings.[6] Luo suffered the misfortune of surviving. For years he was carted around, his leg in a plaster splint, exhibited and beaten before howling multitudes.

Still there was no sign that the Liu family understood what was under way. Liu, Deng Xiaoping, and Peng Zhen had tried to defend Luo Ruiqing without success.

Now Mao, still far from Beijing in his flowery palace beside West Lake in Hangzhou, was picking his next targets: Peng Zhen, Deng, and Liu. Liu told his children that he had telephoned Mao again and again, trying to persuade him to come back to Beijing and take charge. He explained to Mao that he was not familiar with a "Cultural Revolution"; he was trying as hard as he could to learn. Mao offered no advice. Liu and Deng discussed the situation with Zhou Enlai. No one seemed to know what to do. They could get no advice from Mao. Often he didn't pick up the telephone. He was seeing more and more of Kang Sheng, who was rapidly becoming his closest adviser. Mao began to turn his malevolent thoughts toward another victim, Lu Dingyi, his veteran propaganda chief, a Long March comrade. Mao suddenly denounced Lu Dingyi as "the king of hell." Lu's offense seemed to be that he was opposing Chen Boda, Mao's deputy.

At this critical point Liu Shaoqi left China on a diplomatic foray to Pakistan, Afghanistan, and Burma. By the time he got back in mid-April, a new and devastating attack on Luo Ruiqing had opened, charging that his suicide attempt was an act of treason. Just ahead lay a blast from Lin Biao: the claim that Lu Dingyi and General Yang Shangkun, the longtime Party General Office chief, had conspired to wiretap Chairman Mao.

The allegation of a plot was devastating. Yang Shangkun was sent to prison, where he remained in high-security custody and then in forced residence for thirteen years. Peng Zhen and the Beijing leadership were removed and subjected to terrible torture. Tian Jiaying was a genuine suicide. Luo Ruiqing died about three years after his failed suicide. The fate of Lu Dingyi was the worst. He was turned over to hysterical teenage Red Guards. They tied separate ropes around each ankle and each arm, then swung him wildly and repeatedly through the air in gyrating fashion, breaking his spine and turning him into a paraplegic. The Red Guards were severely reprimanded for this — not for beating Lu, but for injuring him so badly he could not be hoisted up and made to suffer beating after beating before mobs of up to a hundred thousand howling spectators.

On the testimony of the Liu children it was June 1, 1966, before an alarm rang in their quiet house. Each day the children sat around the dinner table and told their parents what was happening at school — the hysteria, student meetings, wild oratory, big-character posters, or *dazibao*. Sometimes their father and mother asked questions, but they seldom volunteered any comment.

The children didn't understand what was happening. Nor did they get much enlightenment. Soon students were assaulting principals and teachers, throwing them out of their offices. A *dazibao* was put up at Beijing University by a student named Nie Yuanzi (probably a friend of Jiang Qing's). She attacked the university president and "dark forces" allied against Chairman Mao. Kang Sheng and Chen Boda ordered the text read on the radio and published all over the country. They didn't bother to tell Liu and Deng what they had done.

Within three days every school and college in Beijing was erupting, and "work teams" began to be assigned by Liu and Deng to the Beijing universities. Work teams were a standby Party device — when things got out of hand, you sent in a small group of Party workers to take charge and guide people onto the proper track. The Liu children came home and asked their father to assign a work team to their school. They found their father cautious. "I don't have any experience in leading this kind of movement," he told them. "I have thought that our Party would rectify our incorrect work style and I thought I would watch for a while and see what I should do."

Turmoil spread. Students began to assault professors and teachers. Some were beaten to death. Others killed themselves. The first stages of anarchy had unfolded. Liu and Deng realized they had more on their hands than they could handle. Mao would have to help. They flew to Hangzhou and found him basking amid the flowers. They asked him to come back; things were out of control. "I have no plans to come," Mao said; "solve the problem according to the situation in the movement." What did he mean? The words were empty. He had left them on their own.

The pair flew back to Beijing and ordered more work teams into the schools. The trouble was that Liu and Deng didn't know how the work teams should guide people. Mao wouldn't tell them.

Liu Shaoqi came out to the high school attached to the Beijing Normal School where Pingping was studying. He talked to the students about the Paris Commune, Marxism, the 1917 Bolshevik revolution, and Mao Zedong Thought. The Cultural Revolution? He didn't know it very well. But he had high hopes it would lead onward and upward and that bureaucracy would be left behind.

Liu said that as best he could make out, the objective of the Cultural Revolution was to liberate proletarians and all people so as to create a perfect Socialist era. To students who thought the objective was "Overthrow everything!" his words were a revelation.[7]

In early July Mao wrote Jiang Qing that the Communist cause was at stake, as was his own leadership. Now, Mao said, he might be smashed. The higher you rose, the harder you fell. "What does that matter?" he asked. "Matter is never destroyed, only crushed. Even Marx and Lenin have been crushed — what does it matter if it happens to me?" He felt the apocalypse was near. On July 16, with thousands cheering (and some drowning) in the swift waters of the Yangtze, Mao swam or let himself be carried by the current across the river at the great Wuhan Bridge, a symbol of New China. Then he returned to Beijing.

Liu Shaoqi heard that Mao was back in Zhongnanhai and rushed to the Study of Chrysanthemum Fragrance. It was early evening. The windows blazed with light. There were Red Flag limousines parked outside. Mao was receiving visitors. But the guards told Liu that Mao had been tired when he got back and had gone to bed. Snubbed, Liu Shaoqi went home.[8]

The next day Mao met Liu Shaoqi, Deng Xiaoping, and Zhou Enlai. He denounced them for sending work teams into the schools and universities, even though he had expressly approved the teams in a telegram to Liu. "Who would suppress students' movements?" he asked. "No one who suppresses students' movements will come to a good end."[9] At a public meeting at the Great Hall of the People, Liu and Deng and Zhou had to make public self-criticisms. Liu told the audience: "How do you carry out the Great Proletarian Cultural Revolution? You don't know very clearly. If you ask me, I'll say honestly I don't know either." Mao strolled out of the meeting as the audience rose and sang: "Rely on the Helmsman When Sailing the Seas."[10]

A week later Tingting, then fourteen, ran into "Auntie" Cai Chang, a saint of the Party, in Zhongnanhai. She and her brother had formed a trio with Mao in the earliest Changsha days. No one had been closer than she and her brother to Mao, although he seldom saw her now.

"How is your mother?" Cai Chang asked.

"Oh, she's doing fine," said Tingting. "She is selling food in the students' dining hall in Qinghua University."

"Silly child!" Cai Chang replied. "You still don't know anything!" She burst into tears and hurried off. Within a month two wall posters within Zhongnanhai would vilify Cai Chang and Zhu De's wife, Kang Keqing. Their crime: crying when they saw Red Guards shearing off a woman's hair and shaving her skull.[11]

A little after dawn on August 18, 1966, Tiananmen Square was already jammed with young people wearing the red armband of the Red Guards. At that early hour, the sun streamed red down Chang-an Avenue from the east, a visible symbol of the song the Guards loved to chant: "The East Is Red."[12]

Mao Zedong suddenly appeared, walking briefly among the Red Guards to cheers of "Chairman Mao is here! Chairman Mao is here!" He raised his hand in salute and vanished back into Zhongnanhai. He, of course, had been up all night.

The throng swelled and filled the square with, it was said, a million people. A couple of hours later Mao returned, garbed as he had been since Army Day, August 1, in military tunic. With his associates he stood on the red-and-gold-lacquered rostrum at the Gate of Heavenly Peace. Marshal Lin Biao, thin, dyspeptic, was at Mao's side.

Only two of the men were not in military dress. One was Zhou Enlai, who wore his customary summer dress, a white shirt open at the collar, a cotton jacket loose around his shoulders. The other was Liu Shaoqi, in civilian tunic, standing apart from his colleagues with Deng Xiaoping. At the last moment Mao had sent word to all —

except Liu — that he would wear military dress. All faithfully followed Mao's lead, but Liu, unaware of the change, appeared in his civilian tunic, face unmoving, silent. No one spoke to him. He spoke to no one.[13]

Mao's face was custard blank. He showed no sign that he heard the cheers of the hundreds of thousands. Some commented on his heavy-lidded eyes, gray flesh, and slumped shoulders. They did not realize that he had been awake all night. It was past his bedtime. He did not speak.

Lin Biao, ill at ease, shuffling his papers, screeched to the multitude in a voice as high-pitched as that of Hitler to "beat down" Mao's enemies, the capitalist roaders, the monsters, the traitors within the Party, and the Four Olds — old thought, old culture, old customs, and old habits.[14]

Not one in one hundred thousand Red Guards assembled in Tiananmen Square could have explained how they happened to be there or how they had become Red Guards. Nor could those on the podium. Of the mysteries of Mao's Great Proletarian Cultural Revolution, none equals the organization, proliferation, and objectives of the Red Guards.

To the ordinary Chinese the Red Guards had simply appeared in high schools and colleges in late spring 1966 and spread across the country like a prairie fire, spewing violent rhetoric and violent actions in their train. Their primary targets were those in authority in the Party, in the government, in educational institutions, in industrial establishments, in society as a whole, in the courtyard houses of a *hutong,* in the palaces of the government, and in the gray and dreary villages of the countryside. Every cry, every blow, every act of death or destruction, was undertaken with the name of Mao Zedong on their lips. They were the most faithful of the faithful, and they saw Mao's enemies everywhere.

But who were they? Who organized them? Who directed them?

One man knew the answers. He stood at Mao's side on the Gate of Heavenly Peace, a curious smile playing about his lips, saying nothing, his figure a blur against all the other figures on the platform. The man who knew the secrets was Kang Sheng.

In the early spring of 1966 Mao had talked with him. As he often did, Mao spoke in allegorical terms, citing the classical Chinese fairy tale "Monkey," in which a monkey folk hero wins over all his enemies by magic and tricks. "We must overthrow the king of hell," said Mao, "and liberate the little devils. We need more Monkeys to disrupt the royal palace."[15]

Kang Sheng understood Mao's ellipsis. Mao had launched the Cultural Revolution against the high command of his own Communist Party and his own government. Now he wanted young daredevils to assault heaven. In that obscure and mystical conversation were born the Red Guards. Not the hint of an official hand was shown, but as wall posters went up in universities and schools suddenly, as if spontaneously, young people began to form Red Guard units, donning red armbands and vowing to defend Chairman Mao to the death and to drive out his enemies, whoever and wherever they were. The movement spread so fast that in many places Red Guards were soon fighting other Red Guards, each claiming to be the legitimate defenders of Mao.

It was not as spontaneous as it seemed. Kang Sheng had primed the pump. He had vast numbers of undercover agents, young students themselves in high schools and universities. He spread the word to them, and they quickly got the movement going. When many young teenagers had no notion of what categories of individuals to attack, Kang Sheng was ready there as well. Orders went out through the police to provide the Red Guards with names, places, locations, tactics — whatever they needed to ravage Mao's stated targets.

Until this August assembly there had been no formal recognition of the Red Guards by the government. But now they took on official status. The Central Cultural Revolution Group, composed of Jiang Qing and her three associates, gave them guidance, paving their way with access and information. Quickly they became Mao's official if anarchical weapon in the destruction of those elements in society that he decreed must go.[16]

In a matter of weeks Red Guards were to be found in every nook and cranny of China. Especially in remote rural areas and in minority regions like Mongolia and Tibet, they demonstrated an affinity for violent racial chauvinism, often ganging up with ethnic Red Guards to ravage temples, murder priests, and slaughter minority peasants.

On that August day in Tiananmen, Mao shook hands with Red Guard leaders, with the students of Qinghua University Middle School, with the students of the Beijing Girls' Middle School (the first unit to petition him to abandon entrance exams[17]), with Nie Yuanzi, who had put up the first big-character poster (Mao had now written his own, which said "Bombard the Headquarters!"). Chen Boda spoke.

Shortly after noon Mao, tired, left the high balcony. He had not spoken a public word. Solemnly his associates followed one by one until Liu Shaoqi was left alone. Again and again the crowd shouted: "Bring back Mao." But Mao did not return. Liu Shaoqi stood for hours in his civilian dress, the Red Guards milling below him, casting angry glances and angry words at him. He was the last to leave. No one had given him permission to go.

Mao retired to Zhongnanhai, to his new Swimming Pool House. While he stood on the rostrum his aides had put the last details into place, moved his last possessions out of the Study of Chrysanthemum Fragrance. When he left the Gate of Heavenly Peace he went directly to his new home. He had left Liu Shaoqi dangling slowly, slowly in the breeze.

27

A Small Soldier

THE PAINTED GREEN DOOR at number 19 Feng Fu *hutong* leads into a small entry courtyard, and beyond another heavy wooden door lies a larger courtyard, which in late summer 1966 was ablaze with chrysanthemums.

Feng Fu *hutong* was a quiet place, a place where a writer could find peace and a chance to think about the meaning of life. Lao She bought it in the spring of 1950 from Cheng Jieyin, a writer who had decided to go back and live in his native Taiwan.[1] The house gave Lao She an island of old Peking in New China, the Peking in which he grew up as a weedy, poor, often hungry son of a Manchu soldier of the fourth rank who had been killed in 1900 defending the imperial palace against allied troops during the Boxer rebellion. Lao She was only a year old at the time.

Lao She was a wanderer. He had gone to England in 1924, stayed until 1930, come back to Peking (as it still was called), moved to Jinan and Qingdao, spent the war years in Chongqing, then gone off to America. He was living in the United States when he got a letter from Zhou Enlai asking him to return. Eight days after Mao Zedong stood at the Gate of Heavenly Peace on October 1, 1949, Lao She arrived back in Peking. He was fifty then and in the prime of his career, China's best-known writer in the West (with the exception of his friend Lin Yutang), known all over the world for a book called *Rickshaw Boy,* a best-seller in the United States, Japan, and Europe. He returned to his four grown children and his wife, Hu Jieqing, a talented painter of flowers in the Chinese tradition, pupil of the famous painter of the genre, Qi Baishi.[2]

Lao She found old Peking much changed. He had been born in a small gray courtyard house and grown up in the northwestern part of the city, a peaceful enclave, near the Xin Jie Kou Bridge over the moat beside the city wall. Just over the wall and across the bridge lay Taiping Pond, drowsy, unattended, a realm of frogs and eels. Lao She and his friends had rambled barefoot around the pond in the hot Peking summers and taken dips in its cool waters. The area had been an old Manchu quarter and still was when Lao She was a boy. The Manchus were warriors when they took over China in the mid-seventeenth century and had never lost their martial status, but with the years the palace stipends of silver taels dwindled. By the time Lao She was growing up many lived on the edge of poverty.

With his best-seller's profits Lao She had been able to afford the very old courtyard house in Feng Fu *hutong,* with its curious geometric decorations just under the ceiling. Lao She liked owning his house, liked being different from writers beholden to the government for an apartment in a new Russian-style eight-story complex. It gave him a feeling of independence and a link with his past. Within his courtyard he re-created old Peking amid the flowers that he potted and repotted. He called it the House of Abundance.

On the fifth day of the fifth month of the lunar calendar, usually in early June, Lao She would invite his friends and they would sit in his courtyard, eating *zhongzi,* sticky rice wrapped in reeds and wrapped again in red paper, to celebrate the anniversary of the death of the Chinese poet Qu Yuan. In 278 B.C., Qu Yuan tied a great stone around his neck and leapt into the Miluo River in Hunan, taking his life in protest against the injustice and terror of what he called "the nation of beasts." For twenty-three centuries the people of China had marked the death of Qu Yuan by making little packets of sticky rice and throwing them into a river, symbolically feeding the fish so they would not feed on Qu Yuan's body.

As Lao She and his friends ate the *zhongzi* and tasted *xing ren doufu* (a kind of almond jelly), they would recite the poetry of Qu Yuan:

> Endlessly the road goes on —
> How long! How long!
> Ever seeking in high places and low
> I plod on.
>
> For what my heart loves —
> I would die
> Nine times over
> With no regret.

In late summer of 1966, the courtyard garden shimmering in brown, white, yellow, and purple, Lao She gathered his friends for the moon festival. They ate smoky figs, a kind of peanut brittle called *yupidou,* corn chips, and *kaikoule,* the cracked sesame seed cakes shaped like greedy mouths that were the traditional holiday sweetmeats.[3] They spent the day and evening eating and drinking, breathing the crisp fragrance of the chrysanthemum blossoms. Lao She was looking forward to the autumn festival, the timing dependent on the lunar calendar. It is doubtful that he knew Mao had moved out of his study dedicated to Chrysanthemum Fragrance into the chlorine-scented Swimming Pool House.

Lao She was resented in Beijing's artistic circle for his success, his comfortable life, the attention paid him by the government, and what some called his fawning on the regime. Long after his death many still spoke bitterly of the author of *Rickshaw Boy*. But Lao She did not find it easy adjusting to the new government. He was used to a bohemian life. In America he had been close to the author Lin Yutang and Anna May Wong, the successful Chinese film star. Ernest Hemingway and Pearl Buck were his friends. In China his closest ties were to Ba Jin, the Shanghai writer; Guo Moruo, the court poet; and Mei Lan Fang, the celebrated female impersonator of the Beijing Opera.

Lao had become head of the Beijing Federation of Writers and Artists, a member of the National People's Congress and the Standing Committee of the People's Consultative Congress, and vice chairman of the Chinese Writers Association. A car and chauffeur were at his disposal. He was not a Communist, but he dutifully supported the regime and appeared on platforms at congresses. He was a cultural ornament, and when foreign writers visited Beijing he was trotted out to greet them and attend the banquets.

Lao She's writing had not flourished in the years since he purchased the house he called Abundance. He had produced one major work: *Four Generations Living Under One Roof,* a lengthy family panorama in the style of John Galsworthy's *Forsyte Saga.* The official critics called it an epic, but privately many found fault. The scenes of life under Japanese occupation — when Lao She had not lived in Peking — seemed more cardboard than flesh, and the praise for the new regime was heavy-handed.[4] His play "Teahouse of the August Moon" had won international success, but his Beijing critics carped. Lao She had wanted to write the story of the decay of the Manchu warriors in Beijing, the life of his father and his friends. He embarked on this enterprise, a large-canvas novel called *Beneath the Red Banner* (the banner was not the red banner of Communism, but the name the Manchus gave their fighting legions). As Mao's purges of the intelligentsia succeeded one another, Lao put it aside, aware that it could not be published during the Great Leap Forward and the anti-rightist drive. In 1961 he put it in a drawer, where it reposed, half-finished, at the time of his death. Only after Mao died was it retrieved and a fragment published, which proved to be the best work of his life.

Lao She was also a fine painter, and now he and his wife spent more time with his flowers, planting and replanting, catching the brilliance of their blossoms in paintings that possessed a reality he could no longer capture in words.

Lao She was sixty-seven and not in good health in the summer of 1966. In the first days of August he had attended a meeting in the Great Hall of the People, one of those dedicated to the denunciation of Liu Shaoqi and Deng Xiaoping. There he had encountered Ba Jin, up from Shanghai for the ritual, and had asked him to tell his friends in Shanghai that "I have no problems," using the euphemism of the day to indicate that, so far, he was not being persecuted. The day after the meeting Lao She had awoken in the night, spitting blood. His family had rushed him to the Anti-Imperialist Hospital, as the Capitol Hospital was called in that time. He had had a hemorrhage and spent a fortnight under doctor's care. When he was discharged the doctor had told him he needed rest and advised him not to go back to work.[5]

Heedless of the doctor and his family's protests, Lao She headed for work on the morning of August 23, 1966. His car and chauffeur took him to the office.

The streets of Beijing now were wild with Mao's Red Guards, spreading destruction and terror. Only the day before they had raided the opera, traditional theaters, and museums, seizing truckloads of costumes and stage props, priceless garments of silk and velvet worn by past mandarins and emperors, ancient swords, rapiers, halberds, pikes, scepters, banners, dynastic flags, chamberlains' staffs, old muskets, the treasures of hundreds of years.

On the morning of August 23, Mao's adolescent gangsters busied themselves trucking China's ancient cultural relics to a central spot for the culminating act in the task set them by Mao — the destruction of the Four Olds — old thought, old culture, old customs, old habits.

This great task was being carried out by the Red Guards of the Numbers 2, 12, 23, and 63 middle schools and those of the Central Academy of Fine Arts, youngsters who until a few weeks earlier had been regarded as the hope of China's future. Now, vicious as a wolf pack, they began to truck their booty to Guozijian, the old Imperial College whose classic courtyard was next to the Temple of Confucius, with which it was connected.

The building had been known in Mongol times as the Hall of Classics. From the days of Emperor Qian Long, the emperors had come each year to the hall at the time of the second moon and lectured on the classics. On the lovely yellow porcelain arch of the central hall was inscribed: "All under heaven receive benefit by instruction."

In the cloisters of the courtyard had been erected three hundred stone tablets chiseled with the words of the classics so that they might not be lost by lunatic destruction, as had happened after the rise of Emperor Qin. The stone tablets had been relegated to a storehouse even before the time of the People's Republic. This was a citadel of learning, now used as the capital library. Here the sixteen- and seventeen-year-old arbiters of China's fate heaped up a mountain of books, rare manuscripts, and trunks of precious cultural heirlooms.

They then pounced on the Beijing Bureau of Culture and kidnapped the artists, writers, and officials whom they found there, thirty in all.[6] When Lao She came out to see what was going on, a female student shouted: "That's Lao She. He's an arch-reactionary. Grab him and put him on the truck."[7]

The truck carted Lao She and the others to the Imperial College. On the ancient stones, before the Gate of Highest Scholarship, beside the Jade Disc of Biyong Hall, the pyre of historic artifacts towered temple-high.

Mao's thugs forced the victims to their knees, produced dull-bladed shears, slashed off their hair in yin-yang style (one side of the head shaven, the other left untouched), and poured bottles of black ink over their heads. The pyre was set afire. As greasy black smoke filled the courtyard the victims, hands bound behind them, were kicked into the borders of the fire, heads enveloped in smoke and flame, to shouts of "Feel the heat! Feel the heat!"

The boys and girls picked up the ancient swords and pikes, the scepters and the poles, and rained blows on the heads and backs of their victims. On their victims the teens hung placards that read "Black Clique Rightist," "Monster," "Reactionary Academic." They used their brass-buckled belts as whips on Lao She until his head and face streamed with blood. He collapsed on the courtyard stones and lost consciousness, but the Red Guards yanked him to his feet, shouting that he had a "bad attitude."[8]

Once on his feet Lao She refused to bow his head. Blood spurted from his wounds and turned his torn white shirt carmine. The crowd shrilled: "Bow your head! Bow your head!" He held it higher, his face ashen, his eyes gleaming with what a spectator thought was an uncanny light. A new placard was hoisted around his neck: "Active Counterrevolutionary."

As the Guards continued to beat and kick him, Lao She worked his hands free and silently raised the placard from his neck and hurled it to the ground, striking a glancing blow at one tormentor. They closed in with blows so savage one of the other victims feared Lao She would be beaten to death. Night was falling.[9] An employee of the Cultural Bureau convinced the pack that as an "active counter-revolutionary" Lao She must be turned over to the police for official inquiry (and execution). The crowd dragged him to the Xidan police station, still beating him, as the police looked on with indifference.[10]

A telephone call was made — although not by the police — to Hu Jieqing, Lao's wife. She hurried to Xidan and found him lying on a table, almost unconscious. He could hardly raise his head. Blood was oozing from multiple wounds; his clothes were torn and saturated with blood. She called a rickshaw and helped Lao She to his feet. The police warned him that he must be in his office at eight the next morning to "receive criticism" and answer for "his crimes." He must bring his "Active Counterrevolutionary" placard.

The rickshaw was small. Hu Jieqing propped her husband in the seat and huddled on the floor. They got to the House of Abundance at 2:00 A.M. Hu took the torn, bloody clothing off Lao She. His body was a mass of wounds and bruises. She found the net fabric of his cotton undershirt beaten into the flesh. She washed the wounds, made him some tea, and fed him a little boiled rice. He had had no food since morning.

Neither Lao She nor his wife got much sleep. They talked. He kept saying that everything would be all right. "The people understand me," he told her. "The Party and Chairman Mao understand me. The premier [Zhou Enlai] understands me best."[11]

In the morning he insisted that his wife go to work as usual. Otherwise she would be criticized. The car and chauffeur that ordinarily picked up Lao She did not appear. He tottered to his feet and again told his wife she must not accompany him. "Just give me some money," he said, "and some grain coupons" (rice was still rationed). Lao said he knew how to get to his office by bus.

Hu Jieqing left her husband. The house called Abundance fell silent.

As Lao She crossed the courtyard to leave, his placard under his arm, he called to his three-year-old granddaughter, Shu Yi's child, to come to the window. He bent down and said: "Say good-bye to Grandpa."[12]

Later that morning the Red Guards, swinging their brass-buckled belts, descended on the house. They plastered posters on the walls and swarmed about the *hutong* and courtyard, overturning pots and benches, trampling on the chrysanthemum blossoms. They pulled the house apart hunting for their victim, climbing into the attic, clambering onto the roof, smashing cupboards, pulling books from shelves, upending beds. Where had Lao She hidden himself?

When it began to dawn on them that Lao She was not there, they vanished. Shu Yi, who had been hidden, watching in horror, slipped on his father's bloody shirt, put on a jacket, and rushed to the State Council offices to advise Zhou Enlai. He pulled back his jacket, showing the bloodstains to a secretary, and gave him a note explaining what had happened. A few hours later Zhou Enlai's secretary telephoned to say that Zhou had ordered a search for Lao She and would call with news.

Hours went by. There was no word. So passed the evening of August 24. No word on the morning of August 25. In the afternoon Shu Yi was asked to go to Lao She's offices. He was handed a note that said: "This is to certify that Shu Sheyu [Lao She's real name] of our Federation has alienated himself from the people." A clerk told Shu Yi to go immediately to Taiping Pond, just outside the Desheng Gate, and dispose of Lao She's body. He was not to inform his mother.

It was late afternoon when Shu Yi walked down a dirt path beside Taiping Pond. The August sun was dropping in the west, and its rays blinded his eyes. Ahead loomed a bright splotch of yellow. As he came nearer he saw that it was a straw mat. A young man stood there impatiently. Nearby was a car and the chauffeur who each day for years had driven Lao She to work.

The young man and the chauffeur wore red armbands with the characters *hong wei bing* in yellow, the insignia that meant "Red Guard." The official asked Shu Yi to state his name and show his identity card.

He inspected the paper closely, then said, waving at the straw mat that half covered Lao She's body, "You must dispose of him as soon as possible." The chauffeur leaned out as they drove away and added, "Dogs come here at night."[13]

Not until late that night, during a rainstorm, could Hu Jieqing, hiring another rickshaw, manage to get her husband's body to the state crematorium at Babaoshan. They accepted the body but refused to give her the ashes; the ashes of enemies of the people were not returned to the survivors.

For a time there was speculation that the Red Guards had seized Lao She, beaten him again, and suicided him in Taiping Pond. That seems possible but unlikely. The number 5 bus line runs not far from Feng Fu *hutong* to Desheng Gate. Lao She probably boarded the bus for his old neighborhood. Whether he paid a last visit to the *hutong* where he was born or to the nearby house of his mother will never be known. The gatekeeper at Taiping Park remembered "an old man" sitting all day on a bench on August 24. There was no one else around. He sat quietly from morning to evening, gazing at the brackish water, speaking not a word.

Perhaps Lao She was writing. The next morning the gatekeeper found a few scraps of paper floating in the water — poems by Mao Zedong, each character about the size of a walnut, in Lao She's hand. Whether he wrote a last poem was not disclosed.[14]

Very early on the morning of the twenty-fifth, while Taiping Pond was still covered with mist, an actor who lived nearby came to the shore to do his morning exercises. Looking out on the pond, he saw a dozen paces from the shore a strange object floating on the surface.

As the mist lifted he saw that it was a human head with the yin-yang cut. He ran to a cottage nearby, where a fisher family came to his aid. They managed to bring the body to shore and after a time found beside a bench a neat pile: Lao She's jacket, glasses, fountain pen, cane, and identity card. Still clutched in his hand was a scrap of paper. The paper was not with the other effects when in June 1978 a memorial ceremony was held at Babaoshan and the possessions returned to the family.[15]

Quickly students from nearby Beijing Normal College, many of them lovers of Lao She's writing, appeared on the scene. The police came. The medical examiner came. Representatives of the municipal federation came. But Zhou Enlai did not telephone the widow. Word did not reach her of her husband's death until nine that night.

A few days later a student at the Normal College chiseled out on a piece of stone the characters "This is the place where Lao She left the world" and placed the stone at the spot on the shore where the body had been dragged up.

The stone did not remain long in place. It was bulldozed under a mountain of rubbish used to fill in Taiping Pond less than a year later, in order, it was said, to create space for a materials depot for the subway then under construction. A woven-wire fence was put up around the place where Taiping Pond had been. Perhaps it is sheer coincidence that the pond was filled in so quickly after the death of Lao She. In the months after his death a good many more bodies were pulled from the pond. It had become a place where intellectuals took their own lives rather than waiting for Mao's murders.

The word *taiping* means "peaceful."

Strolling along the old moat, now lined with a cement surface, and gazing at two optimistic fishermen trying their luck in the late spring of 1988, Lao She's daughter paused in the bright sunshine. A thought had struck her. Why not put up a replica of the student's rough-hewn stone on this bank, a grassy knoll beside a busy traffic thoroughfare, and chisel on it words Lao She had once suggested as an epitaph: "In memory of a small soldier of the literary world who has fallen and is now sleeping here"?

Nothing, of course, has been done. But someday perhaps China may honor a man who, like Qu Yuan, gave his life to stir the conscience of fellow citizens of "the nation of beasts." A peaceful lake would seem a fitting place for such a memorial.[16]

28

The Fate of Iron Man Wang

THERE WAS NOTHING accidental about the madman's rage that boiled up in the streets and *hutongs* of Beijing's dusty August 1966. Later some would suppose that the madness was a fever that spontaneously swept China's young people into delirium over Mao Zedong.

That delirium was present, but the fact that it took expression in sadism that knew no bounds was not accidental. It was instigated, managed, aided, and abetted by Kang Sheng. Madness was, in fact, state policy. Mao's order of March 1966 to "liberate the little devils" was carried out literally and specifically by Kang's secret and not-so-secret police.

In a curious letter that Mao sent to Jiang Qing on July 6, probably written for the historical record and to be published after Mao divested himself of his most radical supporters, like Kang Sheng, Lin Biao, and Jiang Qing herself, Mao contended that "great disorder across the land leads to great order."

So, he said, "every seven or eight years monsters and demons will leap out themselves." He referred to Zhong Jui, the mythical champion who adorns tens of thousands of door guards all over China and protects homes against evil spirits.

"I have become the Zhong Jui of the Communist Party," he asserted, intimating that he was being used as a cover by Lin Biao and the others who were leading the Cultural Revolution. But, of course, it had been Mao himself who set the "little devils" free to attack the organized society over which he presided.[1]

Mao's wishes had been translated into precise orders and issued by the Ministry of Public Security in the latter part of August. Speaking to a meeting of top security directors, Xie Fuzhi, their chief, officially relieved them of the responsibility of obeying existing regulations on public order. "I am not for beating people to death," he said. "But when the masses hate the bad elements so deeply that we are unable to stop them, then don't try. . . . The police should stand on the side of the Red Guards and establish contact with them, develop bonds with them, and [emphasis added] *provide them with information about the people of the five categories* [landlords, rich peasants, reactionaries, bad elements, and rightists]."[2]

Security officials within twenty-four hours transmitted the order to their subordinates, who in turn passed the word to the Red Guard organizations. Transmittal of the orders coincided to the day with the auto-da-fé staged in the Imperial College that led to the suicide of Lao She.

Had Lao She not drowned himself on the night of August 24 he would — almost assuredly — have been beaten to death the next day by the Red Guards of Middle School Number 65.

As rapidly as the police orders were transmitted, Red Guards, armed with lists of names and addresses provided by the police, seized their victims by the hundreds and the thousands.

On August 26 the police in Daxing County, on Beijing's northern outskirts, gave the local Red Guards lists of names, telling the adolescents these people were "dangerous elements." By August 27 the beatings had gotten under way. Within a week more than 125 people in the county had the life beaten out of them in the streets and public squares before raving crowds. The toll reached 300 within days. The oldest "enemy" beaten to death was an eighty-year-old grandmother, the youngest a thirty-eight-day-old baby. A single blow to the head was enough to split their skulls and leave them lifeless corpses in the dust. Twenty-two families were wiped out.

The police-triggered terror went on mercilessly. Village gendarmes gave the swaggering youngsters the names of former residents who had moved into the city. They were summoned back. As they descended from the trains, village bullies clubbed them down and finished them off in minutes. For them there were no trials or struggle sessions. Two elderly sisters who had lived quietly in a Beijing *hutong* for twenty years (once concubines or servants in a landlord's house) were called back. They were dead almost before the locomotive of the train that brought them could let off the steam from its boiler. Red Guards set upon them as they kowtowed for mercy. The louts beat the women on the head, on the bosom, on the back, and hurled them into a pit, half-dead, tossing shovelfuls of earth on the heaving bodies.[3] Some 5,000 were killed by these savages in the regions adjacent to Beijing.

No place in China was secure from the terror. In distant Guangxi an estimated 67,500 people were killed. In Mongolia the toll ran to hundreds of thousands. In Tibet and Sichuan it was much the same. One eminently knowledgeable Chinese estimated the total victims of the ten years of madness at 4 million. "No one else will tell you that," he said. "I will."[4]

Although official statistics estimate the toll at 729,500 "persecuted" and 34,000 killed, with the largest single total of deaths — 16,222 — given for Inner Mongolia, independent estimates by Chinese sources place the casualties at several hundred times the official figures.[5] The social historian Yan Jiaqi, who made the most informed investigation to date of the Cultural Revolution (and after Tiananmen became an exile and dissident), refused to estimate the total number of deaths. Asked whether there had been 1 million, 2 million, 5 million, 10 million, or even 20 million deaths, he said, "The actual death total may not even reach those figures. The greatest damage was to human character. That was much worse. Even in Hunan it did not reach genocidal totals. But there were instances — children of landlords and landlords themselves. And, of course, in Inner Mongolia."[6]

Beating sessions in Beijing were organized at sports stadiums. Many theaters, including the famous Jixiang, were requisitioned for the public murders, a new performance every night by Mao's beardless bullies. There was no style about the beating parties, nothing like the brio with which Rome hurled Christians to hungry lions. Beijing's sport resembled a pack of jackals setting on a crippled deer. The victims were bound hand to foot, dumped on a floodlit stage. The audience would shout and drool as the murderers set about their act. Often there were no cries for mercy. (In Shenyang one of the onlookers, a young woman, had her throat slit so that her screams would be stilled.) Gags were stuffed in victim's mouths.

To Chinese suffering from the red-eyed disease, it was heaven. A penciled denunciation (unsigned) would deliver their enemy to the public stage, where they could watch the death agonies on an ensuing night.[7]

The daughter of one of China's distinguished scholars, looking back on these times after twenty years, said with eyes hard as flint: "We became beasts. There was not a human being left in China. We were

worse than beasts. At least beasts do not slaughter their own kind."
She was not aware that she was echoing the words of the poet Qu
Yuan.

In the China of the 1960s it would have been impossible to find a
more universal symbol of Mao Zedong's era than Wang Jinxi. Wang's
rugged face and his nickname, Iron Man Wang, became commonplaces
from Heilongjiang to Hami. He was the personification of Mao's
doctrine of enabling China to lift itself up by its bootstraps.

A talkative, outgoing man who adulated Mao, Wang Jinxi, forty-
three years old in 1966, had been plucked out of nowhere and lifted
to the stage of the Great Hall of the People, made a member of the
Central Committee of the Communist Party and an icon of the regime.
He stood beside Mao on the Gate of Heavenly Peace on state occasions. Wang himself could not have counted the speeches he had made,
the times he had been photographed, the number of documentaries
that had been filmed, the interviews he had given in praise of Chairman
Mao.

Iron Man Wang was a paradigm of the metamorphosis of China
as Mao led it from the old life of poverty, disease, ignorance, and
superstition into the new world of modernity. The fact that Wang
could not read or write and had to issue orders to his production team
by scrawling pictures on a notebook was kept as secret as was the
work in which he was engaged.

Wang was thirteen when he went to work in the Yumen oil field
in Gansu Province, a dirt-poor peasant lad. He was thin as a scare-
crow — his family often went without rice — but he laughed a lot.
He and his friend Xue Guobang, two years younger, liked to wrestle
in the hard-packed dirt courtyard beside their quarters on summer
evenings. Wang was not particularly strong, but he was agile. Xue
Guobang was a bit taller and heavier. It was an even match.

The youngsters worked hard, and the owners — it was a KMT
government-owned operation — provided skimpy rations and low
pay. Neither Wang nor Xue knew anything about the world beyond
Yumen. There was no political talk among the workers. Most, like
Wang and Xue, were illiterate. Of what was happening in the China
or the Europe of the late 1930s they hadn't a clue.

Troops patrolled the perimeter of the oil fields. Just as soldiers were
shanghaied into Chiang Kaishek's army, many of the workers had
been shanghaied to the site by Nationalist "recruiting" squads — they
were grabbed, bound, and dumped into the fields. If they tried to

escape they were shot or beaten. When a worker was caught trying to run away, the others were lined up, given clubs, and compelled to beat their comrade. Each man had to hit the victim three times, hard. If you hit lightly you were beaten yourself. Not infrequently the runaway was beaten to death. Beating was a way of life — and death — in China.

Wang and the other workers lived in caves with few sanitary facilities. The diet could hardly have been worse: No rice, no wheat, only millet gruel mixed with sand and a few red peppers. It didn't take long for a man to lose his strength and come down with scurvy. The water was as bad as the food. Almost every day one or two workers died of typhoid.

Twice there were half-hearted strikes. Once Wang and Xue joined in. They grabbed the oil field manager and threatened to throw him over a dam. That evening the KMT sent troops into the camp. When they set up machine guns and trained them on the workers, the strike fell apart. The ringleaders were sent away, probably to be shot.

The guards and field troops belonged to the notorious Ma clan, a Moslem force famous for ferocity. In the days of the Long March it had fallen upon a Communist battalion of two thousand female soldiers, wiping them out, killing, torturing, raping, and selling the survivors into slavery.

No one in the field had heard of the Revolution until the PLA arrived. The manager paid each KMT soldier three silver dollars to leave peacefully so that there would be no destruction of the refinery and wells.

The new Communist regime gave the workers a test, and Wang was classified a "skilled worker." He quickly became head of Drilling Team 1205. Wang was a good leader, full of enthusiasm. He put forward a slogan: "Drill a thousand yards a month and twelve thousand a year."

"By this time," Xue Guobang recalled, "we were too busy to wrestle anymore. We were wrestling the earth to give China its riches."

Wang's Team 1205 became famous. He made speeches, got written up in the papers. He was sent with other teams to Xinjiang Province, where they found some oil but not a lot.

Although in 1959 Wang was not yet Iron Man Wang, he was invited to Beijing to attend an assembly of "worker heroes." He spoke at the Great Hall of the People, and he and the others were received by Chairman Mao. The next year Wang was feted at a gathering of ten thousand workers in Beijing. As a worker hero he rode a white horse, holding a bouquet of red flowers and wearing a red silk sash. Party secretaries led the horses of the worker heroes by the reins.[8]

The Japanese had found traces of oil in Manchuria during their long occupation, and in 1958 the Chinese sent a geological team to explore a promising area about one hundred miles north of Harbin. On September 26, 1959, they brought in a gusher. Top drilling and production teams were put together to exploit the site, most of them from Yumen. Wang and his Drilling Team 1205 were bundled on a special train (no Pullmans, just converted freight cars with bunks) on March 15, 1960. They arrived at Sartu station, the nearest to the proposed drilling site, on March 21. The area, known as Daqing, was one of the bleakest in China. In winter the temperature dropped to 30 degrees below zero Fahrenheit and the soil froze to a depth of six feet. When the men from Yumen stepped off the train, the temperature was below zero, much colder than what they had been used to. Frost bit into their padded jackets and padded trousers. A constant wind tugged at their fur-lined caps. There were no barracks, no huts, nothing but a small reception shack. Wang and his crew slept there on the night of March 21, without electricity or heat, huddled together for warmth. There was a well, but they had to break the ice.[9]

Next day they went on to the proposed drilling site, SA 55. There they slept in a huddle in a peasant hut. Their baggage had not arrived; neither had their drilling equipment. The ground was frozen and covered with snow, the land flat and empty. No villages relieved the landscape, only an occasional hut. The region was called the red grasslands because of the rusty color of the scraggly grass. Here and there a few animals grazed, but there were no cultivated fields. The growing season was too short. The area was, in fact, a wasteland. The workers lived in tents or sod houses when the weather warmed enough to cut the sod, recalling the pioneer days in the Badlands of South Dakota.[10]

Food was as scarce as warmth. The whole of China was starving in the aftermath of the Great Leap Forward, but conditions were worse in the Manchurian wilderness. Wang and his men ate cornmeal mush. Wild lily buds from the fields were mixed with the gruel. "It was one quarter cornmeal, three quarters lily buds," recalled Tian Runfu, who came in March 1960 to run the local paper. "I got so sick of it I have never tasted it since."[11]

This did not stop Wang. Propaganda accounts later described him as leaping from the train, shouting: "Where is the place where we are to drill the well?" That was legend. The truth was more dramatic. There was no crane to lift the drilling gear, so Wang used pipes and logs to ease it off the flatcars. Inch by inch, Wang moved the gear onto trucks. His men had to lift the heavy equipment six feet, moving it only two or three inches at a shove. Wang had thirty-two men on his team plus two cooks. All heaved at the machinery. It took a full day to unload and reload. In all, they moved sixty tons of equipment by hand.

That feat earned Wang the sobriquet of Iron Man. But he was not really that muscular, his friend Xue said. He was not as strong as the younger men on his team. What he had was an iron will.[12]

Iron Man Wang drilled well after well. Photographs were taken of him tugging the drills off the flatcars and onto the drilling site. A film was made. But all this was done in secret. There was not a word in the national press about Wang or Daqing, nothing on the radio, nothing to tell the outside world that China was developing its first major oil field. That — like so many things in Mao's China — was a military secret, Mao's ace in the hole.

Not until 1964 was the news released of China's great oil strike. Now Mao blazoned the triumph with a slogan: "In industry learn from Daqing." Daqing became the model for the country, and Iron Man Wang was its symbol. This was how China would do it. Iron Man was the brawn, Mao the brains. The old man would move the mountain. New pictures showed Iron Man up to his armpits in a pool of cement, mixing it with his feet in a heroic effort to cause it to set quickly around a balky pipe. Iron Man traveled everywhere. He became a cadre, a deputy director of the Oil Drilling Company. He married and fathered four children, two boys and two girls.[13]

China's leaders came to Daqing to praise Wang and be photographed with him. Zhou Enlai came three times. Deng Xiaoping came. So did Liu Shaoqi. He and his wife, Wang Guangmei, spent some time in Daqing during a tour of the north. They sought out Iron Man, praised him, had pictures taken with him. Years later Wang Guangmei mused about the possibility that their support of Iron Man had played some role in his tragic fate. Mao had never come to Daqing. He didn't care for the rough oil field life. He preferred the perfume of Hangzhou.

In the spring of 1968 the blow came. At a meeting in Daqing, Iron Man Wang was denounced by Red Guards sent from Beijing to ferret out "traitorous elements." Wang and his friend Xue Guobang were pilloried at a struggle session held in an outdoor tent on the red prairie. They were, the hit squad shouted, members of the "number 101 Reactionary Group." They were KMT spies. Why? Because they had worked at the Yumen field while it was under Nationalist control. All who were over thirty-five and had worked at Yumen were classified as traitors.[14]

Red Guards put a fool's cap on Iron Man's head and hung a sign around his neck proclaiming him "Traitor-Worker." They made him do the airplane takeoff stance, his hands fiercely pulled behind him and his head bowed as he had never bowed it in his life. He was made to stand in this posture as they beat him head to ankle with heavy clubs. They hauled him about Daqing on a truck, halting here and there for more beatings, more exhortations, and the rallying of crowds. At one period Iron Man Wang was given no food. The Red Guards did not believe in feeding their enemies. A cook took pity on him and slipped him a bowl of noodles with two eggs in it.[15]

The Red Guards beat Iron Man Wang and then beat him again. Their formula for extracting a "confession" was identical to that employed by Stalin's Beria against the old Bolsheviks — no secret psychology, no truth drugs, just "beat and then again beat."[16]

Adjacent to the tent where most of the beatings in Daqing were administered was a great rectangular pond into which human excrement was poured for fermentation before being pumped into honey carts and spread over the flat, red Daqing fields as fertilizer. The green wastes bubbled and churned, and noxious vapors rose in the air. The Red Guards hurled Iron Man Wang into this pit and left him to drown. He struggled to keep his head above the human offal but gradually lost consciousness and sank under the surface. He did not die. His head bobbed up. Perhaps the wooden placard that labeled him a traitor-worker saved his life. A cook in the mess hall had watched the thugs throw Iron Man into the stew of disintegrating shit. When they left, he rushed to the pool and pulled Iron Man out. He dragged the semiconscious man to his kitchen and helped wipe off the worst of the sediment. He splashed water over Wang's sodden clothing and matted hair.

Later Iron Man told his friend Xue what followed. Wang made his way to the site SA 55, now Well Number 1, pumping as steady as a heart (as it still did in 1987) in a remote corner of the oil field. Iron Man knelt down and drank oily water from the sump of the first well that Team 1205 had drilled at Daqing.

His mind was a red blur. He had a single impulse: to get back to the little railroad station where he had arrived at Daqing on March 21, 1960. He would wait in the shadows for the first train that roared by and throw himself under its iron wheels. He had given all he could for China. He could not live in such shame. If China adjudged him human refuse, he would remove himself.

He huddled beside Well Number 1, his eyes unfocused, his body broken. His lungs wheezed like an old bladder; his nostrils were saturated with excrement. Hour passed after hour. He did not move. No one came near the well. Finally, he rose to his feet and headed to his barracks home.

Iron Man survived — but barely and not for long. His body did not recuperate. He was permitted to resume some duties. In October 1970 he went to a conference in Yumen. Wang had felt ill every day since he had been hurled into the pit. He felt worse in Yumen. Instead of going back to Daqing he went to a hospital in Beijing, where doctors found he had cancer of the stomach. He did not linger long. He died on November 15, 1970, no longer hailed as a national hero, his death not generally reported. His friend Xue (who had undergone beatings almost as severe as those inflicted on him) brought the ashes to Daqing. A quiet ceremony was held in April 1971. There was no wreath from Mao Zedong.[17]

Jiang Qing bore direct responsibility for the death of Iron Man. On March 12, 1968, she, in the company of Lin Biao's wife, Zhou Enlai, and others, met in Beijing with students, including representatives of the Petroleum College at Daqing. The college had refused to support Jiang during February 1968 protests by the military against the Cultural Revolution. Now Jiang Qing denounced Daqing as harboring a nest of supporters of Liu Shaoqi's. The assault on Daqing's leadership and Iron Man followed swiftly.[18] Jiang Qing's fight against Daqing went on and on. It was even revived in 1975 in her struggle against Deng Xiaoping.

There is something curious about the death of Iron Man Wang and that of Lao She. Lao She committed suicide — the evidence suggests — by throwing himself into Taiping Pond. His body was retrieved adjacent to the grounds of the Beijing Normal College. The school boasted one of the most ferocious Red Guard units in China. The unit that came to Daqing and hurled Iron Man Wang into the fermentation pool was from that same school. Connection or coincidence? Who can say?

29

Heaven Above and the Earth Below

IN THE EARLY 1960s the village of Dazhai, its eighty-three families and three hundred members, struggled from before dawn to after sunset grubbing a living from the brown loess plateau of southeast Shanxi, a village like ten thousand others.

A traveler does not see Dazhai until he has cleared the last barrier of hills, which are devoid of water, huts, trees, streams, and people. The desert is punctuated here and there by a dusty track leading to infinity.

This was midcentury China, living just above the abyss, little hope, no escape, endless toil, the people enduring as they had for hundreds of years. So they lived until 1963, when the sky opened up and the rain fell like Noah's flood, washing away fields, paddies, caves, mud-and-wattle huts, creating a Wagnerian setting for Maoist tragedy.

When the rain was over, the peasants found all was gone. They possessed their sodden clothes, and little more. The huts were puddles of clay, the caves collapsed into lumpy dough.

As a sickly sun rose on the empty landscape the people, gaunt as rails, gazed at the rubble of their lives. Nowhere to live, nowhere to sleep, nothing to eat, no crops, no fields.

That morning Chen Yonggui, a vigorous man of forty-eight, sloshed through what had been his village, taking stock. He was the Party chairman, a stubborn, straight-backed man, leader of the Dazhai commune, a man of the Shanxi countryside who had risen from the dust of Xiyang County, the mud of autumn, the frost of winter, the blast of summer. He and his father had been beggars. They roamed the loess hills, with no place to lay their heads, no place to work, no home. They had come down from the barren Shishan Mountain, and when they got to Dazhai they went no farther. They settled, began to scratch a little corn from the flinty soil.

Now Chen Yonggui had been chairman of Dazhai for the past ten years. He was proud of his work. No one in Dazhai ate well, but no one had starved since he became leader. Even in the terrible years after the Great Leap Forward, when most of Shanxi was dying of famine, Chen had built Dazhai into one of the best communes in the county. But all that had been lost in one night.

What to do? Chen Yonggui knew how grim the times were all over China. It was not just hardscrabble Dazhai. The Leap had been a disaster. There had been drought, famine, crop failure, flood, and the pullout of the fourteen thousand Soviet experts. Chen was no ideologue, but he knew what China was passing through. The hopeless conditions put his back up. Part of his determination to reverse the misery came from his dedication to what he thought were the goals of Chairman Mao and the Party, part from patriotism, and part, no doubt, from the stubbornness of his character.

Chen was not going to give up. Dazhai would fight its way out of the slough and do it on its own — no government handouts, no appeal for disaster relief, no emergency petitions, no loans, no financing, no begging. He and his father had had enough of begging. It was Dazhai's life, and Dazhai would put it back together with its own hands.

Three decades later that sounds like bravado, pure and simple. The fact is that Chen bullied, cudgeled, and fast-talked the peasants into doing what every man and woman in Dazhai knew was not possible.

He convinced them not to worry about the mud pies that had been their homes. Get the paddies terraced again, get the fields planted with new crops. Get the farm operating and then worry about the soil-retching blankets, the corn-husk mattresses, the rice-husk pillows, the buried pots and pans, the missing stools and bedsteads. Forget tea. Flavor the hot water with a willow twig or drink "white tea" — boiling water, the standby of the peasantry. Get by. Work the fields by day, start on the houses at night. First and above all, get the farm going. Show China and the world Dazhai can do it.

It took a lot of rhetoric, but Dazhai followed Chen's lead. The town had to have money. Chen wouldn't touch state money, as did other stricken villages. He persuaded the peasants to cash in their pitiful savings and pool them to buy cement for new grain bins, seed to replace what was lost, tools to replace those that were carried God knows where by the waters. Chen had been busy in the years before the flood. He had put Dazhai on the map by bringing in harvests in the years of trouble. Dazhai was beginning to be known in the county and beyond, and Chen had already gotten a reputation as a can-do, gung-ho chief. Now Dazhai would show its grit.

That was the beginning. Within a year all of China — and even some of the rest of the world — was ringing with slogans about Dazhai, the puritanical, independent, self-reliant commune. It fitted Mao's needs so well he might have invented it. But, so far as intensive investigation disclosed, it was Chen Yonggui's idea. He launched it with his own homegrown slogan of the Three No's: "Ask for no shelter. Ask for no grain. Ask for no money." The bedraggled people slept in sheds or tents. They lived a communal life, ate from a common rice pot, worked the fields in common, pooled their soggy grain and dried it for seed. Everything was done communally — cultivation, building, housekeeping. It was Mao's dream of the rural commune come to life. More than anything else it resembled the earliest Pilgrim settlements in Massachusetts. But Dazhai's faith was in Mao Zedong, not the Old and New Testaments.

Soon Chen came forward with another slogan:

> Take care of the fields
> Before you take care of your own.

That is, production first, private needs second.

Mao's delight was tremendous. He brought Chen to Beijing in 1964. Chen spoke to the National People's Congress and was received by Mao. Mao (or Chen Boda) created a new slogan:

> In agriculture learn from Dazhai
> In industry learn from Daqing.

It was catchy. It had rhythm. Soon it would blare from one end of China to another. It spelled the beat of Mao's China in the mid-1960s and for years later.

Before the flood, Dazhai had been known as the place of seven ditches, eight riches, and one slope. The slope was too sharply inclined for planting. It had to be terraced and leveled. No longer was that a problem. Beautiful masonry was laid to hold the contoured soil in place. Water to irrigate the fields and terraces had been a problem. Not anymore. Aqueducts were built to carry water from reservoirs near the Qinzhang River, twenty miles away. Pipes and tiles were laid under the fields. Dams were put in place to prevent new floods. Dazhai was beginning to undergo a magical transformation.

Peasants from hundreds — even thousands — of miles away came to "learn from Dazhai." The buses followed each other like elephants in a circus parade, circling around and around the new curving hard-surface roads built so visitors could see every aspect of the new utopia, the maze of terraces and paddies, ever growing. The peasants joked that if they didn't get to work by 7:30 A.M. they would lose a day's work — after that hour the traffic jams blocked their way to the fields.

Never had the country seen such propaganda. The publicity, the speeches, the tours, the crowds, grew and grew. The leaders of China (except for Mao) came to Dazhai. Zhou Enlai summed up the meaning of Dazhai: "The principle of putting politics in command and advanced ideology, the spirit of self-reliance and hard work, the work style of loving the country and the collective."

This was what Dazhai symbolized. It was the spirit of Mao Zedong in action.

There was such an influx of visitors to Dazhai that the peasants no longer had any real role. To the spectators who gazed in awe from the buses, they were like animals in a zoo. Each year the residents of Dazhai reported more and more spectacular results. They put up new housing, neat brick and mortar, no more caves and huts. Scores of propaganda guides learned the Dazhai spiel and lectured the visitors. Films and slide shows were presented. Documentaries circulated through the country. Short courses were offered. Barracks were built to house the peasant visitors, black-topped parking lots appeared, and finally a massive five-story hotel with a Shanxi-style inner courtyard surrounded by simulated cave dwellings with big circular windows and latticed panes, just like the one Mao inhabited at Yanan, was put up. Special trains steamed out from Beijing southwest to Shijiazhuang, capital of Hebei, and then into Shanxi Province to Yangguan. There the crowds detrained at a glorious nineteenth-century red-brick station right out of Manchester. The VIPs entered Red Flag limos; the peasants loaded onto trucks and buses. It was an hour's drive to Dazhai over a new macadam highway across the wind-eroded loess.

Come they did, twenty thousand a day at the peak. Dazhai was a Chinese Disneyland, the hottest ticket in the country, Cultural Revolution or no Cultural Revolution. No Red Guards came to Dazhai to bully or murder the leaders. There was no interruption in the sensational production gains, no "educated youth," city boys and girls uprooted from their Red Guard careers and sent down to tend pigs, no individuals with "bad histories" compelled to do the airplane and stifle in closet prisons. The residents called Dazhai "an island of peace and harmony." No one drowned in the sewage ponds.

The establishment kept on growing — the 120-room hotel and its dining hall a block long, first-class communal quarters, auditoriums, movie halls, a people's hotel (no beds, just straw mats on bare floors), mass squat toilets.

Chen Yonggui shot up like a rocket. He spoke all over the land, and Mao put him into the Politburo and made him vice premier. He didn't get back to Dazhai very often. The Dazhai crop yields, chiefly corn, soared with Chen Yonggui, zooming from 600,000 jin (a jin equals 1.3 pounds) in 1964–65 to 720,000 in 1975 and 970,000 in 1979. The 4,700 plots of land (much of them private) were consolidated into 240 segments, all state-owned and communally farmed. No more private plots. Dazhai was a wonder. Production per mu (one sixth of an acre) rose from 600 jin to 1,000 between 1964–65 and 1979.

Six great stone-lined reservoirs were built. Two aqueducts poured in the water. No one had ever seen such a thing. Powerful pumps moved the water up to Dazhai's reservoirs in the hills above the farms. Spray systems and underground water pipes moistened the fields and terraces. There was nothing that Dazhai lacked. Delegations presented Dazhai with gifts: a team of horses, three or four cows, a breed sow, three rolls of barbed wire, a dozen bags of cement, steel bars for retaining walls, bags of fertilizer, even tractors. What Dazhai needed, Dazhai got.

The national lecturers broadened their pitch. "Learn from Dazhai" didn't just mean learn to plow the Dazhai way. It meant build as Dazhai built, learn Dazhai's slogans, teach as Dazhai taught, use Dazhai's calligraphy, keep books the Dazhai way, conduct propaganda Dazhai-style, trim sheep as Dazhai did, raise pigs the Dazhai way. Dazhai became a way of life, the way Mao had dreamed China would live. Mao liked to call his leading models "banners." Dazhai was Mao's banner of banners.

Zhou Enlai first came to Dazhai in May 1965 with an Albanian delegation. He returned in the early 1970s. He made his last visit in 1975 for the First National Learn-from-Dazhai Conference. Deng Xiaoping accompanied Zhou Enlai on two visits. Chen Yi was in the 1965 party. Li Xiannian, then China's president, came in 1975. So did Hua Guofeng, just emerging as Mao's stand-in.

Jiang Qing paid her first visit in 1975. She wore a gray cadre suit, a finely tailored jacket and trousers, and a white towel wrapped as a turban on her head. The turban, worn by central Chinese peasants as they work in the fields, is a cliché to be seen in every Chinese peasant play. "Why does she wear that?" the Dazhai workers asked. "She's not a peasant."

Jiang Qing came a few days before the Learn-from-Dazhai meeting, was put up in the deluxe VIP quarters, and staged performances of revolutionary operas that had been created under her direction. And she lectured the peasants about China's classic *The Water Margin* (known in the United States as *All Men Are Brothers*). The peasants had read *The Water Margin* but couldn't understand Jiang Qing's criticism of it, which, in fact, was an attack on Zhou Enlai. By finding fault with one of the outlaws in *The Water Margin* who plotted against his leader, Jiang was suggesting that Zhou was plotting against Mao Zedong.

When the meeting opened, Jiang Qing proposed that the state forgive the loans that recently had been advanced to Dazhai. (These were not the original flood-induced loans of peasant savings, which were still outstanding, not a fen of interest having been paid. Not until three years after Mao's death did the Dazhai peasants get back the savings that they had contributed to Dazhai's rebuilding, and even this came from their own pockets — the profits from their pig farm.)

Deng Xiaoping angrily objected to Jiang Qing's proposal. The conference had no authority over government loans. "This question must be taken up by the State Council and the Politburo," Deng said. "The Learn-from-Dazhai Conference has no right to interfere." Deng and Jiang had a short shouting match, which Deng won. He understood that Jiang's proposal was a trap. If he went along, he would be accused of usurping the power of the State Council. If he objected, she could accuse him of hostility to Mao's favorite banner.

Jiang Qing threw a temper tantrum and cursed Deng in front of the Dazhai leaders. Then she had another idea. Chairman Mao, fearful of war with the Soviet Union, had uttered the slogan "Prepare for War. Dig Tunnels." Jiang Qing instructed the villagers to dig a maze of trenches crisscrossing the commune so that they would be ready to repulse invaders. The villagers pointed out that the terrain was very favorable to the defenders in guerrilla warfare — hilly, rough, hard for organized troops to maneuver around. Dazhai could defend itself better from the hills than from trenches in the fields.

Finally Jiang settled for a symbolic trench, running about sixty feet across the valley. When it was done she complained that it was too shallow and not wide enough. Workers did some more digging until they got it three feet deep and three feet wide. Jiang Qing had her photo taken digging the trench (probably the main purpose of the operation) and planted a peony bush at one end. She told the villagers to put up a tablet commemorating the event. Then she posed with some peasants who were pruning a pepper tree.

Jiang Qing left, and the peasants sighed with relief. One of their projects in the year that followed was to set up a small pig farm. The best location was where the trench had been dug, between one of the circular irrigation pools and the orchard. By putting the pigsty in Jiang's trench, it would be easy to shovel up the pig manure and dump it around the apple trees. Never thinking they would see Jiang Qing again, they obliterated the trench and put in their pig farm.

But in late summer of 1976, a second Learn-from-Dazhai Conference was convened, and Jiang Qing came back. Trouble erupted before she even got to Dazhai. Her train arrived at Yangguan at dusk, and she made her chauffeur drive slowly, with only his low lights, complaining that the high lights hurt her eyes. She would not ride in the front seat because she was fearful the glare would damage her eyes. Every half hour the car was stopped for a rest.

When Jiang finally got to Dazhai she refused to use the VIP quarters. Instead she wanted to stay in the interior caves of the state hotel courtyard, and she ordered the walls broken down so she could move from one cave to another without going into the courtyard. This was too much for the stalwart leader of Dazhai, who refused to break down the walls lest the caves collapse. Jiang Qing had to make do with the VIP quarters.

Jiang flared with anger. Believing that her security was at stake, she demanded that police and troops block all roads leading into Dazhai. The area already was swarming with special agents of Kang Sheng's. More were put out, and the access roads were sealed off.

Next morning Jiang mounted a horse and inspected what she seemed to regard as "her" Dazhai. When she discovered that her trench had been replaced by a pigpen she was furious. No ditch, no plaque, no peony, not even the pepper tree she helped prune. It was, she snorted, "the work of Deng Xiaoping." A campaign against her was being carried out "with the support of Deng Xiaoping," she proclaimed. But in the midst of the Learn-from-Dazhai Conference she hurriedly left for Beijing. It was early September. Word had come that Chairman Mao Zedong was in critical condition.

*   *   *

Dazhai is the story of Mao's dream come true. Dream it was. A nightmare, a fraud, a lie, a deceit. The flood was real. The effort by Chen Yonggui and his people to lift Dazhai out of the mud by sheer hard work — that was real. Nothing more.

From the moment Mao, Chen Boda, and Mao's gang grabbed Dazhai, they corrupted it. Mao pumped millions of yuan into Dazhai to make it suit his dream. He ordered People's Liberation Army units again and again to construct facilities for his new utopia. They built the aqueducts that marched across the ghoulish landscape, elevated on circular pylons strong enough to support the Brooklyn Bridge. The army built the beautifully crafted cut-stone reservoirs. It built the new highway from the railhead. It erected the vast hotel. China had not seen such colossal diversion of public funds since the empress dowager Ci Xi built her marble boat in Kunming Lake at the Summer Palace.

Mao knew it was a fraud; he built it himself. He turned the self-sacrifice of the peasants and the bulldog will of Chen Yonggui into a charade. Dazhai had been a hardworking, modest peasant village. Mao ravaged it with funds from his nonaudited secret budget. He signed the chits that made Dazhai tick. Mao's deceit made Count Potemkin and the village he built in the Ukraine for Catherine the Great look like a schoolboy's trick. Potemkin fooled an empress. Mao fooled millions.

Surely Zhou Enlai and Deng Xiaoping knew what Mao was up to. They knew who paid the bills and that the production figures were faked as well. As a latter-day Dazhai official sadly said, "It was an era of unhealthy exaggeration."

The production figures were made up from year to year, always showing higher and higher yields. Indeed, with the vast infusion of capital funds, the irrigation, the fertilizer, the terracing, the yields *did* rise, but not enough to satisfy Mao. No other commune was permitted to offer higher yield figures than Dazhai. Although other farms could show gains due to their adoption of "Learn from Dazhai," their figures always showed Dazhai leading the pack.

Nor had Dazhai been the "island of peace and harmony" its residents liked to describe. Even before the Cultural Revolution — as the *People's Daily* disclosed in 1987 — more than one hundred people had been clubbed to death or strangled in the Dazhai countryside.

What of Chen Yonggui? No one in Dazhai twelve years after Mao's death considered him part of the scam. The villagers insisted it was not Chen's fault. He had been made to go along, convinced that Mao knew what was best for the country. He never had had any doubts about Mao even in the "era of unhealthy exaggeration." Dazhai didn't believe rumors of corruption by Chen. Residents looked askance at reports that Chen's son was guilty of wrongdoing and had been expelled from the Party.

When Mao died, Dazhai's corn yields dropped to reasonable figures. It remained among the leading producers in Shanxi but was slow to adapt to Deng Xiaoping's new system of private rural enterprise. Chen Yonggui lost his Politburo seat and returned to Dazhai; he never again talked about state or Party business. Gradually Dazhai got into the rhythm of the new life. The slogan "Learn from Dazhai" was dropped in 1977. No more tours. No more visitors. No more foreign delegations. The village was declared off-limits to foreign correspondents.

The peasants began to set up small woodworking establishments and a metal shop. The orchard and forest plantings flourished, thanks to the irrigation system. The population grew from 83 to 130 families, about 500 people; the growth was a natural increase and did not result from any immigration. Some residents had borrowed from the government and gone into trucking. It's a good way to make money, they said. Dazhai even had a few ten-thousand-yuan families, rural "millionaires." The egalitarianism of the Mao days had vanished with the propaganda.

Many peasants had color television by 1988, but it was hard to keep the young people home. They wanted to go to the cities. The old Dazhai residents were not enthusiastic about higher education. It just took the young people away.

They often talked about the old days when life was hard. They had had to struggle, as they said, "against heaven above and the earth below." They worked from five in the morning until ten at night.

"We believed that if you didn't cut off the tail of capitalism you would never get to Socialism," Jia Jincai said. He was the Party secretary before Chen Yonggui and had seen it all. In 1988 he was seventy-eight years old. Now they had divided the fields again and given them back to the peasants. Weren't they replanting capitalist tails? Well, he didn't think so, but he confessed no one really knew what a capitalist tail was. That was just an expression of the Beijing propagandists. It was, he thought, "a historical tragedy" that the whole country had tried to learn from Dazhai.

Life was better now. If only the young people wouldn't listen to those sexy tapes from Hong Kong. In one a cowboy sings, "I'm riding for you." "I'm hot for you," the cowgirl sings back. The young girl singer herself admitted it was corrupt. Yes, the Dazhai slogans had been corrupt. Were they that bad?

It was quiet now in the great hotel; no delegations or VIPs were arriving. Once in a while a county meeting might be held there. The people's hotel had been turned into an art center. But there was no way of filling the block-long dining hall of the big hotel. The chef had been trained in Beijing and then sent by the Foreign Ministry to the Bonn embassy. He was a native of Dazhai, and when he came home from Bonn he took a job at the hotel. He was still waiting for guests.

Chen Yonggui died in 1987. His tomb was built by the peasants on the high hill where Jiang Qing liked to ride, overlooking the village. All the work had been done by Dazhai, not by anyone from the outside. Not fake, all real.

30

The House of Good Fortune

THE MANSION of Liu Shaoqi in Zhongnanhai was an exquisite creation of the Qing dynasty, built in the time of the great emperor Qian Long. It was called Fu Lu Jü, the House of Good Fortune. Emperor Guangxu, nephew of the formidable dowager empress Ci Xi, used Fu Lu Jü for birthday celebrations. It had not brought him much good fortune. The old Buddha arrested him in 1898, confining him to the Ocean Terrace in Nanhai Lake across a marble bridge from the House of Good Fortune.

The house seemed perfect for the large and active Liu family. Four children lived there with their parents in 1966 — Pingping, eighteen;

Yuanyuan, seventeen; Tingting, fourteen (all in high school); and Xiaoxiao, six. Wang Guangmei's mother taught in the Zhongnanhai kindergarten and lived there too. Liu had four grown-up children from his earlier marriage, two working in Beijing and two in Inner Mongolia.

The House of Good Fortune was roomy and comfortable, with two courtyards, one in front and one to the rear. Liu had his offices in front. His wife had a small adjacent office. There were a library and study for Liu in one wing, and the dining room and offices of the secretarial staff in the other. The children lived to the rear. The house had one bathroom.

Mao insisted that his associates live inside Zhongnanhai. The exception was Lin Biao, who lived just outside, his house connected by an underground passage. Another passage led to the Defense Ministry in Iron Lion Lane. The enclave stood atop a burrow of tunnels and air raid shelters, the biggest under Coal Hill. They were linked to an escape route to the Western Hills.

No house in Zhongnanhai sat closer to that of Mao than Liu's. Youyongchi, Mao's Swimming Pool House, had been built so that the Lius' rear wall was only inches from Mao's fortress.

To live in Liu's house in 1966 was to live on the edge. Liu Shaoqi was still president of China. He went to his office every day. His secretaries reported for work. But the telephone never rang. The in-basket was empty. No one knocked at his door. No papers were sent for his signature.

Liu was "standing behind the line," as the Chinese put it, suspended from duty, drawing his pay, holding his title but in limbo, suspected of everything, charged with nothing.

The Liu children could not understand. Like their schoolmates, they joined the Red Guards. They proudly wore the red armbands and went out to smash the Four Olds. One evening Pingping and Yuanyuan, the two eldest children, said they were going off to search a house for "evidence." Liu listened with horror. He took down a volume of the laws of the People's Republic.

"I am the president of the Republic," he said. Tingting always had trouble with her father's thick Hunan accent, but she understood this. "I am responsible for its laws." Although he could not prevent them from breaking into someone's house, they should know the facts. The youngsters did not go out that night. They never went again.[1]

*   *   *

Pingping, Yuanyuan, and Tingting went with their classmates on a tour of the provinces. They were shocked to see *dazibao* everywhere attacking their father. When they hurried back to Zhongnanhai they found him cheerful. He had given a self-criticism in the Great Hall, and Mao had approved, making a note on it: "This is well written and very serious, especially the last part."

Liu thought Mao had come to his aid, but he was wrong. Liu's "confession" was circulated with Mao's comment snipped off. It fueled the campaign against him. *Dazibao* appeared within Zhongnanhai. Every morning the children on their bicycles whirled out to look at them and reported back to their parents. Liu himself strolled about to see what was being said.

The high walls of Zhongnanhai no longer kept out the Cultural Revolution. Posters went up attacking Zhu De as a "Big Warlord" and "Black General." He Long was called a robber and a warlord. Deng Xiaoping, like Liu Shaoqi, was set aside, waiting in his house for a call that never came.

Liu talked to Zhou Enlai. He told Zhou he wanted to resign, assume responsibility for all the "mistakes," let the Cultural Revolution take its course, and free Party members from constant agitation. Zhou was sympathetic, but he told Liu resignation was not an option. He would not be allowed to quit.

Liu had now lost touch with two of the four children from his earlier marriage. Liu Rongbin and his sister Liu Aiqing had been exiled to the deep countryside. Both had studied in the Soviet Union. This, in the hysteria of the day, exposed them to the charge of being Soviet spies.[2] The next son from that marriage, Liu Rongruo, was working in rocketry in Beijing. He would be charged by Jiang Qing as a spy, arrested on January 9, 1967, and confined to Number 1 Prison. The fourth child, Liu Tao, a woman only seven years younger than Wang Guangmei, had turned into a vitriolic pawn of Jiang Qing's.[3]

It got worse. On January 8 a telephone call came from a hospital. An unknown voice said that Pingping had been injured in an automobile accident. Her leg was broken, and she must be operated on immediately. Zhou Enlai had warned Wang Guangmei never, in any circumstance, to set foot outside Zhongnanhai. But in what appeared to be an emergency, she and her husband rushed to the hospital. They were met by Yuanyuan and Tingting, who had also been told of an injury to Pingping. There was no sign of Pingping. "It's a trick!" Yuanyuan shouted. "The Red Guards want to catch you." It was too late. The Red Guards had already surrounded Wang Guangmei. She told her family to go home and turned to face the Guards. Late that night Zhou Enlai managed to persuade them to set her free.

Less than a week later, January 13, 1967, with a revolutionary crisis reigning in Shanghai and the country seemingly about to explode, one of Mao's secretaries appeared in the Liu courtyard. Mao wanted to see Liu. Liu drove with the secretary in Mao's old Varshova car, a gift from the Poles, to the Great Hall of the People, where Mao received him.

Mao greeted Liu Shaoqi warmly. "How's Pingping?" he asked. "How is her leg?"

Liu responded, "It was a trick. There was nothing wrong with her leg."

Liu told Mao he had made mistakes and asked him to let the ordinary Party workers go about their work; put the blame on him and he would resign. He suggested that he go back to Yanan or Hunan. He would take Wang Guangmei and the children and start farming.

Mao drew on his cigarette. Finally he began to talk. He thought Liu Shaoqi should do some reading. He named an obscure work by Hegel and one by Diderot.

"Study hard," Mao said. His last words were "Take care of your health."

That was their final meeting. Mao liked to call in his victims, have a cozy chat, and send them to their fate. It was a device Caligula would have admired.

Liu came home with relief. The chairman had been so nice. He had told Liu to study hard and look after his health. Within two days a wild mob stormed Liu's office. They plastered it with *dazibao* and, for an hour, forced Liu and his wife to balance standing on one leg, atop a desk, while they shouted obscenities.

After midnight on January 16, the telephone rang. It was Zhou Enlai calling Wang Guangmei. "You must be strong, Guangmei," he said in a tender voice. "Get ready for the worst."

Later Wang Guangmei thought of a thousand things she should have said. All she uttered was "Oh, Mr. Premier, you are so nice."

Four days after Liu's talk with Mao, Red Guards returned to his office and took it over, ripping out his telephones. No longer could he communicate with the government that he still headed.[4] Liu wrote Mao. He got no answer.

At midnight one evening Han Miao — the children called him Uncle Miao — was arrested. For years he had been the family cook.

He was held for six years and periodically deprived of food and water. He lost his rotund figure, developed heart disease and high blood pressure. "They tried to persuade me to admit that Liu Shaoqi had been corrupted by my cooking and turned into a revisionist," he said.

Uncle Miao was lucky. Half a dozen elderly men, each in the final stages of cancer or heart disease, were tortured to death in an effort to extract evidence that Liu and his wife were spies.[5]

Liu sensed the end was near. He called Wang Guangmei and the children to his side. "After my death," he said, "please spread my ashes in the sea as was done for Engels. This is my will that I leave to you."

"What if they won't give us back your ashes [after cremation]?" asked Wang Guangmei.

"They will," Liu said. He was wrong.

Mao and Lin Biao left Beijing for Hangzhou in July 1967, and the Red Guards set up tents outside Zhongnanhai and began a siege that would last until the end of September. Its duration was approximately the same as that of the 1989 student occupation of Tiananmen Square. The Red Guards, like their 1989 descendants, were equipped with permanent bunking quarters, portable camp beds, and sleeping mats in their tents. They had cooking pots and built campfires all around Zhongnanhai to prepare their meals. It was in every sense a siege situation.[6]

The Red Guards blasted the compound with loudspeakers night and day. They targeted all of the older leaders — Zhu De, Deng Xiaoping, Tao Zhu (the only member of the Politburo to oppose the Cultural Revolution), and their wives; Marshal Chen Yi, still foreign minister; Li Xiannian, president-to-be; Wang Zhen, who would emerge very late in life as a vociferous reactionary); Marshal He Long, whose wife was hated by Lin Biao's wife; Liu Bocheng, Deng's old partner; and countless others.[7] The Red Guards surrounded the Zhongnanhai gates, urged on by Jiang Qing and Chen Boda. They intercepted governors and high officials.[8] Chen Boda had invented an imaginary Marxist party headed by Zhu De, backed by the Soviet Union, which Chen claimed was trying to overthrow Mao, and the Guards picked up on this fabrication as they hurled taunts through their loudspeakers.

Chen Boda's scenario was nonsense, but the danger was real. The Red Guards hammered at the gates. Zhou Enlai rushed to the scene. He tried to quell the crowd at the North Gate, the Gate of Magic Light. Jiang Qing ran to the West Gate to whip up frenzy. When

Zhou followed her to the West Gate, she rushed to the North. It was a Chinese Alice-in-Wonderland, except it was being acted by real people. For the moment Zhou prevailed.

Soon a new battle erupted. The target was Chen Yi, hauled before a struggle session to be slandered and beaten. Zhou came to the session, took Chen Yi by the arm, and led him out. The crowd did not interfere. A few days later Zhou was surrounded in the Great Hall by hundreds of thousands. He was held captive for eighteen hours, without food or rest. He talked his way out, talked the raging gang down. Not one hand was raised to protect him — not by a security guard, not by a platoon from the 8341 detachment assigned to protect the leadership group, not by a battalion of Lin Biao's troops. There was no word from Mao. He was enjoying the pleasures of Hangzhou. So was Lin Biao.[9]

Liu Shaoqi and Wang Guangmei believed their three older children would be able to fend for themselves. But Xiaoxiao was too young. Wang Guangmei wondered if she could take her to prison, as Mao's wife Yang Kaihui had taken her son Anying in Changsha. No, said Liu Shaoqi, she could not depend on her comrades for humanity. Wang Guangmei said good-bye to Xiaoxiao and gave her to her nurse to keep.

On the morning of July 18, 1967, the Liu children went to breakfast in the Zhongnanhai dining hall. They saw a huge *dazibao* announcing a public meeting that night to "criticize" Liu. Liu realized this would be the climax. He went to his desk and took out two documents. For the first time he showed the children Mao's note commending his self-criticism, as well as another note in which Mao praised the report Wang Guangmei had made after investigating rural conditions in Tao-yuan. "Now you can see your father and mother never lied to you," he said. Astonishingly, as Liu revealed to his children, not since 1949 had Mao signed any memorandum from Liu. Papers came back marked with a small circle to indicate Mao had read them, but there was never any mark of approval or disapproval. Since the founding of the People's Republic, Liu had had to guess with every document whether Mao was for or against it.[10]

That night Liu and Wang Guangmei were dragged to the meetings, as were Deng Xiaoping and his wife, Zhuo Lin, and Tao Zhu and his wife. The victims were taken to separate struggle sessions, conducted *within* Zhongnanhai. Once Zhou Enlai had guarded the gate. Now the Red Guards freely moved within the citadel.

When Liu and his wife were brought back to the House of Good

Fortune, Liu was put under guard in his office. Wang Guangmei was confined to the rear courtyard, the children to the middle rooms. Speaking and communication of any sort were forbidden. But the children managed to whisper to Liu that Wang Guangmei was in the rear.

This had been the curtain raiser. A bigger, more violent spectacle was staged on August 8. Zhongnanhai had been turned into a torture park. A hundred thousand yelling savages outside, thousands inside in the torture halls. The Liu children, even Xiaoxiao, were compelled to watch Mao's knights drag the half-dead victims onto a stage. A film crew videotaped the performance for screenings around the country. Liu and Wang Guangmei were forced into the airplane position. Guards raised Liu up and then dropped him to the floor like a sack of flour. They beat him in the face and head. They kicked and punched him. One soldier yanked Liu by his white hair and pulled his head back while a camera clicked.

The crowd watched breathless. Suddenly a cry rang out. It was seven-year-old Xiaoxiao screaming in terror. Yuanyuan dashed for her. Soldiers tried to halt him, but he forced his way to her and cradled the child in his arms. "What do you think you are doing?" one lout shouted. "Can't you see Xiaoxiao is crying?" Yuanyuan retorted. The act of human kindness enraged the crowd. For two hours, it exhorted the Red Guards to beat the Lius again and again.[11]

Finally the family was brought back to the House of Good Fortune. They paused in the courtyard. Liu and Wang Guangmei were forced to kowtow before posters of Red Guards. Liu was bleeding from the nose, his face swollen. He had lost his shoes and stood in stocking feet on the cobbles. Wang Guangmei thrust her hand to her husband. He clasped it in an iron grip. The two looked deep into each other's eyes. The Guards aimed down more kicks and blows. The children looked on as their parents said what would be their last farewell while four stout guards tore the couple apart and escorted each to separate quarters.[12]

The torture and beatings did not halt. Wang Guangmei's head was badly injured, but each day in the rear courtyard she was made to lug twenty-five-pound stones from one side to another. Liu, his right leg crippled, could hardly walk. He clung to the wall as he stumbled along. A secretary was still in attendance in his office. One day he dictated another letter to Mao. No answer.

On September 13, 1967, an army truck pulled into the courtyard.

The children were ordered out of the house. They packed bags, hoisted their bicycles up, clambered in, and were driven to their schools. Pingping and Tingting were given quarters in a dormitory where there was no heat. Trying to keep warm, Pingping put copies of the *People's Daily* under her thin mattress, but a classmate found a picture of Mao in the paper and Pingping was beaten for insulting the chairman. Yuanyuan had to sleep in a mop closet under the stairs at his school. Soon he was sent to Shanxi, where he would have starved but for friendly peasants. Pingping was shipped to Shandong to plant and harvest rice. Xiaoxiao was beaten when she arrived to start her first-grade class. The other youngsters called her an enemy of the people. The Liu children did not know that their mother had been arrested and thrown into Qincheng Prison.

The children of Deng Xiaoping, Peng Zhen, the Mongol leader Ulanfu, Bo Yibo, Yang Shangkun — all were treated the same way. Once, penniless, Yuanyuan and Fu Yang, the son of Peng Zhen, went to a hospital to sell their blood. The first time the hospital bought their blood. The second time it refused. Theirs was "black blood," for children of the victims of the Cultural Revolution were "black kids of reactionary parents."

Within Zhongnanhai the tragedy deepened. Liu's sleeping pills were seized. He could sleep no more than three hours a night — all his revolutionary life he had worked, like Mao, at night. The medication for his diabetes was taken away. He got no exercise and began to suffer muscular atrophy. With only seven teeth left, he could not chew the kitchen scraps he was fed, nor could his stomach digest them. He lost so much weight he was little more than a skeleton. His hands trembled. He could not get food to his mouth with chopsticks. An old wound in his arm became infected. It took him two hours to put on his clothes and an hour to walk the short distance to the eating hall.

Still the furor raged. Jiang Qing shouted to a mass meeting on September 18, 1968, "I'm in charge of the most important case in China," that of Liu Shaoqi. "He deserves a slow death by a thousand cuts, ten thousand cuts." "Flog the cur that has fallen in the water," yelled Zhang Chunqiao, one of her Gang of Four associates.[13]

More than five hundred investigators opened fifteen archives and examined 2.5 million documents; hundreds were arrested, beaten, tortured, starved, and killed, as the Gang tried to drum up evidence against Liu. He was still a member of the Party, still president of

China. Obscure professors were driven to death because they could not give evidence that Wang Guangmei (whom they had never heard of) was an American spy.

On October 8, 1968, Liu Shaoqi burst into tears. He wept and wept without control. He could no longer swallow and had to be fed through a tube in his nose. His hands turned into claws. When he clutched an object it could not be pried from his fists. The nurses put two small plastic bottles in his hands. He was still clutching them when he died a year later.

Jiang Qing and Kang Sheng became frantic. What if Liu should die before he was expelled from the Party and removed as president? They ordered medical care increased. The Twelfth Plenary Session of the Eighth Party Central Committee was convened on October 11, 1968, and expelled Liu.

Liu was not told of the expulsion. On his birthday, November 24, he was "accidentally" permitted to hear a radio broadcast telling of the Central Committee action.

The macabre charade went on. Liu became so ill a special hospital team was put in charge of him. He no longer spoke. His veins were so raddled that there was hardly a place to insert a hypodermic. Zhou Enlai directed two special nurses to care for him. They could not get him to respond. He showed only one sign of life: He called the names of two young guards, and when they came to his bedside he smiled at them.

On October 17, 1969, Lin Biao, now in command of China as Mao's heir, issued what he called Order Number 1. Fearing war with the Soviet Union, Lin ordered the removal from Beijing of surviving high-ranking victims. Deng Xiaoping and his wife and stepmother were flown to Nanchang. Liu Shaoqi, on feeding tubes and drip medication, was wrapped naked in a cotton blanket, loaded onto a plane, and flown to remote Kaifeng, the old capital of the Taiping rebellion, in Henan Province. He died there on November 12, 1969, lying naked on the cement floor in the basement of an old prison. The special team of doctors and nurses had been withdrawn and sent back to Beijing, taking Liu's personal medication with them. Unshaven, his hair uncut for months, Liu had died of pneumonia.

He was cremated at midnight, twenty soldiers surrounding the crematory. The special task team on the Liu Shaoqi case made out the death certificate in the name of "Liu Weihuang — occupation: none; cause of death: disease." On the line for next of kin it was signed "Liu Yuan, son." The ashes were placed in an unmarked jar and a banquet was laid on. The special task team drank wine and announced: "We have completed our task successfully."

Before dawn one morning after Liu Shaoqi had been sent off to Kaifeng, an army crew entered Zhongnanhai. They attacked the House of Good Fortune with picks and axes. By the time the sun rose, only a heap of rubble was left. No sign remained that the irrepressible clan of Liu Shaoqi and Wang Guangmei had inhabited Zhongnanhai.

After the Ninth Party Congress, April 1–24, 1969, Lin Biao drew up a list of those to be executed immediately by his closely controlled PLA. At the top of this list was the name of Wang Guangmei. The list was submitted to Zhou Enlai, who signed it and took it to Mao. Mao removed the name of Wang Guangmei. "Spare the prisoner and save the knife," he told Zhou, quoting a Chinese aphorism. The knife was used in executions to cut out the heart of the condemned person. "Oh, Mr. Chairman," exclaimed Zhou, "you are so generous."

So, thanks to Mao, the life of the woman whom he had permitted to be tortured to the edge of death, wife of the man whom his minions murdered with all the cruelty they could muster, was spared.

The death toll in the Liu family, including Liu himself, was four. Wang Guangmei's mother died in the Number 1 Prison, endlessly tortured to make her link her daughter with espionage. Liu's eldest son, Liu Rongbin, was beaten to death in Inner Mongolia. His battered body, with a forged suicide note attached, was placed on a railroad track and run over by a freight train. It took the other children years to discover that their half brother had, like so many others, been suicided.

The second eldest son, Liu Rongruo, spent eleven years in Number 1 Prison. He was kept in darkness most of the time, fed little, given no vitamins, allowed no sunlight. He contracted tuberculosis of the spine. When he was released in 1978 he could hardly stand. He died within three months.

The eldest sister, Liu Aiqing, was beaten and sent to the most primitive area of Mongolia, but she survived and regained her health.

Wang Guangmei remained for years in Qincheng Prison. The children had seen her occasionally, a skeletal figure, dazed, hardly able to talk after years of solitary confinement. Finally, in 1979, she was released and within weeks began to flower extraordinarily in the warmth of her remarkable children.

*   *   *

For years the Liu children searched for their father's ashes. Finally, in September 1976, just after Mao's death, they found an unmarked box at Babaoshan, the Beijing crematory. It was covered with a flag and had been placed to one side of a room where the ashes of Kang Sheng, the architect of Liu's death, stood in a place of honor.

The children removed the flag from the nameless box and found it spattered with long-dried spittle and scarred with cigarette burns. It could be their father's — but at any rate, it was that of a victim of the Cultural Revolution.

The day before October 1, 1976, they took a handful of ashes and made their way to Tiananmen. They crossed onto the marble bridge between the two *hou* — lion-dogs of the dynasties — and tossed the ashes into the Golden River that encircles the Forbidden City. The ashes were started on their long journey. They would flow through the heart of China and move slowly from stream to stream to reach the ocean and, as Liu had asked, carry a fleck of his being to the seven seas.

After Wang Guangmei was released from prison, in 1979, she and her children boarded a naval vessel one day, carrying an urn with the rest of Liu Shaoqi's ashes, which they scattered in Bohai Bay.

31

Moon over the Yan

WHEN THE SUN went down over dusty Yanan and the desert began to cool, the men and women of Mao's band — the men outnumbering the women eighteen to one — would come out of their caves and stroll along the river Yan, the men on the right bank, the women on the left, a trickle of water flowing in the rocky middle.

They walked slowly, the men mostly older and often from peasant backgrounds, poorly educated, and the women younger, high school and college graduates, just arrived from Shanghai, Beijing, or Nanjing, eager to take part in the Revolution.

The men smoked their homemade cigarettes, in goat's-leg-shaped holders they had carved from willow twigs, talking of guerrilla tactics and how to fight the Japanese. As the moon rose over the river the thoughts of the women turned to romance. The men thought romance was silly. They called the moon an old bean cake. The men were realistic, the women poetic.

To most of the young women the men were too old, they thought, to make good husbands. They had spent too much of their strength in warfare to be good lovers. Nonetheless, many young ladies set their caps for the men of Yanan, particularly the commanders.[1]

One of the young women who liked to stroll along the Yan was Jiang Qing, who by 1938 had managed to curl her way into the bed of Mao Zedong. Two other strollers — Xue Ming and Ye Qun — would capture two of Mao's most famous generals, He Long and Lin Biao, future marshals of the People's Republic. He Long was the black-bearded Robin Hood of the army, Lin Biao a solitary genius who in a few years would turn China upside down.

Different as the three ladies were, they would have one aspect in common — each would win her husband by displacing the woman who was his wife before they met. Jiang Qing did it with Mao, slipping into the bed left empty when He Zizhen, ill and troubled, went off to Moscow; Xue Ming filled the vacancy when Jian Xianren, the great revolutionary heroine, left He Long to study in the Soviet Union; and when Lin Biao returned from Moscow to China and left his wife, Liu Ximing, behind, Ye Qun took over.

The young revolutionary women knew each other well, and in fact, Xue Ming and Ye Qun were best friends. The three lives became fatally intertwined in the Great Proletarian Cultural Revolution. Jiang Qing and Ye Qun formed a working partnership.[2] As Jiang Qing put it to Ye Qun: "You go and get this enemy of mine under cover of all the chaos. If you have enemies I'll get them for you."[3]

In their Yanan days Ye Qun and Xue Ming worked together, lived together in the same cave, and got their first sight of He Long together. They went to a paper lantern rally in Yanan on the evening of November 7, 1938, outside West Gate, celebrating the anniversary of the Bolshevik revolution. They almost swooned at the sight of He Long, his great black beard, his ruddy complexion, his fiery eyes and dashing appearance, the "living dragon," as the people liked to call him, fresh from the battlefield.[4]

During the Cultural Revolution Jiang Qing spent much time, effort, and the blood of countless victims in a vain attempt to eradicate witnesses to and evidence of her not very revolutionary past, a task in which Ye Qun helped her. Jiang Qing aided Ye Qun in the same kind of endeavor and especially in the persecution (to death) of He Long and in the vicious torment of both his wives, past and present, high on her enemies list.

The son of a factory owner in Hubei Province ruined by warlord extortion, Lin Biao had middle-class roots. The Lin family turned toward radical solutions for China's ills.[5] Many in Yanan thought Lin Biao the most gifted of Mao's commanders. Lin had served first with Zhu De and then in 1928 under Mao directly. He had graduated from the Whampoa military academy at the age of twenty and by 1927 served as a colonel in the joint Communist-Nationalist Northern Expedition from Canton to Shanghai.

Lin Biao's military credentials were impeccable, but his relations with fellow commanders were not warm. They regarded him as a loner, and after his fall many came forward with stories of his selfishness in combat, claiming he sometimes exposed his associates to disaster. But no PLA general disputed Lin's brilliance.

There was another side to Lin Biao. He was moody, withdrawn, and, many thought, a hypochondriac and a neurotic. When Lin went to Moscow in 1939 he insisted he had not recovered from a freak wound suffered as a result of an uncharacteristic prank. He had captured a KMT general and, on a whim, donned the general's cap and greatcoat, flourished his gilt-handled sword, and ridden full tilt into a village. A sentry, thinking him a KMT general, opened fire, wounding Lin Biao in the shoulder. George Hatem, the American doctor serving in the Red Army, insisted that Lin Biao's wound was not serious and had healed before Lin went off to Russia. Dr. Nelson Fu, a Chinese missionary doctor who headed the Red Army's medical service, had the same view. Nonetheless, Lin Biao went to Moscow for medical treatment and stayed there with his new wife, Liu Ximing, for nearly two years.[6]

In Russia, Lin lived in a rambling dacha at Kuntsevo, a pleasant summer community about twenty miles from Moscow. The dacha was a boardinghouse where Stalin put up the Chinese who came for rest, study, or medical care. It had been the estate of a prominent Moscow family. The house was set in the obligatory birch grove, surrounded by a high wooden fence, painted green, and topped by barbed wire. It was, as one resident recalled, commodious by Chinese standards, with a little park to walk in, a Ping-Pong table, a volleyball court, benches where one could sit and enjoy the sun when the weather was good. In the library were Russian classics — Pushkin, Tolstoy, Dostoevsky, Turgenev, and Chekhov — a few European authors, lots of Marx, Engels, Lenin, and Stalin. No Chinese books.

Lin Biao took courses with the others, all given at the dacha. They seldom went into Moscow. The menu was made up of sturdy Russian dishes: borscht, plenty of kasha, occasional beef Stroganoff or shashlik, Russian black bread, and *smetana,* sour cream. No rice or chopsticks were found at the table. The tea was black Russian tea with strawberry jam, served in thin glasses with metal holders, not pale China tea in porcelain cups.

The Chinese got to know each other well — except for Lin Biao; no one got to know him. Sometimes he would be absent for a week or two or three. He never told them why or where he went.

The Chinese quickly got bored and yearned for their homeland. As one recalled, "Russia was at peace. China was at war. We longed to get back and take part in the struggle."[7] It took about eighteen months of fighting Soviet red tape to get permits and passage back to China. But Lin Biao stayed in Moscow until early 1942, and when he returned home he left his wife behind.

During much of Lin Biao's Moscow stay, Jian Xianren, He Long's first wife, lived in the same Kuntsevo dacha. She had known Lin Biao for years, but there was no intimacy. Jian Xianren was an extraordinary figure in the Chinese revolution. She had joined the guerrillas in remote Hunan while hardly out of her teens. Her brother, even younger, had already been fighting with He Long's command. He Long told the young man that he was so good-looking, he wished he were a girl. The brother replied that he had a sister who was even better-looking, and he introduced Jian to He. He Long enrolled her in the Fourth Army, as he called his ragtag outfit, the only woman in a company of a thousand. Within a month they were married.

Jian bore He two daughters. The first died of cold and hunger in the Hunan Mountains, where Jian was snowbound. The second was born three weeks before He Long and Jian joined the Long March. Jian brought her safely to Yanan; she was the only infant to make the whole march. She called her Jiesheng, the rough equivalent of Victoria.[8]

At the dacha Jian Xianren roomed with He Zizhen, the unfortunate second wife of Mao. He Zizhen knew that Jiang Qing (that "low-class artist," as He called her) was trying to win Mao's favor. While in Moscow she gave birth to another of Mao's babies, her fifth or sixth; more had died in infancy on the Long March and during guerrilla operations in the wilderness. This child, a boy, died within months, of undiagnosed measles.

Lin Biao's wife, Liu Ximing, also gave birth in Moscow, to a daughter, Mou Mou. Birth control was not practiced by Chinese of this generation.[9]

While Jian was away in Moscow, Xue Ming and He Long became, as Jian put it, "very friendly." He Long took an interest in the attractive young recruit from the KMT-controlled white areas but was, in the recollection of Xue Ming, then in Yanan, as shy as John Alden. He sent a succession of Party leaders to plead his case. Xue Ming was twenty-two, He Long forty-two. She thought He Long too old. Finally Peng Zhen (one of the oldest leaders) told her that age should not be a barrier. He swore that He Long was still strong and capable, as Peng Zhen put it, "of leading an energetic life." "Could you fight for ten days without sleep?" Peng asked the young girl. "He Long can. Can you do the same?"[10]

A few days later He Long called on Jian Xianren, back from Moscow, and told his first wife he was divorcing her. Jian was not surprised, but she was shocked at the abruptness. Divorce was easy in Yanan; all that was needed was a simple declaration. He Long gave his to Jian on July 28. On August 1, 1942, the anniversary of the founding of the Red Army in 1927 at Nanchang, He Long and Xue Ming were married.[11]

When Lin Biao got back from Moscow in 1942, he laid siege to Ye Qun. He didn't think she took him seriously and got his friend He Long to help. Lin Biao had written a formal proposal to Ye Qun, which she showed to her friends. Lin Biao thought they were giggling at him. He Long told Xue Ming that Ye Qun should respond to Lin Biao and stop showing off his letter.

Xue Ming and Ye Qun went for a stroll along the river Yan. "She didn't seem much interested," Xue Ming recalled fifty years later, "when I told her about Lin Biao. She didn't say whether she would keep the letter private or not. She didn't say one way or the other. She just kept skipping stones over the river." Despite Ye Qun's seeming indifference, she and Lin Biao were soon married. They did not invite Xue Ming and He Long to the wedding feast.

In the days when Xue Ming and Ye Qun had lived in Nanjing, before coming to Yanan, Ye Qun had gotten a job in the Central Broadcasting station run by the Chiang Kaishek government and she had won a speaking contest on the theme "There Is Only One Party in China [the KMT] and Only One Leader [Chiang Kaishek]." When the girls came to Communist Yanan, Xue Ming thought Ye Qun ought to tell the Party about this. Ye Qun broke into tears, refusing to admit her secret. Now, in 1942, Mao launched a "rectification" drive to turn up dark spots in personal histories. Xue Ming told He Long about Ye Qun, and He Long informed Lin Biao.

"My wife is a young woman. So is yours," He Long said. "Both are students and come from the white areas. If my wife did something wrong there, I'll be happy if your wife reports it." Lin Biao didn't seem very happy with He Long's report. The Party ordered both young women into special courses to set their Party thinking straight.

That seemed to be the end of a very petty affair. It wasn't. It resurfaced when Mao put the Party through the wringer again, in 1945. Lin Biao waved away the charges against Ye Qun and took her with him on his new assignment to Manchuria.[12] But from 1945 to 1965, the former Yanan roommates Ye Qun and Xue Ming didn't speak. When the Cultural Revolution started, it became evident that the innocent strolls along the left bank of the Yan had begotten consequences far from innocent.[13]

The Cultural Revolution was not a litany of murder, torture, and crimes committed solely for personal vengeance, but there was more of this kind of vendetta than anyone would have guessed.

Lin Biao and Ye Qun plotted together in the dark days of the terror Mao had sanctioned. Sometime in 1966 Lin Biao directed his subordinates to prepare allegations against He Long. Ye Qun took a hand in this, and Mao soon got a letter denouncing He Long. Mao called the marshal to the Swimming Pool House on September 14, 1966, and gave him the letter, which called He Long a "black character" who was plotting to seize power.

Mao told He Long not to worry. He knew He Long very well. "I stand by my past evaluation of you," Mao said. "You are loyal to the

Party, loyal to the people, merciless to the enemy, and good at keeping close contact with the masses."

It was just the kind of gesture by Mao that put his victim at ease — and softened him up for quick destruction.[14] Mao told He Long that he would be He Long's "royalist" — the code word used in the Cultural Revolution for a supporter of an accused man.

Mao had another talk with He Long a few days later. Not to worry — the problem had been taken care of. Famous last words. Mao suggested that He Long pay a visit to the concerned comrades, and, he implied, the whole thing would be put to rest.

He Long went to confer with Lin Biao. Lin Biao told him his "problem" could be serious or not serious. He Long should be careful about whom he supported and opposed. It was a faintly concealed way of saying You support me and I'll support you.

He Long didn't take the hint. Instead of welcoming Lin Biao's invitation, he simply said he would oppose anyone who opposed Mao. Lin decided that wasn't good enough.

Soon Jiang Qing joined in. She called in He Pengfei, He Long's son, and warned him that his father had "big problems" and that she might have to "shake him up a little." She told him his mother had problems, too. Kang Sheng, then working closely with Jiang Qing and Lin Biao, concocted the scenario of a military coup d'état in which He Long played the leading role. Shortly thereafter Red Guards began ransacking He Long's house.

Zhou Enlai gave He Long and his wife refuge, taking them into his little Zhongnanhai palace. However, agitation by the Red Guards and the Central Cultural Revolution Group got so bad that Zhou invited Jiang Qing and her aides to a formal meeting with He Long. Jiang refused to attend and mounted a racket of Red Guards armed with loudspeakers outside Zhongnanhai, which made the meeting impossible. Deciding He Long was not safe in Zhongnanhai, Zhou sent him and his wife to the Western Hills, where they could be under the protection of the PLA. He had his own bodyguards accompany them and had them change cars on the way to throw off pursuit.[15]

But soon Lin Biao, Ye Qun, and Kang Sheng took command of the area where Zhou Enlai had tried to hide He Long. Since, Kang Sheng said, He Long was too tough to be broken by "struggle sessions," medical means would have to be used in what Kang called "a reverse way." That meant that He Long, who suffered from diabetes, was given glucose and deprived of insulin, a fatal switch.

He Long and Xue Ming were held in a courtyard house and

forbidden to go outside. Their water supply was cut off, and they were dependent on what they could catch from the rain. With the heat of July and August, He Long suffered severely.[16]

He Long was taken to a hospital on March 27, 1969, but the doctors said he was shamming illness. He Long told his wife "they just want to kill me slowly — murder without bloodshed." He violently objected to being returned on June 8 to the same hospital where they had said he was not ill. Although he was vomiting constantly, he was conscious and clearheaded. The doctors claimed he was in a diabetic coma and insisted on taking him away. Xue Ming was not permitted to accompany him.

"Six hours later," Xue Ming said, "he was dead. I have no idea what the doctors did to him."[17]

Xue Ming and He Long's children were informed separately of He Long's death and were taken to the hospital to view the body. He Jiesheng, He Long's irrepressible daughter, broke away from the attendants and lifted the sheet covering He Long's body to see if there were visible wounds. She was grabbed by guards before she could be certain.

That was not the end. In November 1969, Ye Qun telephoned an aide of Lin Biao's and said: "Xue Ming knows too much about me. Remove her to a place farther from Beijing and put her in air force custody."[18]

Xue Ming spent six years in prison in Guizhou at forced labor. Her name was concealed; she was known only as "a mysterious old lady of the mountains." Xue Ming's youngest daughter, He Liming, seventeen, accompanied her to Guizhou. He Pengfei and his sister He Xiaoming were evicted from He Long's house and put in prison.

He Long's first wife, Jian Xianren, heroine of the Revolution, was drawn into the skein. The Red Guards tried to get her to testify against He Long. "He has already abused you," they said. She refused. She was beaten and her grandchildren frightened. She was "put into the cowshed": confined in a dirty hovel, made to clean latrines, put under twenty-four-hour-a-day watch, and given slops for food. One Red Guard said: "You're an old lady putting on the airs of a reactionary." They took her belt and hairpins away lest she commit suicide. They removed her chair and made her stand continuously. Then they left her for days "to think it over." She decided she liked that better than being at home, since she was left alone and felt more secure. The Guards wrote a letter to the Politburo saying she was "against the Revolution." The Politburo told the Red Guards to send her back to her workplace. They did — after nine months. Only then was Jian Xianren informed of He Long's death.[19]

When Jian went back home, her eighty-nine-year-old mother was deep in grief over He Long's death. "Mao should have known of this," she said. "But it seems that he did nothing."

An old friend told Jian that her mother had sat day after day before the portrait of Mao Zedong on the wall talking to him. "Chairman Mao, Chairman Mao, what has happened? Almost all of my family died for the Chinese revolution. Only my two daughters are left. Where are they? Where are they?"

What happened? Jian could not be sure. But, she said, in later years Mao Zedong had secluded himself from the people. He had lived within red walls, the red walls that were the symbol of the ancient dynasties of China.[20]

The question is often asked: How much did Mao know about the tortures carried out in his name? The answer is that he knew a lot but interpreted it in his own way. In 1967 he asked an old peasant leader, Ji Dengkui, whom he had elevated to the Politburo, what it was like to do the airplane, hands sharply thrust behind, head and shoulders bending forward almost to the floor.

Ji had been roughly handled by the Red Guards but tossed the posture off as "nothing much. It might be good physical exercise," Ji said. Mao roared with laughter, tried to do the airplane himself, then laughed some more. Wherever Mao went for months afterward, he told and retold the story. It would have been difficult to find many of his victims who shared his sense of humor.[21]

32

The Shadow of Lin Biao

THE ENIGMATIC FIGURE of Lin Biao cast a deeper and deeper shadow over the Beijing of the late 1960s. For years his character had seemed different from that of his comrades. In retrospect it is clear that the differences were clinical.

Lin Biao had long been known as a complainer about his health. He had been under the general care of Dr. Nelson Fu, the missionary-educated physician who for years was head of the Red Army's medical service. Fu very early on had become aware that Lin Biao's problems were something more than ordinary. Lin had told Dr. Fu that he had become afraid of light, water, wind, and loud noises. His sensitivities were not unlike those that compelled Marcel Proust to immure himself in a soundproof chamber. Lin Biao grew increasingly more agitated. He finally told Dr. Fu, "I'm going to die. You must save me."[1]

The significance of these problems had become acute in the weeks leading up to China's intervention in the Korean War, when, contrary to Mao's wishes, Lin had refused to take command of the Chinese forces, pleading poor health. Despite Mao's entreaties, he flew off to Moscow for medical consultation, as he had done many times previously.

Lin came back from Moscow still obsessed by his phobias. His condition seemed to be deteriorating, and Mao became alarmed. He instructed Dr. Fu to assemble a team of China's best doctors and try to determine the cause of Lin Biao's symptoms.

Dr. Fu brought in doctors from Shanghai, Tianjin, and Beijing. Xiao Hua, an outstanding PLA general, was designated by the Party Central Committee as liaison with the medical group.[2] Lin Biao and his wife, Ye Qun, had a private word with Dr. Fu before the consultation, asking him to certify that Lin Biao was suffering from a serious illness.

But, although the doctors gave him every kind of test, they could find nothing functionally wrong. They did, however, find a plenitude of symptoms of psychological disorientation and plain evidence of drug usage.

Dr. Fu gave Lin Biao and Ye Qun a detailed report. He advised Lin to get outdoor exercise, take frequent walks, eat more vegetables and fruit, drink more water — and stop using morphine. Dr. Fu reported his findings to the Central Committee and in a private talk with Mao told him tactfully that Lin Biao was a drug addict.

The news did not seem to surprise Mao. He indicated that he had known about the drug taking for a long time. Mao copied off a poem by Cao Cao, founder of the state of Wei, one of the heroes of *Romance of the Three Kingdoms,* Mao's favorite, and sent it to Lin Biao:

> It does not depend upon heaven
> A man can live forever if he knows
> How to take care of himself.

It was a gentle hint to Lin Biao. Mao might better have reminded Lin Biao of Cao Cao's fate. He had summoned a great physician, Dr. Hua, to treat his injured head. Hua said, "The pain arises from wind and the seat of the disease is the brain." He then proposed to operate. Cao Cao, scenting a plot, threw the doctor into prison, where he soon died. A bit later Cao Cao succumbed.[3]

Dr. Nelson Fu paid the same price as Dr. Hua. When the Cultural Revolution broke out he was arrested at the orders of a close ally of Lin Biao's. Big-character posters denounced him as an enemy of Mao Zedong's and Lin Biao's. He was paraded through the streets, tortured, and reviled. Fu was seventy-two years old. In 1934 he had saved Mao's life when the chairman was critically ill in Ningdu.[4]

Hoping for a pardon, Fu wrote to Mao and recalled those days: "I saved your life. That at least I did right. Now I hope you will save my life."

Mao wrote on Fu's letter: "This man holds no power and has committed no serious crime. It seems that he should be protected." Thin gruel for a man who saved Mao's life. Fu was not protected. Three days after Mao received Fu's letter he was thrown into a solitary cell and beaten until his ribs were crushed. On March 13, 1968, Jiang Qing said: "Fu Lianzhang [Fu's Chinese name] is a scoundrel. He actually dared to spread information about Chairman Mao's health. Arrest him." Fu, now seventy-four, was unable to digest rough prison food. He was handcuffed, kicked, beaten, given no toilet. His guards wrote in the prison daybook: "The wretch acts like a lunatic." Fifteen days later when they entered Fu's cell they found his body, stiff and cold, on the cement floor.[5]

The revelation of Lin Biao's drug addiction casts a lurid light on many events in the Chinese political scene. It also raises the questions of whether drug addiction was confined solely to Lin or was shared by other leaders, at least for certain periods of time, and of whether the problem could have been serious enough to affect policy.

In Lin's case there are telltale signs of morphia-induced delusions in his concepts and ideas. The possibility cannot be excluded that such personality changes could have occurred in others within the leadership group and particularly in Mao.

As a standard textbook on addiction reports, "Opiate addicts demonstrate appreciable psychopathology, including high levels of neurotic personality and psychotic characteristics, although no common pattern is apparent. Personality characteristics and behavior patterns result in part from the interaction of the addict and the drug in the sociocultural environment."[6]

Clearly Mao's companions were not addicted to the point of stupefaction. They were vigorous and active. No trace of addictive conduct can be seen in Zhou Enlai or Deng Xiaoping, for instance. Mao is another problem. Beginning with his entry into Zhongnanhai, he more and more fell into a pattern of lengthy disengagement from the world, lolling for days, weeks, and months on his pyramid of pillows, whether in Beijing, Hangzhou, or some other resort. These periods were broken by frenzied activity, meetings, conferences, new grandiose schemes, "inspection trips" through the countryside.

The taint of opium could be suspected in the dreamlike quality of Mao's speculations and ideas, remote from reality, his boundless flights of fancy that were transmuted in one form or another into domestic or foreign policy.

How Lin Biao and other leaders could have become addicted to drugs is significant. No other social problem was better known to Mao and his men. Some, like Zhu De, the great old man of the Red Army, had been addicts themselves. Zhu acquired the habit in Yunnan in his days as a warlord. He kicked it by compelling himself to take a long trip down the Yangtze on a British river steamer where not a pinch of opium was available.

Almost everyone had a father, an uncle, a son whose life had been ruined by opium. One of Deng Xiaoping's uncles, a brilliant man dedicated to education and good works, had his career damaged by the remorseless pipe.[7] Mao knew opium and how it transformed character. They all knew the tragedy that the poppy brought to their land and their people.

The Long March had taken the Red Army through China's opium country — Guizhou, Sichuan, and Yunnan, where the poppy fields bloomed pastel pink to the horizon. There everyone smoked: men, women, and ten-year-old boys. Babies were put to sleep sucking sugarcane smeared with opium dust. "Black gold" was the currency of the land. When the Red Army passed by, soldiers broke open the opium barns and distributed the black, round opium cakes to the peasants. The peasants huddled naked in their courtyards, eyes glazed by the drug, deep in opium dreams. They hardly saw the troops.

The Red Army had the strictest of rules: No addicts could enlist. But army doctors used opium medicinally, since there was no other anesthetic in the backcountry. When a wounded man had to have a smashed leg chopped off, he was given an opium pellet.

Mao and his commanders worked by night, slept by day. They stayed up until dawn receiving messages from far-flung units and sending out battle plans for the day. Exhausted, they fell into litters and were carried on these swaying beds during the Long March. Without sleeping pills they could not manage. To a man they became sleeping-pill addicts. Those pills were morphine, codeine, or plain opium capsules. Nothing else was available.

The reliance of the Long March leaders on sleeping pills and the habits of night work were intimately related. No one bothered to count how many became addicted to morphine or other opium derivatives. The leaders maintained their revolutionary working hours in peacetime. Zhou Enlai, like Mao Zedong, made a habit during his long career of working through the night, often getting no more than two or three hours of sleep. He made no secret of his sleeping-pill addiction.[8] George Hatem, the American doctor who served many years with the Red Army, recalled being told by Dr. Fu that he had obtained sleeping pills for Zhou on the Long March, smuggled from Shanghai. These were a German-patented codeine derivative.[9]

During the Cultural Revolution there was no torture more cruel than to deprive a man of his sleeping pills. Liu Shaoqi was almost driven out of his mind. He Long got no sleep. Peng Dehuai's curses lifted the roof off his cell.

No one was more addicted than Mao. He joked in his speeches about taking seven or eight or a pillbox full. Even so, his sleeping hours averaged fewer than four in twenty-four.

Mao's remarkable constipation was well known, and as a standard handbook notes: "Highly tolerant addicts will continue to demonstrate pupillary constriction and constipation."[10]

Whatever addiction's effects on Lin Biao, they did not prevent him from working incessantly to strengthen his position with Mao. He had invented the "little red book" of Mao's sayings — *Quotations from Chairman Mao* — and placed it in the hands of every man, woman, and child in China. Surgeons operated with a scalpel in one hand, the book in the other. Marksmen shot at targets, their aim sharpened by the little red book. Women went into labor reading Mao's sayings; it eased the pain, they reported.

Now Lin Biao produced another triumph: "Long Live the Victory of the People's War." This pamphlet, released in 1965, proposed that China could win the world by mobilizing the people of backward countries just as Mao had mobilized the poor peasants to win China. As Mao, the Red Army, and the peasants had surrounded China's advanced urban centers, so the peasants of the world would surround and triumph over the United States, England, France, and Japan. Mass action, Mao's adored cliché, would win the world.

Lin Biao's strategy was as windy and divorced from practicality as Mao's vision of the Great Leap Forward propelling China into the modern world in three years. The idea, like Mao's, seemed in cold daylight to have been blown out of a pipe. Since the days of Thomas De Quincey's *Confessions of an English Opium Eater,* published in 1822, the literate reader had been familiar with the manner in which the drug-distorted vision had lifted the victim into a cloudy state in which anything seemed possible. It was De Quincey who put the expression "pipe dream" into the language. The concept of Mao's Cultural Revolution — a revolution against the Revolution, destruction of Party and state, creation of *luan* (chaos) in order to produce a new utopia — reeks of the same delusion-prone psyche.

These mirages were being acted out against a backdrop of something very real and dangerous — the threat of nuclear war with the Soviet Union. There is some evidence that Lin Biao tried to divert the drift toward war with Russia, but he could not fight the anti-Soviet emotion that emanated from the Swimming Pool House. He was unable to keep Mao's favor and oppose Mao's obsessive hatred for Moscow.

Lin Biao supported Mao's naive program for preparing for nuclear war: the mass destruction of city walls and ancient buildings to provide stones for pell-mell construction of underground tunnels and deep shelters under Beijing, Shanghai, Tianjin, and all other great Chinese cities. Mao's slogan was "Prepare for War. Dig Tunnels." Dig they did — everywhere, leaving scars on the land that China could never efface.

The remains of Beijing's wondrous walls went. Every street was piled with stones, brick, steel supporting rods. Mao's mass action was put into continental effect. Everywhere people turned from productive work to dig tunnels. "Bad elements" — so branded by the Cultural Revolution — were mobilized. Workers left their factories. School children stopped lessons and "volunteered."

No one bothered to ask whether, indeed, the ramshackle shelters would protect the people from nuclear bombs or simply provide convenient ovens in which they would be incinerated.

Then Zhou Enlai won a breathing spell from the threat of war. He met Premier Aleksei Kosygin at Beijing Airport in September 1969 and after a six-hour talk got a standstill agreement for negotiations to ease the crisis. Lin Biao took advantage of the cooling off to race ahead toward the pinnacle of power. He had gotten his official anointment as Mao's successor at the Ninth Party Congress, in April 1969, when he was named sole vice chairman and Mao's official heir. There was no rival in sight, with the possible exception of Premier Zhou Enlai. Deng Xiaoping was in forced residence deep in Jiangxi; Liu Shaoqi was dead.

Lin Biao watched Zhou Enlai carefully. Zhou appeared again and again onstage with Jiang Qing, Kang Sheng, and Lin Biao all through the Cultural Revolution. Not a word did he speak in public to oppose Mao's wildest fancies. Zhou courted Jiang Qing as meticulously as the nobles at Versailles attended Madame de Pompadour. Zhou was self-effacing. He took no credit for himself. He did not seem a credible challenger.

Lin Biao could see the Dragon Throne on his horizon. Only a few paces and it would be his. Just a short walk from the beautiful old house of the Yu family, where he lived, to the Forbidden City. He would bypass Zhongnanhai. He had no wish to occupy the Swimming Pool House.

Lin knew he had to move fast. Whether or not he completely understood Mao's Machiavellian tactics, he could not fail to realize that the most dangerous relationship one could have with Mao was to be his closest associate. Lin had read enough Chinese history to understand that no emperor trusts his heir.

Professor Hu Hua, who spent a lifetime analyzing Mao, believed he had developed a crafty mechanism to bridle his heirs — he secretly put in place means for their downfall at the very time he elevated them.

Mao had planted a time bomb under Lin Biao. In the quizzical letter he wrote to Jiang Qing on July 6, 1966 (it is not known if it was ever sent), he made clear that he did not trust Lin Biao. He called him "my friend" but said he was going too far. For the first time in his life, Mao claimed, he had been compelled *unwillingly* to go along on major questions: "I have to do things against my own will." He was "quite uneasy" at Lin Biao's speech to an enlarged Politburo meeting of May 16, 1966, in which Lin devoted his time to warning of the danger of a "political coup at the highest level" of the Communist Party. "There has never been any address like his before," Mao said. The letter, produced after the downfall of Lin, was intended to demonstrate Mao's wisdom in never trusting Lin Biao from earliest days.[11] Mao had also set down his private concerns about Liu Shaoqi years before he broke with him openly and denounced him. He did the same with Deng Xiaoping.[12]

Lin Biao knew that Mao was like quicksilver. You thought you had him in your hand, but when you looked again he had slipped through.

To secure his position, Lin now advanced a grandiose new proposal — a theory of greatness. Only once in a hundred years did a true genius appear in the world, perhaps only once in three hundred years. Mao was that genius. Such a man should not be troubled with the mundane affairs of everyday life. He should be honored by his nation as none other. Lin Biao suggested that a new office be created for Mao — that of president. Not the lowly presidency of Liu Shaoqi but a superpresidency fit for a living god, a philosopher-emperor. In this role Mao would commune with heaven and bestow on his grateful people the blossoms of his visions of a new Middle Kingdom, as high above the old Middle Kingdom as it had been above barbarian earthlings. It was a concept more lofty than any other Lin Biao had floated, one to appeal to every fiber of Mao's poetic self-image. Did it evoke the sickly sweet odor of the pipe?

Mao turned it down. Poet, philosopher, and dreamer he was. But he possessed a crafty core of plain politics. Lin Biao's scheme would take the levers of power out of his hands and give them to Lin Biao. Mao may have considered himself a god. But he was not turning the keys of China's Tammany Hall over to anyone else.

Lin Biao's stratagem probably sealed Mao's decision that it was time to begin to remove Lin.

These arcane maneuvers could hardly be missed by Zhou Enlai. He had been around too long and had seen too many favorites fall from power. No one had been more appalled by the danger into which China had been propelled by the quarrel with Russia. No one knew better that China had faced nuclear holocaust nakedly. Its few nuclear weapons could only sting the Soviets. China had not an ally to its name except Albania, North Korea, and, nominally, North Vietnam, then rather busy with the United States.

Zhou Enlai won Mao's approval to try to correct this vulnerability. The only power that could be a counterweight to the Soviet Union was the United States. Although China had been technically at war with America since Korea, Mao had no objections to reopening relations. His fear, suspicion, and hatred of Moscow were intense. Since 1946 or earlier he had preferred an arrangement with the United States, but in those days that was beyond achievement.

Quietly Zhou turned to his task. Not a public word was said. Zhou had one hidden asset. He had picked up the first indications that President Richard Nixon and Henry Kissinger were interested in an opening to China. In August 1969 Nixon and Kissinger visited Bucharest and dropped hints of a change in attitude toward China. For the first time an American president referred to the "People's Republic of China" and indicated that talks were no longer precluded.

Mao offered cryptic encouragement. When Edgar Snow, Mao's old friend from Yanan, came to China in 1970, Mao invited him and his wife to the high balcony at Tiananmen for the October 1 celebration. Mao told Snow two months later that Nixon was welcome to come to China, either as president or as a private tourist.[13]

The signal was a long time in reaching the White House. For several reasons, including prejudice against Snow, his interview with Mao was not published until April 1971. Even then, as Kissinger later admitted, he was slow to realize its significance. There is no doubt that Lin Biao caught the signal immediately and saw it as a dangerous one. If Zhou should achieve a rapprochement with the United States, the effect would be disastrous to Lin Biao. Zhou Enlai as author of the biggest shift in Chinese policy since 1949 would possess a prestige that would oust Lin Biao from his perilous seat as the heir apparent.

What to do?

33

Project 571

EXACTLY when Lin Biao set in train a fallback position against being dumped by Mao — a putsch — cannot be pinpointed. It may have been as early as the first months of 1970, well before any outward sign of the rift.

The Soviet nuclear threat had forced Lin Biao and the leadership to take practical measures for survival. They began to improve and make nuclear-proof the underground city below Zhongnanhai and to expand the secret rail network. This expansion got under way in 1969. The new network provided connections with the Bank of China, so gold reserves could be evacuated, and linkage to the north edge of the Forbidden City, with access to Lin's tunnel from the old Yu estate and the Defense Ministry in Iron Lion Lane.

The network also included new underground spurs to link the Great Hall of the People with an escape route to the Western Hills. It was bombproofed and connected to the trunk metro leading to the northwest corner of Beijing. There it was extended in a new high-security tunnel to the cavernous PLA complex blasted out of solid rock in the Western Hills, which would be the command general headquarters in case of Soviet attack.

All these facilities were replete with power generators, air filters, communications installations, hospitals, independent water and food supplies, and heat. At the same time they provided Lin Biao safe, almost instant access from his headquarters to the Western Hills redoubt, which he, as head of the armed forces, controlled. If he ever had to leave town in a hurry, he could make a quick, safe getaway.[1]

These underground facilities were elaborate and expensive. There were others, none of which was more comprehensive than the one Lin Biao built at West Lake, in Hangzhou, adjacent to the villas he and Mao occupied. It was called Project 704, a numeral that indicates the date when work on it began: April 1970. By this time Lin Biao and his wife, Ye Qun, probably had detected the symptoms of Mao's changed attitude toward them. Project 704 was not built specifically with any plot in mind, but it could be adapted to many uses.

The West Lake construction was almost an underground Pentagon. It covered a fifty-acre site between two hills in the northwest quadrant of the lakeshore. There were two large aboveground buildings — one, very beautifully done, was apparently a palace for the Lin family, and the other, even larger, may have been intended for Mao or for personnel at the base.

The underground complex was a complete military facility capable of being used as an independent command post or as a backup in case the Western Hills site was captured or destroyed. It was built to withstand nuclear attack, with heavy blast-proof glass on exterior windows and triple-plate glass on the inside, and to operate under siege or nuclear bomb attack, with its integrated generators, light and power systems, air-conditioning, hospital, and food and water supplies. Within the compound were a war room with a high-tech communications room adjacent, a map room, and more than thirty individual conference rooms, many with two-way mirrors.

One feature attracted attention. Although as of today Project 704 is said to have been Lin Biao's, it included a magnificent indoor swimming pool, 60 by 120 feet, with excellent ceramic tile walls. Lin Biao was never known to have ventured into a swimming pool; Mao could hardly live without one. Lin obviously expected — or hoped — to have Mao in residence there. Mao spent on the average more time in Hangzhou than he did in Beijing. Perhaps Lin hoped to lure him to 704 under threat of a supposed Soviet nuclear attack, then keep him as a hostage in his new nuclear-safe gilded cage. It sounds improbable, but everything about the Lin conspiracy sounds improbable, and it is consistent with the fact of Lin Biao's addiction.

Project 704 required a construction force of seven thousand, all "volunteers," whose security checks went back three generations. Having volunteers kept costs down. They got minimum pay and a couple of rice bowls a day and slept on the site. Even so, the complex was said to have cost 21 million yuan, about $10 million at the exchange rate of the time. It took fourteen months to complete the buildings. The interior fittings had not been finished at the time of Lin Biao's death.

The great establishment eventually became a white elephant. It was not finished until 1975. After Mao died a year later, nobody knew what to do. Finally Project 704 was turned over to the Zhejiang Hotel, which opened the aboveground buildings as luxury tourist hotels. Sightseers could visit the underground structure by boarding a number 27 bus in downtown Hangzhou and paying a yuan for an admission ticket.[2]

Once again — August. Once again — Lushan. August 1970, not 1959, the ascent of the mountain as arduous as always, the cool at the top delicious. Mao Zedong had assembled his fellows yet again at this island of repose. He did not, so far as is known, write a poem to commemorate this meeting. But he was far from idle. Something about Lushan lifted his energy levels.

This time he did not stay in Chiang Kaishek's house. Now he had a house of his own, a palace, newly built, as much like the Study of Chrysanthemum Fragrance as his architects could build — with a swimming pool.

From this bower of contentment Mao launched Jovian shafts. The target was no longer the hapless Peng Dehuai, living out his last days in an army hospital, his body broken. Mao had a new target, hardly unexpected by those who understood the Mao style. It was Lin Biao, heir to the throne. Any reader of *Romance of the Three Kingdoms* could have guessed at this turn in the endless scrolls of the Chinese dynasties. Had Mao died, Lin Biao would already have succeeded him. But Mao had not died. And in the summer of 1970 he was filled with vigor.

Not once did Mao mention Lin Biao's name in his Lushan speeches. Ostensibly he aimed his shafts at Chen Boda, the ugly spark plug of the Cultural Revolution. He and Chen, Mao confessed with mock humility, had had some disagreements. Some people thought that as a result "Lushan mountain would be blown flat. They needn't worry. This will not happen. The world will continue to turn." Mao shot down a new effort by Lin to declare him the "genius of the world" and make him a figurehead. He was an old fox. No one had to read Mao's lips to know that the honeymoon of the new heir had ended. "What will happen to the succession?" Ye Qun exclaimed.[3]

At Lushan it was obvious that once Mao had Chen Boda in his

sights, Lin Biao and Ye Qun would be next. Lin had said of Mao: "Once he thinks someone is his enemy he won't stop until the victim is put to death; once you offend him he'll persist to the end — passing all the blame on to the victim, held responsible for crimes committed by himself."

Lin Biao and Ye Qun had planned to attack Zhou Enlai at Lushan. It never happened. Zhou was sailing ahead with his minuet that was to lead Henry Kissinger to visit Beijing in July 1971.

If the Lin dynasty was to be saved, it was time to act. Unknown to the world, unknown to all but three or possibly four participants, preparations for Project 571 commenced. As pronounced in Chinese, 571 is a homonym for "armed uprising."

The official government version of Lin Biao's plot, later to be leaked out, is fuzzy as to when and how active work started. Possibly it was in December 1970, more likely in Suzhou in the spring of 1971, when Lin, Ye Qun, and their twenty-six-year-old son, Lin Liguo, were vacationing there. The "planning" had little practical reality; once again the odor of the pipe could be detected. The three discussed a coup d'état using paratroopers, in which Lin Biao would act to save Mao Zedong during a feigned attack. In this psychodrama Zhou Enlai, Jiang Qing, Kang Sheng, and some key military would be "neutralized," or killed, leaving Lin Biao supreme, the hero of the land for saving Mao from the enemy.

That got nowhere. Lin did not have the numbers to carry out anything so elaborate. A palace coup seemed the limit of his resources.

The official report contends that much of the planning for the coup was put into the hands of Lin Liguo, who had by dint of his father's influence become deputy chief of operations of the air force. His use of code names with a kind of Dick Tracy flavor betrayed his still-adolescent nature. The conspiratorial organization was called the Joint Fleet and his command the Flotilla. Mao was code-named B-52 or Emperor Qin. Ye Qun was the Duchess, the Central Committee the Big Battleship. Young Lin bragged that in numbers the Joint Fleet equaled that with which the Bolsheviks carried out their October 1917 coup in Petrograd. This was possibly true, but the Bolsheviks had resources of intellect and revolutionary experience that the Joint Fleet would never match.

There was a suggestion in the official version of the affair that some predecessor of the Joint Fleet antedated Project 571, that there had been a kind of college fraternity of dissident young military men to which Lin Liguo had belonged. The air force was regarded as the main component of the coup. In general Lin Biao depended on the armed forces, which he had busily stuffed with his supporters in the years since he replaced Peng Dehuai.

A notable feature of the plot, as outlined in government documents, was the lack of connection with Jiang Qing and the Gang of Four. The implication was that they were not involved, that there had been a split between them and the Lins. Some have suggested that the "split" hinted at by the documents might have been an arbitrary line drawn by Mao so that it would not appear that his whole establishment was conniving against him.

Nothing came of the sketchy military operation. Very late in the day the plotters' focus turned to assassination.

Mao had set off in August 1971 for a tour of south and central China to visit military provincial headquarters and military bases and to rally the armed forces to his side. He had been carrying out extensive reshuffling of commands in order to weaken Lin's control. Mao knew that Lin's principal strength had to be in the armed forces. Now he was putting reliable men in place. He gave a series of talks, often alluding openly to his differences with Lin Biao. Lin Biao got a stream of reports on Mao's progress and watched it with apprehension. He could feel his support melting away. Mao's special train carried him from point to point with frequent stops for speeches, inspections, and heart-to-heart talks. It was due to bring him into Shanghai about the middle of September.

Faced with Mao's fast-moving and apparently successful effort to turn the tables, the conspirators began to improvise an assassination plot. In two or three days, beginning about September 8 (so the official accounts contend), Lin Liguo and his chums tried to put together a plot of unbelievable complexity. They would bring to bear such fire-power on Mao that the aging chairman would simply vanish in a storm of fire and bullets.

An attack would be made on his special train as it approached Shanghai. A heavy dynamite charge would be smuggled aboard to blow up the train, a plane would bomb it from above, and a battery of 100-millimeter antiaircraft guns would fire point-blank and blast it to bits. Then a squad of rocket men and soldiers equipped with flame-throwers would move in for the kill. Another unit would blow up a bridge to bar the train's passage, and a plane would bomb the Shanghai oil storage park to create such a confusion of flame and smoke that no one would· be able to tell what was happening. If all this failed and Mao survived the fire, the bombs, and the bullets, a fearless gunman would enter the train and shoot him dead with a .45 Colt.

It was an *Apocalypse Now* scenario. Only juveniles or drug-sotted minds could have contemplated anything so bizarre. Yet, if we believe the government's version, that is precisely what they did contemplate, meeting in a conference room at the Beijing West Airport, shuttling back and forth to Shanghai, and trying to put the final touches on the attack in an all-day meeting on September 11. A dozen witnesses testified so at the trial of Jiang Qing, the rest of the Gang of Four, and the surviving Lin Biao conspirators, which opened on November 20, 1980, in Beijing. The witnesses included the chief of the air force, the chief of staff of the army, and the head of the navy. All were described as close collaborators of Lin Biao's. None offered any substantive evidence of his role in the harebrained schemes.[4] Not one of the melodramatic scenarios was carried out.[5]

The only attempt at an explanation for why the conspirators abandoned their plans is a hint that somehow Mao got wind that a plot was afoot. One account says that the dynamite on Mao's train was discovered. If, as the official accounts claim, Mao sped through Shanghai, changing his schedule to clear the city a day or two early, this would support the notion of a tip-off.

None of the evidence disclosed by the government suggests that Lin, Ye Qun, or Lin Liguo and his friends had advance warning that Mao would arrive early in Shanghai and speed right through the city.

At the September 11 all-day conference, Lin Liguo and his group consulted the commander of a special unit equipped with rockets and flamethrowers. One of Lin's group said: "This is just the right stuff to attack a train." The commander objected that he couldn't move his units, but the conspirators airily replied that they could get another outfit to carry out the job. They thought they still had time to put together the assassination attempt. They did not know time had run out.[6]

Lin Biao and Ye Qun were at their villa at the seashore resort of Beidaihe, about 130 miles east of Beijing, that evening of September 11. They were relaxed. Ye Qun was stretched out, reading, on a divan. The telephone rang. Lin answered. Mao's train had already passed through Shanghai and was moving north at high speed. Ye Qun sighed loudly. She got up from the divan and started to pack her bag. She, at least, knew that it was time to go.

She picked up two dictionaries: English-Chinese and Russian-

Chinese. She added two conversational readers, one with phrases in English, one in Russian. Whether they went to Hong Kong or Moscow she was prepared — more prepared for Moscow, perhaps, because she had been there several times and had studied the language.[7]

Mao arrived in Beijing, according to the government account, on the morning of the twelfth. There is no official report on what Lin Biao, his wife, and their son did during the crucial hours before late evening of September 12. The missing hours from midnight of the eleventh to almost midnight of the twelfth constitute a blank page, the biggest hole and the most questionable ellision in the official version. It is not conceivable that Lin and Ye Qun simply puttered around the seashore house, went for a dip, and sunned themselves while their lives and future hung in the balance. Could they have fallen into post-high inertia?

One vague report suggests that Lin Biao may have been in Beijing on September 12. What he was doing there is not explained. The flight and drive to Beijing from Beidaihe take about an hour, so he could easily have traveled to the capital the next day. Another report indicates that Lin Liguo may have flown to Shanghai on the night of the eleventh and flown back to Beijing on the morning of the twelfth.

During those critical hours the plotters must have engaged in frantic efforts to salvage their scheme. One official version suggests that with the failure of the assassination plan, Lin and Ye Qun tried to activate the earlier scheme for an armed uprising, based in Canton. If so, not a shred of evidence of this has been produced. And, in hard fact, Lin didn't have the troops, the organization, or the allies for anything on that scale.

What is known is that late in the day of the twelfth Lin Liguo flew from Beijing to Beidaihe in a Trident three-motor plane, number 256, and landed at the Shanhaiguan Airport. The plane had been assigned for Lin Biao's personal use. The crew of three, which had been assigned the plane on September 6, had often been detailed for VIP flights and was experienced. Investigation later showed no "problems" in their personal backgrounds.

The plane landed in Beidaihe about 5:00 P.M. Lin Liguo told the crew that Lin Biao would be using the plane in the morning. They should wake up at 6:30 A.M., have breakfast at 7:00, and be at Lin Biao's disposal. They were not told where Lin Biao might be flying.[8]

The plane stood on the tarmac during the evening of the twelfth, its presence noted and recorded by air traffic controllers.[9]

*   *   *

That same evening Premier Zhou Enlai was working in the Fujian Room of the Great Hall of the People, not his usual workplace. He had postponed a meeting with a Japanese delegation and was said to be working on a report for an upcoming meeting of the People's Assembly.

At 10:20 P.M. his secretary informed him that Security Unit 8341 was on the telephone. Something unexpected had happened. Zhou lifted the receiver and was told that Lin Biao, Ye Qun, and Lin Liguo appeared to be getting ready to leave the country. Their baggage was being placed aboard a plane at the Shanhaiguan Airport. Immediately Zhou telephoned Wu Faxian, air force commander and a Lin Biao intimate (later to be charged with complicity in the plot), and Li Zuopeng, deputy chief of the General Staff and commissar of the navy. He ordered them to see that the Trident did not take off.[10] Within the next half hour he ordered all planes in China grounded.

At about this time, Lin Liguo called Lin Liheng, Lin's daughter by his first wife. Lin Liheng was twenty-nine, three years older than Lin Liguo. Like him, she was in the air force, but in a minor job. Her nickname was Dou Dou, "Little Beans," an allusion to her father's fondness for them. Dou Dou and Lin Liguo had never gotten on. She had been alienated by his "tournament of girls," his search in Shanghai, Hangzhou, and Suzhou for a beauteous bride. All China had heard and savored the lascivious details of the search, whether true or not. He had, in fact, finally married a very beautiful woman named Zhang Ning.[11]

Lin Liguo told Dou Dou that he and her father and stepmother were taking off. He told her to hurry; the plane was leaving soon (it is not clear where she was at this time). It was later claimed that Dou Dou then called Zhou Enlai, telling him what was up — but did she? Many in Beijing were skeptical of this claim; others were not.

It is certain, however, that Zhou had gotten a flicker, probably from someone in the air force, about the unusual flight of the Trident to the seashore airport. One account holds that Zhou telephoned Lin and his wife at Beidaihe, inquiring about their health. Ye Qun answered the phone and said her husband had gone to a concert. Perhaps it was this call that alerted Lin. Whatever it was, the Lins decided to run for it. Zhou and Mao were too close on the trail. This factor may have caused them to try for Mongolia rather than Hong Kong or Canton. Ulan Bator was closer, and Lin Biao had good relations with the Russians. The Chinese government even charged later that he had planned to coordinate his uprising with a move over the border by Soviet troops.

At midnight on September 12 or shortly before, the three airmen were awakened in their quarters and suddenly told to prepare for immediate flight. It can be presumed that they knew their passenger would be Lin Biao. While they were fueling the plane, Lin Biao appeared, followed by his party of five, including his wife and son and three others, whose identities are not known. In all there were nine aboard the plane.

The crew halted the fueling, supposedly at the insistence of Lin Biao for an instant takeoff. They still, it is said, did not know where they would be flying. The party boarded the plane, and it took off immediately.[12]

The end came quickly. At twelve minutes after midnight the Trident had lifted off and headed for Mongolia. Mao was at the Swimming Pool House. Zhou had alerted him that something was up. Now Zhou came to Zhongnanhai — only two minutes' drive from the Great Hall — to tell him that Lin's plane had taken off. At that moment they were crossing the Mongolian border, heading straight for Ulan Bator. But, said Zhou, the plane was still within range. The Chinese could shoot it down. Mao said no.[13]

"Since it is unavoidable, let nature take its course," Mao said, on the word of Ji Dengkui, an alternate member of the Politburo and the peasant protégé of Mao's from Henan Province who was with him that evening. Mao called Ji "old friend," trusted him, liked his company, and had personally brought him into the top ranks so that he could counsel with him. They had been talking about the countryside when Zhou burst in with his dramatic news.

"If we shoot the plane down," Mao said, "how can we explain it to the people of the whole country?"

Mao was sitting back on a sofa, his eyes closed, his head resting on a pillow. He told Zhou Enlai to let him know immediately if any information came in from the Soviet side.[14]

It was a long wait. The Chinese ambassador to Ulan Bator, just on post twenty days (relations between Mongolia and China had been badly strained by the Sino-Soviet conflict), said the first indication he had of anything unusual came a day later, September 14, when he was summoned to the Mongol Foreign Office, a couple of miles from the Chinese embassy. He arrived at 8:20 A.M. and was told that a Chinese aircraft had violated Mongol airspace and crashed at 2:00 A.M. the day before. The deputy foreign minister demanded an explanation.

The ambassador, Xu Wenyi, promised to call Beijing immediately, but there was a difficulty. The direct telephone line between the embassy and Beijing had been cut during the period of bad relations. The telegraph office said it would take at least four hours to dispatch a telegram to Beijing. The ambassador finally persuaded the Mongols to restore the phone line. It took a half hour to hook up; the Mongols first had to hunt for keys to remove padlocks. But when the ambassador called Beijing, he found the line disconnected at that end too.

Finally Xu Wenyi sent an urgent ordinary telegram asking the Foreign Ministry to hook up the phone line in Beijing: He had an important matter to report. It was 12:25 P.M. on the fourteenth before the telephone was connected and he was able to pass on what he had been told by the Mongols.

Beijing had no immediate explanation. The Mongols were insisting that the ambassador come to the site of the plane crash. Xu Wenyi asked Beijing for instructions. Only at 6:00 P.M. did Beijing tell him to go to the site with his assistant. They took off with the Mongols for the long jeep ride over the open steppe to the crash site.

The Mongols kept pressing Xu Wenyi for an explanation. When he said that it must be a case of mistaken navigation, the Mongols wanted to know if that was an "official explanation." Xu couldn't help much: He had no information. Where had the Trident taken off? the Mongols asked. The ambassador confessed he didn't even know that. He began to get alarmed. Why were the Mongols asking so many questions? What really had happened?

Beijing had instructed him to have the bodies of the victims cremated. If that wasn't possible, they could be buried and returned later for cremation in Beijing.

At the crash site Xu Wenyi found there were nine bodies, none identified. All had been burned, and all had lost their shoes. The bodies were scattered about the wrecked plane. The plane apparently had attempted to land but came down tail first, bounced up, fell back, smashed both wings, and caught fire.

On September 20 Xu Wenyi and his deputy took a train to Beijing. They were received by Zhou Enlai at the Great Hall of the People, had dinner with Zhou, and reported their findings. The Mongols had given them the documents recovered from the wreckage. Zhou did not tell them that it was Lin Biao's plane. The pair went back to Ulan Bator.

As China's October 1 holiday approached, the Mongols said they were going to issue an announcement of the crash. On the eve of October 1 Beijing sent a private message to the Mongols, for the first time naming Lin Biao and the others as the crash victims and telling the Mongols that they had been in flight after their plot against Mao had been discovered. This notification coincided with Mao's first private word to top officials about the affair and Lin Biao's death.

When the initial news came to Zhongnanhai that the Trident had crashed near Öndör Haan, in Outer Mongolia, about 150 miles east of the capital of Ulan Bator, Mao exclaimed with joy: "This is the most ideal ending!" The official account reported the Trident had run out of fuel. Ji Dengkui later said he had heard several explanations for the crash but could vouch for none. Mao, he stated, did order the interception of helicopter number 3685, on which a number of Lin's confederates attempted to escape, carrying documents later used in their trial. Among them were two lists of ninety-three persons who made up the core of the conspiracy. Mao put Ji in charge of rounding them up. Within a few days he had all ninety-three in hand.

Ji later added a comment about the way Mao had allowed Lin Biao to become hoist by his own petard: "Ingenuous as he was, Mao could make the most authoritative, effective and appropriate response to [such problems]."[15]

News of the Lin Biao case was withheld from the public for months. The October 1 military celebration in Tiananmen Square was canceled in favor of singing and dancing by children. Extremely tight security was observed for months. Air traffic was not resumed for several days. The name of Lin Biao did not immediately disappear, but his pictures were removed from stores, as were his books.

At long last the government began to circulate internal documents on the case, letting out information bit by bit. It was a year before the secret was disclosed to the foreign press. When a group of American newspaper editors met with Zhou Enlai in 1972, he was indignant at questions about the "Lin Biao mystery." What mystery? he exclaimed. The government had released all the facts. There was nothing mysterious about it. Not nearly so mysterious, he added, as the assassination of President John Kennedy.

Ji's comment about Mao's mastery of propaganda as demonstrated in the Lin Biao crash probably held the clue. Mao's version gradually took hold, although the most violent and contradictory rumors circulated, such as stories about Lin Biao's having been invited to dinner by Mao. When he and his party left, they were gunned down by rocket fire. Other versions had the plane being shot down by Chinese fighters. Some said there had never been a conspiracy; Lin Biao had simply been murdered by Mao and an elaborate fiction made up to confuse the public.

The difficulty that Mao faced, if Ji's comments are valid, was in explaining to the Chinese people that the man he had called his heir, his closest comrade at arms, his true supporter, the author of much of the Mao cult, had, in fact, been an enemy, a traitor, a man who plotted Mao's death.

The government was at pains to keep a firm lid on information about the plot. Dou Dou may have blown the whistle, but she was arrested and kept in custody until after Mao's death and the rise of Deng Xiaoping. She had a very hard time. Zhang Ning, wife of Lin Liguo, was arrested and detained for a considerable time. When she was finally released she, like all those connected with Lin, was ordered to change her name. She didn't. The only one who did was the air force chief, Wu Faxian. He changed his to Wu Chengqing.

In the end such a tangled trail was left that no one could really be sure what had happened. In 1988, seventeen years after the crash, the Chinese published a detailed, almost hour by hour report by Xu Wenyi. It was accompanied by a briefer report by his deputy, Sun Yixian. These accounts seemed to be factual, representing the knowledge of the Chinese representatives in Mongolia about the affair at the time. Clearly they had no advance knowledge of the overflight, nor did they know that Lin Biao or his party was on the plane until on or about September 30. The accounts leave little doubt that a three-engined Trident jet bearing the designation 256 crashed in Mongolia on the night of September 12–13. On the key point of whether Lin Biao and his party were aboard, the evidence of the diplomats is far from conclusive. Perhaps the most curious fact reported by the Chinese ambassador is that not until May 1972 did the Chinese send an official delegation of experts to examine the crash site and (presumably) the wreckage of the plane. The inquiry, it was said, established that there had been no gunfight aboard and no midair explosion and that no one aboard had been armed.[16]

Equally curious is the supposed fact, asserted by Xu Wenyi, that the Mongol authorities handed over to him all of the papers carried in the plane, which presumably must have given the identity of the parties and clues to the nature of the flight. It is possible, of course, that these papers were far from complete, since the aircraft burned after landing and one would suppose most of the paper would have been consumed. Another oddity: Although the Chinese consistently claimed the 256 had been attempting to land because it had run out of fuel (the fueling having been interrupted at the Shanhaiguan Airport), the experts concluded that the plane was still carrying two and a half tons of fuel when it crashed. Two Mongol diplomats asserted in 1990 that they had positive knowledge that Lin Biao was not aboard the plane and that no evidence of his presence turned up. The reliability of this report is not certain. The Chinese embassy officials claimed that their first instructions from Beijing called for immediate cremation of the bodies. This, of course, would have precluded positive establishment of their identity. A Soviet report contended that Russian specialists had had a look at the bodies and identified one as Lin Biao's by his bridgework, which had been done in Moscow. The gaps in the evidence suggest the best verdict is the old Scots one: "Case not proven."

Twenty years later an atmosphere of unreality clung to the case. In part this may have been imposed by Kang Sheng and his minions, who "investigated" it. There was not a word in the government accounts of the affair about Jiang Qing, who had been Lin Biao's right hand in the army, brought in by Lin as his ally to handle army propaganda, dressed by Lin Biao in a PLA uniform, called by Lin "our Jiang Qing." Every work published by the army propaganda establishment was cleared by Jiang Qing. The notion that Jiang Qing and her associates received no clue of Lin Biao's plans is preposterous. Indeed, evidence existed that Jiang Qing would be offered a high position in Lin Biao's regime.[17] Lin Biao might have cut Jiang Qing out of the loop for some details, fearing a double cross, but there could be no doubt that Wang Dongxing, the security chief, then closely associated with Jiang Qing, possessed some knowledge of what Lin Biao was up to. Kang Sheng — very much alive, very active, also closely associated with Jiang Qing — could not have failed to pick up echoes of the plot.

One cannot examine these questions without speculating on Mao's role and the dreamlike quality of the whole affair. Did it come out of an opium pipe? Most knowledgeable survivors of the Mao coterie believe that Lin Biao died more or less in accordance with the official version. As to what came before they are not so certain. Did Lin Biao plot to kill Mao, or did Lin get wind of a plot by Mao to kill him? The question may never find an answer.

*   *   *

As Zhou Enlai awaited news of Lin Biao's fate, he summoned to his Zhongnanhai house several close associates. He told them briefly what had happened — that Lin Biao had plotted against Mao, that he and his wife and son had taken off by plane toward Outer Mongolia.

Mao, he told them, had ordered that the plane not be shot down. How, Zhou quoted Mao as saying, "could we ever explain it to the army and the people?" Mao ordered that the plane be permitted to proceed. Zhou believed that Lin Biao was flying to Moscow and that when he reached his destination he would issue a statement. Zhou had convened his colleagues so that an official Chinese communiqué could be prepared and issued the moment they had word from Moscow.

Amid the discussion Zhou was called away. He returned smiling. "The problem has solved itself," he said. "Lin Biao's plane has crashed in flames in Outer Mongolia. All the passengers are dead."

After a moment's thought Qiao Guanhua, deputy foreign minister, responded with a poem based on a verse by a famous Tang dynasty poet, Lu Lun, about a rebel tribe that had fled north after an unsuccessful attempt on the emperor's life. A cavalry troop was sent through heavy snow to try to catch the plotters.

Lu Lun had written:

> In the dark of the night swallows soar on high.
> The Chengyu are trying to escape
> And cavalrymen are about to gallop after them.
> Heavy snow blows over the swords and armor of the soldiers.

Qiao Guanhua improvised:

> In the dark of the night swallows soar on high,
> Lin Biao is trying to escape.
> No need to send the cavalry after him
> He has burned himself to death.

Qiao's verse was so brilliant and so apt that his listeners made him copy it down with an ink brush on fine paper. He gave it to Zhou, who framed it and hung it on his wall.[18]

Whatever questions remained about the Lin Biao affair, one thing was certain. It left Zhou Enlai in a commanding position. Lin was gone. Jiang Qing and the Gang were crippled. Mao was stunned. Never had he been so weakened. The shock was so severe he took to his bed. The hour of Zhou Enlai had dawned, and the end of the age of Mao was at hand. That of Deng Xiaoping was not far distant.

34

A Master of the Arts

AIR FORCE ONE touched down at Beijing Airport at 10:30 A.M. on February 21, 1972. It taxied up to the red carpet, the door opened, and President Richard Nixon stepped out. Smiling, Nixon extended his hand to Zhou Enlai as John Foster Dulles had refused to do eighteen years before at Geneva. It was Zhou's finest moment in forty years of diplomacy and survival.

No one in the American party, and few in the world, knew what Zhou knew — that Lin Biao had died in Mongolia the previous September; that Liu Shaoqi had expired on a cold cement floor in Kaifeng; that Peng Dehuai had been broken into a human hulk, barely alive in an army hospital; that Deng Xiaoping labored in a grimy machine shop in distant Jiangxi; that China had been turned into a wasteland, millions dead, population stunned, factories in cobwebs, schools a shambles. Only a handful knew that Mao Zedong had collapsed after the Lin Biao affair and lay dozing in bed or in a lounge chair, his heart and lungs unable to provide enough blood to his brain.

Zhou led the presidential party through a Beijing of broad, empty streets (security police had seen to that) to their quarters in the sprawling Fishing Ledge Park, or Diaoyutai, where Jiang Qing and Kang Sheng had retreated to prepare the terror, the torture, and the atrocities.[1] No American knew that, but Zhou did.

No whisper of hidden concern flickered across Zhou's face as he directed respectful words to Nixon and bantered with Henry Kissinger, whose secret visit to Beijing in July 1971 had started the ball rolling.

Zhou had been an actor in college at the American-founded Nankai University. He had played women's roles; his wife played men. Today, as for decades, Zhou needed every actor's skill he possessed.

No one seemed more in command than Zhou Enlai, and for the first time in his forty years in the Chinese leadership, he *was* in command. Tactfully, purposefully, quietly, he had taken over; Mao was still alive, Jiang Qing and her followers were still in place, but Zhou held the initiative.

Mao had suffered his first critical attack in spring 1971. He had been prone for years to colds and influenza at the change of the seasons and spent much time in Hangzhou to escape Beijing's fierce winds of spring and autumn. This seizure came just about the time of his famous invitation to American Ping-Pong players to come to China, the opening gambit of the move toward détente with the United States. The attack had been the worst of his life. His body was shaken with fierce and constant coughing that no treatment could halt. Although the doctors gradually brought it under control, there were symptoms of heart damage.[2]

That summer Mao had regained much of his energy, but, as his secretary-nurse Zhang Yufeng noted, he was seventy-seven years old, white-haired and noticeably feeble, pale, no longer glowing with health and vigor. Still, he was clearheaded and sometimes humorous.[3]

Mao had managed to mount his devastating campaign against Lin Biao, but the struggle took a toll, physically and psychologically. His collapse in autumn 1971, following Lin's death, was worse than that of the spring.[4] There seemed to be no way of controlling his cough. Every effort of his staff to cut down or end his consumption of cigarettes failed — he refused to give them up. When he made up his mind, no one could oppose him. His temper became terrifying. As for his consumption of sleeping pills, with their possible opium-derivative base, there is no record.

The doctors diagnosed Mao as suffering from lobular pneumonia. They tried to ease his work load, but he refused. He was, Zhang Yufeng declared, extraordinarily stubborn and did not have confidence in the doctors. He turned down many medical suggestions and remained the faddist of his youth. He thought the body's natural functions should repulse disease, but, as Zhang noted, "he was an old man with failing bodily functions" incapable of resisting disease. His illness grew worse because of his refusal to accept treatment. He lay on a sofa day and night, coughing and spitting, breathing with difficulty.

Mao had for some time suffered from Parkinson's disease, caused, his physician believed, by the dysfunction of a gland in the brain. He was treated for the Parkinson's with a powerful drug that worked like magic. Mao would be semicomatose, jaw slack, apparently barely alive. When the drug took hold he would miraculously rise up and for a few hours display vigor. Unfortunately, the medicine worked erratically.[5]

Mao's medical treatment was supervised by Wang Dongxing, head of the 8341 security battalion, and Zhang Chunqiao, one of the Gang of Four. Zhou Enlai watched it closely.

Mao was immobilized until late December 1971, when he gradually showed some improvement but was still convalescent.[6] On January 6, Chen Yi died of cancer resulting at least in part from persecution during the Cultural Revolution. Funeral services were announced for January 10. It was to be a second-class funeral; no high officials would attend. Mao had not been out of the Swimming Pool House for months. After lunch on the tenth he became agitated. Suddenly he ordered his car: He was going to the ceremonies for Chen Yi. Mao was wearing a nightgown and a pair of thin wool trousers. Zhang Yufeng got out his clothes and tried to help him dress, but he waved her away; he would just wear a jacket over his nightclothes. She helped him put it on and slipped his overcoat over his shoulders, and he was on his way.

Mao's car, a 1950s Soviet-made Zis limousine, sped off to Babaoshan, the crematory, where Zhou Enlai, Zhu De, Marshal Ye Jianying, and Politburo member Li Xiannian had hastily assembled. Mao held the hand of Zhang Qian, Chen Yi's widow, and said, "Chen Yi was a good comrade. He was a good man. He made a contribution to China's revolution and world revolution. He won great merit. This is the final conclusion." That was as close as Mao could come to an apology for hastening Chen Yi's death.

Prince Norodom Sihanouk of Cambodia had come to the funeral. Mao spoke to him and for the first time mentioned Lin Biao's death outside the tightest top Party circles. Lin Biao had crashed to his death in Mongolia, Mao said. "Lin Biao opposed me — Chen Yi supported me."[7]

Lin Biao, Mao said, had wanted to undermine him and the veteran comrades. Now many of them were being brought back and given jobs. There was no need to mention their "rightist" tendencies; one should let bygones be bygones. Deng Xiaoping, he said (according to one version), is different from Liu Shaoqi.[8]

Chen Yi's funeral was the last occasion on which Mao was to appear in public.

Perhaps the strain of the visit to the funeral was too much. A few days later Mao collapsed on his bed. He was unconscious and his nurse could find no pulse. The nurse shouted for help, and duty doctors rushed in. Mao was occupying the reception room of the Swimming Pool House. He had been moved there from his cheerless bedroom when illness overtook him in the autumn. The medical team injected heart stimulants three times without result. Mao was propped up in bed, and a nurse rhythmically pounded his back, calling: "Chairman Mao! Chairman Mao!" Zhang Yufeng echoed the call. "Chairman Mao! Chairman Mao!" Presently Mao's eyes opened and he said: "I feel as though I have been sleeping."

Zhou Enlai rushed to the scene. The seizure was diagnosed as cardiorespiratory failure. Not more than half a dozen knew of Mao's collapse. A new supervisory body was set up, headed by Zhou Enlai. All this occurred amid preparations for the Nixon visit. No one, including Zhou, knew whether Mao would be able to meet the American president.

Mao needed a new suit, for he had put on some weight. But he was too ill to have a tailor in for a fitting. The staff took one of his old suits to the Hongdu tailoring establishment (the best in China; they dressed all the top leadership) and asked them to make Mao a new suit in the same style, just a size or so larger. It fitted quite well.[9]

There was also the problem of Mao's shoes. His feet were badly and constantly swollen because of his poor circulation and kidney impairment. He had been shuffling around in slippers for a long time. They got him two new pairs of simple black cloth shoes.

The costume was ready, but could Mao use it?[10]

After lunch on February 21 Mao said he didn't want to take his usual nap. He was restless. Suddenly he said he wanted Nixon to come and visit him — now. The staff had to scramble. They called in a barber. Mao needed a shave, and his hair hadn't been cut for weeks. The barber was fast-moving, unlike Mao's old barber, Wang Hui, who had cut his hair for years. Wang Hui was a tyrant, and once he started work he would not let Mao go. Nor would he hurry no matter how Mao complained or fidgeted. The barber would hold Mao's head firmly and order, "Sit still." Finally Wang would shave Mao's face, like a sculptor putting the final touches on a work of art. Then he would give Mao's face a last pat, step back, and say: "It looks good." Mao would sigh. There was nothing he could do with Wang Hui.[11]

The new man worked quickly and silently. He put some tonic on Mao's hair to give it a little better tone. Zhang Yufeng managed to get Mao into his new suit. "Except for a little swelling and feebleness," she said, "there was no change in his appearance."

Zhou Enlai had dashed to Diaoyutai and told Kissinger that Mao wanted to meet Nixon immediately. Zhou was, as Kissinger noted, on edge and eager not to waste a moment. Kissinger told Nixon the unexpected news, and they set off in Red Flag limousines, sweeping into Tiananmen Square and through the Gate of New China, the usual two sentries on duty, into Zhongnanhai and up to Mao's house. The reception room had been hastily cleared of all evidence that two hours before it had been a hospital room. There was a circle of overstuffed armchairs. Mao, wearing his new "Mao suit," rose from a chair as Nixon entered, hand extended. Mao grasped Nixon's hand in both of his, holding it "for about a minute," as Nixon recalled. Mao apologized for his speech, saying, "I can't talk very well."

Mao told Nixon that "our common old friend" Chiang Kaishek would not approve of the meeting. "He calls us Communist bandits," Mao said.

"What do you call him?" Nixon inquired.

"Generally," Mao said, "we call them 'Chiang Kaishek's clique.' In the newspapers sometimes we call him a bandit. He calls us bandits in turn. Anyway, we abuse each other." Mao added that the history of his friendship with Chiang Kaishek was much longer than that of the Americans'.

Mao's conversation left no doubt in the minds of Nixon and Kissinger that whatever the state of Mao's health (they thought he probably had suffered a mild stroke or two), his mind was functioning sharply. They noticed, of course, that a nurse, Zhang Yufeng, was constantly at his side.

There was banter about Kissinger. Nixon said he had used "pretty girls" as a cover for his secret trips to Paris and Beijing. "So you often make use of pretty girls," Mao said with a sudden display of interest. Nixon insisted that *he* never used pretty girls; it would get him into political trouble. Mao laughed. He did not volunteer anything about his personal experience with pretty girls.

Mao told Nixon that "I voted for you" in the last election but that if the Democrats had won he would have dealt with them. He added, "I like rightists," pointing out that Britain's prime minister Edward

Heath was "on the right." Nixon added Charles de Gaulle to the list. Mao said de Gaulle was a special case and put the German Christian Democrats on his list. "I am comparatively happy," Mao said, "when people on the right come into power."

As he had with Prince Sihanouk, Mao made a point of telling Nixon and Kissinger about Lin Biao. There had been, he said, a group of reactionaries in China that opposed the opening to the United States. "The result was that they got on an airplane and fled abroad." He added — as did Zhou Enlai — that their plane had crashed in Outer Mongolia. Mao wanted Nixon to understand he was speaking of Lin Biao.

Nixon had expected the meeting to be a protocol occasion, taking perhaps fifteen minutes. It lasted almost an hour.

As Nixon rose to leave, Mao shuffled forward and accompanied him to the doorway. He did not step past it. Mao observed that he had not been feeling well. Zhou explained that the chairman had been suffering from bronchitis.

"But," said Nixon, "you look very good."

Mao shrugged. "Outer appearances are deceiving," he said with some emphasis.[12]

The triumph of Zhou Enlai seemed to be complete. True, Jiang Qing was still on the scene. She had, in fact, accompanied by Zhou, escorted the Nixons to the Beijing Opera performance of *The Red Detachment of Women,* one of the eight productions that she had overseen and that now constituted the entire repertoire of the opera.

Nixon had been warned that Jiang Qing was anti-American and that she had opposed his trip and détente with the United States. He and his wife, Pat, found her a bit abrasive, but perhaps to his and Jiang's surprise, he liked *The Red Detachment* — found it dazzling, in fact — and told her so. She made the appropriate Chinese response, asking him for criticism and suggestions. Nixon had none to offer.[13]

Jiang Qing did not push her position. Zhou was in charge. In past times Jiang Qing had made no secret of how she enjoyed talking with Zhou and appreciated his manner. From the earliest times Zhou treated her with respect. He had treated her as a gentleman treats a *lady.* Jiang had rarely been treated like a lady, and she liked the sensation, flirting with him mildly. He repaid the compliment in his courtly style. Jiang Qing's liking for Zhou had irritated Mao. Jiang had praised Zhou's good manners, his breeding, his politeness. She told Mao that Zhou was well educated and had better manners than

Mao, who made a practice of emphasizing his peasant coarseness. She told Mao she wished he would change his habits and be more like Zhou.[14]

Jiang Qing and Zhou understood perfectly that they stood on different sides during the wildest days of the Cultural Revolution. But each was careful to maintain outward relations. Zhou was much too clever a diplomat to press his advantage now that he had the upper hand. He understood that if Mao Zedong should die (as he almost had in January), he and he alone was in a position to succeed him. He also knew that Jiang and her cohorts, while being reined in now by Mao, possessed enormous power in the Party, especially in its propaganda department, an advantage he might not be able to overcome.

So far as Zhou ever indicated, he felt he had done the best he could during the Cultural Revolution. He had gone all out, interposing his own body and daring the Red Guards to trample over him, to protect Zhu De and Chen Yi. He had been more successful with Zhu De, who was still alive, than with Chen Yi, but he had managed to ensure that Chen died peacefully in a decent hospital. Zhou had failed to protect He Long, despite vigorous efforts, and he had expressed his sorrow to He Long's widow and former wife. He had not protected Peng Dehuai or Liu Shaoqi. Perhaps he felt that Mao could not be swayed from these targets. Zhou had had a word of comfort for Liu's widow, Wang Guangmei, but little more. He had not saved Lao She.

Zhou stretched his authority as far as he could. Zhang Ziren, a non-Communist Democratic party leader, had been sympathetic and very useful to Mao and Zhou. He was one of the "four Hunan elders," scholarly men with whom Mao loved to talk. In August 1966 the Red Guards began to harass Zhang in the courtyard house in a *hutong*, behind the Beijing Hotel, that Mao had put at Zhang's disposal. Zhang wrote Mao. Next day Zhou Enlai sent two PLA sentries to protect the house. Acting on this authority from Mao, Zhou managed to send fifteen or twenty other "Democratic personalities" to Military Hospital 301, the top PLA hospital, for care and protection.[15]

If Zhou had a rationale for his conduct, it probably was that he tried. He himself had, after all, undergone savage assaults. His Foreign Ministry had been seized by the most rampant leftists, the British embassy ransacked and burned. Zhou's score was not bad, but he was not a white knight. He was one of the most skilled courtiers the world has seen, always carefully husbanding himself against the day when China entered total chaos and only he, perhaps, could save it.

Yang Shangkun put the case for Zhou Enlai as well as it might be: "He could not oppose Mao directly in the Cultural Revolution. The Gang of Four and Lin Biao would have used this as an excuse to put him away. The damage to the country would have been much worse. He could not oppose Mao openly and save many leading comrades. He tried to handle some of the sectional factions and when he had the power to protect people he used that power. He had to decide how best to protect some comrades. Some he put into prison in order to protect them. These are his merits. He was an esteemed leader."[16]

Zhou Enlai's position concealed a great if hidden weakness: Mao's uncertain backing. Zhou had worked with and for Mao for thirty-five years. He had given him his full devotion. Never in that time, not once, had Mao reciprocated. Mao never went out of his way to speak well of Zhou Enlai. He never paid Zhou Enlai a personal compliment nor thanked him for anything. He did not congratulate him — as any normal person would have — on his brilliant diplomatic triumphs. Mao treated Zhou with the same impersonality with which he treated a piece of furniture. He showed more feeling for his old horse or his bodyguards than he did for Zhou. Never, in the experience of the guards, had he uttered a single positive word about Zhou.[17]

The success of the Nixon visit; the Shanghai communiqué issued at its conclusion; the extraordinary transformation of the United States from perceived deadly enemy to valued friend and ally-to-be; the gesture, so remarkable in Chinese tradition, of the American president traversing sixteen thousand miles to meet Mao in the Swimming Pool House and to quote to the aged leader his own poetry — "Seize the hour" — had given Zhou prestige that in his career he had never before attained.

Zhou now bore almost the whole burden of government. He was conducting not only foreign policy (as always, in line with Mao's general approval), but also the day-to-day operations of the economy. He presided over all of the paperwork and made the selection of documents that flowed up to the enfeebled Mao. He understood that at any moment another "mishap," as Zhang Yufeng called it, might place China in his hands.[18]

Zhang Yufeng thought that Zhou looked fragile and thin when he accompanied Nixon and Kissinger to their meeting with Mao (although neither Nixon nor Kissinger seemed to notice this), but Zhou was energetic. His eyes sparkled. He was dignified and cordial. His movements were quick, and he did not show fatigue although, as she said, "a man is, after all, not made of iron and even an iron man gets tired."

It was more than overwork that caused the frailness that Zhang Yufeng detected. In May 1972 medical examination disclosed that Zhou was suffering from cancer of the liver. The news came as a shock to Mao, still far from well.

Zhou gave no outward sign of the death sentence that now hung over him. But both he and Mao knew that unless able hands were brought in swiftly, the country would be at peril. Their thoughts turned immediately — and inevitably — to Deng Xiaoping.

Zhou's alma mater, Nankai University, in Tianjin, had as its motto (still hanging on a school wall in 1987):

> Face clean, hair cut, clothes neat, buttoned tight,
> Posture straight, shoulders square, chest out, back straight,
> Beware of arrogance, hot temper and idleness —
> In all show amiability, composure and dignity.[19]

Zhou had learned the words nearly sixty years earlier, but they were reflected in the grace with which he now met the world. Serious as was the diagnosis, Zhou kept at his heavy routine: spending most of the day in meetings with state guests, dining night after night at the Great Hall with distinguished visitors, then going back to his office and working half the night.

To those with whom he met he was the same meticulous, urbane, solicitous, witty host as ever. He savored his meetings with Henry Kissinger. There, he felt, he had a diplomatic opponent worthy of his mettle, the best of his career — a compliment Kissinger returned.

On June 15, 1971, Zhou entertained some visiting Americans at the Great Hall; I was among them. I put this note in my journal: "Zhou wore his faultless gray uniform with his single Mao badge inscribed 'Serve the People.' His eyebrows were black as ink, his face looked healthy and freckled. He seemed vigorous and spry, but I thought he let his left arm hang at his side. Looks just as in his pictures and not too different from when I last saw him in 1954 in Moscow."

For almost four hours that night Zhou Enlai talked and argued with his American guests about Vietnam, relations with the United States, cultural exchanges, education, and scientific research. He suggested a joint study of the effects of cigarette smoking; he didn't believe it had any ill effects. When the time came to part, he said it had been a good evening of free discussion, like the days in Yanan when every idea was argued and the talk went on all night. He looked a bit tired as he said good night, but there was no sign of weariness in his bright eyes. It had been four hours spent as he liked to spend them.

Only once did he make a remark that later took on a significance it did not seem to possess at the time. Zhou was invited by his guests to come to America, to pay a visit very soon. He seemed a bit wistful and said he "could not applaud" that suggestion. "Although I believe," he said, "that all the others in this room [six or seven Chinese, mostly from the Foreign Ministry] will go to America, at my advanced age I do not have that hope."

No one took that seriously; no one took him to be at an advanced age.

PART 6

THE CENTER OF THE EARTH

35

Forty Plus Forty Plus Forty Plus Forty Times Forty

THE DRAMATIC EVENTS in Beijing reverberated only dimly in the ears of Deng Xiaoping. He and his wife, Zhuo Lin, and his stepmother Xia Bogan had been packed off to distant Jiangxi Province late in October 1969 under Lin Biao's Order Number 1 for evacuation of all important political prisoners from the capital.

The order had been served on Deng on October 20. When the Dengs arrived in Nanchang, capital of Jiangxi, they were harangued by a provincial army officer who warned that they were under military arrest. They could talk to no one, had no right of communication, and were subject to regulations applying to state criminals.

A few days later the family was moved to the Nanchang infantry academy just outside the city. The grounds were empty and grown up in weeds. The academy, like all educational institutions in China, had been closed by the Cultural Revolution. Even before leaving Beijing the Dengs had been put in what Deng's daughter Maomao called "miserable quarters." Now they were placed in a square bamboo two-story house with a balcony overlooking a large courtyard surrounded by a new wooden fence and protected by a complement of guards who lived in the rear.[1] The quarters had been occupied by the commandant of the academy until it was closed. It was a commodious house with no central heating, just small stoves. Deng was not allowed to leave the compound except on Saturday night, when he went to the public baths.

Deng was sixty-five at the time of his banishment, still active and lively despite three years of harassment following his arrest and dismissal from office in 1969, when his salary had also been cut off. His wife, in her early fifties, suffered from high blood pressure. Deng's stepmother, the illiterate daughter of a boatman on the great Jialing River, was slightly older than Deng. She had lived with the family following Deng's Chongqing days, a capable, hardworking, intelligent woman. It is difficult to imagine the Deng household without her.

Deng himself chopped the wood for the stoves in their new quarters and broke the forty-pound hunks of soft coal into stove-sized pieces. He mopped the floors, swept the halls, and did a lot of other housework, and when spring came he, his wife, and his stepmother planted a good-sized garden. The physical labor didn't bother Deng; it kept him fit. What worried Deng and his wife was the plight of their older son, Deng Pufang, twenty-five, a brilliant senior physics student at Beijing University. Pufang had been taken prisoner by a savage Red Guard detachment and beaten into insensibility in an effort to make him "confess" to the "treason" of his father.

All of the Deng children — indeed, all of Deng's family (including distant relatives) and associates — had been targets of repression and torture, but Pufang's case was exceptional. Beijing University was the battleground of vicious civil war among chaotic Red Guard factions, each claiming to represent Mao Zedong. Pufang was grabbed, confined to a small closet (some of these closets had been painted red with the blood of the victims), and beaten again and again.

Twenty years after the torture Pufang could still not recall all that happened. Much had mercifully been blotted out. But he knew that after his imprisonment in the closet, battered and hardly conscious, he had been dumped in a fourth-floor dormitory room and told he would never get out alive. The room had bare walls and had been stripped of interior woodwork, fittings, and furniture. The window and the window frame had been ripped out, leaving a gaping hole open to the ground four flights below. "That is your only exit," he was told. The Red Guards locked and bolted the doors and left him a bloody bundle on the floor. Pufang lost consciousness. What happened next he did not know. Did he crawl to the edge and hurl himself over? Did he roll out in unconscious agony? Did a torturer return and kick him sprawling into space? He will never know, and as he said: "The process of my being injured was not important. What was important was the consequences of the upheaval. The Cultural Revolution was not just a disaster for the Party, for the country, but for the whole people. We were all victims, people of several generations. One hundred million people were its victims."[2]

Pufang did not die of his injuries. Critical as they were, they could have been treated had he had prompt medical care. He did not get that. He was taken to the Beijing University Hospital, where he got custodial care. Later he was sent to a primitive "welfare" center, a shabby building in the Beijing suburbs, confined to a damp, dark room with ten other crippled patients, unable to move, lying on his back, weaving wire wastebaskets to earn a little food and cigarette money. Had it not been for a young worker named Wang Feng who befriended him, he would have died.[3]

Deng and his wife did not immediately know what had happened to their son. They were under house arrest, cut off from contact with the world, being hauled out to mass shouting sessions, beaten, reviled, spat upon, carted around the streets with great wooden placards around their necks, made to do the airplane. When they did learn of their son's plight they bombarded the authorities with requests for medical help for him. The answer was no. Pufang had been suicided by the Red Guards, but he was not dead. If his injuries were left untreated, perhaps the "suicide" could be made complete. No plea by Deng broke the sadistic determination of the torturers. Pufang received no medical attention. Later, doctors said there would have been a chance of correcting his spinal injuries. But the procedure would have had to be done promptly.

Now, in Nanchang, Deng and his wife were put to work in a small tractor-repair shop. They walked to the workplace, twenty minutes along narrow, muddy paths. During his time in France Deng had worked briefly at the Renault plant outside Paris. Now he was back at the machine lathe. He had not lost his skill. His fellow workers recalled him as a good worker.[4] Zhuo Lin spent her time washing and cleaning coils of wire. They did not get much pay, but it was a help. They sent money to Pufang and put some aside to pay for his transportation when and if they could get permission to bring him to Nanchang.

Deng and Zhuo Lin planted cabbage, beans, chilies, and squash in their garden. They also raised chickens. This provided food for their table, and by selling the eggs they brought in a little more cash to allow Pufang and their other children to join them. The rest of the Deng children had been scattered after undergoing harassment from their Beijing classmates. Maomao and the younger son, Deng Zhifang, eighteen in 1969, had been sent to the countryside, Zhifang to remote Shaanxi.

Not until 1971 did the Dengs receive permission to have Pufang come to Nanchang. They still could get him no medical help. Every day Deng massaged his son's paralyzed back and legs. They could do nothing about the paralysis. They fed their emaciated son and gave him loving care. Pufang later confessed that for the first time he began to know his father as a human being, not as a politician, his mind always busy with state affairs.

"It was down in Jiangxi," Pufang recalled, "that I had the most interflow of feeling with my father. It was very difficult then. But it was then that I realized that he was a true man, a real man, and not like other leaders who are solely interested in politics."[5]

Deng's situation gradually improved a bit. His daughter Maomao, his youngest, was allowed to come to Nanchang, as well as Zhifang. Deng had a few visitors. The prohibition against speaking to people wore off. Deng had made friends among the workers in the machine shop and the local peasants. They didn't think of him as a state criminal. They showed him respect.

The Dengs slept in the upstairs bedroom next to the balcony, and Deng used the room below as a study. He had always been too busy to read much. He had brought books with him — Marx and Lenin, Chinese classics and histories. He wrote a few letters, never knowing whether they would reach their destination. And he thought — he thought a great deal about China and its problems. He tried to understand the events of the past few years and what the future could be.

Every day in late afternoon, after he had hoed the garden and done his chores, he would walk around the perimeter of the courtyard, around and around, next to the fence, until he wore a deep path in the red soil. Deng had broken his leg in the 1950s and exercised regularly to keep it limber. He took forty turns around the courtyard every day. That was forty paces to a side — forty plus forty plus forty plus forty — multiplied by forty, almost four miles a day.

From a window Maomao saw her father: "Watching his sure but fast-moving step I thought to myself that his faith, his ideas and determination must have become clearer and firmer, readying him for the battles that lay ahead."[6]

What to do once the turmoil was over? How to solve the enormous problems? How to harness the infinite capabilities of China — and what would he do should he once again take his place at the helm?

Deng did not talk about his ideas. He kept them to himself. Instead he talked of daily affairs. He had no partners for bridge, but he played a lot of solitaire, sitting at his desk in his study. He read the newspapers and each evening listened to the radio. He tried to keep abreast of events. It was not easy. The newspapers were bland, the radio even more so. You had to guess at what was happening by what was not said.

Deng spent much time with Pufang, hoping somehow for a miracle that would end the paralysis. Both he and Zhuo Lin gave Pufang sponge baths, ran their callused hands again and again over his lifeless muscles. Deng wrote petition after petition asking permission to send Pufang to a hospital in Beijing for examination and treatment. There was never any answer.

On November 8, 1971, everything changed. That day the guards appeared early in the morning and escorted Deng and his wife into Nanchang to a Party meeting, the first they had been permitted to attend since autumn 1966. It was a bare-bones briefing by the local Party on the Lin Biao affair, just a mention of his conspiracy against Mao, his flight across the border, his death in the plane crash in Mongolia — the first installment of Mao's serialized account to the comrades. Deng had suspected something was wrong since the unusual October 1, 1971, anniversary celebration, which had included neither a military parade in Tiananmen nor any mention of Lin Biao.

No one had to tell Deng that it was a climactic moment. The guards brought the couple back to their house about noon. Neither said a word to the children. But as Zhuo Lin made her way to the kitchen she gave a nod to Maomao, who followed her. Zhuo Lin did not speak. She grasped Maomao's hand and traced on it the four Chinese characters that said "Lin Biao *si le*" — Lin Biao is dead.

That was it. Not until the guards left the house did Deng and his wife speak, talking with hushed voices. Lin Biao was dead, but who could say what might happen next. Zhuo Lin could not restrain herself. Good riddance! About time! For a moment Deng was silent, but his children knew he was vastly excited. Finally he spoke: "Justice could not have allowed him *not* to die."

Immediately Deng went to his study and wrote a letter to the Central Committee, commending the denunciation of Lin Biao and declaring his full support. He wrote a second letter, once again requesting permission to send Pufang to Beijing for medical examination and treatment.[7]

That day or the next Deng wrote a formal letter to Mao Zedong, presenting himself as ready in spirit and in strength to undertake any task Mao might set for him. He wanted to get to work, he told the chairman.[8]

From the start there had been hints that Mao held Deng in a different category than Liu Shaoqi. Some said that Mao never intended to take Deng's life. They thought the fate of Liu had been sealed from the beginning. Mao had, according to this theory, always held Deng in reserve — regardless of how he treated him — as a kind of insurance policy.

There is more than one informed Chinese who is certain that Mao told Deng that it was necessary to strike him down once again but also gave him an assurance that his day would come, just as it had in the past. Later, "Deng would be brought back." If this was Mao's intention he made Deng pay a heavy price — the crippling of his son, the ravaging of his home in Guang'an, attacks against every member of his family.

In fact, a second Deng was suicided, Deng Shiping, the youngest of Deng's brothers. When Deng's father died in 1940, Shiping had taken over the family houses and estate.[9] He managed the property until 1949, when he was sent to a Communist Party school and became a Party worker, an able one. Before long he went to Guizhou Province as mayor of a city, possibly Luzë. The Red Guards charged him with KMT connections and with being a member of a landlord family and brother of the number-two capitalist roader. He was savagely beaten and exposed to struggle sessions. Despairing, it was said, of finding a way out of the terror, he committed suicide on March 15, 1967. As in so many cases of suiciding, there is no way of knowing the truth.[10] One report said that Shiping was compelled by the Red Guards to crawl on all fours with a heavy wooden placard dangling from his neck. In despair and humiliation he cast himself into a river and drowned.

Things began to move now. Deng knew that the Nixon visit and the Shanghai communiqué meant that Zhou Enlai was at Mao's side. This was good news. In April 1972 even better news came. At long last Pufang would be permitted to go to Beijing for treatment. His sister Maomao accompanied him.

In Beijing a friend told Maomao that Wang Zhen wanted to see her. Wang Zhen was an old Long March commander, the man whom Deng was to call a big cannon, a blunt, outspoken man renowned to the end of his days for frankness and reactionary overstatement.

Maomao had never met Wang Zhen, but the Deng children in the Zhongnanhai heyday called him "the uncle with the beard." When she called on him at his home, a tall, thin, black-bearded old man greeted her at the door, holding her hand and showering her with questions about Deng Xiaoping and the family.

It was a moving experience after the hostility of the Cultural Revolution. Wang Zhen invited Maomao to dinner and insisted that she stay the night. He had been "set aside," that is, not permitted to work but not cut off like Deng. He was in contact with the leadership and told Maomao that the Central Committee (a euphemism for Mao) "made certain distinctions between Deng" and the other targets of the Cultural Revolution — a confirmation, in a way, of the theory that Mao always regarded Deng as an exception. Wang Zhen said he was writing the Central Committee urging it to let Deng return to Beijing and take a leading position again.[11] Deng was excited when Maomao brought this news.

There were other good signs. Lin Biao's supporters had been cleared out of the Jiangxi government. The new local officials paid a courtesy call on Deng. The armed guards disappeared. People could come to visit. At the end of 1972 Deng and his wife were taken on a trip to Jinggang Mountain, where Zhu De and Mao had joined forces, creating the base of the Red Army in 1927 and 1928. They visited a nearby porcelain center, renowned in Chinese history for the delicacy of its work, and found that Lin Biao had turned it into a factory for making amphibious personnel carriers.[12]

Word came down from Zhou Enlai. If Deng would write a self-criticism to Mao — it needn't be long or detailed — and ask for a chance to go back to work, a job was waiting for him. On August 3, 1972, Deng wrote the letter. He admitted he had made mistakes but swore he was a true follower of Mao's line and loyal to the Cultural Revolution — a basic requisite insisted upon by Mao because he feared that the generation after him would abandon it.

Deng swore to uphold the Cultural Revolution and confessed that he had been wrong in his trademark slogan, that it mattered not whether a cat was black or white so long as it caught the mouse. To Mao that meant ideology and Marxism didn't count.[13]

A visitor dropped in to see Deng in early 1973. He found him perusing *The General Mirror for the Aid of Government*, the identical work that Mao had been reading in the Fragrant Hills as he prepared to leave for Beijing. Like Mao, Deng was paying particular heed to the manner in which power shifted from one emperor to the next, how the Mandate of Heaven passed from the old ruler to the new. The visitor could not help recalling that *The Mirror* had been compiled in the years leading up to 1086, twenty years after the Battle of Hastings, and, of course, dealt with the events of the previous thirteen hundred years. To Deng as to Mao, the annals of China's past had more application to present problems than the words of German and Russian revolutionary theorists. Clearly Deng had an eye on the succession before he packed his baggage for the return to Beijing.[14]

In February 1973, word came from the Central Committee that the Dengs were to return to Beijing. They packed their things. When Maomao went to the tractor-repair shop and told the workers that the Dengs would be leaving, the workers wished them well. "He never seemed like a great state leader," one of the men recalled twenty years later. "He seemed just like one of us."[15]

Indeed, the workers were proud and flattered that the Dengs were living in the community and working in the shop. A delegation of ten arrived at the commandant's house to help carry the Dengs' luggage. But it had already been taken by truck. Deng came to the steps of the house to say good-bye. He embraced the workers, and they gave the little man a hug.

Word had spread that the Dengs were going back to Beijing. When time came to leave, a procession of thirty cars followed them to the train station, where they would embark on the long ride back to Beijing.[16]

Deng Xiaoping was ready to go to work. On March 10, Mao and Zhou formally proposed to restore him as vice premier of the State Council. With no more ado Deng rolled up his sleeves.

36

The Little Man in a Hurry

THERE WAS NO FORMAL announcement that Deng Xiaoping had returned to Beijing and the Party leadership. He simply walked in one evening at a reception for Prince Sihanouk in the Great Hall of the People and began to talk to guests as though he had just returned from a trip to Chongqing. No questions, no explanations.

None knew the necessity for speed better than Deng. He knew that Zhou had cancer. Zhou had given no outward sign, keeping up his ferocious pace, but Deng knew he would be taking over Zhou's duties as fast as he could absorb them. He knew he had Mao's backing — for the moment. He knew how deeply the Lin Biao affair had shaken Mao and how precarious was Mao's health.

And Deng knew, as well as anyone, the extent of Mao's capriciousness and his susceptibility to those around him. The Gang of Four was still in place, still at hand in Mao's circle. Jiang Qing was more quiet, perhaps, but Deng knew she had not given up. The fact that she and her associates had not lost favor when Lin Biao fell was sign certain that they held a powerful hand.

There was everything to be done. Industrial production had not met planned targets for nearly two years. Rail traffic had been brought to a halt by the Red Guards' seizure of critical junctions. Heavy industry was dead or nearly so, having registered no improvement since Lin Biao's death. Workers spent their time reading newspapers, drinking tea, going to political meetings, marching in the streets. The slogan "Make Revolution, Not Production" still prevailed. If a worker tried to fulfill his quota he was denounced as a rightist. Ships stood in the harbor for months; no cargo was loaded or unloaded. Airports dozed in the sun, their waiting rooms caverns of emptiness. A handful of tourists trickled in after Nixon. But only a trickle.

Deng knew what he wanted to do, what he had to do. He had worked it out during those late afternoons when he tirelessly paced the perimeter of the courtyard at Nanchang. To do it he needed power — authority to act in every field, an unlimited transfer of power from Mao. He knew Mao well enough to know he must seem to act entirely in Mao's name for Mao's ends, using Mao's words. And he must have personnel. He had to rid the system of the violent radicals brought in by Jiang Qing and rescue the surviving professionals torn out of government all over the country who were set to minding pigsties and viciously beaten. The Red Guard instructions called for the removal of the two top executives at every level. Deng needed those men back.

Hardly had Deng returned to Beijing than Marshal Ye Jianying called on him. The two sat a few moments in silence. Then both spoke simultaneously, echoing the same thought: "How do you assess the current situation?" Something, each said, must be done to rid the country of the Gang when Mao died, or even before. They stayed in touch from then on. Marshal Ye helped Deng with his household, arranging for staff: a doctor, nurses, servants, a driver. Ye went to Mao and asked that Deng be assigned to the Central Military Committee.[1]

Mao and Zhou had gotten the Party Central Committee to name Deng Xiaoping vice premier in March 1973. In presenting his proposal Mao said: "Deng is a rare talent. He is known in both military and civilian circles for this. He is like a needle wrapped in cotton. He has ideas. He does not confront problems head-on. He can deal with difficult problems with responsibility. His mind is round and his actions are square." Mao meant that Deng possessed tact, skill, a mind that could see problems in the round, and judgment that was solid. From Mao it was a rare and extraordinary tribute.[2]

But this was only the beginning. In August 1973 the Tenth Party Congress named Deng to its Presidium and made him a member of the Central Committee, and on December 12, 1973, he joined the Central Military Committee and became chief of staff of the armed forces. Mao made a self-criticism, saying he had been wrong to listen to Lin Biao and to make He Long and former chief of staff Luo Ruiqing (both now dead) targets of the Cultural Revolution. He reaffirmed that Zhu De was "the red commander-in-chief" and not a worthless adventurer. And he ordered a game of musical chairs for eight regional military commanders, to reduce the chances of a military coup d'état.[3]

However, the return of Deng Xiaoping did not mean that Mao

had abandoned the Cultural Revolution — far from it. He still considered it his most important achievement. At the congress that put Deng on the Central Committee, Mao criticized Zhou. And in December 1973, he criticized both Zhou and Marshal Ye for not paying attention to "political problems." If Mao was trying to drive a wedge between Deng and Zhou, this was not a good omen for the radical changes Zhou and Deng knew had to be made.[4]

Mao personally introduced Deng to responsible members of the Military Committee, saying: "I have invited someone to be your chief of staff. Some people are afraid of this guy. He is very decisive. His life can be viewed as thirty percent negative, seventy percent positive." Mao viewed the Cultural Revolution in the same percentages, 30 percent negative, 70 percent positive.

He also told his listeners that Deng seemed to be soft but was hard as steel inside. Marshal Ye listened with great pleasure. Almost immediately he went over to Deng's house for another talk.[5]

Deng was building a base. Most important, he won Mao's support for release of administrators from tending pigsties and other odoriferous jobs to which they had been assigned.[6] He had managed to pry loose more than three hundred top personnel.[7]

Despite illness Zhou worked tirelessly through 1973, helping strengthen Deng's infrastructure. Mao's health stabilized, but Zhou continued to carry most of the work load. Mao traveled a bit, going south to escape Beijing's spring and autumn winds. Zhou Enlai rebuffed sporadic gambits by Jiang Qing to undercut Deng. Zhou probably knew better than Deng how dangerous Jiang Qing could be. If he moved too swiftly to reverse the effects of the Cultural Revolution she would run to Mao, and Mao might well reverse himself once again.

The spring festival, China's great holiday, of 1974 was hardly over when another blow fell. Mao Zedong complained one day that he was having trouble reading; the characters were all blurred, and his eyes tired trying to bring them into focus. It was the same the next day and the next. He told only one person about his condition: Zhang Yufeng, his nurse-companion. It quickly became apparent to Zhang Yufeng that Mao was going blind.

Mao had won the greatest empire in the world. He held it in the hollow of his hand. Now he could not see that hand if he held it eight inches from his eyes. The deadly secret that Mao was losing his sight (it took only weeks, it seems, for his descent into darkness) burned in the breast of Zhang Yufeng. Mao refused to let her share it with another soul.[8]

By the strictest of Party edicts none of the papers going to Mao or issuing from his study was permitted to be read by anyone but Mao and his private confidential secretary, Xu Yefu. Mao had always strictly observed this rule of secrecy. None of his relatives or children was permitted to see any of his documents. That went for Jiang Qing and for Mao's nephew Mao Yuanxin, who was beginning to move into Mao's entourage. Xu Yefu was an army man who had served Mao for many years. He was, in the opinion of Zhang Yufeng, capable, honest, straightforward, and conscientious, not a man to leak secrets to Jiang Qing, Zhang Yufeng, or Zhou Enlai. But Xu Yefu was in the hospital in the last stages of an incurable disease. He was not then nor would he in the future be able to assist Mao in his blindness.

In the emergency Mao called on Zhang Yufeng to read documents to him, and he dictated his comments to her. The only persons who knew of Mao's blindness were Zhou Enlai (chairman of the special commission overseeing Mao's medical treatment) and Wang Dong-xing, chief of Security Unit 8341. Inevitably a few more people, presumably including Deng and Jiang Qing, became aware of the chairman's new infirmity.

Not until August 1974, when he was in Wuhan, did Mao permit a careful examination of his eyes by specialists. The verdict was senile cataracts affecting both eyes in slightly differing degrees. Nothing could be done except to wait for the cataracts to ripen sufficiently for an operation. How long that wait would be and how it would affect Mao's sight could not be forecast.

Despite his own illness Zhou continued to worry over Mao. He sent Mao a pair of his own spectacles that he said had served him well for years. If they didn't help Mao he would try and find him another pair.

Mao's body was becoming a coven of miseries. He could not see. His speech was increasingly incomprehensible, and he had to have a tablet at hand to scrawl out the characters for words he could no longer enunciate. His heart worked badly. His circulation was poor. He could walk only a few paces. He spent most of his time sprawled in bed on his mountain of pillows or sitting on a sofa. Mao's sofas were hard, Russian-made. Zhang Yufeng got some made with softer cushions, a great help to Mao, whose posterior was sore from long hours on the Russian sofas. Mao had a new sofa made for Zhou Enlai, a rare gesture of thoughtfulness. When Mao received visitors he sat in his chair, his head drooping, or stood for a few minutes, his jaw slack and gaping. His two interpreters — his brother's ward, Wang Hairong, and Nancy Tang, daughter of the publisher of a Chinese newspaper in New York and a Radcliffe graduate — enabled him to convey his thoughts more or less as he expressed them.[9]

Mao's mind remained clear, but his psychological state was affected by his plight. His diet was increasingly bland, since he had trouble with digestion. His kidneys worked poorly. His legs and ankles were chronically swollen. His consumption of sleeping pills continued as he lay awake night after night, contemplating the world he had created and seeking with faltering wits to devise stratagems to prevent his edifice of utopian dreams and Brobdingnagian aspirations from crumbling to dust when he soared to heaven to, as he believed, meet with Karl Marx. Whether he thought Josef Stalin would be sitting at Marx's right hand is not clear.

Mao had rebuked Jiang Qing on November 12, 1974, "Don't show your face too much. Don't write instructions or comments on documents. You are not to form the cabinet from backstage. You have stirred up widespread resentment. You should unite with the majority."

Jiang Qing apologized for "failing to know my limitations" but complained she had not been assigned much work, especially of late. Mao snapped back, "Your job is to study current affairs inside and outside the country. This is an important task."[10]

Jiang Qing would not be put off. She instructed Wang Hairong and Nancy Tang to tell Mao, who had gone to Changsha, that he should put Wang Hongwen, the youngest of the Gang of Four, into a key spot in the National People's Congress.

But the two interpreters would not be the only visitors to Changsha. Deng flew down himself to tell Mao of the trouble the Gang was making. Before he could open his mouth Mao started to criticize the Gang.

"You've set up an iron and steel company," Mao said — his way of saying Deng had created his own power base. Deng said he had indeed. He couldn't stand the mess Jiang Qing and her people had created in the Politburo.

Mao agreed with Deng. "They are imposing things on other people and I'm not happy about that."

Deng told him: "I'm using my iron and steel plant to oppose her iron and steel plant."

"That's good," Mao said. "That's good."[11]

Mao gave the same kind of answer to Wang Hairong and Nancy Tang when they delivered Jiang Qing's message about Wang Hongwen. "Jiang," he said, "has ambitions. She wants Wang Hongwen to be chairman of the Congress Standing Committee so that she herself can be Party chairman." When Wang Hongwen managed to see Mao in Changsha in December, he hinted that all four of the Gang wanted seats in the power structure. Mao blasted the idea, ordering, "Don't form a Gang of Four, don't form factions. Whoever does will trip and fall."[12]

On January 3, 1975, Mao named Deng Xiaoping vice chairman of the Military Committee and chief of staff of the PLA. When the Second Plenary of the Tenth Party Central Committee met on January 8, Deng was named vice chairman of the Central Committee and member of the Politburo Standing Committee. He now had the authority to move fast and hard.

Jiang stormed at Nancy Tang and Wang Hairong and then insisted that they convey her hot words to Mao. They did, and Mao replied: "She thinks highly of very few people, except one, herself."

"What does she think of you?" the women asked.

"I'm nothing in her eyes," Mao said. "One day she is going to break with everybody. Right now people are only humoring her. After I die she will make trouble."[13]

The Fourth National People's Congress met in January 1975. Zhou Enlai, emaciated, pale, face drawn, barely holding himself at the podium, laid before his countrymen his vision of China's paths to the future. It was not a long address; his limited strength did not permit that. But his words staked out an avenue for his country to follow. He called it the Four Modernizations (Chinese have a passion for numerology — the Four Olds, the PLA's Three Main Rules of Discipline and Eight Points for Attention).

The Four Modernizations were Zhou's goals for renewal and advance in agriculture, industry, science-technology, and national defense. They were going to be achieved by the year 2000, a quarter-century ahead. Zhou did not describe a society that would be ideological; not a word was spoken to hint at the egalitarianism of the Cultural Revolution. His program was succinct and specific. More goods, more services, higher production quotas, an end to China's backwardness, and implicit repudiation of the know-nothingism of Jiang Qing and, of course, of Mao himself.

Zhou's program was Deng's program. Deng was the man who would fill it in, insert the figures, provide the drive to bring it into being. If and when it was achieved, the windy, lethal nonsense that Mao had imposed upon his country would be swept away and a New China, free of sloth, ignorance, and morphia-tinged fantasy, would emerge, scrubbed clean by hard-edged pragmatism.

With death gnawing at the heels of both Mao and Zhou, Deng raced ahead. He grew increasingly certain that Jiang would fashion a trap, catch Mao in it, and bring Deng down.

Deng had managed to shake free several young and able lieutenants. One was Wan Li, a deputy mayor of Beijing, the builder of the Great Hall and the new Tiananmen Square, the man who could run 10,000 li, as Mao had referred to him. An attractive, vigorous man with a will of steel, Wan Li had known Deng, worked with him, and played bridge with him since the days in Chongqing. Another was a provincial chief named Zhao Ziyang, then in Guangzhou. A third was Hu Yao-bang, a man as small as Deng and just as full of vitality, leader of the Communist Youth League. These names would more and more frequently be associated with that of Deng.

Thirteen years later Wan Li, by then chairman of the National People's Congress, described how Deng proposed they should deal with the chaos the Red Guards had inflicted on the railway system:

"The railroads were completely paralyzed by the rebels and by factional fighting. Traffic on many main routes was halted completely. One of the worst blocks was Xuzhou, through which traffic to Shang-hai, particularly coal, had to be shipped. Nothing was getting through. It was a very serious situation." In case of war the PLA could not move troops.

Deng, Wan Li said, "came to power at the end of 1974," but the Gang of Four was still in place. It was almost impossible to travel so long as Red Guards controlled the rails. Deng assigned Wan Li to break the blockade.

"I told Deng," Wan Li said, "that the Central Committee must issue a directive to permit the arrest of the key rebels." Deng got the committee to approve Document Number 9, which Wan Li described as his "secret weapon" in the fight to unblock the railroads. The Gang tried to hold him off but failed. Deng spoke bluntly in an address to the Standing Committee of the Politburo: "Regulations are empty unless they are implemented. We must commend those who do good work. We must criticize those who do bad. We must punish those who refuse to work despite repeated admonitions. Strictness must come first. We must go overboard a bit in correcting mistakes."

Deng's words cut like a sword. Wan Li went to Shanghai, where Wang Hongwen of the Gang of Four was boss. He told Wang Hongwen that if supplies for Shanghai were to be unbottled, Wan Li would have to arrest the Red Guard leader who was supervising the blockade at Xuzhou. Reluctantly Wang agreed, and the trains began to run within a week.[14]

Deng specified that half of the new railroad management should be given to the PLA in the interest of national security. But the leaders of the Cultural Revolution had brought army units in to back rival factions. Even the death of Lin Biao did not ease this situation. All over the country army units found themselves opposing other army units. They were part of the problem, and it was hard to get the military to resolve such issues.

"The struggle in 1975 and 1976 was very complicated," Wan Li said wryly (it wound up with his own arrest and detention for two and a half years); in fact, it was not entirely resolved until sometime after Mao's death. But trains rolled. In April 1975 the state production plan was met for the first time in twenty-one months. By June service began to approach normal.

Wan Li was a no-nonsense man. Speaking of the "three bad years of natural disasters" — the standard cliché for the starvation years of 1959, 1960, and 1961 — he said in 1987: "I think we should call these three years of man-made disasters. That would be more appropriate."

Through 1975 Deng raced ahead with meeting after meeting, appointment after appointment. In March it was industrial production. In May it was the steel industry. Using the word "braid" in its Chinese sense — a mistake to be corrected — Deng told steel managers he was like a Uighur girl with many braids in her hair; they could always pull at several braids at a time. He instructed them to hire people who "are not afraid of being knocked down or being overthrown. Find people who dare to insist on principle. People who dare to fight." What was needed were people "strong and bold and competent" — in fact, a description of Deng himself.[15]

Deng carried the day through the spring and early summer of 1975, when Mao authorized the Politburo to criticize Jiang Qing. He told Jiang that it had been eight years since the start of the Cultural Revolution and that it was time for stability, not attacks. Jiang, he said to Deng, had ambitions to replace him. Deng chaired the last two of these Politburo meetings. Marshal Ye Jianying and president-to-be Li Xiannian joined the criticism.[16] Deng fought openly with Jiang Qing in the Politburo. At a stormy meeting on May 27, 1975, he accused her of attacking Zhou Enlai and Marshal Ye when Mao was calling for unity. He said she was good at criticism but not other things. Jiang flashed back that Deng was carrying out "a surprise attack." No way, said Deng. His criticism was less than 40 percent of what he might have expressed, maybe not even 20 percent. At a meeting on June 3, Deng banged on the table. He forced Jiang to make a small self-criticism and won Mao's support. "Jiang Qing should be criticized," Mao told him. "She has never accepted criticism."

Deng said he felt Mao had imposed a very heavy burden on him by directing him to oversee China's recovery, but Mao told him to go forward.[17] In June and July Deng met with the army. In August he called on the defense industry to get into line. He repeated Mao's criticism of the Gang of Four. It was time, Deng said, for production, not revolution. He brought in Zhang Aiping (later to be his defense minister) to oversee "rectification" of the armed forces. And he approved Hu Yaobang's feisty report on science and education.

Then Mao began to balk. The new directions being outlined by Deng and his men were cutting very close to his ideological imperatives, especially Hu Yaobang's blunt words. When Deng convened a big agricultural meeting in September under the rubric "Learn from Dazhai" (he had no intention of moving the Party down *that* road), Jiang Qing mobilized a powerful counterattack with the slogan "Criticize Deng Xiaoping and the Rightists." The lines for battle were being drawn.

On a fine spring day in 1975 a medical consultation had been conducted at the Swimming Pool House. The best of Chinese and foreign medical specialists had been called in to render an opinion on Mao's eyes. One doctor was Tang Youzhi, of the Guanganmen Hospital. When he was introduced Mao said: "Your father must have been a learned man. He undoubtedly named you after Lu Xun's famous poem, '*Youzhi*' [As You Please], written in mourning for Yang Guan."[18] Mao quoted a line or two: "I am mourning for a valiant fighter for the people." Mao recited with a strong Hunanese accent, and his imperfect voice made it impossible for Dr. Tang to catch many words. Mao wrote out the poem and gave it to the doctor.

The doctors decided the cataract on Mao's right eye was ripe for removal. On an evening in mid-August an operating table was set up in Mao's reception room, and Dr. Tang, lead surgeon, prepared for the operation. He thought there was a 70 to 80 percent chance of success.

Mao was in a spirited mood. He asked Zhang Yufeng to play one of his favorite records — a song written to *"Man Jiang Hong,"* a poem by the poet-general Yue Fei, of the Sung dynasty. It was sung by Xue Meiti, of the Shanghai Opera, in a resounding voice.

Echoing the Shanghai star's rendition, Mao walked to the operating table singing:

> "With anger I leaned on the railing, to the patter of rain.
> Raising my head I howled with passion my great aspirations.
> My thirty years of career and honor are like dust and mud.
> I was accompanied only by clouds and the moon on my march of
>   eight thousand li.
> Do not let time pass without accomplishing something.
> Otherwise you will regret it when your hair turns gray."

Mao was eighty-one years old and his hair was, indeed, gray. Did he think of himself still as a warrior preparing for new battle? Probably he did.

The operation took seven or eight minutes. Zhou, Deng, security leader Wang Dongxing, and a few others sat in the lounge and awaited the outcome. Zhou was wan, pale, in pain. He brushed this away. "My illness is not serious," he told Zhang Yufeng. "We must all concern ourselves about the chairman's health."[19]

The bandages were removed a week later. The operation was a success. Mao could see out of one eye after more than five hundred days of blindness. The news on Zhou Enlai was not so good. In mid-October he would have his last operation. The end was a matter of time. He was too weak to carry on real duties. The course of the country, effectively, was in the hands of Deng Xiaoping. But Deng had come under deadly attack.

37

Time Runs Out

DENG XIAOPING'S salvation, and China's, as he saw it, was to outrun the terrible ticking of time, as Zhou Enlai and Mao Zedong lay dying and Jiang Qing rallied her forces in the struggle for succession.

In the summer of 1975, Deng had launched the reorganization and rejuvenation of the People's Liberation Army, the overhaul of basic industries, the rehabilitation of the Party and its cadres. And he moved against Jiang Qing's citadel: her tyrannical control of culture, the arts, writing, music, theater, and propaganda.

Deng had gone head to head with Jiang in the Politburo. He had listened to Mao rebuke her, and he had presided over her personal self-criticisms in Politburo sessions. Deng Xiaoping knew that to confront Jiang Qing was highly dangerous, but he felt that if he did not act now, he risked destruction later. He banged his fist on the table as she shouted. He walked out of the room as she spat words at him.

The issue Deng picked for a showdown was exquisitely tangential. A film had recently been produced about the Daqing oil field. Called *The Pioneers,* it celebrated the workers who descended on the great red wasteland, the barren, windy wilderness, and who lived in sod huts, huddling around potbellied stoves, living on starvation gruel of millet and wild lily buds, wrestling the huge drilling gear into the ground, watching the black oil spout to the heavens. They gave their strength and their lives to what they believed was a patriotic cause.

Mao had made Daqing a national example. He had invented the slogan "In Industry Learn from Daqing." Unless cynicism had totally possessed him, he had to respond favorably to a film about his own popular heroes.

Jiang Qing didn't like *The Pioneers* and forbade it from being shown. But both Deng and Zhou Enlai approved of it. Deng decided on a gamble. If Mao gave the film a green light, Deng could use it as the entering wedge to pry Jiang Qing out of her monopoly on China's creative arts.

Deng moved with caution and cunning. He called upon Hu Qiaomu, Mao's former secretary, who still enjoyed a measure of Mao's confidence, to lead the foray. Deng had set up a political research group for the State Council in order to bypass Jiang Qing's control over the party's ideological organs, and he had placed the wispy, waspish Hu Qiaomu in charge. No one, Deng thought, had more sensitive political antennae than Hu Qiaomu, which is why he gave him the task of bearding Jiang Qing.

Hu Qiaomu had looked into several approaches to breaking Jiang Qing's cultural monopoly. She had just raided the Beijing Hotel, the semi-official hostelry where most distinguished guests were housed, ripping almost all the paintings off the walls and charging that they represented reactionary "black art." Telltale fade marks remained in the rooms for years. Hu considered this action of Jiang's as one possible target. Another was her forbidding the Beijing Philharmonic Orchestra from playing Beethoven's Ninth Symphony. But Hu Qiaomu decided that Deng's choice of *The Pioneers* was a better bet; it offered a chance to enlist Mao's personal sympathy.

Jiang Qing had not only banned the film, she had banned its creators — the scriptwriter, Zhang Tianmin, and his colleagues — from attending the Beijing film festival. She sent them to the countryside to "correct" their thinking.[1]

In the snuggery of the State Historical Museum an upright, fiercely honest woman named He Jiesheng had been placed by Zhou Enlai. Zhou had chosen the museum as a safe haven when He Jiesheng was released from prison after the death of her father, He Long, the famous military commander. Zhou Enlai had tried to slip her into the PLA, but Lin Biao and Jiang Qing had blocked him.

He Jiesheng, a slight woman with sparkling eyes, was a true daughter of her father and his first wife, Jian Xianren. When praised for her courage in fighting for her father's rehabilitation and opposing Jiang Qing, He Jiesheng said reluctantly: "Yes, I have some courage. I dared to do something in my father's case and in the case of *The Pioneers*."

Only a woman of courage could have endured He Jiesheng's life. She had been imprisoned and denied all rights of citizenship for being "in the black line of He Long." In spite of her precautions, new charges would be brought against her for her role in the *Pioneers* affair and for demonstrating in Tiananmen Square after the death of Zhou Enlai, in 1976. Her first husband divorced her when He Long was arrested; her second was beaten to death; her first child committed suicide or was suicided. Red Guards destroyed her home so thoroughly she was left without a bowl for her rice. Her younger brother and sister were enrolled in forced reeducation as children of a "bad family." She did not get her citizen's rights nor Party membership back until after the death of Mao and the rise of Deng.

Hu Qiaomu knew He Jiesheng from the State Museum, and now he delegated to her the preparation of the *Pioneers* case. He Long's daughter took security precautions. She knew how dangerous the enterprise was, and she knew that if Jiang Qing got wind of it she faced prison or death. A writer friend provided a house that belonged to his mother, and the little group assembled by He Jiesheng met there to throw off the scent. Plainclothes police, they thought, were already sniffing around.

The group drafted a report that Hu Qiaomu thought was too strong. So the group decided to persuade the author of *The Pioneers,* Zhang Tianmin, to write a personal letter to Mao defending the film. The writer was frightened and his face paled when they suggested the idea. How could he know, he said, whether Mao would even get the letter? He Jiesheng tried to reassure him. She said they would protect him, and they would spirit him away if Jiang Qing tried to catch him. Zhang Tianmin's wife won the day. She promised him she would take care of the children by herself if he went to jail, and added: "If you don't write that letter our relations will be spoiled." He wrote the letter.

But the question of delivering the letter remained. Zhang Tianmin was asked to make two copies. One was given to Hu Qiaomu to pass on to Deng. The second He Jiesheng gave to Mao's interpreter Wang Hairong to hand to Mao personally. (For some ritualistic reason it was considered less of a crime at Mao's court if your letter was submitted by an intermediary than if you handed it in yourself.) This was a ticklish operation; Miss Wang was not eager to get involved, since she would have to read the letter to Mao, who was then still blind. Finally the interpreter agreed to take on the chore because at this time, He Jieshing said, "she had a lot of complaints against Jiang Qing."

In the end the scriptwriter's letter was read to Mao by Wang Hairong. Mao listened carefully, then wrote a notation on the letter: "This film does not have big mistakes. Suggest giving approval and distributing it. Do not nitpick. Saying it has ten mistakes is excessive and does not favor efforts to readjust the Party's policy on literature and art."[2]

The readjustment to which Mao referred was that initiated by Deng Xiaoping. He had gotten Mao to issue a new directive on July 14, 1975, that encouraged writers to write "as long as they are not hidden counterrevolutionaries." Mao acknowledged that under the reign of Jiang Qing there was a "lack of poetry, novels, prose, literary and artistic criticism."[3]

Beijing is like a bazaar. Nowhere does gossip fly faster. News of Mao's change of heart on the cultural front and of his reprimands of Jiang Qing reached every *hutong*. It moved Kang Sheng, hospitalized with cancer, to call in Wang Hairong and Nancy Tang. He asked them to tell Mao that Jiang Qing and her right-hand man, Zhang Chunqiao, were traitors to the Party, and he supplied them with names of witnesses. The evidence on Jiang Qing, of course, was the same that Kang had airily waved aside when she was admitted to the Party in Yanan. It told of her supposed collaboration in Shanghai with the Chiang Kaishek regime in order to win release from prison.[4]

These were days of the wildest rumors. Word of Jiang Qing's week-long interview with the American scholar Roxane Witke had spread. The interview was described as part of Jiang's plot to make herself empress of China. It was reported that the book resulting from the interview had been translated and read to Mao, who became so upset that he suffered a heart attack.[5] Mao supposedly called Jiang "ignorant and ill informed" and "stupid and benighted." He was, according to gossip, going to drive her out of the Politburo and out of his bed. He would separate from her. Zhou Enlai, it was said, had interceded to win a reprieve for Jiang Qing.[6] Wishful thinking! But the sentiments ascribed to Mao were, in fact, remarkably like many of those attributed to him by his faithful bodyguards. Regardless of the truth of the rumors, people believed them, and this in turn diminished Jiang's power to terrorize. Many people felt she was on the verge of losing her place in power.

The public, of course, and even many in high positions, had no idea of the impaired health of Mao and Zhou. One who did know about their conditions was Ji Dengkui, because he was Mao's improbable personal favorite, the peasant Mao had put into the Politburo, a man who had access to the recesses of Zhongnanhai and knew, almost better than anyone, what was real and what was papier-mâché. He was now vice premier.

Fifteen years after Mao's death and long after he had been summarily ousted from the Politburo and all his offices, Ji Dengkui, old and feeble, painted a picture of the real Mao in his last days. It was unsparing in its flat tone, as devoid of contrasts as a passport photo. Mao, he said, seldom saw any Chinese outside of his personal entourage, and in fact, not many were eager to meet him. They were afraid. His temper was so uncertain they did not know what random word or thought might lead to their downfall. Mao had fallen into a paranoia not unlike that of Stalin as described by Nikita Khrushchev, who recalled Marshal Nikolai Bulganin whispering: "When [a man] sits with Stalin he does not know where he will be sent — home or to jail."[7]

"When we met Mao," Ji Dengkui said, "we were very afraid of what we said for fear of committing an error. It was different from meeting him in the fifties and the sixties. The unhealthy inner Party life was a tragedy for the Party as well as for Mao Zedong."[8] One wonders what drugs might have been administered to Mao on these occasions and in what way they might have affected his rapidly fluctuating moods.

The "inner Party life" had become, in fact, an imperial charade, a pageant of mirrors as might have been staged under the Tang emperors. Mao spoke only in the uncertain voice of his interpreters, Wang Hairong and Nancy Tang. The two acted as though they understood Mao's muffled Hunanese and translated his grunts and slurs into words and phrases, but who could say what relation their words bore to Mao's thought? In fact, if Ji Dengkui is to be believed, Mao was "somewhat not in his right mind." Did on such occasions Wang and Tang fill in his vacant mumbles with ideas or thoughts put in their minds, say, by Jiang Qing? The possibility for manipulation had no limit.

Mao had been propped up, dressed, and put on his feet in 1972 in order to meet President Nixon. He had brought that off remarkably well, considering his disability. The problem now had become more difficult. The task of presenting Mao to visitors was formidable. He could not, in reality, speak. Nor could he stand unassisted. He could not even lift his arm to shake hands.

In Mao's last days, as described by Ji, he received only guests who came from obscure pro-China countries or Communist parties, guests who could be depended upon not to give anything away when they went back home. But even so it was not easy to get Mao dressed, to place him on his feet, to hold him there, to raise his arm so a limp hand could be thrust at the visitor to shake, to fit a simple dialogue to the jumble of sounds that burbled in his throat. The ritual was not often attempted, and it did not last long. Before it began a photographer was in place to snap a quick picture. If after retouching it was deemed not too revealing, it might be printed on page 1 of the *People's Daily*.

Swiftly the tide turned and began to cut the ground from under Deng's feet. In his hurry, it is now clear, he had overplayed his hand. A document submitted in July by Hu Yaobang outlining a new Party program was the first misstep. It aroused Mao's deep fear that his Cultural Revolution might be swept away. Deng either failed to note the telltale symptoms or thought he could override them. He pressed forward with the *Pioneers* case. The symposium in September on agriculture rubbed Mao wrong. Deng's opponents sensed the turn.

At the end of August a new war cry was raised by the Gang. Mao had written a criticism of the hero of the novel *The Water Margin*, a Chinese classic, in answer to an inquiry by a professor at Beijing University. Mao called the novel's hero a "capitulator" who betrayed his leader to win power. The article was a fine example of Mao's tactic of squirreling away criticism of someone whom he had promoted, showing he had suspected the man all along. The *Water Margin* critique had been written in the spring of 1975, just as Deng began to get his campaign under way. Mao offered the piece for publication after, as he said, becoming convinced it applied to Deng.[9]

The intrigue became almost too complex to follow. Wang Hairong and Nancy Tang had begun to feed Mao hints about Zhou Enlai. They reminded Mao that Zhou had not been enthusiastic about the Cultural Revolution. Wang Hairong trod very cautiously. "I have an idea — I don't know whether it is right or not," she said. "In the Cultural Revolution when the rebels built a fire, Zhou was always there to put it out."

Mao was not eager to launch a new campaign. "Sunset is very beautiful," he observed. "But dusk is approaching. The time for me to report to Marx is nearing by the day."

But Wang Hairong persisted, and Mao finally agreed that Zhou was indeed a modern Confucius, always searching for the golden mean. "It is time to criticize him," he said.[10] Although Jiang Qing and Wang Hairong were not on good terms, Jiang Qing shared Wang's enmity for Zhou, and soon the campaign was in full swing.[11] With Mao's permission the Gang launched a drive to discuss *The Water Margin*. The purpose was to make propaganda against "capitulators," among whom they numbered Zhou Enlai and Deng Xiaoping.[12]

Deng plowed straight ahead. "Let them say we are restoring the old order," he said. "Veteran cadres should be resolute in daring to do their work. The worst that can happen is to be overthrown."[13]

Jiang Qing weighed in. "Some Politburo members," she said, "are trying to make Chairman Mao a mere figurehead."

Bad news for Deng was piling up. Worse came shortly. Toward the end of September, Mao got a new general factotum in the person of his nephew Mao Yuanxin, son of his brother Zemin, who had been executed in 1943 by the Xinjiang warlord Sheng Shicai. Mao Yuanxin was thirty-two years old and deputy political commissar of the Shenyang military district, a power in Manchuria. He had spent a good bit of time in Beijing with his uncle, was associated with Jiang Qing and the rest of the Gang and also with "Tiger" Chen Xilian, military commander at Shenyang, a man of deadly violence. Mao Yuanxin had unlimited access. He spoke the Hunan accent.

The negatives he poured into his uncle's ear were echoed in the last words of Kang Sheng, China's evil demon. Before he died in December 1975, Kang managed to rise from the bed of his cancer agony and pay Mao a last call. He told Mao that Deng and Zhou were locked in a conspiracy to sweep away all Mao had created. Every day Deng visited Zhou in the hospital for instructions; Deng paid no heed to Mao.[14]

Mao bought it. His mind fuzzy, his body falling apart, the paranoid yin-yang of his personality in full sway, he moved back into his old orbit. The campaign of Jiang Qing against the hero of *The Water Margin* blossomed into a new campaign simply called "Criticize Deng and the Right." *Red Flag* and the *People's Daily* charged that Deng was trying to reverse the field in education.

On an early November day in 1975 Mao Yuanxin had a talk with his uncle. Mao was coughing. A cold wind was blowing. The nephew said: "The wind outside isn't as strong as another wind."

"What do you mean?" Mao asked.

"I mean the wind of some people to negate the Cultural Revolution."

"Tell me more," Mao said.

"There are a number of questions here — whether the Cultural Revolution was seventy percent good and thirty percent bad or the reverse. How to assess the campaign against Lin Biao and Confucius and whether to continue to criticize Liu Shaoqi."

With a surgeon's skill the nephew touched the most sensitive nerves of Mao's ideological being. Deng Xiaoping was at the root of the problem. Deng, he said, hardly ever mentioned the Cultural Revolution or Mao. He never criticized Liu Shaoqi. He lauded Zhou Enlai. All he talked about was production.

Mao's face darkened. His breath came quicker. He was being betrayed. The warning he'd had from Kang Sheng was true. But perhaps Deng would repent. He asked his nephew to convene a Politburo meeting to consider Deng's position. Mao Yuanxin was not to tell the Gang about it.

The nephew went straight to the Fishing Ledge, where Jiang Qing was living. The Gang met that night, November 4, 1975. When the Politburo next met, Deng refused to back down. He would not change his position. From that moment he was suspended, and by the end of November, Mao had authorized a formal campaign against him.[15]

Deng's drive for change came to a halt. He had raised the gross output of industry and agriculture in 1975 by 11 percent — industry by 4.6 percent and agriculture by 15.1 percent. The increase in 1974 had been a scratch in the sand, about 1 percent. Railroads were running. Factories were beginning to stir. Farmers had gone back to the fields. Food was flowing into the cities. Education was still stymied, but Deng had managed to get a team of veteran administrators back to work. He had laid the foundation. Now Mao had flip-flopped. He first called Jiang Qing's speech about *The Water Margin* "a piece of shit" but by November was leading the chorus in support of Jiang Qing.[16]

Several senior military and party officers — men like Marshal Ye Jianying, Li Xiannian, General Nie Rongzhen, Zhu De, and Deng himself — had monitored Zhou Enlai's condition closely. One or more attended Zhou every day. They had long talks on policy and politics. Sometimes they spent two or three hours with him, but their visits were curtailed as Zhou's condition deteriorated. By the time he had his last one in mid-October he had had thirteen operations, many of them major, in an unsuccessful fight to halt the spread of cancer.

In his final two months Zhou was totally bedridden. His hair grew long and he was unshaven. His voice weakened and sank to a whisper after a bit of talk. In the last weeks he underwent nasal feeding. His bladder function failed. Sometimes there were seven or eight tubes attached to his body. Almost to the end he maintained his interest in the world and international developments, listening to radio reports and to dispatches read to him by his nurses.

In the latter half of December, when Zhou could no longer sit upright and lay in ghastly pain despite large doses of morphine, the hospital team wondered at the wisdom of keeping him alive.

He fell more and more often into a coma in the closing days. His vigilant wife, Deng Yingchao, sought to maintain the arbitrary rules of the Politburo to restrict visitors to those "above the level of the Politburo." Finally she was compelled to permit staff and junior supporters to come to the door of the ward to have a farewell glance. Old marshals were allowed into the room, standing at the foot of the bed in silence as Zhou lay unconscious.

Zhou's last audible words were "Oh, Dr. Wu, give me an injection." This was too much even for Deng Yingchao. "He cannot go on like this," she exclaimed. "It is too much." But Dr. Bian, the duty physician, insisted that Zhou's life was too precious to cut short "even for one more day, even for one more minute."[17]

Mao's condition deteriorated remorselessly. His faithful Zhang Yufeng reported that he could not walk. He could hardly move. She often could not grasp his thoughts from his mumbling lips. She tried lip-reading, but it was no help.

The situation was ripe for manipulation, and Mao himself had clearly set in motion the offensive against Deng and the dying Zhou Enlai. Zhou was almost too feeble to talk after his last, unsuccessful operation. Despite Zhou's condition, Mao's directive to criticize him was obeyed as he lay dying, still telling visitors to say hello to Chairman Mao and worrying over Mao's health.

On the Long March a twenty-year-old commander named Xiao Hua had written a poem about the March that Mao and Zhou had much admired. The poem described Mao as "performing magic" in making his military decisions.[18] The poem had been set to music. Now lying weak and barely conscious in the hospital, Zhou asked that it be played. Permission was refused. Jiang Qing or her representative said the song only praised "black generals" of the old guard.[19]

Instead Zhou Enlai was compelled to listen to a revised rendition of Mao's enigmatic 1965 poem, "Two Birds: A Dialogue." The poem, couched in rough language, had become a verbal grenade to wound or destroy Zhou on his deathbed. Ostensibly directed originally against Nikita Khrushchev, its real target was now Zhou. Its last, inelegant line read: "Don't fart or the heavens will be turned upside down."

The nurses saw Zhou smile when he heard the poem, but later at midnight they found him crying. "What's the matter?" one asked. Zhou choked back a sob and replied: "I'm getting old."[20]

The poem was published in the new version on page 1 of the *People's Daily*, New Year's Day, 1976. Seven days later Zhou Enlai died, at 9:57 A.M. The news was brought to Mao almost immediately by his aide Zhang Yaoci. Mao nodded his head as an indication that he had heard the report. He said nothing. He wrote nothing. His only act was to circle in red pencil his name on a copy of the arrangements made by the Politburo for Zhou's memorial service. He did not attend the ceremony.[21]

At the insistence of Marshal Ye Jianying, Deng Xiaoping spoke at the last rites. His address was formal, as devoid of personal emotion as an entry in *Who's Who*. Only in a few lines did he catch an image of the man to whom China owed its survival in the years of Mao's madness.

The nation, Deng said, should learn from Zhou's "fine style — being modest and prudent, unassuming and approachable, setting an example by his conduct and living in a plain and hardworking way."

Deng added a few lines as enigmatic as any he had ever spoken. He said that in his final days Zhou had "listened attentively" to Mao's poem published on New Year's Day. This, said Deng, "fully showed his indomitable revolutionary spirit." Was there a hidden message in Deng's words; a sign to his listeners that he as well as Zhou understood the despicable act of Mao and/or his minions in launching the poisoned arrow at Zhou as he lay helpless on his hospital bed? To the public Deng's words signified nothing. But to those who knew the inner politics they were redolent of meaning.

So passed from China's scene the greatest statesman of his day, who had given to Mao — and to China — his life and his career, seeing the identity of the land and the man irrevocably as one. Zhou was gone. But his spirit lingered.

It was the last time Deng Xiaoping was to appear in public until after the death of Mao Zedong.

38

The Year of the Dragon

THERE IS a special superstition in China about the Year of the Dragon. It is said to be a year in which bad things happen, and prudent Chinese therefore choose other times to start new ventures, take risks, get married, and embark on long journeys.

The Year of the Dragon 1976 was no exception. It began with the death of Zhou Enlai — what next? Zhou Enlai's passing left the country apprehensive. Jiang Qing and her followers tried to play down the event. Embassies were instructed to lower flags to half-mast for only one hour. Condolences were discouraged. The Gang had even considered having no funeral ceremonies, but Mao grunted his disapproval. The country would erupt, he warned.

Worry had grown in the last weeks of Zhou's illness and Mao's turn against Deng Xiaoping. Marshal Ye Jianying watched the scene with special concern. He was, next to Zhu De (approaching his ninetieth birthday, ill and feeble), China's senior marshal, a tall, still-handsome man, vigorous at seventy-eight. Ye was deadly serious about China's political plight.

In Yanan he had displayed a gay and merry manner. He was fond of Americans and joined happily in the Saturday night dances at the Date Garden. He played the piano and liked American tunes. Later in the civil war he directed guerrilla bands behind Chiang Kaishek's lines. One day in 1946 an American asked Ye what he was doing. He grinned and began singing "I've been workin' on the railroad, all the live-long day."[1] Some spectacular explosions on the tracks followed.

Ye hated the cult of personality around Mao. He confessed that he could not bear to shout: "Long live Chairman Mao!"[2] He had been a member of the original Cultural Revolution group, but his enthusiasm chilled when Red Guards placed his son-in-law's hand in a doorjamb and slammed the door. The hand was crushed and the fingers broken so that the young man could never again play the piano.[3]

No one in China had been a greater ladies' man than Ye, but now he was all seriousness. The fate of his country was at stake. He was devoting his energy to trying to rescue the nation from the plight into which it had been led.

Ye's career had been closely linked with that of Zhou. He had visited the dying Zhou almost daily. Since the death of Lin Biao, in 1971, the marshal had been quietly putting into place a network of senior leaders that might save the country when Mao died.

Marshal Ye was a native of Canton. He had deep roots there and had taken a hand in Canton politics for half a century. Since before the time of Sun Yatsen, Canton had led its own political life, often independent of Beijing. It was the traditional base for insurrection.

Ye lived in the Western Hills in a comfortable villa not far from the Summer Palace. There, too, lived a good many of his colleagues. It was army territory.

Deng Xiaoping worked closely with Marshal Ye. Both he and the marshal knew that it might be impossible for Deng to retain power now that Zhou Enlai was dead and Mao Zedong had turned against him. Deng's ouster might come any day. Nor was there much to be done about it. Jiang Qing had evolved a stranglehold over Mao. Mao Yuanxin oversaw Mao's life. Communications with Mao were handled by the ladies Wang and Tang.

January 31, 1976, was dark, cold, windy. Dust from the Gobi was blowing into Beijing from the northwest. Not for years had Mao stayed in Zhongnanhai for Chinese New Year's, the spring festival. Of all seasons this was the one during which he most often avoided Beijing. He liked to spend the holiday in Hangzhou, with its silky sun, on West Lake, at Liuzhuang, which once had been the residence of the governor-poet Li Bai, or at an adjoining estate that had belonged to a defense minister in the Qing dynasty. Far from the icy winds that clutched his throat and lungs Mao had loved to lounge, to read poetry, to work on some of his massive — albeit never-finished — literary projects, but not this year. He had taken his last journey.

Since the death of Zhou he had lain on his bed in a foul mood. It was true that Mao felt Zhou had become his rival, as he had been long ago in the Central Soviet Zone of the early 1930s, in Jiangxi. It was also true that he understood that Zhou, behind his courtier's manner, had not been sympathetic to the Cultural Revolution and had brought in Deng Xiaoping to reconstruct the country. There was, he thought, at least some truth to the deathbed warning Kang Sheng had given him. Still, he missed Zhou. For nearly fifty years they had worked together.

Some of the time Mao's mind worked; some of the time it didn't. He read a lot, but his hands were too shaky to hold a book. Zhang Yufeng had to hold it for him. The doctor didn't want him to read too much. It might be bad for the eye from which the cataract had been removed. But Mao read anyway. It might not be good for him, but at this stage what was?

The dark day sank into a darker twilight, broken only by the light of the lamp in the courtyard outside the Swimming Pool House. It had been a long time since Mao had been able to enter the pool. It was quiet now.

New Year's is a time for gaiety, for friends, for relatives, for a feast and drinks, for toasts and laughter, for reunion and reminiscence, for dreams. Not a guest entered the door of Mao's villa, not a relative turned up, not a friend. Gone were Mao's old comrades. Some had died naturally; some had not. Gone were Chen Yi, He Long, Peng Dehuai, and a hundred others. Gone were Mao's women. It was too late for them, too late for everything, really. Like his monstrous rival Stalin, China's man of power was spending his last days in solitude, in a world he had gleaned with his own scythe. With his own hand he had swept away — as had Stalin — his people by the tens of millions. To save them, as he thought, he had led them to their death in numbers that made him a modern Emperor Qin. He had unified China and devastated its people as the Yellow River had never managed to do. Of what dreams might have flickered through the dying cells of his eighty-two-year-old brain there is no record. But if he dreamed, it was not of that glittering world he had held in his mind the first night he slept in the Study of Chrysanthemum Fragrance. Only shards of those dreams, of reality, of pain, anguish, feebleness of limb and mind, remained.

Mao was the emperor of China, and he was alone with six bodyguards, two nurses, two doctors, and a couple of servants. There was no New Year's feast on the table. It was not like that New Year's forty-one years before as the Red Army halted before Zunyi, and Mao came back to his quarters through the snow to find the guards had spent hours cooking a feast of which he had only a few bites before they had to get moving again. Tonight even if they had cooked him a feast he could not have eaten it. He could not even lift a pair of chopsticks to his lips. He could hardly open his mouth, and he had no strength to chew. He lay on his side on his bed, as he did day and night, and his faithful Zhang Yufeng spooned a few bits of his favorite Wuchang fish from the Yangtze into his mouth and a few bites of rice, taking care that Mao did not choke, her heart welling up for the sick old man, feeble and alone.

After Mao had eaten, she and her companions — it took four of them — lumbered Mao to his feet and into the reception room, where they sat him on one of the sofas. Mao leaned back and sat quietly, not moving, his mouth open and drooling, staring into space, face blank and drawn. Soon they heard the faint pop-pop-pop of fireworks. Somewhere in Zhongnanhai the new year was being greeted in Chinese tradition. Mao roused himself a bit and looked about. Then he muttered softly. His words, as interpreted by Zhang Yufeng, indicated that he wanted some fireworks "so you young people can have some fun." He wanted to see in New Year's as he had as a boy at Shaoshan. He was going back to his childhood years, just as Vladimir Lenin had done as he lay dying in 1924 at the lovely old estate in Gorki Hills outside Moscow. Lenin the atheist had insisted on having a Christmas tree, as he'd had in his childhood home, on the bluff over the Volga at Simbirsk, and carols for the children.

One of the guards set out and returned with strings of firecrackers. He and another guard came up to the house and lit them outside Mao's reception room. Mao smiled faintly when he heard the crackle. He could not see the guards and the firecrackers because of the high-security windows on his house, nor could they look inside to see the old man whose nostalgia they were satisfying.

These were the last strings of firecrackers Mao would hear in his life. With this episode Zhang Yufeng brought her reminiscences of Mao to an end, drawing a merciful curtain over the anguish of the six months that lay ahead.[4]

Not a word leaked out about Deng's status. Mao had shorn him of power even before the death of Zhou Enlai. But he did not give that power to Jiang Qing or her cohorts. Instead, from some foggy recess of his mind he selected a man named Hua Guofeng, cherubic at fifty-five, as round-faced as Mao. After Mao's death Hua's face was imposed on Mao's in a double medallion that resembled a myopic double pumpkin head. "Pumpkin head" was what some of Hua's detractors called him. But he was no fool.

Mao had found this outwardly amiable man of no particular talent when he went back to Shaoshan in 1959, just before the first Lushan conference. Hua was a rising Hunan politician. He had been county chairman, had spiffed up Shaoshan with a big visitors' guesthouse, new roads, and a rail link to Changsha, and appealed to Mao as the kind of able young country politician he liked to select as a protégé. He brought him to Beijing in 1969, made him a deputy premier and a junior foil to Jiang's Gang, particularly to Wang Hongwen, the young Shanghai factory worker whom Jiang was plugging for the premier's post. Hua was robust and chunky, the opposite of the kinetic Deng, and as a new boy in town was respectful to his elders, especially Mao. He cooperated with the Gang but was sensible enough to keep a little distance. He was, after all, Mao's man, not Jiang's. He was there because Mao put him there, not Jiang. He followed with doglike devotion whatever twist Mao's line took.

Old as he was, feeble as he was, cloudy as his mind seemed, Mao understood the basic precept of his rule — divide and reign. He did not trust Jiang or her comrades. He had not entirely trusted Zhou Enlai for a long time. That was why when Zhou fell ill, Mao fended off Jiang's efforts to put her man into place and reached for Deng instead. But, as usual, Deng had proved too much in a hurry. Now Mao was muttering that Deng was not even a Marxist and never had been (not that Mao was much of a Marxist himself, but that was different).

How this was all going to play out no one — and particularly not Mao or Hua Guofeng — knew. But in early February, with no public announcement, Hua, who had been fifth-ranking vice premier, quietly emerged as "acting premier." He made his initial appearance in that role precisely one month after the death of Zhou. It was reported in the *People's Daily* of February 8, 1976, that Hua Guofeng, acting premier, had received the Venezuelan ambassador.[5]

That was it. If Hua was premier, then Deng was out — or worse. The question that leapt to the lips of Beijing was — Hua who? No one knew him or knew much about him. He had emerged as an agricultural specialist at the first Learn-from-Dazhai Conference, in September 1975. When some of the Gang members protested that he was too unknown, Mao waved them away. "Make propaganda about him," he said simply. There was not a word from Deng. Nor from Marshal Ye. If anyone had any doubt as to where Deng was headed, a blossoming of wall posters on February 10 made it clear — he was being denounced in terms as vivid as those used in the Cultural Revolution. He was still, they proclaimed, the unrepentant capitalist roader he had been in 1966.

Mao's politics, as so often happened, had reversed themselves. The torrent of filth spewed out by the press, the posters, and the radio against Deng left no doubt how dangerous he was to Jiang Qing and the Gang. It was so sensational it began to churn up a public wave of support for Deng. If he had been so bad in the eyes of the Gang, he must have been very, very good.

On the surface Beijing, Shanghai, Chongqing, Nanjing, Wuhan, Tianjin, and the other great cities of China seemed quiet. But in March a great shower of meteors was observed in Manchuria. Falling stars were a folk symbol of the impending fall of a dynasty.

On March 25 the country began to explode. *Wenhuibao,* the so-called literary gazette of Shanghai, the paper that set in motion the Cultural Revolution, printed a savage attack on Zhou Enlai, citing him by name and calling him a capitalist roader.

The article burst like a rocket. Before nightfall the newspaper plant was surrounded by people demanding an explanation. Within a day, news of the article hit Nanjing, China's traditional southern capital, a city where Zhou had spent much time and that regarded itself as a holder of the grail of Zhou Enlai. The Qing Ming festival, the Day of Pure Brightness, was at hand, the traditional occasion when the Chinese sweep the graves of their ancestors, place flowers, pray to the honored dead. Qing Ming became a metaphor for China's feelings, a day of remembrance for the leader who they felt had been true and faithful to his people in a time of China's calvary.

News of Nanjing's tribute was carried to Beijing not by the press, not by radio or television. All official agencies were suppressed, but citizens scrawled slogans on the sides of the Nanjing-Beijing express trains. Authorities were trying to stifle the outburst in Nanjing when the trains carried the word to Beijing. By March 30 wreaths dedicated to Zhou were being laid at the Monument to Martyrs in Tiananmen Square, the same monument that would become world famous as the heart of the great student demonstration for democracy in the spring of 1989, thirteen years later.

Within a day or two, thousands were streaming into the square, laying their wreaths, all of them homemade, and taking out notebooks and copying the epitaphs and poems to the fallen leader. Everyone went. Frantically the Gang tried to stop it. They denounced the demonstration. They denounced ceremonies for the dead. They denounced Zhou Enlai. They denounced Deng Xiaoping. The crowds got bigger and bigger. Not a word of the uproar appeared in the media.

Was there a hidden hand behind the outpouring of sentiment for

Zhou? So the Gang charged. It was, they said, a conspiracy. Deng had the central role. His minions carried out the demonstration, which went on and on. The demonstrators walked down Chang-an Avenue as though they were following a funeral cortege. The pace was slow, the faces solemn. The great white wreaths (white is China's mourning color) sometimes were bigger than the people who carried them.

A bright-faced boy named Shen Tong, seven years old that Qing Ming, lived with his family in a *hutong* off Tiananmen near the great Xidan market. Every day after work his parents took him to Tiananmen. It was a sea of white flowers, paper chrysanthemums made by the people. They strolled with the throngs, and Shen Tong's father, like thousands of others, copied down in a notebook the poems people had posted. It was exciting, and each day Shen Tong could hardly wait for the evening outing.[6]

A young English diplomat, Roger Garside, joined the throngs. While Shen Tong had felt the whole of Beijing was celebrating New Year's Eve, Garside understood that it was much more. One couplet he copied said:

> If there are monsters who spit out poisonous fire
> There will be men who dare to seize them.

Another verse read:

> Devils howl as we pour out our grief
> We weep but the wolves laugh
> We shed our blood in memory of the hero
> Raising our heads we unsheathe our swords.[7]

Marshal Ye Jianying understood as well as Garside that this was no New Year's celebration. He had sent people to mingle in the square as the crowds began to assemble, and he himself drove slowly in his car through the crush to get a firsthand impression. He had poems copied and brought to him.

Ye received reports from Nanjing, Hangzhou, Zhengzhou, and Taiyuan. Everywhere people had taken to the streets, expressing their grief and respect for Zhou, and again and again reviling the Gang. There were denunciations of Jiang Qing and her desire to play the role of empress, and some daring personal aspersions of Mao. The movement was broad and strong throughout China. Because of restrictions on travel, few foreigners were in a position to grasp this fact. But Ye Jianying understood that China was ripe for change and possibly revolution.[8]

By this time Marshal Ye had drawn in the old cannon, Wang Zhen, as his chief agent in maintaining contact with other members of the old guard and with Deng Xiaoping. The fate of Deng was of extreme concern to Marshal Ye and the others. Like Zhou Enlai, they saw him as the only — the inevitable — man to take the helm in China. As popular feeling rose against the Gang, so rose the danger to Deng and his life.

The Gang set up command headquarters in the Great Hall of the People. From this point they could observe the storm rising in the square, just as Deng's cohorts watched from the Great Hall in the spring of 1989 as the student democracy movement burgeoned in the same setting. Loudspeakers were turned on — as they were in 1989 — calling on the crowds to disperse. Sometimes the crowd turned ugly.

On the evening of April 4, security police entered the square with about two hundred trucks. The people had gone home. Swiftly the police bundled up the thousands of wreaths, tore down the inscriptions, and carted them all away. By the next morning Tiananmen looked as it had before the people had risen up.

In the week before, many throngs had come to the square in groups from government ministries and offices, just as they were to do in the closing days of the 1989 demonstration. But on the morning of Monday, April 5, people came as individuals by the thousands. They could not believe their eyes. Police were positioned around the Monument to Martyrs to prevent posting new slogans.

The atmosphere had changed. The crowds surrounded a police loudspeaker van, made the police get out and apologize, and let them go. A handful of student agitators sent into the crowd by the Gang had a narrow escape. They tried to tell the people they owed no homage to Zhou Enlai. The crowd silenced them, and they raced back to the Great Hall. There were more incidents. The crowd overturned a car and set it afire. They burst into a small police command post and did the same. Hundreds of policemen were on the scene, but they acted with restraint. Qiao Guanhua, the foreign minister, for years Zhou's faithful collaborator and now a tool of the Gang (having married one of Jiang's closest friends), came out to the square. He had been ordered by Jiang to quell the mob. He spoke nervously in a high-pitched voice, got angry murmuring in response, then turned and fled back into the Great Hall.

The crowd dwindled with the fall of night and rumors that the police or army would move in. Late that evening, April 5, it happened. The Tiananmen floodlights were switched on (in 1989 they would be switched off). The great gates of the Forbidden City opened wide, and thousands of men wearing the red armbands of the "workers' militia" (almost certainly a mixture of the armed police and security detachments) stormed out, wielding two-by-fours, some armed with iron-tipped staves. They cordoned the square into four segments and relentlessly pressed forward, beating men and women to the ground as they advanced. They dragged hundreds of bleeding demonstrators into trucks and carted them away. Blood and bodies were left in their wake. Before dawn, hose squads cleansed the paving blocks of the stains, and with daybreak Qing Ming was over.

Hundreds had been arrested, hundreds had been wounded, some badly, and word spread that hundreds had been killed and the bodies spirited away by the police. But nearly ten years later, Yan Jiaqi, then a prominent social scientist in the Academy of Social Sciences who, with his wife, carried out the most meticulous inquiry into the Cultural Revolution and its atrocities yet to appear, investigated the Tiananmen affair with equal care. His startling conclusion: Not one person was killed in the square. Perhaps it was this finding that inspired Beijing authorities in 1989 to insist — against all evidence — that not one person had been killed on the night of June 3–4, 1989, in Tiananmen.[9]

On April 10 the Politburo convened and formally relieved Deng Xiaoping of the functions he had actually ceased to perform since the death of Zhou Enlai, on January 8. Tiananmen was declared a counterrevolutionary act for which Deng was responsible. He was dismissed as vice premier, dismissed as vice secretary of the Party, dismissed from the all-powerful Central Military Committee. But he was not deprived of Party membership. Here Mao Zedong drew the line. Perhaps he felt that he might still need Deng. It was a quixotic move by a man whose life had become totally quixotic. He was unable to leave his bed, barely able to speak or write. But he still decreed that Deng keep his Party membership "to see how he will behave in the future." It was a small bet, although a vital one. "Leave him his Party card to show to his descendants," Mao was quoted as saying.[10]

Marshal Ye conferred with Deng, pledging his support come what might and suggesting that the two once again call on Mao. Deng thought that of no use. He said he had had several private talks with Mao: "I think Mao has made up his mind on a change of horses."

Marshal Ye was more sanguine. He thought Deng might remain in office — at least for a while — and only be subjected to criticism.

"I am prepared for the worst," Deng said. "You know my character and my temper. I never make compromises or budge on matters of principle. There is nothing to be afraid of. I have been mentally prepared for a long time. The worst for me would be no more than to be brought down again."

In any event, Ye said, the veteran Party members would go on fighting.

"Yes," Deng said, "we should fight all right but we should be careful about our methods of struggle." Deng revealed that he had discussed the question of removing the Gang and Jiang Qing with Zhou Enlai before Zhou's death. Zhou approved the objective but warned Deng "to be careful about the methods of struggle."

Deng's statement to Ye was the first (and thus far only) revelation that Zhou Enlai had not only persuaded Mao to bring Deng back but had envisaged Deng as a mechanism for ridding China of the Gang.[11]

But now Mao, in the opinion of Marshal Ye, had lost confidence in the Gang. He would not name its members to high office. However, he had also lost confidence in Deng. That was why his choice fell on the inexperienced but neutral Hua Guofeng.

So China tottered into the last months of the reign of Mao Zedong. There were rumors that Deng had been placed under house arrest. He was not to be seen. He had now fallen for the third time.

Quietly Deng slipped out of Beijing and made his way to Canton, there to take cover under the protection of Ye Jianying's powerful political and military allies while awaiting the end of Mao.

By one account Marshal Ye spirited Deng aboard a military aircraft, which landed at the Canton military airport. There General Xu Shiyou, whom Deng had known since the days of the 129th Division, took him under his protection.

The Year of the Dragon raced ahead, reaping its toll. On July 7 the grand old general Zhu De finally died at ninety. More deaths lay just ahead.

39

The Dragon Speaks

A YOUNG MAN name Zhou Wenbin was awakened in the industrial city of Tangshan, a coal-mining center of almost a million, early in the morning of July 26, 1976. Zhou had been bitten by a mosquito, and he got up and ran his hand under the faucet to wash the blood away. Zhou, a jogging fan, decided he would stay up and get in some exercise before reporting for work at the big Kailuan coal combine. He glanced at the clock. The hands were just pointing to 3:40 A.M. He remembered saying to himself: "The whole town is sleeping. I'm the only one who's awake." The thought gave him a sense of secret power.

Zhou never did his jogging. Before he got the blood washed off his hand, the quake hit. He rushed to awaken his wife. He was a foot from the door when the walls caved in and he lost consciousness. A professional team from Kailuan dug him out at 2:00 A.M. on July 27. His wife and children and 53 others of the 163 in the building were killed. So were an estimated 242,000 citizens, including seven of the eleven top executives of the Kailuan mine.

Tangshan is not a pretty town. It is all industry, mostly associated with the vast coal mines. It lies about 125 miles east and slightly south of Beijing and 25 miles from Bohai Bay. The big coal-loading docks are at Tianjin, 60 miles to the northwest. Tangshan is a satellite of the Tianjin complex, one of the great industrial centers of the north.

Tangshan's history is not significant. Its career as a big coal center goes back only to the late nineteenth century, when Chinese and British interests began to develop the field. It was known from the beginning for high-quality coking coal, essential for steel making, a prize hotly fought over by Chinese, British, Japanese, and German concerns, an object of great international intrigue. Just after the Boxer rebellion a young American engineer born in Iowa and fresh out of

Stanford University named Herbert Hoover played a role in this. Hoover's involvement was so complex that volumes have been written on it, and it became a subject of charges of financial manipulation when Hoover went into politics. It remains a tangle, but one thing is certain. Mr. Hoover came out of China with a fortune of several hundred thousand dollars, and the British got control of the field and ran it very profitably until, in 1949, the People's Republic took it over and it became one of the greatest industrial units in the country.

Tangshan exports became a major source of foreign exchange, and much of north China's industry was based on Tangshan coal, coke, and the steel produced there. Tianjin, Dalian, Harbin, Shenyang — all these industrial complexes were dependent upon Tangshan. It was and is the Pittsburgh of northern China.

The geological structure of the coastal plain where Tangshan stands is complex and unstable. China has long been subject to devastating earthquakes, and the roots of Chinese seismology go deep into the dynasties. Chinese scientists were credited with a spectacular and accurate forecast of a serious earthquake at Haicheng, about 250 miles northeast of Tangshan, in 1975. Many thought that China could now predict earthquakes as easily as forecasting the weather. Seismologists knew better, particularly since the Cultural Revolution had crippled their scientific base. In 1976 the seismologists were struggling to get their science back on track.

There had been no significant seismic indications in Tangshan, and seismologists had been lulled by the occurrence of a stiff quake in Helinger, in Inner Mongolia, north of Tangshan. They believed the Helinger shock had relieved tensions in the tectonic plates underlying the Bohai Bay area. It was not likely, they thought, that there would be another shock soon.

Around July 20 a group of seismologists had arrived at Tangshan to collect data for a data base in the area. They had no concerns about current quakes.

The six scientists were put up at the municipal guesthouse in Tangshan. They traveled around the area, collecting data and consulting local seismologists in preparation for formal meetings at the Shenliqiao Seismic Bureau on July 26. The area of Tangshan was an excellent case study, since it was crisscrossed with fault lines. One fault ran for sixty-six miles, from a point in Nanhe County, just west of the city, to Luanxian County to the east. It lay directly beneath Tangshan. The network of faults was testimony to the fragility of the underlying structure.

Reservations had been made for the scientists to return to Beijing on the twenty-eighth.[1]

Le Chun was a tight-lipped, rather bureaucratic man in his mid-thirties, a Party worker, assigned to Tangshan's Number 1 High School, the pride of the city. The school was located next to the old railroad shops, the first in China to make steam locomotives in the 1880s and still turning them out in 1987. The high school, set in a forty-acre park, was a magnet school for the province, with twenty-four classes, three grades, and two thousand students, half boys and half girls. It had been closed during the Cultural Revolution while the students roamed the land "making revolution." When it first re-opened, a blank piece of paper was a satisfactory answer to an examination, but it was now moving back to genuine education. By 1987 it would be among the premier high schools in China, with a university admission rate among its graduates of almost 90 percent, competing neck and neck with Beijing Number 8, Yucai, and Fuzhen, all of which scored a 100 percent rate, and Nankai in Tianjin, with 90 percent.

On July 25, Le Chun was away from the school. He was occupied all day and into the evening with meetings at the municipal building. He decided to spend the night there, in a second-floor dormitory. He was awakened in the night by what he remembered as a great roar, perhaps like the roar of a dragon. It was, he thought, a storm approaching, and he got up and closed his window. As he sat back in bed he saw what seemed like a huge flash of lightning dazzle across the sky. The floor of the room rose up under his feet. It rose and fell three times.

Tangshan is the site of a fine porcelain works, of which Liu Guanghai was to become vice manager. In 1976 he was a freshman at the Institute of Industrial Technology. On the night of July 25–26 he had watched a movie, then gone to his room to write a report. He didn't finish until about 3:30 A.M. He crawled into bed and was half-asleep when he heard a heavy wind. He got up to close the window and saw a great red ball in the sky. He tried to open the door. It was jammed. As he dove through the window a brick hit him. The building collapsed. Some people said they saw lightning. "I saw a great fireball," he said.

It was an earthquake. The dormitory was about forty miles from the epicenter. There were almost 400 students in Liu Guanghai's freshman class. Thirty-eight were killed.

*   *   *

Wang Shirong was deputy director of the Ceramics Corporation, which had a work force of 15,000. During the Cultural Revolution it was one of the biggest producers of Mao badges in China — one of the few items on which production was maintained. In the earthquake 1,320 workers and staff members were killed, including 410 department chiefs and Party workers. The whole plant was destroyed. The inventory — hundreds of thousands of porcelain and ceramic objects — was turned to shards, among them priceless early Ming five hundred years old.

In the early morning of July 26, Yan Xixing, a wiry man in blue jacket and striped pullover, foxy little face, was working the night shift in the foundry of the old locomotive works. It was hot in the big shop, with the charcoal beds and molten iron running in rivulets. Yan had stripped to his shorts. The earth began to move under his feet. He thought it was the shock wave from a new blast of molten metal. People began shouting "Earthquake!" and the roof fell in, the lights went out, and he and his comrades ran for their lives in the eerie light of the glowing streams of metal. He stood under a steel girder for safety, but an overhead car fell, killing three men beside him and knocking him unconscious. When he regained his senses he didn't worry; he thought someone would come to his aid quickly. He also thought only his shop had been hit. He was wrong on both counts. Yan got out at 10:00 A.M. He left a friend behind, pinned by the girder. There was no crane to lift it off. At home he found his wife alive, his one-month-old son dead. The brick walls had toppled in. They lived in a shelter made of blankets for a long time.

The boardroom of the Kailuan Coal Mining Combine could be located at 40 Wall Street. A marble staircase leads to a room half-paneled in discreet teak. The designer table is oval, the chairs finished in black leather, a crystal chandelier and recessed lighting above. At one end there is a slightly raised platform for dog and pony presentations. A push-button screen comes down for slides and films. Kailuan is big business, and Herbert Hoover would have felt at home in this room.

In 1987 Zhang Ruji, a big man, broad face, broad shoulders, slightly battered pug nose, ran the complex. There was no doubt of who was boss. It was hard to imagine the dynamic chief of Kailuan being made to do the airplane in the Cultural Revolution. But he was, and his chief engineer was suicided. Zhang had eleven great mines under his big hands, one of them bauxite, the rest coal, a work force of 135,000, and a community of half a million people. They had their own powder plant, their own explosives, their own chicken farms, lobster and shrimp canneries, breweries, forty primary schools. His mines turned out high-quality coking coal — some for North Korea and Japan but now most consumed in China's own industries. He was producing 20 million tons a year in 1988 and soon would be up to 30 million. In China only the Datong mines, in Shanxi, where Armand Hammer had just installed a highly automated slurry operation, was in Kailuan's league. When there was start-up trouble with the Hammer mines, Kailuan filled the contracts.[2]

Zhang led the way to the locker room where the mining parties donned their gear: heavy cotton underclothes, cotton socks, jeans, heavy denim tunics, quilted jackets, rubber knee boots, black hard hats, and miners' lamps. Into the cage and down 2,500 feet in three minutes, so smooth only pressure in the ears tells you that you're dropping.

On the night of July 25–26, some twelve hundred men were at work in this particular mine. Stories circulated that thousands of miners had been buried alive under thousands of tons of coal.

No, said Zhang, sweeping his electric lamp over the finely cut walls of the seam, the heavy timbering and the willow basketweave protecting ceilings and walls. This mine, the spot where we were standing, was directly over the great fault under Tangshan. We were at a depth of 1,060 meters, a bit more than 3,000 feet. About five and a half miles deeper, directly under our feet, was the fault that caused the temblor at 3:42 A.M. on July 26. Seven persons had died in this mine. Some were injured. When the power went off, the lights went out, the great fans stopped, the water pumps sighed to a halt, and the water began to rise, the men found their emergency exits, began their long climb, and emerged on the surface to a world of devastation at about eleven that morning. True, small parties were trapped, one for thirteen days. But the mine, deep in the earth, so close to the fault, was the safest place in town. On the surface 1,961 workers and their families were killed, trapped in the debris of jerry-built houses.

Why had the mine been so safe? Because, Zhang explained, as you can see, we have shackled and buttressed every foot. It is quarried out of solid coal and rock. True, the earth trembled; we felt it rise under our feet. But our corsets held tight. There were roof falls, of course. Here and there a wall gave way. But aboveground the shock rattled the buildings down in the first seconds.

What Zhang said was true. The city had been a monument to shoddiness. Almost every building tumbled down. The six seismologists in town to do research went to sleep at the guesthouse. All were killed when its walls collapsed and the concrete slab roof came tumbling down seconds after 3:42 A.M. At Tangshan's Number 1 High School 550 of the 2,000 students were killed. Of staff and teachers, 32 of 139 died. The school was located at the epicenter of the quake.

It was China's greatest earthquake, the world's greatest in modern times, 7.8 on the Richter scale. A total of 242,000 people were killed in Tangshan, roughly another 100,000 outside Tangshan in surrounding towns, in Tianjin and Beijing. Estimates of the dead ran up to and beyond 500,000. This seems an exaggeration, but the stated totals may be an underestimate. To compare: 700 lives were lost in America's worst earthquake, that of San Francisco in 1906; 99,300 were lost in the Tokyo earthquake of 1923, before Tangshan the hallmark of disaster of recent times.[3]

Tangshan's destruction was so universal that it was almost impossible to engage in rescue operations. Beijing was unable to move the army in until days later, since highways and railroads were cut and bridges were down. It took authorities half a day to locate the epicenter — the seismograph needles had been jolted off their revolving drums. Telephone and telegraph wires were severed. Beijing itself had been badly hit, many buildings destroyed, particularly the old *hutong* courtyard houses. The industrial complex of Tianjin was knocked out.

In 1987 Wang Daming was vice mayor of Tangshan. He had worked in the iron and steel plant in 1976 and lived nearby in a Japanese-built house, which was badly damaged in the earthquake but did not collapse. He broke his way out, saved his six-year-old boy, his wife, and all those in the house. Then, half-naked, cut, and bleeding, he went to the steelworks. He was assigned to a group of two hundred along with one hundred army men to collect the tens and hundreds of thousands of corpses. Little clear space remained in which to lay them; everywhere was rubble. Many bodies were broken limb from limb. There was no time to identify them — they had to be disposed of quickly. Wang Daming and his group laid out those they could on the ground and sprinkled lime on them until it ran out. They helped toss them into trucks, which lumbered off to dump the bodies in mass graves.

There weren't any niceties. The survivors camped with the dead on the few flat and open spaces, building their campfires, heating kettles of water for rice and tea amid headless, legless corpses with sightless eyes a half dozen feet away. The living were almost as numb as the dead. Truck after truck piled high with bodies lurched off. Dust and stench filled the air. Wang Daming kept at his task for more than a week. He remembered how red his nose got from the disinfectant. And the smell of the corpses was still in his nostrils. It would stay there for life. To Wang Daming the earthquake was not just a column of statistics. It was the bodies, smell, sights. He knew it was the worst earthquake in China's history — the worst earthquake ever, no matter what the figures said.

About one quarter of the city's population had died on July 26 — but what had become of the bodies? The question so agitated Wang Huili, a diminutive guide assigned to escort a Western visitor around Tangshan, that he came close to hysterics. Five of his family were among the victims. Finally he managed to stutter that the bodies had been placed in an abandoned coal mine. The next day he was persuaded to take the visitor to the burial site. It was not easy to find. Twice Wang Huili lost his way. The ride was a long one, through a desert of broken artifacts of devastation, mile after mile of wasteland littered with junk, great fields in which smashed timber of every age was scattered, a field pockmarked with tree stumps, acres of iron, carcasses of army trucks, jeeps, pleasure cars of the 1930s. Gray mile after mile — litter, broken crockery, broken picture frames, broken pots, broken stones, broken brick, sorted in architecturally neat piles. It was a nightmare: yellow bricks here, red bricks there, old cement blocks just beyond, roof tiles across the road, the wreckage of a speedboat. Beside a Tobacco Road shack, gray with dust, was a sign with an arrow outlined in faded red: "*Qu lajichang* — To the Junkyard." Down a sandy road, a bit more than a quarter mile, a bit less than a half, the landscape spread out. Ahead was a clump of trees, and that was it.

Beyond the clump, patches of water could be seen, tufted here and there by scraggly bushes and brackish weeds. In the distance were Tangshan's newly built skyscrapers. Toward the edge was an occasional slender cement post, heaps of earth near the dusty track. Farther back in the tangle of bushes and scrub trees stood more posts, bare and antiseptic — grave markers that bore no names. It was a landscape of dismal thoughts and hopeless future. As the visitors stood there, a thin, quivering sound echoed over the scene, as though dead souls were keening for their lost lives. This was fantasy, of course. The sound came from a faraway tape deck playing a recording by a Hong Kong pop singer.

This was where the dump trucks had come, day and night. A driver touched a pedal and the truck upended the dead into the sunken mine, day by day, week by week, month by month, as if it never would stop. But finally it had ended, and the bodies decomposed and the bones fell clean and white deep into the pithy marsh. The water from the old minehead rose until it covered, at long last, the surface. The municipality, someone said, had stocked the water with fish. Tangshan water was rich in nutrients.

Mr. Wang, the guide, stood at one side, his head sunken into his chest. His father was buried here. How awful to know that his father was one of the 242,000 whose bones now rested in a tumble together in the old mine.

Two bicycles lay side by side close to the water. A couple was out there among the earthen tufts — looking, perhaps, but for what could one look in this patch of anonymity? Suddenly a tweedy-looking man, wearing a huge pair of rubber waders, a basketwork creel under his shoulder, a rod in hand, brushed past with a brisk stride. He was, he said, going fishing.

Mr. Wang turned away from the spot. Many people, he said, come here on April 5, the Day of Pure Brightness, the day for the dead.

Nothing in Tangshan operated for a year after the quake. Most enterprises were not restored for two, three, or four years. The situation was only marginally better in Tianjin, China's number-three city in industrial output (first in many heavy categories). Port facilities were badly smashed. Port operations had to be suspended. Beijing's enterprises were cut back to even lower levels than those already imposed by the Cultural Revolution. The complex of railroads, bridges, and highways serving the industrial heart of north China was wrecked. For months little but emergency food and hospital supplies got through. The enormous casualties deprived plants of a work force. Many were left without senior officials.

No reliable overall statistics have ever been released. But a sampling of the effects on major industries revealed the dimensions of the blow. The earthquake set back China to well below the level of Deng Xiaoping's energetic 1975 campaign. Beijing was so damaged that two years later much of the population was still living in makeshift huts and tents hastily thrown up along the broad boulevards. Damage to courtyard houses in the *hutongs* and to many shoddily built apartment buildings was still being repaired years later.

Inefficiency and bungling, by-products of the Cultural Revolution, made things worse. The army — with great difficulty — had managed to provide emergency and first aid but was unable to do much more than clear roads and gradually restore power, water, light, and other utilities. It was 1980 before the dramatic consequences of Tangshan began to disappear from China's economic balance sheet.

Years later a shabby bit of human interest propaganda portrayed Li Peng, by then the hard-line premier, as having dashed to Tangshan to direct aid. No one in Tangshan seemed to remember this heroic exploit.

40

The Death of Mao

THE NUMBER 202 building is not one of the scenic spots of Zhongnanhai. It is a plain structure of simple gray brick with a red lacquer door and a little gilt trim, no rival to the survivals of the Ming and the Qing. A one-story courtyard house with a nice terrace, it is much in the style of the Party Secretariat building nearby.

Access to number 202 is not through the Gate of New China on Chang-an Avenue but from the inconspicuous gate at 81 Nanchang Street, on the west side of Zhongnanhai. It is a solid and secure residence, and Hua Guofeng moved Mao Zedong here in the early morning of July 26, 1976, fearful that an aftershock of the great earthquake might shake down Mao's Swimming Pool House.

Here Mao was installed with his nurses, the irreplaceable Zhang Yufeng, the medical team, the bodyguards, the oxygen tanks, the respirator, the feeding tubes, the portable pharmacopoeia with its array of hypodermic needles, emergency heart stimulants and medications, the bedpans, a wheelchair — all the paraphernalia of a final and complex illness.

Mao's perceptions seemed minimal as he lay on the hospital bed that had been moved from the Swimming Pool House. He was usually in a semicomatose state, sleeping or drowsing, no longer able to read. His respiration, heart rate, blood pressure, were constantly monitored. His condition had sharply deteriorated since June, when he may have had a stroke or heart attack.[1]

The doctors had orders to prolong Mao's life regardless of discomfort to the patient. Under these conditions the Politburo members paid their final visit to the dying man in the middle of August. Few had seen Mao for months. Now, it was said, they assembled for the last viewing — all, that is, but Jiang Qing. She was represented by two fellow members of the Gang of Four.

The Politburo members were led to the door of the sickroom, where they huddled like elderly schoolchildren for a farewell look. Mao lay on his back, tubes in his body, his eyes closed, inert, thin, shaved, his hair skimpily trimmed, a skeleton of himself. His breath came in wheezes.

Marshal Ye was ushered to Mao's side and stood for a time looking closely at the wreck of his old comrade at arms. As Ye turned to go, Mao's eyes opened and he seemed to make a gesture. Ye was already leaving the room, but Zhang Yufeng spotted Mao's movement and ran after Ye. "Marshal Ye," she cried. "The chairman wants to talk to you."

Ye went back and grasped Mao's hand. Mao struggled to speak, but no words came out. The two held hands for a while; then Ye left.[2]

Marshal Ye redoubled his preparations to thwart Jiang Qing.[3] He was certain that Mao would be dead in a fortnight or so and that the Gang would kill Deng if they got their hands on him.

Marshal Ye's concern over Deng's safety was well founded. Jiang Qing attacked anything connected with Deng. His hometown of Guang'an (and all of Sichuan) was suffering a famine, and the residents of the area were begging for food in the countryside. One of Deng's last official acts had been to send a relief train loaded with food to his home county. The Gang intercepted the train and turned it back.

The people began to chant a quatrain in the streets:

"We are the beggars of Guang'an
We hate Jiang Qing and the Gang.
Deng Xiaoping, hear our petition
Help to save us from starvation."[4]

Deng was safe for the moment. He was in Canton under the protection of his Long March colleague General Xu Shiyou, a fierce enemy of Jiang Qing's and commandant of the Canton military, and Wei Guoqing, the governor. Both were loyal associates of Marshal Ye's. Xu Shiyou was called Old Ironsides by his men. He was a bluff trooper who would later stalk out of a meeting with his colleagues in Beijing at the time of Mao's death, shouting: "If you don't arrest that woman [Jiang Qing] I'll march north." Deng found refuge in the White Cloud Mountain spa, a dozen miles from Canton, one of China's famous beauty spots.[5]

Marshal Ye's lieutenants knew the Gang was feverishly making military preparations, organizing a special people's militia in Shanghai. They controlled through Mao Yuanxin, Mao's nephew, the troops of the Manchurian command and some of the Beijing garrison as well. Marshal Ye was preparing for any eventuality, including a move by the Gang before Mao's death. Ye's lieutenant in these preparations was Wang Zhen, who served as liaison, moving quietly from group to group, assessing the situation, collecting information, and carrying out Ye's orders.[6]

Ye was nervous about security, convinced the Gang had bugged his quarters. He never carried on a discussion without turning on his radio or letting the water splash loudly from a tap.

One of his conversations with Wang Zhen had been conducted in sign language. With his hallmark bluntness Wang Zhen was speaking to Ye in his villa in the Fragrant Hills. "Why can't we just pick them up?" he started to say. Ye silenced him, then stretched out his right hand in a fist. He put his thumb up, down, then put it up again. Two thumbs up! Then Ye put his thumb down again. Wang grasped Ye's meaning. First, they must wait for Mao's death — then they would act.[7]

There were two individuals whose help Ye needed: Wang Dongxing, commander of Security Unit 8341, and Hua Guofeng, the acting premier. Wang was director of the Party's General Office. He had worked closely with the Gang but was not of it. His appointment to the security post had been made by Mao before the Gang came into power. Wang Dongxing was a powerful man: His security forces numbered between thirty thousand and forty thousand. He was in a position to observe and track almost any movement of Jiang Qing and her aides.

Wang Zhen brought the security chief into contact with Ye and the old guard. By chance, the relationship between Wang Zhen and Wang Dongxing went back to the days when Wang Zhen had been commander of the garrison troops in Yanan and Wang Dongxing had been his lieutenant. Wang Zhen, acting at Ye's instruction, carefully restored this old and close connection. This enabled Marshal Ye to meet privately with the security chief and cautiously begin to explore chances for collaboration.

Hua Guofeng, the titular leader named by Mao, was more difficult. With Deng Xiaoping in disgrace, Hua automatically would succeed Mao upon the chairman's death. First contacts between Marshal Ye and Hua were enigmatic. Hua clearly was not ready to choose sides.

Marshal Ye kept in touch with Deng Xiaoping through his allies. It is probable that the marshal or Wang Zhen flew to Canton for secret consultations. Wang Zhen, not possessing Ye's high visibility, could undertake secret missions that Ye could not.[8]

Most of the conspiratorial meetings were held in the comparative security of the Fragrant Hills. Ye's fellow senior marshal Nie Rongzhen left his residence in Zhongnanhai and moved into a villa next to that of Marshal Ye. The two were able to talk privately in their back courtyards. Ye established contact with Chen Yun, one of Mao's oldest collaborators, now under strict surveillance, and with other seniors like Deng Yingchao, widow of Zhou Enlai, and Li Xiannian, who would be president under Deng.

Participants in the Ye ring changed residence almost as often as had members of the French Resistance. Marshal Ye moved from his Xishan villa to the number 9 building at Yuquanshan, a more secluded and commodious residence. Nie Rongzhen moved back and forth between the Hills and Beijing. He used General Yang Chengwu, a hero of the Long March, to warn Ye of the danger that the Gang might assassinate Deng.[9] Ye met at the number 9 building with other army comrades, including Su Yu, a Long March stalwart.

By the end of August, Marshal Ye's group had reached agreement that the only way to thwart the Gang was by quick arrest authorized by the Politburo, in which Ye had a majority. Ye suggested this action was consistent with Mao's intention, repeating to his colleagues a story Mao had told at the time of the recall of Deng Xiaoping. It was the legend of Queen Lu, whose plot to take power in the Han dynasty

Above: Strolling in the park of Zhongnanhai, the leadership compound of Mao's regime, in the spring of 1953 (*from left*): unidentified (probably a bodyguard); Liu Shaoqi; his wife, Wang Guangmei; Peng Dehuai; his wife, Pu Anxin; unidentified.

Right: Meo Zedong (*far right*) chats with Zhang Wentian (*far left*), his ambassador to Moscow; Foreign Minister Chen Yi (*second from left*); and Zhou Enlai in the courtyard adjacent to his palace in Zhongnanhai, 1956.

Above, from left to right: Mao shakes hands with ten-year-old Tingting as her father and mother, Liu Shaoqi and Wang Guangmei, and brother and sister look on in 1962; obituary photograph, which appeared in the *People's Daily* on December 17, 1975, of Kang Sheng, Mao's chief manipulator in the Cultural Revolution; Mao at a Party rally, about 1966, with Lin Biao, later Mao's heir apparent, shown directly at Mao's left, and President Liu Shaoqi, soon to be tortured to death by order of Mao and Lin, at far right; Wang Guangmei, widow of Liu Shaoqi, with her son and daughters, scatters Liu's ashes into Bohai Bay, sometime after Wang's release from prison in 1979. *Far left:* Mao Zedong (standing) takes the salute of massed Red Guards in Tiananmen Square, October 1966. Tiananmen Gate is to the left. *Near left:* Jiang Qing on trial with the rest of the Gang of Four, 1980. The Chinese sign says "The Accused."

Above: Deng Xiaoping with his family. At his right is his wife, Zhuo Lin, and on her right are her two daughters Deng Rong (Maomao) and Deng Lin. On Deng's left is a granddaughter, whose sweater says "America." The grandson taking the picture is Deng's youngest, son of his younger son, Deng Zhifang; he was born in Rochester, New York, and is thus an American citizen.

Left: Deng, in the courtyard of his Beijing house in Miliangku *hutong,* greeting his American grandson. The woman is Deng's daughter-in-law.

Left: Deng Xiaoping with his wife and three granddaughters.

Bottom left: Deng teasing his granddaughter, saying, "I've grasped your pigtail!" In Chinese this means "I've caught you."

Bottom right: Deng playing bridge with Nie Weiping, a champion at *go,* an oriental board game; he seems to be keeping score. Looking over Deng's shoulder is his daughter Maomao.

Deng Xiaoping with the American entrepreneur Armand Hammer at a meeting in the Great Hall of the People, June 1985.

On the terrace outside Hu Yaobang's villa in Zhongnanhai, seated around the table (*clockwise from left*): the author, John S. Service, interpreter Zhang Yuanyuan, Hu Yaobang, Charlotte Salisbury, and Caroline Service.

Zhao Ziyang visits hunger strikers in Tiananmen Square, May 19, 1989, in what was his last public appearance. Zhao was removed as Party secretary ten days later.

Right: China's president, Yang Shangkun, greets youngsters during his constant travels around China.

The author in Tiananmen
Square on the evening of
June 3, 1989, a few hours
before the massacre.

Bottom left: Jiang Zemin, secretary of the Chinese Communist Party, responding to
questions from reporters a
few weeks after taking office,
in 1989.

Bottom right: Premier Li
Peng addressing the Chinese
People's Congress in the
Great Hall of the People,
1990.

had been smashed by the alertness of two high officials, Zho No and Chen Ping. This tale, Marshal Ye felt, was Mao's way of indicating how to deal with Jiang Qing.[10]

There were no signs of imminent change in the condition of Mao Zedong as of September 1. No crisis seemed at hand. On that day Jiang Qing left once again to visit the model farming village of Dazhai.

Jiang Qing's progress to Dazhai was elaborate. She traveled by special train, bringing with her four horses and a truckload of films. She was in a foul mood, recalled the Dazhai official assigned to escort her. She immediately began to quarrel, particularly when she discovered that the trench she had ordered dug the previous year had been obliterated for a new pig farm, and the peony bush she had planted had vanished. It was, she screamed, a conspiracy by Deng Xiaoping, and she continually berated her escort as an agent of Deng's.

In the evening she showed movies and in the day she rode horses with her bodyguards. She liked to ride up the big hill back of Dazhai. Perhaps it reminded her of riding in the Yanan hills.[11]

Jiang Qing hectored the peasants in an effort to make Dazhai a string to her bow. It was fashionable among Party leaders to have projects such as this under their patronage. The cranky Dazhai peasants, however, found Jiang Qing's temperament beyond them.

Whatever Jiang's expectations, they were cut off by an urgent phone call from Beijing. Chairman Mao was sinking; she must return. While a special train was assembled, Jiang passed the time playing bridge, a fact later cited against her ("Jiang was playing bridge while her husband was dying!"). Hustled off to Shijiazhuang, she there caught a plane back to Beijing. She arrived late in the evening of September 5 and hurried to Zhongnanhai. There was nothing to do. Mao was in his last coma. Jiang looked at the dying man, then went to her quarters.[12]

Just after midnight, ten minutes into the first hour of September 9, Mao died. He was three months shy of his eighty-third birthday. Most of the Politburo was in the wings. Mao had been on a respirator at the end. His medical team, aware of the superstitions of the Chinese court — and with indelible memories of Stalin's Doctors' Plot and the paranoia that arose after Stalin's death — had taken precautions. Every device known to medicine was used to prolong Mao's life. The Mao medical commission of Hua Guofeng, security chief Wang Dongxing, and two members of the Gang, Wang Hongwen and Zhang Chunqiao, was on hand to attest to every move. Jiang Qing rushed in just as Mao died.

The breath had hardly left Mao's shrunken lungs when the Politburo went into session, wrangling over the corpse and the legacy. The first decision was what to do with the body. This split the Politburo. Jiang Qing and the other Gang members wanted the body preserved as a mummy, in the style of Lenin. Marshal Ye Jianying and others pointed out that Mao had strongly favored cremation. Mao had visited the Babaoshan crematory with Jiang Qing and picked a spot for their urns, side by side. The Politburo was deadlocked. It kept its options open, instructing the medical team to preserve the body for a while — at least until the formal viewing period was over, possibly for a fort-night. Later they would decide on its disposition. But the next step was not easy. If Mao's corpse was to be preserved (and there was some doubt about whether it could *be* preserved, given its emaciated shape), there had to be a place to display it. Some Politburo members knew that the identical argument had raged over Lenin's corpse. Lenin had eloquently denounced any suggestion of preservation as catering to medieval superstition. He didn't like funerals either. This meant noth-ing to Stalin, who presided over the embalming of Lenin and the placing of the body in a new mausoleum built in Red Square (under Stalin's feet every time he mounted the mausoleum to review Red Square parades).

The Gang wanted to put Mao into the ground he swore never to tread — the Forbidden City. They proposed to build a tomb just behind the Gate of Heavenly Peace. Their opponents felt it would destroy the traditional geomancy, the *feng shui,* of the city, so metic-ulously worked out by the ancients.

Feng shui does not convey much to the Western ear, but the Chinese have been studying this body of mystic and cabalistic knowledge for five thousand years. Mao knew a lot about *feng shui,* which pervaded the handbooks of sex he studied with assiduity. *Feng shui* taught that by cohabiting with hundreds of women a man could prolong his life to infinity. Mao had worked hard at this goal.

Feng shui affected almost every human act. It dictated the positions of yin and yang, the positions of the stars, the best time to plant, to conceive a boy, to celebrate a marriage, or to kill an enemy. *Feng shui* was defined by the specialist E.T.C. Werner as "the art of adapting the residence of the living and the dead so as to cooperate and har-monize with the local currents of the cosmic breath."[13] When Mao built his Swimming Pool House he followed the practice of *feng shui,* and like all proper Chinese houses it faced south. Mao's superstition against stepping across the threshold of his doorway when receiving guests came from *feng shui,* and so did his razing of the house of his perceived enemy Liu Shaoqi once Liu had been carted away to die in Kaifeng.[14]

It was against this background that those who opposed erecting Mao's tomb in the Forbidden City based their objections. But they did not voice their frank conviction — although they knew that a living Mao would have been on their side, in part because the proposed mausoleum would face north. Their true thoughts would have been "kowtowing to the olds," which the contradictory Mao had forbidden.

Instead they lobbied for burial in the Fragrant Hills, citing Mao's deep love for that place and the suitability of a site that would be dedicated wholly to Mao (actually they hoped that the Mao shrine could be as far as possible away from Beijing), or in Tiananmen Square itself, where he would be "close to the people."

The row went on to an inevitable compromise. Tiananmen Square was selected. And here, too, the tomb would face north, not south. The argument was so prolonged that later on rumors circulated that Mao's body had decomposed to an extent that it could not be properly preserved and had to be lowered each night into a refrigeration chamber. As one young woman said, revealing how accustomed people were to Mao's having the final word on every question, "The argument went on so long that when [Mao] finally decided, it was too late to preserve the body properly." Others claimed that the Rumanians had been consulted and their embalming technique was faulty.[15]

When Mao's body was placed in the Great Hall of the People for the formal mourning rites, everyone brought a wreath. Jiang Qing claimed she had made her white paper flowers herself. She attached an inscription to the wreath: "To my teacher, Chairman Mao Zedong. From your student and comrade, Jiang Qing." She added a list of some — but not all — of Mao's family: his son Anqing; the daughters Li Min and Li Na; a grandson, Yuanying; and his nephew Mao Yuanxin. She did not list Mao's second cousin Wang Hairong, who, when she saw the wreath and inscription, shouted at Jiang, "How dare you!" Jiang replied in the coarse language of the Shanghai nightclubs. The women flew at each other, and when Wang Hairong grabbed Jiang by the hair, it came off in her hand. It was a wig. Jiang was bald as an egg, in the account of Soong Chingling, China's vice president, who witnessed the scene and described it with great delight.

She said the women were finally pried apart and hurried off to a dressing room to repair the damage to their toilettes.[16]

Marshal Ye, meanwhile, was putting into place the last elements of his operation. The marshal came into Zhongnanhai and personally made his clinching argument to the security chief, Wang Dongxing: Did Wang believe he would long survive if Jiang Qing won out? Wang Dongxing was a practical policeman. He knew his chances with Jiang Qing were not much better than, say, those of Deng Xiaoping. Marshal Ye offered survival, no recriminations, a decent future. Wang Dongxing joined up. That simplified Ye's job. Wang Dongxing could keep track of Jiang and her men. His apparatus would be vital for the coup.

The marshal had a harder time with Hua Guofeng. Ye won his case by assuring Hua Guofeng that the army and the old comrades would back him if he came with them. "You will be one of us," Ye said. He met a number of times with Hua in his beautiful old courtyard residence in quiet Shijia *hutong,* just behind the Beijing Hotel, not far from Wangfujing, Beijing's main shopping street.[17] Marshal Ye had one simple question that he put to Hua — Whom do you trust, us or Jiang Qing? After thinking it over Hua decided he trusted Ye Jianying.[18]

Marshal Ye acted as though he hadn't a worry in the world. He took long walks in the Fragrant Hills. When he came upon a hillside he particularly admired, he gave it the name Brave Man Hill in honor of his companions. He proposed to call a pavilion Wind and Rain. Then, finding Jiang's operatives lurking nearby, he changed the name to Fei He, Flying Crane Pavilion, and recited in a low voice to his colleagues a poem about a crane that had been forced to change its nest because there were too many people around.

Recruits were now flocking to Ye. One day Li Xiannian showed up. He told the marshal he had thrown pursuers off the trail by pretending he was going to visit the nearby Botanical Gardens, then slipping off to Ye's villa by a back path.[19]

The Gang moved hurriedly. Jiang tried to get the Politburo to remove Deng Xiaoping from the Party rolls. It refused. She terrorized Zhang Yufeng, Mao's attendant, into turning over a batch of Mao's papers. She was hunting for a last testament by Mao or for incriminating materials about herself. She was forced to return the papers but may have forged a few words to indicate that Mao had given Hua Guofeng instructions to keep on the course set by the Gang of Four. At least so it was charged in Jiang's later indictment.

The Gang was working feverishly to line up military backing, especially in Shanghai. The youngest Gang member, Wang Hongwen, was working in Zhongnanhai to keep in touch with political leaders all over the country. He installed new telephone lines, a direct set for each provincial capital, and kept in hourly contact with Shanghai. After the fall of the Gang it was found he had made 107 telephone calls from his special lines to Shanghai alone. The Gang also launched a fight to keep Mao Yuanxin in Beijing because of his military contacts, particularly in Manchuria. Marshal Ye and his associates saw no reason for the further presence of Mao's nephew in Beijing. The Gang said he had to stay and handle his uncle's papers. But Marshal Ye didn't trust Mao Yuanxin to keep the papers intact; he thought he might tamper with them.

Marshal Ye had asked his confederates to be ready to act on October 10 or 11, but he now had information that the Gang might attempt a coup on October 7, 8, or 9. Taking no chances, he called in Hua Guofeng and Wang Dongxing, and they advanced the action to 8:00 P.M., October 6. Operational plans were completed on October 5, twenty-four hours in advance. Marshal Ye alerted his allies in the Military Committee and responsible commanders in defense headquarters, commands of the army, air force, navy, coast guards, and border guards. They were put on notice to be prepared for action and to report counteraction by the Gang.

Wang Dongxing set up special action groups. A notice was sent out that the Standing Committee of the Politburo would meet in Huairen Hall in Zhongnanhai at 8:00 P.M. on October 6 to approve the final proofs of the proposed volume 5 of Mao Zedong's selected works. That would automatically bring Ye Jianying, Hua Guofeng, and two of the Gang of Four, Wang Hongwen and Zhang Chunqiao, to the hall. A third Gang member, Yao Wenyuan, was specially invited to come to help revise and polish the text.

The evening was peaceful and starlit when Marshal Ye drove in from the Fragrant Hills, accompanied by a staff officer. He got to Huairen Hall a bit early. The lantern lights glowed on the terrace. All was quiet as Ye went in. Hua Guofeng was already there. Security chief Wang Dongxing stood behind a screen off the main hall. He had placed his men inconspicuously about the hall.

The atmosphere was hushed. People spoke in whispers, waiting.

When Zhang Chunqiao walked in, Hua Guofeng rose and read out a brief declaration, an indictment prepared in advance by the Politburo, accusing him of opposing the Party and committing unspeakable crimes. He would be held for investigation without the right of communication while an inquiry was made. Zhang's shoulders slumped and his face went ashen as he was quietly led away, staggering.

Wang Hongwen came next. The same procedure was followed. Wang, young and energetic, fought back. He was wrestled to the floor and hauled off. Last was Yao Wenyuan, who started to protest but was silenced and taken away.

Another action squad knocked at the door of Jiang Qing's bedroom in the palace that she had built near the White Pagoda Temple.[20] She was lying on a chaise longue, reading, and did not look up, calling, "Come in." When the strange agents appeared she shouted for her guards, who had already been taken away by Wang Dongxing. Jiang flew into hysterics but was bundled off. Mao Yuanxin — alerted in some manner — made a run for it. He got to the military airport and tried to board a plane for Manchuria. He engaged in a gunfight with a security detachment, wounding two men and suffering minor injuries before being captured. Other details mopped up, taking over the television and radio stations, going to the newspaper offices.

Marshal Ye drove back to the Fragrant Hills, and an all-night Politburo meeting began at the number 9 building in Yuquanshan at 10:00 P.M. It lasted until 5:00 A.M. the next day. Resolutions were passed approving the arrests and the proposed investigation. Telephone calls were made to the Politburo members who were out of town — and especially to Xu Shiyou and Wei Guoqing in Canton.

Marshal Ye personally telephoned his old comrades, Marshals Nie Rongzhen and Xu Xiangqian; Chen Yun, the senior Party member; and Hu Yaobang, who would be one of Deng's lieutenants. Then Ye called Deng Xiaoping, still technically under house arrest. Now Deng could return to center stage. The path had been cleared for his third comeback. He was ready and waiting.[21]

41

The Million-Man Army

AT THE HEIGHT of the Cultural Revolution, in the winter of 1966–67, the radical leaders of Shanghai attempted a coup d'état. They set up what they called the Shanghai Commune and proposed to turn the whole of China into a commune. This grandiose plan was backed by the "Million-Man Army."

With considerable difficulty Mao managed to outmaneuver his dangerous colleagues, and the commune plan was shelved. But the radical core kept its grip on Shanghai. The Million-Man Army continued to control the city, and only by great effort did Mao keep China from falling into open civil war.

In the waning days of Mao's life the Gang of Four sought to reconstitute that army to back — along with other military forces — their bid for power. Wang Hongwen, the energetic former cotton mill worker, youngest of the Gang, the man who hoped to share power with Jiang Qing, set to work in late 1975 and 1976 to re-create the legendary Shanghai revolutionary army. The new force was based on factory workers and members of local militia and other paramilitary units loyal to the Gang. By the spring of 1976 a shock command of one hundred thousand had been whipped together.[1]

Wang Hongwen commandeered two factories and set them to turning out mortars, machine guns, rifles, revolvers, and hand grenades. His men seized artillery from PLA depots. The new militia possessed deadly potential, especially if the Gang could rally the masses of Shanghai behind them.[2] No one in Beijing could be certain what hidden reserves Shanghai could call upon or whether it might have secret allies in other cities.

Hoping to avoid armed conflict, Beijing stole one of the deceptions that Mao had liked to cull from *Romance of the Three Kingdoms,* in which China's ancient warriors employed winged lies and devilish traps to win their victories.

Not a word of the arrest of Jiang and her partners was permitted to leak. The top Shanghai leaders were unwitting when called to Beijing for an urgent Politburo meeting. They rushed to the capital and were arrested as they got off the plane.

Those left in Shanghai anxiously awaited word from their chiefs. None came. A second group made its way to Beijing to see what had happened. It, too, fell into the noose. But a system of code messages had been agreed upon, and it managed to telephone Shanghai that "Mother is suffering from her old stomach trouble." That meant Jiang Qing had been arrested. The Shanghai group speeded plans for an uprising. It would proclaim Beijing a traitor to the Revolution and raise the country against it. But then came reassuring word from their men in Beijing. All was well; they would return soon. The Shanghai group became confused — what was going on?

Beijing played cat and mouse with Shanghai for several more days. Finally it sent the Shanghai leaders home on October 13 to bring the sad news. It was all over. The Gang of Four, Jiang Qing and the rest, was in the bag. They and the local Shanghai group had bowed to the inevitable.

Beijing had not trusted entirely to stealth. The doughty Canton commander General Xu Shiyou had been sent to Nanjing, where he arrested the local commander, an ally of the Gang's, and readied the troops to move on Shanghai if needed. Other military precautions had been taken quietly. None were needed. Shanghai raised a white flag.

Only then — on October 15 — was the official news released that the Gang had been smashed. Afterward, as a Shanghailander said nearly a year later, "ten million Shanghai citizens rushed to the streets to celebrate." A slight but excusable exaggeration. Ships along the Bund blew their foghorns.[3] It was said afterward that every liquor store in China ran out of *maotai* within an hour or two: in Beijing, Chongqing, Nanjing, Chengdu, Tianjin, Canton, and Shanghai. An editor who had been confined to a pig farm outside Shanghai leapt the fence and didn't stop running until he was well into the suburbs.[4] A young Beijing woman walked off the Shanxi commune where she was carting liquid human fertilizer, climbed on a freight car at a village station, and hung on until she got to Taiyuan. "Black elements" everywhere burst out of cowsheds and made their way back home. China's *misérables,* the survivors of the ten years of persecution, threw off their chains.

Not everyone was set free instantly. Those within walled prisons, high-security institutions like Qincheng, north of Beijing, couldn't get out. Some didn't emerge for months or even years. Some who were released were, incredibly, rearrested.

The Gang was gone. Deng was free. But he did not vault automatically to the top. The man who made the great leap was Hua Guofeng, sleepy-eyed and slick, the countryman of whom Mao had said "With you in charge I am at ease." Hua had cooperated with Marshal Ye. The deal left him in power, and he was not going to give up easily.

Time would make Hua Guofeng the forgettable man of Chinese politics. But he had his hour, and he made the most of it. China was a prize to fight for. If he was to hold it, he must block Deng's comeback. He had allies and he made more — those who had supported the Gang, those who had survived the fall of Jiang Qing, and many bureaucrats who feared Deng's pace was too fast.

Deng's first fight was to regain the posts that had been stripped from him in the spring of 1976: the vice premiership, the vice secretaryship of the Party, the vice chairmanship of the influential Military Committee.

He did not win them immediately. Hua Guofeng procrastinated. He worked to build up the double image of Hua-Mao. He put up posters everywhere, presenting himself as Mao's chosen heir. He reminded the public of Mao's words of confidence in him. He publicized the two decisions he had won from the Politburo that testified to his devotion to the chairman — to erect the Mao memorial in Tiananmen Square and to publish the fifth volume of Mao's works.

Tiananmen Square was half-closed for the rush job of putting up the memorial hall, leaving no chance of another big demonstration (although pro-Deng big-character posters were pasted on the construction fence). In kindergartens children were taught to dance and sing to celebrate the Mao memorial, the fifth volume — and Chairman Hua:

> "Chairman Mao, we are always thinking of you
> You are the red sun in our heart. . . .
> How wise Chairman Hua is
> He smashed the four pests
> We will follow him forever."[5]

Concerts and recitals were given to mark the September 9 anniversary of the chairman's death and the ascension of Hua. In one dance two youngsters pirouetted about a great scroll, bigger than themselves, then solemnly drew the red velvet apart to reveal the chairman's sacred words of the fifth volume. On the scrim behind them the sun rose, gradually dissolving into Mao's broad face.[6]

The cult of Mao was alive and well in the China of 1977, and Hua Guofeng bent every effort to drape himself in its sacred folds.

There were no songs for Deng — neither then nor later — no books, no poems, no portraits, no cult of personality. Deng concentrated on basics: his seat in the Politburo. Mao had left him a powerful lever. Deng had been ousted by the Politburo — not the Central Committee, as Party rules specified — and he retained his Party membership. If, as Deng's advocate Marshal Ye Jianying argued, the Politburo had deprived Deng of his offices, it could vote them back. It was a good argument — particularly when backed by the majority in the Politburo that Marshal Ye and his senior comrades had put together.

Hua fought a delaying battle. Badges sprouted with his double emblem, the Hua face imposed on the Mao face. And, more important, Hua Guofeng offered what came to be known as the Two Whatevers as the basis of his platform: Whatever Mao had decided must be carried on, and whatever Mao had said must be upheld.

Hua had given this pledge to Mao when he was named acting premier (Deng had taken the same oath when Mao anointed him). Hua was willing to abide by the Two Whatevers in order to win the support of Mao loyalists. Deng was not. It had been his refusal to take as sacrosanct what Mao had laid down that led to his fall in 1975. There were rumors Deng would take over at the end of 1976. He didn't. Then it was to be January 1977. Then February or March. Still the decision was delayed as Hua blocked his return. Deng spent much time in Canton with his supporters. Marshal Ye was his manager in the Politburo.

To outsiders there was no sign of political struggle. But the tide moved toward Deng. He won the vote in the Standing Committee and then in the Politburo. The last plenary of the Tenth Party Committee convened in early August 1977, and the decision was confirmed. Deng was back. The Eleventh Party Congress a few days later put its seal of approval on Deng, and fireworks broke out in the streets. Children's choruses led PLA troops to Tiananmen Square for a demonstration. Chairman Mao's memorial was finished. The scaffolding was taken down, and once again the square was open for politics.

A visitor arriving in Beijing on the eve of the Eleventh Congress did not know he was witnessing a triumph for Deng Xiaoping. Hua Guofeng still occupied the place of honor and would for a year to come. But Deng had arrived, even though his name did not go up in lights or on a banner over Tiananmen Gate and he was not the subject of headlines in the *People's Daily*. A few days later he met with a group of American correspondents at the Great Hall of the People. He bounced into the reception room, and the air crackled as though with electricity. He displayed no battle scars. He walked lightly on the balls of his feet like a bantamweight boxer. He shook hands with the air of a presidential candidate at a shopping mart, with a word and a smile for wives and female correspondents. Regardless of kindergarten songs and headlines, he was clearly the man in charge.

Deng dominated the room as the moon-faced Hua Guofeng could never do. He joked with the newsmen (and the American secretary of state, Cyrus Vance, whom he was meeting for the first time). He joked about smoking cigarettes — exercise for the hands, he said, quoting a remark by Chairman Mao. He drank a toast in tea and commanded the scene, the embodiment of a modern politician onstage. No one who attended Deng's premiere at the Great Hall was left in doubt that the resilient little man had already bounced his way back to the top.[7]

The Mao memorial hall opened to the public on September 9, the first anniversary of Mao's death. The lines stretched forever. Volume 5 of Mao's works appeared the same day. But it would take more than a building and a book to keep Hua on top. For the moment an uneasy triumvirate reigned: Marshal Ye, Deng, and Hua. Everyone knew, however, that Deng was Ye's favorite. In any disagreement the vote was two to one against Hua.

But China had not yet found a way out of the age of Mao. It was, as the years would show, doubtful it ever would. Confusions arose at every hand. In Shanghai, China's most famous living writer, Ba Jin, who had been silent for ten years, hounded by the Cultural Revolution, forbidden to write, narrowly escaping execution, now had been restored to favor. His first article was published in *Wenhuibao,* the paper that had kicked off the Cultural Revolution. "I have taken up my pen again," he wrote, "to continue my fight." But the point of his article was "to express my deep love for Chairman Mao and Chairman Hua."[8]

Deng Xiaoping gave priority to assembling a team of first-class deputies. He had gotten a few hundred senior executives released before losing his position in 1976. Some of them, such as Wan Li, had fallen back into house arrest, like Deng. Deng had Wan Li and others freed.

No case was more important in China than that of Liu Shaoqi. Unless that could be reversed, unless Liu Shaoqi could be fully rehabilitated, hundreds of thousands — quite possibly millions — of civil servants would still live under a shadow, some in prison, some not, branded as members of the Liu Shaoqi "clique," enemies of the people, unable to participate freely in the work of the country, pariahs, permanent victims of the Cultural Revolution.

For Party members this case was extremely difficult, because at Mao's insistence Liu Shaoqi had been expelled from the Party "forever." There was not to be any reconsideration of his case, as had not infrequently occurred with other expelled Party members.

The emergence of Deng in his old positions did not automatically revive the question of Liu Shaoqi. Wang Guangmei, his courageous widow, languished in prison. Not until December 1978, simultaneous with the Third Plenary of the Eleventh Party Congress, did a special Party commission undertake the case of Liu Shaoqi.

The special commission worked fast. By the time of the spring festival of 1979 — only two months later — the essential decisions had been made. The trained cadres that Deng Xiaoping would need were freed to plunge into the work. Wang Guangmei walked with her surviving children into the Great Hall of the People, free after twelve years in prison from the nightmare that Mao Zedong had imposed.

Throngs rushed to greet her, to congratulate her, to inquire about her husband, and when would they be seeing him. They did not know that he had been dead for ten years.

PART 7

THE LITTLE EMPEROR

42

"Poverty Is Not Communism"

AS EARLY as 1979 a verse began to sweep China:

> *Yao chi liang*
> *Zhao Ziyang.*
> *Yao chi mi*
> *Zhao Wan Li.*

The translation: If you want wheat, go to Zhao Ziyang; if you want rice, go to Wan Li.

These men, Zhao Ziyang, broad-faced, slow-speaking, looking very much like a successful businessman from Kansas City, and Wan Li, handsome, quick-smiling, with a Western, un-Chinese air, had been sent by Deng Xiaoping to the front line of the war on poverty.

Zhao Ziyang, later to become premier and then Party secretary, had gone to Sichuan. For nine years China's great western province, bigger than most European countries, had suffered famine year after famine year. There was no rain. The rice died in the paddy. Or there was too much rain and the rice was swept away by the flood. Sichuan's peasants begged on the roads with empty rice bowls, shuffling through the dust in brown rags, faces skeletal, lips dried, dying babies in mothers' arms.

The situation in central China's Anhui Province was much the same. There Deng had dispatched his strongest lieutenant, Wan Li, the builder.

Deng had taken charge in November and December of 1978. It had taken that long for him to ease Party and state controls into his hands, deftly nudging Hua Guofeng aside without formally depriving him of office.

Deng had had the strong backing of Marshal Ye and the senior military. When Deng and his family arrived at Marshal Ye Jianying's villa in the Fragrant Hills for Ye's eightieth birthday party, on April 28, 1977, all of China's marshals were gathered there. Marshal Ye took Deng's hands in his and said: "You are also a veteran marshal. Actually, you are the leader of our marshals."[1]

Deng's base was much broader than the military. He had been put into power, as one backer of Jiang Qing declared, by "a military coup."[2] Now Deng had the solid support of the Party seniors, led by Chen Yun, a man regarded by Mao as a financial wizard. In the economic chaos that had followed the Great Leap Forward, Mao had turned to Chen Yun. What the country needed, Mao said, was "a wise wife" to get it out of trouble. Mao envied Chen Yun's economic skills. Once while talking to his secretary Tian Jiaying, Mao banged his fist on the table and exclaimed in exasperation, "Why is it that only Chen Yun can handle the economy? Why can't I do it?"[3]

Now Chen Yun backed Deng, and Deng turned to him for aid in working out the economic schemes he was generating. Later Chen Yun would emerge as a symbol of resistance to reform. But he it was who laid out the plan that Deng used to get China going again. Their only difference in those days was timing. Deng wanted to go fast; Chen Yun favored a slow approach.

Deng was stirring into China a mixture of new, younger, more dynamic personalities, most of them men with whom he had worked closely over the years.

One was Wan Li. He had been with Deng in the early days of the Southwest Command. Wan Li had assisted Deng in the breakneck tasks of building the Third Line. He had become the chief builder of Mao's metaphor, the new Tiananmen, and he had been Deng's right hand in the whirlwind of 1974–75 to rescue China's tangled railroads from the wreckage of the Gang. When Deng sent Wan Li into Anhui Province, it was a measure of the critical nature of the problem.

Wan Li was sixty-two years old in 1978, lithe, intelligent, good at tennis and bridge. He had been born in Shandong in 1916 and joined the Communist Party, seeing it as the only effective force opposing Japan's invasion in 1936. He had worked for years in the countryside. He knew Anhui and adjacent Hebei. He had been a deputy mayor of Beijing before the Cultural Revolution, which had brought him two and a half years in detention. None of Deng's men knew the technical side of China's problems as well as Wan Li nor had his grace for carrying out such tasks.

"I fought against the Japanese," Wan Li said in 1987, "and opposed the 'four big families' of the Nationalists — Chiang Kaishek, T. V. Soong, Kong Xiangxi, and Chen Guofu. If we had not succeeded, I would not be sitting here talking to you.

"Our goal," he said, "is to create a country which is prosperous and happy and without exploitation. Belief [in the cause] is not enough. There must be solid work."[4]

After Wan Li was sent into Anhui in 1977 he went immediately into the country to explore conditions firsthand. He headed for Zongyang County, a center of famine, perhaps the worst in all China. Before the Revolution it had been notorious for poverty. People existed by begging along the roads. Before liberation residents had been exploited by landlords. When Wan Li arrived they were still poor, still begging. Little had changed. The landlords were gone, but the people still lived and died in poverty and starvation. The Party had introduced cooperatives too rapidly. The commune system had been stamped onto the peasants' backs. They lived in mud huts, one blanket to a family, no rice in their bowls.

As Deng Xiaoping had said, poverty was not Communism. Wan Li took the problem into his hands. For practical purposes he wiped out Mao's communes. He gave each family its own plot of land and instituted what he called a household contract responsibility system. The system had been introduced experimentally in the 1950s. It gave each family a share in the profits. The peasants made their own contracts to sell grain to the state. The rest they could sell where they liked at whatever the market would bring. For the first time the peasant had a motive to cultivate his plot well, intensively, profitably.

Wan Li took a chance on the contract responsibility system. "Just go ahead," he told the peasants. Nothing like the plan was authorized by the Party. But when the harvest came in, Wan Li had won his case. The peasants had produced enough food to feed themselves and sell the surplus to the state. As he said, "Hua Guofeng was still in office . . . still following Mao's line of learning from Dazhai. But Deng supported me and the practice spread."

It was not until 1982 that the Party formally approved the system, in Document Number 75. By that time it was going into effect all over the country.

Wan Li succeeded a PLA man as secretary of Anhui Province.

"When I came in," Wan Li said, "I criticized the PLA man as well as the Gang of Four. That's how mixed up the PLA got in the Cultural Revolution and its aftermath. Of course the PLA did many good things, but it had been made to follow wrong policies, wrong policies of Mao Zedong."

Despite the great progress of the Deng program, Wan Li felt in 1987 that the legacy of Mao and the Cultural Revolution had not been wiped out, especially in education, where ten years and more of closed schools and universities and of ideological distortions had left China with almost two generations of young people who were untrained and whose talents had not been utilized.

Wan Li had become one of Deng's chief political lieutenants, a leader in the National Congress, and a close associate. He played bridge with Deng and would continue to do so up to 1990.

"Competition is very keen," Wan Li said. "It is apparent that Deng has more skill than I at cards. Deng has his partner and I have mine. Each side wins and loses but he wins more often even though he is twelve years older than I."

Wan Li also played a lot of tennis with the diplomats in Beijing. He rated President George Bush as "very powerful. I lost a match to him," he said. He did not rate former U.S. ambassador to China Winston Lord so highly. "He is younger but he can't match me." He had played with — and lost to — Prime Minister Robert Hawke of Australia.[5]

One of Wan Li's opponents gave a slightly different rating of his tennis ability. Wan Li, he said, always played doubles and had as his partner one of China's leading young tournament stars.

No one else on Deng's team generated the excitement of Hu Yaobang. Hu would become a political icon, a symbol of liberalism, democracy, and freedom of expression. He had a lively mind that ranged from Camus to Nixon, nibbling at every item that caught its fancy. He had no fear of the new and no hesitancy about rejecting the old, especially clichés of the Mao era. But although public opinion came to present him as a champion of democracy, that was not always his role under Deng. Like Mao and Deng, he liked to browse in the Annals of the Twenty-four Dynasties. Like Mao and Deng, he seemed to find them more interesting than Marx or Lenin.[6]

Hu Yaobang was sixty-two years old in 1978. He had worked with Deng for many years, first in the southwest, as had Wan Li. They had been on the Long March together, Hu Yaobang very young and looking even younger (as did Deng), a wiry youngster just as short as Deng but even more energetic. Both looked more like Little Red Devils, the adolescent messengers and errand boys who attached themselves to the revolutionary army, than full-fledged soldiers. But both were fighters. Hu Yaobang had been wounded in the battle at Loushan Pass near Zunyi.

Hu had worked in the army's political department and had been assigned to Peng Dehuai's Third Front Army. After the Revolution he became head of the Party's youth league. Hu Yaobang had been moving rapidly in the Party until Mao sent him to Shaanxi in 1964, saying "he needs some practical work" — probably because he was too vigorous and not ideological enough — a warning of things to come. When the Cultural Revolution struck, Hu Yaobang was summoned back to Beijing and struggled with.

He became one of the Three Hus whose names were vilified, and who were paraded through Beijing's streets, wearing heavy wooden collars about their necks. The other two were Hu Keshi, number two in the youth league, and Hu Qili, number three in the league, who went on to become one of Deng's lieutenants.[7]

Hu Yaobang was sent to an isolated work site for "reformation through labor" under strict security. He was forced to haul huge boulders by hand, stones so large they bowed him almost to the ground. He was not imprisoned, but his labor would have killed any man less vigorous.

Hu was on Deng's first team. Deng had plucked him out of the work site and brought him to Beijing in his brief sway as leader in 1974–75. When Deng fell in 1975, Hu had fallen too.

He became Deng's secretary of the Party and his putative successor. Hu demonstrated his openness to new ideas, his willingness to break, as Deng did, with the tired old dogmas of Marxism and Maoism.

Zhao Ziyang was not a Red Army veteran. He did not make the Long March. He was fifty-nine in 1978, son of a liberal gentry family, well-to-do and well educated, and he had attended a mission primary school.[8] Still, none of Deng's lieutenants could match his knowledge and experience in rural China. He had been born in the central province of Henan, in Huaxian County, and in his whole career had never ventured far from the endless green paddies of the south and the grain fields of the north. None knew so well as he the tragic failure of Mao's mystical commune policies, policies that transformed prosperous agricultural areas into gray vistas of desolation.

Hardly had the People's Republic been founded than Zhao Ziyang was drafted into the Party rural work department and sent to Guangdong Province, one of China's richest rice producers — but equally rich in population. Long before the twentieth century Guangdong was sending wave after wave of emigrants abroad because there was not enough land or food. Most of China's traditional immigration to the United States (and many other foreign lands) came from over-populated Guangdong. These were the Chinese who built the Union Pacific Railroad.

The Cultural Revolution swept Zhao, like all able Communist civil servants, out of office. He was first sent into a factory and assigned to menial tasks. This did not last long. He was rescued from exile and dispatched to Inner Mongolia, where the Cultural Revolution had devastated people and land, slaughtering the Mongol ethnic leaders and tens of thousands of Mongols, destroying the traditional nomadic sheep-and-horse culture of the Mongol. Inner Mongolia was a shambles. Within the harsh limits of a Party still dominated by Mao and the post–Lin Biao spirit, Zhao attempted to alleviate hunger and distress.

Soon he was shifted back to Guangdong, where he began to tinker with the elements of what was to become the contract responsibility system — a perilous undertaking so long as Mao was alive. Mao regarded it as a giant step back toward capitalism. By concealing it under innocuous names Zhao made a start.

Deng switched Zhao into Sichuan. Sichuan had been a great granary of China before the Cultural Revolution. It had been turned into a disaster region by the Gang, drought, and flooding. The hundred million people of Sichuan had been brought to the brink.

Zhao moved fast. Like Wan Li, he threw the rule book out, disguising what he was doing (when necessary) in language that would not raise the hackles of Mao's adherents. He got fast results with a spectacular rise in food production.

It was Zhao's achievement of making Sichuan self-sufficient once again in grain and Wan Li's in making Anhui self-sufficient in rice that gave rise to the popular verse about the pair.

It took Deng Xiaoping longer to put into place the man who was to become the centerpiece of his new dynasty. Yang Shangkun was still in Qincheng Prison when Deng Xiaoping began to take the levers of power into his hands in 1977–78. Charges of espionage and treason were not so easy to wipe off the books. Not until December 1978 did

Yang Shangkun become a free man. He had spent almost thirteen years in prison and custody — a record among the highest-ranking victims of Mao's insanity.

The complications in Yang's case were the invention of Lin Biao. When Lin became defense minister in place of Peng Dehuai, he set out to eliminate possible rivals. He quickly identified Yang Shangkun as a dangerous threat. It was Lin Biao who fabricated the espionage charges against Yang Shangkun and Lin Biao who urged Mao to use the tape-recording episode to get rid of him.

After Deng Xiaoping pried Yang out of prison, he was sent back to Canton for a breather, probably at the urging of Marshal Ye Jianying, a powerful influence in Canton, but soon was brought to Beijing. Once again he was entrusted with high-level Party responsibilities and placed into the vital Military Committee, which in the Communist hierarchy was the top power nucleus. Gradually Yang Shangkun would take on more and more responsibility until he became almost a second Deng.

Yang Shangkun celebrated his seventieth birthday (his seventy-first by Chinese calculations) shortly after his release. He was in good health, lean and muscular, a robust man, his frame fleshed out, energetic, self-confident. His wife, Li Bozhao, a diminutive onetime actress and playwright, had been compelled during the Cultural Revolution to clean toilets and carry buckets of water up and down stairs until she injured her spine. She died in 1985 of a heart attack.[9]

Deng sidestepped the hobble that shackled Hua Guofeng and that doomed him. Deng simply abandoned the Two Whatevers, which bound Hua to preserve Mao's dicta and Mao's acts untampered. Deng cut loose. In a series of meetings culminating in the Third Plenary of the Eleventh Central Committee, in December 1978, he set forth his program for reform and opening to the West. He ordered the rehabilitation of the martyred Liu Shaoqi and the establishment of commissions to review, liberate, and rehabilitate hundreds of thousands whose reputations had been blackened by the Gang. These acts put at his disposal vast numbers of able men and women, whom he substituted for the toadies of Jiang Qing and the other members of the Gang.

Deng developed an ingenious definition of Mao Zedong Thought. Henceforth it would comprise only the good and "valid" portions of Mao's ideas *plus* good ideas from other Party leaders. This definition enabled Deng to deep-six the Cultural Revolution, the Great Leap

Forward, and other utopian schemes of Mao's. By the device of sub-stituting new questions and answers, the Communist catechism could remain nominally unchanged. Out the window went those dreamy vistas of Mao Zedong "Thought."

The contract, or family, responsibility system in the country pro-vided a stylish example of this approach. Party field-workers had known for years that Mao's communes did not work. They offered no incentive for the peasants to labor. Why work harder? You got no more pay. Peasants finished their quota before noon and slept the rest of the day.

The idea of the contract system was probably first advanced by former agriculture minister Deng Zihui, an old Long Marcher and Central Committee official. He had experimented with it as early as 1957 and cautiously advanced the scheme at the Lushan conference of 1959.

Mao did not catch the drift of what Deng Zihui had in mind, but when he grasped the concept he erupted. It was the first step back into capitalism, he raged. He called it a "bound-foot woman," meaning that it was a return to archaic concepts antedating the "advances" of Mao Zedong Thought.[10]

Mao's thunder did not kill the idea. In the disaster of the Great Leap and the commune system, practical Party men were searching anywhere for ways to get production going. The contract notion was quietly added here and there to farm programs. When Liu Shaoqi, Zhou Enlai, and Deng Xiaoping chaired a great meeting of seven thousand Party workers in the West Building of Zhongnanhai in April 1962, the system, carefully nestled amid nonantagonizing language, surfaced again. The Big Three thought the food and famine situation was so serious they might slip the new approach past Mao. They failed. Mao made a few concessions but not on this point. He called it a rightist move to shovel blame for all the troubles onto his doorstep. He blasted the idea away in September 1962, proclaiming that "class struggle" was still the number-one order of the day.

With Mao gone, Jiang Qing and her Gang in jail, and Hua Guofeng and his Two Whatevers beginning to wane, Deng had Zhao and Wan Li introduce the new scheme, even before the necessary Party language had been put into place. Sichuan and Anhui surged for-ward with a vigor that astounded not only the peasants but the Party.

Deng had demonstrated that money, material incentive, worked. The peasants liked money. They liked making money. They hated the communes. Their achievements in Sichuan and Anhui ensured that Deng Xiaoping could now look forward, not backward.[11]

Deng began to talk about China's historical problems. Communism, he began to say, was the right road for China, but it must be Communism with Chinese characteristics. It could not be the kind that Russia had. China must find its own way. Although capitalism was not China's road, that didn't mean China could not pick out from capitalism good elements and use them to improve its society: elements of solid management, a commodity economy, profit incentives.

Backwardness and poverty, Deng said again and again, did not mean Socialism. China was a big country. It had suffered for a long time. China must liberate minds. He was not promising a quick fix or an immediate solution to age-old ills. With resolution and a creative approach, however, China would make progress. It might take a hundred years, but the nation would move forward steadily to the goal of matching the moderately developed European countries.

To get back into office under Mao, Deng had abandoned his aphorism that it did not matter whether the cat was white or black so long as it caught the mouse. But now his cat was back; the central element in his approach was pragmatism. The *People's Daily* began to suggest that Marx was not possessed of all the solutions. He had never known much about China. He had lived long before the age of the internal combustion engine. He had died before the age of the airplane and modern communications. How could he have answers to the problems of the late twentieth century?

If anyone wanted to know what Deng hoped for China, he had only to go to Sichuan. There in the graveyard of Mao's communes, Zhao Ziyang was creating a laboratory for economic and social experiment. Those whose minds had not ossified (to use Deng's favorite expression) could take a look at the future. From Zhao Ziyang you got not only wheat — you got a whiff of what China was going to be like in the year 2000 if Deng's plans succeeded.

43

The Deng Revolution

ONLY THOSE who inhabited China's backcountry could sense the magnitude of the revolution that Deng Xiaoping set off in the villages, where 80 percent of his people still lived.

The Deng revolution bore little resemblance to that of Mao, whose Red Army had swept across China shouting slogans, singing songs, hanging landlords, and turning the land over to the peasants in a kind of national celebration. Deng brought his revolution into the rice paddies and the wheat fields with understatement, no beating of gongs, no ritual chorus, no one hauled off to the village execution square.

Mao helped the peasants seize the land from the rich — then took it back for the communes. Mao had filled the peasants' rice bowls — then emptied them with terrible famines. Deng gave the land back to the peasants, demolished the commune structure, and watched the rice bowls overflow. He put money into people's pockets, money they earned themselves. With the Deng revolution there was no more barracks life, no more "blue ants," no more egalitarianism.

Under Deng the peasants earned money by their own efforts and spent it on their own (not infrequently wasting it on gambling, wedding parties, and funeral displays). The flow of cash began to surge through the atrophied arteries of China's economy. Deng let the peasants divide the land as they pleased and plant what they wanted. The government contracted to buy bulk food grains, rice and wheat. For the rest the peasants were on their own. They could grow high-priced specialty crops and sell them in the market for what they would bring. They could hire labor, up to eight or ten workers or even more, lease land from a neighbor and farm it for a profit. They could go into small industry — set up carpentry shops, stores, lumberyards, pottery kilns, slaughterhouses, truck and bus businesses, whatever ingenuity and skill suggested. The backcountry began to blossom as never before, not in the age of the richest dynasties or the most prosperous landlords.

When Mao's Long March passed through Guizhou in 1934, none of the women came out to watch. They didn't own a dress or a shift. A family of ten owned only one pair of pants and wore them serially. Only when the fog was thick did women emerge from their huts, letting the mist conceal their nakedness. Girls of twelve got a string and a rag to mark their puberty. Children were weaned on opium; women died as young as twenty-one of tuberculosis, childbirth, or the pipe.

Guizhou didn't change much under Mao. Mao never spent money on roads or highways. His capital went into the Third Line, railroads, and defense. Peasants rode Mao's railroads only in corvées to their slave jobs in the secret factories hidden in the hills. They climbed the mountain ridges by narrow footpaths that ran straight up precipitous cliffs. They lugged their pigs to market on carrying poles. Geese were trussed and swung about their shoulders.

The jingle of Deng's dollars altered all that without words, propaganda, slogans. He pledged that there would be no more hysterical campaigns — no more hyperbole, model farms, model factories, model soldiers, model workmen, model peasants, no more learning from Dazhai and Daqing, no more "command economy," no more "Socialist emulation."

When Deng changed peasant life, he changed the country. Jiangxi had been as backward as Guizhou when Mao Zedong set up his Red Capital at Ruijin. All trade in Jiangxi flowed north and south on the river Gan, since no east-west or north-south roads existed. Razor-sharp mountain ranges splintered the province, and jungles confined peasants to their villages. Deng began to build roads and highways, and the people began to circulate. They turned the new highways into bazaars, selling their handicrafts from roadside stalls — cabinetwork, feather beds or bags of goose down, tools, small tables, needlework, sandals, melons, pumpkins, cucumbers, and tomatoes.

Along the main highway there was almost continuous construction of new houses — not of thatched huts topped by a hole to let the smoke out from the straw fire on the clay hearth, but of two-story brick houses almost as impressive as the old-style warlord mansions. At every hamlet, smoke from the new brick kilns rose, responding to the housing boom. All the construction was private. The government was not building houses. The peasants were, sharing labor with a neighbor or hiring a few carpenters and masons. Sometimes they got a construction loan from the local bank.

On a six-hundred-mile trip in 1984 down the main Jiangxi highways from Nanchang to Ruijin and back, a traveler was seldom out of sight or sound of construction sites. Local fairs seemed to be an everyday occasion at villages and towns, with trails of buyers and sellers hiking alongside the road for eight or ten miles. The village fairs were so jammed a jeep could hardly force a path through the racks of new dresses, coats, suits, boots, cheap lampshades, hats, bonnets, umbrellas, chopsticks, teapots, thermos jugs, sunglasses, herbal medicines, ginger and ginseng, quacking ducks, squealing piglets, baaing sheep. Nothing like it since Chaucer's England. More was for sale now in the hill country than had been in Beijing's main shopping street during Mao's last years.

The roads were new but not well built. They were being widened and extended for miles and miles and bulging with traffic, mostly trucks manned by new drivers. This was not without its cost. Almost every sharp curve in the mountains had taken a toll: a smashed truck, a car over the cliff, collisions, breakdowns, often a dozen in an hour's driving. Sometimes two- and three-truck accidents tied up the roads for miles.

Deng's revolution came to China's villages at different times and in different ways. No village in the country had been longer and more intimately under Communist influence than Liu Lin, Willow Grove.

Located on the great loess plateau a few miles north of Yanan, Willow Grove was small, backward, windswept, poverty-racked, disease-ridden, when Mao and his Red Army were settling down in 1936 for what proved to be a decade's stay.

Mao and the Party fanned out over the Shaanxi countryside, bringing their ideas to the peasants. Willow Grove, like many nearby hamlets, became a laboratory for Mao's experiments. The Communists lived a not much better life in the caves of Yanan than did the families in the caves of Willow Grove. Water was short. Drought was more common than not, and life in the caves was subject to the blister of summer and the frigid winds of winter.

Edgar Snow went to Willow Grove in 1936. There were, he wrote, "very few trees, and it was arid except for swift summer floods and winter snows. Its best asset was a fine dry healthful climate. That alone probably explained why poor people could survive in their tumbledown caves."[1]

Mao and his supporters did not try to change Willow Grove in the early days. There was no talk of communes, no dialectic, no lectures on "line struggle," just friendly help at planting and harvest times by

Red Army soldiers, Party workers reading newspapers to the illiterate (most of the population) and giving a few lessons in reading, writing, and arithmetic. The cadres suggested that the peasants could work more efficiently if they shared their labor. That was all. Willow Grove and Mao's people got along.

Willow Grove was visited again and again by foreigners. Edgar Snow went back in 1960. It had become a sprawling commune by that time, embracing twenty-four cooperatives with five thousand acres of land, nearly sixteen hundred families and twenty-six hundred able-bodied workers. Jan Myrdal, the Swedish journalist and social scientist, spent time in Willow Grove with his wife. At the height of the Great Leap Forward, Willow Grove became the East Shines Red Commune.

The village had been through every twist and turn of Mao's policies. It hadn't been easy. During much of the time since 1948 its director was Feng Changye, sixty-four years old in 1988, a bit more gnarled than he had been at first meeting in 1972, but the same blunt, spare-worded peasant, his face more brown and weatherbeaten, still carrying on, never too hopeful, never too discouraged. It was just as well. He had gone through it all and been called a rightist, a rich peasant, an ally of Liu Shaoqi's. He had been removed from leadership, but they always came back to him. For three months in 1964 during the Four Cleansings campaign he had been struggled with. When the Cultural Revolution came along he was subjected to a whole year of struggle. Feng was struggled with in the evening, but at daybreak he was back in the fields, leading the labor. Although they put a dunce cap on his head, paraded him around with a placard around his neck, and swore at him, he hadn't been beaten — or not much.

"I organized Willow Grove four times," he said in 1988. "Each time the Party changed its line and I had to do it all over again."

Willow Grove was no model commune. Its output was low, although it gradually grew. There were bad years, especially 1959–62, when the Great Leap and prolonged drought brought the village to the verge of starvation.

At the height of the Cultural Revolution thousands of Red Guards, making the pilgrimage to Yanan, straggled past Willow Grove's dusty entrance. The peasants gave food and shelter to some but didn't care much for the Red Guards. They were always fighting.

Feng dressed them down. "Even Chairman Mao isn't in favor of all that fighting," he told them. "If you want a fight, go somewhere else. Join the army." He didn't think the Cultural Revolution times were too bad. He had been through worse. So had the villagers.

Perhaps their attitudes were affected by the fact that they had, as it were, grown up under the wing of Yanan and Chairman Mao. Many of them had met and talked with the chairman and other leaders. They were, so to say, part of the family. The Red Guards were upstarts. The village did not feel beholden to the young invaders.

The villagers had done pretty well in production. They had brought their income up from about 80 yuan a year (about $40) in 1948 to 120 yuan ($60) per year by 1972. In 1980 yearly income had been 300 yuan ($150), and in 1987 it was 450 yuan ($225).

True, they had been laggard in bringing in the new Deng system of contract farming and dissolution of the commune. Willow Grove didn't begin the new system until 1981–82, and it wasn't fully adopted, with the reversion of land to the peasants, until 1984.

Feng didn't spell out the reasons for the delay. But Willow Grove wasn't the only laggard, especially in Shaanxi. The province was run by a leadership loyal to Mao and set in its ways. It was antagonistic to the change and the new Deng program. Starting in the mid-eighties, Shaanxi was rated by many as the most unreconstructed province in China. No part of Shaanxi was more rooted in the Maoist bureaucratic style and command economy than Yanan.

Feng was used to swaying with changes in the line, but he didn't seem too happy with those initiated by Deng in the late seventies. There were problems. Before Deng, everyone earned the same amount of money. It was an egalitarian society. Not so today. Large disparities in income had been created. Now there were the rich and the poor. Willow Grove hadn't many "millionaire" peasants — high-income producers who were the ornament of the Deng regime. It did have one 100,000-yuan family and several in the range of 10,000 to 20,000 yuan (roughly $5,000 to $10,000), an enormous sum by Willow Grove standards. But along with the new rich were the new poor, those who earned only 200 yuan yearly.

That spread in income caused trouble for Feng — and bad feelings among the peasants. There was a lot of the red-eyed disease, jealousy. Many did not admire the big producers. Egalitarianism was deeply rooted. Not everyone felt competitive or able. Many could not or would not take advantage of the new chances to boost income. They preferred the "iron rice bowl" of the past — everyone assured (or supposed to be assured) of a subsistence diet. It might not be much, but it was an insurance policy. And, compared with the days before Mao, the work was not that hard.

The able and competent people, Feng mused, adjusted well. They took advantage of the opportunity to earn more, but the older people and those who couldn't or wouldn't work hard didn't like it. The young people, he swore, didn't like to sweat. They were hard to wean from the "one big pot" and the iron rice bowl.

The young people had begun to leave the land. They went into trade and transportation, all kinds of work that never existed in Willow Grove in the old days. The fact was, Feng said with a wry smile, the actual income of the village from farming had gone down while overall income doubled and redoubled. More and more land was being taken out of cultivation, and more and more people devoted their energy to other pursuits. A lot of peasants just contracted their land to their neighbors. Some land now stood idle.

Everything was changing in Willow Grove. Back in 1972 the village didn't possess a truck. Trucks were regarded as a symbol of capitalism. It had one tractor in 1972, a small machine shop to keep it operating, and a small generator-operated mill to grind the millet and wheat.

By 1988 it boasted four trucks, six tractors, five walking tractors, and six bulldozers — all privately owned. The truck owners quickly became rich. They had bought surplus PLA models from the government at prices as high as 40,000 yuan ($20,000). Within two years the profits repaid the purchase price. The highways were filled with army trucks bought by peasants from villages like Willow Grove. They had networks and regular schedules. You could ship all over China. It was getting to be big business. Most of the tractors were used not in fields but for hauling loads on the highways, usually with a train of little carts loaded with freight or people.

In 1972 Willow Grove had planted an apple orchard on a ridge overlooking the cave houses. Every drop of water for the trees had to be carried up in buckets. The orchard was the pride of Willow Grove. Workers were building a storage house so they could keep their apples until price and demand were highest, in the winter. They were also finishing a whole new row of cave houses, tamping down the soil on the roofs. If there was an idle pair of hands in Willow Grove it was not visible. Willow Grove had its eye on the future.

Sixteen years later there was no bustle in Willow Grove. A row of peasants idled outside the houses that had been built in 1972, sunning themselves in their blue jackets and blue pants, smoking their pipes, chatting or just sitting staring into space. No one had to carry water anymore to the orchard. They had put in four pumps and a sprinkler system. It cost 300,000 yuan ($150,000). But now it stood idle. The orchard was aging and didn't bear many apples, and no one thought of planting new trees. The fine storage shed stood empty. "There aren't enough apples," Feng said, "to make it any use."

Feng was not looking to the future any longer. Willow Grove was dying, a victim, in a sense, of the success of the Deng program. It no longer had a future, not as a cooperative, not as a commune. It stood on the brink of vanishing, being swallowed up by progress. Yanan had crept to its doorstep, the city dwellers buying or leasing land and putting up houses. The Yanan municipality preempted land for factories and apartments. Already much of Willow Grove was gone.

The peasants were paying less and less attention to farming. The most active were busy with private business, like the Mu Sheng family. It had gone into lumber. Mu employed three workmen and bought trees from farmers and towns that were clearing sites for building. Mu's wife still did a bit of farming. The family had a five-acre plot and raised pigs and corn to feed them. Mu was doing well, but he cared nothing about what would happen to Willow Grove. He and his wife were in their early thirties. Their future lay in Deng's new entrepreneurial China. They had no regrets for the passing of Willow Grove.

There was not much collective spirit left in Willow Grove. No one seemed to care about the population problem, although the village had doubled in numbers in the past decade. The one-child-family policy was dead. Feng himself had five children and eight grandchildren, with more on the way. The biggest family in the village had thirty-seven members. The last major effort to control population had been in 1983–84. A fine of 100 yuan ($50) was imposed for a second child, 200 for a third, and 300 for a fourth. Half the women in the county received free IUDs from the government. Now no one paid any attention to birth control. If a fine was imposed they just said, "I'm not going to pay it."

Feng thought the people had been disciplined in the past, even the poor people. "Now they are rich and difficult to manage. They want more to eat. They want everything in their life better," he said. "But they don't work. We are rich but we can no longer exercise leadership in the council of the village. We have no economic leverage. We don't have the power to hold people back. Now they have money."

Since people had become free to manage their own affairs, Feng thought, they were using their fists more to settle quarrels. There was more superstition, more feudalism. If something happened that the villagers didn't think was in their interest, they used foul language and beat up whoever they thought was to blame — even Party workers.

The situation, Feng believed, could not be handled at the grass roots. It was a problem typical of the transition from the old to the new. It could only be resolved at the top. The people were rich, but money did not solve their problems.

A sense of fin de siècle hung over Willow Grove. The curtain was going down. The railroad was coming. The townspeople had pinned so many hopes on the railroad. Now it was advancing with iron strides. It would arrive in 1991 or 1992 and would link Willow Grove and Yanan with Xian and the coalfields to the north, extending all the way into Inner Mongolia. No longer would Willow Grove be landlocked. But the railroad was coming not as a savior, not as the harbinger of prosperity and a better life. Instead it was headed dead-on for Willow Grove itself. The railroad station had already been sited. It would sit on the spot where the Willow Grove arch led off the Yanan highway. Once it was built, Willow Grove would be no more.

No one in Willow Grove, not even Feng, seemed to have raised a voice in protest. Willow Grove awaited the inevitable. Some people thought it would make no difference. They could move to the new housing nearby and go on with their carpentry and their sawmills. Most young people were headed for distant cities anyway. If Beijing decreed the end of Willow Grove, who were they to raise their voices? No one inside or outside Willow Grove had given a thought to the fact that one of the earliest experiments of Mao's revolution was about to vanish from the earth.

44

If It Ain't Broke, Don't Fix It

IN THE LANDSCAPE of the Deng revolution there was no ornament more attractive than the successful village of Doudian in the Fangshan district, fifty miles southwest of Beijing, the most distant area of the expanded Beijing municipal region.

The Fangshan village was a community of about twelve hundred families and a population of forty-four hundred in 1988 that had demonstrated dramatic improvement in the Deng years, so dramatic that a succession of visitors had been drawn to it. The influx was nothing like the numbers that went to Dazhai in Mao's heyday but was still very big for the Deng era. Bo Yibo, a member of the Party Standing Committee, had given the community a scroll in his own calligraphy. Huang Hua, onetime foreign minister, had visited Fangshan a number of times. So had Wang Renzhong, an important Central Committee member, as well as leading Beijing municipal officials. Visitors from abroad also came to Fangshan in increasing numbers, representing forty-seven countries in 1985 and fifty-one in 1987.

Among these visitors was William Hinton, the idiosyncratic American farm specialist who had lived most of his life in China. A Quaker and bib-overalls farmer from central Pennsylvania, Hinton had worked with Chinese peasants since the early Mao revolution, and he returned to China every year of the Deng revolution.

Hinton knew Fangshan intimately. He worked with its directors and gave advice (some taken, some not). He regarded it as a fairly impressive operation — so long as it was not turned into a "monument," a model farm for other peasants to follow.

The farm was located in something less than ideal country, in arid, sandy soil. Before Deng took over it was a poor village, not as poor as Willow Grove, but barely above the subsistence level. A farmer's income was about 20 cents a day, an annual total of roughly $63, or 125 yuan. After ten years of Deng the per capita income had risen to

$600 per year, or about 1,100 yuan. The peasants no longer existed on the thin edge of starvation. They were among the most prosperous in China. It was, director Zhang Zhuliang said, like a miracle. The peasants now had color television, electric washing machines, factory-made overstuffed armchairs and divans, clocks, and sewing machines — "everything that city folks have." One in four households had gas for their kitchens generated by biogas tanks using cattle manure.

The managers attributed the transformation to the Deng revolution. But, in fact, Fangshan's Maoist commune had not been dissolved. It was still in place, still a collective, farming on a share-and-share-alike basis as in the past. Prosperity had come through better farming practices, capital investment, and extensive mechanization. It had also come through pell-mell entry into industrial, nonfarm pursuits. The farm was turned, in large measure, into a cattle-feeding operation, and by 1988 it had twenty-eight subsidiaries, most of them industrial, and was hiring more and more outside labor to man its businesses.

The biggest business was the feedlot operation, based on cattle brought down from Inner Mongolia for fattening for the market. The enterprise in 1988 fed, slaughtered, refrigerated, and shipped 31,000 animals to the Beijing market. It produced quality beef, supplying China Air, the Great Hall of the People, and many Beijing joint-venture hotels that had previously been importing high-grade meat from Hong Kong. That year the community raised or fattened 2,500 sheep and 2,600 pigs. Pig production for the Beijing hotel market was expected to reach 5,000 within a year. The workers had put in 49,000 chickens, a local variety similar to Rhode Island Reds, for egg production and started a dairy to provide milk for the big Yangshan petrochemical plant nearby. To feed their own workers they installed a big carp pond.

The key to the operation was the convenient proximity of Fangshan to Beijing. Shipment was easy, and the patronage of important political figures opened doors to Beijing's glitzy Hong Kong–style hotels, the Great Hall of the People, and Party institutions serving thousands of meals a day.

Conventional farm operations had been restructured to support the cattle feeding. At Hinton's recommendation, the farm had replaced an inefficient three-crop year with two solid crops a year. Winter wheat was planted in the autumn and harvested about June 15. Feed corn was then planted and harvested about September 20.

The farm became a conglomerate. It set up a garment factory

exporting to eight countries, a factory producing cloisonné work, brick and tile kilns, and mills that turned out building materials, and it organized a construction company with eight hundred workers that bid on jobs in the Beijing area and did a lot of work for the expanding petrochemical operation.

Fangshan was a vigorous, profitable, enterprising endeavor. Its ordinary farm operations were almost completely mechanized. It plowed with tractors and reaped with harvesters. It sold the government 1.8 million tons of grain in 1987 against 500,000 in 1977. It boasted the largest concentration of harvesters in the Beijing area, and its tractors were fully engaged in farm chores, never used to pull freight and transport people on the highways. The number of farmhands had been 1,200 in 1977. By 1988 it was 160. There had been 102 on the management staff in 1988. Now there were 14.

Fangshan was presented as an outstanding success of the Deng revolution. Yet the land had not been returned to individual peasants. The contract responsibility system had not been introduced. It was still a collective commune, as in the days of Mao. The managers bragged that they had "permitted" the peasants to keep the old system. No one, they said, wanted to change, because they were doing so well with the commune. Since they had "very strong leadership" they just went on sharing "the common prosperity." Nor was there a whisper of complaint from Deng's staff. This was very much in the Deng tradition. He was not a taskmaster like Mao. He did not indulge in micromanagement. He followed the old tradition: If it ain't broke, don't fix it. So long as Fangshan turned in production and profits, what difference did it make whether it ran as a commune or as an aggregate of private farmers? In more ways than one Fangshan was a prototype of the nonideological Deng style.

The bad old days were gone, the days of the one big pot, so the Party leaders said, the days when they were all blue ants, doing the same task and getting the same pay. Now distribution was according to work accomplished.

It was hardly a coincidence that conservatives like Bo Yibo, Huang Hua, and Wang Renzhong had taken the enterprise under their wing. They had helped to make it successful, employing their influence and connections (so important in all Chinese enterprise) to see that Fangshan got lucrative contracts with joint-enterprise hotels and Party-controlled establishments in Beijing. In a not too subtle way they were able to show it off as a great success of the Deng revolution, at the same time pointing out that it was a success achieved without adopting Deng's innovations — innovations with which they were not in sympathy.

There had been no complaints, so far as could be ascertained, from the Fangshan peasants. They were, after all, fairly isolated. Though the farm was only a little more than an hour's drive from Beijing, there was neither railroad nor bus service. Once in a while a truckload of peasants was treated to a day in Beijing, an escorted outing. No one seemed to have thought of regular service to town. "Why should the peasants want to visit Beijing?" an official asked in genuine surprise.

Since most peasants now worked at animal husbandry or nonfarm jobs, their income went up and up and made the question of land use irrelevant — the peasants were too busy in construction, cutting and fitting, and service trades to worry about how the land was distributed. By leaving the land in collective status, as Hinton pointed out, they could use their tractors and harvesters efficiently on eighty- to hundred-acre plots; small household farms, in contrast, would not be easy to maintain with such equipment. The danger lay in the mania for bigness. Hinton was concerned about the growing size and diversity of Fangshan's operations. As a rural conglomerate, Fangshan was finding farming less and less important. Hinton worried that by concentrating on meat production (as many high-profit rural enterprises were starting to do), Fangshan was leading China toward a much higher-protein diet. It was replacing traditional moist wheat buns with hamburgers that cost more in resources: fertilizer, land, and labor.

The question of land use and care was also worrisome. Fangshan now depended on a costly piping system to bring water to the fields. There were signs that the enterprise was neglecting water conservation and land maintenance — the ditching and damming and plowing practices that kept the soil in balance. This was a hidden cost of the Deng revolution. "You can't get something for nothing," Hinton warned his Chinese farm friends.

The vagaries of shortsighted government brought other hazards. A successful Inner Mongolian cattle farm shipped its stock to the Beijing area to be fattened. Overnight it was put out of business when the Inner Mongolian government levied a prohibitive tax on "export" of cattle from Inner Mongolia. Thousands of animals perished on the Mongolian grasslands, unable to find feed.

The Inner Mongolian action was an aberration. But it underscored an aspect of Chinese provincial disunity that neither the Mao nor

Deng revolution was able to resolve. Each province regarded itself as sovereign and was encouraged to be self-sufficient in food and raw materials. Shipments across provincial lines often had to be negotiated like customs shipments between nations. A province with a coal supply attended to its own needs first, regardless of great industries in adjacent provinces being short of fuel. Each province fed itself before shipping rice or grain to its neighbor. If there was general distribution, it had to be done — in most cases — by the central government. This was provincialism on a par with the states' rights exercised by the thirteen original American states under the Articles of Confederation, which led to the nationally unifying U.S. Constitution. China had a constitution. It had the powerful reigns of two leaders, Mao and Deng, but it had not solved the problem of the relationship between the provinces.

The high priority that the Deng revolution placed on profit aggravated China's problem of overgrazing, which speeded the deadly erosion that had already turned so much of north and northwest China into desert.

If Fangshan had skipped the basic requisites of the Deng revolution — the reversion of land to the peasants and the end of the commune — Party workers did not seem embarrassed. The Deng revolution was not Mao's rigid ideological corset. It was a patchwork: one system here, one system there. Deng made clear that details did not bother him. Results counted, not slogans.

Fangshan was one highly successful example of the patchwork that Deng was promoting, a deliberate blend of farming and small-scale industry. But there were dangers in this approach. The drive for production and for money, regardless of how it was earned, was beginning to change the façade of China's countryside. In the rural areas around all the metropolises the same curious mixture of factory and field was echoed, with little regard for how one would affect the other.

What this could produce was illustrated a few miles from the Fangshan farm conglomerate, at the village of Guce. Guce lay at the base of a dam that had created the Niukouyu reservoir, built to supply drinking water and irrigation to farms in the area. For twenty years the petrochemical complex had been discharging waste fluids into the reservoir, unaware or heedless of the fact that the wastes were a hazardous pollutant to crops and humans. The farmers recognized the problem when they began to come down with respiratory ailments and great blotches on their skin. The reservoir began to stink. Irrigated crops withered and died.

The plant ordered purification equipment from abroad, but in June 1988, before the new equipment had been installed, a crisis arose. Heavy rains filled the reservoir close to overflowing. Officials decided on an emergency release of water into the irrigation systems lest the dam collapse.

Fearing loss of their crops, more than a thousand farmers turned out in a protest that produced China's first ecological riot. The peasants were attacked by local police. Scores were beaten and injured, as were a number of local police. Rumors circulated that many peasants had been beaten to death. One report said a ten-year-old boy was killed with clubs, his body thrown into a canal and recovered some distance away.

A number of villagers were arrested. Once police had control of the scene, the sluices were opened and the polluted water discharged. Farmers would be compensated for their losses, authorities said.

This ecological protest was a sign of the times. The Deng revolution was bringing more and more industry into rural areas. Cities like Beijing, Shanghai, Chongqing, Wuhan, Chengdu, and Nanjing were incorporating into their municipal areas great swaths of countryside.

It was Deng's policy to bring these aggregates of city and country under urban command, to create a new kind of megalopolis, half urban, half rural. Deng and his advisers believed these amalgams solved practical problems. As agriculture was rationalized and mechanized, it created large numbers of unemployed peasants who could easily be channeled into the multitude of small plants and industries springing up under the aegis of energetic town and village leaders. The industrialization process could be carried out without swamping living facilities of the cities. The populations that were shifted to small-scale industry lived close to the source of foodstuffs, eliminating distribution problems. These peasants became part-time farmers, part-time assembly-line workers. This change in job responsibilities translated into a more manageable way of handling circulation and transportation, and it lightened the population weight on the big urban cores. At the same time it brought enormous rural populations under municipal management, which meant that the government could immediately begin to exert influence on the population problem. In the quasi-city environment it was possible to begin to wean peasants from their passion for an almost limitless supply of male children (a substitute for China's largely nonexistent social security). Similarly, problems of birth control and disease, education and political indoctrination, were more easily handled.

It was a practical Deng-type solution to many Chinese problems. But like all "solutions," it spawned its own problems. It stimulated peasants to halt production of basic food grains — labor-intensive and low-profit products — in favor of boutique gardening, specialized farming, or rural industry. The cash returns from those enterprises might be ten times higher per hour of labor.

Thus, the profitability and high cash returns that the Deng revolution brought to the country worsened the chronic Chinese problem of raising enough food to feed the ever-growing population. Cash profits, in turn, aggravated the population problem by giving the newly prosperous peasants increased incentive to produce large families.

The breakdown of population control at this village level and the diversion of farming from food grains to more profitable endeavors — animal husbandry and petty industry — compelled Deng to import ever-larger quantities of grain, depleting hard currency needed to purchase high technology. It was a circular problem of great seriousness, and no worthwhile approach to a solution was forthcoming in the ten years from 1978 to 1988 in which the Deng revolution was in full progress.

The biggest grain harvest of the Deng decade was a crop of more than 400 million tons registered in 1984. All the years since then have fallen short of that high mark (with the possible exception of 1990). In Hinton's opinion, the consistency with which China had fallen below the 400-million-ton mark was a strong indication that the Deng decade had no more solved China's food problem than had Mao. The Deng program continued to depend on costly foreign imports. More dangerous, production did not seem to be keeping pace with population increase. Production of grain constantly fell below what was forecast. Production of children constantly rose above predictions. The food-population ratio was not likely to become critical in Deng's lifetime. But it was the number-one problem on China's agenda for the last decade of the twentieth century and the years beyond. So far as became known, no adequate ideas for meeting the crisis existed among the first-class specialists that Deng had at his command.

45

The Shape of the Future

A TOUGH, big, self-confident man whose 153,000 workers called him "Commander" presided in 1988 over a sandy principality at the mouth of the Yellow River. His name was Zhu Wenke, and he had no doubts that the Shengli oil field was the beacon to China's path into the twenty-first century.

It was no accident that Zhu's employees called him "Commander." He looked and acted like the general of a highly trained army and in a sense he was. Zhu was very much a product of the Deng revolution, as was the Shengli field, although it had gotten a shaky start in 1965 on the eve of the Cultural Revolution.

In 1988, Zhu's corporation occupied about eighteen thousand square miles. It possessed what Zhu's experts believed to be China's greatest oil field. It was expected to produce 38 million tons in 1990[1] and was rapidly overtaking Daqing, long China's premier field. By extraordinary efforts Daqing was still producing 50 million tons a year, but output was dropping. By the turn of the century, Zhu believed, his field would be producing half of China's oil.[1]

Shengli means "victory." The name was taken from a village beside the Yellow River that had won a battle against the Japanese occupiers. Neither Zhu nor any of his aides could remember anything about the battle, but they were confident that Shengli would make its name in the history of Deng's revolution.

Shengli was far more than just an oil field. It was a self-contained economic entity providing its own food from a thirty-thousand-acre farm operated by the families of Shengli's workers. The farm maintained large herds of cattle and sheep, raised chickens, ducks, and geese, and produced so many fish in its ponds that it sold the surplus in the community. The large rice paddies were planted and harvested mechanically with the latest machinery from Japan — not because hand labor wasn't available but because Zhu looked forward to assigning his labor to other high-tech occupations.

Shengli's investment in the future was impressive. Four thousand scientists and technicians were employed in a laboratory network. Shengli possessed 152 grade schools with an enrollment of 22,000 and eight higher-educational institutions, including a university with 3,000 students. Shengli was one place in China where education was at the forefront. Most of its secondary-school graduates went to college, and nearly all came back to work at Shengli.

Zhu had the largest computer in China. He used it to run his plants and to program operations. In 1988 he was about to install a communications system to match it. Shengli had no problem in attracting workers. They came knocking at the commander's door from Beijing, Shanghai, Tianjin, and Wuhan. Inflation and high prices didn't affect Shengli, since it raised its own food. Much of Shengli's equipment was made to order by the best Chinese factories or special ordered from abroad. There was no problem about the foreign exchange. Shengli was a $6 billion enterprise. The government to date had recovered about 177 percent of an estimated investment of $10.1 billion. Zhu employed many foreign specialists and maintained close contact with Dresser Industries, in Texas. He kept on top of the latest technical developments and visited the United States and other oil-producing areas. He had made a special trip to Long Beach, California, which possessed an oil field very similar in characteristics to his own.

The concept of the huge integrated complex suited Deng as well as Li Peng, the Soviet-educated engineer who became China's premier in 1987. Shengli was government-owned and government-operated, but internally it used many of Deng's innovations: contract systems, profit incentives, competitive setups. While the form was not suited to every enterprise, it worked well for Shengli.

Shengli's vast territory could be expanded simply by exercising the right of eminent domain. The land had been barren and almost uninhabited in 1965 when Zhu first saw it. The fields were covered with white deposits of salt and alkaline, and few villages tried to make a living from the inhospitable terrain. The peasants chanted a few lines of doggerel to describe the progress of the seasons:

"The spring fields are white
The summer fields are flooded.
In autumn the fields are barren
In winter we go out to beg."

It was a cold, unpleasant place. The workers had always been hungry, and they froze in the unheated shacks where they lived. Now the land was producing 50 million kilos of grain a year. In 1988 workers earned 2,000 yuan ($1,000) a year, and families got an average of 900 yuan ($450) more, a very high income by Chinese standards.

The Yellow River, which flowed alongside Shengli, was well controlled, and each spring PLA detachments were assigned to man the levees and make certain there were no breakthroughs. The commander did not leave anything to chance. His operation was on the south side of the river, but he had built an impressive bridge to the north and was prepared to extend drilling there as soon as the government gave the go-ahead.

Shengli was a solid operation. It drew water from the Yellow River for irrigation and was building a 1.2-megawatt power plant to serve its own operations and those of the refinery that had been spun off under separate management. The scale of Zhu's operation could be judged by his motor park, which held fifteen thousand vehicles, including, as he said, "only a thousand small passenger cars," the rest being trucks and vans. Only China's largest cities could boast a bigger motor inventory.

Shengli was a vast extended family. Priority of employment went to sons, daughters, and relatives of employees. It was, in a sense, a high-tech iron rice bowl, providing economic and social protection from cradle to grave. There was no item of equipment that Shengli wanted that Shengli did not possess. Shengli traveled first-class. Only the best was good enough. All this was overseen by an iron-willed commander who was a graduate of the Foreign Language Institute at Xian, a specialist in Russian who had taught himself the basics of the oil industry by reading Russian-language petroleum textbooks.

Shengli had always been helped by the PLA. Preliminary work in the early 1960s had been done by three thousand demobilized PLA soldiers, part of a contingent of ten thousand demobilized and assigned to civilian tasks in 1952 by Mao.

There was not much talk about democracy at Shengli. It was, in effect, a benign dictatorship. It enjoyed the patronage in 1988 of Zhao Ziyang, Li Peng, and Deng's associate and rival, the elderly economist Chen Yun. Like a good politician, Zhu did not put all his eggs in one basket.

Zhu's task had not been easy in the early years. It took muscle and endurance to get a big oil field going. The timing could not have been worse. Within a year of start-up the Cultural Revolution hit. Zhu lost his job and was assigned to common labor. He was lucky; two top men at the plant were killed by Red Guard mobs. There was heavy fighting although, as Zhu recalled, no cannon were used. But a dozen or more workers were killed in the combat, and productivity was damaged. Production in 1966, the year the Cultural Revolution started, was 1.35 million tons, and it was not until 1970 that Shengli began to produce in line with expectations — 4.67 million tons. From that time forward it moved ahead rapidly.[2]

The "one big family" concept and that of the extended iron rice bowl were not inspired by Deng, although he had accepted their persistence in many state-managed and state-run industries. The "family" and "rice bowl" represented an extension of Mao's psychology, which strongly appealed to Chinese peasants. But the extended family bred hidden dangers. It encouraged strong Chinese tendencies toward patronage and nepotism.

Nothing so dramatically illustrated the dangers of one big family as the great Black Dragon Forest fire, in China's Heilongjiang (known as the Amur in the Soviet Union) River region. It started on May 6, 1987, and within hours had consumed nearly one third of China's prime conifer resources, the greatest natural disaster of the Deng epoch. It may have been the worst ecological catastrophe of modern times.

The fire burned over China's most valuable timber stand, wiping out an area almost as large as New England. It destroyed about 3.5 million acres of Chinese timber and probably 15 million more on the Soviet side of the Heilongjiang. It was estimated to have consumed 52 million cubic yards of Chinese timber and to have damaged another 20 million. Later inspection indicated that these were underestimates. The dollar loss of timber was placed at upwards of $5 billion or $6 billion. Property losses were reckoned at about $150 million, and the fire took a toll of 220 lives, injuring 250.

There were other dangerous consequences — the speeding of desertification in north China because of loss of forest cover; climatologic change in China and the Pacific littoral, including the American west coast; and ecological damage. These are difficult to assess, since the Soviet government never issued any statement of the extent of the fire on its side of the Heilongjiang River.

The conflagration was so vast and so threatening to population and property that most of two Chinese armies were deployed to assist trained foresters and mobilized citizens to bring it under control. But not until heavy rains came in early June did the Black Dragon finally sputter out. It had been the largest fire in three hundred years of Chinese records, five or six times greater than America's Yellowstone fire of 1988.

Loss of the forest dealt a bitter blow to the Deng program. No large nation is as poor as China in timber reserves, and none more in need of these resources, with its heavy program of housing and industrialization. The blow could hardly have fallen at a more critical time. China was already overcutting its forest to meet the demand.

In the United States so great a disaster would have set off a national inquiry, led by Congress, into its causes, the implications of the losses, and the elaboration of a program to prevent any similar catastrophe. Not in Deng's China. Despite — or perhaps because of — the importance of the issues, no seminal investigation took place. Instead there was a narrow in-house inquiry that avoided all major issues and focused on surface matters: an ignorant brushcutter who spilled some gasoline that caught fire and spread into the forest, three youngsters who lit a campfire that went out of control, a smoker who tossed away a cigarette. Stiff punishment was meted out to the brushcutter and other minor figures. The forestry minister was fired, and a few officials who had tried to escape the fire by commandeering trucks and fire apparatus and fleeing madly with their families were sent to prison.

Not a word was said about the Black Dragon "family" that was the root of the trouble, the Mafia-like corporation that ran the forest as a kind of pleasant feather bed with little regard for safety and knowledge of firefighting. The family was a closed corporation. Outsiders might be taken on as temporaries for a few weeks, but only sons, daughters, close relatives of workers, could get a permanent place on the payroll. The family had come into being with the setting up of the forest company in the 1970s. It represented the one big pot. Once in, you had lifetime tenure; no one could threaten your job. It was a little like a Chinese clan. You were born into the clan, and that determined everything in your life. Nothing was more important in time of trouble.

The forest was not efficient; management was self-centered. When the fire broke out, officials spent almost as much energy barring reporters from the area as fighting the fire. They cut off telephone service, refused reporters hotel rooms, would not serve them in restaurants, and denied them information.

The Forestry Ministry was part of the family. All its comments on the fire were upbeat: It wasn't as bad as it seemed; fire was a natural process; the trees would regenerate themselves; too bad, but these things happened; if it hadn't been for that ignorant outsider, the brushcutter, it wouldn't have started; he ought to be shot (he wasn't, but he got eight years in prison). The theme was the need to keep outsiders out of the forest. The worst crime was that a forestry supervisor had hired this man. Few spoke of lack of vigilance, poor management practices, and inadequate fire protection. It was not pointed out that the company had been so busy maximizing output and profit that it had neglected elementary precautions, that it had let tinder-dry brush pile up in the cutting areas, that fire lanes had not been cut through dense areas, that foreign advice about and aid for fire prevention had not been put to good use, that worker comfort got a higher priority than the preservation of one of China's greatest natural resources.

The forestry workers got higher pay for working in a hardship zone. The company gave them forest clothing, heavy sheepskins for winter, leather boots (unobtainable in stores), and other gear. They had comfortable houses, well supplied with wood fuel, and large garden plots; they were granted free access to gather valuable mushrooms in the forest, to hunt, to fish, to trap. They could sell their forest booty in Harbin or Beijing for premium prices. They had their own schools and hospitals. Working for the company was what the Russians called a bear's corner, but it was a very cozy one, a snug harbor. Although the fire had destroyed the forest, there would always be a payroll. If there were no Chinese trees to fell, they could (and did) hire out to the Russians on a contract basis and cut wood in the Siberian forests north of the Heilongjiang River.

Management didn't bring to public attention its nearly nonexistent communications system, its lack of water-dumping aircraft, or its obsolete watchtower system. Fire spotters often had to spend a day hurrying along forest trails to find a telephone to report a fire. Frequently it was a week or more before firefighters could make their way to an imperiled site. When the Germans and Canadians made generous offers of technical assistance the money was accepted, but no word was published in the press to let the Chinese know how improvident company management had been.

To the family the greatest danger of the Black Dragon fire was that it might upset what Mao Zedong would have called their water-tight kingdom. They needn't have worried. Premier Li Peng toured the area by helicopter and brought in more troops, and eventually the fire burned itself out. To critics who said the forest would not regenerate for two hundred years, the family responded by flying in officials and showing them the green leaves already masking the carbon-scarred forest. They didn't bother to say that the leaves were trash growth; the commerical timber was gone.

If Deng or anyone in his establishment thought there was something wrong with the family, it was not put on public record, nor were fundamental changes ordered. The forest went on as a closed system. Five years later all was quiet. Some new fire-detection equipment was provided by Canada and Germany. After amazing bureaucratic arguments some of it was installed. For a few years the Black Dragon Forest escaped recurrence of the holocaust. The idea that the forest problems were ingrown — that nepotism, featherbedding, the one big pot, and cover-ups had something to do with the tragedy — was silently swept under the rug.[3]

Once Shanghai had been a citadel of Chinese industry. By 1988 this metropolis of 12.5 million was almost dead in the water, just rousing from the Cultural Revolution's devastating slogan of "Make Revolution, Not Production." Its leadership had been swept away in disgrace.

Deng sent in a new team in 1978. One member was Jiang Zemin, whom Deng later brought up to Beijing as secretary-general of the Communist Party when he fired Zhao Ziyang after the 1989 Tiananmen massacre. The other was Jiang's successor as mayor of Shanghai, Zhu Rongji, a brisk, open, Western-style administrator, fifty years old in 1978, who had spent thirty-five years in the State Planning Commission. Zhu was low-key except when thwarted. Then he boiled over like a teakettle.

Not even Mayor Edward Koch in New York, said Zhu in 1988, faced such problems as he did. He had to build a new water system. The old one was decrepit, and the supply from the Yangtze polluted. The city was just getting over an epidemic of hepititis A, which affected 300,000 people. His biggest problem was traffic — 2 million of the city's 8 million workers had to cross the Huangpo twice a day. The traffic problem was worse than Rome's. Rail and air terminals were antiquated.

Mayor Zhu and Secretary Jiang were not fazed. They launched China's biggest development: creation of a whole new industrial city on the east bank of the Huangpu, the largest free-trade zone in China. And Zhu tackled head-on Shanghai's most critical political problem.

The central government was taking 80 percent of Shanghai's revenues into the national treasury. Shanghai was broke. Zhu got the take reduced to 70 percent, with a promise of more as city revenue rose. He negotiated a three-billion-dollar World Bank loan for a subway system and new housing.

In the spring of 1989, when Tiananmen hit Beijing, Zhu and Jiang kept things cool in Shanghai — no riots, no bloodshed, no troops, no martial law.

Deng Xiaoping led a small delegation, including President Yang Shangkun and elder statesman Chen Yun, to Shanghai in late winter 1991 to look over the city and its leadership. Then Deng brought Zhu up to Beijing to be vice premier under Li Peng. Zhu was a man on the rise, with his easy mastery of English, his gray Western-cut business suits, maroon and gray foulard ties, and a son studying meteorology at the University of Wisconsin. He possessed an efficient management style learned in Qinghua University economics classes.[4]

No one would have been more surprised than Chiang Kaishek to hear that Chongqing, his ramshackle capital on the cliffs of the Yangtze, had in the epoch of Deng become China's largest city.

In Chiang's day Chongqing was a cramped wreck, hanging to the sides of the cliffs, badly battered by Japanese air raids, isolated, lacking rail links to Beijing and Shanghai, with a population that refugees had swelled to 1.8 million and little hope for the future.

It was Mao's Third Line idea that touched off Chongqing's explosive growth, and no man was more responsible for it than Deng. Under Deng in the 1950s, Chongqing expanded rapidly. Defense industries were enlarged, and the area around the city was filled with new plants tucked into the hills. A foundation was laid for a high-tech industrial zone north of the city along a broad new highway running close by Deng's native Guang'an. Two spectacular bridges led across the Yangtze, giving access to the Xikou mining area, a region of vast limestone and coal deposits along the river. The fields were the largest in China and extended under the river.

The transformation of Chongqing still was under way in 1988 under the direction of one of Deng's vigorous lieutenants, Xiao Yang, sixty-one years old in 1991, schooled in wartime Chongqing, mayor since 1984. In that year he launched Deng's campaign for reform and an opening to the West. Chongqing under Mayor Xiao Yang was the pilot model of Deng's concept of the Chinese metropolises of the future. The city's population was stated to be over 14 million in 1988, having more than doubled from 7 million by the incorporation of rural areas, the most rapid growth in China. By 2000, Chongqing was expected to reach 20 million.

Xiao Yang's tenure as mayor began with disaster. A year after he arrived, there was a tornado that did great damage. Next year a violent explosion due to accumulation of gas in the sewers took a heavy toll of lives. City residents made up a verse about Xiao Yang, a play on his name, which means To Save the People from Suffering. Zao Yang means The People Must Suffer. The two phrases are pronounced almost identically. The people began to say: "Zao Yang, Zao Yang, *lai le zao yang*" — Zao Yang, Zao Yang, you brought us suffering. Later they added: "Xiao Yang, Xiao Yang, *xiao chu, huo yang*" — Xiao Yang, Xiao Yang, you rescued us from disaster.

As Xiao Yang recalled, these were not the best of times. His first and continuing priority was the dismantlement of Mao's Third Line. By the mid-1980s every economist in China recognized it as a burden on Deng's drive for fast, rational industrial expansion. The army had jurisdiction over defense plants, but Deng's spartan military budget aided cost consciousness. Military officials recognized that the Third Line had saddled them with outrageous fiscal obligations.

Xiao Yang's job was to coordinate these efforts and find uses for the hopelessly ill-sited factories. He recognized at the outset that many plants were good for nothing. No civilian enterprise would take them over.

To convert the Third Line factories was a daunting task. Few conversions were so fortuitous as that of the Jialing machine factory, a munitions plant in Chongqing. Under the direction of the Machinery Group Industry, it had been transferred in 1938 by Chiang Kaishek from Nanjing before that city's fall to the Japanese. It was designed and expanded in 1953 under the Soviet aid program, and after Deng came to power it was designated for conversion. By 1988 only 5 percent of it was still used by the military. The rest had become China's number-one motorbike factory, turning out 225,000 motorbikes a year. The plant had worked in cooperation with Japan's Honda bike division as a result of Mayor Xiao's special expertise.

Xiao Yang had handled foreign joint-venture negotiations in Beijing before being tapped for his post in Chongqing. He had participated in negotiations for the Great Wall Hotel and most notably was part of the Chinese team engaged in a deal to manufacture American Motors Jeeps in China. Xiao Yang had been involved in 357 negotiating sessions with Jeep. "The real difficulty," Xiao Yang recalled, "was that the Jeep enterprise involved fundamental changes in the way China handled economic affairs. Everything had to be changed. I told AMC that they were talking with our whole country. We had a planned economy. Every single rule had to be changed."

The principal problem, Xiao Yang concluded, was the Chinese bureaucracy. It was not only the great obstacle to the Jeep plan and other foreign deals. It was Xiao Yang's greatest problem in trying to push his Chongqing associates onto the road of Deng's policy of reform and opening to the West. Nor was he the only mayor to make this complaint. The mayor of Dalian, a tired, experienced bureaucrat, said he spent more time trying to educate his colleagues about the ways of Deng's New China than about any other pursuit. The officials of Changchun's Auto Plant Number 1, the largest in China, held their heads in their hands over the difficulty of cutting a swath through the bureaucracy.

Xiao Yang was making every effort to employ his expertise, as Deng wanted him to, to bring new foreign investments and joint ventures into the enormous Chongqing base. But the Third Line still was a major headache. "Mao thought that war might break out at any time," Xiao Yang said. "He insisted on the plants being tucked into mountainsides. But now China can meet her defense needs without these hidden plants."

Chongqing's two hundred thousand workers still employed in defense industries were rapidly being released. They formed a potentially superlative high-tech pool of skills for new industries, but they would have to be retrained. Like the bureaucrats, the workers were set in their ways and had trouble switching to a new system of competitive wages and output.

The terrible legacy of the Cultural Revolution also hampered Xiao Yang's push toward a New China. Chongqing had been one of the worst battlegrounds in the country, and the defense plants did not escape the upheaval. Conflict erupted at the Jialing machine plant with rival loudspeaker blasts in June 1967, but by 1968 armed struggle broke out. The presence of so many arms factories enabled the participants to use almost every kind of weapon except atom bombs. They assaulted positions with tanks and bombed each other with low-flying attack planes. Great damage was done to the Jialing plant. There were scores of people, perhaps hundreds, killed. Top managers were tortured. Some were forced to walk across live coals in their bare feet. The torture halted only when general fighting became too intense to leave time for torture sessions. The most fanatic battlers were high school students. The high schoolers of the Cultural Revolution days now were forty-year-old workers. "They will never be the same," felt Hao Zhenkun, director of the Changchun auto plant. He shared the opinion of his fellow directors that they were a lost, a "poisoned" generation.

"The younger generation," said Hao Zhenkun, "had no pre–Cultural Revolution experience. When something goes wrong they revert to that Red Guard pattern. The younger generation feels that life is not so interesting as in the 1960s. They are more poisoned than us. We must try harder to rescue them, but there will always be a portion whom we can't reach."

None of these problems deprived Xiao Yang of optimism. He was building a better and greater Chongqing and was proud of it. And he knew what he would do when he retired: "I told General Yang Shangkun that I would peddle *dandan* noodles [a spicy Sichuan variety] from a carrying pole in Tiananmen in front of the marble bridge over the Golden River."

Yang Shangkun told Xiao Yang he would buy his noodles and bring a folding chair so he could sit at the Golden River Bridge and eat them.[5]

46

The Emperor's Clothes

TO THE END of his days Deng Xiaoping never took on the emperor's clothes. Even as the Deng revolution went to full throttle and he acquired extraordinary power, he remained at heart a small dragon, not a supreme dragon like Mao.

Deng was a man of simple tastes. He acquired no villas at West Lake, no Fragrant Concubines, no fancy for larks' tongues or bears' paws. Mao Zedong had celebrated his emperorship by moving into Zhongnanhai. Deng Xiaoping celebrated his by moving out — but not far out. A rather modest house at the end of a block-long *hutong* called Miliangku, near Zhongnanhai and east of Coal Hill, off Iron Lion Lane, was remodeled for Deng. It was a locale of macabre associations. Dr. Sun Yatsen had died on March 12, 1925, in the adjacent princely mansion that housed the Defense Ministry, and on March 18 of the next year forty-two students were shot down and killed here in a protest against the post–Sun Yatsen government — the greatest student toll until that of Tiananmen in 1989. Each time Deng left or entered his house he passed this spot.

Deng's life at the vortex of Chinese politics had given him an obsession with security. He was convinced that Zhongnanhai was not safe, and he would not live there. He advised his associates to move. One bomb, he warned, could wipe out everyone.

The house he picked was eminently secure. It had been occupied for years by Li Kenong, the deceased Party security specialist. Deng had it rebuilt as a three-story, cement-block-and-steel construction, with steel walls and bullet-proof glass. A visitor said that only a tank could crash the front door. It was protected by a wall both high and thick. Steel gates barred the end of the *hutong*, which was too narrow for one Mercedes to pass another.

Deng's house was comfortable but not stylish. Its most pleasant feature was a wide English lawn at the rear. Sometimes Deng took a turn around it, as he had in the courtyard at Nanchang. Corridors of the house were broad so that the wheelchair of his crippled son, Pufang, could move easily. The traditional Chinese raised doorsills to keep out drafts — and ghosts — had been eliminated to let the wheelchair pass. An elevator allowed Pufang to move from floor to floor. An intercom system enabled him (and his father) to speak to any room in the house without moving.

Mao had also displayed a passion for security. His Swimming Pool House was like a fortress. The windows of his great bedroom were skyed so no one could take a shot or toss a grenade at the emperor. Nor could the emperor look out.

Deng's house was more secure and much more pleasant. He had an auditorium seating one hundred, convenient for intimate, off-the-record Party confabs. Deng liked to show movies here. There were overstuffed armchairs for himself and his visitors like those in Stalin's private movie-screening room in the Kremlin, which Deng had probably seen.

Deng didn't care for Chinese-made films. He took an obligatory look at ideologically sensitive productions, but his taste was for American movies. He invited his family and close friends to join him. Like most Chinese he enjoyed *Rambo*. Blood and macho behavior didn't upset him.

Deng had not lost his love for bridge. He played often with his old partners at the club. The club had no name; it was just the club. All the senior members of the Party and army belonged.

Among Deng's five children, Pufang was his favorite. Deng had not had much time for his children until Nanchang. Then he devoted himself to Pufang, and now Pufang lived with his parents.[1] In appearance Pufang resembled his mother more than his father. He had his mother's broad face and her solid frame. Despite his paralysis (he could not move from the hips down) he was a robust man, his shoulders and torso strengthened by therapeutic exercises. He made two of his diminutive father.

Pufang's long struggle with his crippled body had turned his mind to the human condition in a philosophical way not often found among Chinese. He had become a passionate believer in humanitarianism and resolved to devote his life to helping his fellow men. Amazingly, in a civilization thousands of years old, humanitarianism had never found a warm welcome in China. Neither Confucius nor Buddha had paid it much heed. Marxism was violently opposed to it, claiming it was a kind of pap ladled out by capitalists to weaken the resolve of the proletariat to throw off its chains.

Deng Xiaoping was no humanist, but he was sympathetic to Pufang's ideas and displayed interest in them. However, he would not spend any state funds to help the crippled, the blind, and the unfortunate. China was too poor, he thought, to afford the "luxury" of being kind to the lame and the halt. Nevertheless, he did not block Pufang's efforts to win China to the humanitarian idea. It was hardly an easy task. Charitable inclinations had very spindly roots in China. True, monasteries, great families, and princes had spread feasts for the poor at the spring festival and other great holidays. But that was about it. The only people who had really taken an interest in the unfortunates were Christian missionaries. For years the Party had denounced them for trying to create "rice Christians" — Chinese who accepted Christ for the sake of a free meal.

The Chinese response to the disadvantaged was cruel and brutal. Small children mocked lame old women and imitated their wobbly gait, often caused by having had their feet deformed by binding in their youth. Peasants spat at cripples to ward off the evil eye. Lepers were driven out of villages and clubbed to death. Female infants were drowned or thrown on garbage heaps (and still were in 1991). Helpless old people, no longer able to do chores, were led out and left to die in winter snow — a painless death, the peasants said. Emperors were renowned for cruelty, not benevolence. The Chinese world was a rough one. Perhaps the great writer Lu Xun overstated it when he said: "China is a hell full of beasts." But many who survived the tortures of the Cultural Revolution found the statement apt. The only excuse for ignoring the suffering of others was that millions lived on the edge of starvation; they had not a crust to spare. But now the Deng regime had banished starvation, or nearly so. It was time to found a new society with a heart and a soul and a philosophy dedicated to man helping man.

Deng Pufang set himself to change the Chinese tradition. He would start small. He would not ask for a penny of state funds. But he would try to awaken China's conscience to bring people to understand that even a crippled or blind man possessed abilities and rights.

Deng Pufang turned to friends he had made in his life as a cripple, and particularly to Liu Xiaocheng. Liu had lost both legs in an accident. The two founded the China Welfare Fund for the Handicapped and began to make speeches, raise money, and call for action — simple things that did not require state funds. The disabled and the blind were barred from most schools. They were not even permitted to take examinations for entrance into higher-level institutions and universities. Pufang went from ministry to ministry with his message: The handicapped are people with the same rights to education, care, and state services as the able. To deprive them is discrimination as bad as that of the landlords, and it is not constitutional under China's laws. Deng Xiaoping did not help Pufang in his campaign, but the fact that Pufang was his father's son gave him entry to high places.

Pufang put the argument as he had to his father. It was time for China to join the mainstream of world humanitarianism. Its ideas had been skewed by distorted Marxism. China had never passed through capitalism, and its views were still feudal. It did not understand that humanitarianism was not a cheap device but an ethical body of thought, idealistic in nature, that spoke to man's obligation to his brother. It was not anti-Communist or anti-Marxist. Marxists preached about their duty to lift mankind from the abyss. How could it see humanitarianism as an enemy? If, said Pufang, nuns in a capitalist society devoted their whole lives to bettering the lot of man, why could not Communists do the same?[2]

To organize and present his case cost money. Although Pufang had attracted some contributions, more were needed if he was to build treatment centers to give practical support to his rhetoric.[3]

Just how the idea of Kanghua Enterprises was born is not clear. Deng Xiaoping or one of his bridge-playing cronies could have suggested it. Later on Pufang took personal responsibility, but he is an unlikely candidate, given his idealistic and rather innocent mind. As he said, "I know nothing of business." But an idea like Kanghua was in the air of China in the years from 1984 to June 1989.

China at that time was becoming a bazaar. Everything, or so it seemed, was for sale. It was the age of the deal. Everyone was in on it. As the daughter of one of the most distinguished of the old Long March veterans said, "What's wrong with making money? I'd like to be a millionaire." Banners went up in villages: "To Be Rich Is Glorious."

In Beijing, Shanghai, Wuhan, every city of any size, Hong Kong–style hotels sprouted like condominiums in Florida. All were the products of international deals. Big trade and manufacturing operations were initiated too, but they weren't as glamorous or as easy as the hotel deals. A Rockefeller office opened in Beijing. Many American banks sniffed around for easy money. International law firms opened branches.

Deng Xiaoping was quite frank about all this. As the new free-trade zones were set up, as area after area was opened to foreign tourists, foreign trade, and foreign investment, Deng conceded that the old rules were going to be broken. There were going to be bad things as well as good: speculation, crime, prostitution, gambling, corruption, influence peddling. They represented the price that had to be paid for a rocket journey from feudalism into the new high-tech era. A small price, he thought, to achieve great goals.

China had to have the money to buy the new technology. To get it, Deng created government entities to play China's hand in the big casino. The biggest organization was CITIC, set up with billions in government funds and headed by Rong Yiren of the great Rong clan of Wuxi. Rong became one of the "national capitalists" and worked equally for the Rong family and the Communists until the Cultural Revolution, when he fell into the hands of the Red Guards and was tortured. He survived, and Deng asked him to take over China's finances. Rong demurred, saying he could do better making money for the new empire.

He established CITIC. Deng bankrolled it, and Rong entered the world of international finance as a major player. He made deals all over China and all over the world. He bought a couple of timber companies in the United States and Canada, a steel mill in West Virginia, and countless properties in Hong Kong. By 1991 CITIC probably owned as much of Hong Kong as the Hong Kong and Shanghai Bank. Rong held a big family reunion in Beijing in 1987 and gathered relatives from almost every continent. Deng Xiaoping attended, telling the family, "The Rongs are all right." Rong was once again the first name in Chinese finance, the pacesetter, known in Wall Street and in London's Threadneedle Street. The Japanese came to Rong for big syndications. Rong became a synonym for "fast track" in the Deng revolution.

The idea of Kanghua Enterprises fitted the times. It was organized by three men, old hands in the Deng government: Tang Ke, retired petroleum minister and minister of metallurgy; Gao Yanwen, former minister of the coal industry; and Han Guoxin of the Power Ministry. These men were specialists in *guan xi,* "connections," with the Deng government, and in *hou men,* the "back door." There was not much they did not know about wheeling and dealing. They understood the potentials of Kanghua Enterprises, and it did not take them long to put to work the powerful influence they represented.

There is no evidence Pufang understood that his idealistic organization had been put up for sale to the highest bidder. His only idea, as he said in 1988, was to get a better return on his China Welfare Fund's small amount of capital than the low interest paid by the Bank of China. By 1987 Kanghua had paid over to Pufang's society 8.9 million yuan (about $4.5 million). Kanghua was getting to be known as a force. If you dealt with Kanghua, the implication was, you had bought a direct line to Deng. By 1988 Pufang had gotten nervous. He knew nothing of business, but he knew something was wrong. People had begun to talk. He began to disentangle himself.[4]

China had entered an era of glitz in which Donald Trump would have felt at home.

On April 24, 1988, Armand Hammer celebrated his ninetieth birthday, in China. It wasn't his real birth date, but in 1988 he had three birthday celebrations, each in a different country. This was his Chinese birthday. (By the Chinese calendar Hammer was ninety-one.) Each of Hammer's parties was arranged and paid for by his Occidental Petroleum Corporation's public relations staff, but the host for this party was General Yang Shangkun, China's president. Nothing was more symbolic of the era than the festivities at the Great Wall Hotel in Beijing. The hotel had gone through several changes. It began as an American-Chinese venture. Now it was supposedly owned by French and Hong Kong interests. Sheraton was running it.

Armand Hammer was acting out the legend of his life in his last years. His father, the son of a Russian immigrant to America, had been a doctor and pharmacist with Bolshevik sympathies and had sold pharmaceutical supplies to the struggling Soviet government in its early years. At age twenty-three, Hammer returned to Russia in part to see what he could recover of the Hammer property the Soviets had seized. It was an auspicious moment. Lenin needed capitalists to get the country going. He welcomed Hammer with open arms. The statuette of the three monkeys that Hammer gave Lenin was still on Lenin's desk in the Kremlin in 1991, even as debate arose about keeping Lenin in the mausoleum in Red Square.

Hammer had made (or said he had) millions from his Russian connection. Now he had become big in China. His coal venture in Shanxi and Shandong, an automated mine and slurry to move the coal to dockside for export to Japan and the world, was China's biggest foreign project. No matter that the slurry line had failed and had to be shut down. Now no coal was being moved, and older Chinese mines had to fill the Hammer orders, crippling important plants and causing horrendous losses to Deng's economy. Regardless, Hammer in 1988 was displayed as a dazzling example of the success of the Deng revolution.

Anyone who was anyone in China's entrepreneurial world was at Hammer's birthday celebration or was represented, riding up the great escalators to the grand ballroom, opened to its full capacity for the occasion. There was hardly a great family in Deng's Beijing that was not represented. Chen Yuan, the son of Chen Yun, Deng's sometime rival and conservative economic critic, was in attendance. He had a big deal going to develop a large site in the Xidan market area for an office building and stores — a project that ultimately fell through. Peng Zhen's son Fu Yang was also there — the one who had sold his blood with Liu Shaoqi's son Yuanyuan to get something to eat in the harshest days of the Cultural Revolution.

Armand Hammer glowed in the atmosphere of the Great Wall

Hotel. Not many men at age ninety ran a world-class corporation with their own dictatorial hand. Of course he had his detractors. He had an answer for them — stacks and stacks of his new autobiography, a few in English, most in the new Chinese edition. Smartly dressed young women in brocaded *qipao*, the traditional skirt slit almost up to the hip, passed out books to the guests. There were at least six hundred, including ministers, high officials, men on the make. United States ambassador Winston Lord and his remarkable wife, Bette Bao, sat with Hammer and Yang Shangkun at the head table.

Hardly a member of Deng's inner circle did not have a son or a daughter on the payroll of CITIC and the other venture groups. Sons and daughters of the Zhongnanhai circle had fought for jobs as desk clerks when the Great Wall opened. In fact, there were so many scions of the powerful on the payrolls of the new corporations that the *Wall Street Journal* had run a Who's Who, which disturbed the inner circles of Zhongnanhai a good deal.

There were a few words from Yang Shangkun and Hammer (although not a word about the breakdown of the Hammer slurry). A musical program arranged by Hammer's staff followed. A Chinese tenor sang "Ave Maria," and the "Chinese Shirley Temple" and thirty-three young ballet dancers danced some Christmas sequences from Tchaikovsky's *Nutcracker* to honor the great Jewish patron of the Russian and Chinese revolutions.

Some of the younger entrepreneurs had flown in from San Francisco, New York, or Singapore. All came from Canton families with a rich tradition of commerce. No other region had plunged so wholeheartedly into Deng's program for making China rich. Canton had set up a free-trade zone in Shenzhen that had swallowed the little farming village that once existed, with its ducks and hens, at the edge of Hong Kong's New Territories. Now that village had sprouted a forest of skyscrapers. It looked like next-door Hong Kong. Almost everyone at the birthday party hoped that when Hong Kong reverted to China in 1997 it would prove the role model of the future with plenty of money for all. So many Hong Kong businessmen were serving within Deng's government as advisers and specialists helping the Communists to take "the capitalist road" that many dreamed of a day when Hong Kong would be running China.

Among the young Chinese entrepreneurs at the celebration was one from New York who was proposing to build a "Chinatown" adjacent to Disney World, in Orlando. He was certain it would be a big money-maker, and he had come to Beijing to negotiate with

Kanghua. Kanghua, he said, was ready to take off. It was already the fourth-largest investment operation in China. Soon it would be number one. He was one of many investors who had brought a briefcase of plans to the Great Wall. He didn't see how he and Kanghua could miss. He might even put up a "genuine replica" of the Forbidden City. There should be lots of money in it, he thought, and it would be a big help to the building of Deng's China.

In such an atmosphere of obvious wealth and economic opportunism, several members of China's younger generation would not have felt at home. It was the last place to find Pufang. Liu Yuanyuan, son of Liu Shaoqi, was also absent. Like Pufang, he had resolved to devote his life to China, not profit. He had gone to Henan Province, where his father had worked (and died, in Kaifeng), and swore he would work in the countryside. He had been sent to rural Shanxi in the Cultural Revolution, and as he said in 1988, he would have died there had not the peasants been so kind. He had now gone to Henan as an ordinary Party worker. No one knew who he was. He worked simply and quietly and won his way to the peasants' hearts by helping them with practical problems. He dressed in the same blue pants and blue blouse as they did. When they found out who he was, the peasants said Yuanyuan couldn't be the son of a high official; he was too direct, too straight. They told him, "You are too honest. No one can survive in the countryside if he does not lie — at least a bit." Yuanyuan smiled. He had not gone to the countryside to tell lies. He was the only one in his university class who had opted to go into peasant China. "I had to do it," he said. "I owed it to my country.

"A few problems that have existed in the countryside for two thousand years have been solved," Yuanyuan said. "The peasants are happy. It really is their golden time. They can't think of anything better. But there is lots more to do. They don't understand commodity trading. Their big fear is that policy might change and bring back the bad days. We must work with them, help to guide them. But no orders, no commands, no force."[5]

Yuanyuan was far from Beijing on the night of Armand Hammer's party. He was rising in the bureaucracy. He had just been named vice governor of the province, the youngest in China (not entirely a good thing politically; the older politicians were jealous). But Yuanyuan kept his head down. No one in China was more modest. He was the pride of his mother, Wang Guangmei, now living in the great Muxudi apartment complex on West Chang-an Avenue, close by the Fuxingmen Bridge. Prominent widows and retired members of government lived there, in the heart of the new skyscrapers that were transforming the city's centuries-old dusty architecture, the courtyards and the *hutongs*. On East Chang-an was the large diplomatic quarter where the U.S. embassy was sited, the Friendship store where fresh white bread, Chinese caviar, choice beef (from the Fangshan farm), were sold for foreign currency. Here CITIC was putting up the tallest high rise in Beijing, a twenty-two-story skyscraper. There were new hotels everywhere — the Shangri-La, the Lido, the Kun-Lun. The Wangfu, or Palace Hotel, was a joint venture of the PLA and Hong Kong investors, managed by the Peninsula group, and was Beijing's only five-star hotel. It was one of the many enterprises the army got into to make up for Deng's deep cuts in arms spending. Another was selling Silkworm missiles to Middle Eastern countries.

In this world Liu Yuanyuan had no part. Nor did his sister Pingping, just getting a graduate degree at Columbia and returning to Beijing to take a job in nutrition with the Beijing municipality. Pingping's sisters were abroad, both in banking, one in New York, one in Germany, dedicated to the ideals of their father and extraordinary mother. Deng or his aged associates still worried about Wang Guangmei. She was too brilliant. She knew *everything*. Quietly they blocked her from going abroad, even when invited by Madame Mitterrand of France.

But even the Liu family was not without its representative in Deng's new business world. Wang Guangmei's brother was in Hong Kong with Everbright Corporation, the mainland's leading trading company there.

Chinese parties usually end about 9:00 P.M. Everyone at the Great Wall left, a copy of the Hammer book under his arm, a bit after nine. Some were humming a song China's Shirley Temple had sung, "Don't Let the Stars Get in Your Eyes."[6]

PART 8

THE MANDATE SHAKEN

.

47

The Road to Tiananmen

IT BEGAN in the autumn of 1986 with the events leading to the fall of Hu Yaobang. Chinese politics is a tough game, and one of its cardinal principles, as Mao would have put it, is that there can be only one sun in the sky.

Deng had put together a coalition to back himself. He had the support of the military, the old Party leaders, and a vigorous band of younger men whom he had attracted by his attitude toward reform, an opening to the West, and a willingness to break with clichés.

But the coalition had begun to develop strains not always visible from the outside. The stress centered on economics — the contrast between Deng's drive for speed and pragmatism and Chen Yun's stand for careful change and respect for precedent.

In the Chinese tradition, as set forth in the Annals of the Twenty-four Dynasties, no one can challenge the emperor with impunity. If the challenger is allowed to stand, it means the challenger is more powerful than the emperor and signals the loss of the Mandate of Heaven.

Deng was governed by this tenet. If he saw himself challenged, he was bound to destroy the challenger. This had been Mao's rule. It was Deng's.

To avoid so sharp a face-off, Chinese politics traditionally employed surrogates. No one attacked Deng in 1986. When the Party elders felt that Deng's freewheeling policies were wavering out of control, their point of attack was his Party deputy, Hu Yaobang.

Hu Yaobang was a much easier target. He was eccentric. He didn't talk like a Marxist. He carried on a private correspondence with

Richard Nixon, served French snails at dinners, and introduced the works of Albert Camus to the Chinese literati. Now he had launched a campaign to do away with chopsticks and replace them with Western knives and forks. Hu was the perfect symbol of all that the elders found distasteful and dangerous in Deng's conduct of affairs.

They did not attack Deng's economic policies openly. His abolition of the communes and his joint ventures had increased the circulation of money on an unprecedented scale. These policies were doing what they were supposed to do. But they were also stimulating inflation, increasing prices, and putting many items in short supply.

And, as the elders told each other, God knew what was going on in the new trade zones. They had, the elders thought, become cesspools of immorality and corruption — typical capitalist nests. To feed these prejudices some reactionaries organized an excursion to Shenzhen, the lively trade zone between Canton and Hong Kong's New Territories. Some of the more conservative elderly leaders, such as Deng Yingchao, the widow of Zhou Enlai, were taken to Shenzhen to see these libidinous sights in an effort to add emotional force to hard-liners' caveats against the "Hu Yaobang program."

This conflict might have been a tempest in a teapot had it not coincided with an upsurge of protest by the students. Unrest among students was always simmering, and in late fall of 1986 it burst into flame.

Deng was never comfortable with protest. When he had come into power he had encouraged Democracy Wall, a two-hundred-yard expanse at the corner of Xidan and Chang-an Avenue, just down from Tiananmen Square, that had turned into the greatest arena of free expression China had ever known, featuring exhibitions of big-character posters, small-character indictments, passionate appeals for the four freedoms, and debate of almost any question. It was the most exciting place in Beijing. Deng was nervous about the wall, as were some of his associates, but thought it better to let the steam out than bottle it up.

The more people spoke, however, the closer they came to criticizing Deng and his new Party. Deng ignored the dissent for the moment and went off to the United States in February 1979. But not long after he returned from a success in Washington and touring Texas in a big cowboy hat, he ordered Hu Yaobang to crack down and make the students shut up. Hu loyally did his best. The most eloquent poster writer, Wei Jingsheng, was railroaded to prison on March 29, 1979, and was still there in 1991 despite international protest. By the end of

1979 all the posters were down: Democracy Wall had been scrubbed clean. The brief interlude was over.

Deng's reaction against Democracy Wall was in character. He used the word "democracy" a lot, but there was nothing in his career to suggest that he was a supporter of genuine democracy. When the students became restive in the autumn of 1986, he ordered the crackdown of December 1986 and January 1987, in which he again was aided by Hu Yaobang. Deng was not prepared to tolerate disorder within the Middle Kingdom. He had not become emperor in order to turn his mandate over to the students of Beijing University.

The reaction of the elders to the protests was even stronger. Although they were superannuated and were being shuffled off the stage by Deng, they still had power. Two of their number, the aged Chen Yun, Deng's rival, and President Li Xiannian, held posts in the five-man Standing Committee of the Politburo. They had their allies in the bureaucracy. It was time, they thought, to crimp Deng's policies and take a commanding stand for conventional Communist authority and Marxist economics.

Once again it was not a direct attack. They followed the tactics that Mao had made so successful in the Long March, of feint and deceit, of surprise and trap. Their attack was not against Deng. It was against Hu Yaobang, who was rapidly gaining adherents. Hu and his associates had begun to spread unconventional ideas that had aroused the students. Hu had allies all through the Party. Even the Party organ, the *People's Daily,* could no longer be relied upon for conventional opinions.

A fresh-voiced young astrophysicist at the University of Science and Technology at Hefei named Fang Lizhi had emerged as a kind of Pied Piper for the students. They filled his classes to overflowing, and in Beijing the *People's Daily* published a series of his articles in October and November 1986. Fang seemed to express the spirit of the times, and it sent a shudder through the Party elders. His words, they felt, lay behind the student demonstrations, which had started at his university at Hefei and spread to Beijing in January 1986 and elsewhere around the country. The students were bearing banners announcing "A Dream of Freedom" and talking about democracy as if it were a new religion. Here was an issue on which Deng and the elders could see eye to eye. An aroused Deng stamped out — or thought he stamped out — this dangerous tendency. He fired Hu Yaobang as secretary-general in January 1987 and replaced him with Zhao Ziyang, the premier who was regarded as a sound, safe, conventionally thinking man. But Deng took out a small bit of insurance. Mao had not deprived Deng of Party membership when he ousted him in 1976. And now Deng did not deprive Hu of Party membership or his place in the Politburo. It was a gesture — just in case he might need him again. Whether Deng's reading of the Annals of the Dynasties supported this decision is not clear.

In his helter-skelter way Deng had never carried out a real purge of Maoist, Cultural Revolution elements in the Party. He had made no "secret speech," as Nikita Khrushchev had done, effectively closing the door on a resurgence of Stalin's men and policies. The Gang of Four had been imprisoned. A handful of secondary elements had been similarly treated. Perhaps some of the worst offenders had been shot. But even in Shanghai, nest of the Gang, the cleansing had been very light. Perhaps Deng thought a thorough job was beyond his capability. After all, of the twenty million–odd members of the Party at the time of Mao's death almost all had been idolatrous backers of Mao's, and a vast majority had swallowed the Cultural Revolution without a qualm. If he had attempted to purge all these people he would have been left with a shambles in the Party. Best to let bygones be bygones.

But this left him with a Party full of unreconstructed Maoists and Gang supporters. These people were in place, and many still thought the Gang was right and Deng wrong. Not a few had been guilty of torture or sending people to their death. They were not anxious for their crimes to be dug up or to be prosecuted. They walked the streets untouched, and their surviving victims knew their identity. Sometimes a Gang supporter died a mysterious death, the vengeful act of a son or daughter of a victim. But there were others. As late as 1990 they were even to be found in the United States on missions of one kind or another, their American associates wholly ignorant of their true nature.

Common sense suggested that within Deng's close circle there were bound to be those who thought well of Mao. Mao had evaluated himself as 60 percent correct, 40 percent negative. The Party had taken the same position. Deng evaluated his own record at 50–50 and said he was satisfied with that. There could well be those in his circle who put his score lower and Mao's higher. And even Deng did not think Mao wrong on many counts. Like Mao, he tried to follow the precepts of the Annals in the exercise of power. He knew the importance of divide and conquer. And he knew you could not wield power without demonstrating a willingness to use that power.

*   *   *

Removing Hu Yaobang did not solve Deng's problems. A strenuous campaign was opened against "bourgeois liberalization," a dangerous virus that, it was said, had entered China due to Hu Yaobang's lack of vigilance. The disease seemed to resemble that manifest in Mao's anti-rightist campaign and in the Cultural Revolution's attack on the Four Olds — at least many of the targets were those who had gone through it before. And the organizer and mainspring of the drive was also an old hand, Deng Liqun, who had pinned labels on victims in the Cultural Revolution and had clung to his propaganda role thanks to the support of reactionaries and Deng's unwillingness to make a clean sweep of Party reprobates. Deng Liqun was not only a reactionary propagandist but had been guilty of personal conduct that should have caused his expulsion years earlier. His continuance in the role he filled was testimony to Lenin's principle that Communist revolutions need the services of a certain number of scoundrels.

Deng Liqun set to work with vigor on the bourgeois liberalization campaign, but a curious thing happened. The fire went out. The campaign died, and not long after that Deng Liqun was summarily removed from his post. Although the circumstance of this twist is not altogether clear, it probably resulted from a belated decision by Deng that the drive was ill timed and counterproductive. But it was not the end of Deng Liqun. By 1991 he was riding high as the oracle of the Party reactionaries.

China now settled down for an interlude of comparative quiet, albeit brief. Tensions began to rise in the spring of 1988 over Deng's economic program. The battle now came out into the open. It revolved around inflation in the cities and price rises in the countryside in basic elements like fertilizer, gasoline, oil, seed, and pesticide.

The annual June pilgrimage of Party leaders to the seashore resort of Beidaihe started as usual in 1988. The sea was warm, the weather pleasant, and talk was easy. But quickly it became apparent that Deng was determined to press his economic program regardless of inflation and discontent. Party secretary Zhao Ziyang outlined Deng's objectives. They must be bold. Prices must be freed. Let the market command whether they went up or down (everyone knew they would go up). Let the market determine which enterprises succeeded and which failed. If old-fashioned Communist factories could not compete with profit-oriented joint ventures, let them fail or be merged. That was what the new bankruptcy law was for.

Deng's program sent shivers down the backs of the orthodox. This was abandonment of the last shreds of Marxism. If you put your state factories into bankruptcy, what would become of the workers? Did they go on jobless lines as in Pittsburgh or Manchester? The key to Communism, as the hard-liners understood it, was job security, the iron rice bowl. What would the masses say?

Before June was over, Beidaihe was full of angry talk. The conservatives vowed they would not preside over the dissolution of Communism. Deng had never been so stubborn. He would not retreat. He didn't have time. His old comrades had retired. He too, so he said, was "on the second line," not in the thick of battle, but he wanted to achieve his goals in his lifetime. He had lost power three times. He was not going to fail this time. He was eighty-four years old and he didn't have time to waste.

Deng lost the round. No decision was made. The Party leaders agreed to reconvene later, in July or early August. It was a pause. When the extended Politburo plenary met again, Deng still did not have the votes and had to accept a compromise: All economic matters would be taken from Zhao Ziyang and assigned to Premier Li Peng.

Li Peng, an engineer, was sixty, which was very young for a top leader. No one had better Party credentials than Li Peng, a dark, almost handsome man with a bustling, no-nonsense manner. When asked in November 1987 about the "new Long March" toward Deng's economic goals, he replied, "We have to hurry. We have to run."[1] Li had been a ward of Premier Zhou Enlai and Deng Yingchao's and had been brought up by them. His father was a Communist revolutionary, shot to death by Nationalists in 1931. They had had to haul him to his place of execution in a cage; he could not walk, because they had broken his leg torturing him to reveal secrets. Before he died he managed to get a letter to his wife saying: "If I should die, do not show too much grief. My only hope is that my son can be properly brought up."[2]

Zhou Enlai took Li Peng into his charge, fearful that both mother and child would be killed by the Nationalists. Li Peng was a bright, obedient student. He was taken by Zhou to Moscow and put into the Soviet educational system, getting a degree in advanced engineering. It was not a happy experience. When Zhou was in Moscow in 1949, Li Peng pleaded to be permitted to return to China. Zhou insisted that Li continue his schooling. Dutifully Li Peng emerged with a brilliant record, so brilliant that the Russians insisted that he remain in Moscow. Finally Li Peng smuggled a letter out to Zhou with a classmate, begging for help. He suggested that Zhou telegraph Moscow that Li's mother was ill and he must return. Zhou did so, and Li escaped to Beijing.

Li's perfect mastery of Russian and intimate familiarity with the Soviet system led many Chinese to feel he was pro-Soviet and inclined to the old Stalinist ways. He did display an affinity for conventional Communist economics, but those who knew him attributed this to his typical engineer's mind rather than Russian influence.

Because he was brought up by Zhou and because of the martyrdom of his father, Li was known to all of Deng's elders. Many thought of him as "our boy," and they rallied to his side when economic affairs were put into his hands.

That summer wild rumors circulated in Beijing and were carried abroad by Chinese diplomats. A prominent specialist who spent much time in China emerged from talks with Beijing leaders and proclaimed: "Deng is finished!" The word was that he had lost control of the country, that China was a shambles, the countryside starving, the cities seething with unrest.

To one who had traveled deeply and extensively in China during spring and early summer of 1988, the report seemed exaggerated, possibly politically designed to provoke a crisis. In travel through remote Sichuan, rural Anhui, Shaanxi, Shandong, Guizhou, Guangdong, Fujian, Hunan, Zhejiang, Henan, and Guangxi during these months, no signs appeared of starvation. Good crops were being harvested, and the peasants seemed satisfied with the Deng program except for complaints about the price of fertilizer. Nor did the cities — Shanghai, Wuhan, Chengdu, Jinan, Fuzhou, Taiyuan, Xian, and Chongqing — show crisis symptoms. In Beijing the situation was a bit different. Here there were many complaints about prices and scarcities. The huge numbers of workers on frozen state payrolls were suffering. Still, it was difficult to believe the situation had deteriorated so sensationally.[3]

On June 14, 1988, Chinese Central Television presented in prime time across the whole country the first of six episodes in a documentary entitled *The Yellow River Elegy*. It was written by two men in their thirties and directed by twenty-six-year-old Xia Jun, a Central Television reporter.

Whether Deng and his associates watched these programs at

Beidaihe is not clear. But an estimated seventy million did, and when they were rerun at the intervention of Zhao Ziyang a month later, every TV set in China was tuned in.

Yellow River Elegy attacked the historical, mythological, social foundations of China — the legend of the Yellow River, the Great Wall, and the dragon. With remarkable photography it laid waste the old images. For millennia the Chinese had proudly described themselves as the Yellow River civilization. On the great and dangerous river China had been born. Here was the birthplace, south of Yanan, of the Yellow Emperor, China's first. On the rich loess plains of the river China had grown great.

The documentary turned the legend into a dirge. It blamed the river and its worship for China's failure to enter the modern world. While the British, the Italians, the Spaniards, and the Portuguese were sailing the blue seas and discovering the world and its riches, China paddled along the silted yellow waters of its birth river, hardly venturing out of sight of land. It built a splendid empire, but by the fourteenth century it was hopelessly out of date. It was a yellow water empire, not a blue sea empire.

The TV scenario tore down ancient beliefs about the Great Wall. It had cost billions in treasure and millions in lives. It was built to keep the barbarians out. It did not. The hordes swept over the stone ramparts and founded dynasty after dynasty. The wall did not keep people out; it kept Chinese in. They did not venture abroad to strange lands, as Europeans did; they sat at home. And they imitated the Great Wall in their cities, their homes, and their minds. They walled Beijing — and kept people in. They walled their courtyards — and kept people in. They walled their minds to keep thoughts out (this was a favorite theory of Yan Jiaqi's, the brilliant social theorist of the Academy of Social Sciences who a year later would be fleeing China for his life[4]).

The dragon was the symbol of the all-powerful emperor who ruled China by grant of the Mandate of Heaven. The role of the dragon in Chinese society had limited the flexibility of China's rulers. They could not share power — there could be only one dragon. While the legend of the dragon persisted, China could not enter the modern world, with a parliamentary system, a free-speaking, free-thinking public. It was doomed to remain a medieval, closed empire.

The lesson of *The Yellow River Elegy* was that China must sweep the superstitious legacy of the dynasties from its mind. The dynasties did not strengthen the land. They perpetuated weakness. So long as the Annals were the "mirror for the aid of government," China was burdened with a legacy that had no pertinence in the modern world.

No more daring, no more explosive, no more controversial syllabus of ideas could have been presented to China. While Deng and the leaders argued about the economy, inflation, the fast track to modernization, the Chinese public was invited to throw off the shadows of myth and seek a modern path to greatness. *The Yellow River Elegy* was as revolutionary as the *Marseillaise,* the *Internationale,* or *The Communist Manifesto.* It employed man's newest technology to undermine hoary fairy tales.[5]

No one, so far as the record shows, thought to contrast the sophisticated epistemology of *The Yellow River Elegy* with the primitive assault led by Mao Zedong in the Cultural Revolution against the Four Olds. Yet, in a sense, each pursued the same objective — the liberation of China from the philosophy and images that had for so long controlled its heritage. But Mao sent out teenagers with clubs and torches to terrorize the people into a state of know-nothingism. The authors of *The Elegy* sought to lift China toward a state of pure reason.

Not a word was spoken at Beidaihe — so far as is known — about *The Elegy.* No one perceived that China was now entering a two-track era. There was the conventional thinking of the Beidaihe reactionary majority, and there was something entirely new, *The Elegy.* Those who saw *The Elegy* suddenly viewed China in a new focus.

To anyone cognizant of the Chinese situation it was clear that a showdown was coming. It would determine China's course for years. To anyone who understood Deng's career it should have been obvious that he was not going to be defeated. He was the emperor, and he would fight by the rules laid down in *The General Mirror for the Aid of Government.*

48

The General Mirror for the Aid of Government

THE BATTLES of Beidaihe did not end when the willows began to turn yellow in 1988 and the temperature in Behai Bay chilled. When cold winds came down from the Gobi, the attacks on Zhao Ziyang were renewed, and again Deng came to Zhao's side.

As a golden October faded into Beijing's gray November, no sign of crisis seemed apparent. The grumbling over prices went on, but slight improvements — salary adjustments and distribution of grain — had been made.

Zhao had surrounded himself with liberal advisers. They gave no indication that they felt the Party secretary's position had been weakened. Deng met foreign guests and often told them that he no longer worked much; two hours a day was plenty. Deng and General Yang Shangkun made a point of emphasizing Deng's good health. At Beidaihe he swam every day, not just bathing on the shore, but doing the breaststroke, much as Mao had. Deng gave the appearance of an active man enjoying excellent health. More items of publicity were printed — a big new Deng album with many pictures taken by Yang Shaoming, Yang Shangkun's son. There were cheery feature stories in the press, pictures of Deng with his grandchildren, portraying a relaxed and contented patriarch. The drive for reform and the opening to the West were going nicely, so it was said. It was not apparent that putting economic affairs in Li Peng's hands had made much difference.

In the inner councils the struggle over China's future went on. Deng gained some ground for Zhao in the autumn. There were more attacks in January 1989. Deng again defended Zhao.

Attention turned to the coming visit of Mikhail Gorbachev. There were predictions that twenty years of hostility would end as a triumph for Deng. The Russians had first mocked Deng's policies. Now they were reexamining his ideas. Oleg Troyanovsky, the Soviet ambassador, was swamped answering Moscow's questions.[1]

A few arrows had been launched at *The Yellow River Elegy,* but its authors were now at work on a major documentary on the May 4, 1919, student movement and how it had changed China.

On April 8, 1989, Hu Yaobang attended a Politburo meeting in Huairen Hall to discuss new education legislation. While Li Tieying, the Politburo member in charge of education, was speaking, Hu suffered a heart attack. No doctor was immediately available, and he was rushed to the hospital. Great efforts were made by Li Peng and others to try to lay to rest rumors that the attack had been brought on by angry argument. Hu made a partial recovery, but on April 15 he died, suffering a new attack while at his morning toilet.

The death of Hu Yaobang changed China's political climate. He was seventy-three years old, and his active career was over. He had not been the hero of the Beijing students when he had brought their demonstrations to an end in 1987. But now, overnight, he became their icon.

When news spread of Hu Yaobang's death, students at Beijing University didn't quite know what to do. Finally one wrote a message on a long strip of computer paper and hung it out a window. It read: "Yaobang is dead. We mourn." On April 17 some posters appeared at Beijing University. One said: "Those who should die haven't; those who shouldn't have."

On Tuesday, April 18, the first, rather timid student delegation of about a thousand set out on the ten-mile march to Tiananmen. An Australian businessman and his wife came out of the Beijing Concert Hall just as the students were assembling outside the Gate of New China, where the Tower of Yearning of the Fragrant Concubine had stood. Just beyond the gate lay Zhongnanhai and Mao's old Study of Chrysanthemum Fragrance, a sight-seeing attraction now for privileged visitors, its big courtyard windows masked with sheets of yellowing plastic. The students did not know that Deng Xiaoping had not lived in Zhongnanhai for years; that President Yang Shangkun did not live there; that, in fact, few of the top leaders did. They, like all of China, thought Zhongnanhai was synonymous with power in China, as it had been in the days of Mao.

That evening, just before midnight, a Beijing student named Shen Tong, whose home was up the block off Xidan, rode to the Gate of New China with a friend. They dismounted from their bikes and walked into a crowd that was gaping at some students sitting silently on the pavement outside the gate. Shen Tong had printed about three hundred leaflets. On them he had placed the characters: "*Yaobang yiyan: Adou wuguo*" — Yaobang's last words: Adou ruins the nation. It was the kind of literary allusion Mao Zedong might have made. Adou was a character in Mao's favorite, *Romance of the Three Kingdoms*. When his father, Liu Bei, died, the very stupid Adou inherited the throne and ruined the kingdom. The students were likening Li Peng to Adou, intimating that he had inherited his high office because he was the adopted son of Zhou Enlai, and talentless as well.

The students threw the leaflets into the crowd. As they ran for their bikes they heard the crowd muttering: "Who's Adou?"[2]

Neither the students nor Deng and his associates grasped that a major confrontation was at hand. Although the students saw the death of Hu as an occasion for a demonstration, they were not clear as to what their objective should be. At first they spoke more about student issues: dormitory conditions, bad food, lack of financial support. There was no leadership, only a loose coalition that emerged as the crisis developed. The government seemed similarly uncertain. It deployed police and plainclothesmen. It put a watch on the students outside the Gate of New China. It circulated warnings. But there was a lack of decisiveness. Neither Deng, Zhao Ziyang, nor Li Peng was acting in accordance with *The General Mirror for the Aid of Government*.

One of the first and most poignant petitions by the students was for justice for Hu Yaobang, reversal of the verdict that had led to his expulsion as Party secretary, and for a full and honorable funeral. But even this demand quickly was swallowed in the confrontations between students and police as the crowds grew. Repeated efforts were made by authorities to regain control of Tiananmen. Tactically, the government had lost the first round. Its failure to act decisively emboldened the students. They had asserted territorial rights to the square — and won. By April 20, the pattern for the future had been squared off, although none knew it. If the government wanted the students out, it had a choice — drive them out by force or yield to demands for negotiation with no certainty that an agreement could be reached or enforced.

The memorial service for Hu Yaobang was held in the Great Hall of the People, on the west side of Tiananmen Square, on Saturday, April 22. To prevent students from demonstrating, it was announced that the square would be closed on the day of the ceremony. The students leapt that obstacle lightly: They came the night before. It was one week since Hu Yaobang's death. Already it was apparent that the government was moving ponderously. The students had a debating society for leadership yet even so outmaneuvered the government.

Yaobang's memorial at the Great Hall mirrored the divisions within the Party. Wang Guangmei, brave widow of Liu Shaoqi, escorted the widow of Hu Yaobang, Li Zhao. Marshal Nie Rongzhen, a gentleman and custodian of the Party's honor, put himself at the widow's service. What could he do? "Clear my husband's name," she said. Zhao Ziyang delivered the memorial address as Deng Xiaoping, Li Peng, Yang Shangkun, and the old cannon, Wang Zhen, looked on. Chen Yun and the conservative Bo Yibo did not attend. Students knelt outside the Great Hall waiting for Li Peng to meet them. He never did.

What might the end be? Student leaders were sharply split. Many saw no reason to continue after the ceremony for Hu Yaobang. They had made their point. As for the other side, there were signs that the government thought talk would be interpreted as weakness. The emperor gave orders and they were obeyed — or he was not the emperor.

It was a grave dilemma. The students did not know that Tiananmen was a play within a play. It was a test of strength not just between students and the government; it was a test within the government. Would Deng Xiaoping regain control of his revolution, consolidate his coalition once more, resolve the simmering conflict between Zhao Ziyang and Li Peng, or would the whole edifice fall apart with the loss of the Mandate of Heaven? This was the real issue.

With its own inexorability the tragedy moved forward. Zhao Ziyang was scheduled to visit Pyongyang, where relations with Kim Il-sung were wavering. Since the war of the early 1950s, North Korea had been a valued Chinese ally. There could be no talk of delay or postponement of Zhao's trip.

Inside the Party the question of what to do was endlessly discussed. Deng backed a forceful crackdown. Zhao Ziyang took a stand for talks. The elders wanted quick, harsh action. Chen Yun, Bo Yibo, Li Xiannian, and — finally — Li Peng took this view.

The clock was ticking. Mikhail Gorbachev was due on May 15. The government already was hard at work on plans for his visit. Tiananmen had to be cleared before he arrived. International eyes were turning to Beijing. Deng's people thought the government looked weak.

Zhao Ziyang was scheduled to leave by train for Pyongyang on the afternoon of Sunday, April 23. Efforts were made to reach a decision about how to handle the students before he left. Zhao's critics claimed he refused to attend a Politburo meeting on Sunday morning and played golf instead. Zhao said he had agreed before he left on a tough approach, but details were not spelled out.

On April 26 the *People's Daily* published an editorial denouncing the demonstration as anti-Party, anti-Government, a "naked grasp for power." It was a "planned conspiracy and turmoil." Again and again the word "turmoil" or "chaos." Again these words, *luan* and *dong luan,* echoed on the lips of Deng's spokesmen, evoking the dread memory of Mao's Cultural Revolution. Zhao Ziyang was in Pyongyang, out of the loop.

The key fact, however, was that the *People's Daily* statement represented the opinion of Deng Xiaoping. He had decided that the emperor must act or lose the Mandate of Heaven.

Zhao came back from Pyongyang and immediately charged that the April 26 editorial had been changed after he had given his approval. This may have been true, but Deng was boss. What mattered was that the editorial had regenerated student energy. On April 27 the demonstrators mounted a huge outpouring — half a million or more in Tiananmen.

Zhao Ziyang moved publicly to take a moderate position. The students concentrated on another big demonstration, for May 4, the seventieth anniversary of the start of the Chinese students' movement, in 1919.

There was no sign of movement on either side that could cool the rising storm.

The first and best opportunity for bringing Tiananmen to an end without a bloodbath came when Zhao Ziyang returned from Pyongyang — or so it seemed on the surface. Probably the infighting between Zhao and Li Peng was already too nasty for a compromise. Among the students there was a strong faction that wanted to pack it up. A flurry of activity got under way. Yuan Mu, Li Peng's spokesman, pretended that the government was ready to talk. He met with some students, but it turned into a pompous "dialogue." Zhao Ziyang spoke to the Asian Development Bank and sent a signal that the government was willing to negotiate. The students were just asking for things the government believed in, he said: democracy, an end to corruption, and combating inflation. No big deal. No conspiracy, as charged by the April 26 *People's Daily* editorial. Zhao called in his propaganda chiefs and told them to relax control of press and TV, to open up a bit on reporting about the students.

This coincided with an enormous influx of international press and

TV reporters, arriving for the Deng-Gorbachev talks. They set up their discs and transmitters, their clear lines to New York and Tokyo, and flooded the world with reports about the students. China plunged into a world video bath such as it had never seen. There is great doubt that Deng or the elders were able to comprehend this fact. In any event, it was obviously too late for Tiananmen action before Gorbachev arrived on May 15.

Neither Deng nor Yang Shangkun, so far as can be ascertained, ever got a personal look at the square. Yang's photographer son, Shaoming, went in and was said to have told his father, "It's a revolution!" Some of the elders were escorted through the tunnels under Tiananmen and up to an observation post on the third floor of the Great Hall of the People, where they could see what was happening with binoculars. The sight of tens of thousands of youngsters, their worn T-shirts, red-inked headbands, the rubbish of weeks living on the pavement, could not have been reassuring. Most of the elders had gone through horrible struggle sessions with Mao's Red Guards. Massed youth sent a chill through their spines. It was not likely that they perceived the idealism and patriotism of the young people. The throngs in Tiananmen were bound to bring to their minds memories of the *luan,* the turmoil Mao had unleashed. The rising of the masses was something they feared above all, as an NBC photographer at the time of the Nixon visit, in 1972, discovered. He was shooting a sequence of crowds in a Shanghai street. As the throng grew, his Chinese escort became hysterical. "Please," he said. "Leave immediately. You are *arousing the masses.*" The photographer saw that his terror was real and desisted. Deng's elders had all faced the masses under Mao. They never wanted that experience again.

The government was not entirely unprepared. Quietly it had studied the tactics of the Japanese and South Koreans in handling mass demonstrations. The South Koreans had killed hundreds but had maintained control. A good many Chinese leaders were impressed by the South Korean model. It might be a way to keep hundreds of millions docile at their jobs even when a little more freedom was permitted.

The Public Security people had imported riot control gear — tear gas, stun guns, concussion grenades, helmets, and metal shields, but not, apparently, water cannon and high-pressure hoses.

Special detachments like that defending Zhongnanhai had received riot training. Small video cameras had been installed on high poles in Tiananmen and at street intersections. An electronic board at security headquarters on Chang-an Avenue monitored everything and taped it for later inspection and identification of faces. Large sections of this black-and-white footage were ultimately run on Chinese TV and some on American TV as well.

The army, too, had taken precautions. For the past two or three years none of its personnel had been allowed to read newspapers, listen to the radio, or watch TV. Only controlled army information was permitted. The army wanted no conflicts of duty among recruits called to put down civil unrest.

Why the Public Security troops did not employ water cannon and rubber bullets instead of machine guns was never explained.[3] The inference was that someone in command wanted to "shed a little blood," as Deng Xiaoping was known to have said. He had a choice. If he had not wanted blood, the army and armed police would have followed orders.

When Gorbachev arrived on May 15, Deng made no secret of his humiliation at not being able to welcome him with the traditional Tiananmen ceremony. The students were in full possession of the square and had started a hunger strike. American TV was paying more attention to the hunger strike than to Deng and Gorbachev. The world, thanks to electronics, was now perched on Tiananmen's doorstep. It is not likely that Deng understood this, and months later repeated efforts to impress the point on Yang Shangkun failed. That China had become part of the global village was not recognized.

The students turned out to be at home in the new electronic world. Many had lived in the United States. They knew the potential of instantaneous communications as men like Deng and Chen Yun never could. They still thought of communications in terms of the brass key Morse transmissions and inky duplicating machines.

The army had installed for its own urgent purposes a state-of-the-art telephone system from France to replace the old hit-or-miss Chinese system. The students used this fine equipment to set up a fax network to Cambridge, Oxford, the Sorbonne, Harvard, Caltech, Berkeley. The whole student world knew what was happening in Tiananmen before Deng's secretaries could tell him. The demonstrators were able to relay news all over China before the Xinhua News Agency could bumble into action. The student version of events got to people well ahead of that of the government.

Gorbachev left Beijing for Shanghai on May 17. Before he left, Zhao had told him what the whole world had long known — that Deng

Xiaoping was still boss. The Central Committee in 1987 had agreed that no important decision would be made without giving Deng the right of veto. Later Zhao was accused of revealing to Gorbachev a "state secret."

It is tempting to speculate, in the light of what was to occur in both the Soviet Union and China, about what might have happened had the meeting of Gorbachev and Deng proceeded according to plan. Each man was the symbol of change and reform. Each, and particularly Deng, had counted on the high summit not only to commemorate the end of more than twenty years of cold (and sometimes hot) war; each looked to it to strengthen his position against reactionary forces and give new impetus to the remolding of an archaic political and economic system. This was not to be. Tiananmen's first and most dire blow — unperceived, unwanted by either Gorbachev or Deng — was to their separate but converging concepts of the future.

The pace quickened. A million people had filled the square the day before Gorbachev left. Deng and Yang probably moved into the PLA's nuclear-safe bunker in the Western Hills about this time, and Deng flew to Wuhan to meet with his regional army commanders. He didn't want any surprises when he called them to action. He knew they would not all be happy at the orders he would give. The mystique of "the army loves the people; the people love the army" was deeply embedded in both.[4]

By now the students had captured the hearts of Beijing. China had never seen anything like it — hundreds of thousands of people parading to the square, housewives carrying food, medical teams arriving to care for the hunger strikers, government workers carrying banners proclaiming their departments: the Ministry of Petroleum, the Coal Ministry, State Planning, the Foreign Ministry. Even civilian Defense Ministry employees came. The *People's Daily* sent a contingent. So did state television. Young TV workers chanted: "We tell lies. Don't believe us." Capitol Steel and Iron, the biggest industry in Beijing, sent a group, as did Beijing Jeep and the trade unions. "I am there every day," said the wife of a very high-ranking official who lived at the Muxudi complex on Chang-an Avenue. "So are my friends. We are all with the students." CITIC's director, Rong Yiren, gazed benignly from his twenty-two-story skyscraper on the demonstrators. Some said he sent a personal contribution.

During the early days of the protest Li Peng had been the target. Deng's liberal reputation gave him some protection. The students had waved little bottles (Xiaoping means "little bottle") when Deng came to power and had shouted "Hello, Xiaoping!" as though he were a friendly football coach. Now they began to smash little bottles in Tiananmen Square, and signs appeared in the demonstrations: "Down with the emperor."

The students made a distinction between Emperor Mao and Emperor Deng, the Great and the Small. A Chinese of impeccable family, whose grandfather had been a minister under the empress dowager, said: "Mao was a true Son of Heaven, but Deng on Tiananmen seems more like a last emperor." It was a cruel reference to the ineffectual Henry Puyi. But it bore some truth. Deng no longer comported himself with imperial grandeur. Mao seemed like a Son of Heaven even while committing the Jovian act of invoking *luan* to change the world. Deng's use of the term *dong luan* seemed like a cheap imitation. Mao had said in a poem in 1963, "Seize the day, seize the hour!" Deng missed both day and hour.

49

Tiananmen

IN THE WEEKS of Tiananmen several exits from the climax of bloodshed and massacre presented themselves. Deng took none of them. As late as the third week in May a window of opportunity for peaceful talk existed. It was brief, but a settlement might have emerged from it. Deng had gone to Wuhan to consult his military commanders, and in his absence Li Peng and Zhao Ziyang visited the hunger strikers in the hospital, Li Peng rigid, Zhao sympathetic. They were trying to get the students to end the strike, the obvious first step to negotiations. Next day Li Peng met with students at the Great Hall, a bristling, abrasive session whose main purpose again was ending the hunger strike so talks could begin.

Among those present was one man who could have broken the deadlock. This was Yan Mingfu, formerly Mao's Russian interpreter. Unknown to the world, Yan had been talking to the students in Tiananmen and at private meetings in his office since May 13. Yan was an intelligent, sympathetic man with outstanding Party credentials as minister of United Front organizations, son of one of Zhou Enlai's closest underground associates, and protégé of Peng Zhen's, the ultraconservative elder. Yan had been given a mandate to open a line to the students to prepare the ground for talks.

Yan Mingfu came close to success despite the intractability and unpredictability of the students and stonewalling by Li Peng. He won the confidence of the students but in the end lost that of Deng Xiaoping, probably because of sabotage by Li Peng. Li had pinned his political hopes on winning a confrontation. He did not want conciliation.

Zhao Ziyang was taking a soft line and swore he would go into Tiananmen and talk directly to the students. At about 5:00 A.M. on May 19 a highly emotional Zhao made his way into Tiananmen, climbed into a bus where hunger strikers were being cared for, and, close to tears, begged their pardon for coming "too late." He said that the students only were supporting causes the government itself favored. There was no talk of *luan* or confrontation. He begged them to end the hunger strike before it took the lives of any students.

Li Peng stood beside Zhao for a few minutes, grim-faced, then left the square. He had insisted on coming because he feared some unexpected move by Zhao.

That was Zhao's last public appearance. He did not attend a Politburo session later in the day, and within ten days he lost his position as Party secretary.

The students, at low ebb, perceived the split between Li Peng and Zhao Ziyang and saw Zhao was losing strength. That evening they called off the hunger strike. Had the government seized the moment, the demonstration could have ended in hours. But the opportunity was rejected.

The Deng of 1978 would have taken advantage of the chance for peace but not the rigid elder that Deng had become by 1989. He blundered into a declaration of martial law to combat the *luan*. In a confidential speech to top generals, Yang Shangkun devoted himself to the subject of *luan*, sounding like a man trying to convince himself that the peril existed. As an example of the threat he described a train being delayed between Wuhan and Guangdong (the students had seized the railroad bridge across the Yangtze). It was hardly an impressive example to those who remembered that rail service to Shanghai had been blocked for more than a year by Red Guards during Mao's *luan*.

Defiance was the response of the students and citizens to Deng's decree of martial law. Ignoring the precept of *The General Mirror for the Aid of Government* that action must be swift and decisive, Deng did nothing to put martial law into effect. Students staged another enormous demonstration. However, soon word spread of quiet troop movements from the provinces to Beijing and within the capital region.

By the weekend of May 27–28 the air had fizzled out of the Tiananmen balloon. Students were drifting back home. Most of those remaining came from the provinces. A vote was taken on the square — 220 schools voted to pull out, 160 to stay. Many leaders felt the demonstrations were coming to an end. The beautiful firebrand Chai Ling, heroine of the hunger strike, decided to leave. She spent a day and evening saying good-byes, then agreed to stay a bit longer. The dynamic but erratic Wu'er Kaixi made up his mind to pull out. So did Wang Dan, more phlegmatic and businesslike. The students had begun to quarrel among themselves. One faction tried to kidnap Chai Ling to question her about how donations had been spent.

Never had conditions been so favorable for a peaceful settlement. But the government did not move. Deng was going to make plain he had the force and the will to use it. As the imperial edicts had said in the past, the people must *"obey — and tremble!"*

The studios of the Central Academy of Fine Arts are located just east of the Forbidden City. Its students had participated in the demonstration from the beginning. Now the Tiananmen leaders came with a request. In Shanghai the students had carried a replica of the Statue of Liberty in their parades. Could the academy make one for Tiananmen — fast?

The leaders knew that unless something was done immediately the demonstration would collapse. It was already May 26. Could the academy make a statue in three days? The sculptors agreed to try. It would not be a copy of the Statue of Liberty. It would be a Chinese Goddess of Democracy.

The young sculptors had no time for frills. As a model they took a four-and-a-half-foot clay study of a nude man grasping a pole with both hands. They cut off the bottom end of the pole, transformed the upper part into a torch, straightened the figure to give it better posture, and turned the man into a woman. She was given breasts, a Caucasian face, and a flowing robe. This became the design for the finished thirty-seven-foot statue. They constructed it of Styrofoam over wire netting and smeared on a thin layer of plaster for better texture. They cut it into four segments, loaded it onto four flat-topped bicycle carts, and peddled it down Wangfujing Street to Chang-an Avenue, past the Beijing Hotel and into the square, before the astonished eyes of shoppers and policemen. No one lifted a finger to interfere.

The statue reached Tiananmen about 10:30 P.M. on the twenty-ninth. It took the students all night to mount it on a six-foot pedestal in true alignment directly in front of the Mao portrait on the Tiananmen wall. Every TV shot of the Goddess had Mao's ovoid face as a backdrop.

This was a last move. If it didn't give the demonstration a lift, the leaders would have to call the protest off. On the evening of May 30 thousands of Beijingers flocked back to Tiananmen. The hemorrhage of participants slowed but did not halt entirely. The TV cameras loved it. Clips of the Goddess flashed around the world. The message was: The demonstration in Tiananmen is alive! It is going forward! But the statue sent a different message to the elders. It was the last straw. Orders were issued to speed preparations to clear the square.

The Goddess of Democracy gave a boost to the tired, worn, frustrated student leaders. Yet even they realized the end was approaching. The numbers of protesters continued to fall. On June 2, the square was half-deserted by late afternoon. It would have been almost empty that evening but for the arrival of the Taiwan rock star Hou Dejian. Hou had left Taiwan for the mainland a few years earlier and was extremely popular. Now he announced he was joining the hunger strike (actually already canceled) and that evening would sing and play from his repertoire. That brought out several thousand young people, but after the concert they went back home.

It was perhaps the lowest point for the students since they had marched into Tiananmen on April 18. For a week the city had been filled with rumors of troop movements. On May 29 and May 30 troop convoys appeared on the streets close to Tiananmen. As soon as a column appeared, people swarmed into the street and halted it, telling the soldiers that they were the People's Army and should not harm the people. The soldiers, young and provincial (some didn't even know they were in Beijing), were embarrassed. Some burst into tears. Often the soldiers dismounted from their trucks and disappeared.

The decision to move on Tiananmen over the weekend of June 3–4 was probably taken on Friday, June 2. Deng Xiaoping had approved it but left the details to Yang Shangkun. The Twenty-seventh and Thirty-eighth armies would carry out the operation. The Twenty-seventh was one of the PLA's best, stationed at the great Shijiazhuang base, southwest of the city. The Thirty-eighth was Beijing's garrison army. Its commander was not in sympathy with the action and was removed after it had taken place. The armies were strengthened by units from each of China's military districts. If blood was to be spilled, all would share in the spilling.

Word was circulated in Party channels that the troops would move over the weekend. Most informed people believed the strike would come at midnight, Saturday, June 3. Reports traveled through Muxudi and other government enclaves emphasizing the peaceful nature of the impending military operation. If a drop of blood was shed, people said, the whole country would be aroused. The army would not attack the students, but Tiananmen would be cleared.

"Evil elements" had penetrated the ranks of the students, the government claimed, creating *luan*. Neither then nor later were the evil elements identified. There were vague references to foreign agents — presumably the CIA, Taiwan, and Hong Kong. In fact, such agents were spotted in the square, but no evidence indicated they played any role except possibly as a conduit for funds from Hong Kong.

One element in Beijing began to emerge as troop columns moved about the city. This was jobless youth. An estimated one million young people with no work or hope of work, mostly from the provinces, had congregated in Beijing. When violence broke out they joined in some of the worst riots. Their participation was never alluded to by the government.

There was another presence in Tiananmen, never mentioned in government statements but infinitely alarming to the elders — the rapid rise in participation by factory workers and ordinary office workers of the vast bureaucracy. As these critical elements began to join forces with the students and young people, the old-line Marxist-trained veterans of the Party began to have nightmares of what had never happened in *their* revolution: a genuine rising of the proletariat against — and not for — Communism.

Around midday on June 3, a busload of military officers came into the square from the west and drove to the Gate of New China. There it was surrounded by demonstrators. A smartly trained detachment of security troops emerged from the gate, hurled canisters of tear gas, rescued the officers, and sheltered them through the gate. The troops bludgeoned several young people in the process. In early afternoon a detachment of a thousand PLA troops sallied out of the west entrance of the Great Hall of the People. Their intention was not clear, because they were so quickly enveloped by a mass of people. Tear gas was used here, too, but the troops could not break out and, one by one, went back into the hall.

The incidents reinforced the impression that the structures around the square — the Great Hall, the two museums facing west, the Forbidden City, and Zhongnanhai — were stuffed with troops brought in by the tunnel network below Tiananmen Square.

Early in the evening of June 3, a warm, summery Saturday night when many Beijing residents were shopping or strolling in parks and along the boulevards, the martial law command set in motion its operation to bring an end to the demonstration.

The forces they deployed were not those that Beijing citizens had seen on previous days. These were armored divisions, tanks, armored gun carriers, armored troop carriers, masses of them. When they began to roll down Beijing's broad avenues, tracks clanking, motors revving, they filled the world with sound. The noise was reinforced by the firing of their cannon, crisp and heavy. At major intersections, especially in the city center, citizens had placed barricades made of buses skewed across the lanes, reinforced with upended taxis, passenger cars, and trucks.

As the armor roared down the boulevards, the troops fired from two or three blocks away at the barricades, killing and wounding many. Beijingers clogged the streets, using the human-wall tactics that had halted the truck convoys of previous nights. This did not work with the armor. The tanks plowed right through, leaving a train of bodies behind. The racket was so loud the troops could not hear what the people shouted at them.

The first encounters of the armor with human masses occurred far from Beijing's center, and they were witnessed by neither foreign nor Chinese journalists. By chance two Chinese Radio employees saw one episode in the neighborhood where they lived in western Beijing. They were outside their apartment building, squatting in the dust, talking about Tiananmen. Masses of people were ready to block any military columns.

They heard a column coming and rushed into the boulevard, several thousand people together. But this was an armored column. It fired directly into the crowd and, advancing at thirty miles an hour, rammed straight through.

The men saw the tanks run through the screaming people, hardly even slowing. The witnesses thought at least a thousand people had been killed, perhaps an exaggeration. Hospitals in the area overflowed with victims, and this was but one of many such encounters.

Savage combat occurred at Muxudi. A heavily armored detachment was moving down Fuxingmen Street, firing ahead at the intersections. It became stalled at the corner of Sanlihe Lu, just beside the big government apartment complex. The tank commander did not know he was at the doorstep of some of China's most distinguished citizens. He directed random fire into the buildings, and there were half a dozen victims, including the son of a diplomat and a retired Foreign Ministry official. A fierce battle ensued as angered citizens hurled Molotov cocktails. Many became so outraged they wanted to lynch the PLA men. A quick-witted civilian saved many lives. "Let the men take off their uniforms," he shouted. "Then they won't be soldiers anymore." The soldiers shed their uniforms and stood around in their underwear. Kindhearted Beijingers took pity on them and led many to their quarters, where they gave the frightened men tea and sympathy. Then they set fire to the armored vehicles with Molotov cocktails.

On the mall beside Muxudi stood a statue of one of China's Olympic champions. On Monday, June 5, students put a black armband on the statue and dropped a bloody shirt at its base, turning it into a shrine for the fallen. Some PLA men were cleaning up the street. "Why are they honoring that statue?" one asked. Next morning the armband and shirt were gone, and a squad of PLA men stood guard. Someone wiser than the cleanup squad understood.[1]

A bit closer to Tiananmen, near the Minzu Hotel, another bloody battle broke out. An Australian businessman had taken his wife to dinner near the Beijing Hotel. He sent her home by taxi and tried to bicycle home. He was trapped in a cross fire of AK-47 blasts, Molotov cocktail barrages, and fire from arms stolen from army supply trucks. Crawling on hands and knees, he made his way into the Minzu and soon was helping bring the dead, dying, and wounded into the hotel lobby. They placed the wounded and the dead in rows until ambulances could come to a rear courtyard and begin moving them to the hospital. Many victims were members of the armed police, their faces and often their skulls crushed by savage beatings. At intervals daring young men emerged from the shrubbery outside the hotel, dashed into Chang-an Avenue, hurled a flaming grenade into an army vehicle, and scurried away under intense rifle fire. Finally the battle died down, and at 3:00 A.M. the Australian went back to the intersection where he had left his bike under a decorative palm tree. There were hundreds of abandoned bikes heaped in small mountains along the boulevard. Finally he found his, still under the palm tree, put his key in the padlock, turned it, mounted the bike, and pedaled home through the litter of battle, soaked in sweat and the blood of the dozens of victims he had helped.

It was nearly 2:30 A.M. before the first troops entered Tiananmen. Several thousand demonstrators awaited them, many huddled in the bedraggled tent city, some sleeping, some ill. The students had no doubt of what lay ahead. Couriers had brought word of the bloody progress of the tanks. They believed that thousands of citizens had already been killed, and they expected no mercy.

A number of correspondents and TV reporters, including a few Americans, had stayed in the square to record the last act. The Monument to Martyrs, where student headquarters had been set up, was the focus. The demonstrators gradually moved from other parts of the square and congregated there. Television reporters with walkie-talkies communicated with news desks in Beijing hotels. They sometimes were patched directly into networks in New York to record minute-by-minute action in the square.

Once in the square, the troops moved cautiously. They had orders to keep the violence and bloodshed away from the view of witnesses and cameras. That made TV cameras a prime target. Two CBS men lost their cameras and were beaten and held overnight in the Forbidden City. Others, including Hong Kong and Taiwan reporters, were arrested and not released until early Sunday. Nevertheless, even under conditions of darkness, confusion, and danger, cameras continued to roll and videotape to record. Not much was missed.

The PLA carried out a slow squeeze, knocking the Goddess of Democracy to the pavement (recorded by daring TV photographers), tearing down the tent city, steadily taking over the square segment by segment. Fear rose of a final solution in which students jammed around the Monument to Martyrs would be mowed down. Efforts to negotiate safe passage out of the square got nowhere. Finally, as light began to filter in from the east, Hou Dejian, the rock star, took it on himself to try to prevent the bloodbath. He persuaded the military commander to let the demonstrators exit from the southeast corner of the square. There was a pitiful last-minute squabble among the handful of leaders, some of whom had determined to give their lives rather than leave. About 6:20 A.M. on Sunday, June 4, the students lined up and filed away under the eyes of the PLA.

As the demonstrators left they were herded into a narrow *hutong* that abuts the entrance to the square. What happened there is not known. Many on the scene insisted that after the students turned into the narrow street, volleys of machine-gun fire erupted. Others swore that some whom they watched turn into the *hutong* were never seen again.

The question of casualties quickly became a political issue. The government claimed no one had been killed in the square. The volume of gunfire in and around the square made this ridiculous. The government said not a word about the hundreds or thousands of ordinary civilians shot down in the streets. At first it claimed only two PLA men had been killed. Then day by day its estimates of PLA casualties escalated into the hundreds. Best guess: between 1,000 and 2,000 killed in Beijing, perhaps 300 in and around Tiananmen.[2]

The shooting went on for days. The PLA set up a picket line at Tiananmen with machine gunners deployed across the breadth of Chang-an Avenue. All day on June 4 and during most of June 5 the PLA swept the avenue with machine-gun fire every five to ten minutes. A score of citizens moving up Chang-an toward Tiananmen were killed on Sunday, at least two within sight of those watching from the Beijing Hotel. The rumble of tank and antitank guns echoed over the city for days. The streets were clogged with burning trucks, buses, and military vehicles. It was impossible to move through the central district. People threaded their way on foot through the maze of *hutongs*.

Beijing had been given its lesson. On June 9, Deng Xiaoping showed his face to congratulate the PLA on its bravery in putting down the *luan* that, he said, had threatened the Party and the nation and, by implication, himself. He was accompanied by a beaming Yang Shangkun as he shook the hands of commanders who had not hesitated to fulfill their orders to shoot down anyone in their path — man, woman, or child. Special medals were struck to honor the troops. Tiananmen remained in army control for months; martial law prevailed for about seven months. Deng Xiaoping had demonstrated his will but in that demonstration had revealed his weakness. Quite soon he retired deeper into the shadows. He appointed Jiang Zemin Party secretary to replace Zhao Ziyang. Jiang was a robust Shanghai leader, able, obedient, not too aggressive. Deng referred to him as the core of the new younger leadership group.

For months the reactionaries who had taken over the propaganda apparatus of Party and state growled about wanting to put Zhao Ziyang on trial as the creator of the *luan*. But Deng put his foot down. Any trial of Zhao would cut too close to him. After all, Zhao had been his man and, if the truth be known, only carried out his orders. Deng and his longtime rival, Chen Yun, agreed that the Party had been through enough strife. Better put everything on hold and try to heal the wounds. Stress unity and, above all, stability — no more *luan*.

50

"Facts Written in Blood"

THE GENERAL MIRROR for the Aid of Government makes clear that the Mandate of Heaven can be transferred in many ways — by a drop of poison, a dagger thrust, or, in modern times, a bullet at the base of the skull. It can be lost by conquest of the realm, by plot, or by the slow decay of a dynasty, as in the case of the Manchus.

Mao Zedong won the mandate in classic fashion as leader of a peasant revolt, but he did not found a dynasty with an heir of his blood. Had not Anying been killed by a U.S. bomb in Korea, he might have followed his father in true dynastic succession.

There was nothing irregular about Mao's being succeeded by one of his chief lieutenants. This had happened again and again, as *The Mirror* recorded. Deng Xiaoping won his mandate fair and square, and it had been ratified by popular acclaim. But who was to succeed him?

No precedent cited by *The Mirror* offered a clue. There was no mechanism in the structure of Deng's New China whereby an orderly succession was assured. The absence of such a mechanism had long been a critical defect in the "Marxist" states of the twentieth century. Almost invariably the search for a successor degenerated into an old-fashioned power struggle.

As in medieval France, the crown went to the candidate who possessed the ability to hold it. In this art, more was to be learned from *The Mirror* than *The Communist Manifesto*. Machiavelli remained a better tutor than Marx or Mao. Deng's lip service to democracy changed nothing.

Thus it was not chauvinistic historicism that impelled Mao to pore over *The Mirror* during a lifetime; that drove Deng to its pages during his enforced sojourn in Nanchang; or that caused Hu Yaobang to abandon Albert Camus in favor of *The Mirror* after he lost his job as secretary of the Chinese Communist Party in January 1987.

The reality of China was that when no one held a clear advantage, a "time of trouble" was bound to ensue. China had endured nearly forty years of civil strife from the fall of the Manchus, in 1911, to the rise of Mao, in 1949. Eight regimes rose and fell in the interim. Now Mao and Deng had given China forty years of stability, barring only the *luan* of the Cultural Revolution and Tiananmen.

As *The Mirror* noted, during an interregnum military power becomes decisive. Military power had brought Mao to the Gate of Heavenly Peace. Military power put Deng in office and kept him there. *The Mirror* would have approved of Mao's doctrine that all power comes from the barrel of a gun. Common sense dictated that military power would play a prime role in the future. No one, not even students and intellectuals like Fang Lizhi, believed China was likely to be ruled in the twentieth century by some variant of democracy. Few believed that the two billion Chinese who would inhabit the earth in 2050 could be ruled by a Western-style democracy with rival political parties, free speech, free press, and free assembly. This was an ideal, but China would probably not achieve it by the year 2100.

Most politically sophisticated Chinese believed Deng could have lost his mandate at Tiananmen. Had Yang Shangkun been ten years younger, had Li Peng been ten degrees bolder, Deng could have been sent into honorable retirement to play with his grandchildren and peruse the Annals of the Dynasties to see where his political footwork had gone wrong.

After Tiananmen, Deng slipped further from the public eye, but he firmly held the cords that manipulated the other political players. Just as the dowager empress Ci Xi had controlled the political stage from behind a silken curtain, so Deng with the aid of Yang Shangkun directed events in the Great Hall of the People and within the Central Committee at Zhongnanhai. A whisper was enough. Even so, anti-reformist bureaucrats and reactionary elders could wreck Deng's political and economic objectives. No one spoke now of the Deng revolution. Instead, in lengthy talks in 1991 with Party leaders, the author found that even the name of Deng was mentioned more frequently by interviewer than interviewee.

Gradually it became more and more apparent that the big loser at Tiananmen had been Deng Xiaoping himself. He had saved his mandate at the price of mortgaging its content to elderly men and women opposed to his objectives. He had been willing to abandon the reality of Marxist practice in order to jump start China on an accelerated path to the high-tech future. Now, it seemed, he had sold his future for the sake of a fuzzy present.

Had Deng been younger he could have cut his losses and gone ahead fast-forward. But he could not quite grasp what had happened. Nor could Yang Shangkun. Both men listened with impatience to friendly foreigners trying to explain how television's pictures of tanks smashing into the attractive young men and women of Tiananmen gave China an image so ugly it could hardly be overcome. Trying to justify the brutality only made it worse.

Again and again Deng and Yang Shangkun tried to convince themselves and others that China was the victim of an international conspiracy. But to those who had seen the television coverage the only conspiracy was that of the government. China's great writer Lu Xun had written on March 18, 1926, after Beijing's police opened fire on unarmed students, "Lies written in ink can never conceal facts written in blood." The leaders scrubbed and scrubbed, but they could not erase the blood from the paving blocks of Tiananmen. They were still at it in April 1991, nearly two years later. The government announced that the Monument to Martyrs would undergo "restoration." Chisels and sandblasting had not eradicated the marks left by the steel tracks of the tanks that crunched up the pediment in the early hours of June 4, 1989.

What Deng and Yang Shangkun could not realize was that the world had sat in on Tiananmen. Television had shown it what the beleaguered elders in their Beijing bunkers had never seen.

These tragic images were not the only ones that had been lost to China's memory. No one could any longer recall hearing about a young woman in Changsha in the Cultural Revolution. She, like her fellow classmates, had joined the Red Guards, an adoring believer in Mao Zedong. Her unit of Guards split into deadly factions. The young woman was kidnapped by one faction and tortured to the edge of madness to make her confess "secrets." She had none to confess. The guards bound her to crossed poles, stripped off her clothes, plunged shards of glass through her breasts, her throat, and her genitals, and carted her about the streets, chanting and roaring "The East Is Red" until she died of loss of blood. No monument to this Chinese Maid of Orléans was erected. No one in authority ever heard of her case. No one was punished.

In fact, no one was punished for torturing Deng Pufang. No one was punished for the murder of Liu Shaoqi, He Long, or Peng Dehuai. No public court was held on the Cultural Revolution. The trial of Jiang Qing and the other Gang members was open only for brief glimpses. Most of the testimony was taken in camera. No official black book was published. No bronze plaques honoring the martyrs were erected. No monument to them was put up beside Mao's jumbo in Tiananmen. And, of course, no list of the victims of Tiananmen was published, nor were memorials erected at the universities. No squares in the Beijing suburbs bore names of those who died beneath the tanks.

The people of China murmured that there could never be another Cultural Revolution. But human memory was fallible. China lagged behind the Russians, who exposed the crimes of Stalin and Lenin. China's rulers kept the dark crimes of Mao locked in the archives. There was little to prevent the rise of neo-Maoism.

*　　　*　　　*

Deep resentment was expressed in official China when foreigners cut investment funds and nations slapped on economic sanctions after Tiananmen. Tourist traffic dropped to a dribble. Rong Yiren did his best to encourage new investment, but except for South Korea and Taiwan the response was scarce. Loss of foreign exchange was severe: $7 billion or $8 billion in tourism, probably an equal loss in Hong Kong trade. New investment from the United States, Europe, and even Japan dropped precipitously. The glitzy hotels in Beijing and Shanghai, devoid of customers, became halls of gloom.

The price Deng paid for Tiananmen was greater than he could have imagined. Only the peasants went on in indifference. They lived well, with plenty of food, plenty of cheap consumer goods. They worried that policies might change, but they did their best to make hay while the sun shone.

Deng began to feel that events had passed him by. He was uneasy about the alliance with the elders. These were the people he had pushed aside to get his revolution going. Now they were calling the shots. Deng didn't mind bringing in the PLA at Tiananmen. These were his people. They had put him into office. Naturally, he turned to them.

What Deng worried about was the future. He still believed in his revolution. He believed China had to break with constraints. He did not think the command economy that China had inherited from Russia would lead China into a high-tech world. But he — and China — were caught in a dilemma. The breakup of Communist Eastern Europe had inspired real fear among bureaucrats and the elders. They had not cheered when the Berlin Wall went down in 1989. The throngs that toppled Communism in Czechoslovakia and Hungary had not inspired Zhongnanhai. Worst was the fate of Nicolae Ceausescu. No one had been a closer ally. When TV showed the last moments of Ceausescu and his wife on Christmas Day, 1989, as they huddled in overcoats against a bare wall, then lay in a pool of blood in a courtyard outside, a shudder went through the leadership. There, but for the grace of Tiananmen, they would have been.

The Götterdämmerung of Communism came home to the elders. Then Moscow fell, and fear in Beijing became panic. Could China withstand the crumbling of the Communist world? China had survived for years in isolation, but there had always been the Soviet Union. Somehow in the worst of times it had still been a bulwark. Could China live as the surviving Marxist state? No one knew. No one knew what might arise north of the Heilongjiang if Russia became a rogue fascist military dictatorship.

Since Mao's last days China had possessed another friend: the United States. It had felt comfortable with that relationship. America was not an ally, but it was a friendly neutral. Then came the Gulf War, or the Nintendo War, as some Chinese had begun to call it. The Chinese were glued to TV; a monitor tuned to CNN sat beside the desk of every ranking official, including Deng and Yang Shangkun. The message of the smart bombs brought something close to terror.

It had been a long time since Lin Biao and Mao Zedong and the theory of the "people's war," human waves triumphing over technology. The theory was invalid, but China's military had progressed very little under the two Communist emperors. Now, realistically, they could see no possible way in the next hundred years to match Nintendo. Suddenly the Chinese military felt naked in a world beyond its reckoning.

In the months after the United States unveiled the Nintendo War in the Gulf, the Chinese military became incredibly active. It set up a crash program in advanced electronics, specializing in missile-guidance systems. For the first time in twenty-five years there was a flurry of high-level Soviet-Chinese military consultation, with defense ministers and chiefs of staff flying back and forth between Beijing and Moscow. Less than a week before the August 19, 1991, abortive reactionary coup in Moscow, some of China's military chiefs of the Tiananmen crackdown were deep in talks with their Soviet counterparts, the men who would bungle the attempted takeover. Almost certainly this was no coincidence.

Failure of the Moscow coup and the crash of Soviet Communism brought something close to hysteria to Zhongnanhai. An archreactionary cabal, headed by Chen Yun, launched emergency steps to batten down hatches. A new Western bogey was unveiled — "peaceful evolution."

The origins of "peaceful evolution" were traced back to John Foster Dulles. It was, the arch-reactionaries insisted, an American plot to dissolve the Communist world by means of propaganda, insidious wooing of the young (especially students), and cultural exchanges. China must be transformed into a "Jinggangshan," a citadel against this conspiracy. Waves of propaganda suffused the PLA. Internal security was tightened throughout the country. Once again the United States was emerging as the putative enemy while the elders tried to arouse the Party elite to a sense of personal danger should China follow Russia into abandonment of the doctrine of the hammer and the sickle.

No Chinese — not Deng Xiaoping, Yang Shangkun, or Jiang Zemin — saw any solution for these problems in the twentieth century. Nor to the greatest danger of all: the population explosion. Despite the most drastic, but needed, measures, human reproduction in China was again out of control. The prosperity Deng had brought to the villagers had set them to breeding traditionally again, producing boys and again more boys. Could the genie of fertility be put back in the bottle? Or would China drown in a tidal wave of babies? No one knew.

The death of Deng began to be mentioned in 1991 as a political fact that soon must be reckoned with. Deng himself had taken steps looking to the future. He brought in two able new men as vice premiers, one close to Li Peng and one close to Jiang Zemin. They were Zou Jiahua, head of State Planning and an engineer like Li Peng, and Shanghai mayor Zhu Rongji, Jiang's closest ally in that city. Both were pragmatists, neither a student of *The Mirror* or *Das Kapital*.

On a tipsters' sheet both would be listed as the kind of men who would be prepared to lead China back to the Deng Xiaoping time of incentives and profit making. But to get back to that path would be a formidable task in the reactionary tide set in motion by the Moscow events. Only time would determine whether China had the heart for it. No one familiar with the gap between China time and Western time was likely to start marking off days on the calendar. But the path still awaited.

The watchwords of Deng's terminal administration became caution, stability, don't rock the boat, don't disturb the urban masses, and at all costs don't destabilize the peasants. Talking of the future in 1991, Yang Shangkun sounded like a man trying to tiptoe into the twenty-first century without wandering into a mine field. There was not a single new idea in the first five-year plan of the nineties, not an upbeat prediction for the year 2000. The brave visions of the early Deng revolution had faded into gray. China, Yang insisted, was still "on course." If true, the course had taken a detour into a Sargasso Sea.

But after 2000, new soundings might be taken. Not to worry, a cheerful intellectual said. The change would not take long, possibly less than a hundred years.

Chronological Highlights

c. 5,000–
4000 B.C.: Yellow Emperor, legendary progenitor of Chinese civilization.

221–210 B.C.: Reign of Emperor Qin Shi Huang, historic founder of the Chinese empire.

A.D. 618–907: Tang dynasty.

907–960: Five Dynasties.

960–1279: Sung dynasty.

1270–1368: Yuan dynasty.

1368–1644: Ming dynasty.

1644–1912: Qing dynasty.

1662–1722: Rule of Emperor Kang Xi.

1736–1799: Rule of Emperor Qian Long.

1835–1908: Dowager Empress Ci Xi.

1839–1842: Opium War.

1850–1864: Taiping Rebellion.

1893: Mao Zedong born December 26.

1894–1895: Sino-Japanese War.

1898–1901: Boxer rebellion.

1904: Deng Xiaoping born August 22.

1911: Sun Yatsen revolution.

1919: May Fourth student demonstration, Beijing.

1920: Deng Xiaoping goes to France on work-study program.

1921: Sun Yatsen returns to power in Canton.

1921: Chinese Communist Party founded on July 1, Mao a founding member.

1925: Sun Yatsen dies.

1926: Nationalist-Communist coalition launches Northern Expedition from Canton.

1927: Chiang Kaishek turns against Communists; thousands slaughtered April 12 in Shanghai.

1927: Deng Xiaoping enters Shanghai Communist underground.

1927: Mao Zedong leads unsuccessful Autumn Harvest Uprising, retreats to Jinggang Mountain, in Jiangxi Province.

1929: Deng Xiaoping sent to Guangxi to organize peasant revolt.

1931: Deng Xiaoping arrives in Ruijin, capital of "Central Soviet Zone," in Jiangxi, founded by Mao and Zhu De.

1932: Soviet-oriented faction ousts Mao as Communist Party leader.

1934–1935: Long March, Communist Red Army's six-thousand-mile retreat from Ruijin to Yanan, northern Shaanxi. Mao regains command at Zunyi, January 1935. Deng makes march as supporter of Mao.

1935–1946: Mao and Communists establish base in Yanan.

1946–1949: Mao Zedong defeats Chiang Kaishek and drives him from the mainland to Taiwan.

1949: Mao proclaims Chinese People's Republic, October 1; visits Moscow.

1950: Korean War starts June 25; China enters war in October.

1950: Deng, Mao's regent for southwest China, launches Third Line project.

1952: Mao brings Deng to Beijing to handle major national tasks.

1956: Soviet leader Nikita Khrushchev's "secret speech" exposing Stalin's crimes; Mao's speech "Let a Hundred Flowers Bloom."

1957: Mao begins anti-rightist campaign, visits Moscow.

1958: Mao initiates Great Leap Forward, resulting in famine and national catastrophe.

1959: Lushan conference; Mao denounces Marshal Peng Dehuai, spreads fear in upper Party ranks.

1962: Deng and Liu Shaoqi take over China's economic affairs.

1966: Mao launches Great Proletarian Cultural Revolution; Liu Shaoqi and Deng Xiaoping named main targets as "capitalist roaders."

1969: Lin Biao issues Order Number 1, sending Liu Shaoqi, Deng, and others out of Beijing.

1969: Liu Shaoqi dies November 12.

1971: Lin Biao, his wife, and son die September 13 in plane crash in Mongolia after his conspiracy to assassinate Mao is exposed.

1972: President Richard Nixon visits China, February 21.

1972: Premier Zhou Enlai diagnosed as suffering from cancer.

1973: Zhou Enlai brings Deng Xiaoping back to Beijing.

1974: Deng resumes official posts.

1975: Deng accelerates drive to get China going again.

1975: Mao becomes alarmed at Deng's program; Jiang Qing and Gang of Four come back into power.

1976: Zhou Enlai dies January 8; Marshal Ye Jianying lays plans for Deng Xiaoping to succeed Mao, now totally bedridden.

1976: In Tiananmen Square, mass demonstrations for Zhou Enlai and against Jiang Qing and Gang of Four break out at Qing Ming mourning ceremony for the dead.

1976: Deng formally dismissed and blamed for Tiananmen manifestations, April 10; Hua Guofeng named to his place.

1976: Zhu De dies July 7; Mao virtually comatose.

1976: July 26, Tangshan earthquake strikes, the greatest of modern times; 242,000 killed in Tangshan, another 100,000 elsewhere.

1976: Mao dies September 9; Marshal Ye accelerates efforts in behalf of Deng.

1976: Jiang Qing and associates arrested October 6; cleanup officially announced October 15.

1977: Deng gradually takes over from Hua Guofeng.

1978: Deng outlines his program for reform and opening to the West at the Third Plenary of the Eleventh Central Committee in December.

1979: Chinese-U.S. diplomatic relations established; Deng visits America, January 29–February 5.

1986: Autumn student demonstrations; criticism of Party Secretary Hu Yaobang.

1987: Hu Yaobang dismissed in January, replaced by Premier Zhao Ziyang. Li Peng becomes premier.

1988: Party struggle between conservatives and Deng Xiaoping over inflation, corruption, foreign deals; Deng defends Zhao Ziyang, but economic control given to Li Peng.

1989: Party controversy continues; Hu Yaobang dies April 15; Tiananmen student demonstrations; Tiananmen massacre June 3–4; Zhao Ziyang dismissed as Party secretary, replaced by Jiang Zemin, Shanghai Party chief.

1990: Deng's economic program slows; rising influence of President Yang Shangkun.

1991: Economic slowdown continues; hard-liners' influence continues.

Personages

Bo Yibo: Member of the Standing Committee under Deng and a specialist in finance and economics.

Chen Boda: One of Mao's secretaries, who became a major figure in the Cultural Revolution in alliance with Kang Sheng, secret police chief, and Jiang Qing. Chen Boda was responsible for some of the cruelest acts of the Cultural Revolution. He fell from power before it ended and died not long afterward.

Chen Yi: Born in 1901 in Lochi, near Chengdu, Sichuan, into a moderately wealthy magistrate's family. One of China's ten marshals, Chen became Mao's foreign minister and was persecuted in the Cultural Revolution, dying of cancer on January 6, 1972.

Chen Yun: Born in 1900 into a Shanghai working-class family, he started life as a typesetter and became a daring guerrilla, undertaking underground and dangerous secret assignments. Under Mao he won a reputation as an economic wizard. Chen was the author of many of Deng's basic economic reforms, even though he was cautious while Deng was impetuous. Chen threw his influence to Deng after Tiananmen to prevent any violent Party purges or expulsions.

Chiang Kaishek: The firstborn — October 11, 1887 — of a moderately well-to-do family. An ardent supporter of Dr. Sun Yatsen, he became the chief military figure in the Nationalist cause after a murky period in Shanghai, when he was involved with the underworld. Chiang led the Communist-Nationalist coalition in 1927 but turned on the Communists in Shanghai, April 27, 1927, slaughtered thousands, and started a feud that raged for twenty years. After World War II, when Mao won China, Chiang and remnants of his forces retired to Formosa (Taiwan), where he died in 1975.

Deng Pufang: First son of Deng Xiaoping, crippled when he fell or was pushed from a four-story window during torture by Red Guards in the Cultural Revolution. He became a crusader for aid to China's handicapped and for a more humanitarian approach to China's problems.

Deng Xiaoping: Born August 22, 1904, at the Deng family village, Paifangcun, to a prominent provincial family. He started the Long March as a private and later shared military leadership in the 129th Division and the Second Field Army, which destroyed more than a million of Chiang Kaishek's troops. Mao entrusted him with the vast and secret Third Line defense industry operation but cut him down in the Cultural Revolution of 1966. In 1973 Deng had regained favor and replaced the ailing Zhou Enlai, only to fall again, in 1976. Marshal Ye Jianying led a coup after Mao's death that put the country in Deng's hands. For more than ten years he led an eclectic revolution which lost momentum when Deng called out the troops to fire on students and citizens in the 1989 Tiananmen affair.

Deng Youmei: Chinese writer, friend of the author, host on a visit to a typical backward village, his own Deng village, in Shandong Province.

Gao Gang: Mao's early viceroy for Manchuria and his favorite lieutenant until, in 1954 — after Stalin's death — it was discovered that Gao Gang had become a secret ally of the Russians. Gao Gang committed suicide rather than face certain death on charges of treason.

He Long: Born in 1896 in the mountains of Hunan, he began his revolutionary career by attacking a government tax assessor with a butcher's cleaver. He led his brigade against Dr. Sun Yatsen's Nationalist Army and joined Communist ranks in 1926. He fought in the Long March, the Japanese war, and the civil war. In 1955 he was named one of China's ten marshals. Lin Biao saw him as an enemy and when the Cultural Revolution broke out Lin and Jiang Qing targeted him. He died June 8, 1969, in the hospital to which he was taken despite his protest "they just want to kill me."

Huang Hua: Radical Beijing University student who acted as Edgar Snow's interpreter on Snow's famous 1937 trip to the Communist stronghold in Pao-an and Yanan. Long close to Zhou Enlai, he had a distinguished diplomatic career, becoming China's first representative to the United Nations and foreign minister.

Hu Hua: Leading Party historian, associated with the People's University of Beijing; died in 1987.

Hu Qiaomu: An important secretary to Mao Zedong from 1941 until the Cultural Revolution and in 1991, at the age of eighty-four, an important Party conservative. At a critical point during the Cultural Revolution he aided Deng Xiaoping but in later years became a hard-liner.

Hu Yaobang: Deng's Party secretary whose free-wheeling approach frightened Party hard-liners. He lost his job in January 1987. His death on April 15, 1989, at seventy-three, touched off a series of events that led to the student and civilian protest in Tiananmen Square, crushed by the army on Deng's orders.

Jiang Qing: Mao Zedong's third wife. He married her over the protest of his associates with the promise she would not take a political role for twenty years. A B-grade actress in Shanghai, she made her way to Yanan in 1937 and wiggled into Mao's bed, assisted by Kang Sheng, Mao's sinister police agent, and Yu Qiwei, an idealistic student who became a prominent Communist. She was used by Mao to mobilize the Cultural Revolution and herself used the Cultural Revolution to persecute those whom she hated and feared. Eventually overthrown by Party elders who restored Deng to power, she allegedly committed suicide in Qincheng Prison in 1991, at the age of seventy-seven.

Jiang Zemin: Shanghai Party chief, picked by Deng in 1989 to fill the Party secretaryship vacated by Zhao Ziyang after Tiananmen.

Kang Sheng: Mao's chief of secret police and shadowy figure behind many plots and intrigues, a major figure in the Cultural Revolution, often a collaborator with Jiang Qing, whom he had known since their early days in Shandong. He was born around 1900 into a well-to-do Shandong provincial family, died December 16, 1975, of cancer.

Kim Il-sung: North Korean dictator, placed in power by Stalin at the end of World

War II. In June 1950, initiated the Korean War by attacking South Korea. Still in power in 1991 at the age of seventy-nine.

Lao She: China's great contemporary writer, author of *Rickshaw Boy*. Committed suicide in the Cultural Revolution after being savagely beaten and tortured by Mao's Red Guards.

Lin Biao: Born October 7, 1907, in a Lin family village in Huanggang County, Hubei Province, where his father ran a small factory that was ruined by warlord extortion. Lin became a Communist, attended Whampoa military academy, and emerged as a brilliant Red Army commander on the Long March, against the Japanese, and in the struggle with Chiang Kaishek. In 1959 Mao made him defense minister and later his legal successor. Lin took a leading role in the Cultural Revolution, but Mao's favor began to ebb. Lin plotted to assassinate Mao and take power. He failed and, with his wife and son, fled China by plane, crashing to a fiery death in Mongolia, September 13, 1971.

Li Peng: At sixty-three in 1991, one of the youngest in the inner circle. He had been premier since 1987 and had solidified his post by taking a very hard line at Tiananmen.

Liu Bocheng: Born in Sichuan in 1892. "One-Eyed" Liu, with Deng Xiaoping, directed the 129th Division, the best division in the PLA, against the Japanese. When the 129th was expanded into the Second Field Army, Liu led it against Chiang Kaishek.

Liu Shaoqi: Born in 1898 in Ningxiang County, Hunan, to a prosperous family. He first joined Mao in organizing miners and was sent in 1921 to Moscow to study at the Comintern's Sun Yatsen University, where he joined the Communist Party. Back in China by 1925, Liu joined the Russian anti-Mao faction but came over to Mao's side and in the Long March was a commander and political commissar. Liu Shaoqi rose to become president of China and nominal successor to Mao, but Mao in 1966 removed him from power, along with Deng Xiaoping. Liu died in Kaifeng Prison, deprived of food and medical attention, November 12, 1969.

Lo Man (Li Weihan): Prominent Communist who led a violent polemic against Deng Xiaoping in Ruijin before the Long March. He later married A Jin (Jin Weiyin), Deng's second wife, who had divorced Deng.

Mao Yuanxin: Nephew of Mao Zedong, a military officer, he came to Beijing in the summer of 1975 and by October had become liaison between the bedridden Mao Zedong and Jiang Qing and the Gang of Four. Arrested after Mao's death, he was still in prison in 1991.

Mao Zedong: Leader and one of the founders of the Chinese Communist Party. He was the son of an upwardly mobile peasant father and a devout Buddhist mother. Born December 26, 1893, at Shaoshan, Hunan Province, he died September 9, 1976.

Nie Rongzhen: Born in 1899, close by Chongqing, into a prosperous family, which sent him to France on the work-study program in 1920. There he fell under the influence of Zhou Enlai, joined the Communist Party in 1923, and went to Moscow, where he spent six months in military study, returning to China to work in the Whampoa military academy under Zhou. Nie made the Long March, emerging as chief of staff of the First Front Army under Lin Biao. In 1955 Nie was named one of China's ten marshals. As head of the Academy of Science he had responsibility for China's nuclear arms program. The Cultural Revolution cost him his job, but he worked with Marshal Ye Jianying in the post-Mao coup d'état that ousted Jiang Qing and the Gang of Four and brought Deng to power. In 1991 he was alive, at the age of ninety-two.

Peng Dehuai: Born in 1898 in Hunan, where his youngest brother died of starvation. He hired himself out to a warlord army as a private at $2.50 a month and after a dozen years' experience joined the Communist Party. On the Long March many regarded him as the top Communist commander. He led the Chinese troops in Korea when Lin Biao refused the post, pleading illness. Along with Chen Yi, one of two men who called Mao the familiar "Lao Mao," Old Mao, never "Chairman." After Peng told Mao that his Great Leap Forward was causing widespread starvation, Mao accused Peng of heading "a military club" plotting against him. Peng was beaten — 130 times — before he finally died November 29, 1974.

Peng Zhen: Born in 1899 into a declining gentry family, he attended a teachers' institute and was caught up in the May Fourth students' movement. He joined the Communist Party in 1926 and worked with Liu Shaoqi in the underground. For years he played a central role in Beijing, as mayor from 1949 and as Party boss. A bold critic of Mao's policies, on May 16, 1966, Peng was denounced and spent the next twelve years in prison and exile. He returned December 28, 1978, and created the basis of law on which to found Deng Xiaoping's revolution.

Rewi Alley: New Zealand sheepherder who went to China about 1930, became an industrial inspector in Shanghai, and for more than fifty years was an adherent of the Chinese Communist revolutionary movement. Personal associate of Mao Zedong's and of most of the top leadership until his death in 1987, at the age of ninety.

Rong Yiren: A member of China's premier pre-revolutionary banking and industrial family, who became director of CITIC, the large government-financed investment trust.

Soong Chingling: Born in Shanghai in 1895, one of three daughters of Charlie Soong, onetime Bible salesman who amassed a fortune. Chingling, sister of Meiling (who married Chiang Kaishek), married Dr. Sun Yatsen in 1914. Herself a non-Communist, she supported the Communists rather than the Nationalists and became vice president of the People's Republic. She died May 29, 1981.

Sun Yatsen: First president of China, leader of the Chinese Nationalist movement, and founder of the first Chinese Republic, in 1911. Married Soong Chingling in 1914, died in 1925.

Tian Jiaying: One of Mao's secretaries, an idealist who long enjoyed a relationship of extraordinary intimacy with Mao Zedong. He committed suicide on the morning of May 23, 1966, after being informed of false charges brought against him.

Wang Guangmei: The brilliant widow of Liu Shaoqi, regarded by Jiang Qing as a personal enemy and rival, Wang was persecuted in the Cultural Revolution despite some protective efforts by Zhou Enlai. She was born in Beijing in 1921 into a prominent family, her father a high-ranking government official. She and Liu were married in 1948 and had four children; all were persecuted in the Cultural Revolution, but all survived.

Wang Jiaxiang: Participant in the Long March, an anti-Mao, pro-Soviet Party activist who came over to Mao's side and for many years was Beijing's representative in Moscow.

Wang Ming: Born in 1907 in Anhui Province, he became the principal Chinese follower of the Russian anti-Mao line until his death in the 1970s. In the years before the open split between Moscow and Beijing, Mao often used Wang Ming as a stand-in for Stalin, directing remarks at him that were actually meant for the Soviet leader.

Wang Zhen: Born in 1909 in Hunan, he became a railroad worker and joined the

Communist Party in time to make the Long March as political commissar with General Xiao Ke's Sixth Army. While under house arrest during the Cultural Revolution, Wang acted as an intermediary in bringing Deng Xiaoping back from exile in 1973. Wang also played a critical role in returning Deng to power after Mao died. He was alive, very reactionary, and remarkably vigorous in 1991 at the age of eighty-two.

Wan Li: A close lieutenant of Deng's since the days when Deng was in charge of southwest China and the Third Line. Builder of many of China's great construction projects, including the massive Tiananmen Square. In 1991, at seventy-five, Wan Li was one of Deng's most liberal advisers.

Yang Shangkun: Born in 1908 in Suining, Sichuan, into a wealthy landowning family, Yang entered the Communist Party in 1926, studied in Moscow, and became a supporter of the Soviet faction in the Party but quickly gravitated to Mao's side. Although he made the Long March and for years was head of the Party General Office, Mao turned on him before the Cultural Revolution. Yang spent nearly thirteen years in confinement before emerging to become Deng Xiaoping's alter ego and ultimately president of China, a post he still held in 1991.

Ye Jianying: Born April 28, 1897, into a well-to-do merchant family north of Canton. An instructor at the Whampoa military academy, he met Zhou Enlai and remained close to him during his entire life. He joined the Communist Party in 1924 in Germany, came back to China, and rose ultimately to become one of China's ten marshals. He survived Mao's purges, paid lip service to Jiang Qing and the Cultural Revolution, but led the conspiracy of generals and Party seniors that overthrew Jiang Qing and the Gang of Four and put Deng into power. Ye died October 22, 1989, at the age of ninety-two.

Zhao Ziyang: One of the most able provincial secretaries of the late Mao era, recruited by Deng as premier in 1978. Deng replaced Party Secretary Hu Yaobang in 1987 with Zhao, who in turn was removed after Tiananmen.

Zhou Enlai: Born March 5, 1898, into an impoverished mandarin family in Jiangsu Province. Bright, attractive, outgoing, Zhou was sent to the American-missionary-sponsored Nankai school in Tianjin, where one of his teachers was novelist John Hersey's mother. Zhou studied briefly in Japan, returned to China, was caught up in the May 4, 1919, student movement, and quickly moved into the mainstream of China's student radicalism. He sailed for France in 1920 to join the work-study movement and in Paris set up a European branch of the Chinese Communist Party in 1922. He narrowly escaped execution in Chiang Kaishek's 1927 Shanghai massacre of Communists and soon was off to Moscow, the first of many trips. When he came back he sided with the Moscow sympathizers and emerged as a rival to Mao Zedong. But once the Long March began, Zhou moved to Mao's side and never left him again. When he fell ill with cancer in 1972, he persuaded Mao to return Deng Xiaoping from exile to take his place. As Zhou neared death, Mao turned against him (and Deng). Zhou died January 8, 1976.

Zhu De: Grand old man of the Red Army, long Mao Zedong's closest collaborator. Born December 18, 1886, in Hunan Province, Zhu De came from a poor family in which only eight of fifteen children survived. Zhu De became a successful warlord general. He acquired an opium habit, which he subsequently cured. After studying in Germany, he met Zhou Enlai and soon became a Communist leader. Peasants often thought the Communists were led by "Zhu Mao," a single person. By 1949 Zhu's role was more ceremonial than active, but in the Cultural Revolution he was attacked as a "Black General." He died July 7, 1976.

Zhu Rongji: Born in 1928, in Changsha, a native of Hunan and graduate of Qinghua

University. Zhu emerged from the State Planning Commission in 1987 to become successor to Jiang Zemin, Party secretary of Shanghai, when Jiang was elevated to China's Party secretaryship in 1989. Zhu jumped to vice premier in 1991, a fast-track, pragmatic executive who as mayor of Shanghai piloted the city through the Tiananmen crisis without bloodshed or use of troops.

Zou Jiahua: Born in Shanghai in 1927, educated in the Soviet Union, spent most of his career in industry. The son-in-law of the late marshal Ye Jianying and brother-in-law of Ye Xuanping, powerful Canton leader. He was named vice premier simultaneously with Zhu Rongji.

On the Writing of *The New Emperors*

IN 1984 my wife, Charlotte, and I made a 7,200-mile trek through China's backcountry retracing the paths of Mao Zedong and his Red Army on their 1934–35 Long March of 25,000 li (about 6,500 miles) to escape Chiang Kaishek's Nationalist forces.

Almost every important survivor of that epic — the men still running the People's Republic of China — was interviewed, as well as scores of other survivors. That work provided the genesis of *The New Emperors,* the story of the era of Mao Zedong and Deng Xiaoping, the leader of that Long March and one of his young lieutenants.

The New Emperors is the product of years of travel, interviews, and research in China, the United States, and (to a lesser extent) the Soviet Union. In every case possible I have gone back to the original sources, the men and women who participated in the events described, and to original documents and memoirs describing and analyzing them. The book represents a palimpsest of materials, hundreds of interviews, and thousands of miles of journeys into every corner of China.

Neither of the "new emperors" sat for his portrait. Mao was beyond interviews when I first went to China, in 1972, and Deng, from some sense, perhaps of caution, always proved elusive. But these lacunae were more than filled with extended discussions, often ranging over years, with men who knew them intimately, their peers, and in the case of Mao, five men who knew him as only secretaries and interpreters come to know a man: Li Rui, whose biography of Mao's early years gives unique insight into his character formation; Hu Qiaomu, an enigmatic survivor still playing a major role in reactionary Chinese politics in 1991; General Wu Xiuquan, at Mao's side during the Long

March and his specialist and interpreter in the Russian field for many years; Shi Zhe, Mao's interpreter and adviser in Soviet affairs during the Stalin years; and Yan Mingfu, whose career spanned the Khrushchev period and who took a leading role under Deng and in the tragic 1989 Tiananmen affair.

General Yang Shangkun, who assumed China's presidency in 1988, devoted countless hours in the years from 1984 onward discussing and interpreting Deng Xiaoping, for whom he had become an alter ego. Even after the Tiananmen massacre and my harsh appraisal of his and Deng's actions then, he continued to meet with me and explain and seek to justify China's policies. He was invaluable in facilitating research for both an earlier work of mine, *The Long March: The Untold Story,* and *The New Emperors,* possessing an affinity for objective history of the dramatic events of New China's birth, events in which he himself was, of course, a major figure. He made no effort to dissuade me from my conclusions even when they were violently different from his own.

No more frank glimpses of the reality of Chinese politics at the top could have been given than those of Soong Chingling, widow of Dr. Sun Yatsen, vice president of the People's Republic, warm friend of Zhou Enlai's, and vitriolic critic of Mao's Cultural Revolution. After sinking into her final coma before death, on May 29, 1981, Madame Soong was said to have been "converted" to the Communist Party, which, in her conscious life, she had always refused to join. More conventional images of life at the top were provided by Li Xiannian, president of China until Yang Shangkun took over.

Two general secretaries of the Chinese Communist Party, Hu Yaobang and Zhao Ziyang, both later to lose their posts, provided insight into the character of Deng Xiaoping and a peek at their own during dinners in Zhongnanhai, in the villa where Mao Zedong died. Members of Deng's family helped to flesh out the personal qualities of the "little emperor."

The charming and brilliant widow of China's martyred president Liu Shaoqi, Madame Wang Guangmei, herself driven close to death by Mao, painted an extraordinary picture of the imperial court, although she would not use those words. Her son, Yuanyuan, a vice governor of Henan Province, and his sisters Pingping and Tingting told of growing up under Mao's terror.

The nature of Jiang Qing, Mao's wife, and of the sinister Lin Biao was limned by many of their victims, notably the former wife and the widow of He Long, the great martyred military leader: Madame Jian Xianren, herself a daring guerrilla of early Communist days, and Xue Ming, onetime confidant of Jiang Qing's and Ye Qun's, wife of Lin Biao. General Xiao Ke, brother-in-law of He Long, was of great assistance on this and many other questions.

A penetrating view of Mao, Jiang Qing, and the inner circle in the last days was provided by Zhang Hanzhi, widow of Foreign Minister Qiao Guanhua, who gave Mao English lessons and was herself within that circle. Another view was provided by Zhu Zhongli, widow of Wang Jiaxiang, who helped Mao regain power on the Long March. A physician, Madame Zhu sometimes treated Mao and with her husband belonged to the inner circle until Mao turned on them.

Non-Chinese sources included George Hatem (known in Chinese as Ma Haide), American-born physician who spent his life at the side of Mao and the Chinese leaders, and Rewi Alley, a New Zealander, who did the same. Helen Snow, widow of Edgar, shared knowledge of the Yanan days. The scholars Roxane Witke and Ross Terrill helped with the role of Jiang Qing.

On the Soviet side, Sergo Mikoyan, son of Anastas, and Sergei Khrushchev, son of Nikita, should be mentioned. Also of great aid were Oleg Troyanovsky, sometime ambassador to Beijing, and my old friend Pavel Novokshinov, who knows Siberia so well.

No one could have contributed more than Cui Lie, former diplomat and in 1991 a Beijing publisher. He traveled thousands of miles at my side and performed incredible feats of translation and digging out materials. This book could not have been written without his heroic aid. The same goes for the interpreters and translators who provided priceless background — Zhang Yuanyuan, Yao Wei, Li Zhengjun, Mao Guohua, Wu Jun, Zhang Wei, Wang Tieli, Mei Yan, Mei Shan, Robin and Betty Ting, and Zhang Quidong. "Brilliant" is the only word for the assistance of Liu Yadong, a rising diplomat and scholar.

The late Hu Hua of the People's University of Beijing, who devoted his life to study of the Revolution, put his expertise at my command. So did his colleague Xiang Qing, of Beijing University. Chen Hansheng, who devoted a lifetime to the service of Mao and the Chinese revolution, shared his realistic and often sardonic insights.

I am indebted to the writers Zhang Jie, Wang Ming, and Han Suyin for sensitive knowledge, and especially to Deng Youmei, who with difficulty obtained permission for me to accompany him on a visit to his native village, in Shandong. Hu Jieqing, the widow of Lao She, the great Chinese author of *Rickshaw Boy,* and his daughter and son, Shu Ji and Shu Yi, told me the terrifying details of his death. Eva Siao, photographer and widow of the writer Emi Siao, friend of Mao in their youth, gave me the story of his (and her) torture.

The list of political figures interviewed (often repeatedly) constitutes a litany of contemporary China: Deng Pufang, Deng's crippled son; Deng Liqun, Cultural Revolution hanger-on and arch-reactionary of post-Tiananmen times; Wan Li, Deng's leading liberal supporter; Li Ruihan, dynamic former mayor of Tianjin, now a member of the Politburo Standing Committee; Defense Minister Qin Jiwei; Mayor Zhao Weibin, Tangshan; Zhang Ruji, boss of the great Kailuan coal complex, who showed me the earthquake epicenter at the bottom of his mine; Minister of State Reconstruction Gao Shangquan; Kang Keqin, widow of Marshal Zhu De; Wei Fuhai, mayor of Dalian; Zhu Rongji, former mayor of Shanghai, now vice premier; Wu Bangguo, who became Shanghai Party secretary in 1991; Yuan Mu, Li Peng's spokesman; Li Shenzhi, vice chairman, Academy of Social Sciences; Li Miao, American specialist, Academy of Social Sciences; Wang Lidin, vice chairman, Hebei Province; Liu Yuan, vice chairman, Henan Province; Zhang Chenyuan, vice governor, Guangxi Province; Wu Bacai, vice governor, Shanxi Province; Liang Guoting, Party secretary, Shandong Province; Sun Daren, vice governor, Shaanxi Province; Hou Jie, former governor, Heilongjiang Province; Zheng Fengyu, vice governor, Jiangxi Province; Xiao Yang, former mayor and in 1991 Party secretary, Chongqing; Rong Yiren, chairman, CITIC; Chen Zhutou, general manager, Auto Plant Number 1, Changchun; Han Xu, former ambassador to the United States, president of the China Friendship Association; the late Wang Bingnan, diplomat and associate of Zhou Enlai's; the late Zhang Wenjin, former ambassador to the United States; Huang Hua, former foreign minister, who with his wife, He Liliang, gave extraordinary assistance; Li Luyu, former ambassador to the United Nations; Gao Liang, Party information officer.

Deng Xiaoping's career and character were illuminated by extended visits to his home village of Paifangcun, in northern Sichuan, and the remote Guangxi region of his first battles. Two specialists of the Sichuan Foreign Office, Wang Rougang and Shen Zaiwang, were of special help, as was Chan Xingde, Nanning Party historian. Deng's role in the great Huai-Hai campaign of 1948–49 was analyzed by

Zhang Zhen, president of the National Defense University, and my old friend of the Long March, General Qin Xinghan, former director of the Revolutionary Military Museum, and his research chief, Yang Jingtong.

Great light on China's role in the Korean War was provided by historian Hakjoon Kim and other specialists in Seoul, General Qin, Yao Wei, and Soviet specialists.

Insight and information came from Paul Lin, onetime secretary to Zhou Enlai; the saintly Sister Huang Roushan of the Ching Ling leprosarium, deep in Guangxi; Drs. E. Grey Dimond, George Mc-Cormack, Peter Schrag, Wu Weiran, and Peter Gott; Walter Sullivan; Israel Epstein; John Melby, who saw Peking fall in 1949; William Hinton, who knows more of China's agriculture than the Chinese; Frank Coe, American economist long resident in Beijing; Sol Adler; the late Anna Louise Strong; John King Fairbank, who understood the role of China's emperors long before this writer came on the scene, and his prescient wife, Wilma; the long-suffering peasants of Willow Grove and Dazhai; An Wei of Xian; Yan Jiaqi and his brilliant wife, Guo Guo, whose understanding of the historical roots of Chinese conduct is without equal; Professor Zhang Zhi, Beijing's dynastic scholar, who first opened my eyes to the importance of Ssu-ma Ch'ien, *Shi Ji*, and *The General Mirror for the Aid of Government;* Chung-lu Tsen of Geneva, who illuminated the continuity of Chinese tradition and put Tiananmen into context; David Kidd, who knew Beijing when it was still Peking.

By chance I was present in Beijing and Tiananmen Square when the 1989 massacre occurred. This account has been augmented by the impressions of my companion, Yunichi Takeda of Japan's NHK television; William Hinton, also on the scene; Robin Munro, intrepid China Watch observer, who spent the night in the square; John Taylor, Australian businessman, who was trapped in the Minzu Hotel; Kyle Gibson, ABC correspondent who bravely broadcast heedless of bullets; and Doug Leiter, young Minnesotan, who spent almost twenty-four hours a day with the students. His unpublished Tiananmen narrative is the best I have seen. Liu Binyan and his wife, Zhu Hong, contributed to my interpretation. Yang Shangkun laid out the government view to me in January 1991. It was repeated ad nauseam by Yuan Mu, Li Peng's mouthpiece.

My friend and companion of the 1984 Long March, John S. Service, contributed his wisdom and knowledge to these pages, as has my wife,

Charlotte, who accompanied me on almost every expedition to China, except, thankfully, that which embraced Tiananmen.

I offer special thanks to Susan Levin, who has typed most of these pages, and to Deborah Jacobs, who has copyedited the manuscript with extraordinary skill and patience. To my editor, Roger Donald, cheers!

Source Notes

CHAPTER 1. THE OLD CAPITAL

1. Ke Fei came to a tragic death, either by her own hand or by murder. She may have been "suicided." She had rejected the advances of Emperor Qian Long, who had captured her in a battle in which he killed her husband. There are several versions of the story of her death. In one, it occurred at the winter solstice when Qian Long was absent, carrying out observances at the Temple of Heaven. Qian Long's mother, the dowager empress, was outraged by Ke Fei's rejection of her son. She called in Ke Fei and gave her an ultimatum — either submit to the emperor or kill herself. Ke Fei chose suicide. Another version has it that the dowager had Ke Fei strangled by two eunuchs (Arlington and Lewisohn, *In Search of Old Peking*, 94–104; *Nagel's China*, 522–523). A less romantic explanation of the Moslem quarter is that it was a compound built by Qian Long for his Moslem troops; the "mosque," in reality, was a tower where the Moslem officers lived (Dorn, *Forbidden City*). Ke Fei's name means Stranger Concubine. She was also called Xiang Fei, Fragrant Concubine.

2. By 1990 the Jade Fountain's flow had been reduced to a trickle. The water feeding the chain of lakes came from the Beijing municipal water system. No longer was it of the traditional purity. Residents of Zhongnanhai turned aside suggestions that they had ever bathed in the lakes. "They're no longer fit for swimming," they said (personal conversations, 1988).

3. General Zhang Zhen (president, National Defense University), personal interview, May 11, 1980, Beijing.

4. Liu Shaoqi, Zhu De, and Dong Biwu had set up headquarters at Xibaipo in April 1947. Mao, Zhou Enlai, and Ren Bishi went to nearby Chengnanzhuang in Hebei Province, where General Nie Rongzhen had his headquarters, in March 1948 and moved to Xibaipo two months later (Shi Zhe, personal interview, September 1988, Beijing). Mao's wife, Jiang Qing, who accompanied him to Xibaipo, said the date of their arrival was May 27, 1948 (Witke, *Comrade Chiang Ching*, 218).

5. Melby, *Mandate of Heaven*, 300.

6. Bodde, *Peking Diary*, 55.

7. General Qin Xinghan, personal communication, January 18, 1988.
   Lin Biao's north China force comprised the 3rd, 4th, 5th, 7th, and 11th columns of the North China Military Area.

8. General Qin Xinghan, personal communication, January 18, 1988.

9. Ibid.

10. Mariann Clubb, personal interview, August 25, 1988, New York.

11. Bodde, *Peking Diary,* 103.

12. Mariann Clubb, personal interview, August 23, 1988, New York.

13. George Hatem, American-born physician of Lebanese descent, who became a Chinese citizen and took the name of Ma Haide, entered Beijing with the Army General Headquarters staff. They came in by Qianmen Gate; Tiananmen was too cluttered. Half a dozen generals, including Marshal Ye Jianying, who had been named commandant of the city, took the salute from the Qianmen Gate tower. Hatem recalled that the troops were completely equipped with U.S. military supplies, weapons, uniforms, armor, helmets, jeeps. "We were every inch American," he said. Mao and the top leadership remained in the Fragrant Hills (George Hatem, personal interview, May 1, 1988, Beijing).

14. Bodde, *Peking Diary,* 175; *Zhongnanhai,* 18.

15. Soon after the Western Hills were captured, in mid-December, the Communist siege headquarters of Lin Biao were transferred to Songzhuang village, Tongxian County, just east of Beijing (General Qin Xinghan, personal communication, January 18, 1988).

16. Wang Chaoyiu, *Beijing dangshi baogao.*

17. Li Rui, foremost Mao scholar, believed these works played an enormous role in Mao's intellectual development. He also cited the ideas of Li Zhi, Wang Fuzhi, and Yan Yuan as important influences (Li Rui, personal interview, January 30, 1987, Beijing). Even on the Long March, the Red Army's six-thousand-mile retreat through China's backcountry, Mao was reading and studying *The Mirror* and discussing it with Xu Teli, his old teacher, who accompanied him on the march (Li Ruqing, *Xiang Jiang zhan yi*). Mao continued reading these dynastic works almost to the day he died. An excellent discussion of these works can be found in De Bary et al., *Sources of Chinese Tradition,* 231 et seq.

18. Zhu Zhongli, *Shan guan de hong ye,* 141–142; Zhu Zhongli, personal interview, January 29, 1991, Beijing.

19. Yan Changlin, *Jue zhan de rizi,* 231–236.

20. Ibid., 242–248.

21. Li Ruihuan, personal interview, May 1988, Tianjin.

22. Li Dazhao was executed in 1927 in Beijing by the Manchurian warlord Zhang Zuolin.

23. Zhou Shachen, *Beijing,* 122–123.

24. The *People's Daily* of March 26, 1949, reported Mao's arrival and the airport ceremony, naming Liu Shaoqi, Zhu De, Zhou Enlai, and Ren Bishi as being present.

25. Zhu Zhongli, *Shan guan de hong ye,* 146–147.

26. Li Yinqiao (Mao's chief bodyguard), *Hebei Daily,* May 20, 1988.

CHAPTER 2. THE POET OF THE FRAGRANT HILLS

1. Some Chinese historians and some survivors, among them Hu Qiaomu, long a secretary to Mao, recall no debate. To Hu Qiaomu, Beijing *was* the capital of

China. It had been the capital of the Mings and the Qings. With the overthrow of the Manchus, in 1912, the Republican government established itself in Beijing and set up headquarters in the imperial city (Hu Qiaomu, personal interview, May 21, 1988, Beijing). Professor Xiang Qing believed no serious consideration was given to Nanjing or any site but Beijing (Xiang Qing, letter to author, September 28, 1988). Professor Hu Hua, leading Party historian, was not so certain. He believed some of Mao's associates were not entirely pleased at setting up shop in the old imperial locale (Hu Hua, personal interview, October 1987, Beijing; Kidd, *Peking Story*, 198–199).

2. Among the warnings received by Stalin of the imminent Nazi attack on June 22, 1941, was, incredibly, one from Yanan. Precise details of the date, hour, and outline of the offensive had been obtained by Yan Baohang, a friend and associate of Zhou Enlai's, from a KMT officer; as an underground Communist, Yan had close ties to the KMT. The KMT officer, in turn, had gotten the information from the Japanese military. The warning was transmitted to Moscow on June 20, two days in advance of the attack, but, like all the others, was ignored by Stalin. Yanan received an acknowledgment of its message and an expression of appreciation sometime after the German attack from Vyacheslav M. Molotov, acting chairman of the Soviet Defense Committee. Unbeknownst to the Chinese, Stalin had fled the Kremlin and barricaded himself in his suburban villa about 8:00 A.M. on June 22. He did not return until about three weeks later, when he gradually assumed direction of the war.

   Yan Baohang was the father of Yan Mingfu, Mao's Russian interpreter, and died in Qincheng high-security prison on May 22, 1968, during the Cultural Revolution (Yan Mingfu, personal interviews, April 29 and May 6, 1988, Beijing).

3. Stalin referred to his 1946 warning to China not infrequently. However, few details of this early communication have been published, almost none from the Chinese side.

4. Nikita Khrushchev made several references in his memoirs to the fact that under the Yalta agreements the Soviet Union was obligated to turn over military materials seized in Manchuria to the Chinese (that is, the Chiang Kaishek) government. He claimed the Soviet military would assemble the war materials in convenient places where the Chinese Communists could seize them. In reality, most of the arms fell into KMT hands (*Khrushchev Remembers: The Last Testament*, 237–239).

5. Yan Mingfu, personal interview, April 29, 1988, Beijing.

6. Mao Tse-tung, *Selected Works*, vol. 4, 300–307.

7. Yang Shangkun, personal interview, November 8, 1984, Beijing.

8. Wang Fangmin, *People's Daily*, January 2, 1979.

9. Mikoyan made so many secret trips to China that it is no wonder witnesses are confused. Perhaps the most authoritative report about Stalin's 1948 warning not to cross the Yangtze is that of Liu Xiao, Chinese ambassador to Moscow between February 1955 and October 1967. Zhou Enlai briefed Liu before he took up his post in Moscow. He told him Mikoyan came to Xibaipo in May 1948 to convey Stalin's demand that the PLA not cross the Yangtze. Stalin, Zhou said, had opted for a two-Chinas, North-South-dynasty solution. Zhou cited this as an example of the Soviets' mistaken understanding of the world situation and of their fear of war with the United States and of jeopardizing the Yalta agreements (Liu Xiao, *Chu shi Sulian ba nian*). Mao's own version of the warning had long been accepted in Beijing until Shi Zhe, his Russian interpreter, offered a later date, saying Mikoyan came to the main Red Army base of Shijiazhuang on January

31, 1949, and left February 7. Shi Zhe said he met him at the airport and escorted him to Xibaipo. Mikoyan had conversations with Mao, Zhou Enlai, and Ren Bishi (then a Party secretary) every evening, Shi reported, often until midnight. But he insisted the purpose of the visit was to inform Moscow of Mao's plans for his government and not to deter Mao from crossing the Yangtze. The archives were said to support Shi Zhe (Xiang Qing, letter to author, September 8, 1988; Shi Zhe, personal interview, September 1988, Beijing). Shi Zhe's view was supported by diplomat Yu Zhen and Zhang Yuanyou, writing in *New China Diplomacy* in May 1990, a publication of the Foreign Office historical section, 15–21. Yu and Zhang asserted that Mao and other Chinese leaders had never talked about the 1948 or 1949 warning from Stalin. They claimed that in 1958 Mao had told Pavel Yudin, Soviet ambassador, that in 1945 Stalin wanted the Chinese Communists to make peace with Chiang Kaishek and form a coalition government. Mikoyan was present at the 1958 talk, at which Mao said that when Mikoyan had come to China he had lectured the Chinese "like a father lectures his children" — but Mao didn't mention a 1948–49 warning. The writers Yu and Zhang also said that Zhou Enlai, in a long résumé of Soviet-Chinese relations at a Beidaihe conference in 1960, covering relations from Lenin to Khrushchev, mentioned the 1945 warning by Stalin and also Mikoyan's visit to Xibaipo but said nothing of a later warning. They wrote that Stalin, in a meeting with Georgi Dimitrov, the Bulgarian Comintern representative, and a Yugoslav representative, on February 10, 1948, referred to his earlier warning to the Chinese. "I didn't think the Chinese could win," Stalin said. "So you can see I can also make mistakes." The authors noted that if Stalin admitted his earlier warning was incorrect in February 1948, it was not likely he had repeated it a few months later. Sergo Mikoyan, son of Anastas Mikoyan, believed after examining Mikoyan's archive that the Yangtze question was discussed (Sergo Mikoyan, personal interview, December 6, 1988, New York). Mao's chief bodyguard, Li Yinqiao, placed the Mikoyan visit at "the end of 1948." Mikoyan stayed about a week, and Mao dined with him twice. Mikoyan told Mao that when victory was attained China must send Moscow some cooks "to teach us how to make tasty Chinese food." Mao responded: "China's medicine and her cuisine are her two big contributions to the world" (Quan Yanchi, *Wei shi zhang tan Mao Zedong*). Lei Jieqiong, in 1948 a teacher at Yenching University and member of the Association for Promoting Democracy, was invited in December 1948 to go to Shijiazhuang and Xibaipo in a delegation of democratic representatives. They met with Mao at Xibaipo in January. Mao's remarks reflected the discussions with Mikoyan. According to Lei, Mao said that "some circles" were advocating the division of China into two parts, north of the Yangtze and south of the river. That would produce "a North and South dynasties situation." He said such a division would mean abandoning the Revolution, half finished, and giving Chiang Kaishek a chance to heal his wounds and to suddenly pounce on the country. Quoting a Chinese fable, he said, "Never take pity on snakelike scoundrels" (Zhong Wenxian, *Mao Zedong*). Party historian Hu Hua specifically said Mikoyan came to warn Mao not to cross the Yangtze (Hu Hua, personal interview, August 9, 1987, Beijing).

10. Malraux, *Anti-Memoirs*, 363.

11. Shi Zhe, personal interview, September 1988, Beijing.

12. In fact, Stuart, ignoring repeated instructions from George Marshall, then secretary of state, had engaged in a variety of unofficial efforts to bring about a compromise or coalition between the Communists and the Nationalists. To a certain extent the State Department turned a blind eye to Stuart's activities; to

a certain extent Stuart simply did not tell the department (or anyone) what he was doing. Zhou Enlai and the Communists were well aware of Stuart's activities and his undeviating efforts to bring an end to the civil war in China. It was in this context that Stuart's invitation to Beijing was extended. See Melby, *Mandate of Heaven,* for a detailed discussion of Stuart's activities. Melby was in the U.S. Embassy in Nanjing and, in general, sympathetic to Stuart's moves, although skeptical that they could succeed. Huang Hua, who first encountered Stuart as a student at Yenching, was sent by Zhou Enlai to Nanjing in late April 1948 as the Chinese Foreign Ministry representative and met with Stuart several times. In his version Stuart was trying to "strengthen Chiang Kaishek's regime through political tricks" (Huang Hua, *Beijing Review,* 32–35).

13. Lum, *Peking 1950–53,* 57–58.

14. Barnstone, ed. and trans., *Poems of Mao Tse-tung,* 128–129.

15. Mao Tze-Tung, *Poems,* 46–47.

16. The official version of Mao's life has long recorded that he came to Beijing in June 1949, taking up residence at that time in Zhongnanhai. Only a whisper of Mao's romantic attachment sifted through. The first official indication that Mao had spent more than seven months in his Fragrant Hills hideaway was a small card posted in his Villa of the Two Wells (now a museum) recording that Mao lived there from March to November 1949. Mao's lengthy absence from Beijing was confirmed by Zhu Zhongli, widow of Wang Jiaxiang. Both Zhu and Wang had been high-ranking Party members closely associated with Mao since the time of the Long March (Zhu Zhongli, personal interview, January 29, 1991, Beijing).

CHAPTER 3. "DON'T UNDERESTIMATE THAT LITTLE FELLOW"

1. Zhang Zhen, personal interview, May 11, 1988, Beijing.

2. *Khrushchev Remembers: The Last Testament,* 253.

3. Zhang Zhen, personal interview, May 11, 1988, Beijing.

4. Deng did not accomplish this single-handed, but he was the mainspring of the Central Front, secretary and director of the Command, which included himself, One-Eyed Liu Bocheng, and Chen Yi. The Front Command worked under the Communist Executive — Mao Zedong, Zhou Enlai, Zhu De, Liu Shaoqi (ultimately killed by Mao), Peng Dehuai (who suffered a similar fate), and General Yang Shangkun (incarcerated almost thirteen years by Mao). Mao set the main lines of the battle, and the generals translated them into units of force, timetables, and logistics, and passed them down to their lieutenants. The importance of Deng's role in the Command was well known and well established, but it was not until after his ascent to power and Mao's death that it began to be detailed in print. Earlier accounts consistently mentioned Liu Bocheng's role in the Second Communist Field Army, yet neglected that of Deng. This oversight was particularly noticeable in accounts by foreign correspondents who spent some time with the Second Army.

5. Quan Yanchi, *Wei shi zhang tan Mao Zedong.*

6. Harrison E. Salisbury, *Long March,* 121; Li Rui, personal interview, October 26, 1984, Beijing.

7. Quan Yanchi, *Wei shi zhang tan,* chap. 4.

The Soviet observer P. P. Vladimirov, who spent 1942–45 in Yanan, was convinced that Mao and Kang Sheng, his police chief, attempted to kill Wang Ming by medical mismanagement, compelling him to swallow quantities of decomposed calomel as a medicine for a stomach ailment. Moscow intervened with alarming inquiries about Wang Ming's health, and he gradually recovered. The mirror-image reports about Wang Ming reflect the mutual paranoia in Soviet-Chinese relations even at this early date (P. P. Vladimirov, *Osobii raion Kitai 1942–1945,* 103–211).

8. Mao Tse-tung, *Selected Military Writings,* 395.

9. Landman, *Profile of Red China,* 21.

10. When Mao and Stalin met in Moscow in December 1949, Stalin questioned him regarding the delay (as he saw it) in taking Shanghai. Why hadn't Mao called on the proletariat of Shanghai to rise up and take the city? Mao explained that the city had a population of millions and he did not want to take on the responsibility of feeding it. Later Stalin cited this to his Russian comrades as evidence that Mao was not a real Marxist and did not believe in the proletariat.

CHAPTER 4. THE SUNSHINE BOY

1. Li Rui, personal interview, October 26, 1984, Beijing.

2. *Hsin Wan Pao* (Hong Kong), Beijing dispatch, quoting Jilin Publishing House, Foreign Broadcast Information Service (Washington, D.C.), December 11, 1989, p. 25.

3. Li Rui, personal interview, October 24, 1984, Beijing.

4. Li Shenzhi (vice chairman, Academy of Social Sciences), personal interview, May 2, 1988, Beijing.

5. Quan Yanchi, *Wei shi zhang tan Mao Zedong,* chaps. 2, 6.

6. Notes of personal visit and interviews, April 1988, Guang'an.

7. Alley, "Guang'an," 8.

8. Personal observation, April 1988.

9. Dan died in the autumn of 1989.

10. Dan Yixing, Yang Erhe, personal interviews, April 8, 1988, Paifangcun.

11. The wooden boat from Guang'an was too small for sleeping. Deng and his uncle stopped at an inn at Hechuan the first night and at Beipei the second. At Chongqing passengers took a train-ferry for Shanghai (Chen Mingxian [Chinese Writers Association], letter to author, March 11, 1989). Madame Chen was born at Guang'an and took the trip as a child.

12. The program originated in 1912 as the Association for Frugal Study in France, under liberal sponsorship. It was supposed to inculcate knowledge of modern technology and industrious work habits. About fifteen hundred Chinese students went to France between 1918 and 1921, when the program came to an end. Deng, sixteen years old, was one of the youngest. His traveling expenses were paid by the head of the Chongqing Chamber of Commerce. Deng's arrival in France coincided with the postwar economic slump, which made jobs very scarce. There was great suffering among the Chinese students and even deaths from starvation. Soon some, including Mao's closest friend, Cai Hesen, challenged the whole philosophy of the movement and led public demonstrations, which French authorities met by closing down the program and deporting many agitators, including Cai. There is no record of Deng's participating in these political events (Bailey, "The Chinese Work Study Movement in France," 441–461).

13. Huang Hua, personal interview, March 18, 1984, Beijing.

14. In the 1920s, Yang Sen's base was Chengdu. However, he lost Chengdu in the battling among rival warlords and shifted to Chongqing, where he was active during World War II. He ultimately went to Taiwan and died there (John S. Service, telephone interview, January 12, 1991).

15. Interviews with Guang'an residents, April 1988.

16. Dan Yixing, personal interview, April 15, 1988, Paifangcun.

17. Notes of personal visit and interviews, April 1988, Guang'an.

18. The Huaying Mountain range lies just east of the river Qu, rising to an elevation of more than six thousand feet south of Guang'an, about twenty-three miles from the Deng residence. The guerrillas, sometimes acting as bandits, sometimes as Communists, maintained a foothold in the mountains for years. One of Deng Wenming's tasks was to protect the local well-to-do against guerrilla attacks. There was a legend in contemporary Guang'an that Deng's stepmother Xia Bogan once gave them some financial aid (interviews with Guang'an residents, April 1988).

19. Dan Yixing, personal interview, April 15, 1988, Paifangcun.

20. Perhaps that's why in 1988, when I met Uncle Dan, he immediately told me about the bad pains in his back and asked me if I couldn't send him some medicine for his backache — not from America, he cautioned, but from Beijing.

CHAPTER 5. INTO THE WILDERNESS

1. Lo Xuexiang (Donglan Party historian), personal interview, June 6, 1988, Donglan.

2. Zhang Chanyuan (governor of Guangxi), personal interview, June 9, 1988, Nanning.

3. Ya Meiyuan, personal interview, June 6, 1988, Donglan.

4. Ibid.

5. Chan Xingde (Nanning Party historian), personal interview, June 8, 1988, Nanning; Yan Jingtang (PLA historian), personal interview, October 1984, Beijing; Wu Xiuquan, personal interview, March 28, 1984, Beijing.

6. Huang Zhang, personal interview, June 8, 1988, Nanning.

7. Many facets of Deng's career in Guangxi are obscure, in part due to fragmentary records. The memories of veterans of his operations are not precise, and none of the officers and higher Party officials seems to have survived. In 1976 Deng composed a document of thirty thousand Chinese characters that he called *My Own Recollections*. The document has not been made public, nor is it generally accessible to historians. However, one Guangxi historian familiar with it said that Deng reported that before leaving Shanghai for Guangxi he was instructed to establish what was called the "Two Rivers Revolutionary Base," using the revolutionary peasants as its framework. Deng was designated Party secretary of the Front Committee and Party commissar. His instructions, he said, were to carry forward the agrarian revolution, consolidate the bases, recruit personnel, gather grain to feed the military group, and, if he was not able to hold out, to make his way to Jinggang Mountain and join Mao and Zhu De. When Deng Gong (no relation) came to the area to advise him of the new Party line and criticized him for carrying out a "rich peasant policy," Deng retorted that he was carrying out the line of Chairman Mao (Chan Xingde, personal interview, June 8, 1990, Nanning).

8. Given the complex politics of the Communist underground, it is perfectly possible that the "Bolsheviks" sent Deng to Ruijin, thinking they were infiltrating an ally into Mao territory. If this was what they supposed, they were quickly disillusioned. In another version Deng was assigned in Ruijin to a military school that was being organized in the summer of 1931. General Wu Xiuquan recalled finding Deng in command of one of the four companies of the school in late July 1931 (Wu Xiuquan, personal interview, March 28, 1984, Beijing).

9. Li Ruqing, *Xiang Jiang zhan yi,* Nanjing, 1989; Foreign Broadcast Information Service (Washington, D.C.), January 24, 1991.

   The plot was a figment of overheated imaginations. There had been an AB organization within the Nationalist ranks in the days of Nationalist-Communist collaboration. Some young students belonged to the ABs, but the group had no political consequence. When these students joined the Communists, they openly listed membership in the ABs in their Party bios. The idea of the plot may have been spread by clever Nationalist agents.

10. A man named Luo Ming, leader of adjacent Fujian Province, also came under attack. He lost his Party secretaryship, as did Deng, who was shunted into a menial job in the county propaganda department. By April 15, 1932, the anti-Deng campaign was in full cry. Mao Zetan, Mao's brother, and Xie Weijin, who had helped Deng stamp out the AB hysteria, were also targets. Both Mao Zetan and Xie Weijin were left behind when the Long March started — the practical equivalent of a death sentence.

11. In the winter of 1927 Deng had married Zhang Qianyuan. He was then twenty-three years old. She had worked in the Central Soviet Zone of Jiangxi and was transferred to Shanghai, where she and Deng met and married. She died eighteen months later, in labor. In 1932 Deng, aged twenty-eight, married Jin Weiyin, whose Party nickname was A Jin. She divorced Deng after a few months and married Lo Man. A Jin and Lo Man made the Long March to Yanan, where Lo Man divorced her. In poor health, she went to the Soviet Union in 1937 for treatment and disappeared. In 1987 the son of Lo Man and (probably) A Jin, Li Tieying, was named to the State Council in charge of education.

12. Harrison E. Salisbury, *Long March,* 141.

13. In later years Deng could not remember whether he attended the Zunyi meeting. Documents were confused. Yang Shangkun initiated an inquiry, which turned up personal notes by Chen Yun listing Deng as being present and representing the Red Army paper (ibid., 121, 306).

CHAPTER 6. THE STUDY OF CHRYSANTHEMUM FRAGRANCE

1. Bodde, *Peking Diary,* 213.

2. Liu Tingting, personal interview, October 8, 1990, New York.

3. David Kidd, Fulbright scholar resident in Beijing at the time and author of *Peking Story,* recalled the controversy (*Peking Story,* 198). So did Paul Lin, Canadian-born son of a Chinese missionary. He was in Beijing during this period, working as a junior secretary to Zhou Enlai. He recalled the argument as heated (Paul Lin, personal interview, April 29, 1988, Beijing).

4. Cui Lie, personal interview, September 1988, Beijing.

5. Li Rui, personal interview, May 23, 1988, Beijing.

6. Ross Terrill, author of a biography of Mao, says that this wing was once called the Small Palace of the Fragrant Concubine, but no record of this seems to exist.

7. One who knew Mao's bedchamber well commented on the room as now exhibited: "They have changed a lot. The [old] bed was twice as big. It almost filled the room. The furniture has been rearranged and new furniture brought in. It creates a very different atmosphere" (Li Rui, personal interview, October 10, 1986, Beijing).

8. Rewi Alley, personal interview, October 21, 1987, Beijing.

9. Rewi Alley, personal interview, January 21, 1987, Beijing; Li Rui, personal interview, June 17, 1988, Beijing.

10. Almost to the end of his life Mao was trying to learn English, taking lessons as he had off and on for twenty-five or thirty years. His first teacher had been Lin Ke, his English secretary. He never made too much progress, but in 1950 he engaged in a three-language conversation — Chinese-Russian-English — with his son Anying and Anying's wife, Liu Songlin. Anying expressed surprise: "I never heard you talk English before," he told his father (Zheng Yi, *Mao Zedong sheng huo shi lu 1946–1976*, 108). Beginning in the 1960s Mao took English lessons from Zhang Hanzhi, daughter of an old friend. In his final days he was said to have tried to take lessons from his second cousin, Wang Hairong, who had herself learned English (imperfectly) from Zhang Hanzhi.

11. This story may be apocryphal. Wang Hongshi, first vice chairman of Party archives, was in charge of Mao's books and wrote a book about his reading (Hu Hua, personal interview, August 31, 1987, Beijing). Zhang Raxin was in charge of the philosophy and sociology collection (Li Rui, personal interview, May 25, 1988, Beijing). Zhang Zhi, classics specialist at the Beijing National Library, thought it might have been Mao himself who suggested putting some Marx and Lenin on his shelves (Professor Zhang Zhi, personal interview, May 5, 1988, Beijing).

12. Zhu Zhongli, personal interview, January 22, 1991, Beijing.

13. Li Rui, personal interview, June 17, 1988, Beijing.

14. Siao-yu, *Mao Tse-tung and I Were Beggars,* 190–191.

15. For Mao's encounter with the young girl we have the detailed account of Siao-yu (ibid.). Mao took a negative view of Siao's reminiscences. Perhaps he found them too revealing. The story of the monk may be apocryphal, but it gained wide currency among ordinary Chinese, who delight in soothsaying. One version has the monk prostrating himself when Mao appeared at the head of his troops evacuating Yanan in 1947, then employing the nom de guerre of Li Desheng to conceal (lightly) his identity. Mao's biographer Li Rui pointed out that this version was implausible, since the Buddhist monks had left the temple in the early 1940s and it was later used to house a printing establishment (Li Rui, personal interview, June 17, 1988, Beijing). Moreover, Mao's retreat from Yanan did not take him to Qingliming. Of course, Mao had crossed the Yellow River near the monastery earlier, in fighting the Japanese. Liu Binyan said he had heard that Mao sent an inscription in his calligraphy to the temple. In another version Mao was said to have sent a contribution every year to the monks. Obviously, the story grew in the telling. Mao's nom de guerre means Sure of Victory. Zhou Enlai called himself Hu Bichang, Sure of Success.

16. Liu Tingting, personal interview, October 8, 1990, New York.

17. Sometimes secretaries and guards retrieved from Mao's wastebasket poems he had dashed off in his fine calligraphy, to catch a vagrant mood or thought, and then tossed aside. Not a few of these ephemeral jottings rest quietly and unknown in various private drawers (Li Rui, personal interview, June 17, 1988, Beijing). Li Zhisui, a physician attached to Zhongnanhai, believed Mao kept a personal record of his activities, including notations on his sexual experiences. Li considered Mao a sex maniac.

18. Hu Hua, personal interview, August 2, 1987, Beijing.

19. Li Rui, personal interview, October 20, 1987, Beijing.

20. The printing of the special large-character edition of the Annals for Mao was confirmed by Xu Heming, director of the Number 2 Xinhua printing house. At the same time the large-character edition of the Annals was printed for Mao, Xinhua also printed at his order a large-character edition of a three-volume

biography of Napoleon and a one-volume collection of Chinese jokes. What kind of jokes was not specified (Xu Heming, personal interview, May 1988, Beijing). According to Mao's daughter, Li Min, Mao paid for books printed specially for his use with funds from his own book royalties, which amounted to millions and were kept in a special account by an agency of the Central Committee (*Zhongguo Tongxunshe* [Hong Kong], February 10, 1989; Foreign Broadcast Information Service [Washington, D.C.], February 15, 1989, p. 20). At some point "late in life" Mao expressed regret that he had not been able to complete his reading of the Twenty-four Annals (Li Shenzhi, personal interview, May 2, 1988, Beijing).

CHAPTER 7. THE GATE OF HEAVENLY PEACE

1. The terrace and lounge in 1988 were opened to visitors for a fee of 10 yuan (about $3), payable only in foreign exchange certificates, effectively limiting visitors almost entirely to foreigners. In 1988 the gate revenues totaled about 500,000 yuan. Ticket holders, carefully watched by plainclothesmen, could view the strollers in Tiananmen Square, drink tea, spoon ice cream, buy Tiananmen T-shirts, and imagine Mao standing precisely where they stood, taking the salute of a million hysterical Red Guards. The tourists could loiter on the terrace through late afternoon and early evening as a tape deck softly played China's favorite golden oldies, watching the crowds and, on holidays, firework displays. Refreshments were supplied by the adjacent Beijing Hotel (personal observation, May 1, 1988). In the spring of 1989, as the students took over Tiananmen Square, the terrace was closed to visitors and remained closed, except to special groups of tourists, during the ensuing long period of martial law.

2. Kidd, *Peking Story,* 68.

3. Ibid., 61–63.

4. Mao Tse-tung, *Selected Works,* vol. 5, 19–20.

5. Li Rui, personal interview, June 13, 1988, Beijing.

6. Zhang Zhen, personal interview, May 21, 1988, Beijing.

7. Ibid.

8. A rage for pool and billiards swept China in 1988, possibly stemming from Deng's love of billiards. It even drew official denunciation in the Party press.

9. Deng switched to bridge not long after 1949, when he was in charge of Chongqing. Like many Chinese, he loved cards, and he encouraged others to play. Bridge became such an addiction among Chinese college students in the late 1970s and early 1980s that many played from morning to midnight, ignoring their studies. Newspapers began to carry bridge news, including Jacoby's syndicated column. Well into his eighties, Deng played bridge until 1:00 or 2:00 A.M. "I don't like to work too hard," he said. "Two hours of work is enough for a day." In February 1989, at the age of eighty-four, Deng received the golden honorary medal of the World Bridge Federation for his contribution to the game (*China Daily,* February 27, 1989). In 1990 he was still playing excellent bridge and complaining about the death of some of his former partners (Kathrine Wei, personal interview, July 18, 1990, New York).

10. *China Pictorial,* December 1986, p. 6.

11. *China Pictorial,* December 1980, p. 6.

12. Deng took to mentioning this to foreign visitors, and the Chinese press published stories about his excellent health. They also described President Yang Shangkun on his ceremonial visits to foreign countries as displaying great energy and endurance. Probably this meant that rumors to the opposite effect were being circulated.

13. Rewi Alley, personal interview, October 21, 1987, Beijing.

14. Kidd, *Peking Story,* 70–73.

15. Yao Wei, personal interview, June 1972, Yanan.

CHAPTER 8. A MISSING FACE

1. Perhaps the scene was not quite so romantic. Ross Terrill, in *The White-Boned Demon,* says that Mao and Jiang Qing left Yanan crammed into a captured U.S. jeep with two bodyguards (177). However, Jiang described to Roxane Witke (the scholar who interviewed her in 1972) traveling by horseback on this expedition.

2. Harrison E. Salisbury, *Long March,* 42–43.

3. Witke, *Comrade Chiang Ching,* 224–225.

4. Ibid., 225–326; Mao Tse-tung, *Selected Works,* vol. 4, 401–402.

5. Quan Yanchi, *Wei shi zhang tan Mao Zedong,* chap. 6.

6. Ibid.

7. Ibid.

8. Li Rui, personal interview, October 10, 1987, Beijing.
   Zhu Zhongli, wife of Wang Jiaxiang, Mao's trusted representative to Moscow in that time, was close to both Mao and Jiang Qing and dated the rift between the two to 1942, when they had a violent quarrel in Yanan. Zhu and her husband tried to effect a reconciliation between Mao and his wife but failed. Mao in 1942 was refusing to live with Jiang because she had contracted tuberculosis. He made her stay in another cave. Zhu's recollection in 1991 was that Mao opposed Jiang's going to Moscow but that Jiang insisted on it (Zhu Zhongli, personal interview, January 28, 1991, Beijing).

9. Rewi Alley, personal interview, November 1987, Beijing.

10. Ibid.

11. Helen Snow, telephone interview, March 1988; Terrill, *White-Boned Demon,* 44–49.

12. Wang Fushih, the original translator of *Red Star over China* and publisher of the first abbreviated Chinese edition of the book, estimated that nearly three thousand young people made their way to Yanan in 1937. The first Chinese translation was published in March 1937 (report at Edgar Snow symposium, Beijing, 1988).

13. Liu Ying, personal interview, June 6, 1984, Beijing.

14. Salisbury, *Long March,* 174.

15. Details about He Zizhen from ibid. and from subsequent interviews with Liu Ying (June 6, 1984, Beijing) and Jian Xianren, He Long's widow (October 1988, Beijing).

16. Helen Snow, *Inside Red China,* and personal telephone interviews, 1987 and 1988; Terrill, *White-Boned Demon;* Li Rui, personal interviews, May and June 1988, Beijing; Hu Hua, personal interviews, June 1984 and September 1988, Beijing.

17. Jian Xianren, personal interview, October 1988, Beijing.

18. Edgar Snow, *Red Star over China,* 472.

19. Jian Xianren, personal interview, October 1988, Beijing.

CHAPTER 9. SATURDAY NIGHT DANCES

1. Quan Yanchi, *Wei shi zhang tan Mao Zedong,* chap. 10.

2. Cui Lie, personal interview, March 10, 1989, Beijing.

3. A bodyguard once asked Mao for a raise. Mao said he'd pay it from his special

royalty account for his books. The guard asked, "What about the future?" (He didn't dare say "What happens when you die?") Mao replied that he didn't know how to give the guard a raise; the money would have to come from Mao's bank account (Quan Yanchi, *Wei shi zhang tan,* chap. 5).

4. Notes of visits to Zhongnanhai, November 1987, April and June 1988.

5. Cui Lie, personal interview, June 1988, Beijing; Li Rui, personal interview, June 15, 1988, Beijing.

6. Kates, *Years That Were Fat,* 176–177.

7. Arlington and Lewisohn, *In Search of Old Peking,* 100.

8. Kates, *Years That Were Fat,* 186–187.

9. Mao Zedong's speech of September 11, 1950, to Enlarged Session, Military Affairs Committee, quoted by Schram, *Chairman Mao Speaks to the People,* 154–155.

10. Li Rui, personal interview, May 25, 1988, Beijing.

11. Visit by author to Taiyuan, May 10, 1988.

12. Personal observation, January 29, 1991.

13. Mei Yan, personal interview, April 23, 1990, New York.

14. Kidd, *Peking Story,* and personal interview, April 10, 1990, New York.

15. Visit by author, 1985.

16. Charlotte Y. Salisbury, *China Diary,* 118.

17. Witke, *Comrade Chiang Ching,* citing Yan Changlin, *Great Turning Point* (Beijing, 1962), 92–93.

18. Cai Hesen was captured and executed on direct orders from Chiang Kaishek in 1927. His sister, Cai Chang, lived on in Zhongnanhai until her death, in 1990. Despite Mao's closeness to her during their youth, he had little to do with her after the early years of the People's Republic and did not protect her from harassment during the Cultural Revolution.

19. Harrison E. Salisbury, *Long March,* 85–86.

20. Ibid., 85.

21. Quan Yanchi, *Wei shi zhang tan,* 351.

22. Li Rui, personal interview, June 17, 1988, Beijing.

23. Li Rui, personal interview, June 13, 1988, Beijing.

24. Ibid.

25. Quan Yanchi, *Wei shi zhang tan,* chap. 3.

CHAPTER 10. MAO'S FEUD WITH STALIN

1. Stalin's naming of Roshchin as ambassador to the new Chinese government was a deliberate affront. When Roshchin's name was presented to Zhou Enlai, his face fell. He excused himself and hurried to Mao's office. He returned after fifteen minutes and said China would accept Roshchin. Mao and Zhou both knew Roshchin well as Soviet military representative to Chiang Kaishek during World War II in Chongqing and knew he was a high-ranking intelligence officer in the Soviet military apparatus (Tikhvinsky, "Kitai v moei zhizn" [April 1990]: 103–112).

2. Ibid.

3. Orlov, *Secret History of Stalin's Crimes,* 344–345; Scholmer, *Vorkuta,* 134; Korovyakovsky, *Kitaitsy — Zhertvy Stalinskikh repressii,* 142–145.

4. Edgar Snow, *Random Notes from Red China,* 1–5.

5. Not until 1972 was the episode of the proposed visit of Mao and Zhou Enlai pieced together in a magnificent bit of historical detective work by historian Barbara Tuchman. Roosevelt got only distorted versions of the proposal, which was deep-sixed by the State Department. Neither the public nor Vice President Harry Truman ever heard of it. Almost the same thing happened to a communication from Ho Chi Minh to Truman. Ho had worked closely with American intelligence officers in the Office of Strategic Services in the Indochinese underground against Japan. With the liberation of Indochina, Ho came to power in Hanoi. Through his American friends he sent a letter to Truman proposing that he come to Washington and negotiate a relationship with the United States similar to that of the Philippines and the United States (the Philippines had not yet won full independence). Ho's communication was intercepted by State Department officials dedicated to restoration of French rule in Indochina, and Truman never heard of it (Tuchman, "If Mao Had Come to Washington").

6. The text of Stalin's telegram to the Chinese Central Committee (published here for the first time) was as follows: "No civil war should be waged in China. If civil war breaks out in China it will bring the danger of complete ruin to the Chinese nation. Mao Zedong should go to Chongqing for peace talks." It was signed "Stalin, August 22, 1945." Chiang had invited Mao to come to Chongqing on August 14. The official Japanese surrender was announced August 15. Chiang sent a second telegram on August 20, urging Mao to come. The Stalin telegram came on August 22, and on August 23 the Politburo approved in principle Mao's engaging in talks with Chiang. A third invitation arrived from Chiang on August 23. On August 28, Mao left Yanan for Chongqing in the company of U.S. Ambassador Patrick Hurley (Central Archives, Communist Party of China).

7. The book was published under various titles, among them *Dawn over China* and *Tomorrow's China*.

8. Anna Louise Strong, letter to author, August 4, 1956.

9. Harrison E. Salisbury, *American in Russia*, 24–30.

10. Anna Louise Strong, letter to author, August 4, 1956.

11. Shi Zhe, personal communication, November 1988; Cui Lie, personal interview, November 1988, Beijing.

12. Much of this detail comes from Shi Zhe, Mao's Russian secretary and interpreter (personal interview, June 1, 1988, Beijing). Moscow, like much of the world, had mistakenly supposed that Mao's abandonment of Yanan reflected Communist weakness. In fact, it was an integral part of Mao's diversionary, guerrilla-style strategy, which was designed to defeat Chiang by rejecting positional warfare in favor of sudden massing of mobile forces to confront Chiang's dispersed troops serially with surprise attacks by overwhelming numbers.

13. Shijiazhuang had been captured on November 12, 1947 (Cui Lie, personal interview, November 1988, Beijing).

14. Yan Mingfu, personal interview, April 23, 1988, Beijing; Dedijer, *Tito*, 322.

15. Mao suspected his poor relations with the Kremlin might have been caused by a secret clause in the Yalta agreements that the Russians refused to discuss (Yan Mingfu, personal interview, April 23, 1988). Stalin had demanded an agreement with Chiang Kaishek in 1944 recognizing Mongolia as part of the Soviet sphere. Chiang repudiated this agreement in 1946. Mao refused to acknowledge it. The matter was still in dispute in 1988. Mao may have suspected that the Big Three — Stalin, FDR, and Winston Churchill — had given Stalin something of a free hand in China or even that the three had agreed to back Chiang Kaishek against Mao. Moscow, in the recollection of General Yang Shangkun, never briefed China on

the Yalta agreements. The Chinese did not know what arrangements they contained (Yang Shangkun, personal interview, November 3, 1984, Beijing).

16. Harrison E. Salisbury, "How America and Russia Lost China."

17. Yan Mingfu, personal interview, April 23, 1988, Beijing.

18. But in 1955, when China first announced its charges against Gao Gang, editors of Moscow's *Bolshaya Sovetskaya Entsiklopediya* ordered subscribers to remove an adulatory biography of Gao Gang from volume 10 and mailed them a substitute page. Moscow was then following the official Beijing line on Gao Gang. When Moscow and Beijing began trading polemics after 1959, the Russians made plain their close relationship with Gao Gang. It is probable that Mao was personally sensitive to the Gao Gang affair. His secretaries believed that Gao Gang had been his favorite among the Party leaders and that his paranoia about and distrust of the Russians were probably increased when he learned of Gao's betrayal (Li Rui, personal interview, June 17, 1988, Beijing).

CHAPTER 11. STALIN'S BIRTHDAY PARTY

1. Fedorenko later became ambassador to Japan and to the United Nations.

2. Tikhvinsky, "Kitai v moei zhizn" (April 1990): 104.

3. Nikolai Fedorenko, personal interview, April 21, 1990, Moscow; Fedorenko, "Stalin i Mao," 150.

4. Shi Zhe had studied at Kiev and in Moscow, at the University for the Toilers of the East. In 1933 he married a Russian woman, by whom he had two children. He left them behind when he returned to China. For reasons that he did not disclose, he was later removed from duties as a Russian interpreter and from Russian affairs and sent to Shandong as Party secretary.

   When interviewed in 1988 at the age of eighty-five, Shi Zhe had to be assisted into an armchair. His mind remained clear, but his recollection of details was not always correct. Shi Zhe spent thirteen years in prison during the Cultural Revolution as a "Russian spy" (Shi Zhe, personal interview, June 1, 1988, Beijing).

   Mao had a second interpreter of Russian, a young woman named Sun Weishi, a protégée and adopted daughter of Zhou Enlai's. She had accompanied Zhou and his wife when they flew to Moscow in 1939 for medical treatment. She stayed on in Moscow during the war, returning to Yanan in 1945. Later she became an actress and director of the Beijing Youth Theater (Yan Jiaqi, *Wenge shi nian shi,* 79).

5. Yan Mingfu, personal interview, April 29, 1988, Beijing; Cui Lie, letter to author, March 10, 1989; Shi Zhe, "Seprovozhe Predsetatelye Mao," 142.

6. Shi Zhe, "Mao Zedong tong zhi chu fang Sulian," Beijing Radio, January 16, 1989; Foreign Broadcast Information Service (Washington, D.C.), January 26, 1989, p. 9.

7. Stalin may have sampled the kumquats. He was quoted as calling them "the king of oranges" (Yan Mingfu, personal interview, April 29, 1988, Beijing).

8. Shi Zhe, personal interview, June 1, 1988, Beijing.

9. Shi Zhe, "Mao Zedong tong zhi chu fang Sulian."

10. Ibid.

11. Fedorenko, "Stalin i Mao," 151–152.

12. Years later Shi Zhe confessed he had seen *The Red Poppy* a couple of times previously and had not noticed anything offensive. Now, he affirmed, he was as offended as Chairman Mao. He must have dozed through the earlier perfor-

mances. Or perhaps the sense of offense stemmed from Mao's response (Shi Zhe, personal interview, June 1, 1988, Beijing).

13. Ibid.

14. Yan Mingfu, personal interview, May 6, 1988, Beijing.

15. *Khrushchev Remembers,* 463, 465.

16. Shi Zhe, personal interview, June 1, 1988, Beijing.

17. Possibly because he grew up in the sultry south, Mao was like a child when it snowed. His guards learned not to sweep his Zhongnanhai courtyard after a snowfall. He once flew at a guard whom he found sweeping a courtyard for the second time. "No, no," he cried. "Don't sweep it again. The snow's wounds have hardly healed." Mao wrote one of his most famous poems about snow in the Beijing spring. He loved to walk in the snow and hear it crunch under his feet. His habit was to interrupt his work at intervals for a ten-minute walk in the fresh air. His guards learned to let the ten minutes extend to double that when there was snow on the ground. Marshal Chen Yi understood Mao's passion for snow. He kept his Zhongnanhai courtyard unswept too (Quan Yanchi, *Wei shi zhang tan Mao Zedong,* chap. 5). Young people at Zhongnanhai skated on the lakes in winter but not many elders. Mao never tried it, probably thinking it below his dignity.

18. Shi Zhe, personal interview, June 1, 1988, Beijing.

19. Ibid.

20. Shi Zhe was apparently confused as to which dacha Mao occupied. He called it Dalny, "far away." But Stalin's daughter, Svetlana Alliluyeva, remembered that Mao stayed at the Kuntsevo dacha, which Stalin remodeled for Mao's use, adding a second story to the conventional one-story Russian country bungalow (Svetlana Alliluyeva Peters, telephone conversation, March 10, 1989).

21. Shi Zhe, personal interview, June 1, 1988, Beijing.

22. In return for the uranium deposits, the Russians gave the Chinese the large store of arms and ammunition that they had piled up in Xinjiang. This was not mentioned in the communiqué.

A picture was published of the signing ceremony. It showed Zhou and Foreign Minister Andrei Vishinsky signing the documents with Mao and Stalin looking on. Three years later, at the time of Stalin's death, March 5, 1953, the photograph was republished in Moscow in retouched form to make it appear that three men looked on: Mao, Stalin, and Georgi Malenkov, Stalin's would-be heir. All the others, Chinese and Soviet, were neatly airbrushed out. Despite the symbolism of the retouched photograph, Malenkov was quickly ousted as Soviet Party secretary and his place taken by Nikita S. Khrushchev, who did not appear in the original photograph. A Chinese witness of the signing noted that Stalin, who was considerably shorter than Mao, deliberately took a pace forward when the photo was taken, thus changing the perspective and making himself look taller (Shi Zhe, "Mao Zedong tong zhi chu fang Sulian").

23. Ibid.

24. On the evening of the sixteenth, their last night in Moscow, Stalin gave a small banquet at the Kremlin for his departing guests. Ho Chi Minh was present and, after the Sino-Soviet toasts, got up and proposed that since Stalin had just signed a treaty with Beijing, he should sign one with North Vietnam as well. Stalin said he couldn't do that because Ho was in Moscow on a secret mission. Ho persisted, suggesting that Stalin put him in a helicopter, fly him around Moscow, then land officially at Moscow Airport with a fanfare of publicity. "Oh, you Orientals!"

Stalin replied. "You have such rich imaginations" (Wu Xiuquan, *New China Diplomacy,* 153).

25. Fedorenko, "Stalin i Mao," 54–55.

CHAPTER 12. THE TRIPLE CROSS

1. Quan Yanchi, *Wei shi zhang tan Mao Zedong,* 2.
2. Li Rui, personal interview, May 25, 1980, Beijing.
3. Ibid.
4. Quan Yanchi, *Wei shi zhang tan,* chaps. 3, 4, 6.
5. Edgar Snow, *Red Star over China,* 146–147.
6. Notes of visit to Nanning, June 1988.
7. Li Rui, *Beijing Review,* May 7, 1984, p. 28.
8. Quan Yanchi, *Wei shi zhang tan,* chap. 6.
9. Yang Shangkun, personal interview, June 1988, Beijing.
10. Reference News Service, now published in both Chinese and English, is still going strong. The circulation has swollen to five or six million. Each day's bulletin comprises dozens of pages. It still follows Mao's rule: no editing of original transmissions. The man who actually set up Reference News Service and oversaw its production for years was General Yang Shangkun.
11. Li Rui, personal interview, October 19, 1987, Beijing.
12. Georgi Arbatov, director of the USSR's Institute for the USA and Canada, told a meeting of historians in Moscow in autumn 1990 that Stalin opposed Kim Il-sung's invasion plans but was compelled to go along when Mao Zedong approved the project. The reverse appears to be true (Stephen E. Ambrose, *New York Times,* December 27, 1990).
13. Stalin probably mentioned to Mao that Kim Il-sung hoped to reunite the Koreas by military means but put no stress on this. Yan Mingfu said "we were informed" of Kim Il-sung's intentions, although Beijing received no advance warning of the date (Yan Mingfu, personal interview, April 29, 1988, Beijing). In January 1950, Kim asked China to repatriate Korean nationals then serving in the Chinese Army. Some fourteen thousand were combed out and sent back to North Korea in January and February 1950 (when Mao was still in Moscow negotiating with Stalin). A last batch went home in April 1950. These men were placed in North Korea's Fifth, Sixth, and Seventh divisions and totaled nearly half of Korea's first-line forces (Kim, "International Trends in Korean War Studies," 342–344). At this time China was rigorously repatriating all foreign nationals, especially White Russian emigrés long resident in Shanghai, Harbin, and Shenyang.
14. Kim Il-sung passed through Beijing on his way back from Moscow after getting Stalin's approval for the attack. He gave the Chinese no indication that anything was brewing. Citing unnamed informants, the writers Hao Yufan and Zhai Zhihai reported that neither Stalin nor Kim informed China of what impended. Marshal Nie Rongzhen estimated that 1.4 million PLA men had been ordered demobilized on May 20, 1949. Demobilization was under way when war broke out. The bulk of the PLA not earmarked for Taiwan and Tibet had been assigned to agriculture (Hao Yufan and Zhai Zhihai, "China's Decision to Enter the Korean War," 94–99).
15. *Khrushchev Remembers,* 367–373.
16. Vorontsov, "Mikhail Borodin," 112–114.
17. Slavinsky, "Koreiskaya Voina 1950–1953 gg," 80–90.

18. Support for the theory that Mao was cut out of the information chain comes from Li Sang Cho, deputy chief of staff of the North Korean forces, who became Pyongyang's ambassador to Moscow and later was a political refugee in Moscow. He said the plan was devised by Kim Il-sung and approved by Moscow. He made no mention of Mao (quoted by Soviet scholar Mikhail G. Nosov at Korean War symposium, Seoul, September 12, 1990). Khrushchev revealed that the Soviet general staff assisted the Koreans in planning the attack. He blamed Stalin's parsimony for Kim Il-sung's failure: Tanks for one more armored corps would have ensured Kim's success, Khrushchev thought (*Khrushchev Remembers: The Glasnost Tapes*, 145–146). The initial North Korean assault was carried out by seven North Korean divisions and the 145th Armored Brigade, attacking at 4:00 A.M. on June 25 (*Moscow News*, July 15–July 22, 1990). A meeting of historians in Seoul in 1990 concluded that the Russians deployed protective forces and anti-aircraft units in adjacent Soviet areas north of Korea.

19. Andrei Gromyko adds a bizarre twist to the Korean affair. He reports that on Sunday, June 25, Stalin telephoned to ask what the Soviet Foreign Office proposed to do at a meeting of the United Nations Security Council on Korea the next day. Gromyko replied that it intended to bar any action with a veto. Stalin said he did not want the Soviet Union to participate in the meeting. Gromyko warned Stalin that in the absence of the Soviet delegate, the United States would cause the UN to intervene and send American and other forces to Korea. Stalin held to his position. The Soviet Union was not represented at the meeting, and UN intervention was assured (Gromyko, *Memoirs*, 102). Gromyko did not interpret Stalin's motive, but if Stalin had wanted to ensure U.S. involvement in what he calculated would be an American military disaster, this was the way to do it.

20. Kim, "International Trends," 363.

21. Qin Xinghan, personal communication, April 11, 1991.

22. The order setting up the Northeast Border Command was issued by the Central Military Committee on July 13 (Chai Chengwen, Beijing Radio, February 7, 1989). Hao Yufan and Zhai Zhihai give the date as July 7, 1950, citing *Major Events of the Chinese People's Liberation Army*, Beijing, 1985. The 13th Army Group comprised the 35th, 38th, 40th, and 42nd armies; the 1st, 2nd, and 8th artillery divisions; and one antiaircraft and one engineering division. It began movement from Henan, Guangdong, Guangxi, Hunan, and Heilongjiang provinces, where the units had been stationed, toward the northeast border area fairly rapidly (Qin Xinghan, personal communication, April 11, 1991). Nie Rongzhen, chief of staff at the time, stated that Deng Hua was alerted to prepare to go to the border area "in July." All preparations for action were to be completed in the month of August, whereafter he was to await orders. Nie Rongzhen confirmed these instructions on August 6. On August 18 Nie sent another telegram, telling Deng Hua to complete all preparations by the end of September (Nie Rongzhen, *Hui yi lu*, 733). This suggests that Chinese deployment was slower than had been presumed.

23. Details of Chai Chengwen's meeting with Zhou come from *Qiaobao* (*China Press*), New York, August 24, 1990, article signed with the nom de plume "Wenhuishi," probably a version of Chai's own report from the Foreign Ministry archives. The North Korean ambassador to Beijing, Lee Joo-Yun, had presented his credentials to Liu Shaoqi on January 28, 1950 (Kim, "International Trends," 350–351).

24. Some detail is from Russell Spurr, *Enter the Dragon*, 47–69. However, Spurr's informant seems to have confused the August 6 meeting with the later conference of October 1–4, which is described by Hao Yufan and Zhai Zhihai ("China's

Decision"), *Qiaobao's* "Wenhuishi," and in Peng's own account (*Memoirs of a Marshal*, 472–473), which does not mention the August 6 meeting.

25. Li Rui, personal interview, October 20, 1987, Beijing.
26. Chai Chengwen and Zhang Yangtian, *Ban men dian tan pan.*
27. Wenhuishi, "Daozhi Zhongguo xiang chaoxian pai zhi yuan jun shijian ji shi."
28. Yusov, "Kto napravil Kitaiski dobrovoltsev," 108–111.
29. Hao Yufan and Zhai Zhihai, "China's Decision," 94–115.
30. Nie Rongzhen, *Hui yi lu,* 717.
31. Yusov, "Kto napravil."
32. Ibid.
33. Peng, *Memoirs.*
34. Nie Rongzhen, *Hui yi lu.*
35. The theory that the Korean War was directed by Stalin and that its target victim was primarily China, not the United States, was spelled out by this writer in a book called *War Between Russia and China* in 1969. Premier Zhou Enlai ordered the book translated into Chinese and published in an internal edition that was compulsory reading for Foreign Ministry personnel. The book became the object of a dispute between the Soviet and Chinese delegates at diplomatic talks in the early 1970s when the Soviets accused the Chinese of stirring up propaganda against them. The Chinese said they had nothing to do with the book; the author had not been to China nor talked to Chinese officials. Somewhat later I mentioned to a Soviet diplomat that I had heard of the row in Beijing. "There you are!" he said. "We agreed not to say one word about what went on in the conference room. Now the Chinese have again broken their word. You can't trust the Chinese about anything."
36. Most of the above from Yusov, "Kto napravil."
37. Ibid.
38. Wenhuishi, "Daozhi Zhongguo."
39. Yusov, "Kto napravil."
40. Wenhuishi, "Daozhi Zhongguo."
41. Hao Yufan and Zhai Zhihai, "China's Decision."
42. Spurr, *Enter the Dragon,* 116–119.

CHAPTER 13. A LOVELY DAY IN NOVEMBER

1. Spurr, *Enter the Dragon,* 118.
2. Harrison E. Salisbury, *Long March,* 361.
3. Zhong Wenxian, *Mao Zedong,* 222.
4. Ibid., 233.
5. Salisbury, *Long March,* 361.
6. Quan Yanchi, *Wei shi zhang tan Mao Zedong,* chap. 10; Zhong Wenxian, *Mao Zedong,* 231, 236; Liu Songlin, *China Daily,* December 28, 1988.
7. Quan Yanchi, *Wei shi zhang tan,* chap. 10.
8. Zheng Yi, *Mao Zedong sheng huo shi lu,* 116–119.
9. Quan Yanchi, *Wei shi zhang tan,* chap. 10.
10. Ibid.
11. Ibid.
12. Liu Songlin, *China Daily,* December 20, 1988.

13. Zhong Wenxian, *Mao Zedong*, 230.

14. Songlin went to Moscow to study after Anying's death. Mao urged her to remarry, but she refused. When she returned from the Soviet Union in 1957, Mao renewed his persuasion, introducing her to two possible suiters, whom she refused. Finally she fell in love with Yang Maozhi, a thirty-one-year-old air force officer, just back from study in the Soviet Union. They married in 1962. In 1988 Yang was a major general and deputy chief of research in the Air Force Institute. Mao presented them with a congratulatory poem and 300 yuan on their wedding day, saying: "I have never gone shopping and I don't know what to buy. You'd better buy yourselves a gift with this money." In 1972 the couple was arrested in Shanghai and spent ten months in prison because they had expressed public disapproval of Jiang Qing's conduct. Songlin wrote Mao four times, but all her letters were intercepted, and he knew nothing of the case (Liu Songlin, *China Daily*, November 26, 1988).

15. Speaking to the Lushan conference on July 23, 1959, Mao said he had suffered "one son killed [Anying] and one son went mad [Anqing]" (Schram, *Chairman Mao Speaks to the People*, 143).

16. Spurr, *Enter the Dragon*, 314.

CHAPTER 14. DENG TACKLES HIS BIGGEST JOB

1. Deng's failure to return to his birthplace may not be as curious as it sounds. Mao Zedong did not return to Shaoshan for thirty-two years. Yang Shangkun did not go back to his home county for sixty-two years.

2. Central Committee, CPC, *Deng Xiaoping*, 49.

3. Ibid.

4. It was in the course of retracing in 1984 the route of the Red Army's Long March through China's backcountry that the author first saw and learned about the enormous installations of the Third Line. Many were still operating in their original mountain and valley sites. To this day knowledge of the Third Line and its vast proportions is virtually nil inside and outside of China.

5. Barry Naughton, "Third Line," 351–385.

6. Ibid., 351–363.

7. *China Daily*, October 20, 1988.

8. Wang Denglin, *Liang Shuming he Mao Zedong*, 15–16.

9. Cui Lie, personal communication, April 1990.

10. The death of Xia Bogan, on November 17, 1990, was reported by the Hong Kong press. Xia Bogan's grandson Deng Pufang said that the report was false and that she was alive and well (Deng Pufang, personal interview, January 30, 1990, Beijing).

11. Central Committee, CPC, *Deng Xiaoping*, 50.

12. Edgar Snow, *Red China Today*.

13. Garside, *Coming Alive*, 307.

14. There was general agreement among Mao, Liu Shaoqi, Zhou Enlai, and many others that national capitalism would last at least fifteen years. But, as it developed, the concept was abandoned after two or three years (Li Rui, personal interview, October 30, 1987, Beijing).

15. Rong Yiren, personal interview, August 31, 1987, Beijing.

16. Li Shenzhi, personal interview, June 1988, Beijing.

17. Li Rui, personal interview, May 25, 1988, Beijing.

CHAPTER 15. MAO ZEDONG TESTS DENG XIAOPING

1. Zhang Yufeng, "Mao Zedong yu Zhou Enlai de yixie wan nian qu shi," December 26, 1988.
2. Li Rui, personal interview, April 17, 1988, Beijing.
3. Li Rui, personal interview, October 10, 1987, Beijing.
4. Shi Zhe (Mao's principal Russian translator), personal communication via Cui Lie, September 28, 1988.
5. Personal inspection of Zhongnanhai, June 19, 1988.
6. Yan Mingfu, personal interview, April 23, 1988, Beijing.
7. Ibid.
8. Li Rui, personal interview, October 18, 1987, Beijing.
9. Goldman, "Vengeance in China," 8; Mirsky, "Empire Strikes Back," 21; Deng Xiaoping, speech of February 29, 1980, to the Fifth Plenary of the Eleventh Central Committee.
10. Liu Binyan, personal interview, April 1990, Cambridge, Mass.; Mirsky, "Empire Strikes Back," 21.
11. Hu Hua, personal interview, September 1987, Beijing.
12. Deng Xiaoping, *Selected Works,* vol. 1, 228–229.
13. Yan Mingfu, personal interview, April 23, 1988, Beijing.
14. Among the lower-ranking officials with whom Mao met in the preliminary consultations on the Great Leap Forward were Ke Qingshi, Party secretary of the Eastern Bureau; Li Jingquan, Party secretary of the Southwest Bureau; and Tan Zhenlin and Wang Renzhong, Party secretaries of Hebei Province (Li Rui, personal interview, May 25, 1988, Beijing).
15. No one in the Yanan days had the slightest notion that Deng might someday rise to power. George Hatem, when asked whether he had anticipated that Deng would become China's leader, replied: "I never gave it a thought. But those days I never thought Mao would either. We didn't think the Revolution would come in our time. It would be the next generation" (George Hatem, personal interview, March 9, 1984, Beijing).

CHAPTER 16. KARL MARX PLUS EMPEROR QIN

1. Li Rui, personal interview, June 17, 1988, Beijing.
2. Chen Hansheng, personal interview, October 22, 1987, Beijing.
3. Li Rui, personal interview, May 25, 1988, Beijing.
4. Li Rui, personal interview, June 17, 1988, Beijing.
5. These meetings were held all over China, involving many districts and persons, high provincial officials, and ministry officials. They lasted ten to twenty hours. Mao didn't attend to any of the details. He simply handed Deng a list of subjects to be discussed and the geographic locale. Sometimes Mao would appear, but often he did not, leaving Deng in charge of the proceedings (Li Rui, personal interview, May 25, 1988, Beijing).
6. Li Rui, personal interview, October 19, 1987, Beijing.
7. Li Rui, personal interview, October 30, 1987, Beijing.
8. In 1987 Chen Hansheng was unique among surviving Chinese revolutionaries for breadth of experience and understanding. Returning from the United States, England, and Germany, where he was educated, Chen arrived in China in 1924.

He became an underground member of the Communist Party and an open member of the Kuomintang (then collaborating under Dr. Sun Yatsen). He joined the underground Comintern, the Moscow-sponsored international revolutionary organization, and studied and worked in Moscow, constantly moving between China, Russia, and the United States and maintaining energetic academic interests in each country, as well as working for revolution in China. He settled permanently in Beijing in 1951, but his talents were underutilized in the growing bureaucratic structure of the People's Republic. He was arrested in the Cultural Revolution and taken by two guards for a "final visit" to his home. His wife had just died of cancer and was laid out on a plain plank in the gutted house. As Chen sobbed for his wife's death, one guard casually looked over the book-strewn floor and appropriated a finely printed atlas. The other pried a ring from Chen's wife's lifeless finger. When Chen begged to have it back, he shrugged and put it in his pocket (Chen Hansheng, *China Daily,* April 14, 1987, March 21, 1989; Chen Hansheng, personal interview, October 22, 1987, Beijing).

9. Li Rui, personal interview, October 19, 1987, Beijing.
10. Li Rui, personal interviews, October 19 and October 30, 1987, Beijing.
11. Quan Yanchi, *Wei shi zhang tan Mao Zedong,* chap. 4.
12. Ibid., 1.
13. Li Rui, personal interview, October 30, 1987, Beijing; Quan Yanchi, *Wei shi zhang tan,* chap. 4.
14. Li Rui, personal interview, October 30, 1987, Beijing.
15. Ibid.
16. Li Rui, personal interview, October 19, 1987, Beijing.
17. Chen Hansheng, personal interview, October 22, 1987, Beijing.
18. In his letter to Chairman Mao delivered at the Lushan conference in July 1959, Marshal Peng Dehuai estimated that by the autumn of 1958, ninety million peasants were engaged in steel production and that in 1959, seventy million had turned out to work on water conservancy projects (Peng Dehuai, *Memoirs,* 499).
19. Hu Hua, personal interview, August 24, 1987, Beijing.
20. Quan Yanchi, *Wei shi zhang tan,* chap. 6.
21. Li Rui, personal interview, May 6, 1988, Beijing; Rewi Alley, personal interview, October 21, 1987, Beijing.
22. Chen Hansheng, personal interview, October 22, 1987, Beijing.

CHAPTER 17. AT WATER'S EDGE

1. Yan Mingfu, personal interview, April 29, 1988, Beijing.
2. Li Yueran (vice president, Chinese Translators Association, one of Mao's translators at the 1957 Moscow meeting), personal interview, January 30, 1991, Beijing.
3. Li Yueran, Beijing Radio, March 14, March 20, March 21, March 27, 1989; Foreign Broadcast Information Service (Washington, D.C.), April 17–21, 1989.
4. Yan Mingfu, personal interview, April 23, 1988, Beijing.
5. Yan Mingfu, personal interview, April 21, 1988, Beijing.
6. Li Rui, personal interview, October 19, 1987, Beijing.
7. Yan Mingfu, personal interview, April 29, 1988, Beijing.
8. Ibid.
9. Ibid.
10. In an article about this meeting, at which he acted as Soviet interpreter, Nikolai

Fedorenko made no mention of the swimming pool, although in conversation thirty years later he was still amazed at what had happened there. His article did not mention Khrushchev being shunted off to Jade Mountain. He delicately referred to the Soviet party's being taken to a "recently built region in the Beijing suburbs" where the Soviet delegation was quartered (Fedorenko, "Vizit N. Khrushchev v Pekin," 131–132).

11. Ibid., 123.

12. Yan Mingfu, personal interview, April 29, 1988, Beijing.

13. *Khrushchev Remembers: The Last Testament,* 255–275.

14. It is quite clear from Gromyko's account that he understood Mao to be proposing a surprise Soviet nuclear attack to wipe out U.S. armed forces and that he told Mao firmly that the Soviet Union would not consider such a proposal (Gromyko, *Memoirs,* 251–252).

15. Yan Mingfu, personal interview, April 29, 1988, Beijing.

CHAPTER 18. IN THE YELLOW RIVER COUNTRY

All details of Deng village are based on a visit by the author in spring 1988 and on interviews with Deng Youmei.

1. Account of Zhu Hong (wife of Liu Binyan), as related to her by peasants of the village, personal conversation, May 4, 1990.

2. Liu Binyan, personal interview, November 22, 1988, Cambridge, Mass.

3. Quan Yanchi, *Wei shi zhang tan Mao Zedong,* chap. 3.

4. Ibid.

5. Li Rui, personal interview, June 17, 1988, Beijing.

6. Yu Qiuli (PLA propaganda chief), personal interview, November 4, 1984, Beijing.

CHAPTER 19. ASCENT OF MOUNT LU

1. By the time of World War II there were 250 houses atop Kuling, almost all occupied in summer by missionary families. The name Kuling seems to have been invented by the mission families as a Chinese-American pun (Service, ed., *Golden Inches,* the memoir of Service's mother, Grace, who spent the summer of 1912 there).

2. Rice, *Mao's Way,* 165.

3. Pan Xianzhi, *Mao Zedong he tade mishu Tianjiaying,* 27 et seq.

4. Quan Yanchi, *Wei shi zhang tan Mao Zedong,* chap. 3.

5. Li Rui, *Huai nian,* 3.

6. Ibid.

7. Ibid.

8. Pan Xianzhi, *Mao Zedong he tade mishu Tianjiaying,* 27.

9. Peng Dehuai, *Memoirs of a Marshal,* 216–237; Chen Hansheng, personal interview, October 22, 1987, Beijing.

10. Peng Dehuai, *Memoirs,* 487–488.

11. An extremely careful analysis based on available Chinese data, random utterances by Mao Zedong and Zhou Enlai, and the work of skilled foreign agricultural specialists estimates grain yields in 1958 from 194 million tons to 250 million tons. The official figure was finally put at 215 million tons of unprocessed grain, 172 million tons of processed grain. For 1959 the estimates ranged from 168 million

to 270 million tons. The official figure was 192 million tons of unprocessed grain, 154 million of processed grain. Figures for 1960 were 161 million tons of unprocessed and 129 million tons of processed grain (Swamy and Burki, "Food Grains in the People's Republic of China," 58–63).

12. Quan Yanchi, *Wei shi zhang tan*, chap. 2.

13. Barnstone, ed. and trans., *Poems of Mao Tse-tung*, 95.

14. Zhou Lipo, "Visit to His Home Town," in Zhong Wenxian, *Mao Zedong*, 233–238.

15. Quan Yanchi, *Wei shi zhang tan*, chap. 3.

16. *Case of Peng Teh-Huai*, 1.

17. Schram, *Mao Tse-tung*, 277–278.

18. Charles, "Dismissal of Marshal Peng Teh-huai," 66–68; Schram, *Mao Tse-tung*, 280–281; Rice, *Mao's Way*.

19. Han Suyin carefully examined the Peng Dehuai case in the second volume of her biographical study of Mao Zedong, based on research completed before Mao's death (and greatly handicapped by the circumstances of the Cultural Revolution). She concluded that the Soviet angle played a major role in Mao's case against Peng; that Mao believed Peng had been working intimately with the Soviet military; and that he shared Khrushchev's prejudices against the Great Leap in many ways. In the Cultural Revolution era, much was made in the propaganda against Peng of the Moscow "connection." Of course, all this was put forward in the heightened atmosphere of Soviet-Chinese antagonism (Han Suyin, *Wind in the Tower*, 143–165).

CHAPTER 20. THE GREAT DIVIDE

1. Hu Hua, personal interview, October 1987, Beijing.

2. Peng Dehuai, *Memoirs of a Marshal*, 488–490; Quan Yanchi, *Wei shi zhang tan Mao Zedong*, chap. 3.

3. Peng Dehuai, *Memoirs*, 490.

4. Quan Yanchi, *Wei shi zhang tan*, chap. 3.

5. Li Rui, personal interview, April 25, 1988, Beijing.

6. Peng Dehuai, *Memoirs*, 490–491.
   Mao had been extremely fond of Zhou Xiaozhou, who was his secretary during the anti-Japanese war. Mao personally named him Party secretary for Hunan Province, saying he was the only man who could bring Hunan's harvest back to normal. When he was charged with being a "rightist," he wrote Mao a note saying he would choke in his own tears if he confessed to so false an allegation. Zhou Xiaozhou committed suicide in 1966 after burning all his books (Li Rui, *Huai nian*, 74).

7. Peng Dehuai, *Memoirs*, 492–493.

8. Ibid., 494.

9. Li Rui, *Lushan huiyi shilu*, 345.

10. Ibid., 126, 128.

11. Peng Dehuai, *Memoirs*, 494.

12. Li Rui, *Lushan huiyi shilu*, 93, 121.

13. Peng Dehuai, *Memoirs*, 303–304.

14. Ibid., 494–504, 505.

15. Li Rui, *Lushan huiyi shilu*, 145.

16. Witke, *Comrade Chiang Ching,* 301–302.

In theory, Jiang Qing was still covered by the Party edict of the 1930s prohibiting her from any involvement in Party politics. Actually, this decree had been circumspectly violated more and more frequently. From the time of the move into Zhongnanhai and her return from Moscow, Jiang was under Central Committee regulations. She could not visit Chairman Mao except by Party permission and appointment. Presumably these rules were enforced by the Party Secretariat, under Mao's control. Mao's secretary Tian Jiaying, who deplored Jiang Qing's influence on Party affairs, believed that she was firmly under Mao's control. However, during the Cultural Revolution she was able to freewheel in her own style (Pan Xianzhi, *Mao Zedong he tade mishu Tianjiaying,* 130).

17. Peng Dehuai, *Memoirs,* 494.
18. Quan Yanchi, *Wei shi zhang tan,* 12.
19. Schram, *Chairman Mao Speaks to the People,* 131–140.
20. Quan Yanchi, *Wei shi zhang tan,* 4.
21. Schram, *Chairman Mao Speaks,* 146.
22. Quan Yanchi, *Wei shi zhang tan,* 12.
23. Su Xiaokang, *Wutuobang ji.*
24. Li Rui, *Lushan huiyi shilu,* 130 et seq.
25. Su Xiaokang, *Wutuobang ji.*
26. This was reported by Ross Terrill in his *Mao* (276). He attributed it to the Current Background Reports of the U.S. Consulate General in Hong Kong.
27. Wang Bingnan, personal interview, March 20, 1984, Beijing.
28. Quan Yanchi, *Wei shi zhang tan,* 4.
29. Li Rui, *Lushan huiyi shilu,* 276, 286, 348.
30. Li Rui, personal interview, April 25, 1988, Beijing.
31. Witke, *Comrade Chiang Ching,* 302.
32. Terrill, *White-Boned Demon,* 238.
33. Han Suyin, *Wind in the Tower,* 184.

CHAPTER 21. MAO'S METAPHOR

1. Mao Zedong's speech of September 11, 1950, quoted by Schram, *Chairman Mao Speaks to the People,* 146–147.
2. Ibid., 147–157.
3. Ibid., 154–156.
4. Zhang Yuanyuan, personal interview, July 1990, New York.
5. Nikolai Fedorenko, personal interview, May 21, 1990, Moscow.
6. Yan Mingfu, personal interview, May 6, 1988, Beijing.
7. Ibid.; Han Suyin, *Wind in the Tower,* 168–169; *Khrushchev Remembers,* 472–473.
8. There were several explanations for why the park was called the Wu Family Gardens. One was that Wu Sangui, the Ming garrison commander who let the invading Manchus through the Great Wall and into Beijing, lived in the villa with Chen Yuanyuan, a famous concubine of the day. Others thought it got its name from Wu Dingchang, secretary-general of Chiang Kaishek, who bought it during KMT days (Cui Lie, letter to author, October 20, 1990).
9. Ibid.
10. Peng Dehuai, *Memoirs of a Marshal,* 10.

CHAPTER 22. SEEK TRUTH FROM FACTS

This chapter is based largely on Pan Xianzhi, *Mao Zedong he tade mishu Tianjiaying,* supplemented by materials from Yan Jiaqi, Li Rui, and Yang Shangkun.

1. *Renmin Ribao,* June 1, 1990.

2. Pan Xianzhi, *Mao Zedong he tade mishu Tianjiaying,* 84. Pan Xianzhi was himself a longtime associate of Mao's and Mao's secretaries'. He worked in Mao's personal library from 1950 to 1966, when he, too, fell victim to the Cultural Revolution (Xinhua News Agency [Beijing], June 10, 1991).

3. Quan Yanchi, *Wei shi zhang tan Mao Zedong,* chap. 3.

4. Ibid.

5. Pan Xianzhi, *Mao Zedong he tade mishu Tianjiaying,* 26–27.

6. Li Rui, personal interview, May 25, 1988, Beijing.
   Mao was given to such grandiose projects, few of which were ever finished. He launched a plan for a series of works on "the heights of Chinese culture" in 1965, working in Hangzhou with secretaries Chen Boda and Hu Qiaomu. It was not completed. He wrote the Constitution of the People's Republic in the same way, in the same place, with the same secretaries, although that project was completed. He embarked on a great agricultural encyclopedia but never finished it (ibid.). For some years Mao worked on a book that he called *The Strategic Question of the Chinese Revolution.* He began while still in Yanan, before the Xian Incident of 1936. He put it aside, went back to it occasionally, but never finished the last few chapters (Hu Qiaomu, personal interview, May 21, 1988, Beijing). Hu Qiaomu worked with Mao on the study.

7. A brief version of a "Speech at Hangzhou, December 21, 1965" is included in Schram's *Chairman Mao Speaks to the People.* These rambling remarks may be excerpts from the much longer disquisition presented to the group of five.

8. Pan Xianzhi, *Mao Zedong he tade mishu Tianjiaying,* 134.

9. Wang Li emerged in January 1989 with an article in the Shanghai press in which he tried to plead innocence of what the Gang of Four was up to. His claim of victimization by Jiang Qing and Kang Sheng got short shrift among those who had witnessed his brutal operations during the Cultural Revolution (*Renmin Ribao* [Beijing], February 2, 1989; Foreign Broadcast Information Service [Washington, D.C.], February 10, 1989).

10. Pan Xianzhi, *Mao Zedong he tade mishu Tianjiaying,* 83.

11. Ibid.

CHAPTER 23. THE MAKING OF A STATE CRIMINAL

This chapter is based largely on personal interviews with Yang Shangkun, beginning in 1984 and extending through 1991.

1. Pan Xianzhi, *Mao Zedong he tade mishu Tianjiaying,* 115.

2. Yang Shangkun, personal interview, October 24, 1984, Beijing. A KMT report of the event claimed that Yang Shangkun had been killed.

3. One of Yang's first acts after regaining a position of authority under Deng Xiaoping was to collect the "confessions and life stories" written by Peng Dehuai under torture. At Yang's direction the documents were pieced together into a dramatic account of Peng's bravery and resolve. Peng, as Yang wrote in his introduction to the volume, "spared neither life nor limb fighting for the Chinese Revolution"; he was "a man of integrity and uprightness," "loyal and incorrup-

tible." A poem, Yang recalled, tells of a mighty river "which swept many a notable into oblivion," but nothing could blot the bright image of Peng Dehuai from China's history (Yang Shangkun, Introduction to Peng Dehuai, *Memoirs of a Marshal*).

4. When Yang Shangkun was growing up, Suining had been a small county town. Located on the Fu River, it was roughly forty miles from Nanchong and a little more than one hundred from Chengdu. In the 1980s Suining began to expand rapidly, having been selected as a site for regional industrial development. It was reorganized to incorporate five counties with a population just under one million.

5. In 1988 Yang Shangkun had four living younger brothers. The senior was Yang Baibing, director of the political department of the PLA, who came to prominence after the 1989 Tiananmen massacre, playing a very active role in army affairs, giving rise to Beijing gossip about the "Yang family gang." A graduate of the Anti-Japanese War College in Yanan, Yang Baibing had been an officer in the famous 129th Division. Yang Shangkun had had five sisters by his father's first wife, plus a stepsister given by a relative to the family, to raise. There was also a stepbrother, son of an uncle. "My family was regarded as very good at bringing up children," Yang said (Yang Shangkun, personal interview, May 23, 1988, Beijing).

6. Hu Hua, the now-deceased scholar of Party history, said the tape recordings were of great value, since they represented the only record of many of Mao's conversations. They were not, he said, in the state archives but possibly were being preserved in some top-secret Party file. He believed that Yan Mingfu, Mao's Russian interpreter and later minister of United Front Work, was arrested with Yang Shangkun in this affair. Yan served a prison term as long as that of Yang (Hu Hua, personal interview, August 31, 1987, Beijing).

7. Yang Shangkun was also charged with being an American intelligence agent, based on his having met with the American Dixie Mission in Yanan in 1944. Yang had two sons and a daughter, all of whom were persecuted during the Cultural Revolution. The oldest was already in the army. The second was a senior at Beijing University, and his daughter was in high school. "I consider myself lucky," Yang observed. "No one in my family was killed" (Yang Shangkun, personal interview, April 3, 1984, Beijing).

CHAPTER 24. THE ZOO CAPER

1. Arlington and Lewisohn, *In Search of Old Peking*, 240–241; Zhou Shachen, *Beijing*, 163; Rice, *Mao's Way*, 182–183.

2. Personal observation, July 1972.

3. Han Suyin, *Wind in the Tower*, 180.

4. Rice, *Mao's Way*, 180.

5. Mao Zedong's speech of January 30, 1962, quoted by Schram, *Chairman Mao Speaks to the People*.

6. One whom Mao named was Pan Hannian. Mao called him a counterrevolutionary. Actually Pan was a Communist of impeccable credentials who had carried out dangerous missions in the underground. He had smuggled in a wireless set for the secret communications center maintained by Soong Chingling, Sun Yatsen's widow, for the use of Communist couriers. The false charge may have originated in Pan's connections with the Russian-sponsored Comintern.

7. Hu Hua, personal interview, August 29, 1987, Beijing.

8. Li Rui, personal interview, October 19, 1987, Beijing.

9. Yan Jiaqi, *Wenge shi nian shi*, 1; Edgar Snow, *Long Revolution*, 17.

10. Han Suyin, *Wind in the Tower*, 225; Rice, *Mao's Way*, 197.

11. Hu Hua, personal interview, August 29, 1987, Beijing.

CHAPTER 25. POISONED PAPER

1. Li Rui, personal interview, June 17, 1988, Beijing.

2. The tradition of Latinizing the sexual passages was carefully followed by Arthur Waley, the great translator of classical Chinese and Japanese works. Much of this data on the role of erotica in China derives from the study of R. H. Van Gulik, *Sexual Life in Ancient China*. Information on Mao's collections was provided by two of his surviving secretaries. Information on Kang Sheng's role was given by Yan Mingfu in personal interviews in Beijing in 1987 and 1988. Details on Mao's sexual partners came in part from the late Rewi Alley, in a long conversation on October 21, 1987, in Beijing.

3. Van Gulik, *Sexual Life in Ancient China*, 189.

4. Ibid.

5. Kim San, whose underground name was Chiang Chi-rak, in 1937 was in Yanan, where Helen Snow, wife of Edgar Snow, interviewed him extensively and made him the subject of a book called *Song of Ariran*. Kim had lived and worked underground in China and had become a member of the Chinese Communist Party and a Chinese citizen. He had undergone arrest, imprisonment, and torture at the hands of both the Japanese police and those of Chiang Kaishek and was in precarious health. Kang Sheng came to Yanan after Helen Snow had departed, and one of his first acts was to cook up a case against Kim San as a Trotskyite. Kim San was subsequently shot (Helen Snow, telephone interview, August 13, 1990). Allegations of Trotskyism were a vicious weapon often used in Yanan political quarrels. After publication by Edgar Snow of his classic *Red Star over China*, a charge that he and his wife were Trotskyites was leveled by Hans Shippe, a German Comintern operative in Yanan who wrote under the name of Asiaticus. Shippe tried to get *Red Star* suppressed. He carried his case to Mao, who told him to shut up and get out of Yanan (Helen Snow, telephone interview, September 1984). The use of the Trotskyite smear was part of Moscow's continuing campaign to discredit Mao and the Mao brand of Communism. In 1990 a propaganda campaign to picture Shippe as a correspondent "friend of China" was initiated by former foreign minister Huang Hua and a statue erected on the spot where he lost his life while attached to the Eighth Route Army during a battle with the Japanese.

6. Yusov, "Kang Sheng," 111–121.

7. Harrison E. Salisbury, *Black Night, White Snow*.

8. Yan Mingfu, personal interview, May 8, 1988, Beijing.

    P. P. Vladimirov, a Soviet intelligence officer stationed in Yanan between 1942 and 1945 and almost the only non-Chinese present much of that time, claims Kang Sheng was the principal agent of Mao's Party purge of 1942–43 and that among its targets were Wang Ming, leader of the Russian faction in the Chinese Party, Zhou Enlai, Yang Shangkun, Bo Gu, Gao Gang, and Zhang Wentian (Luo Fu). Vladimirov contends that Wang Ming became seriously ill as a result of Chinese poisoning. Vladimirov's diary, published at the height of Sino-Soviet polemics, tends toward exaggeration (Vladimirov, *Osobii Raion Kitai*).

9. Rewi Alley, personal interview, October 21, 1987, Beijing.

10. Confidential source, February 26, 1991.

11. Chen Hansheng, personal interview, October 22, 1987, Beijing; Laffont, *Kang Sheng,* 454–459.

12. Bonavia, *Verdict in Peking,* 204.

13. Liu Yuanyuan, personal interview, May 16, 1988, Jinan.

14. Jiang Qing, so it was rumored, had many lovers during the Cultural Revolution. Another was said to be Zhuang Zedong, the handsome table tennis champion of China.

15. *Ming Pao* (Hong Kong), January 15, 1979.

16. Yan Mingfu, personal interview, May 8, 1988, Beijing.

17. Li Rui, personal interview, October 30, 1987, Beijing.

18. Hu Qiaomu, personal interview, May 21, 1988, Beijing.

19. Li Zehou, "Qing nian Mao Zedong."

20. Li Rui, personal interview, May 28, 1986, Beijing.

CHAPTER 26. "SILLY CHILD! YOU STILL DON'T KNOW ANYTHING!"

1. Liu Tingting, personal interview, October 8, 1990, Beijing.

2. Liu Pingping et al., *Shengli de xianhua xian gei nin.*

3. Furen gradually became dominated more by German Benedictines than American. With the coming of the People's Republic, it moved to Taiwan.

4. Liu Tingting, personal interview, August 21, 1990, New York.

5. Wu Han and his wife and daughter, like so many who fell victim to the Cultural Revolution, committed suicide rather than accept almost certain death by beating and torture. The history of Wu Han and Hai Rui and its antecedents are well told by Garside, *Coming Alive.*

6. Suiciding was not invented by Mao or the Red Guards. It was long established in Chinese tradition, often employed in the dynasties. The so-called Pearl Concubine of Emperor Guangxu was hated by the dowager empress Ci Xi. She had her nephew's consort suicided in a well near the rear gate of the Forbidden City adjacent to Coal Hill (Kates, *Years That Were Fat,* 120).

7. Liu Pingping et al., *Shengli de xianhua,* 23.

8. Yan Jiaqi, *Wenge shi nian shi,* 12; Liu Pingping et al., *Shengli de xianhua,* 4.

9. Mao's admonition (hypocritical though it was) was based on the great prestige that student demonstrations had acquired in China, beginning with that of May 4, 1919. It was a warning that did not seem to be remembered by Deng Xiaoping and his fellows on June 4, 1989, at Tiananmen.

10. Yan Jiaqi, *Wenge shi nian shi,* 14.

11. Liu Pingping et al., *Shengli de xianhua,* 6.
    Cai Chang died in Beijing on September 11, 1990, at the age of ninety, after several years of illness and blindness. The obituaries did not mention the remarkably idealistic friendship she and Cai Hesen, her brother, had had with Mao Zedong, nor did the surviving grand old ladies of the Party — Deng Yingchao, widow of Zhou Enlai, or Kang Keqing, widow of Zhu De — attend the funeral ceremonies or, so far as was reported, send wreaths. Perhaps they, too, were ill.

12. Garside, *Coming Alive,* 46.

13. Xiao Fang, personal interview, July 1990, New York.

14. Garside, *Coming Alive,* 47.

15. Rice, *Mao's Way,* 248.

16. Bridgham, "Mao's Cultural Revolution," 1.

17. The senior third class of the Beijing Girls' Middle School, located adjacent to Zhongnanhai, had on June 6 petitioned Mao and the Central Committee to abolish entrance examinations, which they said "reactionary elements" were employing to control the young people. A week later the State Council abolished university entrance examinations (Xiao Fang, personal interview, July 1990, New York; Han Suyin, *Wind in the Tower*, 281). A young student named Zhang Tiesheng of Shenyang won instant national fame because he turned in a blank piece of paper instead of answering questions for his college exam. Like so many Cultural Revolution folk heroes, he fell swiftly and was sentenced to fifteen years in prison for counterrevolutionary activity. He studied veterinary and general medicine in prison and vowed that when he emerged he would devote himself to free practice for local citizens (*Zhongguo Tongxunshe* [Hong Kong], quoting Shenyang press, November 22, 1988; Foreign Broadcast Information Service [Washington, D.C.], October 28, 1988).

CHAPTER 27. A SMALL SOLDIER

This chapter derives in great part from repeated conversations with Hu Jieqing, widow of Lao She, and with his children, especially his daughter Shu Ji.

1. Lao She paid for the house with two hundred bales of cotton cloth, something over eight thousand yards. He paid in cloth instead of money because the new People's Republic's money was nonconvertible abroad. The exact value of the cloth is impossible to calculate (Shu Ji, personal interview, October 20, 1990, Beijing).

2. *Rickshaw Boy* was published in the United States in 1945 and became a Book-of-the-Month Club selection. The English translation was by an American in the Tianjin consulate using the nom de plume Evan King. He made many deletions and changes and added a romantic happy ending (Hu Jieqing, personal interview, September 29, 1987, Beijing).

3. Ibid.

4. Lao She wrote the first two volumes while he was in wartime Chongqing. The third was completed in the United States and the fourth in Beijing. The shifts in Lao She's locale and viewpoint can be detected in the completed version (ibid.).

5. Shu Yi (son of Lao She), "Lao She's Last Two Days," 2–3; Shu Ji, personal interview, September 1, 1987, Beijing.

6. Yan Jiaqi, *Wenge shi nian shi*, chap. 3.

7. Shu Yi, "Lao She's Last Two Days," 2.

8. Yan Jiaqi, *Wenge shi nian shi*, 16.

9. Shu Ji, personal interview, October 18, 1987, Beijing; Shu Yi, "Lao She's Last Two Days."

10. The Xidan police station, in the heart of the Xidan market area, became known worldwide at the time of the June 1989 Tiananmen crackdown. It was a center for the armed police. Many student demonstrators were dragged here, and some killed.

11. Shu Yi, "Lao She's Last Two Days," 5.

12. Ibid., 6.

13. Ibid., 1.

14. Ibid., 7.

15. Ibid.; Shu Ji, personal interview, May 2, 1988, Beijing.

16. In 1989 Hu Jieqing, then eighty-five years old, was moved from the House of Abundance to a new four-room apartment by the Chinese Writers Association. The famous old courtyard was no longer habitable, and the Beijing municipal authorities were still debating action to make Lao She's house a memorial museum, as Hu had long hoped. She wanted to preserve it just as it had been in Lao She's day. The association also was dragging its heels about preserving this important cultural site, although Lao She had been fully rehabilitated after the Cultural Revolution and was officially considered one of China's four major modern writers. Meantime, a Chinese entrepreneur opened a "Lao She Teahouse" in Beijing, featuring acrobatic performers and catering to Taiwan businessmen (*China Daily*, September 9, 1991).

CHAPTER 28. THE FATE OF IRON MAN WANG

This chapter is based largely on two visits by the author to Daqing, one in 1977 and the other in September 1987.

1. Han Suyin, *Wind in the Tower*, 227–229.

2. Yan Jiaqi, *Wenge shi nian shi*, 17.

3. Liu Zongren, *Tanyin Alley*, 113.

4. Chen Hansheng, personal interview, October 22, 1987, Beijing. After an appearance and speech by Chen Boda at Tangshan, just east of Beijing, on December 26, 1967, a new wave of persecution put 84,000 persons under interrogation and resulted in 2,953 deaths (Bonavia, *Verdict in Peking*, 89).

5. *Great Trial in Chinese History*, 20–21.

6. Yan Jiaqi, personal interview, May 2, 1988, Beijing.

7. Ibid.

8. Xue Guobang (Wang's fellow worker), personal interview, September 8, 1987, Daqing.

9. Ibid.

10. Tian Runfu (Daqing newspaper editor), personal interview, September 7, 1987, Daqing.

11. Ibid.

12. Xue Guobang, personal interview, September 8, 1987, Daqing.

13. Wang's first son was in the army. When demobilized, he went to work at Daqing and became head of the union in the machinery repair department. In 1987 his second son worked, as he had, with a drilling team. One daughter worked at Daqing, and one was in the army. His widow was alive but in poor health in 1987 (Xue Guobang, personal interview, September 8, 1987, Daqing).

14. Ibid.

15. Ibid.

16. Nikita Khrushchev's secret speech of February 25, 1956, quoted by Jacobs, *New Communist Manifesto*, 78–130.

17. During a brief revival of the practice of setting up "role models" in 1990, Party Secretary Jiang Zemin proposed reviving the cult of Iron Man Wang. After a few brief mentions the notion was dropped. It is doubtful if Jiang Zemin, who was in Shanghai at the time of Iron Man Wang's fall from grace, was aware of the tragic fate of this worker hero.

18. Witke, *Comrade Chiang Ching*, 350.

CHAPTER 29. HEAVEN ABOVE AND THE EARTH BELOW

This chapter derives from material gathered in Dazhai on May 8–9, 1988.

CHAPTER 30. THE HOUSE OF GOOD FORTUNE

Much of this chapter is based on extensive conversations with the surviving members of Liu Shaoqi's family.

1. Liu Pingping et al., *Shengli de xianhua xian gei nin*, 5; Liu Tingting, personal interview, October 13, 1990, New York.
2. Wang Guangmei, personal interview, October 22, 1987, Beijing.
3. Liu Tao claimed that her mother had disclosed to her a great deal of material that gave evidence of Liu Shaoqi's basically bourgeois nature (Fokkema, *Report from Peking*, 59).
4. Liu Pingping et al., *Shengli de xianhua*, 11.
5. *Great Trial in Chinese History*, 41–46.
6. Fokkema, *Report from Peking*, 132.
7. *Great Trial.*
8. Liu Pingping et al., *Shengli de xianhua*, 17.
9. *Great Trial.*
10. Liu Pingping et al., *Shengli de xianhua*, 20; Liu Tingting, personal interviews, September 14 and October 13, 1990, New York.
11. Liu Pingping et al., *Shengli de xianhua*, 21.
12. Ibid., 20.
13. *Great Trial*, 35, 39.

CHAPTER 31. MOON OVER THE YAN

1. Xue Ming, personal interview, September 4, 1987, Beijing.
2. Ibid.
3. The enemy to whom Jiang Qing was referring was Sun Weishi, the goddaughter of Zhou Enlai. She had worked as a fourteen-year-old in a Shanghai theater troupe with Jiang Qing and in Yanan had taken a role in a play, *Blood Baptism of Shanghai*, in which Jiang Qing had the lead. Sun Weishi stole the show, and Jiang Qing developed a fierce hatred for her, based partly on envy and partly on the fact that Sun knew too much about Jiang's background. Sun and her husband were arrested and tortured in the Cultural Revolution. Sun died on October 14, 1968. Why Zhou Enlai was unable to save his goddaughter is not clear. Her brother Sun Yang was also killed (Yan Jiaqi, *Wenge shi nian shi*, 74–75).
4. Xue Ming, personal interview, June 16, 1984, Beijing.
    Quoted from Bo Yibo's reminiscence. Bo Yibo recalled an argument he once had with He Long, who had criticized a Shanxi Party leader, Nie Yinguan, for lack of firmness in supporting criticism of his landlord father. The father had actually done good things, said Bo Yibo. He Long didn't know that the peasants had put an iron wire through the old man's nose and forced the son "to herd the cow," making the old man get on all fours and be led around the stable (*Renmin Ribao* [Beijing], March 9, 1989; Foreign Broadcast Information Service [Washington, D.C.], April 7, 1989, p. 20).
5. As Lin Biao was entering the Whampoa military academy, established by Dr. Sun Yatsen, his cousin Lin Yuying joined the Communist Party in 1922, shortly after its founding. He did underground work in Shanghai, Hankou, and Tianjin

and went to Moscow in 1932 as China's representative in the Profintern, the Communist international labor organization. He came to Yanan in 1935 on an important mission — to restore Moscow's contact with Mao and to try to work out an armistice in the intraparty conflict between Mao and his chief rival, Zhang Guotao. Lin Yuying died in 1943. A younger brother, Lin Yunan, also engaged in Party work (Harrison E. Salisbury, *Long March*).

6. Jian Xianren, then wife of He Long, agreed that Lin Biao had entirely recovered from his wound. But, she said, "all of us were in bad health and got attention from Soviet clinic doctors" (Jian Xianren, personal interview, October 7, 1987, Beijing).

7. Ibid.

8. Ibid.

9. Largely based on personal interviews with Jian Xianren (August 11, September 13, October 6, October 8, October 9, October 12, and October 15, 1987, Beijing), Xue Ming (June 16, 1984, September 4, 1987, Beijing), and Xiao Ke (1984, 1987, 1991, Beijing).

   Jian Xianren, daughter of the operator of a dye works in Cici County, Hunan Province, was born in 1909. He Long was the hero of the countryside, renowned for his help to the people. Everyone knew how he led his first guerrilla attack armed only with a butcher's knife. Jian's brother introduced her to He Long in July 1929. He Long and Jian celebrated their marriage by inviting some friends and toasting the event in "white tea." Then they hastily left to keep ahead of a KMT outfit that was chasing them. Their daughter Jiesheng was born October 30, 1935. He Long joined the Long March on November 19, 1935. Jian's sister, also a beauty, married another Long March hero, Xiao Ke. Jian's sister gave birth to a boy on the Long March who the Red Army called "the Long March Baby." The child was safely brought to Yanan but was killed a couple of years later in a Japanese bacteriological air raid, or so the parents believed (Jian Xianren, personal interviews, 1987; Xiao Ke, personal interviews, 1984, 1987; Salisbury, *Long March*).

10. Xue Ming, personal interview, June 16, 1984, Beijing.

11. Jian Xianren, personal interview, September 13, 1987, Beijing.

12. Xue Ming, personal interview, September 4, 1987, Beijing.

13. Mao may have deliberately encouraged rivalry between He Long and Lin Biao in 1964. Mao assigned He Long, in place of Lin Biao, to preside over the Central Military Committee and the Military Working Commission. Mao praised He Long's work and invited him to attend Politburo sessions. Lin Biao was not always notified of these sessions (ibid.).

14. Yan Jiaqi, *Wenge shi nian shi*, 35.

15. Ibid.

16. Xue Ming, personal interview, May 16, 1984, Beijing.

17. Ibid.

18. Bonavia, *Verdict in Peking*, 191.

19. Jian Xianren, personal interview, October 6, 1987, Beijing.

20. Ibid.

21. Wang Lingshu, "Ji Dengkui tan Mao Zedong," *Liaowang* (Hong Kong), February 6–13, 1989; Foreign Broadcast Information Service (Washington, D.C.), February 14, 1989, p. 24.

CHAPTER 32. THE SHADOW OF LIN BIAO

1. Yan Jiaqi, *Wenge shi nian shi,* 52–54.
2. Xiao Hua had been a brilliant Red Army commander in the Long March and commander of the 2nd Division in Lin Biao's First Army. He had written a poem about the Red Army much admired by Mao Zedong and Zhou Enlai. When the Cultural Revolution began he was director of the PLA general political department and was quickly subjected to attack. He was finally put in prison for seven and a half years. It is probable that his knowledge of Lin Biao's addiction was the root of the trouble. He was lucky to survive (Harrison E. Salisbury, *Long March,* 334).
3. Giles, *History of Chinese Literature,* 179–181; Yan Jiaqi, *Wenge shi nian shi,* 51.
4. Edgar Snow, *Red Star over China,* 369.
5. Yan Jiaqi, *Wenge shi nian shi,* 55.
   On May 17, 1975, commenting on the release of another prisoner, He Cheng, Mao noted: "He Cheng is not guilty. He should be rehabilitated. He is lucky to be alive. Fu Lianzhang is already dead. What a pity" (Zhang Tuosheng, *1975 nian de quan mian zhengdun*).
6. Cecil and Loeb, *Textbook of Medicine,* 2017.
7. Notes of visit to Guang'an, April 1988.
8. Li Rui, personal interview, June 17, 1988, Beijing.
9. When Hatem joined the Red Army medical service in 1936, he discovered it possessed no anesthetics. He had brought a small medicine chest with him, but this could not fill the gap. The army was then using a mixture of opium and alcohol as an operating anesthetic. One of Hatem's first lessons was in making tincture of opium (George Hatem, personal interview, March 10, 1984, Beijing).
10. Cecil and Loeb, *Textbook of Medicine,* 2017.
11. Kau, *Lin Biao Affair,* 118–123.
12. Hu Hua, personal interview, August 31, 1987, Beijing.
13. Edgar Snow, *Long Revolution,* 171–172.

CHAPTER 33. PROJECT 571

1. *South China Morning Post,* October 23, 1989.
2. The Hangzhou area and West Lake were closed to tourists, diplomats, and correspondents during 1975 and 1976 and only gradually reopened in the later part of 1977. This may well have been connected with the high-security construction work on Project 704 (visit by author to Hangzhou, September 1977).
3. Han Suyin, *Wind in the Tower,* 343–345.
4. *Great Trial in Chinese History;* Bonavia, *Verdict in Peking.*
5. A young woman who, along with several friends, knew Lin Liguo personally scoffed at the notion that he could have been put in charge of the plot details by Lin Biao. "Lin Liguo was only interested in girls," she said. "He spent all his time chasing them. To think that this young man was capable of putting together a serious plot against Mao is just silly" (Jeanette Sui, personal interview, April 12, 1983, New York).
6. Bonavia, *Verdict in Peking,* 166.
7. Yusov, "Khronika gibeli Lin Biao."
8. Sun Yixian (deputy chief, Chinese embassy, Ulan Bator), *New China Diplomacy,* 195.

9. *Great Trial.*

10. *Great Trial;* Bonavia, *Verdict in Peking,* 167; Yusov, "Khronika gibeli Lin Biao," 97.

11. *The Mirror* (Hong Kong), 1989.

    A score of years after the Lin affair, Zhang Ning was still a handsome woman. After her husband was killed with his parents, she had several offers of marriage. Mao himself took an interest in her. Mao Yuanxin, Mao's nephew, who in Mao's last period became his go-between with the world, wanted to marry her, but she turned him down. His proposal was not based on any desire to cover up what inside details she might have possessed about the plot, but simply on his attraction to her beauty (ibid).

12. Sun Yixian, *New China Diplomacy,* 195.

13. According to one version, Zhou tried vainly to contact the pilot of the Trident by wireless, but he would not respond. Finally Zhou told the operator: "Tell them to come back. I will personally meet them at any airport they specify." There was no response (Yusov, "Khronika gibeli Lin Biao," 97).

14. Wang Lingshu, "Ji Dengkui tan Mao Zedong," *Liaowang* (Hong Kong), February 6, February 13, 1989; Foreign Broadcast Information Service (Washington, D.C.), February 14, 1989.

15. Ibid.

16. Xu Wenyi, *New China Diplomacy,* 153 et seq.

17. References to Lin Biao's plans vis-à-vis Jiang Qing existed in the archive left by Mao. Jiang Qing and her associates made frantic efforts to get control of Mao's papers when he died, fearful that among them would be evidence linking them with the Lin Biao affair and others (Fan Shuo, "Feng lei ji dang de shiyue," 17).

18. Confidential source, March 6, 1991, New York.

CHAPTER 34. A MASTER OF THE ARTS

1. The Nixon party was housed in two of the Diaoyutai palaces: numbers 18 and 12. Nixon was in 18, the biggest. The park had been laid out by the emperor Zhang Zong, of the Jin dynasty, in the twelfth century so he could go fishing on the large lake. It stood in ruins for many years but in 1958 was refurbished by the People's Republic. Jiang Qing took over number 17 in preference to her "separate but equal" quarters in Zhongnanhai. There are now eighteen palaces on the grounds. Some smaller ones are rented to Japanese businessmen at $1,000 a night; smaller suites rent to ordinary travelers at $140 a night. Number 18 was completely redecorated for the visit of Queen Elizabeth in 1986.

2. Zhang Yufeng, "Mao Zedong yu Zhou Enlai de yixie wan nian qu shi," December 26–29, 1988.

3. Zhang Yufeng's reminiscences give the best insight into Mao's late days. She had been a tea lady on Mao's special train. He became fond of her and was rumored to have fathered her child. In Mao's final years she acted as a nurse-secretary on twenty-four-hour duty. She was abominated by cultured Chinese, who regarded her as illiterate and a scandal. But her reminiscences reflect an intelligent and thoughtful person. She was married and had two sons, the younger possibly sired by Mao.

4. It was historian Hu Hua's information that Mao took to his bed shortly after hearing the news about Lin Biao and stayed there for more than sixty days.

5. Dr. E. Grey Dimond, personal interview, October 26, 1989, Kansas City, Mo.

6. Hu Hua, personal interview, August 31, 1987, Beijing.

7. Zhang Yufeng, "Mao Zedong yu Zhou Enlai."

8. Hu Hua, personal interview, August 31, 1987, Beijing.

9. The Hongdu Fashion Corporation was managed in 1972 by Tian Atong, who learned the tailor's trade in Shanghai in a British-owned shop before the Revolution. Neither he nor any of his tailors ever gave Mao a fitting, although they made all his clothes — and the suits of other leaders, such as Deng Xiaoping, Peng Zhen, Li Xiannian, Zhao Ziyang, and Li Peng. In Mao's case, Tian Atong said, his secretaries always came to the shop and told them what he wanted. They kept the measurements (*New York Times*, December 5, 1987).

10. The version is that of Zhang Yufeng, "Mao Zedong yu Zhou Enlai."

11. Quan Yanchi, *Wei shi zhang tan Mao Zedong*, 9.

12. This account follows those of Nixon (*RN*) and Kissinger (*White House Years*), with slight additions from Zhang Yufeng, "Mao Zedong yu Zhou Enlai."

13. *RN*, 571.

14. Quan Yanchi, *Wei shi zhang tan*, chap. 5.

15. Zhang Hanzhi, "Wo yu fuqin Zhang Shizhao," April 1988, pp. 6–21.

16. Yang Shangkun, personal interview, January 3, 1984, Beijing.

17. Quan Yanchi, *Wei shi zhang tan*, chap. 8.

   The question of Zhou Enlai's uncritical support of Mao Zedong has intrigued Chinese scholars. One school of thought suspects Zhou of playing Faust to Mao's Mephistopheles. It suggests that when Zhou Enlai swung his support to Mao at the time of the Zunyi conference, in January 1935, in the midst of the Long March, he gave Mao a written document pledging to back him as long as he lived. This author has encountered Chinese who believed mistakenly he was aware of this secret pact but suppressed it in his account of the Zunyi meeting in *The Long March: The Untold Story*. This theory about Zhou Enlai is remarkably widespread among certain intellectual circles, but no evidence of the "pact with the devil" has been forthcoming.

18. Zhang Yufeng, "Mao Zedong yu Zhou Enlai."

19. Visit by author to Nankai, October 10, 1987.

CHAPTER 35. FORTY PLUS FORTY PLUS FORTY PLUS FORTY TIMES FORTY

1. The place has been considerably improved since Deng's day. The bamboo siding has been replaced by gray brick, the courtyard surrounded by a cement pillar and iron fence, and entrance pillars installed. Trim architectural gardening has superseded the weed-grown courtyard of Deng's time (visit by author, June 1989).

2. Deng Pufang, personal interview, May 9, 1988, Beijing.

   One lurid version widely believed by Chinese young people was that Pufang was placed in the dormitory room and told that he was being exposed to radiation that would cripple him, cause cancer, and kill him. His only escape, he was told, was the hole where the window had been. Pufang was told that the room was an old X-ray laboratory that had been sealed off because of contamination. In another version Pufang jumped from the window, trying to grasp an overhanging roof, but failed and fell twenty-five feet to the ground.

3. Deng Rong (Maomao), "My Father Deng Xiaoping's Years in Jiangxi."

4. Visit to Nanchang, 1989.

5. Deng Pufang, personal interview, May 6, 1988, Beijing.

6. Deng Rong, "My Father Deng Xiaoping's Years."

7. Ibid.

8. Yan Jiaqi, *Wenge shi nian shi*, 77.

9. Some reports, probably mistaken, placed the Deng estate among the largest in Sichuan. Were that true, Shiping, even though a brother of Deng Xiaoping's, hardly could have made so easy a transition from estate manager to Party functionary.

10. Personal interviews, April 1988, Guang'an.

11. Wang Zhen's role in Deng's return to Beijing is one of many reasons that Deng supported Wang Zhen, maintaining him in his government in a position of power even though they represented different political viewpoints, Wang Zhen the most conservative of conservatives, Deng a centrist with liberal leanings.

12. Deng Rong, "My Father Deng Xiaoping's Years."

13. Yan Jiaqi, *Wenge shi nian shi*, 77.

14. Notes of personal visit and interviews, April 1988, Guang'an.

15. Personal interviews, June 1989, Nanchang.

16. Ibid.

CHAPTER 36. THE LITTLE MAN IN A HURRY

1. Fan Shuo, *Ye Jianying zai 1976*, 46–47.

2. Hu Hua, personal interview, October 29, 1984, Beijing.

3. Yan Jiaqi, *Wenge shi nian shi*, 72–73.

4. Zhang Tuosheng, *1975 nian de quan mian zhengdun*, 102–140.

5. Fan Shuo, *Ye Jianying*, 47–49.

6. Yan Jiaqi, *Wenge shi nian shi*, 77–78.

7. Hu Qiaomu, personal interview, May 21, 1988, Beijing.

8. The account of Mao's blindness follows Zhang Yufeng, "Mao Zedong yu Zhou Enlai de yixie wan nian qu shi."

9. Wang Hairong's relationship to Mao was distant and has often been misreported. Her grandmother and Mao's were sisters. Wang Hairong, despite the disparity in ages, was Mao's second cousin. A willful girl, she stole money from her mother, made her way from Changsha to Beijing, and presented herself to Mao, saying she wanted to learn English. She took English lessons from Zhang Hanzhi, Mao's English teacher. A year later she told Mao she had learned English, and he put her into the Foreign Ministry (Zhang Hanzhi, personal interview, February 26, 1991, New York).

10. Yan Jiaqi, *Wenge shi nian shi*, 79.

11. Fan Shuo, *Ye Jianying*, 50.

12. Yan Jiaqi, *Wenge shi nian shi*, 79.

13. Ibid.

14. Wan Li, personal interview, October 7, 1987, Beijing.

15. Yan Jiaqi, *Wenge shi nian shi*, 85.

16. Zhang Tuosheng, *1975 nian de quan mian zhengdun*, 14.

17. Fan Shuo, *Ye Jianying*, 51–59.

18. Yang Guan was a leading Chinese intellectual and liberal who was assassinated by KMT gunmen on June 18, 1933. In translation the poem is usually called "Lament for Yang Guan."

19. This account follows that of Zhang Yufeng, "Mao Zedong yu Zhou Enlai."

CHAPTER 37. TIME RUNS OUT

1. He Jiesheng (daughter of He Long), personal interview, October 5, 1987, Beijing.
2. This account follows that of He Jiesheng. At the same time Mao approved another film banned by Jiang Qing. It was called *Hai Xia* and dealt with guerrilla war on Hainan Island.
3. Yan Jiaqi, *Wenge shi nian shi,* 86.
4. Ibid., 84–85.
5. Mei Yan, personal interview, November 20, 1990, New York.
6. Yan Jiaqi, *Wenge shi nian shi,* 88.
7. Nikita Khrushchev's secret speech of February 25, 1956, quoted by Jacobs, *New Communist Manifesto,* 78–130.
8. Wang Lingshu, "Ji Dengkui tan Mao Zedong," *Liaowang* (Hong Kong), February 6–13, 1989; Foreign Broadcast Information Service (Washington, D.C.), February 14, 1989, p. 26.
9. Hu Hua, personal interview, August 31, 1987, Beijing.
10. After Mao's death Wang Hairong denied having encouraged Mao to start the anti-Zhou campaign. But a tape of the telltale conversation in which Mao agreed it was time to criticize Zhou was turned up (Lin Qingshan, "Mao Zedong zen yang kaishi fan Zhou yundong de," 58–59).
11. Ibid., 58.
12. Zhang Tuosheng, *1975 nian de quan mian zhengdun,* 27.
13. Yan Jiaqi, *Wenge shi nian shi,* 92.
14. Ibid., 93.
15. Fan Shuo, *Ye Jianying zai 1976,* 61–62; Zhang Tuosheng, *1975 nian de quan mian zhengdun,* 31.
16. Zhang Tuosheng, *1975 nian de quan mian zhengdun,* 34.
17. Quan Ye, "Zhou Enlai de zui hou suiyue."
18. Xiao Hua, personal interview, March 16, 1984, Beijing.
19. Harrison E. Salisbury, *Long March,* 70.
20. Liu Yazhou, *Enlai.*
21. Zhang Yufeng, "Mao Zedong yu Zhou Enlai de yixie wan nian qu shi."

CHAPTER 38. THE YEAR OF THE DRAGON

1. Walter Sullivan, personal interview, September 11, 1973, New York.
2. Li Rui, personal interview, October 30, 1987, Beijing.
3. This happened in spite of the fact that, according to General Wu Xiuquan, Marshal Ye's longtime friend and colleague, Mao Zedong "protected" Ye during the Cultural Revolution. Mao's protection was a partial insurance policy at best (Wu Xiuquan, personal interview, March 28, 1984, Beijing).
4. This account is from Zhang Yufeng, "Mao Zedong yu Zhou Enlai de yixie wan nian qu shi."
5. Garside, *Coming Alive,* 18.
6. Shen Tong, *Almost a Revolution,* 20–22.
7. Garside, *Coming Alive,* 119–121.
8. *Yangcheng Wanbao* (Guangzhou), February 10, 1989; Foreign Broadcast Information Service (Washington, D.C.), February 14, 1989.

9. Yan Jiaqi, personal interview, May 2, 1988, Beijing. Yan told the author of his findings, which surprised him as well as his listener. He said they had investigated every case they could find and learned that not one person had been clubbed to death, as was widely believed, although many were severely injured. Many people were persecuted after the affair, he said, and there were a number of suicides.

10. Wu Xiuquan, personal interview, March 22, 1984, Beijing.

11. Fan Shuo, *Ye Jianying zai 1976*, 63–64.

CHAPTER 39. THE DRAGON SPEAKS

This account is based on interviews and observations by the author at Tangshan in October 1987.

1. Mei Shirong (director, Center for Earthquake Research and Prediction), personal interview, October 19, 1987, Beijing.

2. Incredibly, as late as 1991, Kailuan was still being subsidized by the state at the rate of 200 million yuan ($100 million) annually because of the low prices it was compelled to charge domestic users. The subsidy and deficit offered an insight into the complexities of state bookkeeping (*Ching Chi Tao Pao* [Hong Kong] 38–39 [October 1991]: 25).

3. A foreign expert who visited Tangshan a few months after the quake put the toll at 600,000 dead and 600,000 injured, an overestimate but one based on figures collected on the spot. Li Xiannian, then vice president of China, said this must be exaggerated since Tangshan's population was only 800,000, but he offered no official estimate (Li Xiannian, personal interview, August 30, 1977, Beijing).

CHAPTER 40. THE DEATH OF MAO

1. Hua Guofeng told a reporter of moving Mao. He said he thought the number 202 house, a well-built, one-story building, was better suited to survive the earthquake than the Swimming Pool House. Mao stayed at number 202 until his death. The house is now used by the Communist Party general secretary for receiving foreign guests (*Zhongguo Tongxunshe* [Hong Kong], December 26, 1988; Foreign Broadcast Information Service [Washington, D.C.], December 27, 1988, p. 36).

2. Fan Shuo, "Feng lei ji dang de shiyue."

3. Both Fan Shuo, the unofficial historian of Ye's action, and Wang Zhen have been careful to avoid the word "coup" and to stress the care with which legality was observed.

4. Personal interviews with Guang'an residents, April 1988.

5. Harrison E. Salisbury, *Time of Change*, 185.

6. Wang Zhen, *Renmin Ribao* (Beijing), October 22, 1989, p. 28.

7. Fan Shuo, "Feng lei ji dang de shiyue."

8. Ibid.

9. Yang Chengwu had captured Luding Bridge across the Dadu River in one of the most daring feats of the Long March. He was an outstanding Red Army commander. In the Cultural Revolution he briefly replaced Luo Ruiqing as PLA chief of staff but quickly fell victim to Lin Biao and was imprisoned for seven years on charges of giving orders to beat Jiang Qing (Yang Chengwu, personal interview, March 18, 1984, Beijing).

10. Fan Shuo, "Feng lei ji dang de shiyue," 18.

11. Jiang Qing had developed a passion for riding. For the past several years Beihai Park had been closed to the public so that she could ride there in the morning.

Coal Hill at the back of the Forbidden City was closed at the same time, perhaps because it distantly overlooked Zhongnanhai (Frank Coe, personal interview, August 17, 1977, Beijing).

12. Gao Yiling and others, personal interviews, May 9, 1988, Dazhai.

13. Werner, *Myths and Legends of China*, 54.

14. See De Woskin, *Doctors, Diviners, and Magicians in Ancient China;* Van Gulik, *Sexual Life in Ancient China*, 131–155; W. Allyn Rickett, *Kuan-Tzu*.

15. It is contended by many Beijing purists that Mao's mausoleum, in Tiananmen Square, also disturbs the city's geomancy. However, since the square itself is a grandiose expansion of that which the original dynastic architects, sensitive to the demands of *feng shui,* constructed, the questions seem moot (*South China Morning Post,* April 4, 1989; Foreign Broadcast Information Service [Washington, D.C.], April 4, 1989, p. 55). Xiao Yang, an optics and plastics specialist, was called in by Wang Hongwen and put in charge of designing Mao's sarcophagus. He confirmed the violent row over the placement of the tomb and the central — but unspoken — role that *feng shui* played in it. By 1988 he had become mayor of Chongqing, his native city (Xiao Yang, personal interview, April 17, 1988, Chongqing).

16. Soong Chingling, personal interview, September 1977, Beijing.
    The only senior Party leaders who did not pay their last respects to Mao Zedong were Deng Xiaoping and Wan Li. Both were still under house arrest (Wan Li, personal interview, October 7, 1987, Beijing).

17. In 1990 Hua Guofeng's house was opened to tourists. Rooms could be had for twenty-nine dollars a day and up. Its convenient location, close to shopping and to the palace wing of the Beijing Hotel, with good meals and taxis available, made it an attractive spot.

18. Fan Shuo, "Feng lei ji dang de shiyue," 18.

19. Wang Zhen, *Renmin Ribao* (Beijing), October 22, 1989.

20. *Chen Ming* (Hong Kong), December 12, 1978.

21. This version is drawn in large part from the two accounts written by Fan Shuo.

CHAPTER 41. THE MILLION-MAN ARMY

1. Actually, the turnout for Wang Hongwen's militia was smaller than he expected but certainly more than the twelve hundred men estimated by a post-Gang source in Shanghai in 1977 (notes of visit to Shanghai, September 1977).

2. Yan Jiaqi, *Wenge shi nian shi.*

3. Wu Bangguo (deputy Party secretary, Shanghai), personal interview, June 14, 1988, Shanghai.

4. Notes of visit to Shanghai, September 1977.

5. Ibid.

6. Ibid.

7. Ibid.

8. Ibid.

CHAPTER 42. "POVERTY IS NOT COMMUNISM"

1. Fan Shuo, *Ye Jianying zai 1976,* 315.

2. Yuan Chi Chen, personal interview, October 10, 1976, New York.

3. Li Rui, *Lushan huiyi shilu,* 3, 89.

4. Wan Li, personal interview, October 7, 1987, Beijing.

5. Ibid.

6. Li Xianglu (former Zhao Ziyang secretary), personal interview, August 13, 1988, New York.

7. Huang Bing, personal interview, March 4, 1985, New York.

8. Li Xianglu, personal interview, August 13, 1988, New York.

9. Harrison E. Salisbury, *Long March,* 334.

10. Hu Hua, personal interview, August 3, 1987, Beijing.

11. Hu Hua, personal interview, August 31, 1981, Beijing.

CHAPTER 43. THE DENG REVOLUTION

The account of Willow Grove is based on visits and interviews in 1972, 1984, and 1987.

1. Edgar Snow, *Other Side of the River,* 477–478.

CHAPTER 44. IF IT AIN'T BROKE, DON'T FIX IT

Data on Fangshan gathered in personal visit, June 8, 1988; William Hinton, personal interview, July 9, 1988; Guce demonstration, Agence France Presse (Hong Kong), June 30, 1988, Foreign Broadcast Information Service (Washington, D.C.), July 1, 1988, p. 17; Xinhua News Agency (Beijing), June 30, 1988, Foreign Broadcast Information Service, July 1, 1988, p. 17; and Hinton, *Great Reversal.*

CHAPTER 45. THE SHAPE OF THE FUTURE

All material about Shengli is based on interviews done at the oil field, May 17–18, 1988.

1. First-quarter figures for 1991 indicated Shengli was on target. It produced nearly 9 million tons, about 25 percent of China's total, against 14 million from Daqing, roughly 40 percent of the total. The winter quarter is the lightest of the year (*China News,* April 17, 1991).

2. Some of Shengli's figures for production during the Cultural Revolution years are suspect. No figures were provided by Zhu initially for 1967 or for 1969–81. Those became available after some months of delay. They revealed an unexplained production decline from 1978 to 1985, when the field resumed vigorous expansion (Shengli interviews, May 17, 1988; Shengli management, letter to author, November 1988).

3. Largely based on data collected on inspection of the Black Dragon fire area in autumn 1988; mostly incorporated in *Great Black Dragon Fire.*

4. Largely based on personal interviews with Zhu Rongji (June 14, 1988, Shanghai) and Shanghai deputy Party Chief Wu Bangguo (June 14, 1988, Shanghai), who succeeded Zhu when the latter became vice premier in April 1991.

5. Most details from personal interviews with Xiao Yang (April 17, 1988, Chongqing), and Hao Zhenkun (April 18, 1988, Chongqing).

CHAPTER 46. THE EMPEROR'S CLOTHES

1. A Hong Kong paper published a rather scurrilous report of Pufang's marriage in the winter of 1991, raising the question of why Pufang should marry when his paralysis had left him incapable of consummating the relationship. Pufang said: "Don't believe anything you read in the Hong Kong press" (Deng Pufang, personal interview, January 28, 1991, Beijing).

2. Deng Pufang, speech of October 10, 1984, Beijing, to staff of Chinese Disabled People's Welfare Foundation.

3. In May 1991 a burst of publicity about aid to China's handicapped swept Beijing and other cities, consisting of meetings, interviews, feature stories, and reports on the widespread work of Deng Pufang's organization and new legislation approved by the national legislature to help the disabled. Even old reactionaries like Wang Zhen joined in. It was not clear whether this was an effort to establish in Chinese minds an obligation of society toward the less fortunate or a political maneuver by the conservative politicians trying to curry favor with Deng Xiaoping.

4. Largely based on personal interviews with Deng Pufang, 1986, 1987, 1991, Beijing.

5. Liu Yuanyuan, personal interview, May 16, 1988, Jinan.

6. Personal observation of Armand Hammer birthday celebration, April 24, 1988.

CHAPTER 47. THE ROAD TO TIANANMEN

1. Li Peng, personal conversation, November 11, 1987, Beijing.

2. *Takungpao* (Hong Kong), March 30, 1989; Foreign Broadcast Information Service (Washington, D.C.), April 11, 1989, p. 24.

3. Confidential report, August 18, 1988.

4. Yan Jiaqi, personal interview, May 2, 1988, Beijing.

5. Su Xiaokang and Wang Luxiang, *He shang*.

CHAPTER 48. *THE GENERAL MIRROR FOR THE AID OF GOVERNMENT*

Much of the information in this chapter was collected from personal observation, Beijing, June 1989.

1. Oleg Troyanovsky, personal interview, November 1987, Beijing.

2. Shen Tong, *Almost a Revolution*, 170–171.

3. Later Li Peng would complain that China had no rubber bullets and had to use real ones. It was not true. Some witnesses reported seeing water cannon prepared for use by police outside the city center, but there is no evidence they were ever used. Li Peng said the police had no tear gas. Obviously he was not present in the central squares and along Chang-an Avenue, where the armed police employed the canisters in large numbers.

4. The report of Deng's visit to Wuhan may be apocryphal. The author was in Wuhan on June 6–8, 1989, and found no trace of such a trip. Deng Pufang, however, had been in Wuhan a few days earlier for a meeting concerning his work with the disabled.

CHAPTER 49. TIANANMEN

Most of the detail about Tiananmen is based on personal observation, Beijing, June 1989, and on subsequent interviews with participants.

1. William Hinton, personal interviews, June 27, 1989, Beijing; July 1989, New York.

2. Robin Munro, an English observer for China Watch, spent the night in the square, hurrying from one end to the other, to keep track of all that went on. He later wrote a detailed report based on his observations and interviews with participants. His conclusion was that the government might have been technically correct in its assertion that no one was killed within the precise limits of the square. But this did not cover areas immediately adjacent. No one — except the government — disputed conclusions that a minimum of 1,000 to 2,000 people were killed in Beijing during the military operation.

Bibliography

WORKS IN LANGUAGES OTHER THAN CHINESE

The Administrative Divisions of the People's Republic of China. Beijing, 1981.

Alley, Rewi. "Guang'an: Birthplace of Deng Xiaoping." *Eastern Horizon* (Hong Kong) 1 (1981).

Anderson, Aeneas. *A Narrative of the British Embassy to China in the Years 1792, 1793, 1794*. London, 1795.

Arlington, L.C., and William Lewisohn. *In Search of Old Peking*. Peking, 1935.

Atlas of China (Zhonghua remin gong hequo). Beijing, 1983.

Bailey, Paul. "The Chinese Work Study Movement in France." *China Quarterly* 115 (September 1988).

Barnett, Robert W. *Wandering Knights*. Armonk, N.Y., 1990.

Barnstone, Willis, ed. and trans. *The Poems of Mao Tse-tung*. New York, 1972.

Barrett, David D. *Dixie Mission: The United States Army Observer Group in Yenan: 1944*. Berkeley, Calif., 1970.

Belden, Jack. *China Shakes the World*. New York, 1949.

Bodde, Derk. *China's First Unifier: A Study of the Ch'in Dynasty as Seen in the Life of Li Ssu (280?–208 B.C.)*. Leiden, the Netherlands, 1938.

———. *Festivals in Classical China*. Princeton, N.J., 1975.

———. *Peking Diary*. New York, 1950.

Bonavia, David. *Verdict in Peking: The Trial of the Gang of Four*. London, 1984.

Borisov, Oleg. *From the History of Soviet-Chinese Relations in the 1950s*. Moscow, 1972.

Bridgham, Philip. "Mao's Cultural Revolution: Origin and Development." *China Quarterly* 29 (January 1967):1–35.

Burlatsky, Feodor. *Mao Tze Dun*. Moscow, 1975.

———. *Mao Tze Dun i yevo nasledniki* (Mao Zedong and his heirs). Moscow, 1980.

Cecil, Russel L., and Robert F. Loeb. *Textbook of Medicine*. 17th ed. Philadelphia, 1985.

Central Committee, CPC. *Deng Xiaoping*. Beijing, 1988.

Chapple, Geoff. *Rewi Alley of China*. Auckland, New Zealand, 1980.

Charles, David A. "The Dismissal of Marshal Peng Teh-huai." *China Quarterly* 8 (October 1961).

Chen, Jerome. *Mao Papers: Anthology and Bibliography*. New York, 1970.

Chi Hsin. *Teng Hsiao Ping*. Hong Kong, 1978.

Chin-chun Lee. *The Voices of China*. New York, 1990.

Chin Ping Mei (The golden lotus). London, 1955.

Chin-tu Hsueh. *Revolutionary Leaders of Modern China*. New York, 1971.

Clubb, O. Edmund. *Twentieth-Century China*. New York, 1964.

Confucius. *The Analects*. Shanghai, 1933.

Cottrell, Arthur. *The First Emperor of China*. London, 1983.

Deane, Hugh. *Remembering Koji Ariyoshi: American G.I. in Yanen*. Los Angeles, 1978.

De Bary, William Theodore, Wing-tsit Chan, Burton Watson, and Chester Tan. *Sources of Chinese Tradition*. Vols. 1 and 2. New York, 1960, 1969.

Dedijer, Vladimir. *Tito*. New York, 1953.

Deng Rong [Maomao]. "My Father's Days in Jiangxi." *Beijing Review* (September 1984):17–18.

———. "My Father Deng Xiaoping's Years in Jiangxi." *China Reconstructs* 34 (April 1985):28–30.

Deng Xiaoping. *Fundamental Issues in Present-Day China*. Beijing, 1987.

———. *Selected Works*. Vol. 1. Beijing, 1984.

Deng Xiaoping. Beijing, 1980.

De Woskin, Kenneth J. *Doctors, Diviners, and Magicians in Ancient China*. New York, 1983.

Djilas, Milovan. *Conversations with Stalin*. New York, 1962.

———. *The New Class*. New York, 1957.

Dorn, Frank D. *Forbidden City*. New York, 1970.

Eberhard, Wolfram. *A History of China*. Berkeley, Calif., 1960.

Elegant, Robert S. *Mao's Great Revolution*. New York, 1971.

Esherick, Joseph W., ed. *Lost Chance in China: The World War Two Despatches of John S. Service*. New York, 1974.

Fairbank, John King. *The Great Chinese Revolution: 1800–1985*. New York, 1986.

Fan, K. H., ed. *Mao Tse-Tung and Lin Piao: Post-Revolutionary Writings*. New York, 1972.

Fang, Percy Jucheng, and Lucy Fang. *Zhou Enlai*. Beijing, 1990.

Fang Lizhi. *Bringing Down the Great Wall*. New York, 1990.

Fedorenko, Nikolai. "Stalin i Mao: Besedy v Moskve" (Stalin and Mao: Meeting in Moscow). *Problemy Dalnego Vostoka* (January 1989):149–164.

———. "Vizit N. Khrushchev v Pekin" (Visit of N. Khrushchev to Beijing). *Problemy Dalnego Vostoka* (January 1989):121–132.

Feoktinstov, V. P., ed. *Maosizm bez maskii* (Maoism Without a mask). Moscow, 1970.

Fitzgerald, C. P. *Son of Heaven: A Biography of Li Shih-min, Founder of the Tang Dynasty*. Cambridge, England, 1933.

Fokkema, D. W. *Report on Peking*. London, 1970.

Forman, Harrison. *Report from Red China*. New York, 1945.

The Four Books: Confucius and Mencius. Hong Kong, 1898.

Fung, H. K. *Shop Signs in Peking*. Peking, 1931.

Garside, Roger. *Coming Alive*. New York, 1981.

Gernet, Jacques. *Ancient China*. Berkeley, Calif., 1968.

Giles, Herbert A. *A History of Chinese Literature*. New York, 1928.

Goldman, Merle. "Vengeance in China." *New York Review of Books,* November 19, 1989.

Granet, Marcel. *Chinese Civilization*. New York, 1930.

A Great Trial in Chinese History. Beijing, 1981.

Griffith, Samuel B. *Mao Tse-tung: Basic Tactics*. New York, 1966.

Gromyko, Andrei A. *Memoirs*. New York, 1989.

Guikovsky, Emil. *Mao — Réalités d'une légende*. Paris, 1976.

Hammond, Ed. *Coming of Grace: An Illustrated Biography of Zhou Enlai.* Berkeley, Calif., 1980.

———. *To Embrace the Moon: An Illustrated Biography of Mao Zedong.* Berkeley, Calif., 1980.

Han Suyin. *Wind in the Tower: Mao Tse-tung and the Chinese Revolution, 1949–1975.* New York, 1976.

Hao Yufan and Zhai Zhihai. "China's Decision to Enter the Korean War: History Revisited." *China Quarterly* 12 (March 1990):94–115.

Harrmann, Albert. *Historic and Commercial Atlas of China.* Cambridge, Mass., 1935.

Hinton, William. *The Great Reversal: The Privatization of China, 1978–1989.* New York, 1990.

Huang Hua. "A True Account of John Stuart's Departure from China." *Beijing Review* (October 22–28, 1990):32–35.

Huang Zhen. *Sketches of the Long March.* Beijing, 1982.

Hu Hua. *The Early Life of Zhou Enlai.* Beijing, 1980.

Hu Qiaomu. *Interview with Theodore H. White.* Foreign Ministry Notes. Beijing, 1983.

Hu Yaobang. "The Best Way to Remember Mao Zedong." *Beijing Review* (January 2, 1984):16–18.

I Ching: The Book of Changes. Translated by Cary F. Baynes. Princeton, N.J., 1950.

Jacobs, Dan N. *The New Communist Manifesto.* New York, 1962.

Karnow, Stanley. *Mao and China.* New York, 1972.

Kates, George N. *The Years That Were Fat: Beijing 1933–1940.* New York, 1988.

Kau, Michael Y. M. *The Lin Biao Affair.* White Plains, N.Y., 1975.

Khrushchev, N. S. *Khrushchev Remembers.* Boston, 1970.

———. *Khrushchev Remembers: The Last Testament.* Boston, 1974.

———. *Khrushchev Remembers: The Glasnost Tapes.* Boston, 1990.

Kidd, David. *Peking Story.* New York, 1988.

Kim, Hakjoon. "International Trends in Korean War Studies: A Review of Documentary Literature." *Korea and World Politics* (Seoul) (Summer 1990):326–370.

Kissinger, Henry. *White House Years.* Boston, 1979.

Korovyakovsky, P. P. "Kitaitsy — Zhertvy Stalinskikh repressii" (Chinese victims of Stalin's repression). *Problemy Dalnego Vostoka* (February 1991).

Laffont, Robert. *Kang Sheng.* Paris, 1987.

Landman, Lynn, and Amos Landman. *Profile of Red China.* New York, 1951.

Lao She. *Beneath the Red Banner.* Beijing, 1982.

———. *Camel Xiangzi.* Bloomington, Ind., 1982.

———. *Rickshaw Boy.* New York, 1948.

———. *Teahouse.* Beijing, 1986.

Lenin, V. I. "Detskaya bolezn 'levizny' v kommunizme" ("Left-Wing" communism: An infantile disease). Moscow, 1978.

———. "Dve taktiki Sotsial-Demokraty v demokraticheskoy revolyutsi" (Two tactics of Social-Democracy in the democratic revolution). Moscow, 1978.

Li Jui [Rui]. *The Early Revolutionary Activities of Chairman Mao Tse-tung.* White Plains, N.Y., 1977.

Liu Binyan. *China's Crisis, China's Hope.* New York, 1990.

———. *A Higher Kind of Loyalty.* New York, 1990.

———. *"Tell the World."* New York, 1989.

Liu Shaoqi. *Selected Works.* Vol. 1. Beijing, 1984.

Liu Zongren. *Tanyin Alley.* San Francisco, 1988.

Lo Kuanchung. *Three Kingdoms: China's Epic Drama.* Translated by Moss Roberts. New York, 1976.

Lord, Bette Bao. *Legacies: A Chinese Mosaic.* New York, 1990.

Lum, Peter. *Peking 1950–1953.* London, 1958.

Luo Guanzhong. *The Three Kingdoms*. Beijing, 1981.

Luo Ruiqing, Lu Zhengcao, and Wang Bingnan. *Zhou Enlai and the Xian Incident*. Beijing, 1982.

MacKinnon, Janice R., and Stephen R. MacKinnon. *Agnes Smedley: The Life and Times of an American Radical*. Berkeley, Calif., 1987.

Malraux, André. *Anti-Memoirs*. New York, 1968.

Manach, Etienne M. *Mémoires d'Extrême Asie*. Paris, 1971.

Mann, Jim. *Beijing Jeep*. New York, 1989.

Mao's Poems. Beijing, n.d.

Mao Tze-Tung. *Poems*. Peking, 1970.

———. *Quotations from Chairman Mao*. Beijing, 1966.

———. *Selected Military Writings*. Peking, 1967.

———. *Selected Works*. Vols. 4, 5. Peking, 1975, 1977.

———. "Two Birds: A Dialogue." *Peking Review* (January 9, 1976).

Marx, Karl. *Capital*. Vol. 1. Translated by S. Moore and E. Aveling. London, 1938.

Marx, Karl, and Friedrich Engels. *The Communist Manifesto*. Edited by A. J. P. Taylor. Baltimore, 1969.

Melby, John F. *The Mandate of Heaven*. Toronto, 1968.

Milton, David, and Nancy Dall Milton. *The Wind Will Not Subside*. New York, 1976.

Mirsky, Jonathan. "The Empire Strikes Back." *New York Review of Books*, February 1, 1990, pp. 21–25.

Myrdal, Jan. *Report from a Chinese Village*. New York, 1965.

———. *Return to a Chinese Village*. New York, 1984.

Nagel's China. Geneva, 1968.

Naughton, Barry. "The Third Line: Defense Industrialization in the China Interior." *China Quarterly* 115 (September 1988):351–386.

Nien Cheng. *Life and Death in Shanghai*. London, 1986.

Nixon, Richard. *RN: The Memoirs of Richard Nixon*. New York, 1978.

North, Robert. *Moscow and Chinese Communists*. Stanford, Calif., 1953.

Orlov, Alexander. *The Secret History of Stalin's Crimes*. London, 1954.

Olschki, Leonardo. *Marco Polo's Precursors*. New York, 1972.

Pan, Lynn. *The New China Revolution*. London, 1987.

Payne, Robert. *Mao Tse-tung*. New York, 1989.

———. *A Rage for China*. New York, 1977.

Peck, Graham. *Two Kinds of Time*. Boston, 1950.

Peng Dehuai. *Memoirs of a Marshal*. Beijing, 1984.

Pinto, Fernão Mendes. *The Travels of Fernão Mendes Pinto*. Edited and translated by Rebecca D. Catz. Chicago, 1989.

Polo, Marco. *The Book of Ser*. Translated and edited by Sir Henry Yule. 3rd ed. London, 1929.

Qian Gang. *The Great China Earthquake*. Beijing, 1989.

Reischauer, Edwin O., and John K. Fairbank. *East Asia: The Great Tradition*. Boston, 1960.

Rewi Alley Memorial. Beijing, 1989.

Ricci, Matthew. *The Journals 1583–1610*. New York, 1953.

Rice, Edward E. T. *Mao's Way*. Berkeley, Calif., 1972.

Rickett, W. Allyn. *Kuan-Tzu*. Hong Kong, 1966.

Rockhill, William W., trans. and ed. *The Journey of William of Rubruck to the Eastern Parts of the World 1253–55*. Peking, 1941.

Roots, John McCook. *Chou*. New York, 1975.

Rossabi, Morris. *Kubilai Khan*. Berkeley, Calif., 1988.

Salisbury, Charlotte Y. *China Diary*. New York, 1973.

Salisbury, Harrison E. *American in Russia*. New York, 1954.

————. *Black Night, White Snow: Russia's Revolutions, 1905–1917.* New York, 1978.
————. *China: One Hundred Years of Revolution.* New York, 1983.
————. *The Great Black Dragon Fire: A Chinese Inferno.* Boston, 1989.
————. "How America and Russia Lost China." *New York Times Book Review,* September 19, 1971.
————. *The Long March: The Untold Story.* New York, 1985.
————. *Tiananmen Diary: Thirteen Days in June.* Boston, 1989.
————. *A Time of Change: A Reporter's Tale of Our Times.* New York, 1988.
————. *War Between Russia and China.* New York, 1969.
Scholmer, Joseph. *Vorkuta.* New York, 1955.
Schram, Stuart. *Chairman Mao Speaks to the People.* New York, 1974.
————. *Mao Tse-tung.* New York, 1968.
————. *The Political Thought of Mao Tse-tung.* London, 1963.
Schwartz, Benjamin. *Chinese Communism and the Rise of Mao.* Cambridge, Mass., 1951.
Seagrave, Sterling. *The Soong Dynasty.* New York, 1989.
Service, John S., ed. *Golden Inches: The China Memoir of Grace Service.* Berkeley, Calif., 1989.
Shambaugh, David L. *The Making of a Premier: Zhao Ziyang's Provincial Career.* Boulder, Colo., 1984.
Shen Tong. *Almost a Revolution.* Boston, 1990.
Shi Hai'an and Luo Guangshong. *Outlaws of the Marsh.* Beijing, 1980.
Shi Zhe. "Seprovozhe Predsetatelye Mao." (Accompanying Chairman Mao). *Problemy Dalnego Vostoka* (January 1989):139–148.
Shu Yi. "Lao She's Last Two Days." *Harvest* 2(1989): 2–7.
Siao-yu. *Mao Tse-tung and I Were Beggars.* New York, 1959.
Simmie, Scott, and Bob Nixon. *Tiananmen Square.* Seattle, 1989.
Simonov, Konstantin. *Grazhyushchii Kitai* (Fighting China). Moscow, 1950.
Siren, Osvald. *The Walls and Gates of Peking.* London, 1921.
Slavinsky, S. "Koreiskaya Voina 1950–1953 gg: Sovremennoye peresmylenie" (The Korean War 1950–1953: Contemporary rethinking). *Problemy Dalnego Vostoka* (January 1991):80–90.
Smedley, Agnes. *The Great Road.* New York, 1952.
Snow, Edgar. *Journey to the Beginning.* New York, 1958.
————. *The Long Revolution.* New York, 1972.
————. *The Other Side of the River.* New York, 1962.
————. *Random Notes from Red China.* Cambridge, Mass., 1957.
————. *Red China Today.* New York, 1962.
————. *Red Star over China.* Rev. ed. New York, 1978.
Snow, Helen [Nym Wales, pseud.]. *Inside Red China.* New York, 1975.
————. *Red Dust.* Stanford, Calif., 1951.
Snow, Helen [Nym Wales, pseud.], and Kim San. *Song of Ariran.* New York, 1941.
Snow, Lois Wheeler. *Edgar Snow's China.* New York, 1981.
Spence, Jonathan. *Emperor of China: Self-Portrait of K'ang-hsi.* New York, 1974.
————. *The Search for Modern China.* New York, 1990.
Spurr, Russell. *Enter the Dragon.* New York, 1988.
Stanton, Sir George. *An Authentic Account of an Embassy from the King of Great Britain to the Emperor of China.* London, 1797.
Strong, Tracy B., and Helene Keyssar. *Right in Her Soul: The Life of Anna Louise Strong.* New York, 1983.
Sufei, ed. *Ma Haide* [George Hatem]. Beijing, 1989.
Sun Tzu. *The Art of War.* Translated by Samuel B. Griffith. Oxford, England, 1963.
Swamy, Subramanian, and Sharid Javed Burki. "Food Grains in the People's Republic of China, 1958–1965." *China Quarterly* 41 (January-March 1970):58–63.

Sykes, Sir Percy. *The Quest for Cathay*. London, 1930.
Taching: Red Banner on China's Industrial Front. Peking, 1972.
Teng Hsiao-ping. "Memorial Speech, Chou En-lai." *Peking Review* (January 12, 1976):5–8.
Terrill, Ross. *Mao*. New York, 1980.
———. *The White-Boned Demon*. New York, 1984.
Thurston, Anne F. *Enemies of the People*. New York, 1987.
Tikhvinsky, S. L. "Kitai v moei zhizn" (China in my life: Memoirs). *Problemy Dalnego Vostoka* (February 1987); (March 1989); (April 1989); (January 1990):92–94; (April 1990):103–112; (May 1990):99–108.
Tsao Hsueh-chin. *A Dream of Red Mansions*. Beijing, 1975.
Tuchman, Barbara. "If Mao Had Come to Washington: An Essay in Alternatives." *Foreign Affairs* (October 1972):44–64.
———. *Stilwell and the American Experience in China*. New York, 1970.
Urban, George. *The "Miracles" of Chairman Mao*. Los Angeles, 1970.
Van Ginneken, Japp. *The Rise and Fall of Lin Biao*. New York, 1970.
Van Gulik, R. H. *Sexual Life in Ancient China*. Leiden, the Netherlands, 1974.
Vladimirov, O., and V. Ryazantsev. *Stranitz politicheskoi biografii Mao Tse Duna* (Pages from the political biography of Mao Zedong). Moscow, 1980.
Vladimirov, P. P. *Osobii Raion Kitai 1942–1945* (Special District, China, 1942–1945). Moscow, 1972.
———. *The Vladimirov Diaries: Yenan China 1942–1945*. New York, 1975.
Vorontsov, V. "Mikhail Borodin: Gizhnennii podvig i tragediya" (Mikhail Borodin: His successes and tragedies). *Problemy Dalnego Vostoka* (June 1990):135–147.
Wang Hui-ming. *Ten Poems and Lyrics by Mao Tse-tung*. Amherst, Mass., 1975.
Wang Ming. *China: Cultural Revolution or Counter-Revolutionary Coup?* Moscow, 1972.
———. *Mao's Betrayal*. Moscow, 1979.
Wang Xicheng. *Chin P'ing Mei* (The golden lotus). Translated by Clement Egerton. London, 1936.
———. *Chin P'ing Mei* (The golden lotus). Translated by Arthur Waley. London, 1939.
Werner, E.T.C. *Myths and Legends of China*. London, 1922.
White, Theodore H. *Notes of Hu Qiaomu Interview*. Beijing, 1983.
White, Theodore H., and Annalee Jacoby. *Thunder out of China*. New York, 1946.
Wilson, Dick. *Zhou Enlai*. New York, 1984.
Witke, Roxane. *Comrade Chiang Ching*. Boston, 1977.
Wu Xiuquan. *Eight Years in the Ministry of Foreign Affairs*. Beijing, 1985.
Yakovlev, Mikhail. *17 let v Kitaye* (Seventeen years in China). Moscow, 1981.
Yusov, V. N. "Kang Sheng — Kitaiskii Beria" (Kang Sheng — The Chinese Beria). *Problemy Dalnego Vostoka* (March 1991):111–121.
———. "Khronika gibeli Lin Biao" (Chronicle of the destruction of Lin Biao). *Problemy Dalnego Vostoka* (April 1990):96–102.
———. "Kto napravil Kitaiski dobrovoltsev" (Who ordered the Chinese volunteers). *Problemy Dalnego Vostoka* (January 1990):108–111.
Zhang Wenxian. *Mao Zedong: Biography, Assessment, Reminiscences*. Beijing, 1986.
Zhongnanhai: Center of a Country of One Billion. Beijing, 1981.
Zhou Enlai. *Symposium*. Tianjin, 1990.
Zhou Shachen. *Beijing: Old and New*. Beijing, 1989.
Zhu De. *Selected Works*. Beijing, 1986.

WORKS IN CHINESE

Chai Chengwen and Zhang Yangtian. *Ban men dian tan pan* (Panmunjom negotiations). Beijing, 1989.

Deng Pufang. *Women wei canjiren shiye suo zuo de yi qie nuli* (All our efforts for the cause of the disabled). Beijing, 1984.

Fan Shuo. "Feng lei ji dang de shiyue: Fensui si ren bang ji shi" (Tempestuous October: Chronicle of the collapse of the Gang of Four). *Yangcheng Wanbao* (Guangzhou), February 10, 1989.

———. *Ye Jianying zai 1976* (Ye Jianying in 1976). Beijing, 1989.

Franz, Willy. *Deng Xiaoping*. Lanzhou, 1989.

Gong Yuzhi. "Sixiang jiefang de xin qi dian" (A new starting point in mind liberation). *Wenhuibao* (Shanghai), June 2, 1988.

He Fuchuan. *Shan an shangde Zhongguo* (China in a squeeze). Guizhou, 1989.

He Long. *Huai nian* (Reminiscences). Beijing, 1979.

He Zhangwen. "Deng zhengwei zhihui women xiang qian ken: Xi nan zhanyi shengli hou de zhengzhi jueding" (Political Commissar Deng directs us to look forward: Political decisions made after the victory of the southwest campaign). *Renmin Ribao* (Beijing), July 28, 1988.

Huai nian Liu Shaoqi (Liu Shaoqi memorial). Beijing, 1986.

Huai nian Liu Shaoqi (Liu Shaoqi memorial). Beijing, 1988.

Huang Shaoquan. "Zai zhong yan su qu de rizi li Zhou Enlai zhichi Mao Zedong" (Zhou Enlai supported Mao Zedong during the days of the Central Soviet Area). *Dangshi Wenhui* (Beijing) 2 (1988).

Hu Sizheng. "Xiao San de zui hou sui yue" (The last days of Xiao San). *Xinhua Wenzhai* (Beijing) 4 (1983).

Jiang Shifang. *Wang pai chu jin de Zhongnanhai qiao ju* (The last card of the game of Zhongnanhai). New York, 1990.

Jia Sinan. *Mao Zedong renji jiao wang shi lu: 1915–1976* (Recollections of Mao Zedong's personal relations: 1915–1976). Jiangsu, 1989.

Jing Fuzi. *Mao Zedong he ta de nu ren men* (Mao Zedong and his women). Taipei, 1991.

Jinian Chen Yi yuanshuai (Marshal Chen Yi memorial). Beijing, 1989.

Jinian He Long (He Long memorial). Beijing, 1981.

Lei Shoumei. "Renge de li liang" (The power of integrity). *Zhongguo Funubao* (April 1989):4–7.

Liao yuan zhi huo (The spark that could start a prairie fire). Vol. 10. Beijing, 1982.

Li Deshang. "Huiyi wen ge ri zi li de Zhou Enlai" (In memory of Zhou Enlai in the days of the Cultural Revolution). *People's Daily* (Beijing), March 17, 1988.

Li Guopu and Lan Qixuan. *Deng Xiaoping chuanqi* (The legendary Deng Xiaoping). Beijing, 1989.

Li Ming. *Zhongguo de weiji yu sikao* (China crises). Tianjin, 1989.

Lin Qingshan. "Mao Zedong zen yang kaishi fan Zhou yundong de" (How Mao Zedong launched the campaign against Zhou Enlai). *The Mirror* (Hong Kong) 2 (1989).

"Li Peng de fuqin" (Li Peng's father). *Ta Kung Pao* (Hong Kong), March 30, 1989.

"Li Peng yu ta de fuqin" (Li Peng and his father). *Zhongguo Yingcai* (Beijing) 1 (1991).

Li Rui. *Lushan huiyi shilu* (The true record of the Lushan conference). Changsha, 1989.

———. "Mao Zedong wan nian de sixiang he shijian" (Mao Zedong's thinking and practice in later years). *Guangming Ribao* (Beijing), February 2, 1989.

———. *Huai nian* (Reminiscences). Beijing, 1987.

Li Ruqing. *Xiang Jiang zhan yi* (The battle of Xiang Jiang). Nanjing, 1989.

Liu Pingping, Liu Yuanyuan, and Liu Tingting. *Shengli de xianhua xian gei nin: huainian women de fuqin Liu Shaoqi* (Flowers of victory to you: In memory of our father, Liu Shaoqi). Beijing, 1986.

Liu Xiao. *Chu shi Sulian ba nian* (Eight years as ambassador to the Soviet Union). Beijing, 1989.

Liu Yazhou. *Enlai*. Beijing, 1989.

Li Yueran. *Waijiaa wutai shang de Xinzhongguo lingxiu* (Nine leaders of New China on the diplomatic stage). Beijing, 1989.

Li Zehou. "Qing nian Mao Zedong" (The young Mao Zedong). From *Zhongguo xiandai sixiang shi lun* (History of China's contemporary thinking). Beijing, 1987.

Luo Yingcai. "Shu tu tong gui: Chen Yi he ta de san ge xiongdi" (Reaching the same goal by different routes: Chen Yi and his three brothers). *Zhonghua Yinglie* 5 (1987):126–135.

"Mao zhuxi shi zen yang xiugai shici de" (How Chairman Mao revised his poems). *People's Daily* (Beijing), November 7, 1989.

Nie Rongzhen. *Hui yi lu* (Memoirs). Beijing, 1984.

Quan Yanchi. *Wei shi zhang tan Mao Zedong* (Chief bodyguard Li Yinqiao remembers Chairman Mao). Beijing, 1989.

Quan Ye. "Zhou Enlai de zui hou suiyue" (Zhou Enlai's final days). *Descendants of the Yellow Emperor* 5 (1989):7.

Pan Xianzhi. *Mao Zedong he tade mishu Tianjiaying* (Chairman Mao and his secretary Tian Jiaying). Beijing, 1989.

Ren Bishi. *Xuanji* (Selected works). Beijing, 1987.

Shi Zhe. "Mao Zedong tong zhi chu fang Sulian" (Comrade Mao Zedong's first visit to the Soviet Union). Beijing Radio, January 16, 1989.

Sun Yixian. *New China Diplomacy* (May 1990).

Su Xiaokang. *Wutuobang ji* (Elegy of utopia: Summer of 1959 on Lushan). Beijing, 1989.

Su Xiaokang and Wang Luxiang. *He shang* (Yellow River elegy). Beijing, 1989.

Wang Chaoyiu. *Beijing dangshi baogao* (Beijing reports on party history), no. 1, 1988.

———. *Huanying zhong yang dao Beijing* (Welcome the Central Committee to Beijing). Beijing, Historical Documents of Public Security, no. 3, 1987.

Wang Denglin. *Liang Shuming he Mao Zedong* (Liang Shuming and Mao Zedong). Jilin, 1989.

Wang Lingshu. "Ji Dengkui tan Mao Zedong" (Ji Dengkui on Mao Zedong). *Liaowang* (Hong Kong), February 6, 1989; February 13, 1989.

Wang Nianyi. *Da dong luan de niandai* (Time of the great turmoil). Zhengzhou, 1989.

Wang Xiachui. "Deng Pufang tan guanghua gongsi" (Deng Pufang talks about the Guanghua Co.). *Zhongguo Xinwei* (Beijing), January 18, 1990.

Wenhuishi [pseud.]. "Daozhi Zhongguo xiang chaoxian pai zhi yuan jun shijian ji shi" (Record of actual events leading to China sending volunteers to Korea). *Qiaobao* (New York), August 24, 1990.

Wu Xiuquan. *New China Diplomacy* (May 1990):153.

Xiang Qing. *Gong chan guo ji yu zhongguo geming de guanxi* (The relations of the Comintern and the Chinese revolution). Beijing, 1989.

Xin Zhongguo wai jiao feng yun (New China's diplomatic wind and clouds). Beijing, 1988.

Xu Wenyi. *New China Diplomacy* (May 1990).

Yan Changlin. *Jue zhan de ri zi* (Days of decisive battle). Beijing, 1986.

Yang Chien-yan. "Peng he ta de yi jia" (Peng and his family). *Tzu Ching* (Hong Kong), October 8, 1990.

Yan Jiaqi. *Wenge shi nian shi 1966–1976* (Ten years of the Cultural Revolution 1966–1976). Beijing, 1986.

Yu Zhen. *New China Diplomacy* (May 1990).

Zhang Hanzhi. "Gu Xiangxing — Yi Guanhua" (A trip to the hometown — In memory of Guanhua). *Wenhui Yuekan* (Shanghai), January 1987, pp. 56–62.

———. "Wo yu fuqin Zhang Shizhao" (My father Zhang Shizhao and me). *Wenhui Yuekan* (Shanghai) (March 1988):3–11; (April 1988):6–21.

———. *Shui shuo cao mu bu tong qing — Yi Guanhua* (Who says that trees do not understand human feeling? — In Memory of Guanhua). *Family* (Guangzhou) (January 1986):11–13.

Zhang Kai. "Yi Yaobang Shu Shu" (Uncle Yaobang). *Chinese Youth* (April 1989):10–11.

Zhang Yuangyou. *New China Diplomacy* (May 1990):15–21.

Zhang Yufeng. "Mao Zedong yu Zhou Enlai de yixie wan nian qu shi" (Anecdotes of Mao Zedong and Zhou Enlai in their later years). *Guangming Ribao* (Beijing) (December 1988–January 1989).

Zheng Yi. *Mao Zedong sheng huo shi lu 1946–1976* (Eyewitness accounts of Mao's life, 1946–1976). Nanjing, 1989.

Zhongguo gongchandang da shi nianbiao (Chronology of CPC history). Beijing, 1987.

Zhang Tuosheng. *1975 nian de quan mian zhengdun: Yi chang fan dui zuo qing cuo wu he dui si ren bang de zhong da douzheng* (The overall rectification of 1975: A major struggle against the leftist erroneous tendency and the Gang of Four). Beijing, 1990.

Zhong Wenxian. *Mao Zedong*. Beijing, 1986.

Zhu Zhongli. *Shan guan de hong ye* (The glittering red leaves). Changsha, 1986.

Illustration Credits

For illustrations between pages 176 and 177:

1 *Top and bottom*: Courtesy of Central Party Literature Publishing House.

2 *All illustrations*: Author's collection.

3 *Top*: Courtesy of the Museum of the Revolution. *Bottom*: Ringart's Collection.

4 *Top*: From Huang Zhen, *Sketches of the Long March*, Beijing, 1982. *Bottom*: Courtesy of Central Party Literature Publishing House.

5 *Top*: From *Edgar Snow's China*, by Lois Wheeler Snow. Copyright © 1980 by Lois Wheeler Snow. Reprinted by permission of Random House, Inc. *Bottom*: Courtesy of Harrison Foreman, *Triangle*.

6 *Top:* UPI/Bettmann. *Bottom:* Courtesy of Central Party Literature Publishing House.

7 Courtesy of Le Centre Recherches Asiatiques.

8 *Top*: Courtesy of Foreign Languages Press, Beijing. *Bottom*: From *Zhongnanhai: Center of a Country of One Billion*, China Pictorial.

For illustrations between pages 368 and 369:

1 *Top and bottom*: From *Zhongnanhai: Center of a Country of One Billion*, China Pictorial.

2-3 *Top, from left*: Courtesy of Chinese Communist Party Research Office, Xinhua News Agency; AP/Wide World Photos; Courtesy of Central Party Literature Publishing House; Courtesy of Chinese Communist Party Research Office, Xinhua News Agency. *Bottom, from left*: AP/Wide World Photos; Courtesy of China Photo Service.

4 *Top:* Yang Shaoming (son of President Yang Shangkun). *Bottom:* Xinhua News Agency.

5 *Top and bottom right:* Xinhua News Agency. *Bottom left:* Yang Shaoming.

6 *Top*: Courtesy of Central Party Literature Publishing House. *Middle:* Author's collection. *Bottom*: Vu Agency.

7 Xinhua News Agency.

8 *Top*: Author's collection. *Bottom left and right*: AP/Wide World Photos.

Index